UNEXPE

!

TRANS-
FORMATION

UNEXPECTED

!

TRANS-
FORMATION
Being Conformed to the Image of Christ

Bob Leland

Xulon Press

Xulon Press
2301 Lucien Way #415
Maitland, FL 32751
407.339.4217
www.xulonpress.com

© 2020 by Bob Leland

All rights reserved solely by the author. The author guarantees all contents are original and do not infringe upon the legal rights of any other person or work. No part of this book may be reproduced in any form without the permission of the author. The views expressed in this book are not necessarily those of the publisher.

Unless otherwise indicated, Scripture quotations taken from the Holy Bible, New International Version (NIV). Copyright © 1985 by Zondervan. Used by permission. All rights reserved.

Printed in the United States of America.

ISBN-13: 978-1-5456-5851-2

DEDICATION

To all my brothers and sisters in Christ who desire
more than anything else

TO BE CONFORMED TO HIS IMAGE.

ACKNOWLEDGMENTS

I am eternally indebted to Mrs. Roberta Jaeger from UFM (Unevangelized Fields Mission – now CrossWorld) for her cover design on the 1979 UFM Conference booklet which launched me into a life-changing study of the characteristics of Christ.

I am also grateful to Miss Elsie Johnson of Presque Isle, Maine, and my wife, Amber, who spent long hours going over the manuscript for this project, giving suggestions and making corrections.

My gratitude is also extended to many friends who encouraged me in this undertaking and expressed the blessing they already received from some of the material shared with them.

PREFACE

When I first began this study, it seemed to lend itself to a daily devotional structure. Others have encouraged me to put it into lesson format for use in Bible schools or Bible study groups. The resulting format of the lessons, with both study and application questions, I believe will serve both purposes. Some of the subject material, being too lengthy for one devotional or lesson, has been spread over several lessons to allow for adequate treatment. As the APPLICATION sections at the end of each devotional or lesson could be pretty high-powered if taken on a daily basis, I suggest that the reader take them at his own pace thus being free from the "pressure" to do one a day.

Where I have included a number of examples of others who have demonstrated one and another of Christ's characteristics, there is a wealth of untapped material "out there" of which I am unaware. Any additional examples are always welcome and will serve to strengthen the particular lessons to which they apply.

This is not an exhaustive study since much more could be said about each characteristic, name or title of Christ and no doubt there are more that could be added. But I will leave these further details to the reader as the Holy Spirit applies the Word and enlightens the mind.

Unexpected Transformation / ix

TABLE OF CONTENTS

DEDICATION v
ACKNOWLEDGMENTS vii
PREFACE ix
GLOSSARY xix
ABBREVIATIONS xxiii
SUMMARY xxvii
INTRODUCTION xxix

GOD'S LOVING SOVEREIGNTY 1
GOD'S GOAL FOR HUMANITY 4
OUR REACTION TO GOD'S GOAL FOR HUMANITY 6
HE IS THE IMAGE OF GOD 9
HE IS OUR EXAMPLE 11
HE IS THE WAY 13
HE IS THE TRUTH 15
HE IS THE LIFE 18
HE IS SUBMISSIVE TO THE FATHER 23
HE IS THE FORGIVING ONE 26
HE IS THE COMPASSIONATE ONE 32
HE IS TENDERHEARTED 34
HE IS RIGHTEOUS/JUST 36
HE IS GOOD/BENEVOLENT 38
HE IS THE RECONCILER 41
HE IS HOLY 44
HE IS THE PURE ONE 50

Unexpected Transformation / xi

HE IS THE PURIFIER	53
HE IS A MAN OF PRAYER	57
HE IS THE WITNESS	60
HE IS THE PEACEFUL ONE, THE PEACEMAKER	72
HE IS THE KING (the Governor/Ruler)	87
HE IS THE KING (the Servant)	89
HE IS THE KING (the Scepter)	94
HE IS THE KING (the Prince)	96
HE IS THE KING OF KINGS	99
HE IS THE KING (over Satan)	101
HE IS THE KING (over Sickness)	104
HE IS THE KING (over Circumstances and Death)	107
HE IS THE KING (over Self)	109
HE IS THE KING (over the World)	112
HE IS THE KING (with Authority)	116
HE IS THE KING (over Sorrow)	118
HE IS THE VICTORIOUS, THE TRIUMPHANT ONE	119
HE IS THE TEMPTED ONE	129
HE IS THE BURDEN-BEARER/COMFORTER	133
HE IS A COUNSELOR	141
HE IS WONDERFUL	144
HE IS THE GOOD SHEPHERD	148
HE IS THE LAMB	152
HE IS OUR ADVOCATE	159
HE IS OUR INTERCESSOR	161
HE IS OUR MEDIATOR	163
HE IS OUR HIGH PRIEST	165
HE IS OUR MASTER/TEACHER	184
HE IS THE LOVING ONE	187
HE IS THE GRIEVED ONE	191
HE IS THE BROKENHEARTED ONE	193
HE IS THE LONELY ONE (THE DESERTED)	195
HE IS THE ROOT OF DAVID/THE NAZARENE	199

HE IS THE PREEMINENT ONE	203
HE IS THE UNCHANGEABLE ONE, THE ROCK	205
HE IS THE CORNERSTONE	207
HE IS THE CHOSEN ONE	209
HE IS THE PRECIOUS ONE	211
HE IS OUR FRIEND	213
HE IS THE ZEALOUS ONE	216
HE IS THE STUMBLING STONE, THE ROCK OF OFFENSE	218
HE IS THE STONE REJECTED	221
HE IS THE ACKNOWLEDGED ONE	223
HE IS THE ANOINTED ONE	225
HE IS THE APPOINTED ONE	228
HE IS THE AUTHOR AND FINISHER OF OUR FAITH	230
HE IS THE LIGHT	232
HE IS AN ANGEL	238
HE IS THE MESSENGER OF THE COVENANT	240
HE IS THE SAVIOR, THE DELIVERER	242
HE IS THE PRESERVER	244
HE IS THE PROPHET	246
HE IS THE LIVING STONE	249
HE IS THE LONGSUFFERING ONE	251
HE IS OUR DEFENDER, PROTECTOR	253
HE IS THE HONORED ONE	258
HE IS THE LORD OF SABAOTH (LORD OF HOSTS)	262
HE IS THE MAN	265
HE IS MERCIFUL	267
HE IS THE ONLY BEGOTTEN SON	269
HE IS THE MESSIAH, THE CHRIST	271
HE IS THE COMMANDER	273
HE IS THE COVENANT	275
HE IS DAVID	278
HE IS THE DAYSPRING (SUNRISE)	282

HE IS THE DAY STAR 284
HE IS THE DEW 286
HE IS THE DISAPPOINTED ONE 288
HE IS THE DOOR (GATE) OF THE SHEEP 290
HE IS OUR RANSOM, OUR SACRIFICE 292
HE IS THE SIN-BEARER 294
HE IS OUR CONFESSOR 297
HE IS THE BEGINNING OF GOD'S CREATION,
   THE CREATOR 299
HE IS THE SUSTAINING ONE 303
HE IS THE BELOVED ONE 305
HE IS THE OBEDIENT ONE 307
HE IS THE BLESSED ONE 309
HE IS THE PATIENT ONE 311
HE IS THE TRUSTWORTHY ONE 313
HE IS THE PERSECUTED, THE AFFLICTED ONE
   (Background considerations)...316
   (Lack of Privacy, Hangers-on) 319
   (Misunderstood, Rejected) 321
   (Criticized, Despised, Ridiculed) 323
   (Laughed at) 325
   (Hated, Falsely Accused)...327
   (Homeless, Deserted, Overtly Opposed) 330
   (Satanic Attack) 333
   (Psychological, Emotional Turmoil, Fear and
      Dread of the Worst Thing Happening)................................335
   (Oppressed, Betrayed) 338
   (Seizure and Arrest, Denounced, Forsaken) 341
   (Falsely Tried, Condemned, Target for Jealousy).....................345
   (Imprisonment, Curiosity Piece) 348
   (Hauled before Authorities, Beaten, Scourged)........................350
   (Mobbed, Hit, Spit upon) 353
   (Disfigured, Marred, Pierced, Crucified)...................................355

 (Property Confiscated, Mocked, Humiliated) 357
 (Cursed, Thirsty) 360
 (Killed, Christ's Attitude) 362
 (Conclusion) 365
HE IS OUR PROVIDER 368
HE IS THE REDEEMER 371
HE IS OUR REFUGE 373
HE IS THE REPROVER 375
HE IS THE RESURRECTED ONE 377
HE IS THE RESURRECTION 379
HE IS THE LAMP 381
HE IS THE REWARDER 383
HE IS THE SAME 385
HE IS THE SECOND MAN (ADAM) 387
HE IS THE SEED OF ABRAHAM 389
HE IS THE SEED OF DAVID 391
HE IS SEPARATE FROM SINNERS 393
HE IS THE BABE 395
HE IS THE YOUNG CHILD, THE BOY JESUS 397
HE IS SHILOH 401
HE IS THE SOIL 405
HE IS THE SON OF ABRAHAM 407
HE IS THE SOVEREIGN ONE (of the Universe) 409
HE VALUES PEOPLE MORE THAN THINGS 411
HE IS THE POSSESSOR OF ALL THINGS 414
HE IS THE POWER OF GOD 420
HE IS THE PREACHER 424
HE IS OUR PROPITIATION (Atoning Sacrifice) 426
HE IS THE SON OF MAN 428
HE IS THE SON OF GOD 431
HE IS GOD 433
HE IS THE SON OF DAVID (The Offspring of David) 435
HE IS HUMBLE ONE 437

Unexpected Transformation / xv

HE IS THE SELF-DENYING ONE	444
HE IS THE LIFE-GIVING SPIRIT	446
HE IS THE LION	448
HE IS THE FEARED ONE	455
HE IS THE FIRSTBORN FROM THE DEAD, THE FIRSTFRUITS OF THE DEAD	457
HE IS THE FORERUNNER	459
HE IS THE FOUNDATION	463
HE IS THE HARMLESS ONE	468
HE IS THE HEAD OF THE CHURCH	470
HE IS THE HEALER	472
HE IS THE GIFT OF GOD	474
HE IS THE BRANCH	476
HE IS THE BREAD OF LIFE	480
HE IS THE BRIDEGROOM	482
HE IS THE BUILDER OF THE HOUSE	489
HE IS THE HEIR	491
HE IS OUR HELPER	493
HE IS THE HORN OF SALVATION	496
HE IS THE HUNGRY ONE	498
HE IS THE INCARNATE ONE	502
HE IS JESUS	506
HE IS THE JOYFUL ONE	508
HE IS OUR GUILT OFFERING	513
HE IS IMMANUEL (GOD WITH US)	515
HE IS THE GIFT-GIVER	517
HE IS THE JUDGE	519
HE IS THE GENTLE ONE	521
HE IS THE LAST ADAM	523
HE IS THE I AM	526
HE THE IS MIGHTY, POWERFUL ONE	528
HE IS ETERNAL	530
HE IS A FATHER	537

HE IS THE GLORIOUS, THE TRANSFIGURED,
  EXALTED, MAJESTIC ONE 540
HE IS THE LORD 549
HE IS THE APOSTLE, THE SENT ONE 553
HE IS THE AMEN 556
HE IS THE ALPHA AND OMEGA, THE FIRST AND
  THE LAST, THE BEGINNING AND THE END 558
HE IS THE MIRACLE-WORKER 560
HE IS ONE WITH THE FATHER 571
HE IS THE OVERSEER (BISHOP OF OUR SOULS) 578
HE IS THE HORN OF DAVID 580
HE IS OUR PASSOVER 582
HE IS THE ANGRY ONE 584
HE IS THE BRIGHTNESS OF THE FATHER'S GLORY 587
HE IS THE COMING ONE 589
HE IS THE CONSOLATION OF ISRAEL 596
HE IS THE DESIRE OF ALL NATIONS 600
HE IS THE ENDURER 602
HE IS THE FAITHFUL ONE 606
HE IS GREATER THAN THE TEMPLE/ LORD OF
  THE SABBATH 611
HE IS OUR HABITATION 613
HE IS THE HOPE OF ISRAEL 618
HE IS THE MINISTER OF THE SANCTUARY 620
HE IS THE ONE 622
HE IS THE PHYSICIAN 624
HE IS THE REAPER 626
HE IS THE REFINER 628
HE IS THE SEALED ONE 635
HE IS THE SEED OF THE WOMAN 637
HE IS THE SOWER 639
HE IS THE STAR 641
HE IS OUR SUBSTITUTE 644

HE IS THE SUFFICIENT ONE	646
HE IS THE SUN OF RIGHTEOUSNESS	648
HE IS OUR SUPPORTER	662
HE IS OUR SURETY	665
HE IS THE TEMPLE	668
HE IS THE TESTATOR	671
HE IS THE TREASURE HOUSE	673
HE IS THE UNDEFILED	675
HE IS THE WARRIOR	678
HE IS THE WORTHY ONE	682
HE IS THE WISE ONE	685
HE IS THE WISDOM OF GOD	689
HE IS THE WEEPING ONE	696
HE IS THE WEARY ONE	698
HE IS THE WORD	700

APPENDICES
   I. PRINCIPLES IN HELPING US DEAL WITH THE
      WORLD SYSTEM AND HOW TO OVERCOME IT 705
   II. ONE WAY TO SET UP A PRAYER DIARY 711
   III. IDENTIFYING YOUR SPIRITUAL GIFT(S) 716
   IV. HELPFUL BOOKS ON ADMINISTRATION 724
   V. HELPFUL BOOKS ON SPIRITUAL WARFARE 725
   VI. EIGHT REASONS WHY WE GET SICK 727
   VII. POINTERS FOR PERSONAL BIBLE STUDY 730
VIII. OUTLINE OF EPHESIANS 6:10-18 732
   IX. ALPHABETICAL LISTING OF CHRIST'S
      CHARACTERISTICS, NAMES AND TITLES 734

REFERENCE LIST 753
ABOUT THE AUTHOR 757

GLOSSARY

GREEK WORDS

agape (ah-GAH-pay). Love of choice.
aitios (AI-tee-os). That which causes something.
akakos (AH-kah-kos). Blameless.
amen (ah-MAYN). So be it.
amiantos (ah-MI-an-tos). Undefiled.
antheoreo (an-theh-or-RE-o). Carefully consider.
antilutron (an-TI-lu-tron). In our place.
apokekrummenon (apo-ke-krum-MEN-on). Having been hidden.
apostolos (a-POS-to-los). A delegate, ambassador, messenger, one who is sent.
arche (ar-KAY). A beginning.
archegos (ar-kay-GOS). One who leads.
arch- (ark-). Prefix denoting what is of worth.
archo (ar-KO). To be first.
archōn (ar-KON). A ruler.
axios (AHKS-i-os). Worthy.
chorizo (kō-RIDS-o). To put asunder, separate, divide.
diakonos (dee-AH-ko-nos). Minister, servant, deacon.
eleos (EH-le-os). Mercy, compassion.
entimos (EN-ti-mos). To be held in honor, prized; hence precious.
episkopos (e-PIS-kō-pōs). Bishop, overseer.
euangelizo (eu-ang-ge-LEEDZ-ō). To bring good news.
eulogeo (eu-loh-GE-ō). To speak well of.

Unexpected Transformation / xix

exagorazo (ex-ah-gō-ADZ-ō). To buy or to buy out.
fileo (fi-LE-oh). Love of emotion/friendship.
ginosko (gi-NŌS-kō). Knowledge.
homologeo (hō-mō-lō-GE-ō). To assent, consent, admit.
huperetes (who-per-EH-tace). An attendant.
huper lutron (WHO-per LU-tron). To pay on behalf of.
hupo eretes (WHO-pō ei-REH-tace). A sub rower, i.e. one who rows under command of the steersman.
kakos (KAH-kos). Bad, evil.
kaleo (kah-LEH-o). To call.
katartizo (ka-tar-TEEDZ-o). To complete thoroughly.
kechorismenos (ke-cho-RIS-men-os). Having been separated.
kerusso (keh-RUS-sō). To herald or proclaim.
kurios (KU-ree-os). Lord.
leitourgus (lay-tur-GUS). A public servant.
logos (LŌ-gos). The spoken word.
luchno (LUCH-nō). Oil-burning lamp.
lutron (LU-tron). A means of loosing.
lutroo (lu-TRO-ō). To redeem.
makarioi (mah-KA-ree-oi). Most blessed.
para (pah-RAH). Beside.
paraklesis (pah-RAH-klay-sis). Consolation.
piskop (PIS-kōp). Bishop, overseer.
sophia (sō-FEE-a). Wisdom.
suntribo (sun-TREE-bō). Utterly.
synesteken (su-NES-tā-ken). To cohere, hold together.
teleios (te-LAY-ōs). Finished, completed.
telos (TE-los). End.
timā (tee-MAY). Highly esteemed.
xeraino (kse-RĪN-o). Whose it is.

HEBREW WORDS

bereeth (ber-EETH). Covenant.

nazar (naw-ZAR) – (fr. nadar, naw-DAR). Root.
siloh (shee-LO). Whose it is.

INDONESIAN WORDS

Biak (BEE-ahk). Island above the island of Numfoor, a small island about 50 miles east of Manokwari.

Citak (CHEE-tuck). Tribal group of the south coast area of Irian Jaya (W. Papua, Indonesia).

Hatam (HA-tahm). Mountain tribal group of the Bird's Head area of Irian Jaya.

Irian Jaya (EAR-ee-ahn JAI-yah). Island of New Guinea (formerly Dutch New Guinea, now West Papua, Indonesia).

Kayagar (KAI-ya-gar). Tribal group of the south coast area of Irian Jaya.

Manokwari (MAH-no-QUA-ree). Major city in the Bird's Head area of Irian Jaya.

Mayor (MY-or). Clan name of national worker from the Biak-Numfoor tribal group of Irian Jaya.

Merauke (Meh-RAU-key). The major city on the south coast of Irian Jaya.

Numfoor (NOOM-for). A small island about 50 miles east of Manokwari.

Octavianus (Ok-TA-vee-AH-nus). An Indonesian evangelist.

Senggo (Seng-GO). Citak village.

Sentani (Sen-TAH-nee). Town on northern coast of Irian Jaya; location of the school for missionary children.

Tamnim (Tahm-NEEM). Asmat-related village across the airstrip from Senggo.

Yali (YAH-lee). Interior mountain tribal group of Irian Jaya.

LATIN WORDS

in = in
caro (KA-row). Flesh (fr. carnis).

ABBREVIATIONS

EMIS	Evangelical Missions Information Service
ETTC	The Erikson-Tritt Theological College
KJV	King James Version
M.K.	Missionary Kid
NIV	New International Version
NKJV	New King James Version
RBMU	Regions Beyond Missionary Union
TEAM	The Evangelical Alliance Mission
TEV	Today's English Version
T.I.U.	Trinity International University
UFM	Unevangelized Fields Mission

OLD TESTAMENT BOOKS

Genesis	Gen.
Exodus	Exod.
Leviticus	Lev.
Numbers	Num.
Deuteronomy	Deut.
Joshua	Josh.
Judges	Jdg.
1 Samuel	1 Sam.

2 Samuel	2 Sam.
1 Kings	1 Kgs.
2 Kings	2 Kgs.
1 Chronicles	1 Chr.
2 Chronicles	2 Chr.
Nehemiah	Neh.
Esther	Esth.
Psalms	Ps.
Proverbs	Prov.
Ecclesiastes	Eccl.
Song of Solomon	Song.
Isaiah	Isa.
Jeremiah	Jer.
Lamentations	Lam
Ezekiel	Ezek.
Daniel	Dan.
Hosea	Hos.
Obadiah	Obad.
Jonah	Jon.
Micah	Mic.
Nahum	Nah.
Habakkuk	Hab.
Zephaniah	Zeph.
Haggai	Hag.
Zechariah	Zech.
Malachi	Mal.

NEW TESTAMENT BOOKS

Matthew	Matt.
Mark	Mk.
Luke	Lk.
John	Jn.
Romans	Rom.
1 Corinthians	1 Cor.
2 Corinthians	2 Cor.
Galatians	Gal.
Ephesians	Eph.
Philippians	Phil.
Colossians	Col.
1 Thessalonians	1 Thess.
2 Thessalonians	2 Thess.
1 Timothy	1 Tim.
2 Timothy	2 Tim.
Titus	Tit.
Philemon	Phlm.
Hebrews	Heb.
James	Jas.
1 Peter	1 Pet.
2 Peter	2 Pet.
1 John	1 Jn.
2 John	2 Jn.
3 John	3 Jn.
Jude	Jude
Revelation	Rev.

SUMMARY

Many, if not the majority of Christians seem to feel little or no responsibility to represent Christ in their daily lives, much less have a conscious desire to become like him. So they will experience a sudden and unexpected transformation when Jesus appears! As we read in 1 John 3:2, "Dear friends, now we are children of God, and what we will be has not yet been made known. But we know that when he [Jesus] appears, we shall be like him, for we shall see him as he is." Since God has determined to make us like Christ, there is a real need to encourage Christians to take a more serious look at what he wants to do in their lives, and reorient their goals to coincide with his.

In Romans 8:29a we read, "For those God foreknew he also predestined to be conformed to the likeness of his Son." And in 1 John 3:2b, "But we know that when he appears, we shall be like him, for we shall see him as he is." These two verses encapsulate God's goal for us from start to finish – to become like Christ.

But often our goals are other than God's as we try to run our lives according to our own desires. When God introduces upsetting circumstances into our lives, first to gain our attention, then to focus on his plan for us in making us like Christ, we often react negatively and find ourselves fighting both our circumstances and God!

Many books about Christ state that we should become like him, but never tell us how. The purpose of this book is to take the reader beyond the "should" to the "how" as is found in Romans 8:28. God is working for our good in <u>all things</u> (all circumstances – vs.28)

Unexpected Transformation / xxvii

according to his purpose – to make us like his Son (vs.29). Therefore, how we respond to those circumstances will show us where we are like Christ and where we are not.

Once I accepted God's goal for my life as my own, and made it my priority to become like Christ, I found my circumstances no longer to be "enemies" to be fought and conquered, but "teachers" from God's hands to be welcomed as they showed me where I was not like Christ and needed to make some changes.

So, in the following lessons, I have focused on the various characteristics of Christ as indicated by his names, titles and actions, defining each one, and showing where Christ demonstrated it. Then I show how someone else from Scripture, church history or among my acquaintances has demonstrated that characteristic, and conclude with the practical question: "How can I demonstrate this characteristic in my life today?" Thus being conformed to the image of Christ becomes a very practical exercise throughout the entirety of the Christian life.

INTRODUCTION

The mystery of "all things"

Of the many books I have read regarding Christ and his characteristics, I have yet to read one that goes beyond basic Christology and God's decree to conform us to Christ's image, to discussing how we are to be conformed to and reflect his image in our daily living.

Not only is this latter consideration important to me personally in regard to my own spiritual growth, but I have found it to be the basic core for discipleship of believers at various levels of spiritual maturity. No matter how "old" we are in Christ, there is always something more we can learn from his character in application to our living for him.

I love to browse in Christian book stores to see what's the latest. Over several Home Assignments I have noticed a multiplication of self-help titles: how to overcome this and that, the Christian and such-and-such a problem, ad infinitum. As I looked over the titles, a thought came to mind: "If Christians would only obey the principles of God's Word, most of these books would never have had to be written! Even more, if they would pay attention to the character of Christ and begin living as he did, many of their problems would disappear altogether. I want to help them do that." That desire has arisen because of what I have seen happen in my own life as well as in the lives of others with whom I have shared these truths.

My experience as an eighth grade basketball player provides one illustration for the need of this kind of study. We were playing the

Unexpected Transformation / xxix

last game of the season against the toughest school in the village and were losing badly. One teammate and I sat on the bench the entire game, except that he got to play the last two minutes, and I got to watch him! I went home hurt, angry and crying. "Why couldn't the coach have let me play in the last two minutes as well? I couldn't have hurt the team any more than we were already hurting!"

When I told my mother what had happened, she opened her Bible to Romans 8:28 and comforted me with the truth of that verse. Somehow, in some unknown way, God was working even through this disappointment to bring good to me. Perhaps it was so that I would know this verse and be able to lean on it for the rest of my life. I felt comforted.

As some hard knocks came my way, Romans 8:28 was always there to comfort and encourage me. "Somehow, in some way," I thought, "this is working together for my good." But how, I had not the slightest clue. "I guess I'll have to wait for later, when things clear up, before I'll know the 'how.'" So I "toughed out" situation after situation in my Christian life with the hope of Romans 8:28 spurring me on. I suspect that many Christians share this same outlook.

But it doesn't have to be this way. My mother had the key in her hand, but didn't connect with it. One day, after six years on the mission field, I made a startling discovery: Romans 8:29 follows Romans 8:28! Once I put the two verses together, then I discovered the "how" that I was looking for and the key to going through trials with joy and hope rather than with a spirit of toughing it out! Romans 8:29 says, "For those God foreknew he also <u>predestined to be conformed to the likeness of his Son</u>, that he might be the firstborn among many brothers" (underlining mine. All following Bible quotations are from the NIV, unless otherwise noted.). The reason for ALL my experiences in life (the "all things" of vs.28), good or bad, is to make me like Christ. With this realization, I was free to take my eyes off my troubling circumstances and focus on God's using them to conform me to the likeness of his Son! Now my circumstances became my teachers from God's hands, showing me where I was NOT like Christ in my reactions. As my teachers, they were no longer a threat to me, but a help in reaching my new goal to become like him.

This attitude toward our circumstances and their purpose in our lives, to mold us into Christ's image, is a perspective that I sense lacking among many Christians; a perspective which, if adopted, could lead them to greater peace between them and themselves, others, and their circumstances; a perspective that would align them with God's great purpose for their lives. Many problems would literally melt away, and Christians would begin growing as never before, if they would only own for themselves God's goal for their lives.

This possibility is very aptly illustrated by a student in my Life of Christ class at ETTC. At the close of the semester, I found that we had some extra class hours left, so I gave the students five lessons on the characteristics of Christ, emphasizing how we should be reflecting them in our daily living. Two days after the lesson, "He Is the Peace-Maker," a student asked permission to give a testimony. He said, "I am so thankful for the lesson you gave us two days ago about Christ as the peace-maker. Yesterday at the office, one of the workers made me so mad that I doubled up my fists and was ready to punch him in the face. But then I remembered how Christ was a peace-maker and how I, as a Christian, should also be a peace-maker. I unclenched my fists, dropped my arms, answered the worker and turned away. The Lord really helped me. THANK YOU for that lesson." This is what I mean by "many problems would literally melt away"; all the problems the student would have had had he gotten into a fight never happened because he refused to fight.

More recently I heard a Youth for Christ missionary to the street gangs of Chicago say, "Twenty-five percent of all Christians feel no responsibility to represent Christ" (Fitzjerrell, 1994). I was unable to check out his source for that percentage, but, looking at the American scene, I would suspect it to be much higher. Nevertheless, his statement further convinced me of the real need for this book and the desire that it be used to reduce that percentage, whatever it is.

One final statement regarding the need for this book is that so many people have encouraged me to complete it and publish it. I surmised by this attitude that they were expressing a felt need.

How it all started

In the fall of 1979 it was our privilege to be part of the helping staff at the Annual Field Conference of the Unevangelized Fields Mission in Irian Jaya, Indonesia. The theme for the conference was "In His Image." On the back of the conference booklet were printed about one hundred names, titles and characteristics of Christ. That captivated my attention and started me thinking: "If God intends to make me like Christ, then these are the things he is looking for in my life! If so, then I had better start paying attention to them and begin working them into my life in order to bring my efforts and character into line with what God wants for me." That evening I encouraged the UFM-ers to do the same, and promised them a life-changing study. I don't know if any of them did it, but I did, and it changed my life and ministry.

Two key verses for this study are Romans 8:29 and 1 John 3:2. In Romans 8:29 we read: "For those God foreknew he also predestined to be conformed to the likeness of his Son, that he might be the firstborn among many brothers." Then in 1 John 3:2, John writes, "Dear friends, now we are children of God, and what we will be has not yet been made known. But we know that when he appears, we shall be like him, for we shall see him as he is."

Here we find God's goal for our lives stated and the time of its completion declared. In his sovereignty he has ordained that we become like Christ, and in his sovereignty he will carry it out. Since the whole process of becoming like Christ rests upon God's sovereignty, the first several lessons in the book lay the foundation of his sovereignty and our response to it. For if God is not sovereign, then his plan to make us like Christ could abort, and we'd be found striving after the wind. So his sovereignty is absolutely essential to the completion of our quest. In fact, he must carry his plan out or we will never see his face! Hebrews 12:14 says, "Make every effort to live in peace with all men and to <u>be holy; without holiness no one will see the Lord</u>" (underlining mine). The only way we will see God is if we are holy, and holiness lies at the very heart of Christ's character. So we have to be made like him if we are to enter God's presence. It will be done. We read in Philippians 1:6, "Being confident of this, that he who began a good work in you <u>will carry it on to completion</u> until the day of Christ Jesus" (underlining mine). We are going to be made like him. The only choice we have in the matter is whether or not we will work together with God now toward the accomplishment of his goal for us. Some of us will be in for quite a "character shock" when we are changed into Christ's likeness at his coming.

As I read other passages of Scripture, God's plan kept coming into focus. Consider the following in addition to the two mentioned above: "Then God said, 'Let us make man in our image, in our likeness, and let them rule over the fish of the sea and the birds of the air, over the livestock, over all the earth, and over all the creatures that move along the ground.' So God created man in his own image, in the image of God he created him; male and female he created them" (Gen.1:26,27).

God originally made us in his image so that we could have fellowship with him and be a partner with him in governing his creation. This likeness was marred when Adam and Eve sinned, and God has been working ever since then to restore that likeness in our lives. Trench supports this statement, saying, "Sanctification is a process, step by step, by which a person is fitted for the spiritual world into which he has just entered, and in which he now lives and moves; this process is the return to the original character and image of God" (Trench n.d., 34).

In Psalm 17:15 (NKJV), the Psalmist declared: "As for me, I will see Your face in righteousness; I shall be satisfied <u>when I awake in Your likeness</u>" (underlining mine).

Paul says the same thing in 1 Corinthians 15:49: "And just as we have borne the likeness of the earthly man, so shall we bear the likeness of the man from heaven." His purpose in ministry was to form Christ in his converts. He wanted them, more than anything else, to reflect the character of Christ in their lives. So he wrote to the Galatian Christians as "my dear children, for whom I am again in the pains of childbirth until Christ is formed in you" (Gal.4:19).

In 2 Corinthians 3:18 Paul describes the daily process of change that should be taking place and the certainty of that transformation at the coming of Christ. "And we, who with unveiled faces all reflect the Lord's glory, are being transformed into his likeness with ever increasing glory, which comes from the Lord, who is the Spirit." He writes in Colossians 3:9,10: "Do not lie to each other, since you have taken off your old self with its practices and have put on the new self, which is being renewed in knowledge in the image of its Creator." To the Philippians he wrote: "But our citizenship is in heaven. And we eagerly await a Savior from there, the Lord Jesus Christ, who, by the power that enables him to bring everything under his control, will transform our lowly bodies so that they will be like his glorious body" (Phil.3:20,21).

As we look at the Lord Jesus Christ, we are looking at God's blueprint for our lives, his plan for our character. The better we know the Lord Jesus, the clearer will be God's purpose for us, and the easier it will be for us to align our purpose in living with that of God's. Jesus said in Luke 6:40, "A student is not above his teacher, but everyone who is fully trained will be like his teacher." So it stands that the more we are "with" Christ, learning from him, the more like him we will become. This is exactly what God wants. In that path lies a unique freedom from the worries and frustrations that are so common among humanity, a source of victory that I have not found elsewhere, and a blessed sense of the presence of God. This is the underlying answer to the "why" of every problem, and I have found it to be a giant step toward greater spiritual maturity and daily victory when I apply it.

An interesting side benefit of this awareness in my life was a consciousness of the presence of God. For many years I had heard and read about practicing the presence of God, and from time to time I would try it. I wanted to be aware of God's presence. But for me, nothing worked. As soon as I'd get up from my chair and go about the busyness of the day, I wouldn't give God another thought until grace at mealtime! Then I'd feel guilty about not practicing his presence. I finally gave it up as a bad deal and didn't try it any more. Shortly after I began this character study of Christ I discovered to my utter amazement that I was conscious of God's presence in a way I had never experienced before, without even trying! I didn't have to practice his presence; I was experiencing it!

One thing needs to be said about the importance of the role of the Holy Spirit in our becoming like Christ. We read in John 16:13a, "But when he, the Spirit of truth, comes, he will guide you into all truth." The word, "truth," I believe, includes "the character of Christ" since he said of himself, "I am the … truth" (Jn.14:6). So as the Holy Spirit leads us into the truth, he will also be leading us into an understanding and application of the character of Christ in our lives. We continue reading (16:13b,14): "He will not speak on his own; he will speak only what he hears, and he will tell you what is yet to come. He will bring glory to me by taking from what is mine and making it known to you." Thus it is clear that our becoming like Christ depends upon the illuminating work of the Holy Spirit in our lives, teaching us to observe his character and then how to go about adopting it as our own (see again 2 Cor.3:18).

Does it work?

For me personally this has been a life-changing and ministry-creating study. The life changes do not come automatically upon studying the characteristics of Christ, but come about by applying them in our daily living. These changes are the result of faith in accepting God's goal for our lives (to make us like Christ), then determining to work together with him to accomplish it.

Yet I have found that in various situations, even though I <u>know</u> the principles put forth in this book, I am still often reluctant to commit myself to them. Even though I <u>know</u> how I should respond to these situations, often I choose to react in an un-Christ-like manner. So the Lord has to keep repeating those lessons for me until I learn to respond properly. Like all things in the Christian life, I have to really <u>want</u> to do it before I will do it. This study has given me much greater motivation than I had before to <u>want</u> to do it.

Now I find that I must review each characteristic of Christ at greater leisure to begin working them into my life in a more definite way. It's called spiritual discipline.

Several people have come to me to share how the Lord has changed their lives as they have applied what they have studied from the characteristics of Christ. Still others have shared testimony to other blessings they have received through this study. All of this input tells me that "it works."

My prayer is that, as you pursue and apply the truths of this study, your life will change as well as you delightfully discover your life reflecting more and more of Christ's character.

One additional NOTE:

To date I have discovered over three hundred characteristics, names and titles of Christ which I have written up in a devotional format. Each characteristic of Christ was considered from Scripture, followed by an example, where possible, of someone else from the Bible, church history or from among our acquaintances who has already demonstrated that characteristic, and concluded by how we can demonstrate it right now, today.

I wrote up each characteristic using the following outline in general:

1. Study questions to reflect upon.
2. Core questions to be answered by the text:
   a) Define the characteristic and answer the question, "How did Christ demonstrate this characteristic in his life?"
   b) [Where possible] How has someone else demonstrated this characteristic?
   c) How can I demonstrate this characteristic in my life, today?
3. APPLICATION. Each lesson is closed with an APPLICATION section to encourage the reader to put into practice what he has just studied.

In the process of considering what I have listed as Christ's "characteristics," I have become aware of the fact that not all of them can be reflected equally. Some can and must be reflected fully (such as his holiness, meekness, etc.); others can only be reflected in part (such as his being the only way to the Father. We cannot be the way to the Father as he is, but can be ways for others to Christ, hence opening for them the way to the Father); and still others (such as Christ as the persecuted one) can only be reflected indirectly, as persecution is not something we seek in order to reflect him, but seek to reflect his attitude in persecution.

So for the convenience of the reader, I have designated these three categories with the title of each characteristic as follows: [a]Characteristics we must fully reflect; [b]Characteristics we can reflect in part; and [c]Characteristics we can only indirectly reflect.

A parting thought:

In regard to our lives and ministries, my main concern is this: If we misrepresent our Master, others will get a false impression of who he really is and their faith in him or about him will be directly affected. We need to concern ourselves with being true reflectors of his character, so that others will see him in us as clearly as possible and be drawn to him. Now, let's get started.

DAY 1
GOD'S LOVING SOVEREIGNTY

◆

QUESTIONS TO THINK ABOUT:

1. How big is your God?
    a. Is there anything too hard for him to do?
    b. Is there anything too small for him to take notice of?
    c. Is it possible for man or Satan to frustrate his plans?
    d. Can situations get "out of control" as far as God is concerned?
2. How did God prove his love for us?
3. How do you think God's sovereignty and love work together in a person's life?

Genesis 1:1 declares, "In the beginning God created the heavens and the earth." According to Hebrews 11:3 he created all things by his own word, not by anything visible. Anything that came into existence was planned and ordered by God. In fact, the very continuation of the world is dependent upon his word, and its total devastation will be at his word. We read of this in 2 Peter 3:5-7: "But they deliberately forget that long ago by God's word the heavens existed and the earth was formed out of water and by water. By these waters also the world of that time was deluged and destroyed. By the same word the present heavens and earth are reserved for fire, being kept for the day of judgment and destruction of ungodly men."

Therefore we conclude that God is more powerful than all that he has created.

In Luke 1:37 the angel Gabriel says, "For nothing is impossible with God." This statement means that he can do anything he wants, when he wants, and how he wants. There is no obstacle too big for him to overcome, no situation too difficult for him to handle, no man he cannot govern. Solomon says in Proverbs 21:1, "The king's heart is in the hand of the LORD; he directs it like a watercourse wherever he pleases." In Daniel 4:28-37 we see him humbling Nebuchadnezzar, the most powerful king of his day, making him insane for a period of time. Even the nations are said to be no more than a drop in the bucket and counted as dust on the scales in his sight (Isa.40:15)! At the dedication of the Temple, Solomon prayed, "But will God really dwell on earth? The heavens, even the highest heaven, cannot contain you. How much less this temple I have built" (1 Kgs.8:27).

From this we conclude that God is "bigger" than all things, including man.

God also has absolute authority over all things. According to Daniel 2:21, "He changes times and seasons; he sets up kings and deposes them. He gives wisdom to the wise and knowledge to the discerning." In Ephesians 1:11 Paul writes: "In him we were also chosen, having been predestined according to the plan of him who works out everything in conformity with the purpose of his will." God has no need to call together a council of angels to give him advice as to what he should do, neither does he seek counsel from men. God is absolutely sovereign.

But then we read in Romans 5:8, "But God demonstrates his own love for us in this: While we were still sinners, Christ died for us." The sovereign God who is more powerful than all he has created, who is "bigger" than all things and who has absolute authority over everything, loved you and me enough to die for us in the person of the Lord Jesus Christ, to reconcile us to himself even though we were his enemies (Rom.5:10)!

A good illustration of this is found in the Kayagar tribe of Irian Jaya, Indonesia. These men are renowned for their expertise in hunting wild pig. Now hunting wild pig can be very dangerous to one's health! They have this nasty habit of circling around and attacking the unwary hunter from behind. The Kayagar know this, so hunt warily, keeping a good eye on the trail behind them.

Jesus says in John 15:13, "Greater love has no one than this, that he lay down his life for his friends." Now let's say there are three Kayagar men hunting a wild pig. From the spoor they know he's a big one! They keep a wary eye on the trail behind them while they track their quarry. Suddenly, from close behind, the pig breaks cover and charges, all 250 pounds of him. The three hunters, unnerved by the ferocity of the attack, drop their weapons and run. But the pig has the momentum and quickly closes on them. Suddenly, one of the men stops and turns around. The pig crashes into him in a flurry of tusk and limb and the man dies. But his two friends escape. "Greater love has no one than this, that he lay down his life for his friends."

Let's bring this man back again and put him in another situation. Here he is, walking through the jungle on his way to a friendly village. Suddenly he spies three enemies, who, by their actions, are obviously stalking a wild pig. He hides himself, not desiring the hunt to change from the pig to his head, and watches from behind the flanged roots of a big tree. Suddenly, the huge pig charges the hunters from behind, catching them off guard. They drop their weapons and run for their lives. As they pass the tree behind which their enemy is hidden, he sees their terror-widened eyes, hears their screams and smells their sweat. He knows how they feel and before even taking time to think he jumps out from behind the tree and plants himself squarely between them and the charging boar. Soon it's all over. He is dead, and his three enemies escape with their lives. "Greater love has no one than this, that he lay down his life for his friends," Jesus said. But here is a man who laid down his life for his enemies! What kind of love is that? It is the kind of love that God has for us, *agape* love, the love of choice, based upon his own will rather than our character. This love says, "I choose to love you for your benefit, period."

Thus we see God's sovereignty and love inextricably woven together, the one not operating apart from the other. Whatever he sovereignly chooses to do in the life of his child is <u>always</u> done in the context of his love for that child. In his sovereignty, he will do nothing that would violate his love, and in his love, he will do nothing that would violate his sovereignty. Emphasizing the one characteristic to the exclusion of the other will lead us into heresy, for a loving, grandfatherly God who is not sovereign, will be a permissive God. This view of God will lead us into careless living. On the other hand, a sovereign, tyrannical God without love will lead us into legalism.

Whatever God sovereignly chooses to do in our lives is done in the context of his great love for us. Thus in all things, we can fully trust him to do that which is right and best for us, and in turn, we can respond to him with love and submission to his will.

APPLICATION:

1. What steps do you need to take, if any, to correct your faulty or incomplete concept of who God is in his relationship to you personally? You might begin by meditating on such verses as Jer.29:11; Lk.1:37; Phil.1:6; Eph.1:3-6; Rom.5:8; and 1 Jn.4:9 for a start.

2. What do his sovereignty and love mean to you in your own life?

DAY 2
GOD'S GOAL FOR HUMANITY

QUESTIONS TO THINK ABOUT:

1. What is God's goal for humanity?
2. As Christ reflects God's glory here on earth, who should be reflecting Christ's, and how?

3. From whom do we learn how to respond to life?
4. What or who is God's blueprint for our lives?
5. What things can we experience that will not be used by God to accomplish his goal for our lives?

From the fall of Adam and Eve into sin, God's primary goal for us has been to restore us to his moral image which was marred by the fall. So from among all humanity, he has chosen you and me as the objects of his love and grace in order to conform us into the image of his Son. In Romans 8:29a we read, "For those God foreknew he also predestined to be conformed to the likeness of his Son."

Just as God ordained Christ to be his image (Col.1:15; Heb.1:3; Jn.14:9), so he has ordained us to be Christ's image. As Christ reflected God's glory, so we are to reflect Christ's glory. How? By becoming like him. You've heard the saying, "Like father, like son." This is not only true physically, but even more so in terms of personality characteristics. A child learns how to face life and react to it from his parents.

I once heard a story about a mother who always taught her children to pray first whenever faced with a problem. One day the mother was all a-flutter and wringing her hands over something that had happened. Her four-year-old daughter came to her and asked, "Mommy, shouldn't we pray first?"

Even so, we must learn from Christ how to face life and react to it. When we examine his character, we are looking at God's blueprint for ours. When others see us, can they say, "Like Christ, like Christian"?

God has determined to make us like Christ, and, in love, ordains or arranges our circumstances so as to mold us into his image. It is from this fact that Romans 8:28 derives its meaning. All things work for our good because they are tools in the hand of God to mold us into Christ's image.

For example, you no doubt have heard of Joni Eareckson Tada, paralyzed from the shoulders down because of a swimming accident. In her book <u>A Step Further</u>, she describes an evening social in her home. She was sitting on the couch looking very normal – no different than any of the other young people in the room. As she was enjoying everything going on in the room, her friend Betsy turned to her and asked her how she felt being on the couch. "You know what's really interesting?" she replied, "In the short time I've been in this position on the couch, ... I can see how easy it would be for me to forget God if I were on my feet" (Eareckson, 1978, 74).

So, in love, God has permitted that means or circumstance in Joni's life that will keep her "on target" toward becoming like Christ, <u>and</u> he has given her the grace needed to accept her situation.

In our daily lives, the interruptions, nuisances, irksome personalities of other people, frustrations, disappointments, illnesses, accidents, etc. are <u>all</u> permitted by our sovereign, loving God with one main purpose in mind: to glorify himself by making us into the image of his Son. And when you get right down to it, what better gift could he give us than to be like Christ? Is this what you want?

APPLICATION: Pause to thank God for the way he's working in your life to make you like Christ, and covenant to work together with him to accomplish this work.

DAY 3
OUR REACTION TO GOD'S GOAL FOR HUMANITY

◆

QUESTIONS TO THINK ABOUT:

1. What, if anything, can frustrate the accomplishment of God's goal for our lives?

2. What will we lose if we refuse to work together with him to accomplish his goal for us?

3. What will happen if we try to run from his goal?

God's goal for us is to make us into the image of his Son. In his sovereignty, he has determined that this will come about. In 1 John 3:2b we read, "But we know that when he appears, we shall be like him, for we shall see him as he is."

Now what is our reaction to this goal? We still have a free will and a sinful nature. We can choose to work together with God toward his goal for us, or we can resist what he wants to do in our lives. If we resist, we will rob ourselves not only of blessings here on earth, but also of our rewards and responsibilities in heaven. 1 Corinthians 3:11-15 clearly states this choice and its results.

But look also at Luke 19:11-27. Here we find ten servants given a certain amount of money to use wisely while their master was away. All had the same opportunity, but all didn't use their money in the same way. When their master returned, he rewarded his servants according to their faithfulness. One servant gained ten times as much as he was given; he was given authority over ten cities. Another gained five times as much, and was given authority over five cities.

But then there was this other servant. I don't know what possessed him, but his response is <u>not</u> the way to get ahead with one's boss, nor to keep one's job. He said in essence, "Here is the money you gave me. I've kept it safe for you, for I was afraid of you, because you're a hard man, a thief and a swindler!" Like us, this servant had a choice whether or not to work with his master. He chose to do nothing, and his choice robbed him both of his <u>reward</u> and his <u>job</u>, and his potential responsibilities were given to another who was more faithful.

Like these servants, my wife and I also had a choice to make regarding our "stewardship." Our second term as missionaries in Irian Jaya, Indonesia, was very hard. We were getting a pretty rough going over and I wanted out. Had anyone given me a one-way ticket home, I'd have taken it.

But God kept encouraging us through his Word and through people's letters to stick it out and let his purpose be accomplished in our lives. Had we chosen to leave, we would have had to learn the same lessons here in the States that he wanted to teach us there, for God's goal is the same for us no matter where we are. But someone else would have been given our responsibilities and reward. However, we chose to stay and learn the lessons God wanted to teach us so that we'd become more like Christ and experience eventual blessings. One of those blessings was hearing of fifty-five Citak believers burning their fetishes and making the final break with Satan. Our hearts were filled with joy and praise to the Lord for this victory and for the privilege we had in being a part of it. Where would this blessing have been had we quit?

So it would be to our benefit, knowing these things, if we'd work together with God in his plan for us, cooperating with him as he desires to make us into Christ's image, so that we also will have blessings now and a full reward in heaven.

APPLICATION:

1. We can endure almost anything if our goal is clear. What is your goal for your life?

2. Does your goal line up with God's goal for you?

3. If not, then by faith declare his goal yours and agree to work together with him to accomplish it. It will change your life, and that all to the good!

Having considered the sovereignty of God in the process of our becoming like Christ, we're ready now to turn to the various names, titles and characteristics of Christ and how we can reflect each one in our daily lives.

DAY 4
ᵃHE IS THE IMAGE OF GOD

QUESTIONS TO THINK ABOUT:

1. If you are an "image" of someone, what do people expect to see?
2. Some people believe that God's image in mankind was lost at the Fall; others that it was merely marred; still others that the Fall made no difference. How do you respond to these three views?
3. Why is being in his image so important?

In Colossians 1:15 we read, "He is the image of the invisible God." Again in Hebrews 1:3a, "The Son is the radiance of God's glory and the exact representation of his being." And he said to his disciples in John 14:9b, "Anyone who has seen me has seen the Father." What the Father said, he said (Jn.12:50); what the Father did, he did (Jn.5:19). "Like Father, like son" finds no truer example than in Christ.

When God created man, he created him in his image (Gen.1:27). Adam was a perfect reflection of both God's glory and character. God could see himself in Adam and Eve and feel satisfied, fulfilled. When Adam and Eve sinned, that perfect reflection was lost physically and greatly marred spiritually. Then we read in Genesis 5:3, "When Adam lived 130 years, he had a son in his own likeness, in his own image" (underlining mine). According to J. Richard Fugate (What the Bible Says About Child Training, Foundation for Biblical Research, 1980, p.48), "Mankind no longer exists in the state of original creation, but has been altered according to the image of corrupted humanity. This state has been perpetuated through birth." Thus mankind is now reproduced in the "likeness of Adam," rather than in the likeness of God (cf. 1 Cor.15:49).

Unexpected Transformation / 9

Ever since the Fall, God has been at work to restore men and women to his likeness, physically and spiritually.

Physically

1 Corinthians 15:49
"And just as we have borne the likeness of the earthly man, so we shall bear the likeness of the man from heaven." (The context of this verse is concerning the resurrection body – vs.35-53).

Philippians 3:20,21
"But our citizenship is in heaven. And we eagerly await a Savior from there, the Lord Jesus Christ, who, by the power that enables him to bring everything under his control, will transform our lowly bodies so that they will be like his glorious body."

Spiritually

Romans 8:29a
"For those God foreknew he also predestined to be conformed to the likeness of his Son."

Colossians 3:9,10
"Do not lie to each other, since you have taken off your old self with its practices and have put on the new self, which is being renewed in knowledge in the image of its Creator."

2 Corinthians 3:18
"And we, who with unveiled faces all reflect the Lord's glory, are being transformed into his likeness with ever-increasing glory, which comes from the Lord, who is the Spirit."

We reflect Christ's image by becoming like him. To become like him, we must study his character and adopt it as our own. God is more than willing to help us in this quest. In fact, he has gone so far as to guarantee its success! As the Apostle John writes: "But we know that when he appears, we shall be like him, for we shall see him as he is" (1 Jn.3:2b).

Whose image do you reflect right now, Adam's or Christ's?

Let's diligently seek to be transformed into Christ's image.

APPLICATION: As indicated in the Introduction, becoming like Christ is not a blind exercise, but something concrete that we can "see." What we need to do is <u>define</u> the characteristic/name/title of Christ, see how he demonstrated them, then ask ourselves the question: "How can I demonstrate them in my life – today?"

Hopefully, the following devotionals/studies will either corroborate or add to what you discover on your own if you choose to go that route.

DAY 5
[a]HE IS OUR EXAMPLE

QUESTIONS TO THINK ABOUT:

1. What does it mean to be an example?
2. Why are examples important to us?
3. What are some results from being a bad example?
4. What are some results from being a good example?
5. Is it egotistical to say, "Follow my example and you will follow Christ"?

During our time as house parents at TEAM's Hostel for missionary children, one complaint often heard was, "Quit copying me! Uncle Bob, he's always copying what I'm doing. Tell him to stop it." To which we often replied, "Well, that really is a compliment to you that he <u>wants</u> to do what you're doing; for that means that someone else thinks that what you are doing is good."

In John 13:2-15 we read of Jesus washing the feet of his disciples. Picking up the story at verse 12 we read, "When he had finished washing their feet, he put on his clothes and returned to his place. 'Do you understand what I have done for you?' he asked them. 'You call me "Teacher and "Lord," and rightly so, for that is what I am. Now that I, your Lord and Teacher, have washed your feet, you also should wash one another's feet. I have set you an example that you should do as I have done for you.'"

In 1 Peter 2:18-21 we read that Christ left us an example, that we should follow in his steps. The context of this verse has to do with the Christian's attitude toward suffering wrongfully. So often we want to strike back, hurt in return, get an eye-for-an-eye. Yet this was not Christ's attitude. He suffered willingly knowing that it was God's will and that it would provide our salvation. Countless thousands were brought to a saving faith through the unjust deaths of thousands of Christians in the Roman arenas – Christians who accepted their fate without malice, revenge or harsh words toward their persecutors; Christians who fully believed their God and had entrusted their souls to him, even as Christ did (1 Pet.2:22,23).

Paul extends this concept of being an example to all of us. In Philippians 3:17 he says, "Join with others in following my example, brothers, and take note of those who live according to the pattern we gave you." And again in 1 Corinthians 11:1 he says, "Follow my example, as I follow the example of Christ." In Philippians 4:9 he also says, "The things which you learned and received and heard and saw in me, these do, and the God of peace will be with you."

Can we encourage other Christians to do this? Are we following Christ's example in such a way that we can urge others to follow our example and thereby follow Christ? This is not an impossible thing to do. In fact, it is Scripturally necessary for older Christians to provide just such an example to the younger ones (see Tit.2:1-10). Example is the greatest teaching tool we have. We can preach and we can teach. But until others see it work in our own lives, they will remain unaffected and unconvinced. Paul commanded Timothy: "Don't let anyone look down on you because you are young, but set an example for the believers in speech, in life, in love, in faith and in purity" (1 Tim.4:12). This is faith exemplified by works which, in turn, prove to others the reality of that which we say we possess.

As we look at our own lives, can we say, "What I see there, I want others to follow?" Or do we conclude, "You had better not look at me for your example, but at someone else." Well, whether we want to be or not, we all are an example to someone, good or bad. Our example will cause that one to stumble or grow. We cannot live in a vacuum of neutrality that will not affect others. <u>Every day we influence someone, and we are responsible for the example that we set</u>.

What kind of example are you offering for others to follow?

APPLICATION: Jot down one area where you want to become an example to others, and how you will do it. There may be other areas you want to hit as time goes by, but concentrate on only one at a time.

DAY 6
[b]HE IS THE WAY

QUESTIONS TO THINK ABOUT:

1. How can a person's life be a "way" to something?
2. Jesus Christ is "the Way" for the world to the Father; our lives are "the way" for the world to whom?
3. What are the characteristics of a road in disrepair and in good repair? How do our lives reflect these two conditions?

In John 14:6 Jesus told his disciples, "I am the way and the truth and the life. No one comes to the Father except through me."

As we look at Christ, we see a clear road to the Father. There is nothing that would hinder anyone along the way. But as others look at us, what kind of a way do they see: a cluttered way filled with the debris of hypocrisy, double standards, hate, bad habits, immorality, compromise and other such things? Perhaps they have responded to what they see in Christ and begin to move closer toward faith in him, but then begin to stumble and trip over the debris in our lives until they say, "If <u>this</u> is the way, forget it! This is <u>not</u> what I want."

Or do they see a clear road to Christ in our lives? A road not perfect, mind you, but generally uncluttered and attempts being honestly made to get rid of what little clutter there still is. This kind of way will allow many to come to Christ unhindered and we, in turn, will be greatly blessed.

Here is something to think about: Just as Jesus Christ is the way to the Father for the world, so we are the way to Jesus Christ for those around us. In Acts 1:8 Jesus said, "But you will receive power when the Holy Spirit comes on you; and you will be my witnesses in Jerusalem, and in all Judea and in Samaria, and to the ends of the earth."

God has ordained it that through our witness, others will come to Christ, and in coming to Christ be able to approach the Father.

I saw this in my mother at an early age. She loved the Lord and desired to live only for him. Her gracious life was a main factor in drawing me to the Lord. I didn't see hypocrisy or other negative traits in her that would hinder me from coming to him. So when I was ready, there was no hindrance whatever to keep me back.

But the choice of what our "way" is going to be like is ours to make. Romans 12:1,2 brings this truth into focus: "Therefore, I urge you, brothers, in view of God's mercy, to offer your bodies as living sacrifices, holy and pleasing to God – this is your spiritual act of worship. Do not conform any longer to the pattern of this world, but be transformed by the renewing of your mind. Then you will be able to test and approve what God's will is – his good, pleasing and perfect will."

Again in Psalm 119:9,11 we read, "How can a young man keep his way pure? By living according to your word... . I have hidden your word in my heart that I might not sin against you."

And again, in 2 Timothy 3:16,17, Paul tells us that "All Scripture is God-breathed and is useful for teaching, rebuking, correcting and training in righteousness, so that the man of God may be thoroughly equipped for every good work."

You might say that God's Word is like our "repair manual" telling us how we can repair our "way." Our applying the principles of that "manual" will determine what our "way" is like as others try to travel it, whether they will trip and stumble over the debris there, or have a relatively smooth path to the Lord. What is your "way" like?

APPLICATION:

1. What do you need to do to make your "way" unobstructed for others to follow? Perhaps, as a start, you might want to list the things in your life that may be "obstructions" (a sharp tongue, judgmental spirit, etc.) for those wanting to come to Christ. Confess them to the Lord, asking for His help in overcoming them, so that there will be nothing in your life that would hinder others from coming to Him.

2. How can the Word of God help you in this process? With a Bible concordance check out verses that deal with the areas of your concern and ask yourself how they apply to the issue(s) you're struggling with.

DAY 7
bHE IS THE TRUTH

QUESTIONS TO THINK ABOUT:

1. When is it right to tell a lie?

2. What does it mean to live according to truth?

3. What happens when we say one thing and mean something else?

4. When we lie: with whom do we align ourselves? to what "family" are we introduced?

5. Can God ever lie?

In John 14:6 Jesus said, "I am ... the truth." Whatever Jesus Christ did or said, it was true. No man could accuse him of sin and make it stick. Christ said in Matthew 5:37, "Simply let your 'Yes' be 'Yes,' and your 'No,' 'No'; anything beyond this comes from the evil one." Are you living according to truth?

While on home assignments, Amber and I did a lot of interstate driving. Every so often there would appear, between clumps of trees, a car with special markings. At that point, a strange thing happened: people began driving "according to truth" – 65 mph! But what happened when they turned the bend in the road and the police car was out of sight? Accelerators were depressed and truth was forgotten.

One thing that angered us on the mission field was the attempt of parents to use us to get their children to behave. "If you don't sit down and be quiet, the nurse will give you a shot!" An empty threat. No way would the nurse give a shot to a healthy child. But here in the States we find the same thing in different dress: "If you do that again, I'll spank you!" So the child, naturally rebellious, does it again, to which the parent replies, "I thought I told you not to do that again! I'm really going to whack you!" But nothing happens, so the child does it again, upon which the exasperated parent cries, "You're a bad child; go to your room!" In both cases the parents were not living according to truth, but according to falsehood.

What will their children learn from this? First of all, that their parents cannot be trusted to do what they say (which bodes ill for communication of spiritual truth to the child), and secondly, lying is a normal way to respond to life and to get people to do what you want.

A child was playing with a toy truck in his yard. When he was called to come into the house for something, he looked out the window in time to see one of his friends enter the yard and head toward the truck. "Watch out!" he hollered from the window, "There's a spider in that truck!" Upon which the other child withdrew his hand and backed away; and the child in the house smiled, saying to himself: "It worked!"

This situation of living in falsehood places us in dangerous company. In Revelation 21:8 we read, "But the cowardly, the unbelieving, the vile, the murderers, the sexually immoral, those who practice magic arts, the idolaters and <u>all liars</u> (underlining mine) – their place will be in the fiery lake of burning sulfur. This is the second death."

It also introduces us to the wrong family. In John 8:44 Jesus says, "You belong to your father, the devil, and you want to carry out your father's desire. He was a murderer from the beginning, not holding to the truth, for there is no truth in him. When he lies, he speaks his native language, for <u>he is</u> a liar and <u>the father</u> of <u>lies</u>" (underlining mine). So when we lie, it is as if we have excused ourselves from our Father's presence and gone down to visit in the Devil's house for a while. Dare we do that?!

No! If we are to be effective in our living and in our witness, we <u>must</u> live according to truth, i.e. according to the Word of God which <u>is</u> truth (Jn.17:17). Others must know that when we say something, it is always true (as far as humanly possible). Children must see that their parents practice what they preach. I cannot remember a time when my parents ever lied to me. What they said, they did. I could always believe them. The unsaved must also see the same in the lives of the saved. This will draw them to the Savior.

It is impossible for God to lie (Tit.1:2; Heb.6:18). How then, as his children, do we think we have the right to do it? Are you living according to truth?

APPLICATION: In what areas are you not living according to truth?

For instance, do you: fudge on your income tax reporting? color the facts in your favor? say things you really don't intend to follow through on? disobey laws you feel are unreasonable? make empty threats to your children?

Pay attention this week to these and other areas and consciously try to align what you do and say with the truth, with what would be acceptable to God were he visibly present.

DAY 8
ᵇHE IS THE LIFE

QUESTIONS TO THINK ABOUT:

1. What are the signs of physical life?
2. What are the signs of spiritual life?
3. If you were experiencing the full, abundant life that Christ came to give us, what do you think your life would be like?

Again in John 14:6 Jesus says, "I am ... the life." In John 6:35 he says, "I am the Bread of Life." In John 4:10 he offered the Samaritan woman living water unto eternal life (vs.14). And again he said, "I have come that they [his sheep] may have life, and have it to the full" (Jn.10:10b).

As I think of physical life, there seem to be at least five indications that prove the presence of life: (1) the desire for nourishment, (2) growth, (3) movement, (4) the ability to communicate, and (5) the ability to reproduce.

Christ fulfilled each of these indications of physical life: he desired nourishment (Mk.11:12), grew (Lk.2:40), moved (Lk.2:42,43), communicated (Lk.2:46), and had the ability to reproduce (assumed on the basis of his being human, though he never married).

In the spiritual realm, he was also alive, desiring spiritual nourishment, thus spending time with his Father (Lk.5:16); growing (Lk.2:52), ministering (spiritual "movement" – Lk.4:14,15); communicating (Jn.14:9); and reproducing spiritual children (Jn.3:3; 19:38,39). It is this area of life to which we want to pay particular attention.

One day a woman came to me with great concern reflected in her face. "Have I committed the unpardonable sin?" she asked. "Am I really saved?" [**NOTE:** The very fact that she was concerned about her salvation proved that she hadn't lost it, for, according to Hebrews 6:4-6, those who have been enlightened about and then rejected Christ not only cannot repent but don't even want to!] Sometimes when Christians are out of fellowship with the Lord, they begin to doubt and question their salvation. Occasionally, unsaved people who think they are already Christians go through such experiences that they begin to question, "Am I really saved?" That is a good question, and it should cause them to look for indications of spiritual life within them, which, if there, should give them assurance, and if not, should drive them to the Lord in repentance seeking salvation. These indications are the same as we see in Christ's life.

If we have true spiritual life, there will be hunger and thirst for the Word of God. Peter says in 1 Peter 2:2,3, "Like newborn babies, crave pure spiritual milk, so that by it you may grow up in your salvation, now that you have tasted that the Lord is good."

Secondly, there will be growth. Again Peter writes in 2 Peter 1:5-8, "For this very reason, make every effort to add to your faith goodness; and to goodness, knowledge; and to knowledge, self-control; and to self-control, perseverance; and to perseverance, godliness; and to godliness, brotherly kindness; and to brotherly kindness, love. For if you possess these qualities in increasing measure [growth], they will keep you from being ineffective and unproductive in your knowledge of our Lord Jesus Christ."

Thirdly, there is spiritual movement: ministry. After Jesus washed his disciples' feet, he told them that they should do the same for one another (Jn.13:14), and Paul tells us that we have received spiritual gifts from the Holy Spirit in order to minister to each other (1 Cor.12:7). A desire to minister is one good indication of spiritual life.

Fourthly, there is the ability to communicate. There are two kinds of communication we become involved in: communication with God (prayer, see DAY 24), and communication with others (our witness, see DAY 25). Our desire to pray to God and our desire to tell others about him demonstrate the presence of spiritual life.

And fifthly, there is reproduction. Christ prayed in John 17:20, "My prayer is not for them alone. I pray also for those who will believe in me through their message." Also in 3 John 4, the Apostle John says, "I have no greater joy than to hear that my children are walking in the truth."

From our witness, others will come to know the Lord and be born into his family. Apart from the witness of the Holy Spirit (Rom.8:16), one of the greatest assurances of our salvation (proof of our spiritual life) is found in our witness to others and seeing that life take hold in them.

Christ came that we might have life. By this fivefold test, are you spiritually alive?

APPLICATION: Using the five-fold test for life, how do you measure up?

1. Do you desire spiritual nourishment?   Yes ___ No ___
2. Are you growing spiritually?   Yes ___ No ___
3. Are you involved in some kind of ministry?   Yes ___ No ___
4. How is your communication?
    a) Do you pray regularly?   Yes ___ No ___
    b) Do you read the Word regularly?   Yes ___ No ___
    c) Do you desire to be a witness?   Yes ___ No ___
5. Are you reproducing spiritual children?   Yes ___ No ___
    Occasionally ___

NOTE: Not all these indications will be present to the same degree just as a child is not expected to function in every way as an adult. But as long as there is progress, that is the important thing. Then each area will become stronger as you mature.

DAY 9
ᵇHE IS THE LIFE, concl.

◆

QUESTIONS TO THINK ABOUT:

1. How would you describe a full, abundant life?
2. How would the preaching of material wealth and good health play into the "abundant life" theme?
3. By that standard, how would you evaluate Christ's spiritual condition, and that of most Christians?

Christ declared that he had come to give a full, abundant life to his sheep (Jn.10:10). This statement takes us from the indications of spiritual life that we have just considered to the character or quality of that life we possess.

The basis for this life is found in 2 Peter 1:3,4 where we read: "His divine power has given us everything we need for life and godliness through our knowledge of him who called us by his own glory and goodness. Through these he has given us his very great and precious promises, so that through them you may participate in the divine nature and escape the corruption in the world caused by evil desires."

Consider for a moment what we have in Christ, in the full, abundant life he has promised:

1. God's promise to meet every need: material, social and spiritual:
    a) Food, drink and clothing (Matt.6:25-33)

      b) Home, family, business (Matt.10:29-30)
      c) Love, joy, peace, patience, kindness, goodness, faithfulness, gentleness, and self-control (Gal.5:22,23)
      d) Victory over temptation and sin (1 Cor.10:13; Rom.6:11,14)
2. Our psychological needs are met. Among others are:
      a) Contentment (Phil.4:11)
      b) Optimism (Phil.4:13)
      c) Boldness (Heb.13:5,6)
      d) Release from tension and care (1 Pet.5:7; Phil.4:6,7)
      e) Stability (Ps.55:22)
3. Toward the Church we will desire:
      a) meaningful fellowship with fellow believers (Heb.10:25)
      b) to see them grow (1 Cor.14:12; Eph.4:8-13)
      c) to reach the unsaved (Rom.15:20)
      d) to recognize and exercise our spiritual gifts (1 Cor.12:27-31; Rom.12:3-8)
4. And toward God/Christ:
      a) Growth in knowing him (Jn.17:3)
      b) Growth in his likeness (2 Cor.3:18)
      c) A consciousness of his presence (Heb.13:5)

This list is sufficient to bring us to the question: Are you experiencing the full, abundant life that Christ came to give us? I remember a former supporter of ours who is now in Glory, George Joslin, a rivet salesman. He was so full of the glory, joy and wonder of the Lord that it was contagious. He lived the abundant life as found above, and was a tremendous encouragement to us to do the same.

This brings us to a second question: Do others see real life in you, gaining victory over sin and bad habits, freedom from the world's corruption and immoral ways? Do they see us responding with faith, patience and inner joy toward life's hard knocks and heartaches? Or do they see a mirror image of their own defeats, frustrations and bitterness?

The full, abundant life is ours as we trust God and obey him.

APPLICATION: Most aspects of the abundant life are dependent on our relationship with the Lord in terms of our obeying and believing him. If we do not believe his promises and act on them, we will not experience their fulfillment. As for example, in Philippians 4:6,7 Paul tells us not to worry about anything, but to commit everything to God in prayer with thanksgiving; and the peace of God which passes all understanding will guard our hearts and minds in Christ. Now if we choose to worry about something rather than commit it to the Lord in thankful prayer, we will not experience the peace he has promised us no matter how much he wants to give it to us!

From the above list, note those areas where you are weak or not experiencing blessing. Then meditate on the associated verses (and others that come to mind) and begin working on these areas one at a time.

DAY 10
[a]HE IS SUBMISSIVE TO THE FATHER

QUESTIONS TO THINK ABOUT:

1. What does it mean to be submissive?
2. How should childlike faith influence the way we submit to God?
3. How did Christ submit to God?
4. On what basis can we submit to God?
5. If we submit to him, how will that affect our "freedom"?

Unexpected Transformation / 23

A little child, with a "My-dad-can-do-anything" attitude, completely trusts his parents to meet his needs of love and security. Christ touched on this attitude in Matthew 18:3,4 when he said, "I tell you the truth, unless you change and become like little children, you will never enter the kingdom of heaven. Therefore, whoever humbles himself like this child is the greatest in the kingdom of heaven."

Christ demonstrated complete trust and faith in God the Father, and submission to his will. In Luke 22:42 he prayed, while facing the cross, "Father, if you are willing, take this cup from me; yet not my will, but yours be done." This reflects again what we saw in Hebrews 12:2 that he "for the joy set before him endured the cross." There is no joy in what we have to endure, but we can endure almost anything if we are motivated toward a goal. An athlete is motivated to win, and so submits to the regimen set down by his trainer.

As Christians, our motivation should be to become like Christ; so we should submit ourselves to the regimen set down by God to get us there. He will introduce into our lives those things which will make us more like Christ if we submit to him and choose to learn the lessons he wants us to know.

This submissive attitude is also demonstrated by the Apostle Paul on the Damascus road. When he saw the bright light from heaven and heard the voice of Jesus speaking to him, his immediate response was to obey the command given him (Acts 9:1-9). It cost him everything he had (Phil.3:4-9), but he joyfully accepted his lot in order to be in right standing with the Lord.

Soon after Amber and I were married, she came down with a very bad cold which led to bronchitis. In the middle of the night, she woke me up: "Bob! Bob! I can't breathe!" Believe me, I was scared and felt so helpless. ("What do you mean, you can't breathe!" I said to myself. "You can't die yet! We've only been married three months!") The next day I took her to the doctor for medicine and soon she was fine.

Shortly after we arrived in Irian Jaya, Amber came down with another bad cold. My first reaction was fear. We were far from medical help, and if this went into bronchitis again, what would we do?

So I decided to have a day of prayer and fasting <u>so that the Lord would heal her</u> and also meet some needs of other missionaries. It was a great day. But by evening, Amber was worse! (?)

"Well, I'll give You till morning …!" But by morning she was worse yet, and I was both frustrated and angry. (!) "Thanks a lot! After all I did yesterday, giving You my entire day, and <u>this</u> is what I get! Boy! See if I have my Quiet Time today! I'll show You!!" And slammed my Bible shut.

Well, I can't stay angry long; by afternoon I decided that I had better quit this foolishness and have my Quiet Time. After all, I couldn't spend my entire missionary career being angry at God! So I began reading where I had left off the day before in Isaiah, chapter 45, verse 9, where the Lord spoke directly to me, saying, "Woe to him who quarrels with his Maker, to him who is but a potsherd among the potsherds on the ground. Does the clay say to the potter, 'What are you making?'" I repented – fast! and learned a lesson in submission. God had the Creator's right to do with Amber (or me) as he would, and I had no right to complain.

We may not always understand why the Lord permits some things to happen, but we <u>can</u> trust him and submit to his will, for he <u>is</u> sovereign and he <u>does</u> love us deeply. There is no loss in submitting to the will of God. As Paul says in 1 Corinthians 2:9, "However, as it is written: No eye has seen, nor ear has heard, no mind has conceived what God has prepared for those who love him." Do you love him? Are you submitted to him?

[By the way, after teaching me that lesson in submission, the Lord graciously answered my prayer and Amber has never again fallen sick like that. When about ten years later I realized this, my heart just melted at God's graciousness to us.]

APPLICATION: Ask yourself, "How can I demonstrate submission to the Father?"

1. By "convincing" yourself from the Word that God is in total, loving control of all your circumstances, paying special attention to his working in the lives of Bible saints and the results of their obedience and submission to him.
2. By spending time with him in prayer before making decisions.
3. By obedience to what he says/commands.

DAY 11
[a]HE IS THE FORGIVING ONE

QUESTIONS TO THINK ABOUT:

1. In regard to our sins, how fully has Christ forgiven us?
2. Why should we forgive others?
3. Can we bear a grudge after truly forgiving someone?
4. If we pray, "Forgive us our sins as we forgive those who have sinned against us," what are we actually asking God to do if we refuse to forgive someone?
5. How important is forgiveness for you personally?

After all that Christ went through in his crucifixion experience, he prayed, "Father, forgive them, for they do not know what they are doing" (Lk.23:34). That was far different from the bitterness and fear demonstrated by the one thief in verse 39. How could Christ ask for forgiveness for them?

First of all, because they didn't know what they were doing. In their spiritual blindness, they thought they were serving God by putting a blasphemer, a false Messiah, to death. This was what Christ said people would think when persecuting the church (Jn.16:2b): "In fact, a time is coming when anyone who kills you will think he is offering a service to God." In 1 Timothy 1:13 Paul says, "Even though I was once a blasphemer and a persecutor and a violent man, I was shown mercy because I acted in ignorance and unbelief." Many times people sin ignorantly against us, either unknowingly or purposefully but based on a wrong belief which has influenced them to act as they do. These deserve our forgiveness, not our hatred.

When Stephen was being stoned to death (Acts 7:59,60), he also prayed for God to forgive his murderers: "Lord, do not hold this sin against them."

Secondly, Christ could see beyond this act of treachery and hatred against himself to what God was accomplishing through it: redemption for anyone who would receive it. Likewise we must see beyond the offense to what God is accomplishing in our lives. In his loving sovereignty he permitted the offense to happen, first to make us like Christ, and secondly that in our forgiveness toward the ones wronging us, we might be a witness of God's love and forgiveness toward them to bring them to Christ. A vengeful spirit will only confirm unbelievers in their unbelief.

But we must also be willing to love and forgive our fellow believers! In Matthew 18:21, after Christ's discourse on restoring broken relationships between believers (vs.15-20), Peter asks, "Lord, how many times shall I forgive my brother when he sins against me?" Combining the Lord's words from Luke 17:3,4 and Matthew 18:22, we hear him answer, "If your brother sins, rebuke him, and if he repents, forgive him. If he sins against you seven times in a day, and seven times comes back to you and says, I repent, forgive him (vs.22) not seven times, but seventy times seven" (i.e. unlimited, unconditional forgiveness!).

This is indeed hard! But let's stop to think for a moment about our own "besetting sins." How many times have we asked the Lord to forgive us of just that one sin, fully expecting him to do it, and then turn right around and do it again? Shouldn't we then be willing to freely forgive our Christian brothers their offenses toward us? "But if their repentance isn't sincere, wouldn't that be taking advantage of us?" Indeed it would, but don't we do the same thing with God? If our repentance was really sincere, would we continue to commit the same sins over and over again with no progress toward victory over them?

God's forgiveness is free, and we take advantage of it. But ours usually has a price tag: "Well, I'll forgive you this time, but you had better not let it happen again or the results might be different!" The Lord says, "If you want to be forgiven, you must forgive" (Mk.11:25). Paul urges us in Colossians 3:12,13, saying, "Therefore, as God's chosen people, holy and dearly loved, clothe yourselves with compassion, kindness, humility, gentleness and patience. Bear with each other and forgive whatever grievances you may have against one another. Forgive as the Lord forgave you."

How do you use God's forgiveness? Do you forgive others as Christ has forgiven you?

APPLICATION: Read the Parable of the Unmerciful Servant in Matthew 18:21-35 and meditate on the character and need of forgiveness. The next time someone wrongs you, remember, Jesus forgave his persecutors without their asking for it! We must likewise be willing to do the same, hard and unfair as it may seem.

Try to see the other person as God sees him: imperfect, but having all the potential that God will give him if he repents and chooses to live for him. React to that person in such a way as will draw him closer to God, not drive him farther away!

DAY 12
[a]HE IS THE FORGIVING ONE, concl.

QUESTIONS TO THINK ABOUT:

1. If we harbor an unforgiving spirit, what could be some of the consequences?
2. How does an unforgiving spirit influence our relationship with God?

Oftentimes we choose not to forgive someone, but would rather bathe ourselves in self-pity and revengeful thoughts. I remember one time becoming quite angry at our local government officer, and wasted several hours that day trying to think of some way to really let him know how wrong and unjust he was and how to make him feel "hurt" in return. Even that night I spent some good sleeping time daydreaming revenge situations against him!

There is a price that will be paid whenever we harbor an unforgiving spirit. What we must determine is, is it worth it?

The first price we pay is <u>wasted time</u> (as alluded to above). Sadly, some people waste away their entire life-time looking for ways to "pay back" past wrongs. A Hatam pastor we know constantly has to watch out for his life because of people still seeking revenge for something his grandfather had done! Absalom waited two years before killing Amnon, his half-brother, for raping his sister (2 Sam.13:1-29). Then he lost three more years in self-imposed exile, and two more years in Jerusalem without once seeing his father's face. Seven years wasted! And shortly after that his life was taken in a rebellion against his father.

The second price is <u>separation from others</u>. David refused to forgive Absalom (2 Sam.14:21-28), thus estranging his own son. Not only do we estrange ourselves from the ones we refuse to forgive, but also from all those who may "be on their side." Solomon says in Proverbs 17:9 (TEV), "If you want people to like you, forgive them when they wrong you. Remembering wrongs can break up a friendship."

Unforgiveness will also affect one's family life either directly, as in Absalom's case, or indirectly. As revenge is denied or postponed, and as hatred grows over a period of time, bitterness envelopes the unforgiving heart, and that, according to Hebrews 12:15, causes trouble and defiles many: bitterness and hatred, vengeful acts carried out, court, jail or prison, family life disrupted (perhaps permanently), one's own life messed up – there is no end to it.

There are also physical and psychological symptoms which result from an unforgiving spirit. Emotions out of balance can cause a host of physical problems. Bitterness and hatred can cause "nerves," ulcers, loss of appetite and weight, digestive problems, high blood pressure with assorted heart problems; and no doubt any doctor could multiply this list many times. In terms of psychological problems, there is loss of perspective, inability to concentrate and deteriorating social relationships. Even worse, we become enslaved or servant to the ones we hate; for everything we think and do ties directly to them. Their presence governs whether or not we will go to social functions or church. They will not leave our thoughts, day or night. They cause us to lose sleep. They color our friendship with others and tend to polarize our lives – "we" against "them." And even worse yet, we will tend to take on the very characteristics of the ones we hate! Why? Because we tend to become like what we think about the most! Prov.23:7a (NKJV) declares, "For as [a man] thinks in his heart, so is he."

Further, an unforgiving spirit separates us from our fellowship with God (see Matt.18:15-35). We often pray Matthew 6:12, "Forgive us our debts, as we also have forgiven our debtors." If we refuse forgiveness to others, and then pray this prayer, we are actually asking God not to forgive us! Jesus states this in Mark 11:25,26, saying, "And when you stand praying, if you hold anything against anyone, forgive him, so that your Father in heaven may forgive you your sins. But if you do not forgive, neither will your Father who is in heaven forgive your sins." Dare a Christian presume to put himself in such a position?

And lastly, <u>we violate God's standard of holiness</u> in Philippians 4:8 as all of our thoughts and plans of revenge fall short of this standard.

All things considered, is the price of an unforgiving spirit worth it?

APPLICATION: Seven steps to take in forgiving someone.

1. List the names of those in your life whom you have never forgiven for something.
2. Jot down what it is that you are holding against them.
3. Confess to God your sin of an unforgiving spirit asking his forgiveness.
4. Then declare your forgiveness for that person.
5. If you can contact that person, and it's something that needs to be done, then do so at first opportunity.
6. But if the offense is not that important, or might stir up unnecessary problems by revealing it, just keep it between you and the Lord.
7. The important thing is to forgive and keep short accounts with both the Lord and others.

NOTE: Sometimes we take offense when the other person has in no way intended to offend. Then the problem is on our part and only needs forgiveness in the heart.

DAY 13
[a]HE IS THE COMPASSIONATE ONE

◆

QUESTIONS TO THINK ABOUT:

1. What does it mean to be compassionate?
2. How does a compassionate spirit show itself? What keeps us from showing compassion?
3. To whom should we show compassion?

In Mark 6:30-34 we find Jesus and the disciples wanting to "get away from it all." Jesus said, "Let's go to a lonely place and rest a while." So they eagerly got into the boat and left for the other side. But those hotfooted Galileans beat a path around the lake and arrived there before them! Imagine, being dog-tired, exhausted from the ministry, not even having time to eat, and aching for a quiet place away from people – only to find that quiet place crowded with even more people! What would be your reaction? Mine would have been: "Oh no! Go away and leave me alone! Can't you see I'm beat?"

But Christ's exhausted reaction was far different (vs.34): "When Jesus landed and saw a large crowd, he had compassion on them, because they were like sheep without a shepherd. So he began teaching them many things" (underlining mine).

Are you compassionate? When you hear of someone in need, someone suffering, does your heart ache for them? Do you desire to be able to help them? If there is nothing you can do materially, you can pray. But more often than not, there are ways in which we can help if we only look for them. True compassion will motivate us to look for those ways and not merely hide behind a spiritual façade of prayer.

One day Dominggus Mayor, our national missionary, and I were visiting another Citak village and found a man suffering from an infection in his thigh which was swollen several times its normal size. We couldn't take him to the hospital in Senggo (our station) because our boat was already full, so we asked the villagers there in the house if they would take him. They acted as if they hadn't heard us. So we repeated the request more strongly. Still we were met with silence. We were frustrated, angry, and hurt that they could be so cold and uncaring. No compassion. "That's <u>his</u> problem, not ours." So Dominggus lanced the infected area to drain it, and gave him a shot – the best we could do at the moment.

But even in more civilized America, how many stories have we heard of people crying for help, but their cries falling on hearing but deaf ears? "I don't want to become involved because …," and there follows as many reasons as there are people to make them. What it boils down to is plain selfishness. "Leave me alone. I don't want to be bothered with your problems. I don't want you intruding on my plans; it's too inconvenient!"

If Jesus had adopted this attitude toward humanity, where would we be today? Our sin caused him great inconvenience, yet he responded in love and compassion, set aside his heavenly riches and way of life, and came to the earth in poverty to meet our needs. Paul says in 2 Corinthians 8:9, "For you know the grace of our Lord Jesus Christ, that though he was rich, yet for your sakes he became poor, that you through his poverty might become rich."

Jesus Christ is compassionate. Are you?

APPLICATION: How can you show compassion toward others today?

1. First, pray that the Lord would help you gain victory over selfishness which hinders compassion.
2. Then begin to give people that come to you your full attention rather than inwardly wish they'd go away and leave you alone.
3. Look for someone in need with the purpose of helping them. (There are many needs all around us that are going unmet. Don't put yourself on a guilt trip because you can't meet them all. Ask the Lord to guide you to the ones he wants you to help.)

DAY 14
[a]HE IS TENDERHEARTED

◆

QUESTIONS TO THINK ABOUT:

1. What is the difference between compassion and tenderheartedness?
2. How do you feel when things go wrong, and someone comes along with homilies and spiritual clichés to help you resolve the situation, but has never "stood in your shoes"?

The characteristic of tenderheartedness is synonymous with compassion by all accounts. Yet I sense a difference, however slight, between them. Perhaps compassion is directed more toward alleviating the circumstances people are suffering, and tenderheartedness a sensitivity toward how they feel in those circumstances.

Three situations come to mind which illustrate Christ's tenderheartedness. The first one is found in Mark 10:13-16. Parents were bringing their children to Jesus so that he would bless them. His disciples tried to turn them away. In anger, Jesus rebuked them and called the little ones to come to him. Then (vs.16) "He took the children in his arms, put his hands on them and blessed them." He always expressed a special tenderness toward children (Matt.18:1-7).

The second situation occurred when Christ was about to go to Jerusalem for the first time since the beginning of his ministry. He lamented over the city, saying, "O Jerusalem, Jerusalem, you who kill the prophets and stone those sent to you, how often I have longed to gather your children together, as a hen gathers her chicks under her wings, but you were not willing!" (Lk.13:34). And we read in Luke 19:41, near the end of his ministry, that when Christ reached the outskirts of the city and saw it, he wept.

34 / Unexpected Transformation

The third situation occurred near Christ's tomb after the resurrection. Jesus was deeply touched by Mary Magdalene's grief and very tenderly called her name (Jn.20:13-16). Her joy was immediate.

In Ephesians 4:32 the Apostle Paul urges us to be tenderhearted (KJV – "compassionate" in other versions) toward one another in the context of being kind and forgiving – the outgrowth of a tender, compassionate heart. Tenderheartedness is that which motivates us to put ourselves in the other person's shoes, to try to feel what they are feeling. It is that love, that compassion, that kindness in our hearts that responds to others (see also Phil.2:1-4).

Paul himself exemplifies this characteristic as indicated in his attitude toward the Philippians. He writes, "It is right for me to feel this way about all of you, since I have you in my heart; for whether I am in chains or defending and confirming the gospel, all of you share in God's grace with me" (Phil.1:7).

The more we can sense the inner feelings of others, the more tenderhearted toward them we will become. But gaining sensitivity toward their feelings is only done actively, involving ourselves with them, getting to know them, listening to them, being with them, learning where they hurt, where they are weak, and where our strengths can help them. A tender heart will seek to learn why they are the way they are rather than react against what they are. And more, it will seek to find ways to help remake them into the image of Christ. This is love, compassion, tenderheartedness – all nearly inseparable from one another.

How tender is your heart toward others?

APPLICATION: How can you demonstrate a tenderhearted spirit today?

1. Make an honest attempt to put yourself in someone else's shoes to feel what they feel.
2. Ask others how they feel in certain situations so that you can learn what it's like for them.

3. Then as you see others in difficult circumstances, help them in the way you would want others to help you were you in the same situation.

DAY 15
[a]HE IS RIGHTEOUS/JUST

QUESTIONS TO THINK ABOUT:

1. How would you define the word "righteous"?
2. Of what importance is the Word of God in conforming us to his nature and standard of righteousness?
3. What is the difference between positional righteousness in Christ (Rom.4:6-8) and practical righteousness that we experience day by day (Rom.6:12-14)?

In 1 John 2:29 and 3:7 we find statements of Christ's righteousness: "If you know that he is righteous, you know that everyone who does what is right has been born of him." "Dear children, do not let anyone lead you astray. He who does what is right is righteous, just as he is righteous."

If you were asked to define the term "righteousness," what would you say? "Good, upright, just"? According to Vine, "'righteousness' means 'the character or quality of being right or just.' As it pertains to God (Rom.3:5), it 'means essentially the same as his faithfulness, or truthfulness, that which is consistent with his own nature and promises.' A righteous character will produce righteous (good) acts, i.e. 'whatever is right or just in and of itself, whatever conforms to the revealed will of God (Matt.5:6,10,20; Jn.16:8,10). So we could describe a righteous character as 'that which conforms to God's standard (or nature)'" (Vine, 1966, 298).

Christ, as a man, conformed himself to that standard. He said in John 4:34, "My food ... is to do the will of him who sent me and to finish his work." In Luke 2:52 we read that "Jesus grew in wisdom and stature, and in favor with God and men."

As a boy of twelve, he showed a depth of understanding and attentiveness that astounded those around him (Lk.2:46,47). How did this come about? I believe that, first of all, his godly parents encouraged him to study the Scriptures. He obviously took them seriously as this passage indicates. The result? The Psalmist says in Psalm 119:98,99, "Your commands make me wiser than my enemies, for they are ever with me. I have more insight than all my teachers, for I meditate on your statutes."

As Jesus applied these Scriptures to his life, his character grew more and more in its reflection of God's righteous nature.

Our <u>position</u> in Christ is that of <u>being righteous</u>. We read in 1 Corinthians 1:30, "But of him [God] you are in Christ Jesus, who became for us wisdom from God – and righteousness and sanctification and redemption." In Christ Jesus, God already sees and accepts us as being righteous, as having already been conformed to his standard, to his nature.

But in <u>practice</u>, we have not yet reached that point of conformity (always doing what is right), and will not until we are in his presence (1 Jn.3:2). However, that is no excuse for us not to work on developing a righteous character now. For it is God's will that we do this since this is one more step in our being conformed into Christ's image. How does this happen? We become like what we dwell on or think about the most.

To develop a righteous character, the Bible <u>must</u> become the most important book in our lives. Job was perhaps the most righteous man to have lived, and he deeply treasured the words of God to him. He says in Job 23:12, "I have not departed from the commands of his lips; I have treasured the words of his mouth more than my daily bread." God's word to him was spoken, but incomplete. His word to us is written and complete. We need to read it, study it, meditate upon it and memorize it. These activities must be given top priority; otherwise, knowing human nature, they will have no priority, for other "good" things will always crowd them out. We have found, both on the mission field as well as in the States, that we give priority to that which is most important to us at any given time.

Of what actual importance do you consider God's Word in conforming you to his nature and standard of righteousness?

APPLICATION: Prayerfully consider making the following covenant with God:

"Since the Bible is our most important source of information about becoming righteous by conforming our character to God's standard (his own nature), I therefore covenant before God:

1. to give the Bible highest priority in my daily schedule,
2. to read his Word with an eye to obeying it, and
3. to spend adequate time in prayer and reflecting upon what I have read."

Signed: _____ Date: _____

DAY 16
[a]HE IS GOOD/BENEVOLENT

QUESTIONS TO THINK ABOUT:

1. What is your definition of "good works"?
2. What is the difference between "good" and "righteous"?
3. To whom should we do good?

We read in Acts 10:38 that Jesus "went around doing good." Good works, which may be defined as "those which are helpful and beneficial to others," characterized his entire ministry. Everywhere he went, he healed the sick, cured the crippled, and cast out demons. His teachings were good; his example was good; his character was good. He even described himself as the Good Shepherd (Jn.10:14).

Though "good" is nearly synonymous with "righteous," I like to use them in this way: we are righteous (a state of character) toward God; but are good (a state of action) toward others. A righteous character will produce good works (Matt.7:17,18). And God is at work creating us "in Christ Jesus to do good works, which God prepared in advance for us to do" (Eph.2:10).

Gaius, to whom 3 John was addressed, illustrates how we can do good to others. John writes, "Dear friend, you are faithful in what you are doing for the brothers, even though they are strangers to you. They have told the church about your love. You will do well to send them on their way in a manner worthy of God. It was for the sake of the Name that they went out, receiving no help from the pagans. We ought therefore to show hospitality to such men so that we may work together for the truth" (vs.5-8).

Since good works are to be done for the help and benefit of others, it is well to know who these others are so that we can minister to them, and what the purpose of our ministry to them is.

In Galatians 6:10 Paul says, "Therefore, as we have opportunity, let us do good to all people, especially to those who belong to the family of believers."

We find here two categories of people to whom we should do good. The first is to "all people." Here is the Scriptural basis for genuine social action and involvement by Christians. The KJV and NIV say, "<u>as</u> we have opportunity" (underlining mine). We are not to be "blind" to the needs of the world around us, but concerned and aware of what is going on. Then, according to our abilities and resources, act on those needs. We could do much more for the welfare of all people if we had a mind to do so and a willingness to become involved with them.

While we were in Bible School and on very meager income, we became involved with a poor family in the city. We bought them food as we could, took them to the hospital when needed, and helped them in other ways. So no matter how "poor" we feel ourselves to be, there is always something we can do for someone else.

"All people" includes another group of people as well, our enemies! In Romans 12:14 Paul says, "Bless those who persecute you; bless and do not curse." One day I was pondering this verse, asking myself, "What does it mean to bless someone?" Well, a curse is something bad that we wish on someone; therefore, a blessing must be something good we wish for someone. Thinking further, I discovered five ways we can bless our enemies: (1) praying for them (Matt.5:44), (2) loving them (Matt.5:44), (3) doing good to them (Exod.23:4,5), (4) showing compassion toward them (Prov.17:5), and (5) forgiving them (Lk.23:34). Christ did all of these things toward his enemies. Hard as it may be, so must we. And to what purpose? That men might know God and be reconciled to him through Christ. If we hate our enemies, and act accordingly, how will they ever have opportunity to come to the Lord (cf. Rom.2:4 where <u>God's goodness</u> brings repentance)?

The second group to whom we should "do good" and to whom we have the greater responsibility, is the body of believers, fellow Christians. There are those who are poor, or have special needs, or are in sorrow, or suffering, not only in America but also around the world. We must do all we can whenever we can to minister to them, for as we minister to them, we minister to the Lord (Matt 25:40), and build up the Body of Christ (Eph.4:11-16) both physically and spiritually (cf. also Jas.2:15,16; 1 Jn.3:17,18). And the Lord has promised blessing and reward to us as a result (cf. Lk.6:38; Matt.25:34-40; Col.3:23-25). He is no man's debtor!

According to your resources and abilities, what good could you do to others?

APPLICATION: How can you do good to others? Here are several suggestions:

1. Call your pastor, an elder or a deacon to see what needs there are among the church members or others in the community that the church is trying to reach.
2. Prayerfully consider how you can become involved in helping some of these people, then do so according to the resources available to you.
3. As the Lord burdens you, expand your vision to others outside the community and in other parts of the world. Supporting a missionary or contributing to a relief organization could be two outlets for your "extended" help.

DAY 17
ᵇHE IS THE RECONCILER

QUESTIONS TO THINK ABOUT:

1. How did sin affect our relationship with God?
2. What does it mean to reconcile the differences between two or more people?
3. How did Christ reconcile us to God?

Two passages of Scripture come to mind which deal with reconciliation. The first is Romans 5:10 which says, "For if when we were God's enemies, we were reconciled to him through the death of his Son, how much more, having been reconciled, shall we be saved through his life!" The second is 2 Corinthians 5:18-20 where Paul states that God reconciled us to himself through Jesus Christ and has committed to us the ministry of reconciliation.

To reconcile means to effect a change from enmity to friendship. Sin threw mankind into the camp of the enemy, and man was found to be fighting against God. God wanted to open the way for man to return to a right relationship with himself. This way was opened through the death of his Son which satisfied God's justice and wrath upon sin. Thus, those who accept Christ's sacrifice on their behalf have changed their minds and ways from enmity against God to friendship with him; they have been reconciled to God.

The main thrust of Christ's ministry was to bring us back to God. Paul says, "We are therefore Christ's ambassadors, as though God were making his appeal through us. We implore you on Christ's behalf: Be reconciled to God" (2 Cor.5:20). Our ministry is the same. Notice that the message is, "Be reconciled <u>to</u> God," not <u>with</u> God. God doesn't need reconciling because he has never changed in his attitude and actions toward us. It was <u>we</u> who changed, rebelled, and became God's enemies. Therefore, it is <u>we</u> who need to change again and be reconciled <u>to</u> God.

This is evangelism: our attempt, through the Word of God and the power of the Holy Spirit, to effect a change of attitude on the part of the hearers toward sin and toward God. Perhaps the Apostle Paul is the most notable example of this change. He did a compete one-eighty in his relationship with God on the road to Damascus. He persecuted the church, thinking all the while that he was serving God! Being reconciled to God, he then became the main champion of the Church.

In later history, John Newton, one of the most vile of men, a hater of God in every way, and an incessant blasphemer, came to the end of himself and changed his mind about his sin and about God. Subsequently, he became a strong preacher of the Word as well as a hymn writer.

Reconciliation involves resolution of a problem between two or more parties. That means that the one reconciling often has to become judge, jury and lawyer. One day an older married student came to me accusing a younger married student of making a pass at his daughter. He was angry. Knowing this student and the family making the accusation, I doubted the truth of it all until I had talked with everyone involved.

As I was praying about it, the Lord impressed on my heart that this younger student had indeed solicited the girl; and he confessed that to me later that same day. The matter had to get settled, so we set up an appointment with the father. I didn't know what he might demand as payment, but the younger student was prepared for anything, and I <u>prayed much</u> for the Lord to intervene and bring a just resolution to this whole situation. As it turned out, I hardly had to say a thing. After a few introductory words and questions, the young student openly confessed his sin to the father and asked his forgiveness. He was obviously repentant and so open that the father evidently felt he had no other choice than to forgive him. However the Lord worked, the two were reconciled. "Whew! Thank you, Lord!"

God has committed to us the ministry of reconciliation. Are you being faithful in this ministry in your relationship with others and in your witness? Are you a reconciler or a cause of division?

APPLICATION: How can you reflect this characteristic of Christ in your life today?

1. You must be living the kind of life that others respect: honest, trustworthy, and caring for others. No one will choose a hypocrite for the ministry of reconciliation.

2. You must demonstrate wisdom. This comes from being in the Word and from experience.

3. You must respect all parties involved as individuals, envisioning them as God would have them be.

4. You must depend totally on God through the power of his Holy Spirit to guide you and give you wisdom in each situation (whether it is reconciliation between two or more parties or reconciliation between others and God through your witness to them).

DAY 18
ᵃHE IS HOLY

◆

QUESTIONS TO THINK ABOUT:

1. What does it mean to be holy?
2. Why is holiness important?
3. How can you be said to be totally without sin before God?
4. What is God's "Standard of Holiness"?

Before Christ was born, the angel Gabriel announced his birth to Mary, saying, "The Holy Spirit will come upon you, and the power of the Most High will overshadow you. So the holy one to be born will be called the Son of God" (Lk.1:35). Christ was pronounced holy before his birth.

What do you think of when the word "holy" is said – a sanctimonious old man or woman going about with folded hands, a sickeningly sweet smile, and a honey-smooth voice saying, "How are you, sonny? Praise the Lord. It's such a beautiful day today, isn't it? Bless his holy name."? Well, that's not holiness; that's foolishness! What is it then to be holy? There are two commonly recognized meanings basic to the term: one is "to be set apart for a special purpose"; the other, "to be totally without sin." We easily see both in Christ: he was set apart for a special purpose – to become the Savior of humanity (Matt.1:21); and no one could accuse him of sin (1 Pet.2:22). But here comes the crunch. In Leviticus 20:7 and 1 Peter 1:16 we read, "For it is written: Be holy, because I am holy." God doesn't leave us a choice; he commands our holiness. Why? Because "without holiness no one will see the Lord!" (Heb.12:14). It's that important.

In the first sense of "holy," i.e. being separated or set apart for a special purpose, we see this meaning clearly in the lives of John the Baptist and the Apostle Paul. Gabriel announced to Zacharias the general outline and ministry of John the Baptist before he was born (Lk.1:13-17). He was to be the forerunner of the Messiah. At Ananias' objection when told to pray for Saul of Tarsus, the Lord replied, "Go! This man is my chosen instrument to carry my name before the Gentiles and their kings and before the people of Israel. I will show him how much he must suffer for my name" (Acts 9:15,16).

Abraham also was especially called by God and set apart from his people and country in a special relationship with God. Listen to what he said to Abraham in Genesis 12:1-3. "The LORD had said to Abram, Leave your country, your people and your father's household and go to the land I will show you. I will make you into a great nation and I will bless you; I will make your name great, and you will be a blessing. I will bless those who bless you, and whoever curses you I curse; and all peoples on earth will be blessed through you."

Now that is awesome – to be set apart like that and given such a tremendous blessing. But where do we fit in? These men we consider "giants" in the faith. We're just "every-day, ordinary us." According to Ephesians 1:3-6, we have been separated from the world to God just as surely as Abraham was separated from his home country and people to God: "Praise be to the God and Father of our Lord Jesus Christ, who has blessed us in the heavenly realms with every spiritual blessing in Christ. [Talk about tremendous blessing!] For he chose us in him before the creation of the world to be holy and blameless in his sight. [There's the being set apart and the sinlessness.] In love he predestined us to be adopted as his sons through Jesus Christ, in accordance with his pleasure and will – to the praise of his glorious grace, which he has freely given us in the One he loves" (cf. Jn.17:14-16).

And Peter caps this when he writes: "But you are a chosen people, a royal priesthood, a holy nation, a people belonging to

God, that you may declare the praises of him who called you out of darkness into his wonderful light" (1 Pet 2:9).

Holiness is being set apart by God for a special purpose. Have you responded to his call? We respond by what we say and how we live.

APPLICATION:

1. In light of the above discussion, how does your view of holiness need to be corrected?

2. What does being set apart for God's special purpose mean to you?

3. What are you going to do about it? You might begin by asking the Lord what he would have you do, get counsel from your pastor or other mature Christians as to where they can see you ministering, then get involved in whatever area the Lord lays on your heart.

DAY 19
[a]HE IS HOLY, cont.

QUESTIONS TO THINK ABOUT:

1. What is the difference between "positional" holiness and "practical" holiness?
2. What is God's standard of holiness?
3. What role does God's discipline play in our becoming holy?

The first definition of "holiness" is "to be set apart" usually for a special purpose. The second definition of holiness, "totally without sin," is a little harder to accept, for there is not one of us free from sin. Yet, amazingly, Hebrews 10:14 states, "Because by one sacrifice he [Jesus] has made perfect forever those who are being made holy." This verse declares that positionally, we have been accepted by God as perfect (holy) in Christ; but in our experience, we are in the process of being made holy, i.e. being made less and less of a sinner and more and more like Christ as we go along!

To help us in that process, God has given us his Word with some pretty specific instructions. With the command to be holy (1 Pet.1:16) comes also the means by which we can fulfill that command. We read in Philippians 4:8, "Finally, brothers, whatever is true, ... noble, ... right, ... pure, ... lovely, ... admirable – if anything is excellent or praiseworthy – think about such things." This is God's standard for holiness.

What is your reaction to this standard? If it is anything like mine, there is a tacit agreement that it is right and exactly what we should be like, but immediately there is resistance: "This is good, but –." But what? "I'll have to change my lifestyle and I don't want to." "I'll not be able to watch my favorite T.V. shows." "Others will think I'm peculiar or crazy." "I won't be able to indulge myself in my one or two 'allowable' sins." "Life will be a real bore." "This standard really is too narrow, too strict, too Puritan."

From the worldly perspective, this is true, but we need to remember God's goal for us: to make us like Christ who is holy. We also need to remember God's very clear statement in Hebrews 12:14 that without holiness, no one will see him! So he chastens and corrects us in order "that we may share in his holiness" (Prov.3:11,12; Heb.12:4-10). Our miseries and troubles are often God's call for us to consider our ways and return to him in order to have a stronger witness to others.

Joshua challenged the people of Israel one day, saying, "Then choose for yourselves this day whom you will serve" (Josh.24:15b). Today this challenge is repeated to us. If we choose to serve the Lord, then we will serve in accordance with his standard of service: holiness; but if we choose to serve ourselves – and Christians have this option – then we can live any way we like! But that invites

God's discipline to bring us back to himself, and that can prove to be a pretty rough road!

If you had the choice of living a holy life with God's blessing, or living any way you wanted with his discipline, which would you choose?

Well, you do have that choice!

APPLICATION: Pay attention this week to your unholy responses to various situations. Ask yourself, "How is the Lord disciplining me through these things to make me more holy, more like himself?" Then determine to react to them in a more Christ-like manner. It has to be an act of your will in the power of the Holy Spirit. It will never happen spontaneously or by wishing it into existence. You must choose to respond in a holy way, then do it!

DAY 20
aHE IS HOLY, concl.

QUESTIONS TO THINK ABOUT:

1. Why is it so hard to be holy?
2. What is the importance of the Word of God in the process of making us holy?

Two other questions need to be considered before leaving this characteristic: "Why do we as Christians find it so hard to be holy?" and "What is the importance of the Word of God in the process of making us holy?"

One reason Christians find it hard to be holy is that we tend to take a more permissive approach to sin than God does. What was "sin" five years ago is no longer considered sin now. God's standard has not changed, but ours has! Why? Because, contrary to Romans

12:1,2, *we are allowing ourselves to become molded into the world's image*. The Church has more and more adopted the world's standards for "normal" living and getting things done. Through radio, television, literature, and our educational system, we are constantly being bombarded with humanistic thought. We are learning from kindergarten age that we are sufficient unto ourselves. There is nothing we cannot eventually do. Our satisfaction and success come from an abundance of material possessions. Religion is laughed at, if not outrightly ridiculed and misrepresented in our media and educational circles. This is "the lie" which says, "No thanks, God, I can live without your help!"

So as we adapt more and more to the world's system, our values change, and so does our awareness of sin and attitude toward holiness. "Sin" tends to be redefined as "that which is against society" rather than "that which is against God"! And as society degenerates, our view of "sin" goes down with it. Ignoring the Word of God throws out the only rule of thumb by which sin can be measured, and leaves us at the mercy of the world's fluctuating values for moral guidance. This situation was illustrated by a pastor commenting on the problem of Christian young people today not knowing what they believe and not willing to commit themselves to the Christian life: "They do not know the Word of God and have no idea of doctrine. They say, 'Well, I don't know what the Bible says, but I think...'." Thus their thoughts, not the Bible, become the arbiters of what is "right" and "wrong," and they are reduced to living existentially, doing whatever they feel is right, but never really knowing for sure.

Does this way of living reflect your experience? If so, Psalm 119:9 provides you the way out. It asks the question, then answers it, saying, "How can a young man keep his way [life] pure [holy]? By living according to your word." We can only live according to God's Word if we are reading it enough to find out what it says about how we should live. This must be a daily time of reading and reflection so that we will more and more be conformed to his way of thinking, and less and less in tune with the world's (see Rom.12:2).

Christ makes it very clear that we cannot follow him and follow the world at the same time. In Matthew 6:24 he says, in effect, "It's either me or the world; you can't have it both ways." "No one can serve two masters. Either he will hate the one and love the other, or he will be devoted to the one and despise the other. You cannot serve both God and Money."

We cannot serve both because the systems they represent are diametrically opposed (see APPENDIX I). So we must choose either to follow God and his holiness, or the world and all it has to offer.

God says, "Be holy, because I am holy." What is your choice?

APPLICATION: There is no way to become holy apart from filling your mind and heart with the Word of God. If you do not already have a Quiet Time, a time set apart for prayer, reading the Word, meditating on and memorizing Scripture, then it is imperative that you make time for this vitally important exercise. You will never grow spiritually or become holy without it.

DAY 21
[a]HE IS THE PURE ONE

QUESTIONS TO THINK ABOUT:

1. What does it mean to be "pure"?
2. How does one purify oneself?

We read in 1 John 3:3, "Everyone who has this hope in him purifies himself, just as he is pure." In Hebrews 7:26 Christ is described as being undefiled. Were he made of silver and put into the refiner's fire, there would be no dross, no impure scum, only pure silver!

Other synonyms used to describe his pureness are faultless (Jn.8:46; 18:38), guiltless (Matt.12:7), innocent (Lk.23:14,15), spotless (Eph.5:27; Heb.9:14), and sinless (Heb.4:15). No one could ever accuse him of defilement or sin.

Jesus said in Matthew 7:17-20 that a good tree or an evil tree can be known by its fruit (cf. Jn.14:11 where Christ demonstrates good fruit). He also said that a man's works proceed from his heart (Matt.15:11,17-20). If his heart is evil, his works will be evil; if his heart is good, his works will be good. Jesus' works were good, to which the Jews also agreed (Jn.10:32,33).

In 1 John 3:3 above, we read that those who have the hope of Christ's return purify themselves. In 1 Timothy 5:22b we find the command: "Keep thyself pure" (KJV), or, as the NASV translates it, "Keep yourself free from sin." The question is: "How?" Every day we are bombarded by that which is impure, even in Christian circles. We normally have enough trouble with our own thoughts in keeping them pure. But then there is T.V., radio, the magazine racks in stores, DVD's, the internet and the careless dress always before us. As long as we are in the world, we will be besieged by that which supports and promotes the world's values – and these values militate against purity.

It is impossible for us to purify ourselves one hundred percent. But we can make progress toward it. The first step is that of establishing the right attitude toward the world's value system. 1 John 2:15a says, "Do not love the world or anything in the world." We read in Colossians 3:2, "Set your minds on things above, not on earthly things."

The second step is the discipline of our thought life. Philippians 4:8, "Finally, brothers, whatever is true, ... noble, ... right, ... pure, ... lovely, ... admirable – if anything is excellent or praiseworthy – think about such things."

The third step is to obey the Lord and do what we know is right. This is often done in faith rather than by desire, for our hearts are deceitful and desperately wicked (see Jer.17:9). But there is victory in doing what we <u>know</u> God wants us to do. In John 13:17 Christ says, "Now that you know these things, you will be blessed if you do them."

Perhaps these three points can be illustrated as follows. We all know that God's Word condemns impure thoughts. Yet we all succumb to them at one time and another. However, we want to obey the Lord in spite of how we really feel about them. So we choose to reject the world's value system that would cause us to dwell on them. But we need something to put in their place. Here is where memorized Scripture comes into play. I have been memorizing and meditating for some time in Hebrews. Often, when impure thoughts come into my mind, I will begin to reconstruct the book of Hebrews in my mind to see how far I can get before I bog down. By the time I reach the end of what I can remember, those impure thoughts are long gone and I am free. But in the meantime, I have filled my mind with far more constructive and healthy thoughts than those which first tried to dominate it.

We can take much encouragement from the fact that the goal of our purity will be met. Someday Christ will present us before himself "as a radiant church, without stain or wrinkle or any other blemish, but holy and blameless" (see Eph.5:25-27 along with 1 Jn.3:2 and Heb.10:14).

Our purity now is determined by our mindset. Where is your mind set?

APPLICATION: Proverbs 23:7a (NKJV) declares, "For as [a man] thinks in his heart, so is he." What do you spend your time thinking about? That is what you will become! "Garbage in, garbage out" is the proverb. If you are presently filling your mind with impure things, that is what you will become. You can hide it for a time, but in the end you will be known for what you are now thinking. Is that what you want?

Determine to take the steps listed above in cleaning up your mind. Victory will not necessarily be immediate but will come over time as you discipline your thought life. In the end, you will be very glad you did this, for it will save you and others much grief.

DAY 22
[b]HE IS THE PURIFIER

QUESTIONS TO THINK ABOUT:

1. How can a person clean up his life so that there is genuine change?
2. What is the role of the Word of God in this process?
3. Can any lasting, true change be effected apart from the Word of God?

When Malachi was prophesying about the coming Messiah, he wrote: "He will sit as a refiner and purifier of silver; he will purify the Levites and refine them like gold and silver. Then the LORD will have men who will bring offerings in righteousness" (Mal.3:3). He is the Purifier. It is absolutely essential that we be purified, made holy, for without holiness none of us could ever hope to see God (see DAY 19 – HE IS HOLY, and Heb.12:14). Much of the Pentateuch concerns itself with purification from various kinds of uncleanness, and from sin and idolatry. Anyone approaching the LORD to worship in a state of uncleanness was cut off from Israel and therefore from God. Proper steps of purification had to be taken before one could approach the LORD in worship. John the Baptist said of Christ, "I baptize you with water. But one more powerful than I will come, the thongs of whose sandals I am not worthy to untie. He will baptize you with the Holy Spirit and with fire. His

Unexpected Transformation / 53

winnowing fork is in his hand to clear his threshing floor and to gather the wheat into his barn, but he will burn up the chaff with unquenchable fire" (Lk.3:16,17).

The winnowing fan is a wooden fork or shovel used to throw the grain up against the wind in order to separate it from the chaff that resulted from the threshing process. The Lord will thoroughly purge (or cleanse) his threshing floor, that is, it will be so thorough as not to leave one trace of any chaff whatever. When he is through, only pure grain will be left to be gathered into his barn. The chaff will be gathered and burned. Not only will he then separate his own people from the world's people, but he is presently at work in his people to purify them, to separate them from sin. This process, called sanctification, will be completed only when we see him face to face and our sin nature given its final death blow. The method he uses? The Word of God. We read in Eph.5:25b-27, "Christ loved the church and gave himself up for her to make her holy, cleansing her by the washing with water through the word, and to present her to himself as a radiant church, without stain or wrinkle or any other blemish, but holy and blameless." In John 15:3 he told his disciples, "You are already clean because of the word I have spoken to you." And he prayed in John 17:17, "Sanctify them by the truth; your word is truth" (all underlining mine).

The Word of God is indispensable to our purification. Even when the Lord allows difficult circumstances into our lives, it is not those circumstances that purify us, but the Word of God applied in those circumstances. For it is the Word that clarifies to us what the purpose of those circumstances is; it is the Word that tells us what we should do, how we should react, what God has in mind for us. (Look again at and consider Romans 8:28-30.) Again, this emphasizes the importance of our being in the Word each day so that the Holy Spirit can use it as needed in our lives (cf. 2 Tim.3:16,17). We return once more to Psalm 119:9 which asks the question, "How can a young man keep his way pure?" And answers it: "By living according to your word."

What place does the Word of God have in your Christian life? Are you letting it purify you?

APPLICATION: Many times we have returned to the theme of the indispensable role of the Word of God in our lives for victory over sin. If you want your heart to be cleansed from the sin that is there, it can only be done through the operation of the Holy Spirit through the Word (see again Jn.17:17). You need to make it your number-one priority every day to read it, study it, meditate upon it, memorize it, and obey it. You will do it if you really want to.

DAY 23
[b]HE IS THE PURIFIER, concl.

QUESTIONS TO THINK ABOUT:

1. Our purification is actually a cooperative act between several parties. Who are they?

2. What is your reaction to this statement: "If you say that you believe in Christ's coming at the Rapture, but do not attempt to purify yourself in your daily living, you really don't believe he is coming."

3. How should the fact of Christ's coming influence your purity in daily living?

Psalm 119:9 leads us to our responsibility in purifying ourselves by applying the Word of God in the way we live. According to Hebrews 9:14, Christ purges our conscience – gets rid of our guilt before God – by the sacrifice of himself on our behalf. Then as we respond to him in faith, our hearts are also purified (Acts 15:9) and, with mind and heart purified, we literally become new creations in Christ (2 Cor.5:17). Now we have the power to think right and the motivation to do right. So step number one in our purification is to receive the Lord Jesus Christ by faith as our personal Savior.

Step two is found in James 4:8 where we read, "Come near to God and he will come near to you. Wash [cleanse] your hands, you sinners, and purify your hearts, you double-minded" (underlining mine). We must desire to come near to God. This means making time to spend in his presence each day and developing such a friendship/relationship with him that we are conscious of his presence all day long. Consciousness of his presence will help keep us from sin, for we will want to do what is pleasing to him.

Step three is obedience. 1 Peter 1:22a says, "You have purified yourselves by obeying the truth" ["your word is truth" – Jn.17:17]. As the Psalmist says in Psalm 119:11, "I have hidden your word in my heart that I might not sin against you." And someone else has said, "Sin will keep you from this Book; this Book will keep you from sin." As we read the Word of God and obey it, we will be purified and led in the way of true righteousness and holiness.

Step four of our purification lies in the hope we have in becoming like Christ, which will be completed when we see him. In 1 John 3:2,3 we read, "Dear friends, now we are children of God, and what we will be has not yet been made known. But we know that when he appears, we shall be like him, for we shall see him as he is. Everyone who has this hope in him purifies himself, just as he is pure." If we are concentrating on becoming like him, if that is our first priority, then we will be found doing what he would do, saying what he would say, thinking what he would think. "And in him is no sin" (1 Jn.3:5). So as we increasingly become like him, we will be purifying ourselves that much more, and sinning that much less.

I said before that the Word of God is indispensable to our purification. Just as one example, I heard a pastor one day expounding on 1 Corinthians 5:1-7. Verse six says, "Don't you know that a little yeast works through the whole batch of dough?" The meaning was not lost on me: A little sin held on to and enjoyed will influence my entire life and ministry and be a hindrance in my relationship with God. There is <u>no room</u> for sin in the Christian's life (vs.7) no matter how small it is. We must purge it out!

Where are you in the purifying process?

APPLICATION: "The holiness of God is like a consuming fire coming forth from a source of absolute purity" (Gallagher, 1990, Bible Study #18, 1). Our goal is that absolute purity, but it is being thwarted by the "little" sins that we permit to remain in our lives.

What are the "little" sins in your life? Remember, a big storm can destroy a house, but it is more often the work of the termite or dry rot that does the job. A <u>little</u> yeast does its work on the batch of dough. Those "little" sins will "kill" you and make you ineffective as a Christian. Begin to deal with them right now. Don't let <u>anything</u> stand between you and the Lord.

DAY 24
ªHE IS A MAN OF PRAYER

QUESTIONS TO THINK ABOUT:

1. Why don't Christians like to pray?
2. What are some things that keep us from prayer?
3. If God is sovereign and has already determined what is going to happen, then why do we need to pray?

We read in the Gospels of the many times Christ prayed, most often in a solitary place (Lk.5:16), long before daylight (Mk.1:35), all night long (Lk.6:12), and on the mountain (Matt.14:23). John 17 bares his heart in prayer to his Father. Christ talked with his Father as naturally as breathing. The length and place of his prayers depended upon the situation he was facing. But the fact presented in Scripture is that he was a man of prayer. This is what God desires us to be like. He wants us to feel comfortable talking with him – anytime. And he wants us to know that he listens and answers. That is one reason why we call him, "Father."

Paul says in 1 Thessalonians 5:17, "Pray continually." This does not mean that we should be praying non-stop, twenty-four hours a day, but to be continually in the spirit of prayer so that at <u>any time</u> we are free to talk with God. We might be able to paraphrase the verse this way: "Be on continual speaking terms with your heavenly Father."

But here a serious problem arises with most Christians. How can we be continually in the spirit of something which frequently bores us – accounting for the lack of a regular personal prayer time and low attendance at prayer meetings – and "doesn't work anyway"? To support this assertion, how many specific answers to prayer are <u>you</u> aware of? We faced this problem shortly after arriving on the mission field. In our personal prayer lives, we might pray for our families, a friend or two, and our circumstances, but not much more. There really wasn't that much to pray about. In our prayers together, we prayed conversationally every night for the same things until it got to be a game. There were some things I just didn't want to pray for, so I would try to work it out so that Amber would have to pray for those things. (I found out later that she was doing the same thing to me!) I'm sure the Lord was "pleased"! It got to the point where we were both bored to death with our prayer life and knew that we had to do something about it or just quit praying.

So we decided to make a prayer list to help us remember what to pray for and included a section for answers. This was one reason for our boredom: we just weren't seeing prayers answered. Why continue in something that didn't produce results?

We found our prayer list falling into several logical sections: our work, family and relatives, friends, missionaries, countries of the world, and general requests that didn't fit anywhere else. Soon we discovered that we had <u>a lot more</u> to pray for than we realized, and had to exercise care that our list not become too cumbersome!

This change in our prayer life occurred in August 1971. Between then and now (2019), we have seen the Lord answer over 64,500 prayer requests, an average of 125 answers per month. Now you talk about encouragement to keep praying! The list did one more thing: it keeps us in closer contact with the people for whom we are praying since we periodically ask them for answers the Lord has given.

If you are bored with your prayer life, as we were, why not try making a prayer list and also keep track of God's answers? It will encourage you greatly to "see" your prayers working.

One additional thought. There are times when you may want to pray for someone, but you have no specific requests for that person. What then? In 1 John 5:14,15 we read this promise: "This is the confidence we have in approaching God: that if we ask anything according to his will, he hears us. And if we know that he hears us – whatever we ask – we know that we have what we asked of him."

Now, what is God's will in what we pray for? A very profitable exercise would be to read through the Bible jotting down every passage where someone prayed and what they prayed about. Many of these prayers can serve as models for what we should be praying for. Also, in Ephesians 1:15-19, 3:14-19, and Colossians 1:9-12, Paul gives us some specific things to pray about for others. Since this is God's Word, and these things are his will for each believer, as we pray for these things we can <u>know</u> that he will be working in their lives to bring them about. That helps us pray with great confidence.

Unexpected Transformation / 59

APPLICATION: If you are serious about doing something to revitalize your prayer life, I would encourage you to make some kind of list in which you can keep track of the answers to your prayers. A suggested format is found in APPENDIX II. Then use the list as a tool for prayer – do not let it become your master or you will become over-burdened with too much to pray for and find yourself on a guilt trip for "not praying enough."

DAY 25
[a]HE IS THE WITNESS

QUESTIONS TO THINK ABOUT:

1. Who is a witness?
2. What does a witness do?
3. If two or more people see the same incident, their points of view are usually different. How does this difference affect the "truth" of their witness?

According to Webster, a witness is "One who has personally seen, heard, or experienced something" (Webster, 1984, 793). We read of Christ in Isaiah 55:4a, "Indeed I have given him as a witness to the people." And again in Revelation 1:5b, "And from Jesus Christ, the faithful witness." God sent Christ to the earth to be a witness. About what or to what does he testify?

First of all, Jesus himself fulfills the criteria for a witness. In John 3:11-13 he said to Nicodemus, "I tell you the truth, we speak of what we know, and we testify to what we have seen, but still you people do not accept our testimony. I have spoken to you of earthly things and you do not believe; how then will you believe if I speak of heavenly things? No one has ever gone into heaven except the

60 / *Unexpected Transformation*

one who came from heaven – the Son of Man." He personally "saw, heard and experienced" heaven and came to tell us about it.

John the Baptist also affirms this in John 3:31b-34a saying, "The one who comes from heaven is above all. He testifies to what he has seen and heard, but no one accepts his testimony. The man who has accepted it has certified that God is truthful. For the one whom God has sent speaks the words of God."

In John 18:37 Jesus tells Pilate why he came into the world. "'You are a king, then!' said Pilate. Jesus answered, 'You are right in saying I am a king. In fact, for this reason I was born, and for this reason I came into the world, to testify to the truth.'" Pilate's immediate question is also ours: "What is truth?" What is the truth to which Christ was testifying?

Scripture reveals that he gave witness to three things: righteousness (as revealed in truth), sin and judgment. Of God the Father we read in I John 5:20, "We know also that the Son of God has come and has given us understanding, so that we may know <u>him who is true</u>" (underlining mine). He gave us this understanding by personally reflecting the character and works of God. He told Philip in John 14:9, "Anyone who has seen me has seen the Father." God's words also are truth. Christ told his disciples in John 14:24, "These words you hear are not my own; they belong to the Father who sent me." And he also claimed that <u>the Father's word is truth</u> (Jn.17:17).

Furthermore, Christ testified about himself. In John 8:18 he says, "I am one who testifies for myself; my other witness is the Father, who sent me." And in John 14:6 he says, "I am ... the truth." In John 16:13 he calls the Holy Spirit "the Spirit of truth." And so as a witness of the truth, Christ reveals the righteous character of the Triune God.

APPLICATION: "A witness is not called upon to argue and defend; he merely tells what he knows or has experienced." How does this statement influence your thinking about your own witness for the Lord?

DAY 26
[a]HE IS THE WITNESS, cont.

QUESTIONS TO THINK ABOUT:

1. How important are the topics of sin and judgment in our witness? Won't mentioning these things "turn people off" and make our witness ineffective?

2. If we could do the miraculous, how would that affect our witness?

Christ not only bears witness to the righteous character of the Triune God, but also testifies about sin and judgment. In John 15:22-24 he says about the world: "If I had not come and spoken to them, they would not be guilty of sin. Now, however, they have no excuse for their sin... . If I had not done among them what no one else did, they would not be guilty of sin. But now they have seen these miracles, and yet they have hated both me and my Father." As Christ spoke and worked, revealing God's character, man's sin was made plain, for sin is anything that is contrary to the righteous character of God.

Then Christ bore witness about judgment that will come because of sin. What he said bears quoting in full: "Moreover, the Father judges no one, but has entrusted all judgment to the Son... . I tell you the truth, whoever hears my word and believes in him who sent me has eternal life and will not be condemned; he has crossed over from death to life. I tell you the truth, a time is coming and has now come when the dead will hear the voice of the Son of God and those who hear will live. For as the Father has life in himself, so he has granted the Son to have life in himself. And he has given him authority to judge because he is the Son of Man. Do not be amazed at this, for a time is coming when all who are in their graves will hear his voice and come out – those who have done good will rise to live, and those who have done evil will rise to be condemned. By myself I can do nothing; I judge only as I hear, and my judgment is just, for I seek not to please myself but him who sent me" (Jn.5:22-30).

So as Christ bore witness to the truth, he spoke of righteousness (God's character), sin (man's problem) and judgment (man's destiny). These are the same elements in the Holy Spirit's witness to the world (see Jn.16:8-11), and must be the same in ours as well. When Paul was witnessing to the Roman governor, Felix, he "discoursed on righteousness, self-control [sin], and the judgment to come" (Acts 24:25). These same three elements were also present as Peter witnessed to Cornelius and his family (Acts10:34-43): righteousness (vs.38), sin (vs.39) and judgment (vs.42), followed by an invitation (vs.43). In the first case, Felix was afraid, but rejected the message. In the second, Cornelius and his family were glad and received it. Likewise, as we consider our witness, we also must be careful to include these three elements. And if we use tracts, we should be sure that they cover them too.

APPLICATION: As you think about your witness, how can you include God's righteousness, man's sin, and judgment in your conversation? An interesting side-study would be to look at the testimony of the thief on the cross to discover how his testimony also included these three basic elements (Lk.23:40-43).

DAY 27
[a]HE IS THE WITNESS, cont.

◆

QUESTIONS TO THINK ABOUT:

1. Why is it that Christians generally don't witness?

2. Is there such a thing as a "silent witness"? If so, how could that person be considered a witness?

3. How important are our actions in the context of our witness?

In the light of Acts 1:8 where Jesus commands his disciples, and us through them, to be witnesses for him throughout the entire world, there is a question that arises in my mind: "Why is it that we don't witness?" I can think of at least sixteen reasons why our mouths remain shut. Perhaps you will be able to identify with some of them, and hopefully the answers to these problems will help loosen our tongues a bit.

1. <u>Disobedience</u>. The Lord has commanded us to witness for him, and we just don't want to do it! We have other priorities. In Matthew 28:19a, Jesus commanded, "Go therefore and make disciples of all the nations." If we are not faithful to this command, the implication in Matthew 25:28 is that we will lose our reward and it will be given to another. Is disobedience worth this price?

2. <u>We really don't see people as lost souls going to hell</u>. We need to confess our spiritual nearsightedness and ask the Lord to clear our vision to see them as he sees them. There is only one way to heaven. Jesus said in John 14:6, "I am the way... . No one comes to the Father except through me." Everyone not believing in the Lord Jesus and committing their lives to him is on their way to hell!

3. <u>Unconfessed sin</u> in our lives will shut our mouths. The Lord's command to us in 1 Peter 1:15,16 is clear: "But just as he who called you is holy, so be holy in all you do; for it is written: 'Be holy, because I am holy.'" As long as we hold on to some sin in our lives, we are not holy and God cannot use us as effectively as he would. It is like a drain pipe. If it's partially blocked, it cannot function as it was designed to. And as long as that blockage remains, it will function to a degree, though poorly. And if that blockage

is allowed to remain, the drain pipe becomes plugged and totally useless. So it is in our lives when we allow the "blockage" of sin to remain uncleared.

4. <u>Hypocrisy</u> in our lives will shut off our witness as people will not want to hear anything spiritual from us. Our actions and words have already proved our message false. The Lord speaks to this issue in principle when he says in Matthew 5:37, "Simply let your 'Yes' be 'Yes,' and your 'No,' 'No'; anything beyond this comes from the evil one." We should be as good as our word. We should diligently practice what we preach. Then, when we speak, others will listen and not be turned away from Christ because of our hypocrisy.

5. Another reason we fail to witness is <u>the assumption that they are probably saved anyway</u>, especially if they are churched people. Based on Matthew 7:21-23, this assumption is very dangerous, for many very religious people will be turned away from the kingdom of God on that day (i.e. the day of judgment). Jesus says: "Not everyone who says to me, 'Lord, Lord,' will enter the kingdom of heaven, but only he who does the will of my Father who is in heaven. Many will say to me on that day, 'Lord, Lord, did we not prophesy in your name, and in your name drive out demons and perform many miracles?' Then I will tell them plainly, 'I never knew you. Away from me, you evildoers!'" Assuming that that church member or church attendee is saved could be disastrous. Ask them. If they are saved, they will appreciate your concern. If they are not, but think they are, they will most likely become angry at your "judgmental assumption."

APPLICATION: If any of these reasons for not witnessing are true in your life, confess them to the Lord, meditate upon the section dealing with them, and ask the Lord to change that attitude in your heart.

DAY 28
ªHE IS THE WITNESS, cont.

◆

QUESTIONS TO THINK ABOUT:

1. If evangelism is not our spiritual gift, how would that affect our sense of responsibility to witness?

2. How does fear affect our witness? Why do we let it influence us?

6. A sixth reason we do not witness is that <u>evangelism is not our spiritual gift</u>. We become cowed by those who do have this gift and demonstrate an amazing ability to open up conversations and bring people to the point of decision. "I could never do that!" we say.

Perhaps not. But there has to be a planting of the seed, and watering of the seed through the faithful witness of many people. From those who have the gift of evangelism, we can learn how to communicate our faith to others more effectively. Then, in God's own time, some to whom we have witnessed will come to know him. Even as Paul says in 1 Corinthians 3:6, "I planted the seed, Apollos watered it, but God made it grow."

7. <u>Shyness</u> before others will keep our mouths shut. But the Lord didn't say, "All of you, except the shy, shall be witnesses for me." If shyness keeps us from obeying the Word of God, then we must deal with it either as sin or as a problem needing help from a Christian counselor. For shyness implies two basic root problems: a poor self-image and/or fear of people. Perhaps we have a poor self-image because at some time in our lives someone criticized us in an unkind way or did something that showed that we just didn't amount to much. Hurt once, or perhaps many times, we have resolved

never to open our mouths about anything again, or put ourselves in a threatening situation where our supposed inadequacies will be revealed. So we become shy. For improvement of our self-image, mediate on Psalm 139:1-18,23,24, realizing that God, in his loving sovereignty, has made us just the way we are (vs.13-16), and that we don't need to be ashamed of it. He doesn't make mistakes!

8. <u>Fear of people</u> doesn't just afflict the shy; we all have it to one degree or another. Here we need to assure our hearts as to who is stronger, they or God? Then heed God's word to us regarding this problem. He said to Jeremiah: "'Get yourself ready! Stand up and say to them whatever I command you. <u>Do not be terrified by them</u> (underlining mine), or I will terrify you before them. Today I have made you a fortified city, an iron pillar and a bronze wall to stand against the whole land… . They will fight against you but will not overcome you, for I am with you and will rescue you,' declares the LORD" (Jer.1:17-19). Then the Lord Jesus gives us a direct command in Matthew 10:27,28, saying, "What I tell you in the dark, speak in the daylight; what is whispered in your ear, proclaim from the roofs. Do not be afraid of those who kill the body but cannot kill the soul. Rather, be afraid of the One who can destroy both soul and body in hell." Solomon writes in Proverbs 29:25, "Fear of man will prove to be a snare, but whoever trusts in the LORD is kept safe." In other words, our fear of people is overcome by our confidence in God. So we don't need to fear what they might say or how they will react (see also Heb.13:5b,6). If we do, that means that we believe them more than we do God, and that gets us into other problems.

APPLICATION: If any of these reasons for not witnessing are true in your life, confess them to the Lord, meditate upon the section dealing with them, and ask the Lord to change that attitude in your heart.

DAY 29
[a]HE IS THE WITNESS, cont.

◆

QUESTIONS TO THINK ABOUT:

1. How much of the Bible do we need to know before we can witness effectively?

2. How can we overcome the problem of not knowing how to open a witnessing conversation?

9. There is also the <u>fear of rejection</u> that keeps us from witnessing. We read of Christ in John 1:11 that "He came to that which was his own, but his own did not receive him." Yet that did not stop him from proclaiming the message God had given him. His responsibility was to be faithful to God, not to ensure that God's message would be received. This also was the case with Ezekiel. In Ezekiel 3:4,7 God tells him: "Son of man, go now to the house of Israel and speak my words to them... . But the house of Israel is not willing to listen to you because they are not willing to listen to me." But Ezekiel was to go and speak nonetheless, for God's message had to be heard, whether or not it was received.

10. A tenth reason we often don't witness is <u>because of our own ignorance of the Word</u>. Any soldier who doesn't know how to use his gun will be scared to death to face the enemy. As Christians, we must be in the Word daily letting it work itself into us and learning to use it. According to Ephesians 6:17 the Word of God is our sword that we need to learn to use in our spiritual warfare. Paul encouraged Timothy with these words: "Do your best to present yourself to God as one approved, a workman who does not need to be ashamed and who correctly handles the word of truth" (2 Tim.2:15). That Word must have priority in our lives, otherwise we will face the enemy with an empty scabbard – or an empty cartridge chamber!

11. <u>Often we don't know how to begin</u>. The simple solution to that is to ask God to provide the opening in your conversation. Since he has commanded us to witness, he will also open the door of opportunity for us to do so if we want him to. I sat next to a businessman on an airplane trip and wanted to witness to him. But how to begin? We exchanged greetings and names. Then I asked him what he did. He asked me the same. "Missionary." "Oh? What religion?" By that question I suspected, correctly, that he was of the same religion as several of my roommates in college, and that reminded me of one of them who had had a dream one night. Its interpretation was a clear picture of salvation (included in the text below but explained to the businessman after telling him the dream). With that religious bridge connecting this man and my roommate, I was off on the dream story and a witness.

"Let me tell you about a strange dream that my college roommate had. He and two others in the house were adrift on a raft at sea, going nowhere (mankind adrift on the sea of sin). Suddenly they saw an island (heaven) and began paddling with their hands (self-effort) as hard as they could to get there; but the harder they paddled, the <u>further</u> from the island they became! But as soon as they stopped paddling, the current (Jesus Christ) began carrying them toward the island. About 100 yards from the island, they decided to swim the rest of the way (Christians living in their own strength), but a shark (Satan) swimming under the raft changed their minds. He'd have had a quick three-course meal had they dived off! The shark (as only in a dream) also represents the Holy Spirit who keeps us 'on the raft' and committed to Christ. We must depend on Christ, not on our own works, for our salvation." The businessman listened, didn't make a decision, but did receive the tract I offered him.

12. Related to not knowing how to begin is <u>not knowing what to say</u>, how to formulate our witness. Practicing with another Christian will help us get it together. Also going out with another Christian who knows how to witness will help. But many times a memorized or canned presentation is not appropriate, for if we're

interrupted, it is awkward to "get back" to where we left off and takes away our flexibility. Rather it is better to have the basic elements of what we want to say in mind, then count on the Lord to direct the conversation.

APPLICATION: Again, if you feel hindered in your witness by any of the above reasons, prayerfully meditate upon them and take what steps are necessary to correct them.

DAY 30
[a]HE IS THE WITNESS, concl.

QUESTIONS TO THINK ABOUT:

1. Where does our responsibility in witnessing stop, with our witness or in "bringing the person through" to a decision?
2. If we invite a person to accept the Lord and he refuses, does that mean that our witness has been ineffective?
3. To whom should we witness? Are we required to witness to everybody, or to just a select few?
4. How can we be a witness to everybody we meet?

13. Another block we face in witnessing is <u>not knowing how to bring someone to the point of decision and thinking that we have to bring everyone to whom we witness to that point</u>. Let's deal with the second part first by saying that we are not required to bring everyone to whom we witness to a decision. What we are required to do is to witness to them. It's the job of the Holy Spirit to convince them of the truth we've presented and to bring them to the point of conviction to make a decision. Most people we witness to will not receive Christ at that point, but perhaps many of them will later on down the road. Sometimes during the discussion it is obvious that

the person is ready to receive Christ. Sometimes it's not so obvious. But the same question can be used (if the discussion goes far enough for you to "complete" your witness to him): "Would you like to commit your life to Jesus Christ right now and ask him to forgive your sins and be your Savior?" Their response will let you know how to proceed.

14. Some express fear that the person being witnessed to will bring up <u>issues or questions to which they don't know the answers</u>. Many times those questions are a smoke screen laid down to avoid the issue of salvation. Sometimes it's an honest question. If you don't know the answer, you could respond with: "I don't know the answer to that, but I'll check it out and get back to you on it. However, that question really isn't the important issue we must deal with. It is our relationship with God that must receive our primary attention." Thus we get back to the basics.

15. Some have said, "<u>But I meet so many people, I can't possibly witness to them all</u>!" Well, yes and no. Even if we can't talk with them, we can give them a tract after some interaction. We also can be a witness by what we do (see Matt.5:16). Give them a smile and a friendly, "Good morning!" Hold a door open for them. Speak kindly to a disgruntled clerk, etc. Then ask the Lord to give you those opportunities he wants you to use. He will!

16. Lastly, <u>you yourself may be "Christian" but still unsaved.</u> You go to church, give mental assent to the truths taught, etc., but have never made a personal commitment to Jesus Christ yourself. That is why you feel little desire to witness or give more than token involvement in church activities. You have no message to give, nothing to witness about. I would encourage you right now to stop reading, bow your head, and commit your life to Jesus Christ, asking him in your own words to forgive your sins, clean up your life and

Unexpected Transformation / 71

be your Lord and Savior (see Rom.10:9,10,13). Then you will have something to share with others!

By what you say and what you do, you are a witness for Christ for good or ill. What kind of witness are you?

APPLICATION: Looking over the above 16 reasons why we don't witness, which ones apply to you? List them, then set up a plan to deal with them. Perhaps you will need to consult your pastor or a fellow believer who has the gift of evangelism for additional help.

DAY 31
ᵇHE IS THE PEACEFUL ONE, THE PEACEMAKER

◆

QUESTIONS TO THINK ABOUT:

1. What is "peace"? [Absence of conflict – Right relationships – Contentment in turmoil]
2. In what areas of life do we need a sense of peace?
3. What destroys our sense of peace?
4. Why do Christians, after having peace with God through Jesus Christ, often not experience that peace in their lives?

In Matthew 5:9, Jesus said, "Blessed are the peacemakers, for they will be called sons of God." Christ was a peacemaker, and demonstrated this trait in five different ways: between man and God (1 Tim. 2:5), between man and himself (Jn.5,6 – implied by His reactions to false accusations); between man and man (Mk.9:38-40), between man and his circumstances (Jn.16:33), and between man and nature (Matt.8:23-27).

Peace between Man and God

Ever since man sinned, he has been at war with God (Rom.8:6-8), a struggle which only man could lose. Isaiah 57:20,21 states, "But the wicked are like the tossing sea, which cannot rest, whose waves cast up mire and mud. There is no peace, says my God, for the wicked." But God wanted peace between himself and man, so provided it through the death of his Son (Eph.2:14-16) who, by his death, diverted the storm of God's holy wrath against sin from us to himself (1 Jn.2:1,2). Romans 5:1 expresses this peace: "Therefore, since we have been justified through faith, we have peace with God through our Lord Jesus Christ." This is why Isaiah called him, "The Prince of Peace" (Isa.9:6). Now the commission of peace has been passed on to us (2 Cor.5:18-20), that through our witness others may know Christ and be at peace with God.

But often after we have peace with God through Christ, <u>we Christians don't experience that peace</u> in our lives. Why?

1. The foremost reason is that <u>we believe our God is not strong enough nor able to handle our circumstances</u>. A change in our practical understanding of who He really is will change our attitude toward our circumstances (see DAY 34, PEACE BETWEEN US AND OUR CIRCUMSTANCES, for a continuation of this discussion).

2. A second reason that we as Christians don't experience peace with God is <u>because of rebellion in our hearts</u>. Paul says in Colossians 3:15, "Let the peace of Christ rule in your hearts, since as members of one body you were called to peace. And be thankful" (see also 1 Thess.5:18). The command "let" implies a deliberate choice on our part. If we choose to "let" the peace of Christ rule in our hearts in any given circumstance, what is it that we are actually doing? We "let" his peace rule in our hearts by:

a. being sure of who our God is (sovereignty, goodness and love of God),
   b. knowing his promises to us,
   c. believing and accepting those promises and obeying their conditions,
   d. committing our circumstances to God in believing, thankful prayer (Phil.4:6,7),
   e. letting the Holy Spirit rule (Gal.5:22,23), and
   f. avoiding what is displeasing to the Lord (self-discipline).

3.   Thirdly, <u>a lack of prayer and a spirit of thankfulness</u>. Again Paul says in Philippians 4:6,7, "Do not be anxious about anything, but in everything by prayer and petition, with thanksgiving, present your requests to God. And the peace of God, which transcends all understanding, will guard your hearts and your minds in Christ Jesus."

Choosing to believe God will cause us to come to him in believing, thankful prayer, resulting in receiving his peace. Mind you, our circumstances may not change one iota, but with his peace ruling in and guarding our hearts, we can live effectively in those circumstances. This was true of our second term on the mission field. Once we chose to believe God and be thankful in our circumstances, we had peace even though our circumstances didn't change. Then we were able to live and work in that hard situation without the inner turmoil and agitation that had so torn us apart before.

4.   A fourth reason for our lack of peace is <u>because we don't take our Christian life seriously</u>. We too easily compromise our standards with the world's. We want to prosper and get ahead materially. We want our own way! Thus we become worldly in our Christian lives, enslaved to various sins, and subject to continual reproving from the Holy Spirit. The ensuing guilt drives peace from our hearts and lives. The Corinthian Christians were still worldly in their outlook and actions. In First and Second Corinthians, Paul lists at least 41 serious sins that were common, accepted or condoned among them,

and reproved them for their lack of spiritual growth (1 Cor.3:1-3). The worldly mind is hostile toward God, not subjecting itself to God's law (Rom.8:7). Romans 6:11-18 and 12:1,2 give us good guidelines for gaining victory over sin and compromise with the world's standards. But once again, we must choose the direction we will follow; we must choose to obey or disobey these commands. Obedience will bring peace; disobedience will result in continual turmoil and an uneasy spirit. What is your choice?

APPLICATION: Do you have peace with God? If not, there are two things to consider:

1. Perhaps you have never received Jesus Christ as your personal Savior and you need to do that. Then you will have peace with God.

2. If you have received Christ, but are living in disobedience to God, or perhaps are guilty of one of the above reasons for not having peace with him, then identify the problem area and take the necessary steps to correct what is wrong in your relationship with him.

DAY 32
[a]HE IS THE PEACEFUL ONE, THE PEACEMAKER, cont.

QUESTIONS TO THINK ABOUT:

1. What does it mean to "be at peace with yourself"?
2. What kind of things militate against having this peace?
3. If you are not at peace with yourself, what does that say about your attitude toward God?

Peace with Ourselves:

Physically

Now we move on to the second area of peace: peace with ourselves. Nowhere in the Gospels do we find where Christ was not at peace with himself. He was basically concerned with his purpose in life rather than his physical appearance. He was determined to do God's will (Jn.4:34) and to glorify him (Jn.17:4).

Psalm 139:13-18 declares how God, in his loving sovereignty, created us. He made us just the way he wanted. When you look in a mirror, are you happy with what you see? Do you see a "friend" or an "enemy"? Remember, God intends for us to glorify him and, no matter what our shape or "misshape," if we surrender our appearance to him, he will use it in his sovereignty to bring glory to himself.

In Papua there was a single woman missionary (Elinor Young) who was crippled and deformed by polio as a child. Many in her situation would never even consider missionary service, especially in mountainous terrain. And many mission boards would never consider accepting such a person. Yet this woman was burdened deeply for the work of the Lord and bent all her efforts toward that end. The Lord opened the way for her and used her to be a tremendous blessing both to the people to whom she ministered as well as to us missionaries. She could easily have become bitter about her condition and blamed God for it (see Rom.9:20,21), but she didn't. Instead, she demonstrated a sweetness and attractive spirit that drew everyone to her. She glorified God and brought forth praise to him from the rest of us who were amazed at what he was doing in her life. She accepted herself the way she was, and went on from there – in peace.

Spiritually

In addition to being at peace with our physical appearance we must also be at peace with our talents and abilities (or lack of them!) in the measure which God has given them to us (see again

Ps.139:13-18). 1 Corinthians 12:4-31 expands on this idea in the area of the spiritual gifts given to us by the Holy Spirit. He distributes these gifts <u>as he wills</u> (vs.11), and God has placed us in the Body <u>as it pleased him</u> (vs.18).

Just as our body parts are different, so are our positions in the Body of Christ. If we all had the exact same appearance and abilities, we'd go mad with boredom. Just think how you'd feel if every time you turned around, you met yourself, and every time you had a discussion, you literally talked with yourself! Stimulating? Hardly. So spiritually, God has sovereignly given us differing abilities, talents and gifts in order to minister to one another (vs.19-22) and do his work effectively. But every so often we get caught in the trap of wishing we were someone else, having their abilities, appearance or appeal. (Were we to know it, they could well be wishing that they were like us!) As I would look at a fellow missionary who was exceptionally gifted in mechanics, I'd have a hard time "getting victory" over it because I was so limited without mechanical ability. But God has obviously planned it this way so that I would need that fellow missionary, or others like him/her, to help me function as a part of the Body of Christ.

In reading <u>To Perish for Their Saving</u>, by Helen Manning (Victor Press, 1969), the story of Stan Dale and the Yali tribe, I suffered a real spiritual identity crisis. Here was a man totally sold out to the Lord, demonstrating a driving passion to reach the lost, and keep on reaching. I don't even begin to match his drive or passion to reach the lost, and for a while I felt very guilty about it and began to wonder about my own commitment to the Lord. I had fallen into the trap that the Apostle Paul warns us about in 2 Corinthians 10:12b, "When they measure themselves by themselves and compare themselves with themselves, they are not wise." This is the sure way to defeat and discouragement.

What helped me here was the analogy of an army. Like any army, God has His shock troops, infantry, and support personnel.

In an army, the infantry doesn't worry about its effectiveness compared with the shock troops, for their functions are different, and both completely necessary. But without support personnel, without troops to hold and strengthen the ground already taken, the efforts of the fighters in the army would be futile. Stan was a shock trooper. Others, as infantry, enter behind to mop up any remaining resistance and secure the new area taken. Then still others, like myself, become support personnel to consolidate the area, teaching and training the national believers to take their place in the Lord's army. So I have no need to be envious or worried about what others are doing, but to concentrate on what I'm supposed to be doing, according to my abilities and gifts. Now I am at peace with myself.

Whatever our physical appearance or limitations, God has planned each in just such a way so that our potential to glorify him is as great as it can be. Each of us has a function to perform in the Body of Christ. What we need to concentrate on is what that function is and doing it.

Where is your place in the Lord's "army"?

APPLICATION: Remember Paul's apt analogy in 1 Corinthians 12:18-25 regarding our position in the body of Christ. He likens us to various body parts: feet, hands, ears, eyes, head, and so on. Some parts are not as appealing in form as others, yet ALL are essential to the health and well-being of the body.

Find out where God has placed you in the Body and work on serving and glorifying him in that capacity: as a "foot," a "hand," an "eye," or whatever he's chosen. Then you will be at peace with yourself as you concentrate on doing God's will and glorifying him. (See APPENDIX III for some helps on identifying your spiritual gift(s) and your place in the Body.)

DAY 33
[a]HE IS THE PEACEFUL ONE, THE PEACEMAKER, cont.

QUESTIONS TO THINK ABOUT:

1. Why are we so often not at peace with one another?
2. Whose fault is it if there is no peace?
3. What are some steps we could take to make peace between us and others?

Peace between Us and Others

Between Believers and Unbelievers

Now we come to the third area of peace: peace with others. During the major portion of his life, Christ was at peace with those around him (Lk.2:52). But when he began his ministry, and people rejected his teachings and reproof, he was no longer at peace with them. This was not his fault but occurred because they rejected the truth that he presented.

Paul says in Romans 12:18, "If it is possible, as far as it depends on you, live at peace with everyone." The implication here is that it is not always possible, but if there is no peace, don't let it be your fault (cf. Matt.10:34-36 where Jesus says the results of his teachings would not be peace but a sword and division). So peace between the unsaved and the believer is not always possible.

Between Believers

But peace between fellow believers is not only possible, but commanded! The provision for peace between all men was made at the Cross by Jesus Christ (Eph.2:14-18). Here we read of peace between Jew and Gentile, and both to God. Christ urged his disciples in Mark 9:50, "Salt is good, but if it loses its saltiness, how can you make it salty again? Have salt in yourselves, and be at peace with each other." Of all people, Christians are the ones who should be living at peace with one another, which Christ intended to become a powerful witness to the world.

Often Christ's disciples were at loggerheads with one another or with others outside their "privileged circle." One day they were arguing about who would be the greatest among them (Lk.9:46-48). Jesus made a temporary peace among them <u>by teaching</u> them who was really great in the kingdom of God. Evidently that made them feel very uncomfortable, for John answered him with an entirely different situation – perhaps trying to get a word of commendation – about their hindering a man who was casting out demons in Christ's name, but wasn't following him with the disciples. <u>A word of correction</u> followed instead (Lk.9:49,50). Party spirit destroys peace. Later on, when the Samaritans refused to lodge Jesus and his disciples, James and John, wanted to call down fire from heaven to destroy them (Lk.9:51-56). Christ restored peace through <u>a sharp rebuke</u> and <u>a word of instruction</u> as to what his purpose on earth really was.

Unfortunately, the Church today is still marked by these same squabbles of greatness, party spirit, and revenge on both personal and organizational levels. Instead of trying to make peace with the brethren, attempts are made to justify and prove the rightness of one's own position, and the utter wrongness of the other's, thus driving peace that much farther away. A student of a fundamental Bible school told me of the instructions given to their up-and-coming pastors that if they didn't split their churches within a certain period of time after taking a pastorate, they weren't doing the Lord's work! No doubt the idea is that if one is preaching the true Word of God, then there will be those who will reject truth, leave the church and perhaps cause a split. That is true enough, but to make the splitting of the church one's goal is a dangerous exercise indeed. Rather, our goal, through the truth of the

Word of God, should be to lift up the Lord Jesus Christ so that others will be drawn toward him, not driven away from him (Jn.12:32). We must strive to bring peace between them and their Lord, not animosity; peace between them and fellow believers, not strife. All Christians must be peacemakers, and must be willing to step in with whatever word or action necessary to restore peace and a strong testimony.

Christ laid the foundation of this peace in John 13:35 where he says, "By this all men will know that you are my disciples, if you love one another." If there is peace, there will also be love; if there is love, there will also be peace.

The question many have is, "With all our imperfections, how <u>can</u> we love one another as we should? How <u>can</u> we be at peace?" 2 Corinthians 3:18 says, "And we, who with unveiled faces all reflect the Lord's glory, are being transformed into his likeness with ever-increasing glory, which comes from the Lord, who is the Spirit."

The first step toward peace is to look at other Christians as imperfect, but developing images of Christ. Then ask yourself: "Will my reaction to what they are and what they are doing help them or hinder them in this process of becoming Christ-like?" If it hinders them, then your reaction is wrong.

A second step toward peace is <u>gaining the ability to separate the doer from the deed</u>. In Romans 5:8 we read, "But God demonstrates his own love for us in this: While we were still sinners, Christ died for us." Verse 10 states plainly that in such a sinful state, we were God's enemies. He loves the sinner, but hates his sin. Our usual response is to hate both! Amber and I couldn't fully understand how parents could love their child regardless of what that child did. Now that we have been house parents, we can understand. The parents see their child as a person, with the potential of becoming something better than he is now. The child's naughtiness then becomes a hindrance which must be removed by discipline in order for him to reach his potential. They don't hate their child, but certainly hate that which will keep him from reaching his potential. So must our attitude be toward fellow believers.

A third step is <u>a willingness to ask for forgiveness when we are wrong</u>. In Matthew 5:23,24 Christ instructs us: "Therefore, if you are offering your gift at the altar and there remember that your brother has something against you, leave your gift there in front of the altar. First go and be reconciled to your brother; then come and offer your gift." God puts such a high priority on peace between believers that he says reconciliation is more important than worship!

The fourth step is found in Paul's admonishment to us in Colossians 3:12,13, saying, "Therefore, as God's chosen people, holy and dearly loved, clothe yourselves with compassion, kindness, humility, gentleness and patience. Bear with each other and forgive whatever grievances you may have against one another. <u>Forgive as the Lord forgave you</u>" (underlining mine). We are called to peace (Col.3:15).

On all occasions Proverbs 15:1 is a good verse to remember: "A gentle answer turns away wrath, but a harsh word stirs up anger." There was a time when a fellow believer was daily accusing me of wrong-doing, lying to the people we worked with, not keeping my promises, misuse of ministry funds, and so on. I would answer anger with anger trying to justify myself. Being falsely accused was an affront to my pride (another problem) as well as my honesty. My problem was that after I had blown up in return, <u>I</u> had to go to that person to ask forgiveness for my anger, whereas that person should have been coming to me for forgiveness because of the false accusations! One day the absurdity of this continuing drama hit me and I realized that something had to be done to change it. Proverbs 15:1 showed me the way out of my dilemma. So I prayed and asked the Lord to help me give a gentle answer the next time I was accused. A few minutes later the telephone rang, and we were into it again. But this time I gave a gentle answer... . Silence. "Well, uh, goodbye." And there was peace – from that day until now.

Scripture is very clear upon what grounds there can be no peace and when we should separate ourselves from other Christians. Most, if not all of these situations have to do with disciplining wayward believers (cf. Matt.18:15-17; 1 Cor.5:4-7a; Prov.22:24,25; 2 Thess.3:6,7). If there has to be disruption of fellowship, then let it be only on Scriptural, not personal grounds, and only after considerable effort toward reconciliation has been made. After all, we wouldn't amputate so much as a portion of a finger without serious attempts at "maintaining the unity and wholeness of the body," amputating only as the very last resort. Thus should be our attitude and concern for the Body of Christ.

Is peacemaking a central pillar of your life and witness?

APPLICATION: Have you taken the four steps to peace mentioned above toward your fellow believers?

1. See also Ephesians 4:6-18, Colossians 3,4 and Romans 12 for Paul's discussion on peacemaking principles, then prayerfully consider what further steps you need to take to restore peace between you and others.
2. Make a list of those with whom you are not at peace, and list the reasons why. Then pray about these things searching your own heart to discover where YOU may be part of the problem.
3. After that apply the four principles mentioned above in seeking peace with the party(ies) involved.

DAY 34
[a]HE IS THE PEACEFUL ONE, THE PEACEMAKER, cont.

QUESTIONS TO THINK ABOUT:

1. What is the biggest frustration we face in our circumstances?
2. How does Philippians 4:6,7 guarantee us peace in spite of our circumstances?
3. How does faith help us when facing daunting circumstances?

Unexpected Transformation

Peace between Us and Our Circumstances

The fourth area where Christ has made peace is between us and our circumstances. Perhaps this area more than any other, destroys our sense of peace. When Peter, walking on the water, took his eyes off the Lord and began looking at the waves and listening to the wind (his circumstances), he began to sink (Matt.14:24-31)! And Jesus rebuked him, saying, "You of little faith, ... why did you doubt?"

During our first term in Papua, we saw God literally pull us out of several impossible situations. Our faith increased. But then we began looking at our circumstances and began to sink. As we began our second term, we were overwhelmed by our circumstances and began looking frantically for a way out. Needless to say, we had no peace. Our circumstances were bigger to us than God! Then, through his Word, God began to teach us of his sovereignty and we began to see clearly a God strong enough to calm the raging sea, both within and without. We had to come to a point of decision, literally, to choose to believe God or to believe our circumstances and plunge into the sea of bitterness because of our unbelief. We chose to believe God, and our hearts became peaceful even though the outward storm raged on.

Perhaps a review of DAYS 1 and 2 would be appropriate here, for until we believe that God is sovereign, and has all things under his control, and loves us with a deep, eternal love, our hearts will never be at peace with him in our daily lives.

There are two promises, among many that we can claim, in Isaiah 26:12 and 26:3,4. "LORD, you establish peace for us; all that we have accomplished you have done for us." And, "You will keep in perfect peace him who mind is steadfast, because he trusts in you. Trust in the LORD forever, for the LORD, the LORD, is the Rock eternal."

Jesus said to his disciples, "I have told you these things, so that in me you may have peace. In this world you will have trouble. But take heart! I have overcome the world" (Jn.16:33). The foundation of our peace in adverse circumstances lies in the Lord Jesus Christ. Once we settle the fact in our own minds that <u>He is sovereign, having all things under His control</u>, and that He has gone through what we do and came out on top ("I have overcome the world"), we can take our eyes off our circumstances as our source of peace and look to the One who gives peace in spite of circumstances. Once we gain this insight for ourselves, then we can pass it on to others with words of encouragement, and thus bring peace between them and their circumstances too.

APPLICATION: Is your God big enough and strong enough to handle all your circumstances? Take time to reflect on his sovereignty and love, and what these characteristics should mean in your daily life. When you begin to realize just how big your God is, life's circumstances will begin to shrink by comparison, and you will begin to have peace. You might want to review the APPLICATION section from DAY 1 here.

DAY 35
[b]HE IS THE PEACEFUL ONE, THE PEACEMAKER, concl.

QUESTIONS TO THINK ABOUT:

1. How can we "control" or influence nature so as to make peace between it and mankind?
2. How should a Christian be involved in our environment?

Peace between Us and Nature

The last area for peacemaking is that between man and nature. Jesus and his disciples were caught in one of those infamous Lake of Galilee storms, and the boat was filling with water. The disciples were terrified, and pleaded with Christ to do something (Lk.8:22-25). Immediately he arose from his sleep and calmed nature's raging, restoring peace to both his disciples and the elements.

"Stop there!" one may say. "It is one thing to talk about <u>Christ</u> controlling nature but quite another to talk about <u>our</u> controlling nature." Consider the following. On occasion, the Lord permitted man to have direct control over nature: Moses parting the waters at the Red Sea (Exod.14:21,22) when the waters threatened to cut off Israel's escape from Egypt; Joshua during the battle with the Amorites (commanding the sun to stand still – Josh.10:12-14); and Elijah before Ahab, proclaiming that it would not rain until he said so (Jas.5:17,18). I read an account of Indonesian evangelist, Rev. Octavianus, who was just ready to preach when a downpour began. He prayed and then commanded the rain to stop. It stopped instantly, he preached the Gospel, and many came to the Lord (Crawford, 75). On another occasion, during the cornerstone ceremony at a new church site in Merauke, Papua, a rain storm came up threatening to ruin the just-finished cement foundation. The missionary and people prayed for the Lord to stay the rain. He didn't! But what happened was even <u>more</u> amazing. As the rain approached the church site, the clouds split apart going around it, then joined together again on the other side! The church site remained dry while everything around was drenched! God will enable us to do the same if the situation demands it.

But on a more daily level, how can we make peace between man and nature?" By influencing it and its effects upon others. We traveled once by train from Dallas to Chicago, and noticed that wherever people were living near the railroad bed, there was trash, junk, garbage and broken bottles all over the place. It really ruined the scenery and I felt angry, not peaceful. We make peace between man and nature first by respecting God's creation, which includes putting the trash and garbage and junk where they belong, thus preserving nature's beauty and giving others pleasure in what they see.

Human carelessness, negligence and greed destroy thousands of acres of forest every year; contaminate water supplies, killing off water life through chemical and sewage pollution; and contaminate the air, causing acid rains, which in themselves rain down death and destruction of property. Indiscriminate use of water threatens to further lower already low water tables. We are not at peace with nature. But as Christians, our responsibility is first personally, make sure we are not contributing to the problem, then secondly, join with others in combating the man-made pollution and destruction of nature, so as to restore peace between both parties as much as possible, remembering that God's plan was for man to rule over nature, not ruin it.

APPLICATION:

1. What practical steps do you need to take to help create peace between man and nature?
2. Overall, are you a peacemaker, or a disturber of the peace?

DAY 36
ᵇHE IS THE KING
(the Governor/Ruler)

QUESTIONS TO THINK ABOUT:

1. What is the function of a governor?
2. How is a governor also a servant?
3. What does Romans 13:1-7 have to say about those who govern?

In Matthew 2:6 Christ is called the Governor or Ruler (as quoted from Mic.5:2). The term "governor" seems to carry with it the sense of administrative authority in the name of the Emperor or government of the country. In other words, a governor is an administrative government official.

In the Old Testament, the Jews upheld the Lord Jehovah as their King (Ps.47:2; 83:18). Their Messiah therefore would come as a governor under his authority and in his name. This relationship is shown in 1 Corinthians 15:24-28 where we read: "Then the end will come, when he hands over the kingdom to God the Father after he has put all his enemies under his feet. The last enemy to be destroyed is death. For he 'has put everything under his feet.' Now when it says that 'everything' has been put under him, it is clear that this does not include God himself, who put everything under Christ. When he has done this, then the Son himself will be made subject to him who put everything under him, so that God may be all in all."

Seeing Christ as the Governor, an administrative government official, was an eye-opener for me. I hated and feared administration of any kind. It is not my gift. So I fought it every time the possibility of exercising it occurred. Then I discovered that if I am to become like Christ, I must also learn to administrate, since that is a part of his character. "O.K., Lord, I'm ready," I prayed. About three months later, I was asked to be the office administrator for TEAM's Papua field office. I was ready, knowing that here was one more opportunity to become more like Christ, and, because this is God's will for me, he also would give me the gift of administration so that I could fulfill my responsibilities in the office. I found that what once would have cowed me, now was a challenge, and I had great confidence that the Lord and I could handle whatever came across my desk. I had never worked under such pressure before. But the Lord sustained me, strengthened me, and gave me the wisdom necessary for each problem. Once again I learned the principle: "With the Lord's call comes the Lord's enablement."

I also discovered the truth of what Christ told his disciples in Matthew 20:26, "Whoever wants to become great among you must be your servant." The position of an administrator is the position of a servant, for he must constantly deal with the problems and requests of people as well as the desires and commands of his superiors. Thus we find another characteristic of Christ coming out: He is a Servant (which we will consider tomorrow).

APPLICATION: Are you in a position of leadership in some way? If so, are you successfully administrating your responsibility or feel that you are just muddling through? If you need help, there are two things you can do:

1. talk with someone who has the gift of administration to get some good pointers;
2. read some good books on administration in order to better understand its concepts and gain some practical "how to" knowledge (see APPENDIX IV for some helpful books).

DAY 37
[a]HE IS THE KING
(the Servant)

QUESTIONS TO THINK ABOUT:

1. What are the characteristics of a good servant?
2. What is the function of a servant and why is that important?
3. What are the master's responsibilities toward his servant?

Christ came first to serve his Father: "Here is my servant whom I have chosen," God said (Matt.12:18a). He came to serve those under him: "Just as the Son of Man did not come to be served, but to serve, and give his life as a ransom for many" (Matt.20:28). According to Philippians 2:7, he took upon himself "the very nature of a servant, being made in human likeness."

As viewed by his master, a good servant would be:

Characteristics	as seen in Christ	and reflected in us
1. Faithful	Heb.3:2	Heb.3:2; 1 Cor.4:2
2. Obedient	John 15:10	John 15:10
3. Wise/Discerning	1 Cor.1:24	1 Cor.2:7
4. Honest	Matt.5:37	Jas.5:12
5. Trustworthy	John 17:4	2 Tim.4:7,8a
6. Loyal	Matt.4:10	Matt.6:24
7. Able	Matt.28:18 (9:29)	Phil.4:13; John 15:5
8. Selfless (to the point of death)	Phil.2:7,8	Phil.2:17,18
9. Humble	Phil.2:8	Luke 17:10
10. Desire to please his master	John 8:29; Heb.10:7,9	John 8:29; Heb.10:7,9
11. Puts his master's desires ahead of his own	Matt.26:42; John 4:34	Mark 8:34,35
12. Teachable (willingness to listen)	Mark 8:34,35	Mark 8:34,35
13. Flexible	Heb.10:7	Phil.4:11,12
14. Kind	1 Cor.13:4	Eph.4:32
15. Diligent	John 9:4	Eccl.9:10; Col.3:23
16. Thorough	Heb.7:25	2 Tim.4:7
17. Cheerful	Heb.12:2	2 Cor.9:7

As the servant views his master, he would express toward him:

Characteristics	as seen in Christ	and reflected in us
1. Absolute trust	1 Pet.2:23	Prov.3:5,6
2. Utter devotion/love	John 15:10	Ps.37:4; Matt.22:37

As the servant fulfills his obligations and faithfully carries on his work, his master has certain obligations toward him in return: to meet his servant's basic needs. If we are faithfully serving the Lord, then it follows as naturally as breathing that God will meet our needs – even as he has promised (Phil.4:19; Matt.6:33)! These basic needs are for food and drink (Matt.6:25-27), clothing (Matt.6:28-32), shelter (Mk.10:29), health (Ps.103:3), and the tools with which to work (2 Cor.3:5; 1 Cor.12:4-11)! And if we are faithful, there will be reward for faithful service (Eph.6:5-8).

In keeping with the Lord's promise to supply for us, we don't need to worry about those things and so can respond with the writer of Hebrews: "Keep yourselves free from the love of money and be content with what you have, because God has said, 'Never will I leave you; never will I forsake you'" (Heb.13:5). And with Paul in Philippians 4:19 and 11, "And my God will meet all your needs according to his glorious riches in Christ Jesus." "... For I have learned to be content whatever the circumstances." <u>Contentment</u> is the inner expression of total trust in the One wholly capable of meeting our needs at any given time. As servants of Christ, this is our position. Are you content?

APPLICATION: Which of the above characteristics of a servant are lacking or weak in your life? Make note of them and ask the Lord to help you practice them. He will send along such circumstances that will help you develop in those areas.

Unexpected Transformation / 91

DAY 38
ªHE IS THE KING
(the Servant), concl.

QUESTIONS TO THINK ABOUT:

1. How can we be a servant to others?
2. If we open up ourselves to serve others, how can we keep them from "walking all over us"?
3. If we are busy meeting the needs of others, who will meet our needs?

The classic demonstration of Christ as the Servant took place in the upper room where he washed his disciples' dirty, dusty feet. For some reason there were no servants there to perform this task, and it seems that the disciples were more content to eat with dirty feet than to offer to wash anyone else's. Jesus detected this attitude, and, while the meal was being served, he rose up, took off his outer clothing (the disciples look up from their meal, curious), wrapped a towel around his waist, poured water into a basin (by this time his disciples were thoroughly puzzled), and began to wash their feet (and each one turned various shades of red with the realization that Christ was doing for them what they were unwilling to do for one another. In fact, Peter was so embarrassed that he tried to refuse the Lord's offer altogether, but yielded to the Lord's insistence). Then we read: "When he had finished washing their feet, he put on his clothes and returned to his place. 'Do you understand what I have done for you?' he asked them. 'You call me "Teacher" and "Lord," and rightly so, for that is what I am. Now that I, your Lord and Teacher, have washed your feet, you also should wash one another's feet. I have set you an example that you should do as I have done for you. I tell you the truth, no servant is greater than his master, nor is a messenger greater than the one who sent him. Now that you know these things, you will be blessed if you do them'" (Jn.13:12-17).

While at Columbia Bible College, Amber and I sang in the Ambassador Choir. Our director had a servant's heart, and, by both example and encouragement, he instilled that heart in us. Concerts were "easy" because they were impersonal. But after the concerts, the hard work began. He would say to us, "Even though you're tired from traveling and singing, or may not feel well (he directed one whole concert with a very green face!), always be sensitive to the needs of those around you. Seek ways to serve your hosts; be aware of their needs. Pray for opportunities to share Christ with them and encourage them in their Christian life. We are there to serve, not to be served." And that advice has stayed with us to this day.

One final note. In John 15:18-21, Christ told his disciples that if the world hated them, "keep in mind that it hated me first." Then he reminded them (vs.20), "No servant is greater than his master. If they persecuted me, they will persecute you also. If they obeyed my teaching, they will obey yours also. They will treat you this way because of my name, for they do not know the One who sent me." Our lives and witness, as we reflect Christ's character more and more, will tend to polarize those around us. They will be forced either to respond to the truth or reject it, and their actions and reactions toward us will correspond to their response. But ours is not to worry about their responses, but rather to be sure we are faithful servants.

Returning then to Christ as the Governor, he has made it quite clear as to how we should use our position as administrators: "Jesus called [his disciples] together and said, 'You know that the rulers of the Gentiles lord it over them, and their high officials exercise authority over them. Not so with you. Instead, whoever wants to become great among you must be your servant. And whoever wants to be first must be your slave – just as the Son of Man did not come to be served, but to serve, and to give his life as a ransom for many'" (Matt.20:25-28). Martin Luther reflects this statement when he said, "A Christian man is the most free, lord of all, and subject to none [when] he is also the most dutiful servant to all and subject to everyone" (Moody, p.183).

So our administrative authority must be used not as a platform of power, but as a seat of service.

Is your goal to serve or to be served?

Christ came to serve the Father; He came to serve us. Whom are you serving?

APPLICATION: Look around and ask yourself, "Is there someone who has a need that I can serve today?" Then plan to do it. (Don't forget your spouse and children!)

DAY 39
ᶜHE IS THE KING
(the Scepter)

QUESTIONS TO THINK ABOUT:

1. What is the meaning of a scepter in the hand of a king?
2. What does the scepter stand for in regard to the kingdom?

There are at least five different titles given to Christ in Scripture designating his royalty. He is called "The Scepter" (Num.24:17), the "Governor" (Matt.2:6), the "Ruler" (Mic.5:2), the "Prince" (Acts 5:31), and "The King of kings" (Rev.19:16). The last two titles are broken down into several categories which we will consider as we get to them.

In Numbers 24:17, Balaam prophesies about a "scepter" that shall arise from Israel and crush Moab. In context, this is a prophecy about Christ, the Messiah. According to Cruden's Concordance,

"The word originally meant a rod or staff. Thence it came to mean a shepherd's crook, and then the wand or scepter of a ruler. The references to it, save in Esther, are all metaphorical, expressing supreme power." In Isaiah 14:5 we read that "The Lord has broken the ... scepter of rulers." Thus his title of King of kings and Lord of lords can be stated, "Supreme Power above all supreme powers."

Whether planned or unplanned, the story of Esther brings out an interesting illustration of Christ as the Scepter. In Esther 4:8-14, Mordecai persuades Esther to go before the king to intercede for her people. She replied: "All the king's officials and the people of the royal provinces know that for any man or woman who approaches the king in the inner court without being summoned the king has but one law: that he be put to death. The only exception to this is for the king to extend the gold scepter to him and spare his life" (Esth.4:11). She went in, and the king extended the golden scepter to her.

We find this same principle or law operative for anyone presuming to enter God's presence on his own and unbidden; there is but one law for him: "You cannot see my face, for no one may see me and live" (Exod.33:20). In Hebrews 12:14b we are told the reason: "Without holiness no one will see the Lord." In Hebrews 10:14 we read that Christ has made us positionally perfect and thus fit to come into God's presence: "Because by one sacrifice he has made perfect forever those who are being made holy." And we read in Hebrews 12:10 that "God disciplines us for our good, that we may share in his holiness." He thus extends to us the Scepter of Righteousness, Jesus Christ himself, for us to touch. Having touched him, we are accepted by the Father and permitted to enter his presence and live.

The scepter is also the symbol of royal power or authority. So when we read in Hebrews 1:8 that "righteousness will be the scepter of Your kingdom," we know that righteousness will reign supreme in Christ's kingdom. His absolute authority is justified by his righteous character, which guarantees that whatever he does will be good and right. He is totally trustworthy in the use of his power.

As sons and daughters of the King, we also have authority delegated to us that we might act on behalf of our King (cf. 2 Cor.5:18). If that authority is not exercised on the foundation of righteousness, it will be corrupted and misused. We all can recall examples where this has happened. But if we exercise our authority on the foundation of righteousness, then our teaching and preaching will have the ring of Divine approval and people will recognize that we are speaking on behalf of our Lord.

As members of Christ's kingdom, do we reflect the supremacy of righteousness in our lives? Do others see that foundation of righteousness as we exercise our spiritual authority? Through our lives, the world can and should catch a glimpse of the righteous character of Christ's kingdom.

What do they see as they look at you?

APPLICATION: Someday we will be reigning with Christ.

1. What steps are you taking now to bring your life into line with the righteousness that will characterize his kingdom?
2. What further steps do you need to take?

DAY 40
ᶜHE IS THE KING
(the Prince)

QUESTIONS TO THINK ABOUT:

1. What does it mean to be a prince?
2. What authority and responsibilities does a prince have?

3. How does a prince prepare himself to exercise his future authority and responsibility?

4. Can the word "prince" also refer to a king?

The fourth title given to Christ, expressing his royalty, is The Prince (Acts 5:31): the Prince of Kings (Rev.1:5), the Prince of Life (Acts 3:15), and the Prince of Peace (Isa.9:6). The title of prince, as applied to Christ, has two closely related meanings: 1. chief leader, ruler, and 2. author. The same Greek word is translated both ways in various passages. The idea is "one who takes the lead in anything and thus affords an example, a predecessor in a matter" (Thayer, *arche*, p.77).

Thus Christ is:

The Prince	(the Chief Leader),
The Prince of Kings	(Ruler of Kings – to whom all kings, presidents, prime ministers, dictators, etc. will have to give direct account of their governing),
The Prince of Life	(Author of Life – beginner, sustainer and example of life as God intended it to be lived (see DAYS 7,8 – HE IS THE TRUTH and HE IS THE LIFE), and
The Prince of Peace	(The Peacemaker, taking the lead in establishing peace between God and man, man with himself, man and man, man and his circumstances, and man and nature (see DAYS 31-35 – HE IS THE PEACEFUL ONE).

How do we reflect Christ as the Prince? Going back to Thayer's explanation, there are two possibilities: 1. to be a predecessor in a matter, and 2. to take the lead by being an example for others to follow.

When it comes to the Christian life, are we among the first to discover new truths from the Word and to experience their reality, or are we usually among the last? Are we on the cutting edge of faith, or somewhere down the handle? When it comes to Christian living in our community, are we among the first to address social problems, ills and needs, or happy to let others do it? Throughout history, Christians have been credited with the beginning of hospitals, prison reform, establishing orphanages, providing social relief, and so on. We obviously cannot be a predecessor in everything, but are we a predecessor in something where we are?

The second flows logically from the first: if we are a predecessor in something, then it follows that we will take the lead by being an example for others to follow, be it in the spiritual, social, educational, political or economic realm. The Bible speaks to each area, and we as Christians not only should but _must_ be Biblical examples in each one (see DAY 5 – HE IS OUR EXAMPLE). Christians should be setting the standards for others to follow, not vise versa as is usually the case. We know that the world is getting worse and worse. The Bible says that this will happen. But Christians _could_ considerably reduce the pace of decline if they would only begin acting like the princes they are and begin setting godly examples for the world to see.

Are you a visible prince, or a prince in hiding?

APPLICATION:

1. Is there some area where you have an interest in which you can spearhead some effort for the kingdom? What area is that, and how could you develop it?

2. Are you setting a good example for others to follow in their spiritual life?

DAY 41
[a]HE IS THE KING OF KINGS

QUESTIONS TO THINK ABOUT:

1. What does it mean to be "King of Kings"?
2. When will we reign with Christ?
3. How can we reign with him now?

As we consider Christ as King of kings, there are several titles given to him depending upon the perspective taken. He is:

King of the Jews (Matt.2:2, from the Gentile perspective)
King of Israel (Jn.1:49, from the Jewish perspective)
King of Kings (Rev.11:15; 19:16, from the world's perspective, i.e. King of the Gentile nations), and
The Everlasting King (Lk.1:33, from the Believer's perspective) whose kingdom will never end.

Christ came to earth first to establish a spiritual kingdom (Mk.1:15), not an earthly one (Jn.18:36). The physical manifestation of his kingdom will take place at the end of the Tribulation period (Ps.2; Rev.20:6) and last for 1,000 years. During that time, we who are his will reign with him (2 Tim.2:12), and in the eternal state reign for ever and ever (Rev.22:3-5).

But there is another aspect of our reigning found in Romans 5:17. "For if, by the trespass of the one man, death reigned through that one man, how much more will those who receive God's abundant provision of grace and of the gift of righteousness reign in life through the one man, Jesus Christ" (underlining mine). Our position is that of imputed royalty by virtue of our adoption into God's Royal Family (Rom.8:15-17), and we have the authority invested in us to act through our Lord Jesus Christ (Jn.15:16; Acts 1:8, etc.). So, how

Unexpected Transformation / 99

do we "reign in life through ... Jesus Christ"? How do we reflect Christ's character as King day by day?

There are at least nine major areas where we can reign now, where we have authority to act, and can reflect Christ's royalty as King. We will begin here and continue on for several days.

What does it mean "to reign in life"? (All following underlining is mine)

> (Rom.6:12,14) "Therefore <u>do not let sin reign</u> in your mortal body so that you obey its evil desires... . For <u>sin shall not be your master</u>, because you are not under the law, but under grace."

> (Rom.6:6,7) "For we know that our old self was crucified with him so that <u>the body of sin might be rendered powerless</u>, that we should no longer be slaves to sin – because <u>anyone who has died has been freed from sin</u>."

> (1 Cor.10:13) "No temptation has seized you except what is common to man. And God is faithful; he will not let you be tempted beyond what you can bear. But <u>when you are tempted, he will also provide a way out</u> so that you can stand up under it."

I. To reign in life means to reign over sin. It is no longer our master; through Christ we are its master (Rom.13:14). Through prayer ("Lead us not into temptation" – Matt.6:13) and the Word (Ps.119:11) we are armored against it. By God's intervening action (1 Cor.10:13) there is always a way out when we are tempted. Thus there is no acceptable reason for a Christian to sin apart from his own choice to do so. Many times we temporarily hand back our crowns to sin, allowing it to rule over us rather than we over it. Then we suffer from its tyrannical rule until we force it, through repentance, to give the crown back to us. This is foolishness of the highest order. What king could long reign who keeps giving his crown to the enemy, then struggles and fights to regain it again, only to give it back once more another time? Let's stop surrendering our crowns!

APPLICATION: Just as we choose to sin, we can also choose not to sin. According to 1 Corinthians 10:13, the very reason we are tempted means that we can overcome that temptation IF we take the way out that the Lord has provided. One way out is through the Word of God. Psalm 119:11 says, "I have hidden your word in my heart that I might not sin against you." Memorizing verses which deal with your area of temptation can be a tremendous help in overcoming sin and ruling over it. (See HE IS THE TEMPTED ONE, DAYS 53 and 54, for further discussion about this.) Try it.

DAY 42
ᵇHE IS THE KING
(over Satan)

QUESTIONS TO THINK ABOUT:

1. How much influence is the occult exerting on Christians today?
2. What harm is there in a Christian's dabbling in the occult (like tarot cards, Ouija boards, levitation, etc.)?
3. What influence could the possession of occult objects in one's house have on him and his family?

Again we ask, *What does it mean "to reign in life"*? (All following underlining is mine.)

(Jas.4:7) "Submit yourselves, then, to God. <u>Resist the devil, and he will flee from you</u>."

Unexpected Transformation / 101

(Matt.10:1) "He called his twelve disciples to him and <u>gave them authority to drive out evil spirits</u> … ."

(Lk.10:17-19a) "The seventy-two returned with joy and said, 'Lord, <u>even the demons submit to us in your name</u>.' He replied, 'I saw Satan fall like lightning from heaven. I have given you authority … .'"

II. To reign in life means to reign over Satan and his demons. We have authority over him through Christ. While in the city of Manokwari one summer, holding Christian Life seminars in various local churches, we experienced strong opposition from demons. Sunday morning of the last week I had the greatest freedom I've ever had in delivering the Word of God. But Monday and Tuesday evenings were a mess! People kept coming in late causing a disturbance each time, making everyone lose his train of thought (including me). I struggled to give the lessons. Dogs barked, children ran around playing noisily. Roosters crowed just outside the windows. Babies cried. Total confusion! Both nights Amber and I felt exhausted and played out. We figured that four weeks of seminars had finally caught up to us.

Alone with my thoughts and the Lord the second night, I pondered this situation and concluded that it was demonic interference. I prayed, "reminding" the Lord of his promise of fruit (Jn.15:16) and told him that this demonic interference was hindering his promise and keeping the church folk from understanding the Word. Then I turned and rebuked those spirits causing confusion in the name of the Lord Jesus Christ, commanding them to cease their opposition. Wednesday through Friday evenings there were no problems! Everyone came on time, dogs, children and roosters were quiet, and the lessons "got through." Amber and I both felt refreshed and physically strong.

One day the student head of the women's dorm came to me complaining of headaches and inability to concentrate on her studies – strange headaches that would not respond to anything.

Before our conversation ended, she ventured a comment on some strange happenings in her dorm room. Her locked door would be standing open in the morning. The chair under her desk was found out in the room. She could not sleep well nor turn on her bed because "something" was holding her down and making it hard to breathe. The "symptoms" were a clear indication of demonic activity.

After checking to be sure she wasn't involved in anything occult, we prayed, committing her to the Lord and rebuking those wicked spirits in the name of the Lord Jesus Christ. She went back to the dorm obviously relieved. The next day I asked her how things were. She said that her headaches had nearly stopped, and that her room was peaceful. She had had the first good night of sleep that she had had in a long time. Then she said something interesting. "When you prayed for me yesterday, I suddenly felt a rush of wind go around me, but there was no wind. I reached back to feel whatever it was; but there was nothing there. What was it?" "I'm not sure. Perhaps what you felt was the demons departing, or God's angels chasing them away. But whatever it was, it was God's indication that He had delivered you."

There aren't demons "behind every bush," but when you encounter one, you have all the authority in heaven at your command to resist him.

APPLICATION: The conflict between the occult and Christianity is growing. This calls for a greater awareness of our enemy (Satan) and how to resist him in prayer and obedience to the Word of God. Listed in APPENDIX V are some very helpful books which will heighten your awareness of the conflict and give you instructions on how to fight the spiritual battle we are in.

But don't go on "demon hunts" every time something goes wrong. Just be aware of Satan's ways and be prepared to resist when resistance is called for. When you encounter something occultish that is too strong for you, do not hesitate to call upon more mature believers for help and counsel.

DAY 43
[b]HE IS THE KING
(over Sickness)

◆

QUESTIONS TO THINK ABOUT:

1. Why do Christians, or people in general for that matter, often become sick?
2. Some say that it is always God's will to heal us of our infirmities. What do you think?
3. How is it possible to "rule" over sickness if we are NOT healed?
4. How could health become a deadly enemy, and sickness a blessed ally?

What does it mean "to reign in life"? (All following underlining is mine).

(Matt.10:1) "He called his disciples ... and gave them authority ... to heal every disease and sickness."

(Jas.5:14-16) "Is any one of you sick? He should call the elders of the church to pray over him and anoint him with oil in the name of the Lord. And the prayer offered in faith will make the sick person well; the Lord will raise him up. If he has sinned, he will be forgiven. Therefore confess your sins to each other and pray for each other so that you may be healed. The prayer of a righteous man is powerful and effective."

(Jas.1:2,3) "Consider it pure joy, my brothers, whenever you face trials of many kinds [including sickness], because you know that the testing of your faith develops perseverance."

III. To reign in life means to reign over sickness, both in terms of our authority to bring healing and in terms of our patient attitude toward sickness (or physical infirmity) if healing does not come immediately.

During the Christian Life seminars in Manokwari, mentioned yesterday, I shared as a matter of course several experiences of healing that I have had since coming to Indonesia. One morning, the phone rang. I was called to a home to pray for the healing of a sick wife. Frankly, I went with much misgiving. "Why me, Lord? This man talks as if he <u>expects</u> something to happen! I can't do anything. Lord, help me know what to say, what to do."

In sharing the principles of James 5:14-16 with her, it seemed that she had been disobedient to the Lord. From past experience, I knew that if her sickness was discipline from the Lord for sin, then as soon as that sin was confessed, the need for discipline would be over, and she would be healed. However, I didn't know for sure if what she confessed was indeed the presenting cause for her illness, or if something else was at work. So I prayed "broad spectrum," asking the Lord to forgive her sin, rebuking her symptoms in the name of the Lord, and committing her will to the Lord if this sickness was to teach her something she had yet to learn. Within the week she was well and attending the seminar.

But what happens when the sickness isn't immediately healed? Who rules then? If the sickness rules us, we will become disillusioned, bitter and angry at the Lord for not answering our prayers; after all, "we have a right to be healed!" Or we become introspective and begin doubting our faith and relationship to our heavenly Father.

On the other hand, though the sickness may have overpowered our bodies, it need not overcome our spirit. A joyful, indomitable spirit, patient and full of faith, praise and love for the Lord, even in the midst of sickness or physical disability, shows that we truly are reigning over sickness. Healing will come in time, perhaps, but not necessarily according to our schedule. We need to treat sickness as we do other circumstances (as we will be dealing with next): "Lord, what are you trying to teach me in this that will make me more like Christ and a better servant of yours?" We can be certain of one thing: when the Lord has accomplished His purpose through the sickness in our lives, we will then be healed (see APPENDIX VI for eight reasons why we get sick).

One time I had a sickness which made me very weak, and the pressure I felt in my chest made it hard to breathe. When some Christian friends came to pray for me, that pressure hindering my breathing completely and immediately cleared up, yet the basic weakness remained. The Lord indicated that he wanted me to learn to depend upon his strength, and that that was the purpose of this illness. Most of the time, the reasons may not be so clear. It is then that we exercise our faith and patience in the Lord's goodness and love, keeping an open heart to receive whatever his purpose is. Usually we will gain insight and discover "reasons" after we have gone through that trial.

Someone shared this thought with me one day: "We can have victory (reign in life) over the world, the flesh, the Devil and sin whether in sickness or in health. Sickness can be a blessed ally and health a deadly enemy!" (cf. 2 Cor.12:7-10 for an instance of this kind where health would have been a deadly enemy to Paul.)

When sickness attacks, are you reigning, or do you abdicate the throne?

APPLICATION: Look at APPENDIX VI and consider the eight reasons we become sick. Familiarize yourself with these reasons so that the next time you fall ill, you will know how to respond and rule over that sickness.

DAY 44
ᶜHE IS THE KING
(over Circumstances and Death)

◆

QUESTIONS TO THINK ABOUT:

1. How can we be seen to be ruling over our circumstances when everything seems to be going wrong?
2. How can we have joy in our hearts in spite of our circumstances?
3. How can we be said to "reign over death" if we die?

What does it mean "to reign in life"? (All following underlining mine.)

(1 Thess.5:18) "<u>Give thanks in all circumstances</u>, for this is God's will for you in Christ Jesus."

(Phil.4:6,7) "<u>Do not be anxious about anything</u>, but in everything, by prayer and petition, with thanksgiving, present your requests to God. And the peace of God, which transcends all understanding, will guard your hearts and your minds in Christ Jesus."

(Jas.1:2) "<u>Consider it pure joy</u> … whenever you face trials of many kinds."

IV. To reign in life means to reign over our circumstances. James 1:2 carries the basic ingredient for reigning over our circumstances: a rejoicing spirit. In all our circumstances, our attitude will indicate who is ruling – we or they!

One day I needed to get some kerosene from the fuel drum. The pump was corroded shut. It just would not work. I knew what was wrong and how to fix it, but was impatient. I wanted that fuel <u>now</u>, not later. So I tried to force the handle, then hit it with an ax head, then tried again to force it back and forth, back and forth, getting angrier and angrier, until the securing ring at the mouth of the drum broke. Then I exploded.

Who was reigning, I or the fuel pump? If I was reigning, my response would have been to give thanks for this trial to my patience and rejoice, committing myself and the pump to the Lord. [Praying something like, "Lord, reproduce yourself in me right now" is a good reminder to us of God's working through that circumstance to make us like Christ.] Then I'd either fix the pump or use an alternative method to get the fuel. We can always tell who or what is reigning by our attitude toward whatever happens. God is in sovereign control of our circumstances. Since we are hidden with Christ in God (Col.3:3), we too are in control. Are you?

What does it mean "to reign in life"? (All following underlining mine.)

> (Heb.2:14,15) "Since the children have flesh and blood, he too shared in their humanity so that by his death he might destroy him who holds the power of death – that is, the devil – and free those who all their lives were held in slavery by their fear of death."

> (Rom.6:4,8,9) "We were therefore buried with him through baptism into death in order that, just as Christ was raised from the dead through the glory of the Father, we too may live a new life... . Now if we died with Christ, we believe that we will also live with him. For we know that since Christ was raised from the dead, he cannot die again; death no longer has mastery over him."

V. To reign in life means to reign over death. Death no longer has dominion over Christ and we are in him; therefore it has no power over us either! It can no longer hold us as slaves in fear; thus we are free to walk daily in our resurrection life in Christ (see DAYS 51,52 where this subject, along with its application, have been dealt with in greater detail).

APPLICATION: Getting victory over our circumstances is perhaps one of the hardest exercises for the Christian to go through (see DAY 34 – HE IS THE PEACEFUL ONE). More and more I am convinced that it is a matter of personal discipline to force ourselves to stop, ponder God's loving sovereignty in those situations, and give him thanks for what he is accomplishing in our lives through them, then do what we can, if possible, to resolve them. What circumstances are beyond our power to do anything about we must commit to God for him to handle.

DAY 45
[a]HE IS THE KING
(over Self)

QUESTIONS TO THINK ABOUT:

1. How do our thoughts control our words and actions?
2. Is "acting without thinking" spontaneous or learned behavior?
3. Some have thought that the best way to control oneself is to become a monk or nun in a monastery or convent, isolating oneself from the world and its temptations. What do you think about this method of self-control? Is it effective? Does it work? Or is it merely "escapism"?
4. What advantages would a person have in learning to control oneself in the "outside world"?

What does it mean to "reign in life"? (All following underlining mine.)

> (1 Cor.9:25-27) "Everyone who competes in the games goes into strict training. They do it to get a crown that will not last; but we do it to get a crown that will last forever. Therefore I do not run like a man running aimlessly; I do not fight like a man beating the air. No, <u>I beat my body and make it my slave</u> so that after I have preached to others, I myself will not be disqualified for the prize."

> (2 Cor.10:4b,5) "We demolish arguments and every pretension that sets itself up against the knowledge of God, and <u>we take captive every thought to make it obedient to Christ</u>."

> (Jas.3:2) "We all stumble in many ways. If anyone is never at fault in what he says, he is a perfect man, <u>able to keep his whole body in check</u>."

VI. To reign in life means to reign over one's self. The key to self-control is the control of the tongue (Jas.3:2). Question: How does control of the tongue assure us of our ability of self-control? We think in words, then we act. Thus as our words are controlled, so will be our actions. But what fuels the tongue? Our thoughts. So we need to be sure our thoughts are right. How? By obeying Philippians 4:8. "Finally, brothers, whatever is true, ... noble, ... right, ... pure, ... lovely, ... admirable – if anything is excellent or praiseworthy – think about such things."

That is hard. So how do we get ourselves in the right frame of mind to do that? By offering ourselves as living sacrifices to God and not being conformed any longer to the pattern of this world, but being transformed by the renewing of our minds (Rom.12:1,2). And here is the crucial and initial step to reigning over self: renewing (reprogramming) our sinful minds through the Word of God.

"For as [a man] thinks in his heart, so is he" (Prov.23:7 – NKJV). And the Lord said: "You brood of vipers, how can you who are evil say anything good? For out of the overflow of the heart the mouth speaks. The good man brings good things out of the good stored up in him, and the evil man brings evil things out of the evil stored up in him. But I tell you that men will have to give account on the day of judgment for every careless word they have spoken. For by your words you will be acquitted, and by your words you will be condemned" (Matt.12:34-37).

So as we read, study, memorize and meditate upon the Word of God, our minds and hearts are "reprogrammed" and renewed after God's thoughts. Our words will reflect this change, and the more our words are thus controlled the greater will be our self-control in all areas (which, by the way, is also a fruit of the Spirit – see Gal.5:23).

APPLICATION: What do you spend most of your time thinking about? That is what forms your attitudes and influences your words and actions. A very revealing exercise would be to take a "Thought Inventory" for a day and jot down your thoughts by topic and how much time you spent thinking about each one. Maybe you'd want to do this for several days to get a better picture of your thought life. Then go back to Philippians 4:8 and judge each topic by this verse. If you are going to become like Christ, then your thoughts will have to be more centered on him than on other things.

Another help here is to ponder what you are in Christ. Christ always exercised self-control. Now he indwells you and as you yield to him, he controls your "self." So in Christ, we have victory over "self" and thus reign over it.

DAY 46
ᵃHE IS THE KING
(over the World)

QUESTIONS TO THINK ABOUT:

1. What does it mean to "love the world"?
2. How will loving the world affect our love for God and his kingdom?
3. What resources do we have that will help redirect our love toward God and what is pleasing to him?
4. Why will adhering to "kingdom" standards lead to persecution of some kind?

What does it mean "to reign in life"? (All following underlining mine.)

(1 Jn.2:15-17) "<u>Do not love the world</u> or anything in the world. If anyone loves the world, the love of the Father is not in him. For everything in the world – the cravings of sinful man, the lust of the eyes and the boasting of what he has and does – comes not from the Father but from the world. The world and its desires pass away, but the man who does the will of God lives forever."

(Rom.12:2a) "<u>Do not conform</u> any longer <u>to the pattern of this world</u>."

(Matt.6:31-33) "<u>Do not worry</u>, saying, 'What shall we eat?' or 'What shall we drink?' or 'What shall we wear?' For the pagans run after all these things, and your heavenly Father knows that you have need of them. <u>But seek first his kingdom and his righteousness</u>, and all these things will be given to you as well."

(Lk.16:9) "I tell you, <u>use worldly wealth to gain friends</u> for yourselves, so that when it is gone, you will be welcomed into eternal dwellings. (One explanation of this verse is that worldly wealth can be used to help others, whose gratitude will ensure a welcome in eternity [cf. Matt.25:34-40 as an example]. People will stand up and testify on your behalf about how you used your wealth to meet their needs.)

(Jn.16:33) "I have told you these things, so that in me you may have peace. In this world you will have trouble. But take heart! <u>I have overcome the world</u>."

(1 Jn.5:4,5) "For <u>everyone born of God overcomes the world</u>. This is the victory that has overcome the world, even our faith. Who is it that overcomes the world? Only he who believes that Jesus is the Son of God."

VII. To reign in life means to reign over the world's system. We are in the world, but not of the world (Jn.17:11,14). However, being in the world, we are subject to the world's influences. Its methods and ways are human-centered, not God-centered; based on sight, not faith; calculated to pamper, not develop character.

The command of God is for separation from the world's system. "Do not be yoked together with unbelievers. For what do righteousness and wickedness have in common? Or what fellowship can light have with darkness? What harmony is there between Christ and Belial? What does a believer have in common with an unbeliever? What agreement is there between the temple of God and idols? For we are the temple of the living God. As God has said: 'I will live with them and walk among them, and I will be their God, and they will be my people.' 'Therefore, <u>come out from them and be separate, says the Lord. Touch no unclean thing</u>, and I will receive you. I will be a Father to you, and you will be my sons and daughters, says the Lord Almighty'" (2 Cor.6:14-18).

This kind of thing will inevitably lead to suffering, but suffering develops character and patience and hope. Consider 2 Corinthians

4:17,18. "For our light and momentary troubles are achieving for us an eternal glory that far outweigh them all. <u>So we fix our eyes</u> not on what is seen, but <u>on what is unseen</u>. For what is seen is temporary, but what is unseen is eternal."

And Paul's conclusion? "Since we have these promises, dear friends, let us <u>purify ourselves from everything that contaminates body and spirit</u>, perfecting holiness out of reverence for God" (2 Cor.7:1).

From the above verses, we gain the basic attitude of the Christian toward the world: Don't love it; don't conform to it; use it as a tool over which you have mastery, but do not let it master you. Seek what is eternal, not what is temporal. As Paul says in Colossians 3:2, "Set your minds on things above, not on earthly things."

As you view the world, where is your mind-set?

APPLICATION: One sure way to "set your mind on things above" is to determine to "seek first the kingdom of God (that is, strive to do those things that will strengthen and promote God's kingdom) and his righteousness" (living uprightly, doing what is right – Matt.6:33).

List two or three things that you could do right now to help strengthen God's kingdom and how you plan to do them.

DAY 47
[a]HE IS THE KING
(over the World), concl.

QUESTIONS TO THINK ABOUT:

1. Imagine a situation in which you had two bosses. What would your life at work be like?

2. Is it really possible to love God and love the world at the same time?

3. What is the goal of the world's system? of God's?

What does it mean "to reign in life"? As we saw in DAY 46, it means to overcome the world's system.

As Christians we have a choice between following the world's system or following God's. It is impossible to do both as we cannot serve two masters (Matt.6:24. See also APPENDIX I for a comparison of the World's System and the heavenly System). Have you ever been in a situation where you've had two bosses? If so, then you know the frustration of conflicting goals, opposing commands, and the inability to make headway in any direction. It is impossible to obey or please both bosses; the employees must choose which boss they want and stick to him.

Demus found this out and made his choice. Having loved this world, he deserted Paul (2 Tim.4:10). James has a word of rebuke for those in such a state: "You adulterous people, don't you know that friendship with the world is hatred toward God? Anyone who chooses to be a friend of the world becomes an enemy of God" (Jas.4:4).

What we as Christians need to consider seriously is this: How much of the world's system are we following naturally, as a matter of course, because this is what we've grown up with and are used to? Perhaps there are areas of practice we are following which are diametrically opposed to the principles of faith and the Word of God, but about which we are unaware. How do we become aware of these things? By taking the promises of God and the principles of his Word to their ultimate end, not stopping short of that end as we usually do.

As an example, Matthew 6:33 says, "But seek first [God's] kingdom and his righteousness, and all these things will be given to you as well." We read this verse, say, "Amen" to its content, then go out and use our credit cards to buy all sorts of stuff that we <u>think</u> we need instead of waiting for God to provide what we really <u>do</u> need. What happens then is that we end up owing a debt which we would have avoided had we waited for <u>God</u> to supply.

Unexpected Transformation / 115

There is a balance that must be sought – that of <u>using</u> the mammon of this world with wisdom without becoming its servant (Lk.16:13), which will prove us capable of handling true riches (Lk.16:9-12). We must always be its master, and remember that we are on our way to a far better world, so should not be becoming entangled in or enslaved to the world system through which we are passing.

APPLICATION: If you truly viewed this world not as your home, but someplace you were just passing through (see Heb.11:13-16), how would that change your priorities and way of life?

DAY 48
ªHE IS THE KING
(with Authority)

QUESTIONS TO THINK ABOUT:

1. How can a Christian teach, preach or minister in any way with unwavering authority?

2. Is it arrogance on our part if we categorically say in the spiritual context, "This won't work but this will"? "This belief system is not right, but this one is"? Why or why not?

3. How does knowledge of the truth affect our spiritual authority?

What does it mean "to reign in life"? (All following underlining mine.)

(Matt.7:28,29) "When Jesus had finished saying these things, the crowds were amazed at his teaching, because <u>he taught as one who had authority</u>, and not as their teachers of the law." Jesus taught with authority because he knew the truth, and was sent from God (Jn.7:18).

(Acts 1:8) "But you will receive power when the Holy Spirit comes on you; and you will be my witnesses ... to the ends of the earth."

(2 Cor.5:18-20) "All this is from God, who reconciled us to himself through Christ and gave us the ministry of reconciliation: that God was reconciling the world to himself in Christ, not counting men's sins against them. And he has committed to us the message of reconciliation. We are therefore Christ's ambassadors, as though God were making his appeal through us. We implore you on Christ's behalf: Be reconciled to God."

(Jn.16:13) "But when he, the Spirit of truth, comes, he will guide you into all truth."

VIII. To reign in life means to reign in spiritual matters.
When Christ taught, he could teach with authority, because he knew that what he taught was true. God's Word is truth (Jn.17:17). Peter preached the truth of the Gospel with authority in Acts 2 resulting in the salvation of 3,000 people.

As we are led into the truths of God's Word by the Spirit of God, then we can speak and teach with authority as we represent Christ in the world. Teaching the truth, we can expect results as we share it, for God has promised us lasting fruit (Jn.15:16) and that his Word will not return to him empty, but will accomplish the purpose for which he sent it (Isa.55:11). Therefore, we can go forth in great confidence that our mission will be successful in the end.

APPLICATION: If you desire to speak with spiritual authority, there is only one way to do it – through a thorough knowledge of the truth. That truth is found only in the Word of God. In John 17:17 Christ prayed, "Sanctify them by the truth; your word is truth." And, among other things, the Holy Spirit was given to us to lead us into all truth (Jn.16:13). So make every effort to give the Word of truth the priority it deserves in your life. Then, with the Spirit's guidance and your perseverance in the Word, you will be able to speak with spiritual authority.

DAY 49
[a]HE IS THE KING
(over Sorrow)

QUESTIONS TO THINK ABOUT:

1. Is it wrong for a Christian to grieve and be sorrowful? Why or why not?
2. What is the basis for a Christian to be joyful in sorrow?
3. How does a spirit of joy help us through our sorrows?

What does it mean "to reign in life"? (All following underlining mine.)

> (1 Thess.4:13) "Brothers, <u>we do not want you</u> to be ignorant about those who fall asleep, or <u>to grieve like the rest of men</u>, who have no hope."

> (Jn.16:20,22) "I tell you the truth, you will weep and mourn while the world rejoices. You will grieve [sorrow], but <u>your grief will turn to joy</u>... . Now is your time of grief, but I will see you again and you will rejoice, and no one will take away your joy."

IX. To reign in life means to reign over sorrow. When Christ told his disciples that he was going to leave them, they were filled with sorrow (Jn.16:16,20). But he promised that their sorrow would be turned to joy. This happened at the resurrection (Jn.20:20).

As the leaving of Christ brought sorrow to his disciples, so the departure of our loved ones brings sorrow to our hearts. Yet we do not sorrow as the world does because we share with other believers the hope of the resurrection and eternal life.

We read in Neh.8:10b, "For the joy of the Lord is your strength." There is weakness in sorrow; there is strength in joy. The more deeply we get to know the Lord and have fellowship with him, the more we will be filled with joy, the more our faces will radiate his glory. Worldly sorrow indicates despair (hopelessness); joy expresses hope. As we realize that God is in sovereign control and is working all things together according to his omniscient plan, there then is no hopeless situation for the Christian. This is cause for great joy in our hearts.

APPLICATION: To reign over sorrow does not mean that we will not cry, that we will never be heartbroken, that we will never feel empty or lonely. What it does mean is that we can face sorrow with hope rather than despair. We can face sorrow knowing that it is only temporary; the end will be joy because of our Shepherd who is with us. In this we reign, not sorrow.

Christ is King! We are reigning in him right now. Are you wearing your crown?

DAY 50
[a]HE IS THE VICTORIOUS, THE TRIUMPHANT ONE

QUESTIONS TO THINK ABOUT:

1. When someone sins, we have often heard him say, "Satan made me do it." What do you think about that statement?
2. What power does Satan have over us to make us sin?

3. What are several ways we can overcome temptation and sin?

We find in Scripture at least five areas of possible defeat where Christ triumphed: over temptation, sin, the Devil, death and this world's system.

In Matthew 4:1-11, we find **Christ triumphant over temptation**. Satan hit him with the lust of the eyes (vs.8,9), the lust of the flesh (vs.3) and the pride of life (vs.5,6). But Christ overcame these temptations, not through argument or philosophical debate, but by the power of the Word of God! "It is written," he said three times. And three times the Devil-sponsored temptations were beaten. Christ held to the Word of God and thus did not yield to temptation.

We read in Psalm 119:11, "I have hidden your word in my heart that I might not sin against you." The more of the Word we have in our hearts, the less room there will be for temptation to take hold and bring forth sin (Jas.1:14,15. Notice the promise of the crown of life in James 1:12 to those who endure temptation and overcome it). This is one "way out" that God has provided for us in overcoming temptation. We read in 1 Corinthians 10:13, "No temptation has seized you except what is common to man. And God is faithful; he will not let you be tempted beyond what you can bear. But when you are tempted, he will also provide a way out so that you can stand up under it."

Christ overcame sin. We read in Hebrews 4:15b, "But we have [a high priest] who has been tempted in every way, just as we are yet was without sin." Christ was sinless. We are not. But we do have a position of victory over sin in him. Romans chapter 6 makes this very clear. In Christ, we are dead to sin (vs.6,7); this is our clear position. Verse 14 says that sin shall not have dominion over us because we are not under the Law, but under grace. But our practice is sometimes other than our position. We are to reckon ourselves dead to sin (vs.11) and then not let it reign in our lives (vs.12). So when we do sin, we sin by deliberate choice, not by necessity or coercion. Remember, a dead body (vs.6,7) cannot be coerced! So our victory over sin depends upon our choice whether to do it or not – for in Christ we do not have to sin!

We find some very encouraging verses in Scripture concerning **Christ's victory over Satan**. Colossians 2:15 says that on the cross, Jesus "disarmed the powers and authorities," making "a public spectacle of them, triumphing over them by the cross." John wrote in 1 John 3:8b, "The reason the Son of God appeared was to destroy the devil's work." We read in Philippians 2:10 that every knee shall bow at the name of Jesus and every tongue will confess him as Lord. This includes Satan and his demonic hordes. They hate his name, though they must also bow (Jas.2:19).

In the name of Jesus, we have the victory over Satan. As we submit ourselves to God, and resist the Devil in the name of Jesus Christ, Satan has no other alternative than to flee from us (Jas.4:7). This is God's promise to us, and on his ground, we are victorious.

One day I had what I thought to be a "travel" headache. But a rest didn't help; a good meal didn't help; some good fellowship that evening didn't help; and I could not get to sleep that night because of it. About midnight, I examined my heart and confessed what sin I found; still no relief. Aspirin didn't help either. So there was only one thing left; I submitted myself to the Lord for whatever his purpose might be in this, then rebuked the headache in the name of the Lord Jesus Christ. It was gone instantly, and I was asleep in seconds.

In addition to using the name of the Lord Jesus Christ, we can wage successful warfare against Satan and his minions by using the "armor" prepared for us (Eph.6:10-18). Bear this in mind: ours is not a struggle for victory from a position of defeat, but rather from a position of victory! "From victory unto victory," goes the song. We must claim Christ's victory and move on from that to other victories.

Satan is a defeated foe, but acts as if he is winning. Do you let his bluff cow you into defeat? Next time you are tempted, call his bluff by using the Word of God and your authority in the Lord Jesus Christ.

APPLICATION: In what areas are you often suffering defeat at the hands of Satan? Memorize verses of Scripture that deal with those areas and use them whenever you're tempted to sin. You will have deliverance if you really want it. Some know they should not do this sin, pray about it, and memorize Scripture to ward it off, but in their hearts they still want to do it. For them there will be no victory. Something to think about.

DAY 51
ᶜHE IS THE VICTORIOUS, THE TRIUMPHANT ONE, cont.

◆

QUESTIONS TO THINK ABOUT:

1. Have you ever felt the fear of death? How did it influence what you did? what you thought?
2. When we are fearful, what does that say about our attitude toward God?
3. How can one get victory over this fear?
4. For the Christian, what is death?

In the last lesson we considered Christ's victory over temptation, sin and Satan. Now we will consider **Christ's victory over death**.

In 1 Corinthians 15:20 we read a succinct statement of his victory: "But Christ has indeed been raised from the dead, the firstfruits of those who have fallen asleep." Proofs of his resurrection are plentiful both here (vs.18) and in Acts, chapter 1 and John, chapters 20 and 21.

In 1 Corinthians 15:22,23 we read of our ultimate victory over death: "For as in Adam all die, so in Christ all will be made alive. But each in his own turn: Christ, the firstfruits; then, when he comes, those who belong to him." So we have God's own guarantee for our ultimate victory.

But there is a present victory over death that we can experience even now. This is indicated in Hebrews 2:14,15 which says: "Since the children have flesh and blood, he too shared in their humanity so that by his death he might destroy him who holds the power of death that is, the devil and free those <u>who all their lives were held in slavery by their fear of death</u>" (underlining mine). We as Christians can be free from bondage to the fear of death. This is real, present tense victory. Let me share with you an experience I had regarding this.

On July 23, 1979, we were shocked by the news of the crash of MAF's Nomad in which the pilot and our good friend, Jim Lynne, was killed. The plane was found the next day, but it wasn't until after five tension-filled days of searching that Jim's body was found some distance from the wreckage.

Then on July 30th, a week later, we lost one of our national carpenters who fell from a rain-slicked tree and was killed. Petrus was a baptized believer, and well-loved both in his village of Tamnim and in Senggo. His loss was keenly felt and mourned.

These two deaths so close together suddenly brought the reality of death very, very close, and a gripping fear of death began gnawing at my heart. On August 18, five days before our annual Field Conference, I awoke at 5:00 A.M. with my stomach churning and feeling like someone had tied it into a huge knot. I was full of fear and dread with a certain foreboding about our conference flight. I was sure our flight was going to crash. But there was no hope. I couldn't very well not go to Conference just because I was scared. But the fear continued and grew.

Unexpected Transformation / 123

"What's happening to me?" I thought. "From where is this unreasonable fear coming? God has not given me the spirit of fear; but of power, and of love, and of a sound mind according to 2 Timothy 1:7" (NKJV).

During my prayer time that morning, I began thinking about God's sovereignty and love, and how death is only the doorway to heaven and a glorious life. Also the spirit of fear does not come from God, but from Satan; and I was filled with fear, which equals unbelief in all of God's good intentions toward me! So I knew that this fear had to be dealt with.

Then various verses came to mind, like Hebrews 2:14,15 describing the fear of death as slavery. It <u>is</u> a great bondage, influencing every part of one's life; and I was experiencing just how terrorizing it can be. "If I <u>do</u> this, will I die?" or "If I <u>don't do</u> this, will I die?" It becomes an all-consuming fear which robs us of physical and spiritual energy and effectively neutralizes us. We constantly scheme and plan in an effort to outwit our circumstances so as to avoid threatening situations, always trying to do what is very, very safe. Thus we become preoccupied with "staying alive," and all else, including our service for the Lord, becomes secondary. Do you know what I'm talking about?

But Romans 8:15 declares that we "did not receive a spirit that makes [us] a slave again to fear, but [we] have received the Spirit of sonship. And by him we cry, 'Abba, Father.'" God, our sovereign, loving Father, has given us his Spirit of power, love and a sound mind. He has opened the way for us to become his very own. He loves us and is going to care for us as a loving father would his own children. Realizing his sovereignty, we can respond to him in love, knowing that he is <u>more than capable</u> of caring for us. This knowledge in itself will banish fear, as John writes in 1 John 4:18, "There is no fear in love. But perfect love drives out fear, because fear has to do with punishment. The man who fears is not made perfect in love."

Then I thought of Psalm 23:4, "Even though I walk through the valley of the shadow of death, I will fear no evil, for you are with me; your rod and your staff, they comfort me." No sooner had I read this verse, than Psalm 139:16 came to mind with this encouraging and comforting thought: "All the days ordained for me were written in your book before one of them came to be." God has determined the length of our days; he has ordained the years of our life. And when that time comes to an end, he will take us to be with himself. All the scheming in the world will not alter this fact. In Psalm 116:15 we read, "Precious [of great value] in the sight of the LORD is the death of his saints." He does not take our death lightly; but it is a very precious, intimate thing with him. We need not fear what is precious to the Lord! So we can actually be free from worry about death knowing that, until the appointed time, we shall live to serve and worship God here on earth.

How does the fear of death influence your life?

APPLICATION:

1. What steps do you need to take to overcome your fear of death?

First of all, recognize that there is always a *feeling of uncertainty* in any move. That is a normal part of our struggle when facing death and can be fearful at times anticipating it.

Secondly, recognize that the debilitating fear of death (the above *uncertainty* totally out of control) is not from God (cf. 2 Tim.1:7), but from Satan to misdirect your focus and neutralize your life and ministry. That fear leads to desperation on your part to do everything you can to "guarantee" that you will live and not die; and that's a burden none of us can bear.

Thirdly, confess to God your sin of unbelief in his power to protect you and choose to submit to his plan for your life and its length.

Fourthly, meditate on the fact that death is merely the "doorway" to heaven and eternal life (cf. Luke 24:43); freedom from sin and life's trials and struggles and ask yourself, "What's so bad about that?"

Fifthly, your death is precious in God's sight (cf. Ps.116:15) because it is God's "Welcome home!" to you and all the blessings that await you there.

Sixthly, we are more fearful anticipating the process of dying than the actual event itself. But whether it comes slowly or quickly, God's grace will be sufficient for what you need at that time. You don't need "dying grace" now.

Finally, recognize that God has already numbered the days of your life (cf. Ps.139:16), so it's a waste of time and energy to worry about dying when you may have years to go yet.

2. The phrase "fear not" occurs at least 365 times in the Bible (that's one time for every day of the year!), and would make an interesting and valuable study in itself. What does the Bible say that we should not fear?

DAY 52
aHE IS THE VICTORIOUS, THE TRIUMPHANT ONE, concl.

QUESTIONS TO THINK ABOUT:

1. How can freedom from fear of death be a source of great power?
2. What is the key to overcoming the world?

One additional word needs to be said about those who do not fear death: they have a real source of power.

Consider: there is <u>freedom to carry on one's work</u>. I was afraid to go on village visits because if anything went wrong with the outboard motor, I wouldn't know how to fix it; I'd be stranded and maybe would die. Without my fear of death, my fear of the outboard diminished and I found new courage to reach out as occasion demanded.

Also, <u>it is impossible to be intimidated</u>. John Schultz, a Christian and Missionary Alliance missionary who grew up in Holland, spoke of an eighty-three-year-old woman who was arrested by the Nazis, being suspected of harboring Jews. She was not afraid of death. And where others were terrified by that prospect, she was not. There was nothing the Nazis could do to threaten her, so, frustrated, they let her go!

Finally, there is <u>a zest for living</u> which others cannot have, being shackled by fear of death. We can enjoy life because we're not worrying every moment about the prospect of death.

So, the next time you may be tempted to give in to the fear of death, remember: the source of that fear is Satan, not God; secondly, God, in his sovereignty, has ordained the length of your days which will end at their appointed time and not before. Therefore, we need not worry about our death, for that is under <u>God's</u> control (cf. Job 1:12; 2:6). Then we will be free to serve him fully and enjoy life to the greatest degree possible in this fallen world.

Now we come to the fifth area where **Christ is victorious**, and that is **over the world's system** (see DAYS 46 & 47 – HE IS THE KING, for further discussion on our victory over the world's system). In Revelation 19:19-21 and 20:15, we see where he returns to earth, overthrows the Antichrist, false prophet and Satan, and sets up his Millennial Reign. The curse will be gone (Isaiah, chapter 11) and perfect government will rule the nations. Many Old Testament passages describe the character and events

Unexpected Transformation / 127

of this blessed era, during which we also will be reigning with Christ (2 Tim.2:12).

1 John 5:4,5 further states our position: "For everyone born of God has overcome the world. This is the victory that has overcome the world, even our faith. Who is it that overcomes the world? Only he who believes that Jesus is the Son of God." Faith in him puts us on a higher plane altogether, even as he said of his disciples, "They are not of this world, even as I am not of it" (Jn.17:16). The tragedy is that from this exalted position so many Christians choose to descend to the world's level and once again become engrossed in its system. Christ prayed that the Father would <u>keep his own from the evil [one]</u> in the world (Jn.17:15), not take them out of it. Victory in the midst of evil is genuine victory, and that is already ours in Christ.

Paul gives us two verses declaring our victory. In 1 Corinthians 15:57 he writes, "But thanks be to God! He gives us the victory through our Lord Jesus Christ." And again in Romans 8:37, "No, in all these things we are <u>more than conquerors</u> through him who loves us" (underlining mine).

If you were to rate your daily victory from 1 to 10, where would most days fall?

APPLICATION: Since overcoming the world depends upon our faith (1 Jn.5:4), and faith comes from hearing the Word of God (Rom.10:17), then it stands to reason that if we desire to overcome the world, the only way we can do it is by strengthening our faith through the Word. If you have not done so yet, set aside time each day for personal reading and study of the Word. As the Word renews your mind, you will cease being poured into the world's mold as you are changed into the image of Christ.

DAY 53
ʿHE IS THE TEMPTED ONE

◆

QUESTIONS TO THINK ABOUT:

1. From where does temptation come?
2. Is temptation the same as sin?
3. Some say that you have to sin in order to understand the sinner. How would you respond to this view?
4. When we are tempted, what is provided by God for us as a way out?

In Hebrews 4:15 we read: "For we do not have a high priest who is unable to sympathize with our weaknesses, but we have one who has been tempted in every way, just as we are – yet was without sin."

1 John 2:16 clarifies the three areas of temptation we all face: the lust of the flesh ("the cravings of sinful man"), the lust of the eyes ("the craving to have what we see"), and the pride of life ("the boasting of what we have and do"). Christ experienced all three in his wilderness temptation as the devil tried to make him fall into sin (Matt.4:1-11).

Quoting at length from Greene (Greene, pp.89,90, but substituting the NIV for the KJV that he uses), he writes: "What did Satan really tempt Jesus to do? First of all, after He had fasted for forty days and forty nights He was hungry; and Satan tempted Him to turn the stones into bread. From the standpoint of the flesh and the hunger of His physical body, to change the stones into bread did not seem unreasonable. He could have wrought such a miracle – and the flesh was willing to have Him do it" [Lust of the flesh]. "But the Spirit was not willing. The God part of Him said, 'It is written, Man does not live on bread alone, but on every word that comes from the mouth of God!'

Unexpected Transformation / 129

"Then the devil took Him to the Holy City, and had Him stand on the highest point of the temple. 'If you are the Son of God,' he said, 'throw yourself down. For it is written: "He will command His angels concerning you, and they will lift you up in their hands, so that you will not strike your foot against a stone."'

"In the eyes of men, Jesus could have become famous that day" [The pride of life – boasting of what he could do. Actually, the Pharisees had a tradition that the Messiah would descend to earth at the Temple site. What better way for Jesus to prove to them who he was!] "He could have cast Himself down from the pinnacle of the temple – it would not have hurt Him. But He would not yield to the temptation to be spectacular and run His own life apart from the will of God. He answered Satan again from the Word of God: 'It is also written: "Do not put the Lord your God to the test."'

"But Satan did not give up. He then took Jesus up into a high mountain and from that vantage point he showed Him all the kingdoms of the world, and the glory of them" [The lust of the eyes]. "He then said to the Son of God, 'All this I will give you … if you will bow down and worship me.'

"Luke tells us that these kingdoms were Satan's to give to whomsoever he would; but Jesus said, 'Away from me, Satan! For it is written: "Worship the Lord your God, and serve him only."' The devil then left Him, and angels came and ministered to Him."

We will continue with Greene tomorrow, but notice how Satan was beaten by the use of the Word. That should tell us something about overcoming temptation in our own lives.

Have you ever tried using the Word to overcome temptation?

APPLICATION: Select verses of Scripture that apply to your special areas of temptation and memorize them. Then, as you are tempted, recall them to mind. As they center your thoughts on the Lord and away from the temptation, you will find yourself more and more overcoming that temptation.

Two examples will support this statement. I have found Romans 13:14 particularly helpful in the areas of lust and self-indulgence. It has come to my aid numerous times: "Rather, clothe yourselves with the Lord Jesus Christ, and not think about how to gratify the desires of the sinful nature." Malachi 2:15 has been helpful in the area of my marriage when my thoughts are tempted to wander: "Has not the LORD made them one? In flesh and spirit they are his. And why one? Because he was seeking godly offspring. So guard yourself in your spirit, and do not break faith with the wife of your youth."

DAY 54
'HE IS THE TEMPTED ONE, concl.

QUESTIONS TO THINK ABOUT:

1. How can our experiencing of temptation help us in encouraging others?

2. Some say, "The Devil made me do it!" Others, "I just couldn't help myself; I had to do it!" Can we ever be tempted beyond what we can withstand so that we are forced to sin?

3. True or false: "The basic key to overcoming temptation is wanting to in the first place." Why?

In concluding Greene's statement on Christ's temptations, he says, "Jesus faced the temptation to follow His own will and do what the flesh said to do, instead of what the Father said to do. He faced the temptation to live independently of God and create a name for Himself. He came to declare the Father and make known the love of God and God's grace. He faced the temptation to become King and reign on the earth by taking a short cut – but the God-part of Him cried out against it" (Greene, p.90).

Unexpected Transformation

Hebrews 2:18 says, "Because he himself suffered when he was tempted, he is able to help those who are being tempted." His victory, and his willingness to help us when we are tempted, form the basis for our victory over temptation.

We have no trouble in reflecting Christ as the Tempted One in terms of our experiencing temptation – for that comes daily. Our trouble comes in reflecting his victory over temptation! In 1 Corinthians 10:13 we read: "No temptation has seized you except what is common to man. And God is faithful; he will not let you be tempted beyond what you can bear. But when you are tempted, he will also provide a way out so that you can stand up under it."

There are three encouraging truths brought out in this verse: 1. None of us are <u>ever</u> tempted differently than anyone else (no special cases!); 2. The very reason we are tempted means that we <u>can</u> overcome it, for he has promised that our temptations will <u>never</u> be more than we can bear; and 3. For every temptation we face, <u>there is always a way out</u> – which completely eliminates <u>any</u> reason for a Christian to sin apart from his own choice to do so.

How can we then experience victory over temptation? There are at least six steps we can and must take.

First, we have to <u>want</u> to have victory (Rom.6:11,12,16).

Secondly, we must die to self and the desires of the flesh (by faith "forcing" ourselves to acknowledge what <u>God</u> wants in any given circumstance, then doing it – Lk.9:23,24).

Thirdly, we must walk in the Spirit (a life of obedience to the written and revealed will of God); then we will not fulfill the desires of the flesh (Gal.5:16; 2 Tim.2:22).

Fourthly, even as Christ did, we must use the Word of God as a weapon against temptation (Matt.4:4,7,10).

Fifthly, Paul urged Timothy to "flee the evil desires of youth" (2 Tim.2:22) – a very effective way to gain victory – leaving the scene, taking the physical way out that God has provided (cf. Joseph: Gen.39:6-12).

And lastly, we must not make provision for temptation (Rom.13:14). Don't purposely plan to subject yourself to it! I read recently in a Christian magazine a statement I'll never forget. It went something like this: "Don't keep your eye on the temptation while praying to God for victory over it!"

These are the six steps to victory <u>if we want</u> victory. Do you?

APPLICATION: Which of the above six steps do you need to concentrate on right now in order to gain victory over temptation? After choosing those which apply, sit down and plan your course of action in implementing them.

DAY 55
ᵇHE IS THE BURDEN-BEARER/ COMFORTER

QUESTIONS TO THINK ABOUT:

1. Why do so many Christians continue to live with unresolved burdens?

2. What does "casting our burdens on the Lord" imply about our attitude toward God?

In Psalm 55:22 we read, "Cast your cares on the LORD and he will sustain you; he will never let the righteous fall." Again in 1 Peter 5:7, "Cast all your anxiety on him because he cares for you." And Christ further invites us in Matthew 11:28-30, "Come to me, all you who are weary and burdened, and I will give you rest. Take my yoke upon you and learn from me, for I am gentle and humble in heart, and you will find rest for your souls. For my yoke is easy and my burden is light."

All through his ministry on earth, Christ lifted people's burdens: the burden of the father with the lunatic son (Matt.17:14-18), the burden of the desolate widow whose son had just died (Lk.7:11-15), the burden of the hungry multitude (Jn.6:1-12), the burden of the fearful disciples (Matt.8:23-27), and the burden of the anxious for daily needs (Matt.6:19-34). No matter what the burden, the Lord is Master of it and able to resolve it. No one who ever came to him in faith with a burden was ever disappointed.

We read in Hebrews 13:8 that "Jesus Christ is the same yesterday and today and forever." If this is true, then why do so many of us continue to live with unresolved burdens? Perhaps there are several reasons.

The first reason is <u>unconfessed sin</u>. Psalm 66:18 says, "If I had cherished sin in my heart, the Lord would not have listened." Sin creates its own burdens, and these and others will not be lifted as long as we continue to live in unconfessed sin.

Secondly, <u>our God is</u> often <u>not "big enough"</u> to handle our burdens. We can let him handle the small ones all right, but the big ones <u>we</u> need to care for so it will be done right! We <u>know</u> the doctrine of his sovereignty (see DAY 1 – GOD'S LOVING SOVEREIGNTY), but do we really believe it and practice it?

Ideally, in a child's eyes, there is nothing his father cannot do or care for. In his presence, his child has no worries or cares. I can remember, as a child, dreading bed time when I knew my folks would be down in the basement in the print shop. That put one story and the noise of the printing press between them and me; and I <u>knew</u> by the noises of our old, creaky house, that a robber was trying to get in. Many a night I spent under the bed covers, scarcely breathing lest that robber should hear me and come into my room. But let my parents come upstairs to their bedroom, and the house could creak and groan all it wanted. Dad was there, and he wouldn't let anything happen. We need to have this same utter faith in our heavenly Father. So then, when we find ourselves in turmoil, we can often attribute it to a lack of faith in him who is sovereign and surrounds us with his love.

APPLICATION: Are you burdened with unconfessed sin and a lack of faith in your heavenly Father? If so, the first is cared for by confession and repentance; the second by meditating on the meaning of God's sovereignty and love and believing his promises to us. Take time right now to think about these things. (The APPLICATION section from DAY 1 might be helpful here.)

DAY 56
[b]HE IS THE BURDEN-BEARER/ COMFORTER, cont.

QUESTIONS TO THINK ABOUT:

1. Why do we often want to "take back" burdens that we give to the Lord?

2. The Lord has promised to meet our needs; but if a fellow believer closes his heart to the Lord's promptings to help us, could that need go unmet?

In addition to unconfessed sin and a lack of faith in our heavenly Father, a third reason we have unrelieved burdens is because once having committed them to the Lord, we often take them back again, trying to resolve them in our own way. Peter walking on the water illustrates this problem. In the midst of a terrifying storm, he walked on the water toward the Lord, until he let himself be terrified by the storm again; then he began to sink and was reprimanded by Jesus for his lack of faith (Matt.14:25-31). So when we take our burdens back again, we are really saying to the Lord, "I'm sorry, Lord. I know I gave you this burden to care for, but I really think I can handle it better myself, if you don't mind." So he lets us have it back, shaking his head in disappointment.

A fourth reason we suffer unresolved burdens is because of <u>the disobedience of other Christians</u>! God has chosen to meet our needs basically through one another. Elijah being fed by the ravens was an

Unexpected Transformation

exception to the rule. If God directs us to take from what we have to minister to the need of a fellow believer, and we refuse, that need may just go unmet – provided for, for God is faithful, but unmet because of the disobedience of his child.

I once heard a story of an evangelist visiting a certain town, who stayed in the home of a church member. He was totally broke. He couldn't even buy a 3-cent postage stamp, but had a letter that he had to get mailed. He was embarrassed to ask the lady of the house for a stamp, so prayed that the Lord would supply him one. In another room of the house, at that same moment, the lady was in prayer, and the Lord spoke to her in her heart, telling her to give the evangelist a 3-cent stamp. "But, Lord! That's only three cents! Surely he has three cents. No one is so poor that he can't even buy a postage stamp. Besides, he is an evangelist, a servant of yours, and you have promised to supply all his needs; so I don't need to interfere. No, I don't need to give him a 3-cent stamp." So she didn't.

About a year or so later, the evangelist was holding meetings again in the same town, and once again stayed with this same family. During the course of conversation, the topic of the Lord's faithfulness in meeting our needs came up, and the evangelist recalled one time when he prayed for a 3-cent postage stamp because he was flat broke, but the Lord hadn't answered. The lady of the house, in embarrassment and shame, replied: "Sir, the Lord <u>did</u> answer your prayer. He told <u>me</u> to give you that stamp, and I refused." As God directs us to meet the needs of others in answer to their prayers, and we refuse, can you see what that might to do their faith in God's promises when the need goes unmet? It will surely put their faith to the test (as it did for that evangelist), and may cause them to doubt the Lord. Let's not give them that opportunity by our unfaithfulness or disobedience to the Lord's promptings.

So then, to gain relief from our burdens, we must first confess all unconfessed sin, take God and his promises at face value (believing and claiming them), and leave our burdens with him. We must be willing to accept help from fellow believers since God will most often supply our needs through them. Then we can praise God for undertaking for us. Reviewing, meditating upon and living out the promises of God will reveal Jesus Christ as our Burden-Bearer (see DAY 55 – HE IS THE BURDEN-BEARER, paragraph 1).

Are you bearing unnecessary burdens?

Is the faith of others in God's faithfulness being put to the test because you are not responding to God's urgings for you to meet their needs?

APPLICATION: If you tend to take your burdens back again after having given them to the Lord, confess this sin of unbelief to God (for that is what it is) and meditate again on his loving sovereignty. If he is "big enough" to care for the universe, he certainly is big enough to care for your burdens. Leave them there with him, and trust him to work them out in his time and in his way.

In terms of meeting the needs of others, pray, asking the Lord to help you be sensitive to their needs and the Spirit's promptings, then courageous to act on them.

DAY 57
[b]HE IS THE BURDEN-BEARER/ COMFORTER, concl.

QUESTIONS TO THINK ABOUT:

1. Why does the Lord permit us to be burdened?
2. If we have a burden, does that mean that we have sinned?
3. How can our burdens help us minister to others?

Unexpected Transformation

Yesterday we saw why Christians are often burdened from a negative standpoint. Today let us consider at least six positive reasons why we have burdens.

First, **in order to become Christ-like**. Burdens will help develop his characteristics in us if we view them with this in mind (Rom.8:28,29). James says, "Consider it pure joy, my brothers, whenever you face trials of many kinds, because you know that the testing of your faith develops perseverance. Perseverance must finish its work so that you may be mature and complete, not lacking anything" (Jas.1:2-4).

Secondly, **so that we can learn to trust God** with them and learn that he is sovereign over them. If all went well, we'd have no reason to trust him. We need to learn to depend solely upon him, and not upon ourselves and our own resources (Jn.15:5).

One day, soon after we arrived in Senggo, the local government officer gave our doctor a list of demands that we had to fulfill. Some of them were no problem, at worst a nuisance, but others spelled the end of our work there before it had begun. Our doctor and a fellow-missionary made arrangements with the local government officer to go to the nearest government seat on Monday to talk these things over with higher authorities. But it could go either way: for us or against us. Sunday afternoon we had a special prayer meeting about this matter. While we were praying, the Lord gave me faith that the whole matter was already cared for, and the fellows' trip on Monday was a mere formality to confirm what had already taken place. I nearly shouted for joy. Monday afternoon, when they returned, they were beaming. The Lord had indeed worked it all out and saved the local government official's face to boot. So we had another prayer meeting of thanks for what the Lord had done. Had we not had this "burden," we would not have seen what the Lord could do in impossible situations, and our faith for other such times would not have been as great.

Thirdly, some burdens are God's way of **motivating us to do something** that is on his heart. Until we do it, we have no rest. This was Jeremiah's experience: "But if I say, 'I will not mention him or speak any more in his name,' his word is in my heart like a burning fire, shut up in my bones. I am weary of holding it in; indeed, I cannot" (Jer.20:9).

Fourthly, **to cleanse us from sin**, God gives us a burden of guilt and other burdens in the form of discipline to draw us back to himself and a holy life. The Psalmist declared, "It was good for me to be afflicted so that I might learn your decrees" (Ps.119:71). And again Peter reminds us: "… He who has suffered in his body is done with sin" (1 Pet.4:1).

Fifthly, we have burdens **to teach us compassion** toward those with similar trials. In principle, this is what Christ experienced. We read in Hebrews 4:15,16, "For we do not have a high priest who is unable to sympathize with our weaknesses, but we have one who has been tempted in every way, just as we are – yet was without sin. Let us then approach the throne of grace with confidence, so that we may receive mercy and find grace to help us in our time of need." He knows our burdens by experience, and grants us grace in lifting them. That grace often comes through fellow believers who also have suffered and experienced God's grace.

This brings us to the sixth reason why we suffer burdens: **so that we can comfort those who are burdened**. As we identify with their pain and share with them the Lord's comfort, their hearts can experience encouragement and release. Paul says in 2 Corinthians 1:3,4, "Praise be to the God and Father of our Lord Jesus Christ, the Father of compassion and the God of all comfort, who comforts us in all our troubles, so that we can comfort those in any trouble with the comfort we ourselves have received from God."

We can reflect this characteristic of Christ in our lives as we also become burden-bearers. In Galatians 6:2, Paul urges us: "Carry each other's burdens, and in this way you will fulfill the law of Christ."

There are two ways to lift another's burden: one is to take the responsibility for it upon oneself, and the other is to bring words of comfort and encouragement that will help the burdened person get through his trial successfully.

Christ demonstrated both of these ways. On the cross, he bore the entire burden of our sin. We read in 1 Peter 2:24, "He himself bore our sins in his body on the tree, so that we might die to sins and live for righteousness; by his wounds you have been healed." He took the responsibility for all our sins on himself, received our judgment, and made us free. Isaiah foresaw this when he wrote: "Surely he took up our infirmities and carried our sorrows, yet we considered him stricken by God, smitten by him, and afflicted. But he was pierced for our transgressions, he was crushed for our iniquities; the punishment that brought us peace was upon him, and by his wounds we are healed. We all, like sheep, have gone astray, each of us has turned to his own way; and the LORD has laid on him the iniquity of us all" (Isa.53:4-6).

There are times when we have it in our power and resources to take on the responsibility of another's burden. Solomon says, "Do not withhold good from those who deserve it, when it is in your power to act" (Prov.3:27). We can do this in paying a widow's debt, for instance, or by providing meals or food for the hungry, transportation for someone in an emergency or in need, and so on.

The other way to bear another's burden is through encouragement and comfort. In Luke 8:43-48 we find the story of the woman who had an incurable bleeding problem. When she touched the hem of Jesus' garment (vs.44), she was healed immediately. Jesus had taken her physical burden away. But then she was frightened when Jesus singled her out as having touched him. He said, "Daughter, be of good comfort: your faith has healed you. Go in peace" (vs.48). His words brought release from her burden of fear.

I remember Dr. Larry Crabb's course in Biblical Counseling. During one class session, he shared with us how, as a teenager, he was greatly burdened with a stuttering problem. He couldn't say one sentence without stuttering. One time in Prayer Meeting, he was asked to close in prayer. He literally stuttered and stammered through something, and then headed for the door as fast as he could politely go, utterly ashamed and embarrassed. However, an elder in the church blocked his way, put a hand on his shoulder, and said, "Larry, whatever you choose to do for the Lord, I'm behind you 100%!" Those words were a balm to a wretched, burdened soul, and gave Dr. Crabb the grit and determination first, not to disappoint this man of God who expressed such confidence in him, and second, to overcome his stuttering so that he could serve the Lord free from that burden. He did both.

That elder could not take up Dr. Crabb's stuttering, but with a word of encouragement, he lifted a crushed heart and inspired the determination to overcome the burden. This is something we all can do, perhaps more often than we realize.

Are you using your burdens for spiritual growth and service to others?

Do you comfort instead of criticize? Are you a burden-bearer?

APPLICATION: The next time you are burdened, ask yourself, "What is the Lord trying to teach me through this burden?" Check the above negative and positive reasons for clues to the answer; care for whatever needs caring for, then rejoice in that trial and do whatever you need to do in it.

DAY 58
[b]HE IS A COUNSELOR

QUESTIONS TO THINK ABOUT:

1. In what way could everyone be considered a "counselor"?
2. Prov.15:22 states that with many advisors plans will succeed. Why is that true? It often seems that with many advisors there is only confusion.

3. When is the giving of advice meddling rather than counseling?

4. How can you become an effective counselor even though you are not academically trained?

Again in Isaiah 9:6 we read that "he will be called Wonderful Counselor." There are three levels of counseling which Christ used in his ministry, and these levels should be found in varying degrees in the Church. (I am indebted to Dr. Lawrence J. Crabb, Jr. for the outline and basic ideas regarding this characteristic of Christ. See Crabb 1977, 165,173,181.)

The first kind of counseling is "<u>encouragement</u>," <u>to change another's feelings</u>. This is a level at which all Christians can and should operate. We find an example of this kind of counseling in John 14:1-4. Jesus has just told his disciples that he is going to die, and that Peter was going to deny him three times. This news was obviously very discouraging to them and they became troubled. He ministered to them to change their feelings, to encourage them (see also Heb.3:12,13).

A second, deeper level of counseling is "<u>exhortation</u>." The object is <u>to effect behavioral change</u>. Most Christians should be able to operate on this level as well, but will be only as effective as the amount of the Word of God they know. Exhortation often involves reproof, rebuke, or strong urgings to change one's behavior. In Matthew 6:1-15 Christ demonstrates this level of counseling: "Don't do as the hypocrites do (in reference to the Pharisees), but do thus and so, and the Father will reward you." In Matthew 23:13-36 we find the strongest kind of rebuke and a promise of certain punishment leveled at the scribes and Pharisees. Matthew 18:15-18 gives us the proper guidelines for level two counseling in the Church (see also Tit.1:10-14).

The third and final level is that of "<u>enlightening</u>." The object is <u>to effect a change in one's belief system or his thinking</u>. Not all

Christians are equipped to meet and deal with the complex psychological and emotional problems presented by some people. (Many of these problems, by the way, might never have developed had these people been met at levels one and two by other Christians in the church.) Here we encounter problems that must be unraveled and resolved before the persons involved can once again feel at peace with themselves, others and God. Christ demonstrates this level of counseling in John 4:5-30 where he had to break through the woman's outer defensive shells (religious and social) before he could get to her basic need. There are those in each church who have this ability in counseling, and, with training, could become very effective in handling complex problems which otherwise would have to be referred to "professional" counselors.

To be a good counselor at any level, one must be sensitive to others. With today's preoccupation with "number one," sensitivity to others is becoming an increasingly difficult task. 1 John 3:16-18 and James 2:14-17 speak to this attitude on a material level. The immaterial level is not far removed, as is dealt with in Philippians 2:1-4, Galatians 6:1,2 and Romans 12:10.

Are you growing daily in the Word, so that you are becoming more sensitive to the needs of others and thus better equipped to counsel them as opportunity comes?

APPLICATION: Proverbs 25:11 says, "A word aptly spoken is like apples of gold in settings of silver."

1. Ask the Lord to give you "apt" words to speak to others so that they may be encouraged with good counsel from your lips.
2. Ask him to make you sensitive to others' feelings so that you will be guarded from saying the wrong thing though meaning well.

DAY 59
[b]HE IS WONDERFUL

QUESTIONS TO THINK ABOUT:

1. How is it possible for us to be a source of wonder to others?
2. Can you think of some people that you really enjoy being with? Why?
3. What are the characteristics of people whom you hold in wonder, who amaze you? Why do you think they are the way they are? How did they get that way?

In Isaiah 9:6 we read one of the names of Christ: "Wonderful Counselor." He is wonderful, or, as perceived by others, full of wonder. People marveled at his works (Mk.5:20; Lk.4:15) and his teaching, and were astonished at his doctrine (Matt.7:28,29). It was good to be around Jesus, and at one point he had to create a situation to "thin out" the ranks (see Jn.6:26-66).

In the days of the early church, we find accounts of people marveling at the things they saw. They were filled with wonder and amazement at the healing of the lame man by Peter and John (Acts 3:9-11). The Sanhedrin marveled at their boldness, because they were unlearned and ignorant men (Acts 4:13), and they had to conclude that they had been with Jesus. The people at Lystra thought Paul and Barnabas were gods because they had healed a crippled man (Acts 14:8-12).

Throughout church history the works and teachings of men and women empowered by God have been a source of wonder to those around them. Where the Wesleys went, revival broke out; when John Knox prayed, men quaked and answers came; when D.L. Moody preached, souls were saved. People marveled at the dedication and endurance of early missionaries as they faced almost certain death in their quest to take the Gospel to other lands. Today we marvel at the teachings of men like Ian Thomas, Joseph Stowell, Charles Swindoll, Stephen Olford, and others. We leave with the feeling of being fed through their ministry. They preach with authority and assurance. It is good to be in the presence of such men of God and often our desire is to stay there to learn and hear more.

So we marvel at the "greats," but what about the "not-so-greats"? Are we to be of no account? On the contrary, God intends for us to live and work in such a way that others will have cause to marvel. I have felt awe at the grace, peace and joy of fellow believers going through difficult times. I've felt wonder at the spiritual insights of others as they taught a Sunday School class, or were just sharing something from the Word. I have been fed and blessed through the ministry and fellowship of fellow missionaries and national believers. I have been amazed at what the Lord has accomplished through others in their own simple way.

What is the secret? There is no secret. Scripture is very clear: "And they took note that these men had been with Jesus" (Acts 4:13). Today, through the Word of God, we are in the presence of Christ. There he can teach us what he wants us to know, and as we live and share these things with others, they will marvel. The Psalmist says in Psalm 119:99, "I have more insight than all my teachers, for I meditate on your statutes" (cf. Ps.1:1-3; Josh.1:8). In John 16:12-15, Jesus promised that the Holy Spirit will be our teacher, instructing us in everything God wants us to know and share with others; but we must "attend class!"

APPLICATION: Determine to spend more time with Jesus, through his Word and in prayer. There is no other way for his wonderful spirit in your life to become evident to others.

DAY 60
ᵇHE IS WONDERFUL, concl.

◆

QUESTIONS TO THINK ABOUT:

1. Why do you feel more comfortable around some than around others?
2. Recount a time when you "wanted the fellowship to go on forever." Why did you feel that way?
3. Are you aware of others enjoying being with you?

The last statement in the first paragraph of the last study was: "It was good to be around Jesus." People generally had a sense of well-being and security in his presence. It was wonderful to be with him. God wants others to feel the same way in our presence. I have heard of others visiting a saint of God and sensing God's presence in a tangible way, though I myself have not experienced that. Most of my experiences with other Christians have been quite neutral, and, on occasion, negative, although there are a few who cause me to eagerly anticipate their fellowship. We have been in some churches looking for warm fellowship only to find the chief preoccupation to be cutting others down, gossip, hard feelings and self-justification. On the contrary, instead of being ministered to and strengthened in fellowship, we felt emotionally exhausted, physically drained and spiritually polluted. What ministry we had to offer lost much of its effectiveness as we increasingly desired to get away and go somewhere else. There was nothing wonderful there.

We have found other Christians to be more neutral: not unpleasant to be around, but also not very stimulating spiritually. They are friendly and congenial but would rather be anonymous and not "make waves." We heard an interesting song one day entitled, "Evidence." The gist of it was, "If you were ever arrested on suspicion of being a Christian, would there be enough evidence to convict you?" For many Christians, the answer would have to be, "No." They come across as neutral, making no impact one way or another, and thereby lose that aura of wonderfulness that God wants them to have.

Then I can remember a dinner engagement that was far too short. The fellowship we enjoyed talking about the Lord, the comfort and security we sensed in the presence of the others there, really ministered to us. We didn't want to leave. This is as it should be wherever we are.

So let's ask ourselves, "When others are around us, do they sense the presence of God? Do they have a sense of well-being, peace and security? Can they tell a difference without our saying or doing anything?" If they can, then Christ's characteristic of being wonderful is coming through.

Again we must ask, "How can this be done?" We become like what we think about the most. The more time we spend with Christ, the more like him we will become, and the more we will demonstrate his wonderfulness to others. This is not a conscious characteristic so that we can say, "I have it now!" But it is an unconscious characteristic that grows and grows the closer we become to him (cf. Exod.34:28-35).

Are you wonderful to be around?

APPLICATION: What will make others wonder and sometimes fear is their realization that you have been with Jesus. How much time do you spend with him? We make time for our best friends and are willing to sacrifice anything to be with them. As we are with them, we become like them, and others see them in us. The same is true in our relationship with the Lord Jesus. Are you short-changing your friendship with him? If so, what steps do you need to take to correct this situation? He is wonderful, and as you fellowship with him you will begin to take on this characteristic as well.

DAY 61
ᵇHE IS THE GOOD SHEPHERD

◆

QUESTIONS TO THINK ABOUT:

1. What are the characteristics of a good shepherd? (see also Ezek.34:4-16)
2. Why is his relationship to the flock important?

In John 10:11 Christ says of himself, "I am the good shepherd." This statement is found in the context of verses 1-30 in which Jesus describes the qualities of a good shepherd. He:

1. knows his sheep (vs.3),
2. leads his sheep (vs.3,4),
3. protects his sheep (vs.7-9,27-30),
4. provides for his sheep (vs.9,10),
5. gives his life for his sheep (vs.11-18), and
6. seeks for his lost sheep (vs.16).

Let's look at each of these qualities to see how they can apply to us. First, in verse 3, "He calls his own sheep by name." He can tell which one is which by their shape, wool color, actions or sound of its voice. To an outsider, all sheep look alike and are "impossible" to distinguish one from another. This was our experience when we first arrived in Senggo in Papua. All the villagers looked alike to us. But after a time, faces took on names and personalities, and it became easier for us to distinguish one person from another. Some even reminded us of folks back home and we nicknamed them accordingly (just between ourselves, of course). So it is with the shepherd. Because he knows his sheep, he can distinguish them easily from all others, even at some distance.

Almost all Christians, at one time or another, have the opportunity to develop shepherding qualities, either as they assume some leadership role in the church or parachurch organization (1 Pet.5:1-4), or as they marry and become parents (Deut.6:6,7). If you are a pastor, church leader or Sunday school teacher, how well do you know your "sheep"? If you are a parent, how well do you know your "sheep"? And husband, how well do you know your wife? Or are they all comparative strangers to you even though you are in the same church, the same class, or live in the same house? Do you, like a shepherd, spend enough time with them so that you can know them on a more intimate level and where they express confidence in you as their "shepherd"? If not, how can you expect to meet the needs of your "sheep"?

In verses 3 and 4 we read that "he leads them out" and "goes on ahead of them." Jesus, for example, was "tempted in every way, just as we are – yet was without sin" (Heb.4:14,15). He's been there; he's gone ahead of us; he knows what it's like. He will never lead us where he himself has not gone or will not go. Do we as "under-shepherds" try to lead our sheep where we have never been? Do we tell others what they should do, but fail to do it ourselves? If we don't "practice what we preach," we will mislead our sheep and cause them to go astray. Let's be sure that whatever we are telling others to do, we are either doing the same or working on it.

In verses 7-9 we find Christ as the "door of the sheep." A shepherd would gather his sheep in a pasture sheepfold often constructed in a circle of brambles and thorns with only a small opening, the "door." The shepherd would lie down to sleep, blocking the entrance with his body, thus ensuring the security and safety of his sheep for the night. Nothing could pass over him to the sheep without awakening him. In Christ, we find such security (Jn.10:27-30). Is your level of Christian maturity such that others find the same sense of security in your presence? Do you know the Scriptures well enough through personal study and application so that you can "encircle your sheep"

Unexpected Transformation / 149

with a fence of truth? If you know the Scriptures, you will know the truth and thus be aware of false teaching when it is approaching. Our knowledge of the truth will keep our sheep from going astray into the dangers of the cults, world philosophies and other -isms of our time. Thus we, like the shepherd, become their "door of protection."

APPLICATION:

1. What steps do you need to take in order to get to know your "sheep" better? Perhaps spending more time with them; asking them how they feel or what they think about this or that; finding out what their interests are, etc.
2. Are you leading them where you yourself have gone, or are you "pushing" them into areas where you have not yet ventured?
3. Do your "sheep" sense the protection of their "shepherd," or are there gaps in the "fence"? What steps do you need to take to "repair" the fence? Perhaps a good start might be showing more interest and concern for them, or helping them work through problems they're facing, or just being with them and giving them your complete attention, etc.

DAY 62
bHE IS THE GOOD SHEPHERD, concl.

QUESTIONS TO THINK ABOUT:

1. How does a shepherd provide for his sheep?
2. What is his attitude toward his sheep if they are in mortal danger or perhaps lost?

In John 10:9,10 we find that Christ came to give his sheep abundant life (see DAYS 8,9 – HE IS THE LIFE). The shepherd is responsible to provide pasture for his sheep and a place where they can find good water (Ps.23:1,2). Even so, we are responsible to make every provision possible for the spiritual growth of our "sheep." As my wife's "shepherd," I have the responsibility to provide the environment in which she can be nourished spiritually and encouraged to minister to others. Family devotions, mutual sharing, encouragement to take on-line Bible courses, and so on, all contribute to her spiritual growth and well-being.

In verses 11-18 we find that the good shepherd "lays down his life for the sheep." Perhaps this is the hardest concept for us to accept since we tend more and more to resent intrusions into our privacy and our right to do "our thing." Here is where we need a good dose of compassion (see DAY 13 – HE IS COMPASSIONATE) and *agape* love. How much are we willing to "lay down our lives for our sheep"? Seldom does this involve actual physical death, but often involves "dying" to our desires and plans in giving preference to their needs. My parents exemplified this attitude. They would sacrifice whatever was necessary if it would benefit their children. They were totally selfless where we were concerned.

Paul speaks of this attitude in Phil.2:3,4: "Do nothing out of selfish ambition or vain conceit, but in humility consider others better than yourselves. Each of you should look not only to your own interests, but also to the interests of others." The hireling looks out for his own interests first (Jn.10:12,13), and the sheep come to harm.

Even so we have a choice to make: to be willing to sacrifice our desires for the benefit of the sheep, or to put our own selfish desires first to the harm of the flock. What happens to children who are neglected by their parents? To the wife neglected by her husband? To the church people neglected by their pastor? Is the price the sheep pay worth the enjoyment we experience through the selfish indulgence of our own rights and desires?

Finally, in verse 16, Christ declares that he has other sheep to find and bring into the fold. There were others, given him by the

Father (Jn.6:37) who had not yet come to him. Christ was concerned about reaching them. Throughout his ministry he was reaching out to gather in his sheep (Matt.11:1) and instructing his disciples to do the same (Lk.10:1). He closed his ministry with a commission for world outreach (Mk.16:15; Matt.28:18-20). He has delegated the responsibility for reaching "the other sheep" worldwide to the Church. We cannot do it all, but we all can do something where we are (Acts 1:8), and, doing that, we would find many more sheep entering the fold.

How concerned are you about your sheep?

APPLICATION:

1. What steps do you need to take in order to provide more adequately for your "sheep"?

2. If you have problems sacrificing your rights and desires for the benefit of your sheep, try meditating on Phil.2:5-11. How was Christ "repaid" for what he sacrificed?

3. What are you doing to reach "lost sheep"? What more could you do?

DAY 63
bHE IS THE LAMB

QUESTIONS TO THINK ABOUT:

1. What are the characteristics of a lamb?
2. How dependent is the lamb upon its shepherd?

As we look at Christ, we see displayed several lamb-like characteristics: gentleness, meekness, innocence, total dependence, unresisting submissiveness, and recognition of the Shepherd's voice.

There is no animal as meek and gentle as a lamb. By its very nature it is a quiet animal. Jesus said in Matt.11:29b, "For I am gentle and humble in heart." And indeed, he demonstrated gentleness, compassion, and a humble spirit throughout his life and ministry. In like manner must our nature be expressed. Paul says in 2 Tim.2:24, "And the Lord's servant must not quarrel; instead, he must be kind to everyone, able to teach, not resentful" (or "patient when wronged" – NASB).

A lamb is innocent, unable to purpose to do wrong. In John 8:46 Christ challenged, "Can any of you prove me guilty of sin?" No one answered him. 1 Peter 2:22 says of Christ: "He committed no sin, and no deceit was found in his mouth." None of us is innocent from sin, yet God has determined to make us innocent, and has provided all we need to become innocent. Consider carefully the implications and commands of Psalm 119:9,11a; Romans, chapter 6; 1 Corinthians 10:13; Philippians 4:8 and Ephesians 5:25-27.

The more we gain victory over sin, and the more our normal life pattern becomes like that of the Scriptures, the more innocent we will become.

The third characteristic, total dependence, is aptly illustrated by the experience of some missionary friends of ours, Jack and Corky Hook (UFM) who once had a pet lamb. They were absolutely astounded at its total, absolute dependence upon them for everything. We have a cat. Any morning we are late letting it in, she sets up a howl and the whole world knows it! Not so the lamb. It just stood there waiting quietly for something to happen. It ate when given food. If food wasn't given, it just stood there. If Jack and Corky didn't provide for it in everything, it went without, unable to care for itself.

In just such a manner, Christ was totally and absolutely dependent upon the Father for the content of his ministry, and upon the Holy Spirit for the power to perform it. Of his relationship to the Father, he said, "I tell you the truth, the Son can do nothing by himself; he can do only what he sees his Father doing, because whatever the Father does the Son also does" (Jn.5:19). Again in John 12:50b he says,

"Whatever I say is just what the Father has told me to say" (see also Jn.5:30 and 8:28). Of the Holy Spirit's role in Christ's ministry we read that Christ was filled with the Spirit (Lk.4:1), led by the Spirit (Lk.4:1), and worked miracles by the Spirit's power (Matt.12:28). He did nothing on his own.

In the same way, we are totally and absolutely dependent upon Christ. He said in John 15:5b, "Apart from me you can do nothing." However, in this day of technological Christianity, we often act as if without him we can do anything! Proverbs 3:5-7 speaks to correct this attitude: "Trust in the LORD with all your heart and lean not on your own understanding; in all your ways acknowledge him, and he will make your paths straight. Do not be wise in your own eyes; fear the Lord and shun evil." I once paraphrased these verses this way: "Put your complete confidence in the LORD no matter how absurd it seems. In all your ways give way to him, and he shall direct your paths. Don't be a conceited know-it-all; be in reverent awe before the LORD, and flee from the practice of doing evil." What does it mean to acknowledge him? It means that we admit or recognize that he is there with us to help us, then give him the "go ahead" to work, to lead the way.

As we learn total and absolute dependence upon God, we will become more like Christ as the Lamb, and find greater fruit, blessing and power in our daily lives and ministry.

Are you dependent or independent in your relationship with your Shepherd?

APPLICATION: In which areas of your Christian life have you recently "barged ahead" without even a thought about what the Lord thinks? You just went ahead and did it. Meditate upon John 15:5 and begin to make it a practice to pray before making your plans, committing them to the Lord and asking his direction and help. Proverbs 16:3 says, "Commit to the LORD whatever you do, and your plans will succeed."

DAY 64
bHE IS THE LAMB, cont.

◆

QUESTIONS TO THINK ABOUT:

1. Why is it that we so often resist doing the will of God? What are we afraid of?
2. Why do we often resist another Christian when we see him wanting to do God's will?

Next we see Christ as the unresisting, submissive lamb. A lamb is always unresisting and submissive to the will of its shepherd. Whether being led to be sheared or slaughtered, it silently goes to its fate. Even so Christ. He came to do God's will which was food for him. We read in Hebrews 10:7, "Then I said, 'Here I am – it is written about me in the scroll – I have come to do your will, O God.'" And again in John 4:34, "My food," said Jesus, "is to do the will of him who sent me and to finish his work." In the Garden of Gethsemane he prayed, "Not my will, but yours be done" (Lk.22:42b). God, as his Shepherd, was leading him to the slaughter. "He was led like a sheep to the slaughter, and as a lamb before the shearer is silent, so he did not open his mouth" (Acts 8:32). When falsely accused, he said nothing in his defense (Matt.26:59-63). When reviled and suffering on the cross, he "did not retaliate; … he made no threats. Instead, he entrusted himself to him who judges justly" … "leaving [us] an example, that [we] should follow in his steps" (1 Pet.2:23 with vs.21).

In Psalm 100:3 we are called God's sheep. As his sheep, are we as unresistingly submissive to his will as Christ was? Shadrach, Meshach and Abednego were determined to do God's will, even if it meant death (Dan.3:13-18); and others did die, giving rise to Psalm

44:22 and Romans 8:36 which laments, "For your sake we face death all day long; we are considered as sheep to be slaughtered."

Is God's will like food to us as it was for Christ? Job said, "I have treasured the words of his mouth more than my daily bread" (Job 23:12b). Do we willingly subjugate our will to his? Are we willing to follow him wherever he chooses to lead us? Usually the Lord has to make us willing. In Jeremiah and Ezekiel, we read of God forcing Israel out of its land in great wrath but with the promise of returning again to her own land. However, Israel tried to assimilate herself in the lands of her dispersion rather than hope for a return. So once again God had to stir up great wrath to get her moving in the direction he wanted (Ezek.20:32-34). This situation indicates a strange paradox in our lives as God's sheep. A shepherd's sheep follow his voice (Jn.10:4); yet we, as God's sheep, often don't.

Furthermore, a sheep has no rights other than to follow its shepherd. To use a different picture, God purchased us from sin's slave market and we have become his servants (1 Cor.6:19,20). Our relationship to him now is as a bond servant to his master (see Exod.21:5,6). A bond servant, by love and choice, binds himself to his master for life; his only right being to do his master's will. Just as it was totally <u>unnatural</u> for a bond servant <u>not</u> to want to obey his master, so it is totally <u>unnatural</u> for a sheep <u>not</u> to follow its shepherd. Yet, we are sheep who often refuse to follow our Shepherd; bond servants who often refuse to obey our Master's commands! The inconceivable in the natural world we do in the spiritual world!

In his sufferings, our Shepherd did not complain, curse or threaten; yet we often do, or wish we could. In his teachings, our Master commanded us to love one another as he has loved us (Jn.15:12); yet we often bite and devour one another. Paul warns us, "Watch out or you will be destroyed [devoured] by each other" (Gal.5:15b) – sheep acting as if they possessed the nature and heart of wolves!

We need the exhortation found in Colossians 3:12-14 where Paul writes, "Therefore, as God's chosen people, holy and dearly loved, clothe yourselves with compassion, kindness, humility, gentleness and patience. Bear with each other and forgive whatever grievances you may have against one another. Forgive as the Lord forgave you. And over all these virtues put on love, which binds them all together in perfect unity."

May the Lord give us new hearts and softened natures that will, with unresisting submissiveness, respond fully and willingly to him.

In which areas have you been acting more like a wolf than a lamb?

APPLICATION: Confess your un-lamb-like actions to the Lord and ask him to make you more aware of when you are being "wolfish." Then work on developing a lamb-like spirit in those situations.

DAY 65
[b]HE IS THE LAMB, concl.

QUESTIONS TO THINK ABOUT:

1. What do sheep do when a stranger approaches the flock?
2. In what ways can we "hear" God's voice?

According to John 10:3-5, sheep recognize their shepherd's voice, but will flee from a stranger, not recognizing his voice. Christ knew his Shepherd's voice. In John 12:50b he says, "The things I speak, I speak just as the Father has told me" (NASB). Three times during Christ's ministry God uttered his voice so that others could hear it: at Christ's baptism (Matt.3:17), at his transfiguration (Matt.17:5), and just before his crucifixion (Jn.12:28-30). Jesus knew this voice and spoke acknowledging it (Jn.12:30).

Peter knew God's voice (2 Pet.1:17), the Lord's voice (Acts 10:14), and the Holy Spirit's (Acts 10:19-21). Paul recognized Christ's voice although he had never known him (Acts 9:4,5). And we are assured by

Christ himself that "everyone of the truth hears [his] voice" (Jn.18:37, NASB); and again, in John 10:27, "My sheep know my voice."

How do we hear his voice? Primarily through his Word, if we are reading it daily (Heb.1:1,2). Many times his voice is "heard" inwardly, as a conviction urging us to do what is right, or a compulsion to do something. Once, while praying for a sick person, I felt a compulsion to praise the Lord; so I did. And the sick one recovered. But we need to be aware that not all inner voices or compulsions come from our Shepherd. <u>All things</u>, including our "understanding" of the Word of God, <u>must be measured by the Word</u>. If any of them violate or contradict God's Word, then it is <u>not</u> the Lord's voice we are hearing.

Many times the Lord speaks to us through circumstances. When Amber and I were asked to be house parents at our TEAM Hostel in Sentani (after having been assigned to reopen the South Coast Bible School upon returning from furlough), the Lord assured us through our circumstances that reopening the Bible school was not his will for us: no school buildings left, no national teachers, no money to build, little financial support for the school, and little support from the south coast missionaries themselves. The Lord's voice was clear: "Not here! Not now!"

He also speaks to us through others. We are commanded to obey those in authority over us, receiving God's direction through them (as is consistent with his Word): parents (Eph.6:1-3), spiritual leaders (Heb.13:7,17), and government (Rom.13:1,2). When others say or do something to or for us and we respond in an un-Christ-like way, God is saying, "My child, here is a character trait in you that is not like my Son's. You need to work on it." He also speaks to us as others admonish and encourage us.

Less frequently, he speaks to us directly through dreams and visions, (Joel 2:28; Acts 10:10-16; 16:9,10), a word of prophecy (1 Cor.14:1,3), or an audible voice (Matt.17:5).

Do you recognize and follow the Lord's voice when he speaks? If you claim to be his sheep, but are listening to the voice of "strangers," be careful! You may be in the wrong fold!

APPLICATION: Do you frequently find yourself being sidetracked by the latest spiritual fad, or going off on some spiritual tangent? Do you find yourself asking, "What is God's will for me?" when the Scripture is very clear about the situation you're facing? Is it easier for you to listen to the voice of a others than to spend time in the Word of God?

If you find familiar any or all of these questions, then you are listening to the voices of other shepherds than your own. The only remedy I know of is to spend time in the Word of God so that you will "get used to hearing" your Shepherd's voice. Then you will be able to discern the voices of others and know when not to give heed.

DAY 66
bHE IS OUR ADVOCATE

QUESTIONS TO THINK ABOUT:

1. Who is an advocate and what does an advocate do?
2. Why do we need an advocate with God?
3. When we criticize or slander a fellow believer, whose work are we doing?

In 1 John 2:1 we read, "But if anyone sins, we have an advocate with the Father, Jesus Christ the righteous" (KJV). The NIV reads, "But if anybody does sin, we have one who speaks to the Father in our defense – Jesus Christ, the Righteous One." An advocate is "one who speaks to someone else in our defense," "one who pleads another's cause" (Vine, 1966, 1:208). An advocate implies the presence of at least three other people: the defendant (the one being accused), the prosecutor (the one accusing), and the judge (the one who can do something about the case). Scripture is very clear as to who these others are. In Zechariah 3:1,2 we read, "Then he showed me Joshua the high priest [the accused] standing before the angel of the Lord [Christ as attorney for the defense], and Satan [the prosecutor] standing at his right side to accuse him. The Lord said to Satan, 'The LORD [God] rebuke you, Satan! The LORD, who has chosen Jerusalem, rebuke you! Is not this man a burning stick snatched from the fire?'" In Revelation 12:9-11 we see the fall of the dragon (Satan); and it is said in verse 10b, "For the accuser [prosecutor] of our brothers [the defendents], who accuses them before our God [the Judge] day and night, has been hurled down" (all underlining mine).

The background for this court scene is given so clearly by Oliver Greene. He writes: "'The wages of sin is death' (Romans 6:23), physical and spiritual, suffering the eternal wrath of a righteous, holy God. Satan, as a usurper, and exercising that power, continually demands that the sinner pay up. His demands are based upon God's justice, the inflexibility of his law, and the true nature of our sins. But when Christ died in our place, when he was made sin and a curse for us, then all the power of Satan was gone – and now what can Satan say? Jesus endured the penalty of the broken law, and now, since the law is vindicated, sin put away, death swallowed up, Christ Jesus has stripped the devil of his power and wrested from his hands his most awful weapon!" (Greene, 1966(?), 80,81).

Satan tries to accuse us before God, but each time is silenced by the scars and rebuke of our Advocate. Now let me ask a question. When we gossip about, slander or accuse our fellow Christians before others, whose work are we doing? Whose side have we just joined? Whose character are we reflecting?

James 5:9 says, "Don't grumble against each other, brothers, or you will be judged. The Judge is standing at the door!" Galatians 6:1,2 says, "Brothers, if someone is caught in a sin, you who are spiritual should restore him gently. But watch yourself, or you also may be tempted. Carry each other's burdens, and in this way you will fulfill the law of Christ." And Colossians 3:12-14, "Therefore, as God's chosen people, holy and dearly loved, clothe yourselves with compassion, kindness, humility, gentleness, and patience. Bear with each other and forgive whatever grievances you may have against one another. Forgive as the Lord forgave you. And over all these virtues put on love [*agape*], which binds them all together in perfect unity."

Are you an advocate or an accuser of fellow believers?

APPLICATION: The next time you begin to criticize a fellow believer, stop and pray for him instead. Ask the Lord to bless him, give him wisdom, and show him the right way. Ask the Lord to fill your heart with love and compassion for him and enable you to accept him as "a new creation in process" in Christ. Realize that your attitude toward him will draw him closer to the Lord or drive him farther away. Be an advocate, not an accuser!

DAY 67
[a]HE IS OUR INTERCESSOR

QUESTIONS TO THINK ABOUT:

1. What does it mean to "intercede" for someone?
2. What must be the credentials of the "intercessor"?
3. When, if ever, is it right to pray against someone?

In Hebrews 7:25 we read, "Therefore he is able to save completely those who come to God through him, because he always lives to intercede for them." And in John 17, we find Christ interceding for his disciples as well as for all those who would believe on him through their witness.

Intercession is double-pronged. An intercessor is one who pleads with someone either for or against others (Vine, 1966, 2:267). We see evidence of both in Scripture. The whole Jewish community petitioned Festus against Paul (Acts 25:24); Elijah appealed to God against Israel because they killed his prophets and tore down his altars (Rom.11:2,3). In many of the Psalms David pleads to the Lord against his enemies (cf. Ps.5).

On the other hand, we see in Romans 8:27 and 34 both the Holy Spirit and Christ interceding for the saints (for us); and we see Paul interceding for Onesimus, which occasioned his short letter to Philemon. Moses interceded many times for Israel in the wilderness, thus averting from them the wrath of God.

On occasion we may plead the cause of another person before someone; but most frequently we plead the cause of others before the Lord as we pray for them. Paul urges us, as part of our spiritual warfare, to "pray in the Spirit on all occasions with all kinds of prayers and requests. With this in mind, be alert and always keep on praying for all the saints" (Eph.6:18 – "praying" here is primarily "a wanting, a need" [Vine, 1966, 3:200], that is, what we want for them and what they present to us as their needs). And what should we be wanting for them? Paul gives us a running start in Ephesians 1:17-20; 3:16-19 and Colossians 1:9-12. In praying for these things in the lives of fellow believers, we know that we are praying according to the will of God for them, and that he will answer our prayers.

But there are also things we must intercede against. One time we knew of a Christian young lady engaged to a fellow of another religion. We prayed against that engagement, knowing that it was against the revealed will of God in his Word. Praying against sin in a Christian's life is always valid. In our spiritual warfare, we pray against the devil, rebuking him in the name of the Lord. And we also have prayed against those trying to hinder the Lord's work, asking God to bring confusion upon them, at the same time hoping that somehow through this they will come to know Christ, as they recognize God's hand against them (cf. Ezek.33:27-29).

So as intercessors, we have the responsibility to intercede <u>for</u> all men, but <u>against</u> sin. May the Lord give us both wisdom and a right spirit in our intercession ministry, that we may intercede for others according to their need and according to the will of God.

Another thought: If victory in other Christians' lives depended upon our intercession for them, what would happen?

APPLICATION: Since the Lord wants us to pray for others, ask him to bring them to mind, any time, any place, whenever there is a need to be prayed for. You don't have to know what that need is; just pray for them as the Lord burdens your heart. Do you dream at night, then wake up thinking about someone you know (from your dream)? I use that as a prompting from the Lord to pray for that person in the few moments of consciousness before falling asleep again. They may have a need right at that moment. Be alert to intercessory moments throughout the day or night. Eternity will reveal some very surprising things that happened because you prayed.

DAY 68
ᵇHE IS OUR MEDIATOR

QUESTIONS TO THINK ABOUT:

1. How is a mediator different from an intercessor?
2. How can you be a "guarantee" of better spiritual things for others?
3. What are some daily occurrences in which Christians can serve as mediators?

In 1 Timothy 2:5 we read, "For there is one God and one mediator between God and men, the man Christ Jesus." Vine says this about Christ as our mediator: "The word 'mediator' is used in two ways in the N.T., (a) one who mediates between two parties with a view to producing peace, as in 1 Timothy 2:5, ... [and] (b) one who acts as a guarantee so as to secure something which otherwise would not be obtained. Thus in Hebrews 8:6; 9:15 and 12:24 Christ is the [Mediator] of 'the better covenant,' 'the new covenant,' guaranteeing its terms for his people" (Vine, 1966, 3:54).

I would like to add a third factor: (c) one who becomes a bridge of communication between God and man (Heb.1:1,2).

Moses is spoken of as a mediator in Galatians 3:19. Many times in his ministry, he mediated between Israel and God with a view to producing peace (Deut.9:13-20,23-29; 10:10; Num.16:41-48, etc.). All who yet lived of Israel were alive because Moses interceded for them as mediator before God.

We likewise are mediators between God and men as we strive through our witness to bring them into a peace relationship with him (2 Cor.5:18-20 – As mediators, we stand between God and men either to direct them to him or to drive them away! – see DAY 6 – HE IS THE WAY). We also are mediators between fellow Christians. Unfortunately there is too often no peace between them. When that happens, we must be sensitive to the situation and seek ways of restoring peace between the parties involved. Paul did this in Philippians 4:2,3 where he counseled two women to be at peace with one another. He also did this in trying to reconcile Onesimus with his master, Philemon, whom he had wronged. Sometimes though, all we can do is pray. Other times God will use us to effect the peace that is needed. There is a blessing in this as Christ said, "Blessed are the peacemakers, for they will be called sons of God" (Matt.5:9).

In the second meaning of the term "mediator," how can we be "a guarantee so as to secure something for someone which otherwise would not be obtained"? I see this principle at work basically toward believers in two ways: (1) As we pray for them, and the Lord answers, they receive what they otherwise might not have obtained. (Could it be said, "They have not because we asked not!"? – cf. Jas. 4:2b). (2) Through our example, other believers can see new vistas in the Christian life to reach for in their own, and gain encouragement in overcoming sin or gaining victory in other areas. Without our example, perhaps their growth in these areas would not take place or be delayed. Our victory thus becomes a motivation for theirs.

We will consider the third meaning of the term "mediator" tomorrow.

Meanwhile, how are others benefiting from your work as a mediator?

APPLICATION: One good way to act as a mediator is to counter gossip with something positive about the person being discussed. For some, this is a daily occurrence. Then suggest that you all pray for that person in the area being discussed. Two things will happen, maybe three: (1) your friends will stop gossiping in front of you (they will resent your "holier-than-thou" attitude); (2) the person being talked about will definitely be helped as you pray for him or her; and (3) perhaps those gossiping will be convicted about their sin and begin praying for, more than talking about, that person.

DAY 69
bHE IS OUR HIGH PRIEST

QUESTIONS TO THINK ABOUT:

1. How can a Christian become a bridge of communication between God and others?

2. What kind of sacrifices can a Christian, as a priest, offer up to God?

The third area of mediation is that of becoming a bridge of communication between God and man. This is especially true of the office of High Priest which Jesus also fulfilled. We read in Hebrews 5:10 that he "was designated by God to be high priest in the order of Melchizedek." The High Priest, as a mediator, represents mankind in matters related to God, offering gifts and sacrifices for sin (1 Tim.2:5,6; Heb.5:1). Even as the Jewish High Priest entered the Most Holy Place once a year with the blood of atonement for Israel (Heb.9:7), so Christ entered the Most Holy Place in heaven, with his own blood, once for all time, to make atonement for the sins of everyone who would accept it (Heb.9:12,26b).

In 1 Peter 2:5, Peter writes: "You also, like living stones, are being built into a spiritual house to be a holy priesthood, offering spiritual sacrifices acceptable to God through Jesus Christ."

In Scripture it seems that the priest has a threefold function: (1) to make sacrifices that would atone for sin (mediation); (2) to represent men before God (intercession); and (3) to represent God to men (teaching – the "bridge" of communication – cf. Jn.14:8,9).

As priests, we can no longer minister through the offering of blood sacrifices for sin, because the final blood sacrifice was made by Christ himself on the cross. The sacrifices we now offer are spiritual (more detailed discussion follows), among which are:

1. our bodies as living sacrifices (Rom.12:1),
2. doing what is just and right (Prov.21:3),
3. listening in God's presence (Eccl.5:1,2),
4. service to other Christians (Phil.2:17),
5. meeting material needs of God's servants (Phil.4:18),
6. obedience (1 Sam.15:22),
7. showing mercy (Hos.6:6),
8. knowing God (Hos.6:6), and
9. praise, doing good, sharing (Heb.13:15,16).

However intercession, along with teaching, is a continuing ministry. Paul urged Timothy (and through him the church) to pray for everyone, for kings, and all those in authority with the intent that we might "live peaceful and quiet lives in all godliness and holiness," which is pleasing to "God our Savior, who wants all men to be saved and to come to a knowledge of the truth" (teaching is implied – 1 Tim.2:1-4).

Samuel, in his farewell message to Israel, linked the ministry of intercession with that of teaching: "As for me, far be it from me that I should sin against the LORD by failing to pray for you. And I will teach you the way that is good and right.... Fear the LORD and serve him faithfully with all your heart; consider what great things he has done for you" (1 Sam.12:23,24).

Even as Christ taught us about the Father, so we as his priests, must teach others, so that the knowledge of God is passed on from generation to generation (This ministry is dealt with in more detail on DAY 77 – HE IS OUR MASTER/TEACHER). This teaching is not necessarily formal, but a daily example, dropping a word here and a word there, demonstrating one principle or another at appropriate times, sharing the character of God at natural moments. Moses puts it best in Deuteronomy 6:6,7 where he says, "And these words which I command you today shall be in your heart; you shall teach them diligently to your children, and shall talk of them when you sit in your house, when you walk by the way, when you lie down, and when you rise up."

Are you fulfilling the functions of your priesthood as mediator, intercessor and teacher?

DAY 70
ᵇHE IS OUR HIGH PRIEST, cont.

◆

QUESTIONS TO THINK ABOUT:

1. What is a true sacrifice? What is its quality?
2. Do you usually give to God the best that you have, or something of little worth to you?

Peter says in 1 Peter 2:5 that we are "to be a holy priesthood, offering spiritual sacrifices acceptable to God through Jesus Christ." The Scriptures mention at least 17 different sacrifices that we should be offering to him. But first we need to be aware of what a sacrifice is. It is not a cast-away or a hand-me-down, or something used or broken that no longer has any value (see Mal.1:6-8,13,14). A true sacrifice is that which costs us something, that which has value to us. As David said to Araunah when he offered to give David his threshing floor, "No, but I will surely buy it from you for a price; nor will I offer burnt offerings to the LORD my God with that which costs me nothing. So David bought the threshing floor and the oxen for fifty shekels of silver" (2 Sam 24:24).

So where do we begin with the sacrifices we are to offer?

1. We begin with *the sacrifice of ourselves*. Romans 12:1 says "Therefore, I urge you, brothers, in view of God's mercy, to offer your bodies as living sacrifices, holy and pleasing to God – this is your spiritual act of worship." The servant attitude: "Lord, I am ready for whatever you want me to do, anytime, anyplace, with whatever resources I have at my disposal." We need to develop the mind set found in 1 Corinthians 16:19,20 where Paul writes: "Do you not know that your body is a temple of the Holy Spirit, who is

in you, whom you have received from God? You are not your own; you were bought at a price. Therefore honor God with your body." And we do that by making ourselves fit for his service, physically, mentally, emotionally and spiritually.

    2.   The second sacrifice we are to offer is found in Psalm 51:17 where David prays: "The sacrifices of God are *a broken spirit*; *a broken and a contrite heart*, O God, you will not despise" (bold added). This sacrifice implies such a sensitivity to sin that to commit sin brings deep grief and leads to true repentance. It is the recognition that any sin breaks our fellowship with God, and our fellowship with him is such that anything breaking it and causing him grief causes us grief. Generally, we do not take sin seriously enough, forgetting that "a little yeast works through the whole batch of dough" (1 Cor.5:6).

As long as we allow sin to remain in our lives, unconfessed and unrepented of, God cannot and will not use us as he would like to. In this condition, we would become like a chipped chisel in his hand. The results would be uneven and marred. To be useful again, the chisel needs grinding down so that its edge is even and sharp. So God begins to "regrind" us through discipline to make us sharp, even and usable. But some chisels have lost their temper and will not keep an even and sharp edge. Such must be discarded and replaced. Let's not reject God's chastening and refining and so be set aside as unusable tools, our work given to someone else, but rather let us offer to him a broken and contrite heart, turning away from sin in true repentance. Then our fellowship with him will be what we desire, and he will be able to use us as he desires.

    Have you offered your body as a sacrifice to God, along with a broken and contrite heart?

APPLICATION: Are there sins in your life that need confessing and forsaking? According to Psalm 66:18, if you treasure those sins in your heart, the Lord will not hear your prayers, and it follows that he will not use you until the breach in your fellowship with him has been repaired. Keep short accounts with your Lord so that he can use you like a sharpened chisel in his hand.

DAY 71
ᵇHE IS OUR HIGH PRIEST, cont.

QUESTIONS TO THINK ABOUT:

1. How can listening to God be considered a sacrifice?

2. How is a sacrifice made in love different from the same sacrifice made in duty?

3. The third sacrifice we offer to God is ***taking time to listen to him***. We read in Ecclesiastes 5:1, "Guard your steps when you go to the house of God. Go near to listen rather than to offer the sacrifice of fools, who do not know that they do wrong." Why don't they know that they do wrong? Because they are talking so much (their "sacrifice") that they do not give God a chance to say anything to them and to show them their sin. Proverbs 10:8 speaks to this condition: "The wise in heart accept commands, but a chattering fool ["chattering"– a constant stream of idle talk] comes to ruin" (see also Prov.17:28; 29:11 and Eccl.10:12b-14a). We need to take time to be quiet in his presence and let his Word and his Spirit speak to our hearts. Some say, "Time is money!" Sometimes it will cost us to set aside time to be with the Lord, but that is a sacrifice we cannot afford not to make.

4. In Hosea 6:6 we read about the fourth and fifth sacrifices that we offer to God: "For I desire mercy, not sacrifice, and acknowledgment [knowledge] of God rather than burnt offerings." (Let's make the fifth sacrifice, ***knowledge of God,*** number four, since ***the sacrifice of mercy,*** which comes first in this verse, is a result of knowing God and

also will lead us in other directions.) The reason for the third sacrifice of taking time to listen to God is the basis for the fourth: growing in our knowledge of him. The only way we can get to know him better and deeper is to spend more and more time in his presence. Growing to know him takes time, as it does in any relationship – time that many times we would rather be doing something else – or tempted to be doing something else. To grow to know God demands the sacrifice of our time.

5. ***The sacrifice of mercy*** now becomes the fifth sacrifice that we offer to God. According to Vine, mercy (Gk. *eleos*) is "the outward manifestation of pity; it assumes need on the part of him who receives it, and resources adequate to meet the need on the part of him who shows it" (Vine, 1966, 3:60). "As with God toward us: Grace describes God's attitude toward the lawbreaker and the rebel; mercy is his attitude toward those who are in distress" (Ibid., 61). To be moved by the needs of others is compassion; but to act on that compassion by using our resources to meet those needs is mercy.

I saw mercy enacted time and again by my parents toward us children. Many times they sacrificed their own desires and needs in order to meet ours – and they did it joyfully and in deep love. Never once did I ever hear them complain about the sacrifices they made for us. We must do the same for others. Sacrifice made in joy and prompted by love hardly seems like sacrifice to the one showing mercy, for the joy of giving and the blessing one experiences as a result far exceed any sacrifice made.

6. There are four other sacrifices mentioned in Scripture that could easily be sub points to the sacrifice of mercy. In Philippians 2:17 we read of ***the sacrifice of service toward other Christians***. Paul writes: "But even if I am being poured out like a drink offering on the sacrifice and service coming from your faith, I am glad and rejoice with all of you." The Philippians had a need, and Paul expended himself and all his spiritual resources to meet that need. Ministering to fellow believers

will demand the same from us. This sacrifice becomes evident when we have to prepare a sermon or Bible lesson, or are called to the home of a troubled person to give counsel when we would much rather be watching a football game or be out fishing or reading a book.

All of these sacrifices flow out from our knowledge of God. How much time do you spend listening to him and getting to know him?

APPLICATION: One way to spend more time with the Lord in a busy schedule is to memorize Scripture verses and songs and meditate on them in off moments. Verses written on small cards could also be useful. The Holy Spirit will take his Word and open your understanding of it in fresh ways. This is one way to keep getting to know the Lord better and also to be in the right frame of mind to hear his directions throughout the day.

DAY 72
bHE IS OUR HIGH PRIEST, cont.

QUESTIONS TO THINK ABOUT:

1. How would doing good to your enemy qualify as a sacrifice?
2. How is it more blessed to give than to receive?
3. What does our sharing with others tell them about us, and about the Lord?

7. A second sacrifice coming under the sacrifice of mercy is *the sacrifice of meeting the needs of God's servants*. In Philippians 4:18 Paul thanks the Philippian Christians for meeting his needs: "I have received full payment and even more; I am amply supplied, now that I have received from Epaphroditus the gifts you sent. They are a fragrant offering, an acceptable sacrifice, pleasing to God."

Meeting the needs of God's servants is a sacrifice well pleasing to God because this sacrifice guarantees the extension of his kingdom through their ministries. It means that they will not have to work full-time at meeting their living needs and only part-time in the Lord's work, but that they will be able to devote full-time effort in furthering the kingdom. It is through the continuing gifts of God's people that we have been able to concentrate full-time effort in planting the church and training church leaders in Papua. Without the sacrificial gifts of God's people, we couldn't have done it.

8. The third sacrifice under mercy is found in Hebrews 13:16: "And do not forget ***to do good and to share with others***, for with such sacrifices God is pleased" (bold added). Doing good and sharing both involve sacrifice, for as we do good to others it demands the sacrifice of our time, attention and resources. And if it happens to be toward our enemies, it demands the sacrifice of our emotional "druthers." Romans 12:19-21 speaks to this issue quite pointedly: "Do not take revenge, my friends, but leave room for God's wrath, for it is written: 'It is mine to avenge; I will repay,' says the Lord. On the contrary: 'If your enemy is hungry, feed him; if he is thirsty, give him something to drink. In doing this, you will heap burning coals on his head.' Do not be overcome by evil, but overcome evil with good" (the sacrifice of doing good when you'd rather do him in! – cf. 2 Kgs.6:18-23 where Elisha gave food to Syrian raiders when he could have had them killed. They came no more into Israel after that.)

Sharing with others means dividing what we have and giving them a part, which could have surprising results. My parents opened our home to student nurses from the local nursing school as a "home away from home." They could drop in anytime and be welcome. We were eight in our family. One day we had just sat down to eat, when the doorbell rang. In walked two student nurses. Mom invited them to sit down and eat with us. We had a round steak on the platter which was just enough for our family. "We'll just have to have a little bit less," thought Mom as Dad began cutting the meat and serving the plates. The doorbell rang again, and in came three more prospective nurses. As they joined us, Mom silently prayed, asking the Lord to multiply the meat just as he did the little boy's lunch. We were thirteen at the table now. As Dad served, Mom watched in amazement as everyone had a full share of meat with some still left over on the platter!

A national pastor told me that during the dry season of 1992, all the wells around his area of the city were going dry, including his. He prayed and asked the Lord to supply water to his well, and that he would freely share it with anyone needing it. When he went out to his well, it was full and remained full when all others around went dry. So there was water for everyone in the area who needed it.

Sometimes sharing means that we will do without once our portion is gone. That is sacrifice. But other times the Lord will immediately bless our sacrifice and make what we have left sufficient for our needs. How many times have we not seen this power of the Lord in our lives because we have refused to share?

APPLICATION: Sacrifices are best done as a result of our love for the Lord, his servants, and his people, and accomplished as we bury our own desires in putting others first. Pride will keep us posturing as "number one" and make us insensitive to others' needs. Ask the Lord to give you an open heart and an open hand.

DAY 73
[b]HE IS OUR HIGH PRIEST, cont.

QUESTIONS TO THINK ABOUT:

1. What is it that prompts us to give any kind of sacrifice?
2. How can we be a living sacrifice?

3. How can treating others with respect, without partiality, be a sacrifice?

9. The fourth sacrifice under mercy is found in Ephesians 5:2, *the sacrifice of love*, which prompts us in the giving of any sacrifice: "And live a life of love, just as Christ loved us and gave himself up for us as a fragrant offering and sacrifice to God." Christ gave himself for us; Paul gave himself to his converts (1 Thess.2:8), and the Corinthian Christians gave themselves to Paul (2 Cor.8:5). We must likewise give ourselves to those whom we serve.

Christ says in John 15:13, "Greater love has no one than this, that he lay down his life for his friends." There are two ways to "lay down" our lives for our friends: one is, like Christ, to actually die for them if the need arises; but the other is to willingly and joyfully sacrifice anything we have in order to meet their needs. Thus we offer God a living sacrifice and offer our friends a sacrifice of love.

10. Close to these sacrifices are two others found in Proverbs 21:3 which says: "To do what is right and just is more acceptable to the LORD than sacrifice" - *the sacrifice of doing right* (or *the sacrifice of righteousness*). What is righteousness? It is living in conformity to God's holy standard, living in a way that pleases him. It is doing what is right even at personal cost. It's doing what you know should be done even when you don't feel like doing it. It is living according to heavenly values rather than earthly, worldly standards. This puts us in direct conflict with the world, and open to ridicule and persecution: "Hey, don't be weird! Everybody else is doing it, so it must be O.K." "Look, Preach, don't give me that Bible bit. This plan is a neat way to get some extra bucks. If you don't like it, bug out!" Thus righteous living demands sacrifice.

David gave a good description of this kind of living in Psalm 15:1-5. "Lord, who may dwell in your sanctuary? Who may live on your holy hill? He whose walk is blameless and who does what is righteous, who speaks the truth from his heart and has no slander on his tongue, who does his neighbor no wrong and casts no slur on his fellow man, who despises a vile man but honors those who fear the LORD, who keeps his oath even when it hurts, who lends his money without interest and does not accept a bribe against the innocent. He who does these things will never be shaken."

11. As the sacrifice of righteousness deals with our way of life, *the sacrifice of justice* has to do with our treatment of others. God deals with everyone without respect of persons, without partiality. Yet, according to James 2:1-4, we tend to give preference to the rich, to those who could help us get ahead. We want to get to know those influential people who could carry us higher in various social circles or organizations. To honor a poor man, or person of another race equally with a rich man, or someone of importance, will alienate those of higher status from us, and will disadvantage us in terms of promotion, status or financial gain. Thus dealing without partiality, dealing with all men justly, can become a real personal sacrifice. It can also become a real personal testimony. A rather prominent man in the town of Manokwari, (Papua, Indonesia), said of our field chairman, with a tinge of deep respect in his voice, "No matter who came into the office, he was treated with respect. That's not like what we do here."

How does your love prompt you in sacrificing for the needs of others?

APPLICATION: The love that prompts us to sacrifice is *agape* love, the love of choice. It says, "I choose to love you for your benefit, period." Since this love is not based upon feelings, anyone can choose to do it anytime to anyone (see DAY 78 – HE IS THE LOVING ONE, for further discussion on *agape* love). To whom could you show this love today?

Showing partiality in relating to others is always a struggle. But we need to look beyond the cultural and economic differences and get to the person. We need "status blinders" in our relationships with others so that we can minister to all of them equally. Ask the Lord to work this out in your life.

DAY 74
ᵇHE IS OUR HIGH PRIEST, cont.

◆

QUESTIONS TO THINK ABOUT:

1. What is your reaction to this statement: "The Lord would rather have you obey him than worship him"?
2. How can prayer be considered a sacrifice?

12. In 1 Samuel 15:22, we find **the sacrifice of obedience**. "But Samuel replied: 'Does the LORD delight in burnt offerings and sacrifices as much as in obeying the voice of the LORD? To obey is better than sacrifice, and to heed is better than the fat of rams.'" This sacrifice goes hand in hand with the sacrifice of righteousness as it forms the foundation or basis for righteous living. Obedience often involves sacrifice as we must frequently set aside what we want to do to do what the Lord wants, or what anyone in authority over us wants. To couch this verse in modern terms: "To obey the Lord is more pleasing to him than worshipping him."

How can we say that? Look at Matthew 5:23,24 where the Lord says, "Therefore, if you are offering your gift at the altar [worship] and there remember that your brother has something against you, leave your gift there in front of the altar. First go and be reconciled to your brother; then come and offer your gift." Obeying the Lord in seeking peace with your brother is more important to him than your worship!

Look also at Matthew 15:7-9 where Jesus blasts the Pharisees for their hypocrisy: "You hypocrites! Isaiah was right when he prophesied about you: 'These people honor me with their lips, but their hearts are far from me. They worship me in vain; their teachings are but rules taught by men.'" In the Temple or synagogue they professed to be following the commands of God, but in daily practice they followed the commands of men. "Obedience is better than sacrifice."

In Amos 5:21-24, the LORD said the same thing of the nation of Israel: "I hate, I despise your religious feasts; I cannot stand your assemblies. Even though you bring me burnt offerings and grain offerings, I will not accept them. Though you bring choice fellowship offerings, I will have no regard for them. Away with the noise of your songs! I will not listen to the music of your harps. But let justice roll on like a river, righteousness like a never-failing stream" (underlining mine).

Is your worship offensive to the Lord because you are not obeying him?

13. In Psalm 141:2 David says, "May my prayer be set before you like incense; may the lifting up of my hands be like the evening sacrifice." Again in Revelation 8:3 we read: "Another angel, who had a golden censer, came and stood at the altar. He was given much incense to offer, with the prayers of all the saints, on the golden altar before the throne" – *the sacrifice of prayer.*

To really pray takes time. It is not a quick "hello" and "goodbye" to God, but time taken to talk with him. Sometimes it means going to bed earlier so you can get up earlier. Sometimes it means setting aside longer periods of time (Christ prayed several times all night long – Luke 6:12 is one example). Making the effort to attend the regular prayer meeting at church or special prayer meetings being held will demand the sacrifice of our time. Sometimes we will go without a meal or several meals in order to give our full attention to prayer. If we take prayer seriously, we will be willing to take whatever time is needed to pray about any situation that comes up.

Do you enjoy spending time talking with your heavenly Father? Are you willing to sacrifice time in order to do it?

APPLICATION: Do you have any long-standing accounts with the Lord or with others that have not yet been settled? Plan to settle them as soon as possible so that your relationship with the Lord will be right and that he will accept your worship.

Do you like to talk with God? As you spend time getting to know him better, you will find yourself in conversation with him more often, and even making special times to meet with him in prayer. Keep at it!

DAY 75
ᵇHE IS OUR HIGH PRIEST, cont.

QUESTIONS TO THINK ABOUT:

1. Why do we consider it important to give thanks to someone?
2. Why is it we so seldom give thanks to God? Why is it so hard to do this?
3. Why is giving thanks in difficult situations considered a sacrifice?
4. Why do we find it so hard to praise the Lord?

Unexpected Transformation

14. Now we come to *the sacrifice of thanksgiving*. In Psalm 116:17 we read: "I will sacrifice a thank offering to you and call on the name of the LORD." In the belly of the big fish, Jonah prayed, "But I, with a song of thanksgiving, will sacrifice to you. What I have vowed I will make good. Salvation comes from the LORD" (Jonah 2:9).

So often we pray and the Lord answers only to hear us pray again without so much as a "thank you" for what he has done. We rub the "magic bottle" of prayer and expect God to jump out and do whatever we want. No thanks given because he's only doing his job! This example is a bit crude but isn't this the way many Christians treat him? We need to learn to offer the sacrifice of thanksgiving.

What is involved in the offering of this sacrifice?

a) First is <u>submission and obedience to the will of God</u>. We read in 1 Thessalonians 5:18, "Give thanks in all circumstances, for this is God's will for you in Christ Jesus."

b) Secondly, <u>thanking him for the not-so-nice things we go through</u>. This implies that we fully trust him in whatever circumstances we find ourselves, and that we know that in his loving sovereignty, he will take these circumstances, good or bad, and use them to make us more like Christ.

c) The sacrifice of thanksgiving also means <u>making the effort to be aware of God's answers and then thanking him for them</u>. Not only is it polite to say "Thank you," but it is also an admission that we had a need which only he could meet.

d) So saying "thank you" is <u>a humbling of ourselves before him</u>. How do you feel when someone says "thank you" to you for something you have done? What does that expression of appreciation mean to you? The Lord also deeply appreciates our expressions of thanks, and receives them as a sacrifice well pleasing to him.

15. Close to the sacrifice of thanksgiving is ***the sacrifice of praise***. We read of this sacrifice in Hebrews 13:15. "Through Jesus, therefore, let us continually offer to God a sacrifice of praise – the fruit of lips that confess his name." This verse is loaded with meaning. First of all, this is a continuous sacrifice; it is to be going on all of the time. This sacrifice is described as "the fruit of [our] lips," so it involves what we say aloud for others to hear.

There are three ways we can praise others: by telling them how wonderful they are and thanking them for what they have done; by telling others how wonderful they are and what they have done; and by becoming like them, saying and doing what they would say and do.

We saw this time and again when we worked in TEAM's Hostel for M.K.'s at the international school in Sentani, Irian Jaya (Papua). The children not only resembled their parents physically, but spoke and acted like them as well. Thus as we become more like Christ, speaking and acting like him, we literally offer a continual sacrifice of praise to him. (Just a parenthetical thought: lips that are occupied in giving praise to God will have little time for gossip and slander of others. So praise is one way to keep us from sinning with our lips!)

Is your relationship with the Lord characterized by thanksgiving and praise?

APPLICATION: If you have trouble remembering to give thanks to the Lord, keep track of answered prayers and make a "Thank You" list to say to him. If praise comes with difficulty for you, make a "Praise" list also, then use it in your praying. Later on, you won't need these lists as thanksgiving and praise will come more naturally.

DAY 76
ᵇHE IS OUR HIGH PRIEST, concl.

◆

QUESTIONS TO THINK ABOUT:

1. Why is our confession of Christ important?
2. What will we lose if we do not confess him?
3. What do you think is involved in offering a sacrifice of joy?

16. The last part of Hebrews 13:15 reads, "praises – the fruit of lips that confess his name." According to Vine, the Greek word translated "confess" (*homologeo*) means "confess by way of celebrating with praise" (Vine, 1966, 1:224). As we praise him by telling others about him, we are offering ***the sacrifice of confessing his name***; and this can be a real sacrifice indeed. In many countries, including America, one can lose his job for confessing the name of Christ before others: imprisonment, fines, confiscation of property, break-up of family (either the unsaved partner leaves, or the government removes the children from such an "unhealthy" environment), beatings and persecution of all kinds. But we need to weigh the consequences of not confessing his name.

First of all, we will be found in disobedience to the Great Commission where Christ has commanded us to go into all the world preaching the Gospel to everyone (Mk.16:15; Acts 1:8).

Secondly, if we refuse to confess Christ before men, he will refuse to confess us before his Father in heaven. Refusing to confess him evidently means that we don't possess him, hence are not saved. Christ would never deny his own. He says in Matthew 10:27,32, "What I tell you in the dark, speak in the daylight; what is whispered in your ear, proclaim from the roofs... . Whoever acknowledges [confesses] me before men, I will also acknowledge [confess] him before my Father in heaven. But whoever disowns me before men, I will disown him before my Father in heaven" (cf. Matt.7:21-23).

Thirdly, <u>confession is necessary in the process of salvation</u>. Romans 10:9,10 says, "That if you confess with your mouth, 'Jesus is Lord,' and believe in your heart that God raised him from the dead, you will be saved. For it is with your heart that you believe and are justified, and it is with your mouth that you confess and are saved." The point is this: If there is no confession, there is no possession! So the sacrifice of confessing his name is an absolutely essential sacrifice in the Christian's life <u>as it proves the presence of saving faith</u>.

17. Finally, there is *the sacrifice of joy*. In Psalm 27:6 we read: "Then my head will be exalted above the enemies who surround me; at his tabernacle will I sacrifice with shouts of joy; I will sing and make music to the LORD." Where was this sacrifice made? "At his tabernacle," in the place where men could meet with their God. Where is that today? In the church! Do you know what would happen if someone tried to offer this sacrifice to God in the usual church service? He would be labeled "charismatic" or "crazy" and counseled, "We don't do that here!" But his only "sin" was in responding audibly with joy to what the Lord was doing; offering the sacrifice of joyous shouts. We must give one another the freedom for audible expression of joy without censorship and accusations of being what we are not. There are times when my heart is so full of joy for what the Lord has done, that I feel like I'm going to burst. A time like that is the time for the sacrifice of joyful shouts to release that pent-up emotion.

These are the sacrifices that we, as priests of God, should be offering up daily in our worship and service for him.

How well are you fulfilling your office as priest?

APPLICATION: Regarding our confession of Christ before others see DAYS 25-30 – HE IS THE WITNESS for additional help in dealing with problem areas in your witness/confession.

Somehow I don't feel that "Give three cheers for Jesus!" qualifies as a sacrifice of joy. Rather it should be a spontaneous response from an overflowing heart toward God himself and what he has done. If yours is not an "amen" church, then "shout" quietly where you sit. Talk with your pastor about it. Perhaps he will "give permission" to the congregation to say, "Amen" at appropriate times, which, in turn, will give you permission to say it a bit louder. Others may catch on and join you. You never know.

DAY 77
bHE IS OUR MASTER/TEACHER

QUESTIONS TO THINK ABOUT:

1. How can one teach with authority?
2. How powerful is example in a teacher's life, public as well as private?
3. How important is it that the teacher also practices what he teaches?

Again in John 13:13, Jesus declared himself a teacher: "You call me 'Teacher' and 'Lord,' and rightly so, for that is what I am." Nicodemus, who came to Jesus by night, said, "Rabbi, we know you are a teacher who has come from God. For no one could perform the miraculous signs you are doing if God were not with him" (Jn.3:2). Everywhere he went, people called him, "Teacher," as his habit was to teach (Jn.8:2). Let's see what we can learn, then, from his character as a teacher.

1. <u>He taught with authority</u>. In Matthew 7:29 we read, "He taught as one who had authority, and not as their teachers of the law" (cf. Lk.4:32). Their teachers always quoted other rabbis and writings, stating opinions and possibilities. Jesus came along, removing the various shades of gray with a clear "Thus-says-the-Lord" presentation, astounding his listeners and enraging their teachers. Where they hedged and quoted, Christ declared with an air of authority that could not be dismissed.

2. <u>He practiced what he taught</u>. In Matthew 11:29b, he said, "I am gentle and humble in heart." Paul gave proof of this in Philippians 2:5-11 where Christ humbled himself to take on the form of a man and suffer death. In Matthew 20:28 he declared that he "did not come to be served, but to serve, and to give his life as a ransom for many." In John 13:2-14 Jesus did the work of the lowliest servant in washing his disciples' feet. He gave his life on the cross to ransom many (Jn.19:16).

3. <u>He used himself as an example for others to follow</u> so that they would become like him. In John 13:15 he said, "I have set you an example that you should do as I have done for you." Peter declares in 1 Peter 2:21b that "Christ suffered for you, leaving you an example, that you should follow in his steps." And in John 17:11 he prayed that his followers might become one with one another and with him (vs.21). Again in Luke 6:40 he said, "A student is not above his teacher, but everyone who is fully trained [Gk. *katartizo*, "to complete thoroughly"] will be like his teacher." 2 Timothy 3:16,17 mirrors this thought. God gave his Word to us "so that the man of God may be thoroughly equipped for every good work."

4. Lastly, <u>he promised results to those who followed his teachings</u>. In John 13:17 he says, "Now that you know these things, you will be blessed [Gk. *makarioi*, "most blessed"] if you do them."

Unexpected Transformation / 185

Obviously, if his teachings didn't work, we wouldn't be blessed in doing them!

So if we are to reflect Christ as the Teacher, we must first <u>know</u> the Word of God so that we can teach it with authority. I found out in the Theological College that as long as I stuck to the Word, I had great confidence in what I was teaching, and so could teach with authority.

But we also must practice what we teach, for <u>practice</u> is the proof of the principles taught. Then we can let ourselves be used as an <u>example</u> since what we are doing pleases God and <u>works</u> (bears results).

Lastly, because of our experience in <u>practicing</u> what we're teaching and seeing it <u>work</u>, we can promise success and blessing to others who follow our example. Paul urged Timothy to "be an example" (1 Tim.4:12). He also counseled the Philippian Christians to follow him and use him and his fellow helpers as their examples (Phil.3:17). It is not egotistical to encourage others to do something that <u>works</u>. If you want to build a bridge, you must follow the example and experience of construction engineers who have proven that certain principles, if followed, will guarantee success – your bridge will not fall. "If you do it like this, as we have done, it will withstand great stress and be around long after you have gone." They know what <u>works</u>, and if what you are doing in the context of Scripture <u>works</u>, encourage others to follow your example.

You don't have to be a teacher to be a teacher! Every day we're teaching someone by our life and example. What kind of teacher are you?

APPLICATION: Example is one of the best teaching methods there is. Review DAY 5, HE IS OUR EXAMPLE, and take a good look at the example you are giving to others. Do you need to make some changes? Work on them so that by your example you will be a good teacher.

DAY 78
[a]HE IS THE LOVING ONE

◆

QUESTIONS TO THINK ABOUT:

1. What is love? What are its characteristics?
2. What does a person mean when he/she says, "I love you"?
3. How many different kinds of love can you think of?
4. How is love demonstrated?

In the New Testament, there are three Greek words used for our English word "love," two of which are *agape*, the love of choice, and *fileo*, tender affection (the love of emotion). Christ's love is described in terms of *agape* in all but three instances where *fileo* is used: John 11:36 toward Lazarus; John 20:2 toward John; and Revelation 3:19 toward the church of Laodicea. *Fileo* carries the intent of "cherishing the object above all else" (Vine, 1966, 3:22), whereas *agape* is "the love that values and esteems (cf. Rev.12:11). It is an unselfish love, ready to serve" (Ibid., vs.22). Further, it is "an exercise of the Divine will in deliberate choice, made without assignable cause save that which lies in the nature of God himself" (Ibid., vs.21). To put it simply, God chose to love us for no other reason than he wanted to!

Vine says again, "Love can only be known from the actions it prompts" (Ibid., vs.21). Christ said, "No one has greater love than the one who lays down his life for his friends" (Jn.15:13). But according to Romans 5:8,10, Christ willingly laid down his life for us, his enemies! How much greater, then, is his love! We read: "But God demonstrates his own love for us in this: While we were still sinners, Christ died for us... . For if, when we were God's enemies, we were reconciled to him through the death of his Son, how much more, having been reconciled, shall we be saved through his life!"

Unexpected Transformation / 187

Let's illustrate it this way. If you saw someone taking aim with a gun to kill someone you really loved (*fileo*), it wouldn't take a snap of the fingers before you'd try to step between the gun and your loved one. But if some drunken skid row bum had just threatened you and robbed you of everything you had, then turned to go on his way, and suddenly you saw someone pointing a gun at him, what would your reaction be? I think we would stand back and let him "get what's coming to him," right? Christ would have just as quickly jumped between the gun and the man who had just robbed him!

That is *agape* love, the love of choice which is part of the very nature of Christ. And it is this love, *agape* love, that he prayed would be in each of us: "I have revealed you [God] to them [the disciples], and will continue to make you known <u>in order that the love you have for me may be theirs</u> and that I myself may be in them" (Jn.17:26 – underlining mine). That love, which flows from the very nature of God, Christ prays will become a part of our nature. It is a love which, in part, looks at a person not for what he is now, but for what he can become; a love which responds to need, not to personality.

1 Corinthians 13:4-8 is God's measuring stick for *agape* love: "Love is patient, love is kind. It does not envy, it does not boast, it is not proud. It is not rude, it is not self-seeking, it is not easily angered, it keeps no record of wrongs. Love does not delight in evil but rejoices in the truth. It always protects, always trusts, always hopes, always perseveres. Love never fails."

This is *agape* love, God's love. How does your love measure up to his?

APPLICATION: Read over and meditate upon 1 Corinthians 13:4-8, asking yourself, "Am I patient? Am I kind? Am I envious?" etc. Then deal with yourself in those areas of *agape* love that clash with what you are like now.

DAY 79
ªHE IS THE LOVING ONE, concl.

QUESTIONS TO THINK ABOUT:

1. How is it possible for us to fulfill *agape* love when it is impossible for us to feel *fileo* love?
2. How does *agape* love figure in any marriage relationship?
3. How can a person say, "I don't love (*fileo*) you any more" yet still love (*agape*) that person?
4. What kind of love does God command us to have for one another? Why?
5. How is it possible to love (*agape*) your enemies or those you just don't like?

Yesterday we considered *agape* love, the love of choice, which Christ has shown to us and prayed that we would show to others. Today let's consider how we can help answer that prayer.

First of all, we are commanded (this takes the choice out of it) to walk in love (*agape*): "And live a life of love, just as Christ loved us, and gave himself up for us as a fragrant offering and sacrifice to God" (Eph.5:2). Christ said in John 13:34, "A new commandment I give you: Love [*agape*] one another. As I have loved [*agape*] you, so you must love one another" (underlining mine). And not only one another, but he commands us also to love our enemies! "But I tell you: love [*agape*] your enemies and pray for those who persecute you" (Matt.5:44). For the Christian, love is not an option, but a command to be obeyed, a way of life to be lived. With so many of us, it has to be worked at; but with our Lord, it was the normal outflow from his very nature.

Why do we need to work at showing love? Because we haven't truly crucified "self" with its vested interests. As long as any

Unexpected Transformation / 189

part of us remains "number one," we will have trouble with the outflow of *agape* love toward others. Once our selfishness and selfish motives are dead (and they can be put to death, just as any other sin!), then we will be able to express *agape* love as naturally as Christ did. This also is possible since God has commanded it and since it is part of his guaranteed goal for our lives to make us like Christ.

Another area for expression of *agape* love is necessary to consider. Ephesians 5:25 says, "Husbands, love (*agape*) your wives, just as Christ loved the church and gave himself up for her." In our culture (though not in all), the man chooses the woman he wants to marry. That choice may be based on many criteria: beauty, talent, motherliness, social status, wealth, family connections, similarity in interests, gratification of personal need and/or desires, and so on. But once into marriage, things change. Bad or irritating habits are discovered, children come along (or may not), schedules change, circumstances change, beauty is marred by age, accident or bitterness, someone more beautiful or more talented comes along, and the list continues. What then? Expectations fail and you suddenly realize, "I don't love (*fileo*) her!" "I don't love (*fileo*) him!" Two choices remain: (1) to get a divorce, or (2) to endure a bad situation for the sake of outward appearance and/or family.

Or ... there is a third choice: to die to your selfish expectations and the selfish basis upon which you married in the first place, and choose to love your mate biblically with *agape* love, the love of choice. Obedience to the biblical command will bring about guaranteed results and fruit in your own life and may, in God's grace, result in renewed love (*fileo*), stability and spiritual vitality for your family. But remember that many of Christ's own people rejected his love, even as your mate might reject yours. But he loved them anyway! That was his responsibility. He loved to and through the cross. And this is the kind of love we must have for our mates.

Is your love characterized by a-gap, or *agape*?

APPLICATION: Since *agape* love is the love of choice, we can choose to demonstrate it any time to anyone. Sometimes we need to force ourselves to do what we know is right. This is perhaps even more true of *agape* love. Try to take note of times when you should have shown *agape* love and didn't. Then take steps to improve your "performance" the next time. It will make a difference.

DAY 80
ᵇHE IS THE GRIEVED ONE

QUESTIONS TO THINK ABOUT:

1. What is grief?
2. What are some things which cause us grief?
3. What do we do that causes the Lord grief?

One Sabbath day Jesus entered the Temple, and there was a man there with a withered hand. Some of the Jewish leaders were there too, intently watching Jesus to see if he would "break" the Sabbath by healing the man. Then they could accuse him. Having set the man in front of everyone, Jesus turned to the leaders and said, "Which is lawful on the Sabbath: to do good or to do evil, to save life or to kill?" But they didn't answer him. Then "he looked around at them in anger, deeply distressed [grieved – KJV] at their stubborn [hard] hearts" (Mk.3:4,5).

In Psalm 78:40,41 we read: "How often they [Israel] rebelled against him in the desert, and grieved him in the wasteland! Again and again they put God to the test; they vexed the Holy One of Israel." And again in Psalm 95:10,11 God says, "Forty years I was angry [grieved – KJV] with that generation; I said, 'They are a people whose hearts go astray, and they have not known my ways.' So I declared on oath in my anger, 'They shall never enter my rest.'"

Unbelief, hardness of heart, and opposing the work of the Lord always brings grief to his heart – and anger. For some reason, I have been able to identify more closely with this characteristic than with many others. Many, many times, I have been grieved in my heart as God's Word has been presented, but people have been talking, looking around distractedly, or even sleeping. I found myself becoming angry both at them and the distractions because of the dishonor they are doing to the Lord and because they are robbing themselves and others of spiritual blessing and growth. Then, disgustingly, I frequently find myself doing the same thing! Often as someone else is preaching, and especially when they are praying, my mind will wander off on something they have mentioned, or go on some other "journey," and sometimes, minutes later, I "come to" and realize that I've missed something – but it's gone.

We have had the experience where a fellow believer, who could not have his own way in running things, openly threatened to ruin the attempts of others to serve the Lord. The Lord, in his grace, brought all those threats to naught; but he was grieved as were the rest of us. And in anger, it is difficult for us to still love, and not rather "call down fire out of heaven" to consume this enemy of the Lord, professed Christian though he be.

Anything that separates us from the Lord is a grief to him because of his great love for us. Let's stop grieving him and begin to give him joy as we delight in his presence, ignore distractions, and encourage others to do the same.

Are you grieved when the Word doesn't "get through" because of hardened or distracted hearts?

APPLICATION: So often our grief is expressed in anger either at God for allowing something to happen or at others for what they have done or are doing. We need to discipline ourselves to pray instead, committing those situations to the Lord and looking to him for comfort and encouragement. As we commit these things to him (Phil.4:6,7), his peace will flood our hearts, and we will be able to handle the grief that we must bear.

DAY 81
ᵇHE IS THE BROKENHEARTED ONE

QUESTIONS TO THINK ABOUT:

1. How does it feel to be brokenhearted? How does that influence how you feel about the world?
2. What is it that breaks a person's heart?
3. How can/should one minister to a person with a broken heart?

To be brokenhearted is "to have one's spirit depressed; to be crushed by grief or despair" (Webster, 1984). Four times we read of Christ being in this emotional extremity. Perhaps the first is found in Luke 19:41-44 at the time when he was approaching Jerusalem the week before his crucifixion. "As he approached Jerusalem and saw the city, he wept over it and said, 'If you, even you, had only known on this day what would bring you peace – but now it is hidden from your eyes. The days will come upon you when your enemies will build an embankment against you and encircle you and hem you in on every side. They will dash you to the ground, you and the children within your walls. They will not leave one stone on another, because you did not recognize the time of God's coming to you.'" Here Christ's deep grief was two-fold: humanly, he inherited that fierce loyalty and pride in Jerusalem common to all Jews, and the thought of its total destruction broke his heart. Spiritually, he knew what would bring Israel true peace, and saw their utter blindness to it, resulting in their eventual destruction – and that also broke his heart.

Secondly, we read prophetically of Christ's enduring scorn for God's sake. "For I endure scorn for your sake, and shame covers my face… . Scorn has broken my heart and has left me helpless; I looked for sympathy, but there was none, for comforters, but I found none" (Ps.69:7,20). How many times he was scorned and ridiculed during his ministry, and how greatly he was scorned and put to shame on the cross. That scorn broke his heart as he saw men rejecting the only way to peace with God and forgiveness of sin, rejecting the very reason Christ came to earth.

We read of the third time in Luke 22:41-44 as he anticipated the crucifixion: "He knelt down and prayed, 'Father, if you are willing, take this cup from me; yet not my will, but yours be done.' An angel from heaven appeared to him and strengthened him. And being in anguish, he prayed more earnestly, and his sweat was like drops of blood falling to the ground."

Finally, on the cross, crushed by the load of our sins (Isa.53:5b), and God having turned his back on him, he cried out with a broken heart, "My God, my God, why have you forsaken me?" (Matt.27:46).

I experienced that broken-heartedness to the point of tears when writing my Master's thesis on Zionism. It broke my heart to realize that God was moving to return the Jews to Palestine and to reestablish their nation, but that the majority of them were completely oblivious to his working. Oh the blessing and the joy they were missing out on by not even recognizing the hand of God in the events surrounding their homeland!

We read in Psalm 34:18 that "the LORD is close to the broken-hearted and saves those who are crushed in spirit." We also see in Isa.61:1 that Christ came to "bind up" or heal the brokenhearted.

People are often utterly crushed by their circumstances and situations, but the Lord Jesus Christ stands with his arms wide open, ready to welcome and comfort all who come to him: "Come to me, all you who are weary and burdened, and I will give you rest," he says (Matt.11:28). He is the answer to our broken hearts.

Have you come to him? Are you making yourself available to bring comfort to others who are brokenhearted?

APPLICATION: How can one minister to the brokenhearted? The place to begin is by answering the question, "How would I want to be ministered to if I were brokenhearted?" Ask the Lord to make you sensitive toward the feelings of others; to know when to speak a word of encouragement and when to remain silent.

DAY 82
ᶜHE IS THE LONELY ONE (THE DESERTED)

QUESTIONS TO THINK ABOUT:

1. What does it mean to be lonely? Why would one feel lonely?
2. How can one be lonely in a crowd of people?
3. How can love, understanding and faithfulness counteract loneliness?

Let's begin today with some questions: "Have you ever felt lonely or deserted? Have you ever felt like God has left you to make it on your own and isn't even around for advice? Have you ever felt like all your friends and perhaps even your own family have deserted you?" If you have, then you're in good company, for

Christ experienced loneliness on a number of occasions. Let's look at five of them.

At the Last Supper, only Jesus himself knew that he was going to die. His disciples were not aware of it. "Jesus knew that the time had come for him to leave this world and go to the Father" (Jn.13:1b). They also didn't understand when Christ told them he was going to die (Jn.13:33,36,37). They thought he was just going to leave them and were most disappointed at the prospect.

Just previous to this, the disciples had expended much energy and all their attention on who among them would be the greatest (Lk.22:24-27). So Jesus had to settle this dispute which only added to his burden. He was very much alone, even when among his disciples, because, as they argued about their status, they were totally unaware of his distress at what was coming. They didn't even try to console him or meet his needs, for they weren't aware that he <u>had</u> any needs! Can you identify with the loneliness he felt?

Secondly, in the Garden of Gethsemane, Jesus prayed alone while his disciples slept. He had the most important decision of his life to make and wanted at least Peter, James and John to pray with him, humanly, to strengthen him. He had to choose between his own will not to die, or his Father's will which was for him to die (Matt.26:42). But his closest friends left him alone to wrestle with his problem while they slept!

Have you ever struggled over God's will for you, wanting to do it, but afraid to? Or wrestled over some personal or family problem, or a bad situation at work, and deeply desired some counsel or support from your friends, but found, to your dismay, that they did not seem to understand or even care about your problems, and so offered no help, leaving you to make your own way and find your own solutions? The Lord has been there before you!

Thirdly, when Jesus was arrested, everybody turned tail and ran (Matt.26:56), leaving him alone to face that angry mob. The principle Solomon stated in Proverbs 14:20 is true here: "The poor is shunned even by their neighbors, but the rich have many friends." For three years, while Christ enjoyed growing fame and popularity, his disciples found it a good thing to be seen with him. But when the tide turned against him, they vanished like the morning fog on a summer day. No one stayed to help him; all fled, fearing for their lives. If you ever suffer this kind of loneliness, remember, Christ did too!

Can you recall any times you might have left someone alone who needed your help and encouragement?

APPLICATION: Sometimes our loneliness is self-induced. One cure for any kind of loneliness is to become involved with others, meeting their needs or just doing something with them. Look for ways you can become involved in their lives; then do it. Also an enjoyable hobby or special projects can help pass "lonely" time constructively and bring great satisfaction.

DAY 83
ᶜHE IS THE LONELY ONE (THE DESERTED), concl.

QUESTIONS TO THINK ABOUT:

1. What are some things we do that would make others feel lonely?
2. What provisions has God made so that we do not need to feel lonely?

Yesterday we saw Jesus alone in a crowd, left to solve his most pressing problem by himself, and deserted when the chips were down. Now we will consider the last two occasions of his loneliness.

When Jesus was falsely accused before the Jews and before Pilate, no one stood up to defend him, though <u>all knew</u> he was innocent! Talk about injustice! I feel angry just thinking about it.

Have you ever been falsely accused and had no one stand up on your behalf? Have you ever smarted under the unjustness of it all? You might have been demoted, or lost your job, or had your name unabashedly smudged in your social circles or church fellowship. And though your friends felt for you, they didn't have the courage to speak up for you, lest their "testimony" be hindered, etc. It happens. Christ knows that by experience.

Lastly, on the cross, Jesus was literally forsaken by God. He cried out in the anguish of one doomed to hell: "My God, my God, why have you forsaken me?" (Matt.27:46b). David penned these words a thousand years before Christ (Ps.22:1-22) when he felt that God had deserted him. These words echo in the hearts of many Christians when troubles mount up, when prayers "bounce off the ceiling," when victory eludes the grasp. But remember, Christ not only <u>felt</u> forsaken, he <u>was</u> forsaken!

If you have never received Christ as your Savior from sin, there will come a day when you also will experience being utterly forsaken by God – forever. Your sins, unforgiven, will separate you from him who died and rose again to forgive them, if you had only asked him to.

But if you have already received Christ as your Savior, then he himself has promised that you will <u>never</u> have to suffer this loneliness that he suffered. In Matthew 28:20b, he says, "And surely I will be with you always, to the very end of the age." And again in Hebrews 13:5b is the promise: "God has said, 'Never will I leave you; never will I forsake you.'"

But here comes the twist. Do you, by the way you live your Christian life, make Christ lonely all over again? As he enters the Body of Believers, do you remain oblivious to his presence, preoccupied with your plans and ignorant of his, unfeeling for his earnest love and desire for the unsaved? When he wants to meet with you in prayer, does he find you "sleeping" or uncommunicative or "BUSY" hung on the door of your heart? When being a Christian becomes unpopular, do you "run and hide" lest you be discovered and ridiculed? When Jesus' name is maligned and false things said about him, do you remain silent, leaving his name to suffer without defense? By your willful, continued sin, do you make his loneliness that much more for him to bear?

If the Savior was dependent upon your fellowship, how lonely would he be?

APPLICATION: Knowing what causes loneliness, what steps can you take to prevent your being the cause of someone else's loneliness?

DAY 84
ᶜHE IS THE ROOT OF DAVID/ THE NAZARENE

QUESTIONS TO THINK ABOUT:

1. What are the functions of a plant's roots?
2. Which root system is stronger, diffused root or tap root?
3. What is the meaning of the word "roots" in our family tree?

I can imagine your first question: "How are these two names related?" Christ was called a Nazarene (Matt.2:23) because he was from Nazareth, just like Americans are called Americans because they come from America. The primary importance of Christ's being called a Nazarene is prophetical – one more indication of his Messiahship. But there is an interesting point to notice: "Nazareth" comes from the Hebrew word "*nazar*" meaning "root"! And Jesus, as the Root of David (Rev.5:5), indicates not only his relationship to David, but also to Israel as symbolized by David. This is a Jewish name of Christ and must be understood in that context.

Every plant has a root of some kind. Roots are essential to its life process and stability. Before the seedling sprouts, their root has already begun to grow and to absorb nourishment from the soil. As seen in the Psalms, David, as a man, was well-nourished by his faith in God. His roots went deep in his relationship with him.

But in relation to Israel, we have a different picture. Here we have a flourishing tree with deep roots during David's and Solomon's reigns. But then a dry rot sets in, the tree split apart into two sections, withered and died, leaving only a stump. But the roots, their foundation, were still there! And from these roots there sprang forth a shoot (Isa.11:1), new life, even as we have seen happen to tree stumps at one time and another. Isaiah 11:10 says, "In that day the Root of Jesse will stand as a banner for the peoples; the nations will rally to him, and his place of rest will be glorious." (In this verse, Jesus is referred to as "a root of Jesse." Since Jesse was David's father, there is no conflict here; they stand, prophetically as one.) The following verses relate to the gathering together of Israel again and the setting up of the kingdom. So Christ, as the Root of David, assures Israel of future spiritual life and the fulfillment of the Old Testament kingdom prophecies.

As roots provide nourishment for life, they also provide stability for the plant. Have you ever tried to pull up a dandelion plant successfully, root and all? It's hard, for of all roots, the tap root is strongest. Trees with tap roots are the most stable of all trees. Those with a diffused system are more easily toppled. Trees don't need to send down deep roots if there is plenty of surface water and nutrients. Such is the case with trees in Papua. The deepest root system I've seen on 125-foot-tall trees measured only 18 inches! That's not much to keep the tree from falling in high winds! But where there is a lack of water, particularly, trees will be forced to send roots deeper into the soil and rock for nourishment. High winds don't often topple these trees!

The important thing to remember here is that Jesus, as the Root of David, in whom the Gentiles also trust (Isa.11:10), is our sure source of spiritual nourishment, and a deep root which shall never be pulled up (cf. Heb.13:8). Our security lies in him.

APPLICATION: As you drive your roots deeper into Christ through personal Bible study (see DAY 85, APPLICATION), you will become a stabilizing influence for others around you. You also will be able to draw up nourishment for them which will help them send their roots deeper.

DAY 85
ᶜHE IS THE ROOT OF DAVID/ THE NAZARENE, concl.

QUESTIONS TO THINK ABOUT:

1. How can we become rooted in Christ?
2. From where does our spiritual "root system" obtain its nourishment?
3. How is our "root system" strengthened?

Since Christ's title as the Root of David is a Jewish title with particular significance for Israel, how, then, does that title apply to us? Isaiah answers this question: "In that day the Root of Jesse will stand as a banner for the peoples; the nations will rally to him, and his place of rest will be glorious" (Isa.11:10). In his first coming, Christ was rejected by his people (Jn.1:11), but received by the Gentiles (Jn.12:20,21), who then experienced his rest (Rom.5:1)

Unexpected Transformation / 201

which indeed was glorious; peace with God is true rest from the turmoil of a guilty, troubled soul.

Paul then says that we have become "rooted in him" (Col.2:7), rooted in the eternal, stable Root of David. In verse seven Paul also talks about our being built up in him, and strengthened in the faith. The question is, "What kind of a root system are we building?" Nourishment is so easy for us to get. Many churches preach the Word, there are Bible studies and conferences without number, special meetings of all kinds, TV, radio, internet, DVD's and CD's. We don't need to put down very deep roots because of the abundance of ready nourishment. We take in much from others, grow tall spiritually, until – until the "wind" comes, and we are blown about by life's adversities. Having no deep root, we tumble to the ground! This is what happens with a "spiritually diffused" root system.

But if we send down a tap root, taking advantage of the ready nourishment, by going down deeper in personal study and daily meeting with God in prayer and through the Word, then when those "winds" come, we'll be shaken about, to be sure, but will not fall. I like Psalm 1:1-3 in this context: "Blessed is the man who does not walk in the counsel of the wicked or stand in the way of sinners or sit in the seat of mockers. But his delight is in the law of the LORD, and on his law he meditates day and night. He is like a tree planted by the streams of water, which yields its fruit in season and whose leaf does not wither. Whatever he does prospers."

Some of that fruit is brought out in this way: just as Christ nourishes us and helps us grow, so we are to nourish others and help them grow. No matter who you are, there is always someone you can help and encourage in their Christian life. It's called discipleship. The deeper we go in the Word, the greater will be our capacity to help others.

As we need the Lord for our ultimate stability, so he has given us one another for temporal stability. Younger Christians look to older Christians for their example, for guidance, for consistency. As they see the Gospel worked out and lived in the lives of these older in the Faith, they will gain a sense of stability and strength which will encourage them to do likewise (see Tit.2:1-10).

How deep does your root system go?

APPLICATION: In order to send your roots deep into Christ, you must make time for in-depth Bible study. Select any topic you want to know more about in the Bible and go for it. (See APPENDIX VII for comments on how to set yourself up for personal Bible study.) You will make exciting new discoveries (for you) that will heighten your love and enthusiasm for the Word of God, and will strengthen you more and more.

DAY 86
'HE IS THE PREEMINENT ONE

QUESTIONS TO THINK ABOUT:

1. What does it mean to have "preeminence" in something?
2. How do we make Christ preeminent in our lives?

When I was a child, we had written across the front of our church sanctuary:

THAT IN ALL THINGS HE MIGHT HAVE THE PREEMINENCE – Col. 1:18

We find this theme particularly emphasized in the book of Hebrews where Christ is shown to be superior to the prophets (1:1-3), angels (1:4-2:8), Moses (3:1-6), Joshua (4:1-13), the Aaronic Priesthood (4:14-10:18), and the kings of Israel (1:8,9). He is the

Creator of the universe and will still be around when it has vanished (1:10-12).

We also see his preeminence in Revelation 1:5, Colossians 1:18 and 1 Corinthians 15:23 where he is called the Firstborn and the Firstfruits from the dead. He is the first one to have experienced death and to have risen never to die again. He is also called the Firstborn over all creation (Col.1:15), stating his position in relation to all that is created. He has the rights of the firstborn son over all, thus will inherit all. In addition to these things, he is also called the Head of the Church (Col.1:18).

In other words, "That in all things he might be first, occupying the highest place."

How do we reflect Christ's preeminence? By giving him the first or highest place in our lives as we submit ourselves to him, accepting and acknowledging him as Lord (see Rom.10:9,10), choose to obey him and forsake sin (Deut.13:4; Col.3:5-10) and learn to know his desires, his mind, his will. This can only be accomplished by spending time with him: in prayer, in reading, memorizing and meditating on his Word, and in meditating on the Lord himself. Then, with renewed minds, we will be able to know his will and discern his ways (Rom.12:2). The next step follows closely upon the last: to delight ourselves in him. As we do this, he will implant his desires in our hearts (Ps.37:4,5). Then what he wants, we will want; his will becomes our will, his thoughts our thoughts, his ways our ways. Thus we give him first place in our lives, and he is now preeminent.

Any Christian living in such a relationship with the Lord will show his preeminence daily as a matter of course. It is the same as Christ said of the Father, who was preeminent in his life: "What the Father says, I say. What the Father does, I do. I always do those things which please him (Jn.8:29) for I have come to do his will" (Jn.4:34).

Is Christ truly preeminent in your life?

APPLICATION: If you have never consciously made Christ Lord of your life, made him preeminent, then bow your head right now and give him that place. Then follow the steps in paragraph three above.

DAY 87
bHE IS THE UNCHANGEABLE ONE, THE ROCK

QUESTIONS TO THINK ABOUT:

1. How can one be flexible and unchangeable at the same time?
2. How important is consistency in our lives?
3. How important is it to us that God is unchangeable?

In Hebrews we find two clear statements about the unchangeable character of Christ: "[The earth and the heavens] will perish, but you remain; they will all wear out like a garment. You will roll them up like a robe; like a garment they will be changed. But you remain the same, and your years will never end" (Heb.1:11,12). "Jesus Christ is the same yesterday and today and forever" (Heb.13:8).

These statements show that Jesus is the same now as he was while here on earth and as he was before the incarnation. Because he does not change, his teachings do not change, and the truth he uttered while on earth is still truth today. This consistency makes him totally reliable on all points and gives us a solid foundation from which we can judge all things.

Christ is also referred to as the Rock, unmovable, firm, solid (1 Cor.10:4). The more like Christ we become, the more our character will be aligned with truth; the more aligned with truth we are, the greater consistency will characterize our lives. Then we too will become a rock upon which others can find security.

In Matthew 7:24,25, Christ likened a wise man to everyone who hears his words and does them. This wise man built his house on a rock; so when the storms came, his house stood firm. As we obey the truth of God's Word, we will not be shaken by the storms of life, but will remain firm and solid. As the Psalmist said, "Great peace have they who love your law, and nothing can make them stumble" (Ps.119:165). As we stand on Christ, the unchangeable, solid Rock, we are not troubled by "miry ground" or "unstable sand."

Martin Luther provides us an example of being rock-like. Even before the Emperor himself, he solidly, immovably affirmed his absolute faith in the Word of God, and no amount of pressure from the Catholic church could force him to recant. Many Christians have endured torture, imprisonment and other forms of persecution because of their faith – and refused to recant. Rather, they have grown in their faith and have become solid rocks for others to build upon.

Aligning our lives with the truth will also help us remain consistent when it comes to making decisions and plans. Having the guidelines of absolute truth (the Word of God), we will not be wishy-washy in our deliberations, but consistent and sure. This will infuriate some, but most will find it a refuge and place of security, a solid rock on which to stand.

Is your life like sand or a solid rock?

APPLICATION: Identify the areas in your life where you are inconsistent or "weak-willed." Using a Bible Concordance or Bible Dictionary, find out what the Bible says about your particular area(s) of concern, then determine what steps take to strengthen those areas. You may want to enlist the help of your pastor or another mature Christian to clarify the steps you need to take and to whom you can be accountable in taking them.

DAY 88
ᶜHE IS THE CORNERSTONE

QUESTIONS TO THINK ABOUT:

1. What was the original function of a cornerstone?
2. What is the symbolic importance of a cornerstone?
3. How can we function as cornerstones in the Church?

One picture the Scriptures use to show our relationship with God is that of a building. In Ephesians 2:19b-22 we read: "You are ... members of God's household, built on the foundation of the apostles and prophets, with Christ Jesus himself as the chief cornerstone. In him the whole building is joined together and rises to become a holy temple in the Lord. And in him you too are being built together to become a dwelling in which God lives by his Spirit."

In Bible times two kinds of cornerstones were frequently used in construction: one laid in the foundation tying it together, and one set at the top corner of two walls, thus tying all the walls together. This second cornerstone is called the capstone. Old Testament prophecies referred to the coming Messiah as both the corner- and capstone (see Isa.28:16; Ps.118:22,23). The New Testament claims fulfillment of these prophecies in Christ as both the cornerstone of the foundation (Eph.2:19-22) and the capstone of the walls (1 Pet.2:7) which reflect his being the First and the Last, the Beginning and the Ending, the Alpha and the Omega. In other words, as he has begun the building, he also will finish it.

We reflect this aspect of Christ's character through our thoroughness and faithfulness in all that we do as we seek to finish the jobs we've started. But there is another way in which we can reflect him as the cornerstone.

The cornerstone is that which joins the various building sections together to keep them from coming apart. In Isaiah 19:13, the leaders of Egypt are referred to as cornerstones. The national unity of Egypt depended upon them. The same could be said of church leaders. If they are united, the church will be united.

On a higher level, 1 Peter 2:5 calls us "living stones" being built into a spiritual house. In Christ, we are all tied together. Ephesians 2:14-18 tells us how he has done this through making peace between Jew and Gentile. As we make peace among believers, we are like cornerstones, bringing them together and building them up in the Faith.

In 1 Peter 2:6 Christ is called the "chosen stone"; in Isaiah 28:16, the "tested stone." The cornerstone must be closely examined (tested) for any faults or cleavages which would make it weak and therefore unfit for use. For thirty-three years Christ was thoroughly tested and was found faultless (Heb.4:15). In John 8:46 he challenged his listeners, "Can any of you prove me guilty of sin?" No one ventured an answer. Therefore he was "chosen" to be the cornerstone of God's spiritual house.

Even so, before new periods of ministry, God will often put us through a time of testing. If we fail that test, we cannot be "chosen" to do that work he wanted us to do. But if we pass the test, then we are chosen for the job and will reap the blessings and fruit that go with it.

In Isaiah 28:16 and 1 Peter 2:4,6, Christ is called the "precious" cornerstone. Precious infers something of great value to someone. Indeed, the cornerstone is of great value to the house, and as we reflect this characteristic of Christ, we will become "precious" in the sight of others, of great value to them in their spiritual lives and ministries (see DAY 90 – HE IS THE PRECIOUS ONE).

APPLICATION: How can you, as a "cornerstone," help "tie" believers together? One way would be by being a peacemaker (see DAY 33 – HE IS THE PEACEFUL ONE); another might be through counseling (see DAY 58 – HE IS A COUNSELOR); still another by being a friend to someone and encouraging them spiritually (see DAY 91 – HE IS OUR FRIEND). What other ways can you think of to be a "cornerstone" to someone?

DAY 89
[a]HE IS THE CHOSEN ONE

QUESTIONS TO THINK ABOUT:

1. Why would someone or something be chosen for a particular task?
2. What part does testing play in being chosen?
3. How important to being chosen for a task is faithfulness in small things?

In Isaiah 42:1 and again in 1 Peter 2:6, Christ is referred to as "my chosen One," and "a chosen and precious cornerstone." As we considered Christ as the Cornerstone (DAY 88), we saw that the word "chosen" in this passage means that it has been closely examined, thoroughly tested for any faults or cleavages which would make the cornerstone weak and therefore unfit for use. In his thirty-three years of life, Christ proved himself to be without fault, perfectly fit for the work God had for him to do. So he was chosen after being tested (cf. Heb.5:8-10).

In Ephesians 1:11 we find that we ourselves have been chosen in Christ as a part of God's plan from the beginning. And in 1 Peter 2:9 we read that we "are a chosen people."

There are two ways in which we are chosen. The first is in regard to salvation. God chose to save us and make us his people totally apart from any effort on our own. "Not by works, so that no one can boast," says Paul in Ephesians 2:9. The second has to do with our service for God. Christ was tested for a period of time before entering his ministry. In the parable of the servants in Luke 19:12-27, the servants were tested with a certain amount of money to see what they'd do with it. Those who used it faithfully were chosen to have authority over a proportionate number of cities. The one who was unfaithful was not chosen for anything else but to be cast out. He was tested and found wanting.

This is often the case in our lives. God has set us apart for some specific work, but there has to be a time of testing first before we can really enter into that work. If we succumb to our circumstances and quit, we will lose out on the work and reward God intended for us to receive. If we remain faithful in spite of our circumstances, then we will be blessed in our work and receive the reward God wants us to have. I suspect that each new work God gives us to do in itself becomes the "test" for the next work to follow, so that for the faithful servant of God, there is an ever-increasing level of responsibility and reward. As Christ said in Luke 16:10, "Whoever can be trusted with very little can also be trusted with much." And each new level becomes a challenge to trust the Lord in a new way in preparation for the next level to come.

The general principle of testing before blessing is seen in 1 Peter 1:6,7: "In this you greatly rejoice, though now for a little while you may have had to suffer grief in all kinds of trials. These have come so that your faith – of greater worth than gold, which perishes even though refined by fire – may be proved genuine and may result in praise, glory and honor when Jesus Christ is revealed."

If we are faithful, we will be chosen for higher responsibility. Are you being faithful where you are now?

APPLICATION: Are there tasks that you habitually do not finish? Begin the discipline of faithfulness by finishing those tasks; then do your best in finishing subsequent tasks entrusted to you. As you prove to yourself (and others) that you can be trusted in little jobs, you will subsequently be entrusted with bigger ones.

NOTE: A word of caution is perhaps needed here. Those who are faithful in everything they do usually end up with the lion's share of responsibility. Along with faithfulness, you also need to cultivate the discipline of saying, "No." People will often "dump" jobs on you for which you do not have the time, interest, or ability to do. You need to be discerning about which jobs to accept and which to reject.

DAY 90
ᵇHE IS THE PRECIOUS ONE

QUESTIONS TO THINK ABOUT:

1. If we hold something or someone as "precious," what does that mean?
2. How do they or those things become precious to us?

In 1 Peter 2:6,7a Peter writes, "For in Scripture it says: 'See, I lay a stone in Zion, a chosen and precious cornerstone, and the one who trusts in him will never be put to shame.' Now to you who believe, this stone is precious." "Precious" is taken from the Greek word *entimos*, "to be held in honor, prized; hence, precious"; and in this context "precious as a highly valued stone or gem" (Thayer 1977, 218).

There are two points of view here as to Christ's preciousness: to the Father (vs.6) and to us who believe (vs.7). To the Father, he is precious as his one and only Son; he is precious because he was obedient and always did his Father's will and what was pleasing to him. "A wise son brings joy to his father," says Solomon in Proverbs

10:1. God's testimony of Christ, even before his ministry, was, "You are my Son, whom I love; with you I am well pleased" (Mk.1:11).

To us who believe he is precious for other reasons: he is precious as one who has saved another from certain death; his is precious because he is faithful to his own, he is utterly trustworthy and always keeps his promises; he is precious because of his help and because of his blessings to us; he is precious because he understands us and intercedes for us; he is precious because of his love and goodness toward us; he is precious because he won't let us get away with sin, because in him is no sin and he wants us to follow his example; he is precious because he is our peace, providing us peace with God, peace with others, and peace with ourselves; he is precious because he put our interests, our welfare, ahead of his own, giving up everything for our sakes.

In Acts 9:36-41 we meet with a woman who was very precious in the sight of others. Dorcas was "always doing good and helping the poor" (vs.36). She became sick and died. The people called for Peter to come to them quickly. When he arrived, "all the widows stood around him, crying and showing him the robes and other clothing that Dorcas had made while she was still with them" (vs.39). She didn't do these things to become precious, rather, she was precious because she did them. In the same way, we cannot consciously purpose to be precious to others today, for our "preciousness" lies with them, not with us. In fact, more often than not, we are totally unaware of our preciousness in the sight of others – and that is probably just as well. We have trouble enough with pride as it is. But from Christ's and Dorcas's examples, we can know what will make us precious to others: putting others first, meeting needs that they cannot meet themselves, loving them unconditionally, sharing the same attitudes, ideals and principles; obedience, faithfulness, honesty, growing in wisdom, etc. As we become more and more like Christ, inevitably we will become more precious to others whether we realize it or not.

Are you fulfilling these prerequisites for preciousness?

APPLICATION: The important thing here is not that you plan to become precious to others, but that you work on becoming like Christ. The preciousness will come of its own accord as you relate to people like Christ would.

DAY 91
ªHE IS OUR FRIEND

QUESTIONS TO THINK ABOUT:

1. What is the difference between an acquaintance, a casual friend, a close friend and an intimate friend?
2. What are the qualities or characteristics you look for in a close friend, an intimate friend?
3. Why are close friendships and intimate friendships important to us?
4. How would you describe a good friend?
5. What are some of the risks of friendship?

Jesus Christ is described in Matthew 11:19 as "a friend of tax collectors and 'sinners.'" What is a friend? Let's draw a picture from Scripture. Friends are those who:

Unexpected Transformation / 213

Characteristic	Stated	Fulfilled in Christ
1. love at all times	Prov.17:17	Rom.8:35
2. are always loyal	Prov.18:24	Matt.28:19,20; Heb.13:5,6
3. enjoy close communion	Exod.33:11	John 15:15
4. receive honored positions in their relationship	Judg.14:20	John 3:29
5. give counsel to each other	Prov.27:9	Rev.3:18
6. give each other gifts	2 Chr.20:7	Eph.4:7-12
7. pity each other	Job 6:14	Ps.103:13
8. share common values	Prov.22:11	John 17:13,14
9. rebuke one another	Prov.27:6	Luke 9:55
10. stimulate one another	Prov.27:17	Matt.13:36
11. help one another	Luke 11:5-8	John 15:16

In every way, Christ fulfilled these characteristics of friendship. Although he was called "a friend of tax collectors and 'sinners,'" his closest friendships were with those who followed him. Even among them, there were three who were closer yet to him; and among those three, just one was an intimate friend.

There are three general levels of friendship that we experience with others: (1) respect (casual contact), (2) association (ministering contact), and (3) personal (intimate contact).

The first level (casual): is reserved for strangers or for those with whom we have contact for short periods of time. We are polite, show them consideration, and perhaps lend some mutual service, but that is all.

The second level (association) takes place at school, work, church or other organizational activities. Here we enter into more than just "weather" talk as we find out what others are like, their backgrounds and interests. Here we have opportunities to witness, minister to needs and begin to develop level three friendships

The third level (personal) includes that group of people with whom we feel most free, and can share our hearts openly without fear or intimidation. Mutual care, love and concern are expressed most at this level. And within this group, there will be one or two "special" friends to whom we not only open our hearts but our souls as well.

There is a tragedy in our churches where so many of our Christian brothers and sisters are treated as "level one friends" – casually, then dropped. They enter the church looking for personal friendship, only to find casual respect, and leave as empty and "friendless" as when they came in! "Behold, how they love one another" cannot be said for many of our churches. Most believers just don't want to get involved in the lives of others. The price of friendship involves being responsible for someone else; being burdened with their problems and blessed in their joys; but it also means being vulnerable to hurt and disappointment as a friend fails and perhaps even becomes your enemy (see **NOTE** below). Yet the rewards of friendship far outweigh its "hazards" and become one of the greatest and most enjoyable of blessings we can ever experience. Proverbs 18:24a (NKJV) says, "A man who has friends must himself be friendly." Are you?

[**NOTE:** Psalm 41:9 and Matthew 26:47-50. We had a close friend turn against us when disciplined by the national church. I happened to be a member of the board at the time. It hurt deeply that he would do that and at the same time refuse to repent from his sin. We have had other close friends follow different religious teachings, and likewise shut us out of their lives, judging us to be unspiritual, hypocritical and even unsaved!]

APPLICATION: One way to develop close friendships is to show genuine concern for others. That is shown by being a good listener, asking questions and showing interest in who they are, where they are from, what their interests are, etc. An invitation for a meal or to attend an event together will provide a more informal atmosphere in which mutual interests can surface.

Not only do friends enjoy the same things, but they always put each other first. Selfishness destroys a friendship and makes enemies. So work on those characteristics that will create and strengthen friendships. Then, somewhere along the way, something with someone will "click" and you will find yourself moving from the "association" to the "personal" level of friendship.

DAY 92
[a]HE IS THE ZEALOUS ONE

QUESTIONS TO THINK ABOUT:

1. How do you feel when you walk into a pre-service sanctuary full of noise and commotion?
2. Is that noise and commotion necessarily a bad thing?
3. Of what importance is a quiet pre-service sanctuary?
4. What type of activities in a worship service / in a church would tend to drive people away from God rather than draw them closer to Him?

During the first Passover of Jesus' public ministry, he went into the Temple and found it filled with all manner of corruption and filth (Jn.2:13-17). In the heat of holy anger, caused by his consuming zeal for the purity and purpose of his Father's House, Jesus made a scourge of cords and drove everybody and everything out. The Temple was not to be a place of merchandise, but a house of prayer and worship. But alas, the Jews didn't have the same zeal, for we see Christ having to repeat the cleansing of the Temple once again near the close of his ministry (Matt.21:12,13).

In Scripture, the word "zealous" is used in a number of ways: jealousy for the Lord (Num.25:11 – ASV), holding something in high esteem (Acts 21:20), working earnestly on God's behalf (Acts 22:3), greatly desiring something (1 Cor.14:12), working quickly to get something done (Rev.3:19), eagerness to do what is good (Tit.2:14), and a deep concern toward someone (Col.4:12,13). So we find written in John 2:17b, "Zeal for your house will consume me."

Why did Christ feel this way about the Temple? From the very start, the Temple was God's dwelling place on earth ("my Father's house" – John 2:16), a place where man could meet with God and worship him. This was one part of God's plan in restoring his fellowship with man. Because God was there, the Temple was holy. Nothing blemished or unholy could enter. Christ saw that the merchandising enterprises being carried on in the Temple not only hindered worship and turned people away who were seeking fellowship with God, but also gravely violated God's holiness through cheating the worshipers. Often, when a worshiper came with the required lamb, spotless and without defect, the Temple "merchants" would "assess" the animal as unworthy of sacrifice and force the worshiper to buy a lamb from the Temple stock. By these means and others, worship became a burden rather than a blessing, and men's hearts were driven away from God. When Christ saw this, he couldn't hold back. He had to do something to show the people what was really happening. His Father's House was to be a house of prayer, where men and God could meet unhindered.

Are our churches houses of prayer where men and women can meet God unhindered? Unfortunately, many are not. In fact, it is rare to step into a quiet, pre-service sanctuary in order to meditate and prepare one's heart for worship. I heard on the radio one day that a certain producer needed a sound bite for an angry mob. He obtained just what he needed – by taping pre-service conversation in a church! That was hard to believe until several Sundays later I found myself in a church that had such loud pre-service noise that it

Unexpected Transformation / 217

was impossible to meditate, pray or worship. When the minister of music stood to announce the beginning of the worship service, he had to shout into the microphone before he could be heard!

This situation leaves us with several questions to answer:

1. Does our use of God's House make it possible for others to draw near to him in worship, or do our activities hinder the worshiper and the seeker?
2. Are we zealous for God and man to meet and plan our programs and services accordingly, or are we more zealous for our programs which make the church seem alive?

APPLICATION: How are we using the Lord's House? What could you do to help make the atmosphere more worshipful? What do we need to do to create an atmosphere that will draw men and women to the Lord rather than drive them away from him?

DAY 93
'HE IS THE STUMBLING STONE, THE ROCK OF OFFENSE

QUESTIONS TO THINK ABOUT:

1. What things in our lives can cause others to be offended and stumble?
2. How can good things in our lives cause others to be offended and stumble?
3. How can truth bring offence and cause others to stumble? What is it about truth that they resent?

In his first epistle, Peter declares that Christ is "a stone that causes men to stumble and a rock that makes them fall" (1 Pet.2:8). These same words are penned by the Apostle Paul in Romans 9:33, both writers quoting from Isaiah 8:14. Christ became a stumbling stone to them who did not believe (1 Pet.2:8). We see this clearly in John 6:22-69. Many people were following Christ for the wrong motives. Among other things, he had just given them food the day before (vs.1-15), and they all flocked to him again hoping for another free meal (vs.26); but they did not actually believe in him (vs.64). So when he gave them a spiritual lesson requiring faith and spiritual understanding on their part (vs.63), they stumbled and fell as they tried to interpret what he said in a rational and literal manner. All they got was foolishness from what the Lord was saying, felt offended, and left him.

We can expect this same reaction as we try to witness to others and share with them what the Lord is doing in our lives. That is one reason why the Lord warned us not to "give dogs what is sacred; do not throw your pearls to pigs. If you do, they may trample them under their feet, and then turn and tear you to pieces" (Matt.7:6). Usually, beyond a witness to the unsaved, it is not wise to share deeper spiritual truths with them, for they are incapable of understanding them and will inevitably misinterpret them. First Corinthians 2:12-14 declares: "We have not received the spirit of the world but the Spirit who is from God, that we may understand what God has freely given us. This is what we speak, not in words taught us by human wisdom but in words taught by the Spirit, expressing spiritual truths in spiritual words. The man without the Spirit does not accept the things that come from the Spirit of God for they are foolishness to him, and he cannot understand them, because they are spiritually discerned."

However, there is another time in which we must remain silent, refraining from sharing deeper spiritual truth. That is with carnal Christians who are out of fellowship with the Lord, and thus are not interested. Immature Christians who are still on milk rather than the meat of the Word (cf. Heb.5:11,12) are not able to receive deeper spiritual things. And perhaps again with other Christians who, though possessing a knowledge of spiritual truth and doctrine, have not grown enough in their faith to accept and appropriate those things in their experience or they have already "made up" their minds and are unwilling to consider anything else outside that framework! Christ recognized this general problem even among his disciples. In John 16:12,13a he said to them, "I have much more to say to you, more than you can now bear. But when he, the Spirit of truth, comes, he will guide you into all truth." So it's not that we always have to remain silent when with other Christians, but be discerning as to when they are ready to listen to and receive what we have to share with them.

One time a fellow missionary and I shared together a new spiritual insight that blessed us both tremendously. A day or so afterwards, I tried to share the same concept with another missionary. He completely missed the point and gave the whole thing a wrong interpretation. I was disappointed, but learned that it is not always wise to share all you know, even with Christians, for they also can stumble over spiritual truth if they are not ready for it.

Are you eager for new spiritual truth and insight, or do you also stumble when something new is shared?

APPLICATION: When you hear some "new" spiritual truth from someone, be like the Bereans who checked out what they heard from the Scriptures. What is false, reject – what is truth, accept – don't stumble over it.

DAY 94
ʿHE IS THE STONE REJECTED

QUESTIONS TO THINK ABOUT:

1. What happens when we put things "neatly" into a box?
2. Have you ever been "stereotyped"? How did it make you feel?

Near the end of his earthly ministry, it was obvious that the leaders of Israel as a body were set in their rejection of Christ as their Messiah. After the parable of the landowner (Matt.21:33-41) which was obviously meant for the chief priests and Pharisees, Jesus quoted from Psalm 118:22,23, saying, "Have you never read in the Scriptures: 'The stone the builders rejected has become the capstone; the Lord has done this, and it is marvelous in our eyes'?"

God was in the process of building his kingdom. The foundation was already laid and now he was ready to lay the Cornerstone that would tie everything together and provide a solid anchor for the superstructure. But the "builders" (the chief priests and Pharisees) took one look at that Cornerstone and rejected it. It was just an ordinary-looking piece of work, nothing flashy, no sparkle, and certainly not big enough for the kingdom of God's glory. It was the wrong size, the wrong shape, and esthetically unappealing. "No, there must be a mistake somewhere. Set it aside, men. This cannot be the cornerstone. We're looking for something else of better quality." Well did Isaiah say, "He had no beauty or majesty to attract us to him, nothing in his appearance that we should desire him" (Isa.53:2b).

God had a plan, and man had a plan derived from God's plan. Unfortunately something got lost in the translation. Hopes were created and fanned into flame. The Messiah was put into a box of expectations that allowed for no variation in the theme of God's plan. So when the chief priests and Pharisees discovered something happening outside their box of expectations, they rejected it outright. Theirs had to be the right plan!

But let us not judge them too quickly, for if we look carefully enough, we may discover some of the "Pharisee" in our own hearts. We also tend to enclose God in our own "box of expectations" and thus are in danger of doing the same thing as the Pharisees, to our loss.

Consider the following:

Is our church the only one really preaching the truth?

What about methods of evangelism? Are all others either wrong or at best less Biblical than ours?

"Certainly a person can't be a Christian and stay there, no matter what he says!"

"A Christian dressed like that coming to church?! Scandalous!"

"Did you know he raises his hands when he prays? We had better inform the pastor; this could bring a dangerous influence into the church!"

... and so on.

First Corinthians 1:18-31 speaks to this attitude of boxing God in to align with our expectations. Just verses 18 and 21 are sufficient here: "For the message of the cross [God's plan] is foolishness to those who are perishing [because it doesn't agree with their plan], but to us who are being saved [who acknowledge God's plan], it is the power of God... . For since, in the wisdom of God the world through wisdom did not know him [see NOTE below] God was pleased through the foolishness of what was preached to save those who believe."

The Christian life and message is foolishness to the wisdom of the world. So the world will cast it off and us with it, looking elsewhere for what only our message can bring. For example, Christians in communist lands are often fired from their jobs or expelled from school because of their message of peace, justice and equality among men (among other things) which is also part of the communist "doctrine" but couched in different terms. Their message is rejected because it doesn't fit in the "box" that communism has set up, even though communism professes to be seeking the same things.

So when our message is rejected, remember, they rejected the Cornerstone first. But in the end, that Cornerstone became the Chief Cornerstone because the Lord made it that way. In the end, our message will be proven true and no one will be able to refute it.

Have you ever been rejected because of your message? If not, maybe you're bearing the wrong one!

APPLICATION: Jesus warned his disciples many times that they and their message would be rejected (cf. Jn.16:1-3). But their responsibility (and ours) is to be faithful in proclaiming it whether or not it is received. God's responsibility is to bring the fruit (souls) to himself (cf. Isa.55:10,11).

(**NOTE:** See John 8:55 where Christ told the Jews that they did not know God because they were trying to know him according to their own scheme of things. See also Romans 10:1-3.)

DAY 95
[a]HE IS THE ACKNOWLEDGED ONE

QUESTIONS TO THINK ABOUT:

1. Have you ever passed by someone whom you knew, only to be totally ignored by them? How did that make you feel? Why do you think they ignored you?

2. Or, has someone criticized a friend of yours and suddenly you felt compelled to "put your distance" between that friend and yourself? Why did you or might you do that?

3. How can the lives we live be an acknowledgement of Christ?

Both at Christ's baptism and at the Transfiguration, God acknowledged him before men, saying, "This is my Son, whom I love; with him I am well pleased" (Matt.3:17). "Listen to him" (Matt.17:5). After the feeding of the 4,000 (Matt.15:32-39), Christ moved on to the region of Caesarea (Matt.16:13) and there asked his disciples who people were saying the Son of Man is. Then he asked them who they thought he was (vs.15). Peter replied, "You are the Christ, the Son of the living God" (vs.16). Again in Matthew 10:32,33 Christ declares, "Whoever acknowledges me before men, I will also acknowledge him before my Father in heaven. But whoever disowns me before men, I will disown him before my Father in heaven." Then again in Proverbs 3:6 we read, "In all your ways acknowledge him, and he will make your paths straight."

In these verses we see two uses of the word "acknowledge," one as a public confession of our allegiance to Christ as our Master and Lord; the other is "saying hello," as it were, to the Lord as he walks along with us, and giving him the lead. We don't have much trouble with the first, but we definitely have problems with the second as we often blithely go our way without even a thought about how the Lord feels about what we are doing. That is why we need Proverbs 3:5,6 all over again: "Trust in the LORD with all your heart and lean not on your own understanding; in all your ways <u>acknowledge</u> him, and he will make your paths straight" (underlining mine). As he walks along with us, we acknowledge his presence (that's only polite), then his lordship and sovereignty (that is his due), and then his ability to lead us as we go along (that is a MUST).

As we acknowledge the Lord before men and in our own lives, two things will happen: first, Christ will acknowledge us before his Father and the angels (Matt.10:32; Lk.12:8). "Father, here is _____. I died for him and he has loved me and served me with his whole heart." And the Father's thundering voice answers: "Well done, good and faithful servant! You have been faithful with a few things; I will put you in charge of many things. Come and share your master's happiness!" (Matt.25:21).

Secondly, others, friends and enemies alike, will acknowledge that we are Christ's. In Acts 4:13 we read, "When they saw the courage of Peter and John and realized that they were unschooled, ordinary men, they were astonished and they took note (acknowledged) that these men had been with Jesus."

Have you acknowledged Christ publicly <u>and</u> in your private life?

APPLICATION: It would be a good habit to develop that, upon awaking each morning, you stop and acknowledge the Lord, committing the day to him, and asking him to help you glorify him in all you do and say. The highest honor we could ever have on earth is for others to acknowledge that we "have been with Jesus," for that means that they are seeing him in us.

DAY 96
[a]HE IS THE ANOINTED ONE

QUESTIONS TO THINK ABOUT:

1. What does it mean to be "anointed" to a ministry?
2. How has the Lord "anointed" us to serve him?
3. How could the indwelling Spirit be considered God's special anointing upon us for ministry?

4. How could the terms "baptism of the Spirit," "filling of the Spirit," "pouring out of the Spirit upon" and "anointing of the Spirit" be considered synonymous?

In Daniel 9:25,26 Christ is prophetically referred to as "the Anointed One." In Luke 4:18 he quotes Isaiah 61:1 and claims the fulfillment of that prophecy: "The LORD has anointed me to preach" ... etc. And again, in Acts 4:27, the early Christians confessed in prayer that God had anointed his "holy servant Jesus."

In the Old Testament, prophets, priests and kings were anointed with a special anointing oil before assuming their responsibilities (cf. 1 Kgs.19:16; Lev.8:12; 1 Sam.16:13). This was at God's direction and served as a sign of his appointment, qualifying that person for a special work or function. Thus the king was often referred to as "the Lord's anointed" (see 2 Sam.1:14).

To the Jew, an anointing was a serious act as it indicated "a transference to the anointed one of something of the holiness and virtue of" [Jehovah] and "imparted to him a special endowment of the Spirit of Jehovah" (cf. 1 Sam.16:13; Isa.61:1; also I.S.B.E., Vol.I, p.138, "Anointing," no.4). In Acts 10:38 we read that God "anointed Jesus of Nazareth with the Holy Spirit and power."

In like manner, God has also anointed us, imparting a special endowment of his Spirit upon us that we might be fully equipped to live for him and serve him. This is expressed in 2 Corinthians 1:21,22 where Paul says, "Now it is God who makes both us and you stand firm in Christ. He anointed us, set his seal of ownership [i.e. the Holy Spirit – Eph.1:13] on us, and put his Spirit in our hearts as a deposit (Eph.1:14), guaranteeing what is to come." In 1 John 2:20,27 the Holy Spirit is referred to as our "anointing."

In the Old Testament, the anointing ceremonies usually took place just before someone was to begin a special work; although sometimes it preceded the realization of that work by a number of years (as in the case of David) for the purpose of further training before the service begins.

God has given us a special task to perform: to be his witnesses (Acts 1:8) and his ambassadors to plead with the world to be reconciled to him (2 Cor.5:18-20). But before that task can be carried out, there has to be an anointing, a special endowment of his Spirit upon us, a special equipping for the task.

The disciples, who already had the Spirit (Jn.20:22 – but were not yet indwelt by him in New Testament terms), were told to await his coming when they would be <u>baptized</u> with the Spirit (Acts 1:5). In Acts 2:4, when the Spirit came, nothing is said about their being baptized with him as such, but it does say they were "<u>filled</u> with the Holy Spirit." Then Peter explains this event as the "<u>pouring out</u> of my Spirit upon all flesh" as mentioned in Joel 2:28-32. All the elements of an <u>anointing</u> appear here as well, i.e.:

a. God choosing someone for a special task (Acts 1:4,8);
b. Oil poured on the head of the chosen (fire above the heads of those chosen – Acts 2:3);
c. Prophet or Priest doing the anointing (Christ active here – cf. Matt.3:11);
d. Transference of something of the holiness and virtue of Jehovah and his Spirit upon the anointed one (the Holy Spirit begins to indwell and empower the believer – Acts 4:8).

This seems to indicate that the terms <u>baptism</u>, <u>filling</u>, <u>pouring out upon</u> and <u>anointing</u> could be synonymous. The disciples, who had the Spirit (in Old Testament terms), needed his indwelling and anointing (in New Testament terms) in order to perform their ministry.

Following Pentecost, those who received Christ as Savior (with two special exceptions – Acts 8:14-17; 19:1-7) were immediately indwelt and anointed by the Holy Spirit for the work God had for them to do (1 Jn.2:20,27; 2 Cor.5:18-20). The same holds true for us today, but we must daily walk in the Spirit (Gal.5:16) and be filled by the Spirit (Eph.5:18) so that the effects of our anointing can be seen, not only in his power (Acts 3:1-12) but also his fruit (Gal.5:22,23).

Are the anointing, power and fruit of the Spirit evident in your life today?

APPLICATION: Jesus said in John 15:5b, "If a man abides in me and I in him, he will bear much fruit; apart from me you can do nothing." If we are abiding in Christ, we will have all the filling, anointing and authority we need to speak and act in his name as we serve him, and we will experience the truth that with his calling comes his enablement.

DAY 97
[a]HE IS THE APPOINTED ONE

◆

QUESTIONS TO THINK ABOUT:

1. What does it mean to be appointed by someone, and what does that appointment mean?

2. How does knowing that we are appointed by God give us boldness in ministry?

3. How does knowledge of the truth give us authority in what we share?

In Hebrews 3:2 we read that Jesus "was faithful to the one who appointed him, just as Moses was faithful in all God's house." The idea of an appointment (according to Webster) is that of "assigning, designating, or setting apart by authority; to place in office, as to appoint ... to a post." This appointment carries with it the authority of the one appointing. Thus Christ, as appointed by God, has God's authority to act as our High Priest (Heb.5:10), to be Heir of all things (Heb.1:2), and to be King over God's kingdom (Lk.22:29).

We, in turn, have been appointed by Christ (and thereby have his authority) to act as priests in service to God (Rev.5:10), to be joint-heirs with him (Rom.8:17) and to be rulers in his kingdom (Lk.22:29; Rev.5:10). We are also appointed as ambassadors of God to bring to the world the message of reconciliation (2 Cor.5:20).

There is a process involved in gaining an appointment. First there is a time of testing (educating); then, if we pass the test, we are chosen; upon being chosen, we receive our appointment to the task God wants us to perform. We can perform our task with great confidence then, knowing that we are acting in and under God's authority. Thus it is no wonder that the people were amazed at Jesus' "teaching, because he taught as one who had authority, and not as their teachers of the law" (Matt.7:29). So Paul exhorts Titus, "These, then, are the things you should teach. Encourage and rebuke with all authority. Do not let anyone despise you" (Tit.2:15).

To speak with authority, we must have a clear understanding of the will of the one who appointed us and be faithful to his purposes. This understanding only comes from the Word of God which reveals his will to us. Peter hints at this in 1 Peter 3:15 where he counsels: "But in your hearts set apart Christ as Lord. Always be prepared to give an answer to everyone who asks you to give the reason for the hope that you have."

An inherent characteristic of truth is authority. Thus Christ, who called himself "the Truth" (Jn.14:6) also declared: "All authority in heaven and on earth has been given to me" (Matt.28:18). Then He turned to his disciples, authorized them to go and make disciples of all nations (vs.19), and empowered them with the Holy Spirit to do it (Acts 1:8).

Another inherent characteristic of truth is courage. When we know the truth, we have courage to speak with authority. Not knowing the truth breeds uncertainty. "Is this true or not?" In Acts

4:13, "when [the leaders and elders of Israel] saw the courage of Peter and John and realized that they were unschooled, ordinary men, they were astonished and they took note that these men had been with Jesus" [who is the Truth!]. The apostles knew the truth and therefore were certain of their message, thus their boldness and faithfulness in their appointment.

Do you know the truth? Are you being faithful to your appointment?

APPLICATION: The only way to know the truth is to apply it in your own life as you find it in God's Word. Truth always works! When you discover that, and experience the undeniable results of truth, then you will be bold in proclaiming it to others with all confidence and authority.

DAY 98
'HE IS THE AUTHOR AND FINISHER OF OUR FAITH

QUESTIONS TO THINK ABOUT:

1. How could we be the "author" of someone's faith?
2. What can we do to move them along to spiritual maturity?

The writer to the Hebrews describes Christ as "the author and perfecter [finisher] of our faith" (Heb.12:2); in Hebrews 5:9, the "source [author] of eternal salvation for all who obey him."

There are two different Greek words used in describing Christ as "Author." In Hebrews 12:2 it is *archegos*, meaning primarily "one who takes a lead in, or provides the first occasion of, anything" (Vine, Vol.I, p.88, "Author"). In Hebrews 2:10 (where He is called the Captain or Author of our salvation) "the word suggests a combination of the meaning of leaders with that of the source from whence a thing proceeds." So again, in Hebrews 12:2, "He is represented as the one who takes precedence in faith and is thus the perfect Exemplar of it... . Christ in the days of his flesh trod undeviatingly the path of faith, and as the Perfecter has brought it to a perfect end in his own Person. Thus He is the leader of all others who tread that path" (Ibid.).

The second word is *aitios*, denoting "that which causes something." Christ, our exalted and glorified High Priest, is the formal, concrete and active cause of our salvation. Yet "He has not merely caused or effected it, He is, as His Name, 'Jesus,' implies, our salvation itself, Luke 2:30; 3:6" (Ibid.).

The Greek word translated "perfecter" or "finisher" is *teleios*, which signifies a thing having reached its end, finished, complete, perfect (Ibid., Vol.III, p.173). So Christ not only originates and is our salvation, but also takes it to completion and perfection.

The Apostle Paul, through his church planting missionary journeys and many epistles, became the source of salvation and maturity in salvation for thousands of people. He encouraged them to follow his example in the Faith, and in doing so, they would also be following Christ (1 Cor.11:1). He said that if they followed his example, the God of peace would be with them (Phil.4:9).

Like Paul, we reflect Christ as the source of salvation through our witness to others. We become their "source" as we share Christ and the Word of God with them. Then as we exercise our spiritual gifts toward one another, the Lord uses us to build each other up and bring our salvation to maturity (Eph.4:11-13). Our example should be such that as others consider it and follow it, they also will become more like Christ who is the goal of our salvation. In Hebrews 13:7 we read, "Remember your leaders, who spoke the Word of God to you. Consider the outcome [end] of their way of life and imitate their faith." The word "consider" (Greek *anatheoreo*) means to consider carefully, intensively, contemplatively (Vine, Vol.I, p.115).

If others were to think about our lives like this, giving real thought to what they see and the direction we are heading in, would they see a developing and unfolding image of Christ and thus be encouraged to imitate our faith? If it depended upon you, in which direction would they head?

APPLICATION: As you look at your life and all you do, what would you need to change so that as others imitate you and consider the end of your way of life, they would successfully mature in their Christian faith?

DAY 99
[a]HE IS THE LIGHT

QUESTIONS TO THINK ABOUT:

1. As you think of light, what is its purpose, what does it allow us to do, why do we need it?
2. As you think of darkness, what is it like, what does it allow us to do, why do we want it?
3. Is it possible for light and darkness to be in the same place at the same time? Why or why not?
4. How can our lives be a light to others? (cf. Matt.5:16)

In Isaiah 42:6 is a prophecy regarding the Servant of the Lord, whom we understand to be Christ: "I, the LORD, ... will make you ... a light for the Gentiles." And again in Isaiah 9:1,2 and Matthew 4:16, the Jewish people and Gentiles, "the people living in darkness, have seen a great light." In Luke 2:30-32, Simeon praised God when he took the baby Jesus in his arms, saying, "My eyes have seen your salvation, ... a light for revelation to the Gentiles and for glory to your people Israel."

During His ministry, Christ claimed, "I am the light of the world. Whoever follows me will never walk in darkness, but will have the light of life" (Jn.8:12). This verse gives us a clue as to what this light is: it is life, eternal life, a new life, a life of restored fellowship with God who is light (1 Jn.1:5). John 1:4 clarifies it further: "In him was life, and that life was the light of men."

The Chinese have a proverb that a picture is worth a thousand words. In considering Christ as the Light (and that light is his life), and then considering all that that includes, we could branch off into every other subject that has to do with our salvation and the Christian life. The schematic outline below should save the use of many words and allow some brief comments where necessary.

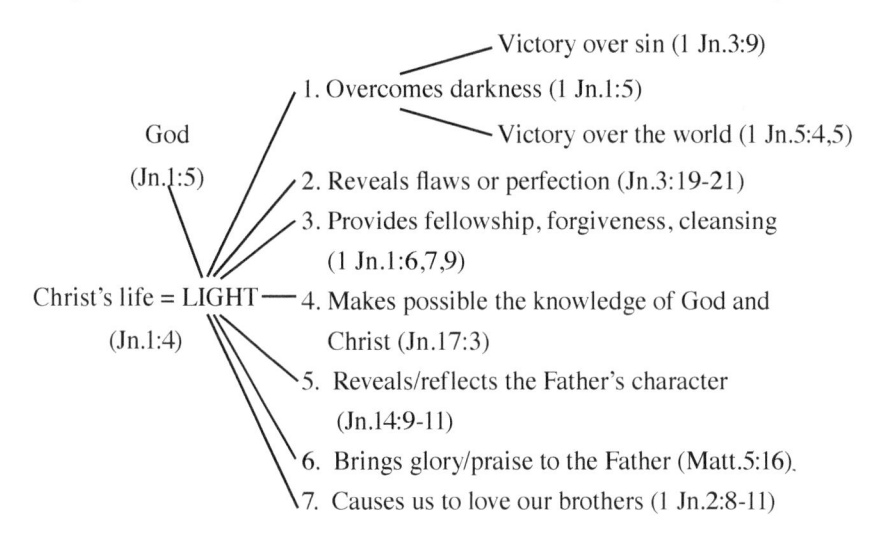

```
                              ┌── Victory over sin (1 Jn.3:9)
                   1. Overcomes darkness (1 Jn.1:5)
     God                       └── Victory over the world (1 Jn.5:4,5)
    (Jn.1:5)     2. Reveals flaws or perfection (Jn.3:19-21)
                 3. Provides fellowship, forgiveness, cleansing
                    (1 Jn.1:6,7,9)
Christ's life = LIGHT ── 4. Makes possible the knowledge of God and
    (Jn.1:4)              Christ (Jn.17:3)
                 5. Reveals/reflects the Father's character
                    (Jn.14:9-11)
                 6. Brings glory/praise to the Father (Matt.5:16)
                 7. Causes us to love our brothers (1 Jn.2:8-11)
```

1. The reason that Christ's light overcomes darkness is that light by its very nature dispels darkness. The picture we get from 1 John is that light pictures holiness (completely without sin), whereas darkness pictures sinfulness. When we received Jesus Christ as our Savior, God, at that point, removed us from the Kingdom of Darkness and placed us in the Kingdom of Light (Col.1:12,13). We are now in Christ with a new nature (2 Cor.5:17) which is incapable of sin (1 Jn.3:9) since it issues from God himself. That is why, positionally,

Unexpected Transformation / 233

we who are in Christ have overcome sin and the world system. Our problem is getting our experience to reflect our position! (see DAYS 46 and 47 – HE IS THE KING – for further discussion).

Does the light of Christ indwell your heart and impel your life?

APPLICATION: If you claim to be a Christian, but sense that you have no light shining from your life, that there is no difference between you and everyone else, then you need to search your heart to see if you have ever made a personal commitment to Jesus Christ. All you need to do is confess your sin to him, ask for his forgiveness, and make him Lord of your life. The sense of joy, newness of life and his presence will confirm to you that his light is in you and now ready to shine brightly to others.

DAY 100
[a]HE IS THE LIGHT, cont.

QUESTIONS TO THINK ABOUT:

1. How does light reveal the character or quality of something?
2. What does it mean to walk in the light? How does that influence the areas of fellowship, forgiveness and cleansing in our lives?
3. How can Christians be considered "color blind" to some spiritual things?

2. Light reveals the character of a thing being examined, whether it is flawed or perfect (Eph.5:13,14). Light generally attracts things to it. When we first lived in Senggo, we had a kerosene Petromax lamp. As we turned it on each evening, we had to get under our 8 x 8-foot room net quickly so as not to be inundated by the myriads of bugs that came flying in, being attracted by the light.

234 / *Unexpected Transformation*

The light of God's life and character should draw all men to it (cf. Jn.12:32), especially when compared with the dismal alternative of darkness. For light is essential to life. Without it, all life forms would perish. Yet we read in John 3:19-21 of two responses to that light; the ungodly hate it because it exposes the true nature of their sinful deeds (Eph.5:11). Thus they hate Christians whose godly lives make theirs an embarrassment. But the godly love the light and come to it, because they live and work according to truth, and feel no shame or embarrassment in having their works examined and revealed for all to see.

If your deeds were examined today, would they be flawed or pass scrutiny?

3. Light also provides for fellowship, forgiveness and cleansing. According to 1 John 1:6,7, if we walk in the light, as God is in the light, we will have fellowship with God and with one another. Why? Because our lives, characterized by light, would have nothing in them that would disrupt fellowship on either plane. And if we do sin, walking in the light as a habit will cause us to be conscious of it immediately and be anxious to confess and forsake it. Then we receive God's forgiveness and cleansing, as well as forgiveness from our fellow believers (vs.7,9), and our fellowship with him and them remains unbroken.

Do you have "long-standing accounts" with God and others, or are you enjoying unbroken fellowship with them?

4. Light makes it possible to know God and Jesus Christ whom he has sent (Jn.17:3). While in Bible School, Amber and I both had the same teacher, but for different classes. Amber was "on his wave length" and did very well on his tests. I was not on his wave length and struggled just to maintain a C average.

There are various light waves all around us, and if we are in tune with them, we perceive colors. But one who is blind is not "on the same wave length," and sees nothing but blackness or perhaps various shades of gray. In this same way, the world is "blinded" to the "light waves" issuing from God (2 Cor.4:4), and, not being on the same wave length, think that what does issue forth from him is colorless and foolish (1 Cor.2:14). But those of us who have received Christ as Savior are "on his wave length," and can "read" him as it were. When he speaks, we know and understand what he is saying and what he wants. Thus, possessing the very same light that is issuing from God himself, we can get to know him better and better as he continues to show us new things about himself.

Are you on the Lord's "wave length"? What is your spiritual color perception like?

APPLICATION: To be able to "see" things as God sees them, all we must do is pray the Psalmist's prayer in Psalm 119:18, "Open my eyes that I may see wonderful things in your law." The Lord will do that because that is his will for each of his children. However, there is a responsibility that comes with additional understanding. Jesus said in Luke 12:48b, "From everyone who has been given much, much will be demanded; and from the one who has been entrusted with much, much more will be asked." But the fruit that results from accepting that responsibility is more than worth the "risk" we might feel in accepting it.

DAY 101
[a]HE IS THE LIGHT, concl.

◆

QUESTIONS TO THINK ABOUT:

1. How can one's character be likened to light or darkness?
2. How does light symbolize our good works?
3. How can loving our Christian brothers and sisters be a proof of our salvation?

5. Light reveals/reflects the Father's character. In 1 John 1:5 we read that "he is light, and in him is no darkness at all." There is no sin, nothing whatever that soils his character. In Hebrews 1:3 we read that "the Son is the radiance of God's glory and the exact representation of his being." And again in John 14:9-11, he tells Philip, "Don't you know me, Philip, even after I have been among you such a long time? Anyone who has seen me has seen the Father. How can you say, 'Show us the Father'? Don't you believe that I am in the Father, and that the Father is in me? The words I say to you are not just my own. Rather, it is the Father, living in me, who is doing his work. Believe me when I say that I am in the Father and the Father is in me; or at least believe on the evidence of the miracles themselves."

So, as the Light of the world, Christ reflects God's character. Thus, as we see Christ's light (character of life), we know what God is like. In like manner, as others see our light (character of life), they should be able to know what Christ is like.

How much of his light are you reflecting?

6. Light brings glory and praise to the Father. In Ephesians 5:8-10 Paul tells us: "For you were once darkness, but now you are light in the Lord. Live as children of light (for the fruit of the light consists in all goodness, righteousness and truth) and find out what pleases the Lord." Jesus said in Matthew 5:16, "Let your light [manner of life] shine before men, that they may see your good deeds and praise your Father in heaven."

This is not unlike the son of a cabinet maker. If he produces excellent work, it directly reflects upon his father. Not only is the son praised but the father is commended for having such a son and for teaching him so well. Likewise what we do directly reflects upon our heavenly Father.

Do others praise him because of you?

7. Light causes us to love our brothers. The Apostle John writes: "Yet I am writing you a new command; its truth is seen in him and you, because the darkness is passing and the true light is already shining. Anyone who claims to be in the light but hates his brother is still in the darkness. Whoever loves his brother lives in the light, and there is nothing in him to make him stumble. But whoever hates his brother is in the darkness and walks around in the darkness; he does not know where he is going, because the darkness has blinded him" (1 Jn.2:8-11).

Love for our brothers is one proof of our walking in the light. Therefore it becomes a source of assurance of our salvation. But if our hearts are full of hatred, then we are walking in darkness and have no part in the light. Thus we have no assurance of salvation, no guarantee that we really know the Lord.

Considered overall, how brightly is your light shining?

APPLICATION: As the lamps of the foolish virgins went out for lack of fuel (Matt.25:7,8), so the lamp of our lives (our witness) will become dim and in danger of going out altogether if we don't keep "fueled up" with the Word and obey it. It is the light of our good works, Jesus said, that will cause others to glorify God, and, hopefully, come to Jesus as a result. If you haven't yet, make time to be in the Word each day, and purpose to obey what you read. You will be blessed – and others with you!

DAY 102
ᶜHE IS AN ANGEL

QUESTIONS TO THINK ABOUT:

1. When you think of angels, how would you describe them?
2. What are the functions and responsibilities of angels?

3. Christ is referred to as being an angel many times in Scripture. Can you think of some instances? Does that mean that he is an angel? (cf. Heb.1:1-14)

4. How can we be said to "be an angel" to someone?

In Revelation 8:3-5 there is described an "angel, who had a golden censer, [and who] came and stood at the altar. He was given much incense to offer, with the prayers of all the saints, on the golden altar before the throne." Evidence (though not conclusive) points toward the Lord Jesus as this angel in that this angel carries out the High Priestly function that Christ now performs.

More conclusive are the various appearances of the "Angel of the Lord" in the Old Testament, "in which, in almost every case, this messenger is regarded as Deity and yet is distinguished from Jehovah [See Gen.16:7-14; 22:11-18; 31:11,13; Exod.3:2-5; Num.22:22-35; Judg.6:11-23; 13:2-25; 1 Chr.21:15-17; 1 Kgs.19:5-7]. There is good reason for thinking that he is the pre-incarnate Logos, his appearance in angelic or human form foreshadowing his coming in the flesh" (The New Compact Bible Dictionary, "Angel of the Lord," p.39).

In Hebrews 1:14, angels are described as "ministering spirits sent to serve those who will inherit salvation." We also find them in both testaments bringing messages from God to men (cf. Dan.9:21; Lk.1:26). As angels are messengers sent to serve, even so Christ is God's Messenger sent to serve (Mk.10:45) and to bring us a message as to who God is (Jn.14:8-14), what our true condition is (Jn.15:22-25), and how the two can be reconciled (Eph.2:11-18). And as God has promised help through his angels (Ps.91:11-13), he also promises help through Christ as the Angel of the Lord (Ex.23:20-23; Phil.4:13).

If someone brings us good news, or helps us in a time of need, we often say, "You are an angel!" Several times King David was referred to as an angel of God, or like one, in terms of doing all things well (1 Sam.29:9), discernment of good and evil (2 Sam.14:17), great wisdom (2 Sam.14:20), and having authority and power to act (2 Sam.19:27).

By their dress and appearance, angels reflect the glory of the Lord (Rev.10:1). Christ reflected the glory of the Father in all he said and did (Heb.1:3). And so we are called upon to reflect Christ's glory (cf. Acts 4:13; 6:15 where Stephen's face is described as being like that of an angel).

So, then, as we serve others as ministers sent from God, as we bring them the good news of his Word and as we reflect the very glory of Christ before them in our lives, we too become like angels to them, which will bring glory, honor and praise to the Lord, which glory will scatter as rays of sunlight upon us as well.

Can others say of you, "You're an angel!"?

APPLICATION: "An Angel" is not a title for which we should strive, nor could we attain it if we wanted to! It is an appellation that will come to us as we concentrate on becoming like Christ and doing that which is pleasing and glorifying to him.

DAY 103
[b]HE IS THE MESSENGER OF THE COVENANT

QUESTIONS TO THINK ABOUT:

1. Of what Covenant was Christ the Messenger?
2. How can we be said to be Messengers of the Covenant?

Christ is referred to as the Messenger of the Covenant in Malachi 3:1,2. To the Jewish reader, this title meant the Messiah, the Coming One, the One who would fulfill God's promises to Israel in abundant blessings and rule the world with an iron scepter. But verses 3-5 make it clear that his coming would not be for Israel's national blessing only, but also for judgment against those in Israel who are living sinful lives and do not fear him.

When Christ came to earth the first time, the gospel of the kingdom was preached. This would have meant the soon fulfillment of the Covenant promises. But Israel rejected the Messenger of the Covenant and crucified him. So instead of national blessing, they brought upon themselves the curse of national judgment and destruction.

Yet Christ was, is, and yet will be God's fulfillment of the Covenant he made with Israel. This fulfillment we see in the New Covenant, experienced by the Church now, and will be by Israel as a nation later (Rom.11:25-27). In Hebrews 8:7-12 God says: "The time is coming, declares the Lord, when I will make a new covenant with the house of Israel and with the house of Judah. It will not be like the covenant I made with their forefathers when I took them by the hand to lead them out of Egypt, because they did not remain faithful to my covenant, and I turned away from them, declares the Lord. This is the covenant I will make with the house of Israel after that time, declares the Lord. I will put my laws in their minds and write them on their hearts. I will be their God, and they will be my people. No longer will a man teach his neighbor, or a man his brother, saying, 'Know the Lord,' because they will all know me, from the least of them to the greatest. For I will forgive their wickedness and will remember their sins no more" (from Jer.31:31-34).

How do we reflect Christ as the Messenger of the Covenant? By being messengers ourselves. Each Covenant, the Old and the New, contains promises of blessing and judgment. Our message also must include both of these. Sin always results in judgment; righteousness always results in blessing even though we may not see either for a period of time. This fact oftentimes causes the sinner to think he's getting away with his sin, and makes the righteous wonder if it's worthwhile being righteous anyway since all they seem to have for their efforts is trouble. (Asaph struggled with this problem in Psalm 73 and overcame it when he was able to look beyond the immediacy of this world and consider the answer in terms of the eternal destiny of the wicked.) But as messengers of the Covenant, we must make its provisions clear so that others will know what they are choosing when they accept or reject it.

The tendency these days is to water down the judgment of God on sin and to emphasize his love and blessings on the obedient. This is not being true to the New Covenant message he has called us to give! The ministry of the Holy Spirit among men is to convince them of sin, righteousness and judgment (Jn.16:8). As messengers of the Covenant, we also must include these three elements in our witness. Deemphasizing any one of them will distort the truth and lead others astray.

What message are others hearing from you?

APPLICATON:

As you think about your witness to others, give serious thought to including the subjects of sin, righteousness and judgment in some way, for these are the essential elements in the New Covenant. Sin: man's rebellion against God; righteousness: God's provision for forgiveness through Christ; judgment: God's pronouncement upon all who refuse the gift of his forgiveness.

DAY 104
ᶜHE IS THE SAVIOR, THE DELIVERER

QUESTIONS TO THINK ABOUT:

1. From what did Jesus come to save us? How did he accomplish that?

2. How can we be considered as someone's savior or deliverer?

When Gabriel appeared to Mary, telling her that she was to be the mother of Israel's Messiah, he said to her, "You are to give him the name Jesus" (Lk.1:31). Later, when it was obvious that she was pregnant out of wedlock, a troubled Joseph saw an angel in a dream who told him what was happening, and then said, "You are to give him the name Jesus, because he will save his people from their sins" (Matt.1:21). The name Jesus means Savior, Deliverer, Preserver.

Israel's history is replete with examples illustrating this name. For a period of nearly 400 years after Joshua, Israel suffered relapse after relapse, going after other gods and ignoring the Lord, that is, until they got into trouble! Then "they cried out to the LORD, and he raised up for them a deliverer" (Judg.3:9, etc.), a savior, one who would rescue them from their enemies. These were men and women of faith, whom God chose for this special task. Their willingness was varied, but God used them nonetheless.

Jesus saved us from the power and penalty of sin. He first announced the gospel (Heb.2:3 – "salvation"), and others have taken up the call, proclaiming what God has done through Christ to deliver them from the bondage of sin. Just as God sent the judges to deliver Israel from her enemies, so he sends us to deliver men from their sins through the Gospel.

The Citak people on the south coast area of Irian Jaya (now called Papua), to whom we first ministered, were bound by their fear of demons, black magic and bondage to sin. As we proclaimed the Gospel, God lifted the veil from their eyes, and many turned to the Lord. One day a believer came to me and said, "You know, we used to see evil spirits all the time; but now we hardly see them anymore" — deliverance, not only from sin, but also from their great fear of evil spirits.

We also are used to keep each other from sin as we daily encourage one another in the faith. Hebrews 3:12,13 admonishes us in this responsibility: "See to it, brothers, that none of you has a sinful, unbelieving heart that turns away from the living God.

But encourage one another daily, as long as it is called Today, so that none of you may be hardened by sin's deceitfulness." One reason for the weakness and failure of the Church is that we're not encouraging one another daily as we ought. We choose to remain silent, not to "interfere," and leave the encouraging, counseling and exhortations to the pastor on Sundays. [But see DAY 58 – HE IS A COUNSELOR, where we find our responsibility to counsel and encourage one another.] In not doing this, we fail to reflect Christ as Savior and Deliverer to one another.

When was the last time you shared the Gospel with an unsaved person or encouraged a fellow believer in his Christian walk?

APPLICATION: Make it a point to be a witness to the unsaved and an encourager to the saved. In that way, the Lord may use you to be someone's "savior" or "deliverer" from whatever might have them in bondage.

DAY 105
ᶜHE IS THE PRESERVER

QUESTIONS TO THINK ABOUT:

1. How does Jesus preserve and protect us?
2. How can we enter into the preservation and protection of others?

In 2 Timothy 4:18, Paul declares that Christ will rescue him "from every evil attack and will bring [preserve] him safely to his heavenly kingdom." Again, Jude expresses this truth in Jude 1, saying, "Jude ... to those who have been called, who are loved by God the Father and kept [preserved] by Jesus Christ." The Lord himself declared this in John 10:27-30, saying, "My sheep listen to my voice; I know them, and they follow me. I give them eternal life, and they shall never perish; no one can snatch them out of my hand. My Father, who has given them to me, is greater than all; no one can snatch them out of my Father's hand. I and the Father are one." Hebrews 7:25 declares: "Therefore he is able to save completely [preserve] those who come to God through him because he always lives to intercede for them."

The Lord is able to preserve us because he always lives and continually intercedes for us, prays for us, pleads for us before the Father's throne (Heb.9:24). In like manner, we can move the hand of God in the preservation of other Christians through intercessory prayer. Paul wrote the Thessalonians: "Finally, brothers, pray for us that the message of the Lord may spread rapidly and be honored … and pray that we may be delivered from wicked and evil men …" (2 Thess.3:1,2). When Peter was imprisoned, many Christians had gathered together to pray at the house of John Mark (Acts 12:12), evidently to pray for him as well as others, since Herod had begun to persecute the Church. They obviously thought he also was going to die (following James, the brother of John – Acts 12:1-3). So we can imagine that they were praying that Peter would have courage and be faithful to the end. That is why they were astonished when he actually appeared at the door (Acts 12:16). But the point is, God worked in answer to their prayers, and delivered Peter from death.

Many Christians have been delivered from death or peril through the intercessory prayers of others. One night my mother awoke and found herself praying desperately for a close missionary friend, that she would not lose her baby. (Mom didn't even know she was pregnant!) She prayed until the Lord gave her peace. On that same night, that missionary wife nearly had a miscarriage, but the Lord delivered her.

One day Amber and I were on an MAF flight from the south coast of Irian Jaya (Papua) to the Bird's Head area for Field Council meetings. The clouds were just above the trees, and we got lost. Finally we were heard far to the north of where we were supposed to be and were radioed that information. We soon landed safely, picked up two other missionaries, and continued our flight, having to cross the cloud-enshrouded mountains. The pilot tried several times to work his way through, but each time had to turn back. Suddenly a narrow "passageway" opened clear to the other side, and we flew through it, the clouds closing in behind us as we went! We came out precisely where the pilot was heading for all along and continued on our way safely. Someone was praying and we were preserved from danger. Later we found out who that was. My mother wrote to us asking what happened on such-and-such a date. She had been praying urgently for our safety at the very time we were flying!

Are you responsive to the urgings of the Lord to pray for others so that they, through your prayers, are preserved from danger?

APPLICATION: Be faithful in praying for the safety and preservation of God's people in whatever circumstance they may be in: missionaries in dangerous places, Christians enduring persecution, Christians under spiritual attack and in danger of losing their faith or ruining their ministry by giving in to temptation. Sometimes you will know specifically who they are; other times you will have to pray generally. Ask the Lord to guide you in your prayers, and for whom you should pray. It just might be your intercession that will make the difference in the end.

DAY 106
ᶜHE IS THE PROPHET

QUESTIONS TO THINK ABOUT:

1. What is a prophet?
2. What is a prophet's ministry?
3. Why is it important for us to listen to the one expounding the Word of God?

In Deuteronomy 18:15,17-19, Moses told Israel: "The LORD your God will raise up for you a prophet like me from among your own brothers. You must listen to him... . The LORD said to me: ... 'I will raise up for them a prophet like you from among their brothers; I will put my words in his mouth, and he will tell them everything I commanded him. If anyone does not listen to my words that the prophet speaks in my name, I myself will call him to account.'"

In fulfillment of this prophecy, the Lord Jesus himself said: "... I do nothing on my own but speak just what the Father has taught me" (Jn.8:28b). And again in John 15:22, "If I had not come and spoken to them, they would not be guilty of sin. Now, however, they have no excuse for their sin." God will hold them accountable for what they had heard. And again in John 12:47-50: "As for the person who hears my words but does not keep them, I do not judge him. For I did not come to judge the world, but to save it. There is a judge for the one who rejects me and does not accept my words; that very word which I spoke will condemn him at the last day. For I did not speak of my own accord, but the Father who sent me commanded me what to say and how to say it. I know that his command leads to eternal life. So whatever I say is just what the Father has told me to say."

A prophet had a dual ministry: first, he foretold the future. This perhaps occupied a fraction of his time. Secondly, he spoke on God's behalf to the people through preaching and proclaiming God's words to them. Christ foretold some coming events (Matt.24 and 25), but the bulk of his ministry was teaching the people about God and how he expected his people to live (Jn.14:9; Matt.5-7).

The same was true of the early Church. There were words of prophecy concerning coming events (Acts 21:10,11; 2 Pet.3:3-10; Rev.1:1,19), but the bulk of the ministry concerned how to live the Christian life. The same is true today. To those who have and exercise the gift of prophecy, the main thrust of their ministry is communicating what God wants to say to individuals or groups about their Christian lives and work. Most of what we need to know about the future is already revealed to us in the Scripture, but occasionally God will encourage us through a personal word. As an example: one time I felt quite ill and some fellow missionaries came to pray for me. One expressed a word of prophecy regarding God's plans for me, in essence: "Bob, I have a work for you to do among the Bible School students. I am preparing their hearts to receive my Word; but you must spend much time with me so that you will know what to give them." That word of prophecy was a great encouragement to me. Not only did I know that I wasn't going to die, but also that a fruitful ministry lay ahead which indeed was the case.

Paul urged the Corinthian Christians to desire spiritual gifts, but especially the gift of prophesying (1 Cor.14:1), for "everyone who prophesies speaks to men for their strengthening, encouragement and comfort, edifying the church (1 Cor.14:3,4). Hebrews 3:12,13 also emphasizes this ministry: "See to it, brothers, that none of you has a sinful, unbelieving heart that turns away from the living God. But encourage one another daily [i.e. talk to each other about the Lord and his Word each day], as long as it is called Today, so that none of you may be hardened by sin's deceitfulness."

There's an interesting verse in Malachi 3:16. "Then those who feared the LORD talked with each other, and the LORD listened and heard. A scroll of remembrance was written in his presence concerning those who feared the LORD and honored his name." And verse 17 adds, "And they will be mine, a valued possession." So let's talk to one another about the Lord, and encourage one another in the Lord, for he is listening, recording our words and holding in high value those who do so.

Are you a "prophet" to those around you?

APPLICATION: Most of us will never be prophets in terms of foretelling the future, but we all can use the Word of God to be an encouragement to one another, to challenge one another, and to keep each other from yielding to sin and temptation. Be anxious to share the blessings of God's Word with others, for you may never know how that ministered to a specific need at a specific time for that person's encouragement.

DAY 107
ᵇHE IS THE LIVING STONE

QUESTIONS TO THINK ABOUT:

1. How can a person be symbolized as a "living stone"? What do these two words imply?

2. What picture comes to mind when you read the words: "You also, as living stones, are being built up a spiritual house"? (1 Pet.2:5a).

3. What does that picture say about the character and function of the stones?

We read in 1 Peter 2:4, "As you come to him, the living Stone – rejected by men but chosen by God and precious to him." Jesus Christ is the Living Stone. We have to go back to the Old Testament to find out in what way he is a living stone. In Daniel 2:34,35b we read, "While you were watching, a rock was cut out, but not by human hands. It struck the statue on its feet of iron and clay and smashed them ... [They] ... became like chaff... The wind swept them away without leaving a trace. But the rock that struck the statue became a huge mountain and filled the whole earth."

In Exodus 17:6 the Lord told Moses: "I will stand there before you by the rock at Horeb. Strike the rock, and water will come out of it for the people to drink." First Corinthians 10:3,4 ties this together with Christ, where Paul says: "They all ate the same spiritual food and drank the same spiritual drink; for they drank from the spiritual rock that accompanied them, and that rock was Christ."

Recall from DAY 8 – HE IS THE LIFE, the five indications of life: 1. the desire for nourishment, 2. growth, 3. ability to work, 4. ability to reproduce, and 5. the ability to give nourishment to others. We find in the two above descriptions of Christ that several of these signs of life are present. The stone cut without hands smashed the image and ground it to powder (ability to work). Then it grew and became a mountain that filled the whole earth (growth). And from the smitten rock in the second passage, a symbol of the suffering Christ, came forth water (the ability to give nourishment).

In 1 Peter 2:5, Peter writes, "You also, like living stones, are being built into a spiritual house … ." So, without stretching things too far, we find the Living Stone fulfilling another sign of life: reproducing after its own kind.

We reflect Christ as the Living Stone as we become more like him. In Nebuchadnezzar's dream there was this stone, just a small thing, but powerful. After smashing the image (world's kingdoms, the world's system), it grew and became a mountain that filled the whole earth. Christ-likeness in our lives begins as a small stone, but a stone empowered by the Holy Spirit. With it we can smash the sin in our lives, we can smash our bondage to the world's system. Then we can grow in our likeness to Christ until his likeness fills our entire lives like a mighty mountain.

There is much condensation that occurs on mountains (rain, snow, fog), and, as it builds up, rivulets, creeks, streams and rivers form, bringing nourishment and life to those living below. The more we become like Christ, the higher our mountain and the greater will be the runoff (the message he has given us) for the nourishment of others. Then, returning to Peter's picture of us as living stones, others also will join us and together we shall be built into a spiritual house in which God will dwell as we strengthen, nourish and uphold one another.

APPLICATION: A living stone has the qualities of hardness (steadfast in faith), usefulness (functioning for the purpose for which it was fashioned [spiritual gifts – see APPENDIX III]), and life (the power to reproduce). Peter says that we should make every effort to add to our faith (2 Pet.1:5-8) the various Christian graces, which include the above three characteristics. A "dead" stone just lies there; a "living" stone is about doing something!

DAY 108
[a]HE IS THE LONGSUFFERING ONE

QUESTIONS TO THINK ABOUT:

1. What do others do that "drive you up the wall"?
2. What do you do to others that "drive them up the wall"?
3. What do you do that would "drive Jesus up the wall" if he were not God?
4. What does the term "longsuffering" actually mean?
5. How should the Lord's patience with you affect your patience with others?

We read in 2 Peter 3:9, "The Lord is not slow in keeping His promise, as some understand slowness. He is patient (longsuffering – KJV) with you, not wanting anyone to perish, but everyone to come to repentance." Verse 15: "Bear in mind that the Lord's patience (longsuffering – KJV) means salvation ... ."

Longsuffering is "that quality of self-restraining in the face of provocation which does not hastily retaliate or promptly punish; it is the opposite of anger and is associated with mercy" (Vine, Vol. III, p.12). This quality is shown when Jesus and his disciples were traveling through Samaria and were refused lodging. James and

John wanted to call down fire out of heaven to destroy these people (Lk.9:51-56). But the Lord rebuked them sharply. They were angry at an inconvenience and at the fact that the Samaritans didn't recognize who Jesus or his disciples were. The Lord Jesus was longsuffering, willing to endure a slight like this and do nothing about it because he was not willing that these people should perish. It is purely supposition, but I imagine that many of these same people did in fact become believers during Philip's evangelistic campaign in Samaria (Acts 8:4-25). Had they been destroyed at the bidding of James and John, they would have been eternally lost. So where the Lord disciplines his own children, he often lets the ungodly go "scott free" for a while, giving them opportunity after opportunity to repent, so that they will have no excuse. In his sovereign election, he has chosen those who will receive him, so bears long with them until they yield (as in the Apostle Paul's case). We are not so patient.

I knew of a man whose wife was a constant complainer. He loved her and was faithful to her. He wasn't henpecked, but quietly endured her griping year after year. We marveled at his great patience with her, his "longsuffering." Until the day of her death, she never changed. One day, when was asked about his patient attitude toward her, he replied: "Well, when you make a mistake, you have to live with it." They were married for 67 years! Anyone nowadays would have sued for divorce on the grounds of incompatibility or mental cruelty. "I have a right not to listen to these complaints day after day. She's driving me up the wall. I don't have to put up with this and I won't." Where is the longsuffering? As long as we have our best interests at heart, we will not have it. But as we put the best interests of others ahead of our own, we will have established the basis for it. As we yield ourselves to the Holy Spirit, he will work longsuffering into our lives as part of his fruit (Gal.5:23). Furthermore, we are commanded in Colossians 3:12,13, that "... as God's chosen people, holy and dearly loved, clothe yourselves with compassion, kindness, humility, gentleness and patience (longsuffering – KJV). Bear with each other and forgive whatever grievances you may have against one another. Forgive as the Lord forgave you."

Is your longsuffering of short duration? If so, then it isn't "long"!

APPLICATION: If you have trouble being longsuffering toward others, just think about how patient the Lord has been with you; how long was it before you learned those lessons you expect others to demonstrate more quickly? Recognizing that others are also a work "in progress," that they are not now what God eventually intends them to be, should help us be more patient. Perhaps this question will be of help: "Will my attitude toward them help them along toward what God intends them to be, or hinder their progress?" Then choose to do that which will move them along.

DAY 109
ᵇHE IS OUR DEFENDER, PROTECTOR

QUESTIONS TO THINK ABOUT:

1. Why do we feel that we need protection?
2. What is it that we fear and from which we need protection?
3. What does Jesus protect us from?

In Psalm 5:11 we read: "But let all who take refuge in you be glad; let them ever sing for joy. Spread your protection over them, that those who love your name may rejoice in you." And again in Psalm 23:4, "Even though I walk through the valley of the shadow of death, I will fear no evil, for you are with me; your rod and your staff, they comfort me."

We find the Lord protecting Peter and other disciples from Satan in Luke 22:31,32 where he says, "Simon, Simon, Satan has asked to sift you as wheat. But I have prayed for you, Simon, that your faith may not fail. And when you have turned back, strengthen your brothers." How did He pray for them? John 17:11,12a give us an idea: "I will remain in the world no longer, but they are still in the world, and I am coming to you. Holy Father, protect them by the power of your name – the name you gave me – so that they may be one as we are one. While I was with them, I protected them and kept them safe ... ."

In his prayer, Christ also mentioned keeping them in God's name. What does it mean to be kept in his name?

I can think of two examples: first, of *the power of a name over the actions of others*. In Matthew 2:19-23, when Herod was dead, an angel of the Lord appeared to Joseph in a dream when he was in Egypt with Mary and Jesus. He was told that Herod was dead and that he could return to Israel. But the mention of a name changed the place where Joseph would dwell: "Archelaus," son of Herod. We read that Joseph was afraid. Why? Because he knew the evil character of Archelaus. When Saul and his army were facing the Philistines, just the mention of the name of Goliath was enough to bring great fear to the Israelite soldiers – and to see him was enough to send them flying! (I Sam.17:10,11,23,24). Why? Because of who he was and his great stature and strength. When the Israelites approached the area of Jericho, the hearts of the populace melted for fear and became as water, for they had heard of the mighty works of Israel's God and were terrified. In the Old West, if the townsfolk heard, "Jesse James is acomin' to town!" they ran for cover. Just his name was enough to spark great fear because of the terrible things he had done and gotten away with.

Secondly, *the power of a name can also carry with it certain rights and privileges*. In the days of the Roman Empire, "I am a Roman citizen" would put a person in a different class altogether and place him under the protection of Caesar himself (cf. Acts 22:24-29).

Here Paul was protected from physical harm through the power of a name. In Psalm 20:1 we read, "May the LORD answer you when you are in distress; may the name of the God of Jacob protect you." Psalm 124:8, "Our help is in the name of the LORD, the Maker of heaven and earth." Proverbs 18:10, "The name of the LORD is a strong tower; the righteous run to it and are safe." Philippians 2:10, "That at the name of Jesus every knee should bow … ." (all underlining mine).

So we are protected as Christ prays for us and keeps us in the mighty name of God the Father. Satan cannot stand before the name of God, nor of the Lord Jesus Christ as he cannot withstand their power nor undo what they have done. The truth of this is expressed in the following poem, "In Your Name Is Authority."

IN YOUR NAME IS AUTHORITY

In Your Name is authority.
In Your Name there is might.
In Your Name there is strength and pow'r.
In Your Name there is right.

In Your Name there is victory.
In Your Name is our song.
In Your Name is deliverance
From all sin, from all wrong.

In Your Name, Satan's pow'r is crushed.
In Your Name, devils quake.
In Your Name, the pow'r of death is gone.
In Your Name worlds will shake.

In Your Name there is hope and joy.
In Your Name there is love.
In Your Name there is rest and peace
As we seek our home above.

Response:

O praise God for His holiness
O praise Him for His grace.
O praise God with one heart and mind.
O praise Him every race.

– R.J.L., Jan.3, 1983

APPLICATION: The power of our prayers is not just closing them with, "In Jesus' name, amen!" but by actually praying "in Jesus' name," i.e. praying on his authority and according to his will as if he were praying that prayer. As we pray asking for his defense and protection, either for us or others, sometimes we don't know what God's will is for that particular situation. But with the same authority Jesus used, we also can pray, "Not my will, but yours be done!" and have the same certainty that it indeed will be done.

DAY 110
ᵇHE IS OUR DEFENDER, PROTECTOR, concl.

QUESTIONS TO THINK ABOUT:

1. Why is it important that we pray for others on the authority of Jesus' name?
2. How can we do it?
3. How else can we protect them from spiritual danger?
4. Why is our experience and example important when ministering to them?

How, then, can we reflect Christ as Defender and Protector? First of all by praying for our fellow believers in the name of the Lord Jesus Christ. Christ prayed that the faith of his disciples would not fail (Lk.22:32). We know from what he said elsewhere that he prayed in the authority of the name of God the Father and according to his will (Jn.17:11,12). How can we pray this way? Let's say, for example, that a Christian friend of ours is caught up in an immoral relationship. We read in I Thessalonians 4:3-5, "It is God's will that you should be sanctified: that you should avoid sexual immorality, that each of you should learn to control his own body in a way that is holy and honorable, not in passionate lust like the heathen, who do not know God." Knowing his will, we can pray confidently, in the authority of his name, for this person and know that God will answer: "Lord, I bring _____ before you. He is involved in this immoral relationship that is contrary to your will. Therefore, in the name of the Lord Jesus Christ, I rebuke these unclean forces who are blinding him to the truth, deceiving him that happiness can be found in sin, and leading him to destruction, and command them to cease their work in his life. I pray that your Holy Spirit would work unhindered to bring him back into a right relationship with you and your people ...," and so on. This prayer will be answered according to the promise given us in I John 5:14,15 that if we ask anything according to his will, he hears us and will answer. It might not come immediately, maybe not for several years, but it will come.

Secondly, we defend and protect fellow believers <u>by giving them the Word of God and being an example for them to follow</u>, demonstrating to them the reality of what we are saying. Someone has said, "Nothing succeeds like success itself." When we see the principles of God's Word working in the lives of others, we are encouraged in our own faith to follow those principles and let them be worked out in our lives. Our national pastor in Papua was a good example of this. He taught in our Bible School. Often on a Sunday, he would share with us some principle he had come across while teaching, and how the Lord had worked it out in his life that very week. Then he would challenge us to do the same, and we were greatly encouraged in our Christian lives. In that encouragement, we were protected from the evil snares of the Devil that we might otherwise have fallen into in that particular area. So we all need to be sharing with one another how the principles of Scripture work out in our lives. We need to pray for one another so that we will be delivered from temptation and sin and grow as Christians.

Are you actively defending your fellow believers through prayer for and sharing the Word with them?

APPLICATION: Look for opportunities to share with others what God is teaching you: a note, a phone call, a casual chat. What you share with them just might be that which God will use to protect them from some spiritual danger or deliver them from temptation or bondage to something you know nothing about.

DAY 111
[b]HE IS THE HONORED ONE

QUESTIONS TO THINK ABOUT:

1. What does it mean to be honored by someone?
2. Why is it not good to seek one's own honor?
3. On what basis will God honor us?

In Hebrews 2:9 we read, "But we see Jesus, who was made a little lower than the angels, now crowned with glory and honor (*timā*) … ." And again in 2 Peter 1:17, "For he received honor and glory from God the Father when the voice came to him from the Majestic Glory, saying, 'This is my Son, whom I love; with him I am well pleased.'" The Greek word, *timā*, means "to hold in esteem of the highest degree." At his baptism, before he had even begun his ministry, we read the same words: "And a voice came from heaven: 'You are my Son, whom I love; with you I am well pleased'" (Mark 1:11). How is it that, at that point, God was well pleased with him?

In his pre-incarnate state, he voluntarily laid aside his riches and glory in order to humbly obey the will of God (see 2 Cor.8:9 and Phil.2:5-8). Submission to the will of God is always pleasing to him. Paul reflects this attitude in Philippians 3:4-9 where he says that nothing is as important as the excellency of the knowledge of Christ for whom he suffered the loss of all things (vs.8), and whom he served. He submitted himself to the will of God first, and all his needs were met (Phil.4:16-18) in fulfillment of Christ's promise in Matthew 6:33, "But seek first his kingdom and his righteousness, and all these things will be given to you as well." When a child submits to and obeys his parents' will, and his parents want what is best for him, they are pleased and proud of him. So it is with God and us. We don't need to fear his will, just do it.

We read in Luke 2:40 that "… the child grew and became strong; he was filled with wisdom, and the grace of God was upon him." How did this happen? Because his parents, though poor and uneducated, were godly people (note Matt.1:19,24; Lk.1:28,30,38,45; 2:22-24,39,41,42) and created a family environment conducive to godliness. Nazareth had a bad reputation (Jn.1:46), but Joseph's family was able to live above it. Joseph and Mary were obviously faithful in teaching Jesus all they knew about God and his Word (cf. Deut.6:6,7). He learned quickly and well. There would have been a school in the local synagogue where Jesus probably attended as a child. There he would continue to apply himself to the study of God's Word and continue to grow in wisdom and understanding. And God was pleased.

Christian parents need to create a godly atmosphere in their homes so that their children will have the optimum opportunities to become godly. But even more, the parents themselves must model godliness and practice it with their children. We once were in a very missions-minded church and got into discussion with some of the parents. "Here we are, a missions-minded church, yet not one of our children is interested in serving the Lord full-time! What's wrong?" After some discussion, it was concluded that the parents' true values were influencing their children away from the Lord. They were "preaching" missions but "living" materialism. Joseph and Mary were godly in what they taught and godly in how they lived, and God was pleased (Lk.1:28).

As God looks at your family life, can he say, "I'm pleased with what I see!"?

APPLICATION: I believe that the secret to God's honoring us is both to know and to do his will. In other words, we must practice what we say we believe. If we don't, we will lose both God's blessing and our friends and families. Generally, others must see the principles of God's Word working in our lives before they will believe them and practice them for themselves.

DAY 112
bHE IS THE HONORED ONE, concl.

QUESTIONS TO THINK ABOUT:

1. How old does one have to be before he can be pleasing to God and be honored by him?
2. What does this imply about our ministry to children?
3. Without being legalistic, what does it take to develop a close relationship with the Lord, and one that is pleasing to him?

The next scene of Jesus' life opens when he is 12 years old, accompanying his parents to the Temple in Jerusalem (Lk.2:42-52). In these verses we see "a youth after God's own heart." He loved

God's House and felt drawn to it (vs.43,46); he had a teachable spirit, displayed a great depth of understanding and an ability to communicate what he knew (vs.46,47); he had a desire to serve his Father and do his will (vs.49); yet he subjected himself to his parents and obeyed them (vs.51). In this position, he continued to grow in wisdom (spiritual and practical insight), and stature (physical growth), and in favor with God and man (vs.52).

David serves as a good example of God honoring a man. He was known to be "a man after God's own heart." In Acts 13:22 we read, "After removing Saul, [God] made David their king. He testified concerning him: 'I have found David son of Jesse a man after my own heart; he will do everything I want him to do.'"

There are several indications from Scripture that illustrate how David was a man after God's own heart and how we can be too. In Psalm 40:8 we read, "I desire to do your will, O my God; your law is within my heart." Psalm 119:11, "I have hidden your word in my heart that I might not sin against you." David's heart was also full of praise and thanksgiving to the Lord. He knew who his God was (see 2 Sam.22; 1 Chr.16; Ps.18,103,105 for several examples). He was full of faith and zeal for the Lord's name (1 Sam.17:26,45). His desire was toward God's House (2 Sam.7), and he exhorted his people to fear God (1 Chr.28). David's heart was toward God, delighting in his presence; and God was pleased. Thus he greatly honored David in the sight of his people Israel.

The Lord created us to have fellowship with him, and is pleased with our companionship when we delight to be with him and live in obedience to his Word. We need to take the time necessary to develop our relationship with him and learn from him. Like Joshua, when he and Moses went into the presence of the Lord, he remained in the tent even after Moses went out to the people (Exod.33:11). He was hungry for God, and the Lord has promised that those who hunger and thirst after righteousness will be filled (Matt.5:6) – not only full and satisfied, but overflowing with God's message to others. As the

Lord fills our hearts with himself and his Word, we cannot keep silent; we must speak, we must share; God is pleased and we are honored.

Then will come that final day when we all stand before the throne of God to receive our rewards for what we have done here on earth. Jesus said that if we confess him before men, then he will confess us before the Father and the holy angels (Lk.12:8). To those who have been faithful to the Lord, they will hear, "Well done, good and faithful servant! You have been faithful with a few things; I will put you in charge of many things. Come and share your master's happiness!" (Matt.25:21). And we will be honored as well before all the saints and angels.

Can the Lord say of you, "My child, in whom I am well pleased!"?

APPLICATION: One thought that has kept me motivated to serve the Lord as faithfully as I can is the way I approached the end of the school semester. After the finals, I wanted to feel, "Whew! I made it!" That motivated me to study the best I could throughout the semester. When I get to heaven, I want to feel the same way: "Whew! I made it!" which motivates me to serve the Lord the best I can now. The honoring is up to him; I just want to feel like I did the best I could in the meantime.

DAY 113
'HE IS THE LORD OF SABAOTH (LORD OF HOSTS)

QUESTIONS TO THINK ABOUT:

1. What is justice?
2. How would it be applied by supervisors/bosses in the work place?

3. How would "do to others as you would have them do to you" affect the attitude of employers toward their employees? of employees toward their bosses?

4. How should we respond to injustices that we might see or be aware of?

In James 5:4 we read: "Look! The wages you failed to pay the workmen who mowed your fields are crying out against you. The cries of the harvesters have reached the ears of the Lord Almighty" (Lord of Sabaoth – KJV). The "Lord of Sabaoth" is the Old Testament "Lord of Hosts." In Romans 9:29 it is used in reference to Jewish Christians. James also wrote primarily to Jewish Christians (Jas.1:1). So again James 5:4 would have special meaning to them. Since the Lord Jesus Christ is the Jehovah of the Old Testament (see DAY 36 – HE IS THE KING [Governor/Ruler]), then we are not out of line in attributing this title, "Lord of Sabaoth," to him, especially in light of the New Testament contexts in which it occurs. "Lord of Sabaoth" means "the Lord Almighty" and in the context of James 5:4, "the Omnipotent Sovereign who is not oblivious to injustice." It is this point that we will consider here.

The Lord hates injustice. Matthew 23:1-36 contains a scathing statement on injustices done through the hypocrisy of the scribes and Pharisees. In verse 23 he outrightly accuses them of committing injustices. In Matthew 7:12 he goes to the heart of injustice saying: "So in everything, do to others what you would have them do to you, for this sums up the Law and the Prophets." That's no guarantee that others will treat us right, but it does guarantee that we will treat others right, and that others will have less reason or cause to do us ill; for this world's system is based on revenge. If there is no cause for revenge, then usually none will be taken.

There are many unjust things that occur in this world. We can't right them all, but we can speak out about those that occur around us. I remember one instance on the mission field where a government

Unexpected Transformation / 263

employee was punishing a group of villagers for some offense. He was forcing them to lie on their backs and look directly at the sun. I was horrified and went to him to protest this type of punishment. A few minutes later a command was given and their punishment was changed. It won't always happen that way, but in reflecting Christ as Lord of Sabaoth, we must speak out against injustices whenever and wherever we meet them. The Lord has placed Christians in all levels of society and government so that the greatest influence for reform could be felt if we would but speak up and do what was in our power to do. There are many injustices about which we are powerless to do anything; but we <u>can</u> pray and trust the Lord's sovereignty in them. The Lord says in Luke 21:12,13, "But before all this, they will lay hands on you and persecute you. They will deliver you to synagogues and prisons, and you will be brought before kings and governors, and all on account of my name. This will result in your being witnesses to them."

So when we can speak out about injustice, let us speak out; when we can do something about an injustice, let us do it; but when we can do nothing, then let us pray to the One who can, and commit that situation to his sovereign will.

If you are aware of an injustice, but it doesn't directly affect you, are you just as willing to let it ride? Is that the kind of attitude you'd hope to see from others if they were aware of an injustice being done to you?

APPLICATION: As you become aware of injustices, the first step always is to pray about them. Then ask the Lord is there is anything you could do about it. If he opens the door, then go through it in faith that he will lead you in what you are supposed to do.

DAY 114
[a]HE IS THE MAN

◆

QUESTIONS TO THINK ABOUT:

1. What does it mean to be human?
2. How do we know that Christ became human?
3. What was the basic difference between Christ and us?
4. As the Holy Spirit empowered Jesus, as a human being, for service, so he empowers us for service. What is the implication of this statement? How it is limited in our experience?

In Acts 17:31 we read, "For he has set a day when he will judge the world with justice by the man he has appointed. He has given proof of this to all men by raising him from the dead." Also in 1 Timothy 2:5 we read, "For there is one God and one mediator between God and men, the man Christ Jesus." In Philippians 2:7,8 we read, "But [Christ] made himself nothing, taking the very nature of a servant, being made in human likeness. And being found in appearance as a man, he humbled himself and became obedient to death – even death on a cross!"

In all of Christ's characteristics which we have studied, this is the only one in which we can say he reflects us! Christ was a man in every way as we are, only without sin. Man was made in God's image with the ability to communicate, think, feel emotion, and make choices. Hunger, thirst and weariness are also common to man; so also is death. We don't have to look far to see all these characteristics of humanness in Christ. He communicated (Matt.28: 18-20); thought (Jn.6:15); felt emotion: grief (Jn.11:35), anger (Mk.3:5), amazement (Mk.6:6), agony (Lk.22:44), joy (Lk.10:21), compassion (Mk.6:34), loneliness (Matt.26:40), and love (Jn.14:21); he made choices (Jn.13:18); was hungry (Matt.4:2), became thirsty

Unexpected Transformation / 265

(Jn.19:28), weary (Jn.4:6), and wanted to be alone (Mk.7:24); he was tempted in every way as we are, yet without sin (Matt.4:1-11; Heb.4:15); he also died (Jn.19:30).

As a man, Christ did not have our sinful nature, but he did have a human nature. He could have chosen, as a man, to sin, otherwise the temptation by the Devil would have had no substance. But he chose rather to listen to the voice of the Holy Spirit and live in obedience to him. According to John 3:34, he was given the Spirit without measure; there was nothing in his life that hindered the fullest operation of the Holy Spirit. We, as Christians, have that same Spirit indwelling us, but because of our sins and sinful nature, the Spirit is hindered in his operations through us. We could say, "We have the Spirit in his fullness, but, because of our sin, he has us only in part." So it would stand to reason that the more we hear his voice, the more we obey him, the more of the full measure of the Spirit we will experience and the less he will be hindered in working through us. We could say that everything that Christ was as a man we can become, the more we listen to and obey the voice of the Holy Spirit. Everything that Christ did as a Spirit-empowered man, we can do as the Holy Spirit gains more and more control in our lives. The Spirit was sent to be our Teacher, Guide and Source of Power (Jn.16:13-15; Acts 1:8). Therefore we must make ourselves available to him so that he can do his work in our lives, even as he did in Christ's.

You already have all of the Spirit. Does the Spirit have all of you?

APPLICATION: Since Jesus became human just as we are (excepting for sin), he knows exactly how we feel, how we are tempted, and how weak we often feel when it comes to ministry and living a godly life. That is why he sent the Holy Spirit to us to be our Comforter, our Strengthener and our Enabler. Our part is to let the Holy Spirit do his work in us by being obedient to what we know God wants us to do, endeavoring to walk closely with him. God has compassion on us knowing that we are but dust (Ps.103:13,14).

That is one reason why he gave us his Holy Spirit to overcome our weaknesses and make our lives fruitful.

DAY 115
[a]HE IS MERCIFUL

QUESTIONS TO THINK ABOUT:

1. What is mercy?
2. What does it mean to be merciful?
3. How does empathy for others play a part in mercy?
4. What role does our own weakness play in our showing mercy to others?

In Matthew 9:27 two blind men approached Jesus and said, "Have mercy on us, Son of David!" In Hebrews 2:17 we read that "… He had to be made like his brothers in every way, in order that he might become a merciful and faithful high priest in service to God … ." To repeat a part from DAY 71 – HE IS OUR HIGH PRIEST on the sacrifice of mercy, mercy is "the outward manifestation of pity; it assumes need on the part of him who receives it, and resources adequate to meet the need on the part of him who shows it… . To be moved by the needs of others is compassion; but to act on that compassion by using our resources to meet those needs is mercy." So Jesus healed the two blind men using his resources in response to their faith (Matt.9:29). Since Jesus was every bit as human as we are, apart from sin (see DAY 187 – HE IS THE SON OF MAN), he can fully sympathize with our weaknesses (Heb.4:15). He knows by experience our needs; and, as our High Priest, he not only intercedes for us because of our weaknesses, but extends to us the resources of his power to overcome those weaknesses and live

Unexpected Transformation / 267

a life of victory (see Phil.4:13 for a start where Paul says, "I can do everything through him who gives me strength."). He also wrote in 1 Corinthians 15:57, "But thanks be to God! He gives us the victory through our Lord Jesus Christ."

Paul wrote about our bearing with one another (Col.3:13) and bearing one another's burdens (Gal.6:2). One thing I have found helpful in bearing with others is remembering how patient the Lord is toward me. Someone asked me one time if we didn't feel impatient toward the Citak believers who weren't showing more maturity in their new faith after several years had passed. I said, "No, not really. It took me 35 years to learn patience, and I had all the resources available to help me had I used them. The Citak believers come from perhaps thousands of years of no knowledge of God and his ways. It takes time for them to understand, accept and then practice this totally new way of life, especially since they have few resources on which to draw for help." So knowing my own weaknesses and God's patience toward me helps me be patient toward the weaknesses of others and more accepting toward them as well. Step one of mercy.

But step two must be taken as well. If we have the spiritual or other resources to help meet their needs, then that becomes our responsibility before God toward them. As Solomon says in Proverbs 3:27, "Do not withhold good from those who deserve it, when it is in your power to act." When Christ says in Matthew 25:40, "I tell you the truth, whatever you did for one of the least of these brothers of mine, you did for me," we understand that our hands also become "God's hands" in meeting their needs, bringing encouragement, giving instruction. So as we show mercy toward others, we will not only feel compassion for them, but also will strive to minister to them with the resources available to us. Thus we reflect Christ as the Merciful One.

Are you merely compassionate toward others, or are you merciful as well?

APPLICATION: Consciously put yourself in the other person's shoes and ask yourself, "It that were me, how would I want others to act toward me and help meet my need?" There will always be those who will "play" to your sympathies and try to get something for nothing. Well, mercy is giving something to someone who is totally undeserving of it! That's what God did for us, so we should offer the same to others, regardless of their motivation. God's goodness led us to repentance; hopefully ours will lead others to repent as well.

DAY 116
ᶜHE IS THE ONLY BEGOTTEN SON

QUESTIONS TO THINK ABOUT:

1. What does the term "Only Begotten Son" mean?
2. When did God "beget" Christ as his only begotten Son?
3. How has God "begotten" us as his children?
4. What does it mean to be a child of God?

In John 3:16 we read, "For God so love the world that he gave his one and only Son, that whoever believes in him shall not perish but have eternal life." And again in 1 John 4:9 we read, "This is how God showed his love among us: he sent his one and only Son into the world that we might live through him."

Even though Christ is referred to as God's one and only Son, or only begotten Son (KJV), before, during and after his incarnation, it seems that the actual time of his "begetting" was at the resurrection. When Paul was preaching in the synagogue at Antioch in Pisidia, he said: "We tell you the good news: What God promised our fathers he has fulfilled for us, their children, by raising up Jesus. As it is written in the second Psalm [2:7]: 'You are my Son; today I have become your Father'" (Acts 13:33). In other words, "Today, when I have raised you up from the dead, I have begotten you. You shall never die again" (vs.34; and see DAY 200 – HE IS THE FIRSTBORN FROM THE DEAD – Col. 1:18). In Romans 1:4 we read that Jesus "through the Spirit of holiness was declared with power to be the Son of God by his resurrection from the dead." Everything Jesus said, taught and claimed for himself hinged on the resurrection. If he died as other men, and stayed dead, then he was no different than any other false messiah. But if death could not hold him, if he arose as he said he would, then everything he said, taught and claimed for himself would be true, and his title as God's only begotten Son would be officially bestowed on him, even though it was used of him before his resurrection.

What does "only begotten Son" mean? "Only" implies "one of a kind"; "begotten" implies "reproducing after one's kind"; and "Son" implies "a special relationship with one's father." How do we reflect Christ as the Only Begotten Son? As he was one of a kind, so are we. There's not one Christian identical with another. We're all different, all unique. All begotten by the Father through the Holy Spirit. "Everyone who believes that Jesus is the Christ is born of God, and everyone who loves the father loves his child as well" (1 Jn.5:1; see also Tit.3:5). In Psalm 139:14a our uniqueness is brought out: "I praise you because I am fearfully and wonderfully made."

In a sense, we who are believers have been "begotten" twice. In Genesis 1:26,27 man was created in God's image; God "reproducing after his own kind." Sin marred and distorted his "offspring," so God once again is "reproducing man after his own kind," i.e. re-generated into the image of Christ (see again 1 Jn.5:1; 3:9,10), hence "born again."

Being born of God spiritually, we then enter a special relationship with him as sons and daughters (1 Jn.3:1). We are no longer of the world, but of heaven. "Therefore come out from them and be separate, says the Lord. Touch no unclean thing, and I will receive you. I will be a Father to you, and you will be my sons and daughters, says the Lord Almighty" (2 Cor.6:17,18).

So as we reflect Christ's uniqueness as the Only Begotten Son of God, we will be emphasizing and using our own uniqueness and abilities God has given us in our service to him.

Are you living as a uniquely begotten child of God?

APPLICATION: Have you been re-generated by God to become his unique child and hence able to reflect Christ as the Only Begotten Son? If not, then now is the time to repent of your sins and ask Jesus Christ to forgive you and become Lord of your life. He will never turn away anyone who comes to him. If so, then you are in a position to reflect Christ's uniqueness as the Only Begotten Son and his other characteristics as well. All you need to do is agree with God in terms of his goal for your life: to make you like Christ (Rom.8:29), then start incorporating his characteristics into your life. As you do, you will begin to reflect him more and more.

DAY 117
'HE IS THE MESSIAH, THE CHRIST'

QUESTIONS TO THINK ABOUT:

1. What does the title Messiah or Christ mean?
2. How are discipline and suffering good preparations for leadership?
3. How do righteousness, peace and joy reflect the kingdom Jesus will establish on earth?

In Hebrew the word "Messiah" means "the Anointed One," which, in Greek is translated, "Christ." The Lord Jesus Christ was God's fulfillment of many prophecies concerning the coming Messiah who would "put an end to sin and war and usher in universal righteousness and through His death ... make vicarious atonement for the salvation of sinful men" (Bryant, "Messiah," p.358). Jesus of Nazareth claimed to be the Messiah, and his disciples acknowledged that claim.

In Luke 4:18-21, Jesus read the prophetic messianic portion from Isaiah 61:1,2, closed the scroll, and announced to his hearers, "Today this scripture is fulfilled in your hearing." In John 4:25,26, when talking with the Samaritan woman, in response to her belief that the Messiah is coming and will clarify everything, he said, "I who speak to you am he." Both in prayer (Acts 4:26,27) and in preaching (Acts 10:38), the Apostles referred to Christ as the Anointed One, the one whom God anointed, hence, the Messiah. About this they had no doubt.

The Jews were looking for a kingly Messiah who would end sin and war and establish a righteous kingdom, delivering them from the Roman yoke; but they were not prepared to receive a suffering Messiah even though Isaiah and Daniel clearly prophesied his suffering (Isa.53 and Dan.10:26). But just as suffering precedes glory (Rom.8:17), so also suffering precedes authority. 2 Timothy 2:11,12 says, "Here is a trustworthy saying: If we died with him, we will also live with him; if we endure [suffer – KJV], we will also reign with him." Christ learned obedience through what he suffered (Heb.5:8). The maxim still stands that "he who would be a good leader must first be a good follower." That implies obedience, and learning obedience often entails discipline and suffering. Paul encouraged the believers in Lystra, Iconium and Antioch to remain true to the faith even when suffering (Acts 14:22), saying, "We must go through many hardships to enter the kingdom of God."

But Jesus Christ is coming again a second time, and this time he <u>will</u> set up his earthly kingdom and usher in a millennium of righteousness. Peace will cover the earth (Isa.65:25) and the knowledge of God will be everywhere (Heb.8:11). In Romans 14:17,18 we read, "For the kingdom of God is not a matter of eating and drinking, but of righteousness, peace and joy in the Holy Spirit, because anyone who serves Christ in this way is pleasing to God and approved by men." So as our lives reflect these characteristics of the kingdom (righteousness, peace and joy), we reflect Jesus Christ as the Messiah.

Do others see the kingdom in miniature in you?

APPLICATION: Righteousness (right living), peace (contentment) and joy (inner delight) are characteristics of the kingdom of God. With Christ indwelling us, that kingdom is already in us, just not yet in the world. So the characteristics of that kingdom should be continually showing and growing in us. As we obey the Word of God, we will be living right (righteousness), which results in contentment (peace) and an unbounding delight (joy) because of what we see God doing in and through us, and often, in spite of us!

DAY 118
ʿHE IS THE COMMANDER

QUESTIONS TO THINK ABOUT:

1. What is the role of a military commander?
2. What is the role of those under his authority?
3. In what ways are we like a commander in our relationship with other Christians?

In Joshua 5:13-15 we read of Joshua's encounter with the commander of the army of the LORD: "Now when Joshua was near Jericho, he looked up and saw a man standing in front of him with a drawn

Unexpected Transformation / 273

sword in his hand. Joshua went up to him and asked, 'Are you for us or for our enemies?' 'Neither,' he replied, 'but as commander of the army of the LORD I have now come.' Then Joshua fell face down to the ground in reverence, and asked him, 'What message does my Lord have for his servant?' The commander of the LORD'S army replied, 'Take off your sandals, for the place where you are standing is holy.' And Joshua did so." This encounter with Deity in the Old Testament is called a "Theophany," that is, an Old Testament appearance of Christ. Here he appears as the Commander of the LORD'S armies.

We meet him again in this role in Revelation 19:11-14: "I saw heaven standing open and there before me was a white horse, whose rider is called Faithful and True. With justice he judges and makes war. His eyes are like blazing fire, and on his head are many crowns. He has a name written on him that no one but himself knows. He is dressed in a robe dipped in blood, and his name is the Word of God. The armies of heaven were following him, riding on white horses, and dressed in fine linen, white and clean."

A commander is responsible for the safety, training and well-being of his troops. He does not throw them away carelessly on the battlefield, nor does he throw them into combat for which they are not trained, nor send them into combat without proper equipment, clothing or food. Thus the Lord has equipped us for battle (Eph.6:12-18), given us a training manual with an Instructor (2 Tim.3:16,17; Jn.16:7-15), and has promised to be with us always (Matt.28:20b).

Now as others come to know the Lord through our ministries and witness, we likewise are responsible to provide for their training and growth (discipleship) so that they might become effective soldiers in Christ's army. We are responsible to provide them food (1 Cor.3:2), clothing (Rom.13:14), and training for battle (2 Tim.2:1-4). In doing these things, we provide the basis for their safety (spiritual stability). But also we will not jeopardize their safety by throwing them into situations for which they are unprepared and ill equipped. That would be spiritual disaster. For example: when Amber and I first went to the mission field, we were asked to do a job for which we had insufficient training, no interest, and, as we found out very quickly, no ability. We were completely on our own with no provision for counsel or help of any kind. After two-and-a-half years of struggling, floundering and no direction, another person was provided to do that job for which we had been responsible. But by that time, we were wiped out, and came very, very close to adding our names to the roster of mission field casualties.

Thus reflecting our Commander, we must use our troops with care and prayerful planning, considering their gifts and training, in order to accomplish the most with the manpower at our disposal.

How are you "commanding" those under your authority?

APPLICATION: We all disciple someone, for good or ill: parents disciple their children; we disciple our friends; church leaders disciple their congregations; many of us disciple new believers. Before committing them to spiritual ministry, we need to carefully consider their spiritual gifts and training for that particular task. Putting people in ministry positions just to "plug a need" can lead to disaster, discouragement and a loss of personnel to ministry. Let's strive to be the best "commanders" we can be wherever God has placed us.

DAY 119
ᶜHE IS THE COVENANT

QUESTIONS TO THINK ABOUT:

1. What is the purpose of a covenant?
2. If a person makes a covenant with someone, what do you expect from him?

3. If God makes a covenant, what do you expect the outcome to be?

4. If we make a promise to someone, how important is it that we keep it?

In Isaiah 42:6 we read a prophecy concerning Christ: "I, the LORD, have called you in righteousness; I will take hold of your hand I will keep you and will make you to be a covenant for the people and a light for the Gentiles." The word "covenant" here is from the Hebrew word "*bereeth*," "a compact (made by passing between pieces of flesh)" (Strong, Hebrew/Chaldee Dictionary, p.24, no.1285). This was a most solemn and binding of covenants. The only place such a covenant is recorded in Scripture is in Genesis 15:9-21. In verses 9-11 Abraham took a three-year-old heifer, a three-year-old female goat, a three-year-old ram, a turtledove and a pigeon. He cut all but the birds in half and laid out the halves side by side. Abraham fell into a deep sleep (vs.12) and God appeared to him, telling him of the next 400 years of his descendants and again promising him the land of Canaan for his own. Abraham saw a smoking fire pot and a blazing torch, symbolizing God's presence, pass between the halved animals, thus indicating that God only was making this covenant (as Abraham did not pass between the pieces). Thus its fulfillment would rest upon God's faithfulness alone.

Christ became as solemn a covenant to Israel as God's covenant was to Abraham. In Christ all of God's promises to Israel are fulfilled. The only difference was that Abraham accepted God's covenant; Israel flatly rejected it. All the blessings of God for Israel were tied in with Christ, every provision for their spiritual and physical well-being and their national sovereignty. Christ was the meeting place for Israel and their God, binding the two together. It was all of God's doing and none of Israel's. God promised because he chose to promise; therefore his promise, his covenant <u>will</u> be fulfilled. Israel will eventually enjoy that fulfillment in national salvation (Rom.11:25,26 with

Isa.44:21-23) and sovereignty (Rom.11:12,15 with Isa.60), but only when they recognize and accept Jesus Christ as their Messiah and Redeemer. Then they will know him as their Covenant.

All who place themselves under God's Covenant, Jesus Christ, are never disappointed: God <u>always</u> keeps his promises. As Christians we reflect Jesus Christ as the Covenant as we fulfill our promises. To those of us who are married, have we forgotten our marriage vows? Many have. These vows were a sacred promise, a holy covenant before God and each other, that, forsaking all others, we would be faithful and true in this marriage relationship to our partner. Have you promised your wife, or your child that you would do something with or for them? Reflecting Christ as God's Covenant to us, you will keep your promise. Did you make a promise to God at one time regarding your life and service for him? Perhaps that promise, that covenant, needs renewing so that you can begin fulfilling it where you are right now.

God made a covenant with Israel; Christ was the embodiment and fulfillment of that covenant.

God keeps his word. Are you keeping yours?

APPLICATION: Think back about all the promises you have made. Have you kept them? Some broken promises are long past and cannot be fulfilled now. But others could be if you choose to do it. As a Christian, you are obligated to fulfill the promises, the commitments that you have made.

As a general rule, it would be good for all of us to follow Ecclesiastes 5:5 which says, "It is better not to vow than to make a vow and not fulfill it." That is, don't make a promise without thinking about its ramifications first; our credibility is at stake if we don't keep our word, and, as Christians, we should be as good as our word! God is.

DAY 120
ᶜHE IS DAVID

◆

QUESTIONS TO THINK ABOUT:

1. What are the similarities between David and Christ?
2. How did they both please God?
3. How is it possible for us to please God?
4. We don't do in order to please him; we do because we want to please him. What is the difference between these two "doings"?

In prophetic scripture, Christ is called "David" which embodies both his being a descendant from David (see DAY 49 – HE IS THE KING [over Sorrow]) and a king like David (Isa.55:3,4; Jer.30:9; Hos.3:5). In these passages, he is called, "David, the King, a Witness, Leader and Commander, My Servant and Shepherd." All that David was to Israel, Christ will be and more. David was a man after God's own heart; so was Christ. Both delighted to do God's will (Ps.40:7,8; Heb.10:7). And God testified to his pleasure in both (Acts 13:22; Mk.1:11).

Is our present way of life pleasing to God? Does he take pleasure in our fellowship with him? Do we delight to be in his presence and do his will even as David and the Lord did?

In all that we do, we should strive to please God. In 1 Thessalonians 4:1 Paul says, "Finally, brothers, we instructed you how to live in order to please God, as in fact you are living. Now we ask you and urge you in the Lord Jesus to do this more and more." In John 8:29 Jesus said, "The one who sent me is with me; he has not left me alone, for I always do what pleases him." And we find an interesting statement in Hebrews 11:5 regarding Enoch: "By faith Enoch was taken from this life, so that he did not experience death; he could not be found because God had taken him away. For before he was taken, he was commended as one who pleased God." Paul prayed for the Colossian Christians that they might "live a life worthy of the Lord and may please him in every way" (Col.1:10). Again in 1 Thessalonians 2:4 Paul says, "We are not trying to please men but God, who tests our hearts."

And he responds to those who try to please him. In Isaiah 56:4-7 we read, "For this is what the LORD says: 'To the eunuchs who keep my Sabbaths, who choose what pleases me and hold fast to my covenant – to them I will give within my temple and its walls a memorial and a name better than sons and daughters; I will give them an everlasting name that will not be cut off. And foreigners who bind themselves to the LORD to serve him, to love the name of the LORD, and to worship him, all who keep the Sabbath without desecrating it and who hold fast to my covenant – these I will bring to my holy mountain and give them joy in my house of prayer. Their burnt offerings and sacrifices will be accepted on my altar; for my house will be called a house of prayer for all nations.'"

Are you consciously trying to please God each day?

APPLICATION: The bottom line of our desire to please God is found in 1 John 4:19, "We love Him because He first loved us" (NKJV). We don't do to please him in order to gain his love; we do because we want to please him in response to his love. There's a difference. Tomorrow we will look at what the Scriptures say about what pleases him.

DAY 121
ᶜHE IS DAVID, concl.

◆

QUESTIONS TO THINK ABOUT:

1. What specific things do you think pleases God in our lives?
2. If God wanted us to please him, but left us in the dark about it, how would that make you feel?
3. So how can we really know what pleases him?

God's Word clearly states what things in our lives are pleasing to him and elicit a positive response from his heart toward us. (All italics mine in the following verses.)

FAITH (Hebrews 11:6) "And without faith it is impossible to please God, because anyone who comes to him *must believe* that he exists and that he rewards those who earnestly seek him."

OBEDIENCE To the Lord. (1 Jn.3:21,22) "Dear friends, if our hearts do not condemn us, we have confidence before God and receive from him anything we ask, *because we obey his commands* and do what pleases him."

To one's parents. (Col.3:20) "Children, *obey your parents* in everything, for this pleases the Lord."

GENEROSITY (Phil.4:18) "I have received full payment and even more; I am amply supplied, now that I have received from Epaphroditus *the gifts you sent*. They are a fragrant offering, an acceptable sacrifice, pleasing to God."

DOING GOOD (Heb.13:16) "And do not forget *to do good and to share* with others, for with such sacrifices God is pleased."

REPENTANCE (Ps.51:17,19) "The sacrifices of God are a broken spirit: *a broken and a contrite heart*, O God, you will not despise… . Then there will be righteous sacrifices, whole burnt offerings to delight you; then bulls will be offered on your altar."

PRAISE and THANKSGIVING (Ps.69:30-32) "*I will praise the name of God with a song, and will magnify him with thanksgiving.* This also shall please the LORD better than an ox or bullock that has horns and hooves. The humble shall see this, and be glad: and your heart shall live that seek God."

SUBMISSION *to what God wants to do in our lives.* (Heb. 13:20,21) "… May … God … equip you with everything good for doing his will, and may he work in us what is pleasing to him, through Jesus Christ, to whom be glory for ever and ever. Amen."

And if there is any doubt about what we should do to please him, we read in Philippians 2:13, "For it is God who works in you to will and do what pleases him." He will show us and give us the will and the ability to do it!

Can God say of us as he did of David and of Christ, "He is a man, she is a woman after my own heart; for he/she always does what pleases me"?

APPLICATION: The only thing I can suggest is that you go over the above-mentioned items that please God and make a personal inventory of each one. Wherever you are lacking, plan steps to take to implement that item into your life. When you know that you are pleasing someone, there is also that sense of pleasure in your own heart which, humanly speaking, makes it all worthwhile.

DAY 122
ᵇHE IS THE DAYSPRING (SUNRISE)

◆

QUESTIONS TO THINK ABOUT:

1. When you see a sunrise, and often its rose-pink reflections in the clouds, how do you feel?
2. What is the significance of the sunrise?
3. If it is a cloudy day, and you don't see the sun rise, how does that affect how you feel?
4. What is the importance of light?

In Luke 1:67-79 Zacharias, filled with the Holy Spirit, prophesied of Israel's deliverance by the Lord. In verses 78,79 he calls Christ, "the rising sun": "… because of the tender mercy of our God, by which the rising sun will come to us from heaven to shine on those living in darkness and in the shadow of death, to guide our feet into the path of peace."

As the sun gives rise to a new day, so the coming of Christ signified the coming of a new relationship between God and man. The entrance of a Christian into any place in society, signifies the coming of a new relationship for those around him and the possibility of their restoration to God.

The sun sheds light on the earth so that men may see where they are going and what they are doing. It delivers us from the bondage and limitations of darkness. Yet some choose to cover their eyes so as not to see the sun! As John says in John 3:19, "This is the verdict: Light has come into the world, but men loved darkness instead of light because their deeds were evil." Christ came to deliver us from the Kingdom of Darkness to the Kingdom of Light (cf. Col. 1:13). As he shines in our hearts, we begin to "see" clearly and understand the true nature of things around us, the true nature of sin, and the truth as it is contained in Christ himself. Thus we begin to understand spiritual truth and can begin sharing it with others to deliver them too.

Sunshine is essential for growth and the sustaining of life. Without sunlight, the photosynthesis that takes place in plant life would cease thus causing the plants to die. It would also mean that the producing of oxygen through photosynthesis would cease, and thus bring about the death of every living thing on earth. As the Lord, through his Holy Spirit, teaches us all things (Jn.16:13), we will grow and be sustained. As we teach others the truths of God's Word, they too will grow and be sustained.

The sun is also a source of limitless energy. Man is just now learning how to begin harnessing that energy. The only limitation is with the type of receptor used. As the receptors (like solar panels) improve, the amount of useful energy from the sun will increase. Jesus Christ is our source of limitless energy. The "receptors" available are the only problem in the release of that energy. The more we become like him and yield to him, the greater will be the flow of his power through us. He has given us his Spirit to equip us and energize us for the work to be done.

What kind of "solar panel" are you? Is your energy capacity growing? It will as you allow yourself to be "remodeled" and "upgraded" by the renewing of your mind and heart (Rom.12:2); for that very power God used to raise Jesus Christ from the dead is available to you as you submit to him and allow him to work through you (see Eph.1:18-20).

APPLICATION: As you spend time in the Word and in prayer, they will gradually renew your mind (i.e. give you the mind of the Lord) so that what you think and do will more and more radiate the Light that is in you. That Light will either repel or draw others from or to the Lord (cf. Matt.5:16 and Jn.3:19). Whichever, it is up to us to "shine."

DAY 123
ᵇHE IS THE DAY STAR

◆

QUESTIONS TO THINK ABOUT:

1. When you see the day star (Venus) before the dawn, what are you thinking?
2. What does it "promise" to us?
3. In what way(s) can Christ be likened to the day star?

In 2 Peter 1:19 we read, "And we have the word of the prophets made more certain, and you will do well to pay attention to it, as to a light shining in a dark place, until the day dawns and the morning star rises in your hearts."

For a time the Jews had the light of the words of the prophets to dispel the darkness around them until the true Light should come. And to that feeble light they did well to give heed. But all this presaged a new day in which the morning star would rise to shine in their hearts.

In Numbers 24:17, Balaam prophesies about the star that will come out of Jacob, a scepter that will rise out of Israel. This parallelism indicates the word "star" to refer to a Ruler who was coming. Its first application was probably to David; but its larger application was prophetic in its reference to Christ. Again in Revelation 22:16b, Jesus himself says: "I am the Root and the Offspring of David, and the bright Morning Star."

The word "day star" comes from the Greek *phosphorus* meaning "light bearing," and is used of the morning star as the "light bringer," the beginning of a bright, new day. Prophetically, it is looking forward to Christ's kingdom and his physical presence on earth. But in the present, it is "the arising of the light of Christ as the personal fulfillment, in the hearts of believers, of the prophetic Scriptures concerning His coming to receive them to Himself" (Vine, I, p.272). And though we have more light now than Israel had then, even yet what we have in Christ is but a feeble reflection compared with that which is coming. As Paul writes in 1 Corinthians 13:12, "Now we see but a poor reflection; then we shall see face to face. Now I know in part; then I shall know fully, even as I am fully known."

Light reveals things, and as Christ, through his Spirit, shines in our hearts, what is it that he reveals to us? He told his disciples that the Holy Spirit would guide them into all truth (Jn.16:13); in reference to God he said, "Your Word is truth" (Jn.17:17); in reference to himself, he said, "I am the truth" (Jn.14:6). As the Lord shines in our hearts, we will learn and come to know the truth. As we have opportunity to teach others from the Word, the Lord will also use us, by his Spirit, to reveal truth to them, to show God to them, that they might know him better and understand what he is doing in his eternal plans. The more we learn to know him, the brighter shines the light of the Morning Star in our hearts.

How bright is that light shining in your heart?

APPLICATON: The day star is actually a planet (Venus) that has no light of its own, but reflects the light of the rising sun. Moses' face shown as a result of spending time in the Lord's presence (Ex.33:11; 34:29, 30). The people saw a reflection of God's glory in his face. As we spend time with the Lord, there will be a "light" about us that others will see and take note of. Someone once commented to my mother, "You're a Christian, aren't you? I can tell by the glow in your face." She spends much time with the Lord.

DAY 124
ᵇHE IS THE DEW

◆

QUESTIONS TO THINK ABOUT:

1. What is dew and what is its purpose?
2. How can Christ be said to be the "dew" in our lives?
3. How can we be the "dew" in the lives of others?

In Hosea 14:5,6 the LORD says, "I will be like the dew to Israel; he will blossom like a lily. Like a cedar of Lebanon he will send down his roots; his young shoots will grow. His splendor will be like an olive tree, his fragrance like a cedar of Lebanon."

To Israel the dew was extremely important. From April to October there is no rain. Were it not for the exceptionally heavy dews characteristic of the area, they would have no summer crops, and would suffer hunger. But the dew is so heavy, that whatever moisture is lost during the day is recouped at night. This is true in the desert places as well. So there is plenty of water available for the growth indicated in Hosea 14:5,6. Thus arose the symbolic meaning of dew in Israel as a refreshing, reinvigorating picture of prosperity (cf. ISBE, Vol.II, DEW, pp.840, 841).

That Christ is the fulfillment of this prophecy in Hosea is seen in Acts 3:19,20 where Peter says: "Repent, then, and turn to God, so that your sins may be wiped out, that times of refreshing may come from the Lord, and that he may send the Christ [Messiah], who has been appointed for you – even Jesus."

There are two things tremendously refreshing: one is the sense of being clean after the burden and guilt of sin have been removed; the other is the encouragement gained from being with people who love the Lord. Through Jesus Christ, the burden and guilt of sin have been removed forever. Thus in him, we have a fresh, new

286 / *Unexpected Transformation*

beginning. "The old has gone, the new has come!" (2 Cor.5:17b). Then there are those Christians who love to talk about the Lord and share with others what he is doing. After such times together, I have felt refreshed and encouraged.

In our ministry in Manokwari (Papua, Indonesia), I had two to three weeks of intense effort to get visa-related papers done and handed in to the government. One Wednesday I was particularly feeling under the pressure of the work. That evening was prayer meeting at the church we attended. Our national brethren there really loved the Lord. As we shared and prayed together, I felt strengthened and release from the pressure I was under. As we left for home, I felt refreshed and ready to "go" again the next day.

Now we've also been with Christians who left us feeling burdened and even discouraged as their pessimism and situation-oriented outlook turned our eyes away from the Lord and onto the problems around us. We each need a holy optimism, rooted in the eternal sovereignty and love of God, full of confidence that "there is nothing my God cannot do!" This knowledge of God will be refreshing to us and will spill over to others, refreshing and encouraging them.

Are you a refreshing dew to fellow believers or a dry wind?

APPLICATION: Dew is the condensation of water vapor already in the air. It can be sensed, but cannot be seen apart from its appearance on the ground and other things. The more we are in the Word of God, and the Word of God in us, the more "water vapor" is available to fall on the people around us as we share that Word with them; and they will be refreshed and encouraged.

DAY 125
ᶜHE IS THE DISAPPOINTED ONE

◆

QUESTIONS TO THINK ABOUT:

1. What is disappointment?
2. What is the effect of disappointment on how you feel about things? about God?
3. What are some of the things that disappoint you?
4. In what ways do you think we disappoint the Lord?

Disappointment arises when our hopes or desires remain unfulfilled. Our Lord Jesus experienced disappointment many times as those around him and closest to him failed to measure up to the faith they could have had and the relationship with God that was possible.

In John 6 Jesus talked to the people about "eating" his flesh and "drinking" his blood, symbolic of their relationship with him (vs.63), but taken literally and offensively by the majority of his listeners. Verse 66 says that "many of his disciples turned back and no longer followed him." Though this did not surprise him, it hurt him deeply and in disappointment he turned to the twelve and said, "Do you want to leave me too?" (vs.67).

Another disappointment of Christ occurs in John 14:7-11 when it is obvious that his disciples still did not understand who he was: "'If you really knew me, you would know my Father as well. From now on, you do know him and have seen him.' Philip said, 'Lord, show us the Father and that will be enough for us.' Jesus answered, 'Don't you know me, Philip, even after I have been among you such a long time? Anyone who has seen me has seen the Father. How can you say, "Show us the Father"? Don't you believe that I am in the Father, and that the Father is in me? The words I say to you are not just my own. Rather it is the Father, living in me, who is doing his work. Believe me when I say that I am in the Father and the Father is in me; or at least believe on the evidence of the miracles themselves.'" He was disappointed in their lack of understanding of obvious truth.

Lack of faith also brings disappointment to the Lord. When the disciples were powerless to heal the epileptic boy, and he was brought to Jesus, his disappointment was obvious. Matthew 17:17: "O unbelieving and perverse generation," Jesus replied, "how long shall I stay with you? How long shall I put up with you? Bring the boy here to me." When the disciples asked him why they could not drive out the demon that was causing the boy's condition, "He replied, 'Because you have so little faith'" (Matt.17:20).

As we become concerned about the spiritual growth and welfare of other Christians, we open ourselves up to disappointment as they fail to respond to the truths of God's Word. Perhaps they are sidetracked, preoccupied, or just not interested. Whatever the reason, they do not respond and we become disappointed – disappointed basically because we realize, up to a point, what they are missing out on and how they are robbing themselves of spiritual blessing and reward.

One real disappointment to us was the national church in Irian Jaya. The people in general, even after some teaching, refused to support their pastors, refused to give a tithe to the Lord for his work. Realizing the hardship that the national pastors and their families were placed in, plus the resultant lack of blessing in the lives of the church members, we were very disappointed.

How much is the Lord disappointed in us as <u>we</u> fail to respond to obvious truth, display a lack of faith, or find ourselves too busy for him?

APPLICATION: We will always be disappointed, let down, by others. But what we have to remember is that they are accountable to God, not us, for their actions. We need to handle disappointments the way the Lord did, and look at them as another lesson from God's hand to make us like Christ. In the meantime, we must do our best not to be a disappointment to others (or God), keeping our word/promises, fulfilling our responsibilities and maintaining our fellowship with God and his people.

DAY 126
bHE IS THE DOOR (GATE) OF THE SHEEP

QUESTIONS TO THINK ABOUT:

1. What is the function of a door?
2. Why is the quality of a door important?
3. How can we become a "door" for other believers?

In describing one aspect of his relationship to his people, Jesus used the picture of a shepherd with his sheep (Jn.10:1-30). In verses 7-9 he describes himself as the gate for the sheep.

The picture Christ evokes here is that of a sheepfold out on the hills, usually an enclosure of rock and bramble topped with thorns. There was no door in the opening, so the shepherd himself would lie down and sleep across the doorway. Nothing could enter or leave the fold without him knowing it. Thus the shepherd was a protection for the sheep. So Christ is our protector. Nothing can get to us except through him. We are secure in him; no one can take us from his hand while he "guards the doorway." He says in John 10:27,28, "My sheep listen to my voice; I know them, and they follow me. I give them eternal life, and they shall never perish; no one can snatch them out of my Father's hand."

Christians who are more mature should be able to offer protection to those who are less mature. I can remember as a boy looking at the older Christians in my home church and gaining a sense of security from them. They loved the Lord and they loved me, and I saw God's faithfulness in their lives. As we share with younger Christians, counsel them, encourage them, stand with them in their trials, we become a "door of protection" to them, and they will be safe.

In John 10:9 Jesus adds, "[They] will come in and go out, and find pasture." In the security of his protection, we have freedom to go in and out. This phrase was familiar to his listeners as it constituted one of the blessings given to Israel if they obeyed the LORD (cf. Deut.28:1,2,6). What is this freedom of which he speaks? Freedom from bondage to sin, freedom from false folds (sects and heresies), freedom from the world's system, freedom to graze contentedly from the Word of God, freedom to enjoy God's presence, freedom to follow him wherever he leads, and freedom to have our needs met.

Mature believers become the "door" of the fold for less mature believers, defending them from attacks from without and keeping them in the fold. Faithful teaching and exemplifying the Word will help keep them from sin and false belief; counsel and discipline will bring them back into the fold if they have "run outside."

A dear pastor family to us had inadvertently become entangled in the occult and the pastor was suffering terribly. His family was also being tormented and harassed. As we shared material with them on the freedom we have in Christ and the victory that is ours through our position in him, this family gained freedom and release from the demons. Through our efforts, encouragements, counsel and prayers, we became as a "door" of protection for them. They were very encouraged and relieved and now are actively helping others who are suffering from the same bondage they had been in. The sense of security that younger Christians feel in the presence of older Christians will encourage them to remain faithful to the Lord and grow in their faith in him. Thus we become "doors of protection" for our fellow believers.

Are you a door for others, or still needing a door?

APPLICATION: Becoming a "door" for another believer implies spiritual maturity on our part. As we grow in the Lord and experience his goodness, we will have that to share with others, both to encourage them and protect them in their Christian walk. Make it a point to keep growing through personal or formal Bible study, regular church attendance, or other venues that will encourage spiritual growth.

DAY 127
"HE IS OUR RANSOM, OUR SACRIFICE

QUESTIONS TO THINK ABOUT:

1. What does it mean to ransom something?
2. Why would you want to ransom anything?
3. Why would God want to ransom us?
4. How could we sacrifice ourselves for someone else?
5. What does it mean to be a "living sacrifice" to God?

Four verses of Scripture state these characteristics of Christ. "So Christ was sacrificed once to take away the sins of many people" (Heb.9:28); "He ... died as a ransom to set them free from the sins committed under the first covenant" (Heb.9:15); "The Son of Man ... [came] to give his life as a ransom for many" (Matt.20:28); "Who gave himself as a ransom for all men" (1 Tim.2:6).

The Greek word for ransom, *lutron*, literally means "a means of loosing." When someone is kidnapped, a sum of money or some other act is demanded as a ransom for the one being held. Once the ransom demands are met, the person is usually set free. In this way, Christ has set us free from the penalty of sin. To paraphrase from Vine, he paid the price for us "in our place" (Gk. *antilutron*) so that we could be loosed from eternal death. In 1 Timothy 2:6 *huper lutron* is used, meaning "on behalf of" all men, indicating that the ransom was provisionally universal; Christ died for all men, yet his ransom was effectual only for those who accepted God's conditions (Vine, III, pp.247,248).

As Christ presented himself to God as a sacrifice for sin, so we must present ourselves to him "as living sacrifices, holy and pleasing to God – which is your spiritual service" (Rom.12:1). The attitude behind this is that of willing, unselfish service for the Lord, even to the point of death. This is why Paul writes in Philippians 2:3-8, "Do nothing out of selfish ambition or vain conceit, but in humility consider others better than yourselves. Each of you should look not only to your own interests, but also to the interests of others. Your attitude should be the same as that of Christ Jesus: who being in very nature God, did not consider equality with God something to be grasped, but made himself nothing, taking the very nature of a servant, being made in human likeness. And being found in appearance as a man, he humbled himself and became obedient to death – even death on a cross!"

As a ransom for others, we sacrifice our time, efforts, our very lives in order to free them from captivity to sin by bringing them to Christ. I read of several Ayore (ay-O-ray) believers in Paraguay who felt burdened to reach an isolated and fierce part of their tribe. They knew it was dangerous, but they just had to try to share with them what they had found in Christ. Five of the party were killed, being suspected of treachery, before the isolated people realized they really came in peace. Filled with remorse for what they had done, they welcomed the rest of the party and listened to the Gospel (Tom Taylor, "The Martyrs of Campo Loro," <u>Moody Monthly</u>, April 1988: 14-22).

Fellow believers are often taken captive by sin and need deliverance. We must be willing to sacrifice our time, efforts, and our very lives in order to "ransom" them from that sin, so that they can come to maturity in Christ. Paul writes of this in Colossians 1:28,29, saying, "We proclaim him, counseling and teaching everyone with all wisdom, so that we may present everyone perfect in Christ. To this end I labor, struggling with all the energy he so powerfully works in me."

Are you willing to sacrifice yourself in order to ransom/deliver others from sin?

APPLICATION: Jesus was willing to sacrifice his life on our behalf in order to ransom us from the penalty of sin and deliver us from the power of sin. We tend to value our lives too highly, giving priority to what we want rather than what God wants. We tend to fear what we might lose if we "give everything" to him. But what shall we as Christians profit if we "gain the whole world" and lose the ministry God intended us to have? We need to confess our wrong priorities and ask the Lord to "make us willing" to do his will whatever the cost. What we have here is temporary; what we have in heaven is eternal. Which would you rather have?

DAY 128
ᶜHE IS THE SIN-BEARER

QUESTIONS TO THINK ABOUT:

1. What did it cost Christ to bear our sins on the Cross?
2. In what way can we bear the sins of others?

3. In what way could we bear the sins of our nation?

When Christ hung on the cross, he bore our sins upon himself and became sin for us so that we could be made righteous. "So Christ was sacrificed once to take away the sins of many people; and he will appear a second time, not to bear sin, but to bring salvation to those who are waiting for him" (Heb.9:28). Again, in 2 Corinthians 5:21, "God made him [Christ] who had no sin to be sin for us, so that in him we might become the righteousness of God." "The Lord has laid on him the iniquity of us all" (Isa.53:6b); "For he bore the sin of many and made intercession for the transgressors" (Isa.53:12b).

Once a year, before entering the Most Holy Place in the Tabernacle to make atonement for the sins of the people, Aaron had to take two male goats for a sin offering (Lev.16:5), one to be used as a sacrifice, the other to be used for making atonement by sending it into the desert as a scapegoat (vs.7-10). The blood of the first goat he sprinkled on and in front of the mercy seat or atonement cover (vs.15), making atonement for the sins "the people had committed in ignorance" (Heb.9:7). Then we read in verses 20-22: "When Aaron has finished making atonement for the Most Holy Place, the Tent of Meeting and the altar, he shall bring forward the live goat. He is to lay both hands on the head of the live goat and confess over it all the wickedness and rebellion of the Israelites – all their sins – and put them on the goat's head. He shall send the goat away into the desert in the care of a man appointed for the task. The goat will carry on itself all their sins to a solitary place; and the man shall release it in the desert."

As the blood of the sacrificial goat "covered" the sins of the people, and the scapegoat "carried" those sins far from them, even so the blood of Christ provides forgiveness for our sins which he then carries away from us forever, never to be mentioned or remembered again (Heb.10:17).

Nehemiah and Daniel illustrate best how we can reflect Christ as the Sin-Bearer. When Nehemiah heard how Jerusalem was still in ruins, he sat down and cried. He mourned, fasted and prayed to God, and took upon himself the confession of the sins of Israel, saying, "I confess the sins we Israelites, including myself and my father's house, have committed against you. We have acted very wickedly toward you. We have not obeyed the commands, decrees and laws you gave your servant Moses" (Neh.1:6b,7). Yet Nehemiah himself delighted in revering (fearing) the name of the Lord (vs.11). Nevertheless, he willingly identified himself with the sins of Israel, "taking" them upon himself as if he himself had committed them.

So with Daniel. Understanding that the 70 year captivity was at an end, he prayed for the promised restoration of Israel, "pleading with God in prayer and petition, in fasting, and in sackcloth and ashes" (Dan.9:2,3). He said, "We have sinned and done wrong. We have been wicked and have rebelled; we have turned away from your commands and laws. We have not listened to your servants the prophets, who spoke in your name to our kings, our princes, and our fathers, and to all the people of the land… . We are covered with shame … because of our unfaithfulness to you" (vs.5-7), and so on. Daniel was probably the most righteous, God-fearing man among the Jews. Yet he humbled himself and confessed the sins of the nation as his own. He was willing to assume the fault of others.

Are we this concerned for our own nation?

APPLICATION: Consider God's promise to us in 2 Chronicles 7:14 where he says, "If my people who are called by my name will humble themselves, and pray and seek my face, and turn from their wicked ways, then I will hear from heaven, and will forgive their sin and heal their land." The first interpretation is to Israel as God's chosen people. But I believe, in principle, that this promise could apply to us as well, for as the Bride of Christ, we are also his chosen people – different from Israel, to be sure, but chosen to himself nonetheless. The Lord honors repentance no matter where it occurs geographically; and though the blessings might be different than what Israel would have experienced, he will still bless – and heal us and our land. What have we got to lose?

DAY 129
bHE IS OUR CONFESSOR

◆

QUESTIONS TO THINK ABOUT:

1. What does it mean to confess something?
2. What are the two meanings of the word "confess"?
3. What does it mean to be a confessor?

There are two ways in which Jesus Christ acts as our Confessor. The first is found in Matthew 10:32 where he says, "Whoever acknowledges (confesses) me before men, I will also acknowledge (confess) him before my Father in heaven." In Luke 12:8 he adds another dimension: "I tell you, whoever acknowledges me before men, the Son of Man will also acknowledge him before the angels of God."

As we confess his name here on earth, he, as our High Priest, is confessing ours in heaven, interceding for us (Heb.7:25). There will also come that day when we will appear physically in God's presence. I have no doubt that at that time we will hear Christ acknowledge us by name before the Father, the angels, and the host of saints, welcoming us into our heavenly home.

How do we confess Christ's name? Through our verbal witness to others, through sharing him with other Christians, and through living consistently and obediently according to the Word of God.

The second way in which Christ is our Confessor has to do with sin. We read in 1 John 1:9, "If we confess our sins, he is faithful and just and will forgive us our sins and purify us from all unrighteousness." We find Christ forgiving sins directly all during his ministry: for example, the paralytic (Matt.9:2-8), the woman taken in adultery (Jn.8:9-11), and the woman who anointed his feet with perfume (Lk.7:47-49).

He also gave his disciples the authority to forgive or retain sins (Jn.20:23) promising that whatever they "bind on earth will be bound in heaven, and whatever [they] loose on earth will be loosed in heaven" (Matt.18:18). The Lord honors the forgiveness we extend to others, and also honors the withholding of forgiveness when that is necessary (as in certain cases of church discipline). It is in line with this authority, then, that James encourages believers to "confess [their] sins to each other and pray for each other so that [they] might be healed" (Jas.5:16). Here, however, forgiveness is not so much the question as it is confession and healing (restoration). "Confession is good for the soul." We all need someone in whom we can confide and to whom we can bear our heart. This presupposes trust and unbetrayed confidences. God, for instance, doesn't broadcast to the world what we tell him in secret. Neither should we broadcast what others tell us in confidence. We must listen carefully to those who confide in us, confessing their sins, by supporting them in their struggle, praying for them, counseling them, and encouraging them in their Christian life. This is for the health of the Church and the purity of the saints.

Are you the kind of "priest" to whom confession can be made?

APPLICATION: Think for a moment about the qualifications of a confessor: empathetic, non-judgmental, a good listener, able to apply the Word to any given situation, trustworthy, able to keep confidences. Come to think of it, these also are characteristics of Christ that we should be reflecting in our daily lives. The more you work on these characteristics, the more you will be able to minister to your fellow believers in their time of need.

DAY 130
'HE IS THE BEGINNING OF GOD'S CREATION, THE CREATOR

QUESTIONS TO THINK ABOUT:

1. Some religions teach that as the "beginning of God's creation," Christ was the first being created. How do you respond to this teaching?
2. What does it mean to create something, or create a new way of doing something?
3. Why do we want to create anything anyway?

Revelation 3:14 (KJV) says that Christ is "the beginning of the creation of God." In the NIV it says that he is "the ruler of God's creation." According to Vine (Vine,. I, pp.110-111, "Begin, Beginning, Beginner," B. Noun), the three meanings are tied together in the same word *arche* which means "a beginning." "The root, *arch–* primarily indicated what was of worth. Hence the verb *archō* meant 'to be first,' and *archōn* denoted a ruler. So also arose the idea of a beginning, the origin, the active cause, whether a person or a thing, e.g. Col.1:18." The same word *arche* is used and transated "beginning" in the NIV.

We have already considered Christ as the Ruler (see DAY 36 – HE IS THE KING [Governor/Ruler]). Now we should consider him as Creator, the beginning or cause of God's creation. We read in Heb.1:10, "In the beginning, O Lord, you laid the foundations of the earth, and the heavens are the work of your hands." In John 1:3 we

Unexpected Transformation / 299

read that "through him all things were made; without him nothing was made that has been made." It was the hand of Jesus Christ that brought everything into being. Even as a masterpiece reflects something of the glory of the artist, so the Lord's creation reflects his glory. "The heavens declare the glory of God; the skies proclaim the work of his hands. Day after day they pour forth speech; night after night they display knowledge. There is no speech or language where their voice is not heard" (Ps.19:1-3).

And in Romans 1:19,20 we read of those who suppressed the truth by their wickedness being subject to God's wrath "since what may be known about God is plain to them, because God has made it plain to them. For since the creation of the world God's invisible qualities – his eternal power and divine nature – have been clearly seen, being understood from what has been made, so that men are without excuse."

God has also given us the ability to be creative which reflects something of the glory we have as people created in his image. Though we cannot create something out of nothing, there are always new ways to present old truths, new inventions to help perform daily tasks, new forms of expression never tried before. In the marriage realm, married couples can "create" new life. In the economic realm we can create new businesses, new services to others, new programs for the benefit of many. There is no end to man's capability of creativity. The Lord indicated as much in Genesis 11:6 where he "examines" the situation at the Tower of Babel and declares: "If as one people speaking the same language they have begun to do this, then nothing they plan to do will be impossible for them."

As our glory shines ever more clearly through our creativity, men will be able to see God's glory more clearly and honor him through us. As Christ said in Matthew 5:16, "… Let your light shine before men, that they may see your good deeds and praise your Father in heaven." This will happen as we use our creativity for his purposes and glory.

What new, creative thing have you come up with lately?

APPLICATION: We can exercise creativity anywhere and in anything we do. Could even the simplest chore be done more efficiently? We had a house helper in Papua who was very creative in how she cleaned the floors: as she swept the floor, she used a damp rag under her feet to take up the dust or dirt left behind! So, basically, she had to go over the floors only once, not twice. And, amazingly, it worked!

DAY 131
'HE IS THE BEGINNING OF GOD'S CREATION, THE CREATOR, concl.

QUESTIONS TO THINK ABOUT:

1. When we say, "Look what *I* did!" what are we actually saying?
2. What is the role of the Holy Spirit in our creativity?
3. What should be our attitude in anything we do?

Something needs to be said regarding how Christ created the heavens and the earth. We read in Genesis 1:2 that the Spirit of God also was active in creation: "Now the earth was formless and empty, darkness was over the surface of the deep, and the Spirit of God was hovering over the waters." Elihu declared, "The Spirit of God has made me; the breath of the Almighty gives me life" (Job 33:4). Christ created all things through the power of the Holy Spirit. In laying the foundation for the new creation at Calvary, he did so by the power of the Spirit. In Hebrews 9:14 we read that Christ offered himself to God through the Spirit, and in Romans 1:4 that he was raised from the dead by the Spirit. Because of the resurrection, we who believe in Jesus have become new creations: "Therefore, if anyone is in Christ, he is a new creation; old things have passed away; behold, all things have become new" (2 Cor.5:17 – NKJV).

Even as Christ created everything through the power of the Spirit, so we can only be creative through the power of the Spirit. In and of ourselves, we have no power to do anything. Jesus reminds us in John 15:5 that without him, we can do nothing. Zechariah declares: "This is the word of the LORD to Zerubbabel: 'Not by might nor by power, but by my Spirit,' says the LORD Almighty" (Zech.4:6). Thus in everything we do, we need to develop a conscious awareness that <u>we can only be creative as the Holy Spirit enables us</u>.

There is a real thrill in facing a job that you don't know how to do, praying about it, and suddenly "thinking" [creativity] of how it can be done, doing it that way, and finding out that it works! all the while knowing that on your own you never would have thought of doing it that way. I am not a carpenter, and yet as I have faced carpentry-type projects that have had to be done, and consciously sought the Lord's help in them, I found myself able to envision what needed to be done and able to do it. Then I could look at the final results and say, "Thank you, Lord. We did this together. It's not a finished masterpiece, to be sure, but it's functional and quite adequate for what I need." In this way I've made a typing table with a drawer, a tool cabinet out of scrap wood, a drum rack for storing packing drums, book shelves, a bucket shower frame, screen frames, a work bench, and picture frames.

There is joy and a sense of accomplishment in creativity. In Job 38:4-7 God asks Job where he was when he created the world, "while the morning stars sang together and the angels shouted for joy." In Genesis 1:31 we read, "God saw all that he had made, and it was very good." He was satisfied. And so it is with us. We have joy and a sense of accomplishment in our creativity, and a special blessing in knowing that we did it with God's help – we did it together with him.

Are you and the Lord in partnership in all that you do?

APPLICATION: What we need to remember is that without Jesus, we can't do anything; but with him, we can do everything he requests of us. We need to develop this mindset consciously and purposely in all that we do. I suspect that in the awareness that he is our partner, we will be more careful in how we do things since a sloppy job will reflect badly on him too!

DAY 132
ᵇHE IS THE SUSTAINING ONE

QUESTIONS TO THINK ABOUT:

1. How does Christ sustain/maintain what he has made?
2. Why is it important to maintain what we have made or what we possess?
3. How does this principle apply to us in the Church? What do we have to "maintain" in it?
4. How does this principle apply to our care of the environment?

The Lord not only created all things, but he sustains what he has created. We read in Col.1:16b,17, "All things were created by him and for him. He is before all things, and in him all things hold together." Again in Hebrews 1:2,3, God "has spoken to us by his Son ... through whom he made the universe. The Son is ... sustaining all things by his powerful word." His word is the "glue" holding the universe together, keeping every atom, every molecule in its proper place. There is coming a time when the entire universe will become "unglued," and completely disintegrate. "The heavens will disappear with a roar* (see ***NOTE** below); the elements will be destroyed by fire, and the earth and everything in it will be burned

Unexpected Transformation / 303

up" (2 Pet.3:10 – underlining mine). John says, "Then I saw a new heaven and a new earth, for the first heaven and the first earth had passed away, and there was no longer any sea" (Rev.21:1).

There are two ways in which we reflect Christ as the Sustaining One. First, Paul encourages us to be unifiers in the Body of Believers: "Make every effort to keep the unity of the Spirit through the bond of peace" (Eph.4:3). How we do it is found in Colossians 3:12-15: "Therefore, as God's chosen people, holy and dearly loved, clothe yourselves with compassion, kindness, humility, gentleness and patience. Bear with each other and forgive whatever grievances you may have against one another. Forgive as the Lord forgave you. And over all these virtues put on love, which binds them all together in perfect unity. Let the peace of Christ rule in your hearts, since as members of one body you were called to peace."

Secondly, as stewards of his creation, we are to do our best to "tend the garden" and keep things in repair. As Christians, we are responsible to do our part to keep nature beautiful and a source of enjoyment to others. Whatever we possess, we should endeavor to keep it in good repair rather than let things go to ruin which shows a spirit of irresponsibility and carelessness that does not typify Christ's attitude as he sustains the universe.

We may not always be successful in either maintaining the unity of believers, saving the environment or in keeping things repaired and in working order. But success is not the issue, it is our reflecting this characteristic of Christ that is important. Any measure of success will come directly from his hand as he blesses our efforts.

Are you doing your part in helping to keep things "glued together"?

APPLICATION: What we don't do is sometimes just as important as what we do do: maintaining the unity of the brethren by not getting into a fight – letting that snub go because it just isn't worth making an issue over; maintaining the beauty of nature by not littering – cleaning up after ourselves. Let's be good "sustain-ers."

[***NOTE:** Scientists say that creation occurred from a "big bang." Maybe ... when God said, "Let there be ..."; but the Scriptures seem to place the "big bang" at the end! (cf. 2 Pet.3:10).]

DAY 133
aHE IS THE BELOVED ONE

◆

QUESTIONS TO THINK ABOUT:

1. What does it mean to be "beloved"?
2. What is the basis of that kind of relationship?

Christ is declared to be loved by the Father, hence, the Beloved One. In Matthew 3:17 we read, "And a voice from heaven said, 'This is my Son, whom I love; with him I am well pleased.'" And again in Ephesians 1:5,6, "In love he predestined us to be adopted as sons through Jesus Christ, in accordance with his pleasure and will – to the praise of his glorious grace, which he has freely given us in the One he loves" [i.e. "in the Beloved One"].

What was it that caused Christ to be so loved by his Father? He gives us a specific answer in John 10:17: "The reason my Father loves me is that I lay down my life – only to take it up again." In verse 11 he says: "I am the good shepherd. The good shepherd lays down his life for the sheep." In a broader sense, "The world must learn that I love the Father and that I do exactly what my Father has commanded me ..." (Jn.14:31). Jesus was beloved because he did the Father's will, even to the point of death.

In John 14:21 Jesus tells us how to be beloved of the Father: "Whoever has my commands and obeys them, he is the one who

Unexpected Transformation / 305

loves me. He who loves me will be loved by my Father, and I too will love him and show myself to him."

In his Word we have his commands. If we willingly obey them, that obedience becomes proof of our love for him. That love will bring forth a special response from God's heart toward us – and we also will be beloved of the Father. Jesus was willing to do God's will even though it involved his death (cf. Phil.2:5-8). To him, doing God's will was more important than life itself (cf. Jn.4:32,34). Is this our attitude as well?

One of Jesus' commands that ties directly into our willingness to do God's will is found in Mark 8:34,35: "If anyone would come after me, he must deny himself and take up his cross and follow me. For whoever wants to save his life will lose it, but whoever loses his life for me and for the gospel will save it." The subject of taking up one's cross and dying to self is never a popular one. Much is made of doing and not doing, giving up this and that, and so on. But I tend to think the answer is simpler than that: it is considering God's will as more important than life itself, and doing his will becomes our most important endeavor. Then we won't have to worry about giving up this or that, or doing something else in order to show to ourselves and others that we are "taking up our cross." Those things will naturally slough off as doing God's will becomes our primary goal and source of ultimate joy.

So as we submit to and obey his will, Romans 12:1,2 takes on fresh meaning: "Therefore, I urge you, brothers, in view of God's mercy, to offer your bodies as living sacrifices, holy and pleasing to God – which is your spiritual worship. Do not conform any longer to the pattern of this world, but be transformed by the renewing of your mind. Then you will be able to test and approve what God's will is – his good, pleasing and perfect will."

Is doing God's will of paramount importance in your life?

APPLICATION: Being "beloved" of God is not so much what you do on the outside, but what you are on the inside. Jesus said that what we say and do proceed from the heart (Matt.12:34,35). We are beloved by God not because of our works, but because of our heart-attitude toward him which prompts those works. As he sees our love for him, he is pleased, and his heart responds to us in return as his "beloved."

DAY 134
[a]HE IS THE OBEDIENT ONE

QUESTIONS TO THINK ABOUT:

1. How do we learn obedience? Why is it important?
2. How does suffering teach us obedience?
3. Which do you think is more important, obedience or worship? Why?
4. What are the results of obedience?

In Hebrews 10:5,7 we read, "Therefore, when Christ came into the world, he said ... 'Here I am – it is written about me in the scroll – I have come to do your will, O God.'" In response to his disciples' urging him to eat because of his weariness, he said, "I have food to eat that you know nothing about... . My food ... is to do the will of him who sent me and to finish his work" (Jn.4:32,34).

Hebrews 5:8 declares that "although [Jesus] was a son, he learned obedience from what he suffered." He had to experience what it meant to surrender one's will, even one's very life, to a higher will. That struggle often involves suffering. In the Garden of Gethsemane, he was in extreme anguish of soul, pleading for deliverance from the horrors of the death he was about to die, yet, in the same agony, surrendering his will to his Father's: "Yet not my will, but yours be done" (Lk.22:42b).

Again in Philippians 2:8, "And being found in appearance as a man, he humbled himself and became obedient to death – even death on a cross!"

When Paul saw Jesus in the vision on the Damascus road, he asked the Lord what he should do. The Lord told him, and he did it. Many years later, he was witnessing to King Agrippa, and said, "So then, King Agrippa, I was not disobedient to the vision from heaven" (Acts 26:19). Throughout his ministry, Paul suffered many things. Yet he remained obedient to the Lord's will.

God places a premium on obedience. He told King Saul though the prophet Samuel: "Does the LORD delight in burnt offerings and sacrifices as much as in obeying the voice of the LORD? To obey is better than sacrifice, and to heed is better than the fat of rams" (1 Sam.15:22). The Lord would rather we obey him than go through a lot of religious ceremony with an unsubmissive, disobedient heart.

Obedience is not always easy. In fact, until <u>we develop it as a patterned response to God</u>, it is never easy, for there is always the tug of the flesh in the opposite direction. One of the hardest choices of obedience I had was in returning to the mission field for a second term. God had not indicated a change of place, so, in fear of the consequences of disobedience, I chose to return. That second term we experienced the birth pangs of our present ministry, and our third term was full of joy and blessing. Obedience delights the Lord, and he will reward and bless us as we obey. Of Christ it is written: "Therefore God exalted him to the highest place and gave him the name that is above every name" (Phil.2:9). As for us, the Lord promises sure reward and blessing if we obey him (Matt.24:45-47).

Are you obeying what you <u>know</u> to be your Father's will?

APPLICATION: Obedience comes from making it a habit. Choose a verse of Scripture that you are presently not obeying and determine how you will start obeying it. For the first 10 or 15 times, you will have to consciously choose to obey it; after the habit is formed, you will find yourself "automatically" doing it without a thought! You will be delighted – and so will God.

DAY 135
[a]HE IS THE BLESSED ONE

QUESTIONS TO THINK ABOUT:

1. What does it mean to be "blessed"?
2. How do we bless God?
3. How do we bless others? (cf. Rom.12:13)

When Jesus entered Jerusalem for the final time, riding on a donkey, the crowds preceded him crying with loud voices, "Blessed is the king who comes in the name of the Lord! Peace in heaven and glory in the highest!" (Lk.19:38).

The word "blessed" comes from the Greek word *eulogeo*, meaning "to speak well of" (*eu* = well, *logos* = a word). It is used in four ways: 1. To praise God; 2. to invoke blessings upon a person; 3. to ask God's blessing on something, and 4. to bestow blessings on someone, hence causing them to prosper, to make them happy. From this Greek word comes our word "eulogy," meaning to give someone high praise (whether living or deceased).

So Jesus was being acclaimed with high praise by the people. There is a future acclamation that he will receive. Yesterday we saw how "he humbled himself and became obedient to death – even death on a cross!" (Phil.2:8). The following verses (9-11) state how

Unexpected Transformation / 309

God blessed him: "Therefore God exalted him to the highest place and gave him the name that is above every name, that at the name of Jesus every knee should bow, in heaven and on earth and under the earth, and every tongue confess that Jesus Christ is Lord, to the glory of God the Father."

The praise Jesus received from the multitudes lasted but a few moments. A week later, he was hanging on a Roman cross. But God's praise is final and eternal, and it is his praise that we should seek.

In Matthew 6, Jesus made it very plain that those who do good deeds "to be seen [praised] by men" have already received their reward, and there is nothing more for them from the Father (6:1,2,4-6,16,18). He also warns us in Luke 6:26, "Woe to you when all men speak well of you, for that is how their fathers treated the false prophets." The false prophets told the people what they wanted to hear, thus caused no waves and confirmed their listeners in their self-righteous ways. But few had a good word to say about the true prophet from the Lord, for he decried their sins and called them to repentance with the dire threat of God's judgment. No one likes to hear how bad they are, but this is what the Gospel does. However, what is important is God's praise, which is final and eternal. His "Well done, good and faithful servant!" will ring forever in our ears and be a continual source of joy for us, knowing that we have been approved of God. What need we ask for more than that?

Are you receiving God's acclamation or hunting for man's?

APPLICATION: I find dying to pride an almost daily battle. Even when I don't want to, I frequently find myself singing, preaching or teaching in order to impress others. It's just there! How do we overcome it? We need to confess our pride to the Lord, then consciously change our focus from others to him. Easier said than done! But it's either that or have our works "burned up" as unprofitable for the kingdom (cf. 1 Cor.3:11-15). We cannot fight pride passively.

DAY 136
ᵃHE IS THE PATIENT ONE

◆

QUESTIONS TO THINK ABOUT:

1. How is patience considered a sign of strength or a sign of weakness?
2. What are some of the results of impatience?
3. Why is patience important?
4. How could selfishness be looked at as the root of impatience?

"The Lord is not slow in keeping his promise, as some understand slowness. He is patient with you, not wanting anyone to perish, but everyone to come to repentance" (2 Pet.3:9). Christ is patient, and God also wants us to be patient.

Long ago I stopped praying for patience, for, according to James 1:3 (KJV), "tribulation worketh patience" and I didn't like to "tribulate"! I figured that I'd let the Lord be the judge as to how much patience I needed, when I needed it, and how I was to learn it. Obviously, he saw that I needed LOTS of it badly, especially during our first two terms on the mission field.

There are two areas in which we must learn patience: in our circumstances and with people. We had to build our house out of iron wood, a very hard wood like oak. It's the kind where one has to drill a hole into it before nailing. Then you have to drill again to get the first drill bit out that just broke! Then you should be able to nail it. I called myself an expert nail bender because many times the nail I hit would bend over! Then, after several times, I'd get frustrated, then angry, and rear back to really hit that nail! I'd show it who's boss! Only I'd miss and put a circular scar on the board! That made me angrier yet. So I'd take another swing and hit the nail. Now I had a bent nail imbedded in the board and had to pry it out with a screwdriver and a crowbar, adding a half-moon

Unexpected Transformation / 311

scar, pry marks, and an indentation from the crowbar in the board. All of this because I was impatient! It took a long time for me to gain patience in this kind of situation. Now, when I'm nailing something, and the nail bends, my response is, "Oh, a bent nail." And I pull it out and begin again.

Being patient toward circumstances is one thing, but toward people is quite something else. Think of the patience Christ had to have with his disciples. For three years he had to put up with Peter's impetuosity (Jn.13:36-38), James' and John's tempers and party spirit (Mk.3:17; Lk.9:49-56), Philip's spiritual insensitivity (Jn.14:7-9), Thomas's pessimism and doubts (Jn.11:16; 20:24-29), hard feelings between Matthew (tax collector for the Romans) and Simon the Zealot (an Israeli patriot). Then there was always the hypocrisy of Judas Iscariot, his opportunism and treachery (Lk.22:3-6). And on the very night of his betrayal, the disciples were arguing as to who was the greatest among them (Lk.22:24-27), and in the time of prayer, fell asleep (Lk.22:45,46)!

How could Jesus do it? He could do it because he could "see" beyond the present circumstances and personality problems to the mature servants of God these men would someday become (excepting Judas). He could envision them ultimately becoming just like himself, and thus was able to view personality problems, etc. as areas where God was working in their lives toward that end. Thus, seeing the end result, Jesus could work together with God through prayer (Lk.22:32) and teaching (Jn.13:12-17) to help the disciples resolve their problems and become that much closer to his image.

In the same way, we can develop patience toward other Christians, knowing that in all their problems and circumstances, God is working to make them like Christ. Then we can pray for them according to God's goal for them, and work toward the same as God gives us opportunity. We need to learn to respond to them even as Jesus did to his disciples.

According to Romans 5:3, patience only comes through adversity. So when adversity comes, through things or people, let us welcome it as God's tool to teach us patience (cf. Jas.1:2,3).

Adversity can be received with a smile or with a frown. Which way you receive it will make a <u>big</u> difference in how you handle it!

APPLICATION: The root cause of impatience is selfishness. We want what we want, when we want it, now! That's putting ourselves and our desires above everything and anyone else. When things don't go the way we want, we erupt in an explosion of impatience: road rage, throwing things across the room, swearing, shouting at someone or everyone in general, physical or verbal abuse, withdrawal, giving the "silent treatment," etc. – not exactly a reflection of Christ's character!

We need to realize that when we put ourselves first, we are taking God's place in our lives, raising ourselves to his position and prerogative. That's not really a good thing to do! Yet we all do it, perhaps more than we realize.

What is the way out of this dilemma? We need to change our focus from "what I want" to "What is God trying to teach me through this situation that will make me more like Christ?" That changes our situations from "enemies to be fought and conquered" to "teachers from God's hand to make me like Christ," which, in turn, changes our irritation to thankfulness; our anger to a grateful spirit. I have personally found this to be the "key" to overcoming impatience – when I apply it!

DAY 137
[a]HE IS THE TRUSTWORTHY ONE

◆

QUESTIONS TO THINK ABOUT:

1. What does it mean to be a man or woman of your word?
2. As you think of "trustworthiness," what comes to mind? What does it imply?

3. How does making a promise, then not fulfilling it affect our relationships and our witness to others?

The term "trustworthy" means "worthy of trust, reliable." Someone is given a job and he sticks to it until it is completed and done to the best of his ability. Trustworthiness is built upon a foundation of several other characteristics: honesty, truthfulness, industriousness, ability, willingness, loyalty, obedience and a servant attitude. We have seen each of these characteristics in Christ in one way or another as we have progressed in our study of him. So when we read in John 17:4, "I have brought you glory on earth by completing the work you gave me to do," we are reading of Christ's trustworthiness. He was given a job to do and he completed it to God's satisfaction.

Paul found such a man in Timothy. When he first met him, he was already known as a disciple of the Lord and was well-spoken of by others (Acts 16:1-5). Paul took him along and was obviously impressed. Soon Timothy was preaching alongside Paul and Silas (2 Cor.1:19) and Paul began to send him back to the churches already established to care for unresolved matters: Corinth (1 Cor.16:10); Philippi (Phil.2:19-23); Thessalonica (1 Thess.3:1-8); and finally left in charge of the work in Ephesus and Asia Minor (1 Tim.1:3). Paul described him as "my fellow worker" (Rom.16:21); as "carrying on the work of the Lord, just as I am" (1 Cor.16:10) and as one who is like-minded with me (Phil.2:19-23). Listen to this last commendation; it speaks for itself: "I hope in the Lord Jesus to send Timothy to you soon, that I also may be cheered when I receive news about you. I have no one else like him, who takes a genuine interest in your welfare. For everyone looks out for his own interests, not those of Jesus Christ. But you know that Timothy has proved himself, because as a son with his father he has served with me in the work of the gospel. I hope, therefore, to send him as soon as I see how things go with me."

I think of two students at ETTC about whom I had the same feeling. I had complete confidence in them both that whatever I ask of them, they would do it cheerfully to the best of their ability. I wasn't disappointed, ever. And I saw this same attitude in whatever they did for others as well. Trustworthiness – an invaluable and rare commodity even among Christians. Paul said he only found this in Timothy. Everybody else was serving Christ from other motives. If Colossians 3:23 characterizes our attitude, "Whatever you do, work at it with all your heart, as working for the Lord, not for men," then others will find us trustworthy and we will be entrusted with responsibilities that others could not be trusted with.

Are you worthy of others' trust?

APPLICATION: If people cannot trust us in the material realm, how will they trust us in the spiritual realm? We read in James 5:12, "Let your 'Yes' be yes, and your 'No,' no, or you will be condemned." As Christians, we must be known for being "people of our word." If we say we will be somewhere at such-and-such a time, that is when and where we will be. If we say that we will do such-and-such a job, it will be done. If something comes up that interferes with what we have promised, we contact the people involved accordingly and make other arrangements. If we are not trustworthy in our actions, others will not believe our words, our testimony for Christ will be neutralized and Christ's name (whom we represent) will be brought into disrespect. According to Psalm 15:4, a godly man "keeps his oath [promise] even when it hurts." We must be men and women of our word! Don't make a promise, then not keep it!

DAY 138
[a]HE IS THE PERSECUTED, THE AFFLICTED ONE

(Background considerations)

QUESTIONS TO THINK ABOUT:

1. What does it mean to be persecuted?
2. Why do we not like to talk or think about it?
3. How is persecution a part of our becoming like Christ?
4. What should be our attitude toward persecution and the persecutors? (cf. Jas.1:2-4; Matt.5:44)

We read in 2 Timothy 3:12 that "all who desire to live godly in Christ Jesus will suffer persecution" (NKJV). That doesn't mean that we will suffer every kind of persecution, but we will suffer some kind of it, sometime.

As the Lord allows us to suffer wrongfully, we all have the opportunity to join with those many Christians of history in using that suffering as our pulpit from which many others may come to know Christ. The world cannot understand love when they expect hate, compassion when they expect revenge, or a soft answer when they expect a tirade. This puzzles them, and perhaps even adds fire to the vehemence of their persecution until they can no longer deny that a greater Power than them is in control. Questions come, followed by answers and conversions. But if Christians respond as the world does, there would be no witness, no revealing of God's glory, strength and love, and no harvest in that part of the field.

I have long avoided this subject of persecution and hardship because I feared it. Who wants to suffer? No one. And it is certainly an unpleasant subject to those of us who have had it easy throughout our

Christian life. Yet we are in the minority. The majority of Christians have and are suffering persecution to varying degrees all over the world. And they suffer without our sympathy or support. Why? First, we can't believe it's really happening since we are so comfortable; secondly, we don't want to admit it is happening because that would open the unpleasant door of it possibly happening to us. Then we might begin to feel more responsible for our suffering brethren which would demand our time in prayer and effort to meet their needs. In this way we actually increase the suffering of our brothers and sisters in Christ rather than support them in their trials (see Papov, p.63).

What changed my attitude and made me willing to deal with this subject was a Sunday School class discussion on Christ as the Glorious, Transfigured One (see DAYS 239-242). In the very first class session, someone brought out the Scriptural principle that suffering precedes glory. In Philippians 2:8,9 we read of Christ: "And being found in appearance as a man, he humbled himself and became obedient to death – even death on a cross! Therefore God exalted him to the highest place and gave him the name that is above every name."

Again in 2 Corinthians 4:17,18 Paul reminds us that "… our light and momentary troubles are achieving for us an eternal glory that far outweighs them all. So we fix our eyes not on what is seen, but on what is unseen. For what is seen is temporary, but what is unseen is eternal." Peter writes: "Therefore, since Christ suffered in his body, arm yourselves also with the same attitude, because he who has suffered in his body is done with sin. As a result, he does not live the rest of his earthly life for evil human desires, but rather for the will of God" (1 Pet.4:1,2).

Suffering is one means God uses to mold us into the character and likeness of his Son since suffering purifies us from sin (even as Christ is pure). I can think of several instances in my own life when God sent physical affliction in order to purify me from some particular sins. One day, while in Senggo, I was enjoying some lustful thoughts. I knew it was wrong, but did it anyway. Suddenly I came down with a severe headache. Not malaria. Wrong symptoms. So I took some aspirin. No help. Later I took two more aspirin. Still no relief. Then I began to question: "It's not malaria, I know that. Usually aspirin knocks my headaches, but this one it's not touching at all. Could my headache be from some other cause?" I didn't have far to look. I knew what I had been thinking and enjoying. So I confessed my sin to the Lord in prayer – and within ten minutes my headache was gone!

We read in Romans 8:29,30, "For those God foreknew he also predestined to be conformed to the likeness of his Son ... and those he predestined, he also called; and those he called, he also justified; those he justified, he also glorified." Suffering rids us of sins and makes us more like Christ. Then we will be glorified, exalted. Paul reminds us again in Romans 8:17,18, "Now if we are children, then we are heirs – heirs of God and co-heirs with Christ, if indeed we share in his sufferings in order that we may also share in his glory. I consider that our present sufferings are not worth comparing with the glory that will be revealed in us."

If our goal is to become like Christ, then we will welcome the suffering God sends our way because that suffering will speed us on our way toward that goal. One day one of our Bible School students came to me and said, "I'm so thankful to the Lord for this physical infirmity I'm suffering, because it keeps me depending on him and keeps me mindful of his purpose for my life."

Now with this background, we are ready to move on to our consideration of Christ as the Persecuted One.

APPLICATION: Prayerfully consider your attitude toward persecution and suffering and choose to align it with the Word of God. We need to remember that God gives us grace to handle whatever comes our way when we need it, and not before. Do not fear and worry about what will draw you closer to him and make you more like his Son.

DAY 139
[a]HE IS THE PERSECUTED ONE, cont.

(Lack of Privacy, Hangers-on)

QUESTIONS TO THINK ABOUT:

1. How do you feel when that phone call disrupts your plans for the day, or interrupts a good night of sleep?
2. How do you respond to people who demand more of your attention than you want to give them?
3. How do you feel about those who "attach" themselves to you just for what they can get out of that relationship?

Jesus reminded his disciples in John 15:18,20, "If the world hates you, keep in mind that it hated me first.... No servant is greater than his master. If they persecuted me, they will persecute you also." In Isaiah 53:7a we read: "He was oppressed and he was afflicted...." Throughout Christ's ministry, he suffered persecution ranging from lack of privacy to attempted murder and finally death. He was maltreated, tormented and suffered adversity at every turn. As we look at Christ's suffering over the next several days, we will discover that our sufferings are no different than what he has experienced!

LACK OF PRIVACY

In Mark 6:31,32 we read: "Then, because so many people were coming and going that they did not even have a chance to eat, he said to them, 'Come with me by yourselves to a quiet place and get some rest.' So they went away by themselves in a boat to a solitary place." Christ was tired, hungry, and wanted a restful break from the pressures of his ministry. He wanted some time alone with his friends. Who among us has not wished for that at one time or another?

However, this was not to be. We read in verses 33 and 34, "But many who saw them leaving recognized them and ran on foot from all the towns and got there ahead of them. When Jesus landed and saw the large crowd, he had compassion on them, because they were like sheep without a shepherd. So he began teaching them many things."

Any missionary, pastor, Christian leader or Christian involved with people will attest to the fact that they suffer from a lack of privacy. There is always that knock at the door, that phone call, that "nosy" reporter, that person with a desperate problem in the middle of the night. We learn to accept that as a part of the ministry, yet many times something within us cries out, "Oh to be left alone! Oh to sink into anonymity!" Yet we minister to them anyway, even as Christ did.

HANGERS-ON

On the mission field we call them "rice Christians." They come to church and make a show of spirituality only for what they can get out of it for themselves. If we can produce the "goods" they want, then no effort is too great on their part to be close to that source.

When Christ fed the 5,000, he faced this very problem. When he had left them and had gone to Capernaum, pretty soon here they came again seeking him. He knew why. They cared nothing for his message, but only wanted a free meal! "Jesus answered, 'I tell you the truth, you are looking for me, not because you saw miraculous signs but because you ate the loaves and had your fill'" (Jn.6:26).

Then he had to further discourage these "hangers-on" with some very strong "medicine," and not only lost them but others too through their misunderstanding of what he said (cf. Jn.6:51-63).

Have you ever been attached to by some hangers-on who only were along for the ride, hoping to get whatever they could from you rather than for what they could learn from you or contribute to the ministry? If so, then you know how Christ felt.

DAY 140
ªHE IS THE PERSECUTED ONE, cont.

(Misunderstood, Rejected)

QUESTIONS TO THINK ABOUT:

1. Have you ever been misunderstood? How did that make you feel? What were the results of that misunderstanding?

2. Have you ever suffered rejection? How did that make you feel? What kind of lasting effects has that had on your life?

MISUNDERSTOOD

To get rid of the hangers-on, Christ told them that they would have to eat his flesh and drink his blood (an appropriate parable for those seeking free meals!), which they interpreted literally, even though he was speaking of spiritual truth (Jn.6:63). Not only were the hangers-on offended, but so were many of his disciples who promptly ceased following him (vs.66). The defection was so great that, humanly, in disappointment, he turned to the twelve and asked how soon they were going to leave too (vs.67)!

There will always be misunderstanding and misinterpretation of what we say by those who are not "on our wave length" (cf. Jn.2:18-21). It is to be expected, and though we try to communicate clearly, what we say is filtered through so many other sets of reference, colored by prejudice, ignorance, knowledge, culture, ambition, etc., as to come out totally different from what we intended. That is frustrating. But the more we are involved with people, the more we will be misunderstood.

Unexpected Transformation / 321

REJECTED

On the heal of misunderstanding comes rejection. We read in John 1:11, "He came to that which was his own, but his own did not receive him." He was rejected by Israel's spiritual leaders (Mk.8:31), and he was an offense to his own family (Jn.7:3-6) and townspeople (Mk.6:1-6). Others came and went.

As soon as Paul of Tarsus, the champion of Orthodox Judaism and pride of the Sanhedrin, was converted and began to espouse the very Way which he had so viciously persecuted just days before, he was dropped like a hot potato by the Jewish leaders and marked for death from that point on (Acts 9:19-24).

Forms of rejection range from passiveness to violence. And as Christ experienced them, so will his followers to varying degrees. Consider the following examples:

"He is raving mad!"	(Jn.10:20)
"Your great learning is driving you insane."	(Paul before Festus – Acts 26:24)
"He is demon-possessed."	(Jn.10:20)
"He (John the Baptist) has a demon."	(Lk.7:33)
Feared and asked to leave.	(Jesus – Lk.8:37; Paul & Silas – Acts 16:39)
Refused hospitality.	(Jesus – Lk.9:52,53; the disciples – Lk.10:10,11)

Christians today are treated in the same way in many lands. Formerly in communist countries, they were "diagnosed" as "insane" and committed to insane asylums. Contacts with families of prisoners were feared (presumed "guilt" because of association). They were shunned even by other Christians, lest they also be arrested and imprisoned (Papov, p.63). If we are Christ's, we will be rejected at one time or another.

DAY 141
ªHE IS THE PERSECUTED ONE, cont.

(Criticized, Despised, Ridiculed)

QUESTIONS TO THINK ABOUT:

1. Criticism can be constructive or destructive. It has been said that hidden inside every criticism is a seed of truth. How should that make us respond to any kind of criticism?

2. Much is being said about bullying today. You don't have to be a Christian to suffer that kind of ridicule. It's easy to talk about those whom you despise; but it's another story to be on the receiving end. If you've ever been on the other end, how did that make you feel?

CRITICIZED

Christ's rejection by the Jews continued to be intensified as his ministry developed. He suffered criticism many times at the hands of the Pharisees: he ate with tax collectors and sinners (Matt.9:10,11; Lk.15:2), his disciples didn't fast and pray as others did (Lk.5:33), they broke the Sabbath by "harvesting" grain (Lk.6:1,2), and he broke it by healing the sick (Lk.13:14)! And on it went.

Mary of Bethany was sharply criticized by the disciples when she anointed Christ's feet with costly ointment (Mk.14:4,5). Much later, Peter was criticized by his fellow believers for going into the house of uncircumcised men to eat with them (Acts 11:2,3). But once they learned the truth, they withdrew their criticism (Acts 11:18). This illustrates the principle that criticism is frequently based upon incomplete knowledge of the facts and is carried forth on the wings of assumption!

Jealousy, doing something "differently than we've always done it," or just plain lack of information or understanding will spawn criticism. When Amber and I began applying to TEAM, we were hit from all sides with criticism about TEAM and finally began to wonder just what we were getting ourselves into. But rather than listen to the criticism and judge from that, we began writing letters to TEAM and interviewing TEAM personnel visiting the Bible College, sharing the criticisms and seeking clarification. Candidate School clinched it for us that these criticisms were just that, criticisms mostly based on unfounded facts, preconceived notions, or hearsay!

One thing to notice: in each of the above situations being criticized, a reason was given for what was being done, but that reason was not always accepted. We need to be prepared for that too. But even more, we also need to take care that we ourselves don't fall into the same trap of criticizing others (see Rom.14:1-12)!

DESPISED/RIDICULED

To despise someone is an attitude of heart in which we make him of no account, we regard him as nothing, we treat him with contempt and reject him as worthless. Ridicule is the action of one whose heart is filled with despite and is evidenced by criticism and mockery of which Christ received more than his full share.

In Isaiah 53:3 we read: "He was despised and rejected by men." He was laughed at for his point of view (Mk.5:39,40), and sneered at for his teaching (Lk.16:14). He was called a glutton and a drunkard (Lk.7:34), a friend of scum (tax collectors and sinners – Lk.7:34), a Samaritan (Jn.8:48 – indicating that he was a despised half-breed, of mixed and impure race and therefore having no spiritual authority; euphemistically used for a demon-possessed person), and of illegitimate birth (Jn.8:41 – Some believed that Jesus was the product of Mary and a Roman soldier!). He was treated with rudeness when visiting a Pharisee who didn't even give him common courtesy upon inviting him for dinner (Lk.7:44-46).

New Christians are often thought strange by their unsaved friends (1 Pet.4:4), who, unable to explain their strange behavior, begin to heap abuse upon them. Paul and Barnabas were subjected to verbal abuse from jealous Jews in Pisidian Antioch (Acts 13:45), and Paul and Silas in Corinth (Acts 18:6). While in Athens, Paul preached Christ and the resurrection at which he became the target of sneers from some (Acts 17:32). Those who reject our message, for whatever reason, will ridicule us and the message to justify their own unbelief and to dissuade others from believing.

Proverbs 17:28 says, "Even a fool is thought wise if he keeps silent, and discerning if he holds his tongue." Sometimes, in the face of criticism and ridicule, it is best to say nothing, but do what Jesus did, entrusting himself to God who judges justly (1 Pet.2:23). If truth is at stake, then we must respond; if not, then remain silent.

DAY 142
[a]HE IS THE PERSECUTED ONE, cont.

(Laughed at)

QUESTIONS TO THINK ABOUT:

1. How does it make you feel when laughed at or mocked?
2. How do you think we should respond to such situations?

LAUGHED AT

One day the daughter of Jairus, one of the rulers of the synagogue of Capernaum, became very ill and was at the point of death. Jairus heard that Jesus was close by so went to him for help. As they approached the ruler's home, when Jesus "saw the flute players and the noisy crowd, he said, 'Go away. The girl is not dead but asleep.' But they laughed at him" (Matt.9:23,24).

On the Cross, Jesus was mocked and laughed at. Psalm 22:7a says: "All who see me mock me" (laugh me to scorn – NKJV). It's the laugh of derision, the laugh of mockery, the laugh that says, "You are a fool; you are crazy and deceived; you are a nothing!"

When Hezekiah sent messengers throughout Judah and Israel with word for everyone to come to Jerusalem to keep the feast of the Passover, they "went from town to town in Ephraim and Manasseh, as far as Zebulun, but the people scorned and ridiculed them" (2 Chr.30:10).

Nehemiah and company were laughed to scorn by Sanballat, Tobiah and Geshem when they were trying to get the wall of Jerusalem rebuilt (Neh.2:19). Job was laughed to scorn by his friends (Job 12:4), for they "knew" that he had obviously committed some great sin and was suffering retribution for it. Throughout history, Christians have been laughed at, ridiculed and mocked for their faith.

1 Corinthians 2:14 is still true today: "The man without the Spirit does not accept the things that come from the Spirit of God, for they are foolishness to him, and he cannot understand them, because they are spiritually discerned." What people consider foolishness, they will laugh at.

I can remember being laughed at twice: once by non-Christians and another time by Christians. While in grade school, I would often ask the other kids not to use foul language when I was around. One day after gym class, I walked into the locker room. Someone called out, "Hey, guys, here's the preacher! Watch your language!" They did, but they also laughed.

The second time I was laughed at was at Bible camp. We were in a "For Guys Only" session. During the discussion, I mentioned that the first time I ever intended to kiss a woman would be when I'm engaged to be married. The staff member leading our discussion broke out in laughter along with everyone else and said, "Well, good luck if you can do it!"

I did it. But their attitude hurt me deeply. I thought that at least their standards as Christians would have been higher and that I would have had support from our discussion leader. To be laughed at by the unsaved is expected; but to be laughed at by fellow Christians is most discouraging.

But to be truly Christ-like will make us sufficiently different from others (Christian or non-Christian) that we will be laughed at from time to time. However, that is a small price to pay for being like Jesus.

APPLICATION: People laugh at and mock what they do not understand or don't want to understand. As long as we know the truth we can persevere as the price of denying the truth is too expensive to pay. We need to pray for those who mock us, that the Lord would open their understanding and convince them of the truth.

DAY 143
[a]HE IS THE PERSECUTED ONE, cont.

(Hated, Falsely Accused)

QUESTIONS TO THINK ABOUT:

1. Hatred takes on a more personal and threatening aspect. How can you face that and not get paranoid?
2. What should be your attitude toward those who hate you?
3. It's no fun to be falsely accused of anything. How should we respond to false accusations?

HATED

People in general do not like to be told they're wrong; and when they get that message either in word or by action (changed life style, etc.), hatred is often the result. When Jesus began showing up the scribes and Pharisees for the hypocrites they really were, this was too much for their pride to bear. Hatred flared (Jn.7:7; Lk.6:11) and they initiated a campaign of spying and harassment (Lk.14:1; 20:20,21) to try to catch him in something for which they could accuse him and get rid of this embarrassment (Mk.3:2).

We read in Luke 11:53,54 that the scribes and Pharisees "began to oppose him fiercely and to besiege him with questions, waiting to catch him in something he might say." They baited him (Lk.20:20-26), tried to trap him in his words (Matt.22:15-22), challenged his authority (Jn.2:18; Matt.21:23), questioned his truthfulness (Jn.6:41-43), and when they perceived a contradiction, they pounced upon it with a vengeance (Jn.5:31,32,36,37; 8:12-14).

Even as Christ was and is hated, so are his followers. Again in John 15:18 he reminded his disciples, "If the world hates you, keep in mind that it hated me first." And again in his prayer for them he said, "I have given them your word and the world has hated them, for they are not of the world any more than I am of the world" (Jn.17:14). Hatred is the result of the enmity that God put between the Seed of the woman and Satan's seed (Gen.3:15).

Paul encountered this hatred many times during his ministry (Acts 21:36; 22:22). Peter and John's authority was questioned (Acts 4:7). And Christians today in many communist and Muslim countries are spied upon and (even in our own country) willfully misquoted in the news media so as to discredit them. Whenever a Christian leader makes a blunder, contradicts himself, or falls into sin, the media get a lot of mileage out of it and people generally seem to enjoy seeing him and other believers (by extension) put down. There's no love lost on the Christian by the world.

When beset by hatred, it is good to keep in mind Jesus' words in Matthew 5:44: "But I tell you: love [agape] your enemies [i.e. choose to act for their benefit] and pray for [not against!] those who persecute you, that you may be sons of your Father in heaven."

FALSELY ACCUSED

Not finding anything for which to accuse Jesus, the Jews had to come up with something to save their pride and keep the fires of agitation against Christ stoked. So they began to falsely accuse him of working miracles through the power of Satan (Matt.12:24), of blasphemy against God in claiming his right to forgive sins (Mk.2:6,7), and in claiming to be God (Jn.10:31-33). He was accused of breaking and dishonoring the Mosaic Law (Matt.5:17 implied), and accused of threatening to destroy the Temple (Matt.26:61).

When the unbelieving Jews of the Synagogue of the Freedmen could not down Stephen in argument or debate, they brought against him false witnesses who accused him of blaspheming Moses (the Law) and God (Acts 6:9-11). Then, before the Sanhedrin, they produced other false witnesses who accused him of speaking against the Temple and the Law (Acts 6:13). The reason? They heard him say that "Jesus of Nazareth will destroy this place and change the customs Moses handed down to us" (Acts 6:14). Evidently Stephen had alluded to Christ's statement found in John 2:19-21 in his teachings, and once again the false witnesses misinterpreted it, or twisted it to their own ends. Either way, it had the same effect.

Peter speaks to the issue of suffering wrongfully in 1 Pet.3 and 4 saying, that if we suffer for what is right, we are blessed (3:14), and to always live "so that those who speak maliciously against your good behavior in Christ may be ashamed of their slander. [For] it is better, if it is God's will, to suffer for doing good than for doing evil" (1 Pet.3:16,17).

It's no fun to be falsely accused. But if it is done because of our good works, then we will have eternal reward stored up for us in heaven – we will be blessed – so can rejoice even as Christ told his listeners in Matt.5:11,12a: "Blessed are you when people insult you, persecute you and falsely say all kinds of evil against you because of me. Rejoice and be glad, because great is your reward in heaven."

Unexpected Transformation / 329

APPLICATION: 2 Corinthians 4:17 is a great encouragement when encountering hatred or false accusations. "For our light and momentary troubles are achieving for us an eternal glory that far outweighs them all." I was able to diffuse one false accusation situation by using Proverbs 15:1, giving a gentle answer in return; another (formal accusation before the National Church Council) by just keeping silent (cf. Matt.26:59-63a]. When trying to answer false accusations or defend ourselves against them, we will often say or imply the wrong things and get ourselves into deeper trouble. Often, like Jesus, it's just best to say nothing.

DAY 144
[a]HE IS THE PERSECUTED ONE, cont.

(Homeless, Deserted, Overtly Opposed)

◆

QUESTIONS TO THINK ABOUT:

1. What does it mean to be homeless? How was Jesus homeless?
2. Why would someone desert you? What does that imply?
3. How do you handle overt opposition in whatever form it takes?

HOMELESS

Throughout his ministry, either because of its itinerant nature, or because of persecution, or disobedience on the part of others (Mk.1:40-45), Jesus had no place to call home (Matt.8:19,20). The same has been true of many Christians down through the ages (Heb.11:38). Even today in many countries, the families of religious prisoners are often forced to move out of their homes with no place to go. Any other Christian offering even temporary shelter is liable to arrest, imprisonment or death – so many do not. In the winter time, this causes great suffering. Friends are forced to ignore friends on the same threat. One day a pastor's wife and children visited the church where her husband had pastored for over 20 years. He had just recently been arrested. No one in the church could even acknowledge her presence, lest they be accused of aiding and abetting an enemy of the State (Papov, p.63). Thus any kind of hospitality to her was hindered. She felt ...

DESERTED

When Christ rid himself of the hangers-on, many of his disciples also left him, saying that his teachings were too hard (Jn.6:66). In the Garden of Gethsemane, Jesus was deserted by the twelve when arrested. Paul felt this to a degree as Demas forsook him leaving only Luke with him (2 Tim.4:10,11). Apart from Timothy, "everyone else" was looking out for his own interests rather than the things of Christ (Phil.2:19-21). And there were just three Jews among Paul's fellow workers at the time he wrote Colossians: Aristarchus, Mark and Justus (Col.4:11) – a real heartache for one who had so earnestly hoped that many from Israel would join the Believers' ranks (Rom.10:1). But the worst was yet to come. During the preliminary hearing for his final trial before Rome, no one came to his aid; everyone deserted him (2 Tim.4:16). Being a Christian in Rome had now become very dangerous since they were being blamed for the burning of the city and everyone was talking against them (Walvoord and Zuck, p.759). Now Paul knew how Christ felt in the Garden ... all alone.

OVERTLY OPPOSED

As Christ's ministry proceeded, the opposition he faced grew bolder and more open. In Luke 4:29 we find him being driven out of his home town, Nazareth, with an attempt on his life. He escaped. He was an increasingly unwelcome commodity among various circles. The Jewish leaders began plotting against him to take his life (Jn.11:53), and other times he was threatened with arrest (Jn.7:32; Lk.20:19) and death (Matt.12:14; 26:4). Two other times people attempted to stone him (Jn.8:59; 10:31-33). And the Jewish rulers did everything they could think of to make his life miserable (Jn.5:16). No wonder we read in Heb.5:7, "During the days of Jesus' life on earth, he offered up prayers and petitions with loud cries and tears to the One who could save him from death, and he was heard because of his reverent submission."

In Acts 13:50 we read of Paul and Barnabas being thrown out of town. Peter and John were severely threatened (Acts 4:21) and plotted against (Acts 5:33). Stephen was stoned (Acts 7:58) and so was Paul after he and Barnabas were threatened with stoning in Iconium (Acts 14:5,19). Paul was strongly opposed by the Jews in Corinth (Acts 18:6) and again in Ephesus, who tried to speak against the Way (Acts 19:9). His enemies successfully poisoned the minds of others against him (Acts 14:2).

Throughout history, Christians have been persecuted, even as Christ said would happen (Jn.15:20), being excommunicated from their places of worship (John 16:2 – We received a letter from some missionary friends of ours sharing how they had been summarily dropped from their home church because they had used the A.S.V. translation of the Bible while speaking there rather than the King James Version!), hunted down like animals (Acts 9:2), pursued from town to town (Matt.23:34), and mistreated (Lk.6:28; Heb.11:37).

We can expect overt opposition when we swim against the tide!

APPLICATION: According to Hebrews 11, some are delivered from persecution; others are not, of whom it is said that "the world was not worthy of them. They wandered in deserts and mountains, and in caves and holes in the ground" (homeless, deserted and overtly opposed). In this kind of situation, we are totally thrown upon the Lord for his provision for our physical and spiritual needs to help us persevere. Once in heaven, all this will just seem like a bad dream, now over, and we will be comforted.

DAY 145
ᵃHE IS THE PERSECUTED ONE, cont.

(Satanic Attack)

QUESTIONS TO THINK ABOUT:

1. According to 1 Peter 5:8, Satan goes about like a roaring lion, seeking whom he may devour. How can one know if he's under Satanic attack?

2. If you sense that you are under attack, what steps can you take to counter it?

3. What exposes one to Satanic attack?

SATANIC ATTACK

Christ suffered at the hands of Satan while exposed to the elements in the desert for forty days where he was without food, had no adequate shelter, and was in danger from wild animals (Mk.1:12,13). On two occasions he was endangered by storms on the Lake of Galilee (Matt.8:23,24; Mk.4:37-39). And we can see Satan's hand in the frequent strife among the disciples (Lk.9:46) and in Judas Iscariot's betrayal of the Lord (Lk.22:2-6).

Christ told Peter that Satan wanted to have him to sift him like wheat (with the idea of destroying his faith – Lk.22:31,32). Paul was in storms at sea and shipwrecked three times (2 Cor.11:25). Once he suffered snake bite (Acts 28:3-6) which was an obvious attempt of Satan to keep him from Rome (as was the shipwreck that brought him to the island in the first place). Job suffered as Satan tried to destroy his faith (Job 1 & 2). As Peter says, Satan is like a roaring lion, prowling about, looking for someone to devour (1 Pet.5:8).

He hasn't changed his tactics. Even today he is prowling about, tempting, alluring, hindering, obstructing, opposing, terrifying, killing, devouring. Paul says, "We are not unaware of his schemes" (2 Cor.2:11), and yet the Church generally seems oblivious to him, allowing him to wreak havoc with impunity. We do not want to give him more credit than is due, for that would exalt him; yet we must recognize his hand in what he does do so that we can resist and overcome him in the name of our Lord Jesus Christ and through the power of his blood.

For instance, one day I came down with a headache. Thinking it was from travel, I thought a good rest, then a good meal, then good fellowship, then a good night of sleep, then two aspirin, might help. Nothing worked. So I searched my heart to see if there was any unconfessed sin there. Still no relief. Finally, at midnight, I tried the only thing left to do. I prayed to God, claiming the blood of Christ, then rebuked that headache in the name of the Lord. It was gone instantly! I turned over and was asleep that fast.

While we were house parents in Sentani at the Hostel, I had a series of meetings in a church on one of the islands in Lake Sentani. Every time I was preparing to go, I experienced some physical symptom of illness. After one or two times, it became evident that Satan was trying to hinder my going to minister to those believers. Each subsequent time, I prayed in the name of the Lord Jesus Christ, rebuking this symptom and that. <u>Every time</u> the symptoms disappeared, some immediately, others gradually over several days. The last time I went, Satan tried again! It struck me so funny, that after all these times of defeat, he <u>still</u> was attempting to do the same thing. As I laughed, the symptom immediately disappeared.

We can expect Satanic attacks as we seek to serve the Lord. So we need to take up and use the armor and weapons God has given us if we hope to have victory over these attacks in our lives.

APPLICATION: There are two avenues of access that Satan uses to attack us: one is through purposeful sin; the other is through our ministry (which threatens his hold on others). The first avenue of attack is cared for by confession of and forsaking our sin. That way, Satan has no foothold from which to trouble us. In dealing with the second avenue, I have found James 4:7 to be very effective: "Submit yourselves, then, to God. Resist the devil, and he will flee from you." In any given physical or ministry situation, when I sense there is a possible Satanic attack (sometimes it's really hard to tell), I follow the steps found in this verse: 1. I submit myself or this ministry into God's hands for his will to be done. He just might want to teach me something through this situation that I might not otherwise learn, and I must be willing to let him do that. Then I rebuke this situation, whatever it is, in the name of the Lord Jesus Christ and command it to cease. When it does, then I know that it was a Satanic attack; if it doesn't, then I know that God has something to teach me through it, so am able to focus on that. Either way, we come out on the victory side!

DAY 146
[a]HE IS THE PERSECUTED ONE, cont.

(Psychological, Emotional Turmoil,
Fear and Dread of the Worst Thing Happening)

QUESTIONS TO THINK ABOUT:

1. Psychological warfare is a very powerful tool. Dictators, tyrants and even religions use it and the fear it produces, to force people to do what they want. How can this fear be overcome?

2. We fear and dread what we cannot control; but what does that say about our faith in God when we give in to it?

PSYCHOLOGICAL, EMOTIONAL TURMOIL

It is no wonder that when we consider Christ's suffering (Heb.5:8), we read that his heart was troubled (Jn.12:27,28) and that he was a man of sorrows, even to the point of death (Isa.53:3; Matt.26:38)!

Paul described his sufferings as an extension of Christ's for the sake of the Church (Col.1:24). In 2 Corinthians 4 he cataloged some of what he went through: a wasting away of the body (vs.16), hard pressed and perplexed (vs.8), persecuted and struck down (vs.9), and under constant sentence of death (vs.10,11). He and others often had been in dangers, sleepless, suffering from hunger and thirst, cold and without proper clothing, and subject to hard labor (2 Cor.11:26,27). He wrote in the same letter, "We do not want you to be uninformed, brothers, about the hardships we suffered in the province of Asia. We were under great pressure, far beyond our ability to endure, so that we despaired even of life" (2 Cor.1:8 – underlining mine).

Referring again to the story of Pastor Harlan Papov, he wrote that many of the prisoners physically could endure the torture and extreme hardships they were put to. But what caused many men to crack emotionally and mentally was the helplessness they felt and the deep frustration of knowing that their wives and children were suffering as much as they were, and that they could not help them; knowing that their families were homeless, starving, going without necessary clothing, being subjected to winter's cold without adequate shelter, being shunned by former friends, and even unable to find work because their husband and father was in prison and they are Christians.

We don't begin to know the pressures of that kind of persecution for the sake of Christ. When Popov's family was able to move to Sweden (his wife was a Swedish citizen), he felt like a new man; no longer could the communists get at him through his family. He felt free and experienced new boldness to preach and witness in prison (Papov, pp.64,77,78).

At the time of Christ's trial and death, culminating his suffering here on earth, Satan pulled out all the stops and did his utmost to completely overwhelm him and conquer his spirit (Lk.22:41-44).

The sufferings of Christians today reflect the full spectrum of suffering that Christ endured, but none of us individually will ever suffer to the extent he did, nor experience all the kinds of suffering he went through. This is God's grace to us.

FEAR AND DREAD OF THE WORST POSSIBLE THING HAPPENING

In the Garden of Gethsemane, Christ, deeply distressed and troubled, said to his disciples, "My soul is overwhelmed with sorrow to the point of death" (Mk.14:33,34). And Luke records that he was in anguish, praying earnestly and sweating profusely (Lk.22:44).

Have you ever feared about the worst possible thing happening to you? It happened to Christ in the Garden and he recoiled from it. "Father, if you are willing, take this cup from me," he cried. (His prayer is a bit bland in written form, but remember Hebrews 5:7 where his prayers are described as loud cries punctuated with tears. "Father!! Take this cup from me! I can't bear it!!!" And his body is convulsed with wrenching sobs and dread. Then, with tears streaming down his face, and sweat pouring out of every pore, he resigns himself to his Father's will: "Yet not my will, but yours be done" (Lk.22:42).

Job experienced this as well. He says in Job 3:25,26, "What I feared has come upon me; what I dreaded has happened to me. I have no peace, no quietness; I have no rest, but only turmoil."

If your worst fears ever come to pass, know that Christ's did also; he's been there before you. He knows what it is like to face something so dreadful that the dread of it alone was enough to bring on death (Mk.14:33,34)!

APPLICATION: We all have our obvious or secret "dreads." Some of them can be cared for just by our taking responsibility to learn what we need to know to guard against any eventuality. Others are beyond our control. Those we have to leave in God's hands, knowing that he knows what is best for us and will only allow those things to touch us. Then he will give us the grace to go through that trial and come out the other side! Jesus said, "Don't worry about tomorrow" (Matt.6:34). So let's not!

DAY 147
[a]HE IS THE PERSECUTED ONE, cont.

(Oppressed, Betrayed)

◆

QUESTIONS TO THINK ABOUT:

1. If one is feeling oppressed, what does that mean?
2. What is the difference between feeling oppressed and being oppressed?
3. Has there ever been a time in your life when you felt betrayed by someone? What did that do to you?

OPPRESSED

Two definitions given in the dictionary bear on Christ's sufferings. In Isaiah 53:7 we read that he was oppressed. "To oppress" means "to burden spiritually as if by weight, to weigh down" (Webster). We read in John 13:21 that Jesus was "troubled in spirit." And in John 12:27 he said to his disciples, "Now my heart is troubled, and what shall I say? 'Father, save me from this hour'? No, it was for this very reason I came to this hour." He was weighed down in spirit because of what he knew was coming.

The second definition is "to crush, burden or trample down by abuse of power or authority; to treat with unjust rigor or with cruelty" (Webster). In Isaiah 53:5 we read that Jesus was "crushed for our iniquities." The whole trial scene of Jesus was a demonstration of abuse of authority as everything the Sanhedrin did was technically illegal. Though innocent, he was treated with unjust cruelty, being beaten, flogged, mocked, spit upon and finally executed.

Stephen was similarly treated. He was falsely accused (Acts 6:11-14) and brought before the Sanhedrin. When his defense brought conviction of sin to their hearts (Acts 7:54), they reacted with hatred and immediately cast him out of the city to stone him.

The Lord warned his disciples in John 15:20, "If they persecuted me, they will persecute you also." The promise to us is that they who live godly in Christ Jesus will suffer persecution (2 Tim.3:12). Why? Because the world cannot stand the conviction of sin that a godly life brings upon them. So we need not be amazed when we are persecuted. Some have claimed that more Christians have perished this century than the sum of all centuries from Christ until now, just because they are Christians. But their lifestyle and beliefs make them "incompatible" with the political/religious systems of their countries. So they are oppressed, afflicted, and killed, even as Christ was. This gives us more urgency in our desire for the world to come, even as Paul writes in Romans 8:22,23: "We know that the whole creation has been groaning as in the pains of childbirth right up to the present time. Not only so, but we ourselves, who have the firstfruits of the Spirit, groan inwardly as we wait eagerly for our adoption as sons, the redemption of our bodies."

BETRAYED

Judas Iscariot, supposed friend and disciple of the Lord's for three years, trusted treasurer among the twelve, sold him for a mere 30 pieces of silver (approximately $12.60!) Considering the daily wage of a penny an hour, this amount would represent approximately

1/3 of a year's wage at 10 cents a day. He supposed, since he loved money, that he could make a tidy profit, the Lord would be beaten and probably released, and all would be well. However, when Judas discovered that Christ was condemned to die, his money turned sour in his bag, he threw it back to the priests and went out to hang himself (Matt.27:3-5).

King David experienced betrayal from his best friend and counselor, Ahithophel, when Absalom overthrew him in a coup (2 Sam.15:31; 17:14; Ps.41:9). It is one thing to be <u>deserted</u> by one's friends, but wholly another to be <u>turned over</u> to one's enemies by them. Yet Christ said that this would happen to his followers, where even those of one's own family will betray the believer to death (Matt.10:21; Lk.21:16)! This is a very common occurrence in lands dominated by communism (Papov, p.25), Islam, Buddhism and Hinduism. Betrayal and death are always a daily threat.

We experienced "betrayal" when a close friend and co-worker up and left the area for another job without telling us a word about it until just before they left. We had to pick up the pieces and move on, but the sense of betrayal still lingers on today, many years after it happened.

APPLICATION: From time to time we will feel oppressed because of betrayal by others. It helps to accept the fact that they will have to give account to God, not to me, for their actions. In spite of the continuing hurt caused, we have to leave it in God's hands and persevere in what he has given us to do. I have found that praying for those who have oppressed or betrayed me has greatly reduced the hurt and even anger I feel toward them. But sometimes I just have to harden my heart against the hurt I feel and choose not to let it bother me. Then I remember the lesson from DAYS 11,12 – HE IS THE FORGIVING ONE, and must pray again, this time to forgive them and thus release my hurt and anger from them once and for all. May we each have the grace and willingness to do this.

DAY 148
ᶜHE IS THE PERSECUTED ONE, cont.

(Seizure and Arrest, Denounced, Forsaken)

◆

QUESTIONS TO THINK ABOUT:

1. When Jesus was arrested, his disciples forsook him and fled. How do you suppose that made him feel?

2. When have you ever been left "holding the bag" while your friends "scattered"?

3. How do you suppose it would feel to be forsaken by God and know it?

SEIZURE AND ARREST

Once Judas had identified Christ to the mob that came with him, they seized, arrested and bound him (Jn.18:12). It was at night, in a quiet place, during a "prayer meeting" (Matt.26:50). Then they led him away (Lk.22:54). How many thousands of times has this pattern been repeated since then! Christ knew what it was to be summoned at night and taken away. And he said that seizure and arrest would also happen to his followers as a matter of course (Mk.13:11). The pattern developed in Acts: Peter and John were seized in the evening and put in jail (Acts 4:3); Stephen was arrested and killed (Acts 6:12); the apostles were arrested and jailed (Acts 5:18); Saul of Tarsus went about dragging people from their homes to jail and death (Acts 8:3); James was arrested and executed (Acts 12:2); Peter was arrested and jailed (Acts 12:3-4); and Paul was arrested, bound and kept in Roman custody (Acts 21:33).

It is no different in many countries today. In Nepal, for instance, Christians are routinely arrested and jailed for witnessing as it is against the law for a Buddhist to change his religion. In many other countries, Christian leaders have been routinely arrested and jailed as "enemies of the state."

DENOUNCED

At his mock trial that followed, Jesus was denounced as a blasphemer even though he had told the truth (Matt.26:63-66). This is not surprising, for those whose consciences have never been renewed by the Spirit of God cannot recognize truth even when it stares them in the face and shouts (1 Cor.2:13,14)!

Early Christians were slanderously reported as saying, "Let us do evil that good may result" (Rom.3:8). The obvious truth of Christianity regarding sin was totally ignored (see Rom.5:20-6:4). Even today the Christian message is misrepresented and denounced as false, impractical, and foolish. Many university students can attest to this attitude vocally expressed in class by their professors. And we all know what happens when Protestant Christianity is portrayed on TV. The singing is usually off-key, the people dressed shabbily, provincial and out-of-date, and the pastor usually wimpy. Thus the world does its best to denounce Christianity as totally irrelevant to modern times.

FORSAKEN

When the chips were down and the end looked dangerously certain, the disciples deserted Christ, leaving him on his own (Mk.14:50). Those who had so boldly confessed with Peter that they were ready to die with him rather than disown him now fled for their lives (Matt.26:35). The only two who had second thoughts were John and Peter (Jn.18:15), the latter following from far off and eventually denying Christ anyway (Lk.22:56-62). John got as close to Christ as he could, but even so Jesus had to endure his ordeal alone.

The climax of desertion occurred on the Cross where Christ, becoming sin for us, was forsaken by his Father, resulting in the anguished cry from his lips, "My God, my God, why have <u>you</u> forsaken me?" (Matt.27:46, underlining mine). Forsaken by man and forsaken by God, Christ was totally, devastatingly <u>alone</u>.

Yet for believers, that final forsaking by God will never happen. Christ suffered that for us so that we will never have to. The Lord's promise to us is, "Never will I leave you; never will I forsake you" (Heb.13:5; Papov, p.33). So even though at times we feel like he has turned away and left us to face life alone, that feeling is <u>false</u>. His promise is sure. We can count on it 100%! We will <u>never</u> have to experience the total desolation and horror of being forsaken by God.

One Christmas we received a Christmas card in which was written the following story (which emphasizes the above point just made):

FOOTPRINTS

One night a man had a dream.
He dreamed he was walking in a field with the LORD.
Across the sky flashed scenes from his life.
For each scene, he noticed two sets of footprints in the sand;
one belonged to him and the other to the LORD.
When the last scene of his life flashed before him,
he looked back at the footprints in the sand.
He noticed that many times along the path of his life
there was only one set of footprints.
He also notices that it happened at the very lowest and saddest
times in his life.

This really bothered him and he questioned the LORD about it.
"LORD, you said that once I decided to follow you,
you'd walk with me all the way.
But I have noticed that during the most troublesome times
in my life,
there is only set of foot prints.
I don't understand why when I needed you most you would
leave me."

The LORD replied, "My precious, precious child, I love you
and I would never leave you.
During your times of trial and suffering,
when you see only one set of footprints,
it was then that I carried you."

(Author not named)

Our friends and family may forsake us, but God <u>never</u> will! So even when we are alone here on earth, he is still with us. The problem is that we can't see him, so we have to take it on faith. But then, he's never broken a promise yet! Prayer, reading or quoting memorized Scripture, meditating on God's character and singing spiritual songs can go a long way in giving us that assurance that God is with us.

DAY 149
ᶜHE IS THE PERSECUTED ONE, cont.

(Falsely Tried, Condemned, Target for Jealousy)

QUESTIONS TO THINK ABOUT:

1. Have you ever been falsely accused of something? How did it make you feel?
2. What would be the motives for false accusation?
3. How should we respond when someone else is jealous or envious toward us?

FALSELY TRIED, ACCUSED AND CONDEMNED

Jesus was taken bound to Annas, who then sent him bound to his son-in-law and High Priest, Caiaphas (Jn.18:12,13). The whole Sanhedrin was assembled together with the purpose of seeking a way to put him to death (Mk.14:55). They were neither interested in justice or the truth. Many false witnesses testified against him, but their testimonies conflicted so badly that it embarrassed the Sanhedrin (Mk.14:55-61). Finally Caiaphas asked him if he were the Christ, the Son of the Blessed One, to which Jesus answered, "Yes." Completely disregarding all evidence from his life and ministry that supported this claim, the High Priest and Sanhedrin immediately accused him of blasphemy and condemned him as worthy of death (Mk.14:62-64). Then the soldiers guarding him blindfolded him and began to mock him and beat him and spit in his face (Mk.14:65).

Early Christians suffered the same fate. Stephen endured an unfair trail and condemnation to death because of racial prejudice and conviction of sin among his accusers (Acts 6:8-8:1). With great fanaticism, Saul of Tarsus arrested and brought to trial every Christian he could find in his attempt to stamp out this "heretical religion" (Acts 8:3; 9:1,2; Gal.1:13). Then, when he himself was converted, he suddenly found himself at the receiving end of such treatment, condemned out of hand and even accused of insanity (Acts 16:37; 22:21,22; 26:24).

During these days, the Lord has much company, especially in many countries where Christians are constantly harassed, questioned, detained, accused of being social parasites, insane, or involved in anti-revolutionary or anti-government activities (witnessing or preaching the Gospel), and summarily imprisoned, committed to insane asylums or executed. Truth and justice never even enter the picture. The authorities, like the Sanhedrin, are only interested in crushing anything that doesn't agree with their purposes or political philosophy.

TARGET FOR JEALOUSY/ENVY

Then the Jews took Jesus to Pilate. We read in Matthew 27:18 that Pilate "knew it was out of envy that they had handed Jesus over to him." Jesus was popular, he was powerful, he taught with assurance and authority, he worked undeniable miracles (even to raising the dead! – see Jn.11:47,48,53). He successfully silenced his critics and the "spiritually undeserving" flocked to him. The Pharisees complained to one another at the Triumphal Entry.

"... This is getting us nowhere. Look how the whole world has gone after him!" (Jn.12:19). They keenly felt their loss of status and authority to Jesus. "How can we get rid of him so that once again we can enjoy the prestige of our position, so that all the world will look to us as the true leaders of the Faith?"

This reaction is forever the same. Whenever power and position are threatened by the truth of the Gospel as people respond to it, envy and jealousy will result in the hearts of those who reject it and feel threatened by it. The apostles experienced this at the hands of the Sadducees and were jailed (Acts 5:17). Stephen experienced it at the hands of the members of the Synagogue of the Freedmen, and was killed (Acts 6:8-11; 7:58). Paul experienced it at the hands of the Jews when the whole city flocked to hear him instead of them (Acts 13:44,45,50). He also experienced it at the hands of other supposed Christians who preached the Gospel out of envy, rivalry, and selfish ambition, hoping to add trouble to him while he was in chains (Phil.1:15,17). And Christians have always experienced it whenever other religions have felt threatened by the truth of the Gospel.

One of our missionaries in Irian Jaya had begun what seemed to be a very successful and appealing radio program for the youth of the town in which he ministered. After only two programs, there were complaints from the local liberal Protestant church, and the program was stopped. They were afraid of losing their young people to "another religion."

So we should not be surprised when it happens to us.

APPLICATION: When falsely accused of something, Jesus gives us a good example of how to respond – with silence. He only replied when truth was the issue (cf. Matt.26:59-64).

How does one respond to someone who is jealous of him? First, pray for him that the Lord would work contentment into his heart, for the root of jealousy is discontent with what one is or has. Secondly, follow the guidelines for church discipline (if this person is a believer) found in Matthew 18:15-17. If the person is an unbeliever, then pray for his salvation and a contented heart. Talking with him might not be an immediate option. Pray also for opportunities to be a help to him demonstrating God's love for him. The Lord has wonderful ways of engineering the circumstances of life to provide such opportunities.

DAY 150
ᶜHE IS THE PERSECUTED ONE, cont.

(Imprisonment, Curiosity Piece)

◆

QUESTIONS TO THINK ABOUT:

1. How could imprisonment be an opportunity from the Lord to extend and strengthen his kingdom?
2. Since the message of the cross is foolishness to unbelievers (1 Cor.1:18,21-23), how will they look at us?

IMPRISONMENT

The only reason Jesus didn't experience imprisonment was that he was so quickly executed after his arrest and "trial." Yet again, he has experienced imprisonment. It might be stretching it a bit, but his three days in the grave would have been a kind of imprisonment to him. But then he says something interesting in Matt.25:36, "I was in prison, and you visited me." Now when was this? "When you visited my brothers, you visited me," he replied (Matt.25:40). As he has promised never to leave us nor forsake us (Heb.13:5), that means that wherever we are, he is there too! Therefore, if Christians are in jail, so is he!

When Harlan Papov was committed to a subterranean cell where no light could penetrate, when he was "at the end" and could endure no longer, he tells about how Christ became visible to him, put his arms around him, comforting and strengthening him (Papov, p.67).

Beginning with John the Baptist (Matt.14:3-5), then with the Apostles (Acts 5:17,18), then Peter (Acts 12:1-5), Paul (Acts 16:24;

24:27), John (Rev.1:9) and others (Heb.11:36), Christians through the ages have been frequent occupants of jails and prisons far more often because of their testimony rather than for any evil done.

I remember hearing about three Indonesian women imprisoned for their faith. They demonstrated God's love to the other inmates by cleaning the filthy toilet areas, doing general "house cleaning" in their cell block, and generally changing the entire atmosphere of their prison area. I don't know if any inmates made decisions for Christ, but they sure got a picture of God's love for them!

TREATED AS A CURIOSITY PIECE

From Caiaphas, Jesus was taken to the Roman government for execution. The Jews' accusations could not be proved and Pilate found him innocent. But hearing that Jesus was from Galilee, "Herod's jurisdiction, Pilate sent him to Herod, who was also in Jerusalem at that time. When Herod saw Jesus, he was greatly pleased, because for a long time he had wanted to see him. From what he had heard about him, he hoped to see him perform some miracle. He plied him with many questions, but Jesus gave him no answer. The chief priests and the teachers of the law were standing there, vehemently accusing him. Then Herod and his soldiers ridiculed and mocked him. Dressing him in an elegant robe, they sent him back to Pilate" (Lk.23:7-11).

The Apostle Paul sensed this type of humiliation. When writing to the Corinthians, he said, "For it seems to me that God has put us apostles on display at the end of the procession, like men condemned to die in the arena.* We have been made a spectacle to the whole universe, to angels as well as to men" (1 Cor.4:9).

As others notice the difference between our lives and theirs, their curiosity will be aroused as to why the difference. Some will be convinced and converted; but most will respond with something like, "Boy, isn't he a curious one! How could he ever believe that rubbish?" Some will try to initiate dialogue or debate, just to hear and laugh at these curious beliefs. If we are different, we will be an enigma, a curiosity piece to those around us.

APPLICATION: Bouncing off Christ's words, "When I was in prison ...," he also spoke about being without clothing, sick, being a stranger, etc. In essence, what he is saying is that in all our afflictions, he is right there with us, going through whatever trial we are experiencing. Why doesn't he deliver us immediately? There are several reasons. 1. We gain eternal reward from our trials (2 Cor.4:17); 2. We gain spiritual maturity in our trials (Jas.1:2-4); 3. God is working through all these things to make us like Christ (Rom.8:28,29); and 4. We gain opportunity to be a witness to those who are persecuting us. Even though our trials are not pleasant, the outcome is well worth it, and for that we can give thanks!

* [**NOTE:** When the victorious Roman army returned to Rome, they would parade their captives through the streets of the city in a triumphal procession. At the end of this procession was a group of captives who were doomed to death in the arena. They were on display to be looked at, jeered at, and exulted over.]

DAY 151
ᶜHE IS THE PERSECUTED ONE, cont.

(Hauled before Authorities, Beaten, Scourged)

QUESTIONS TO THINK ABOUT:

1. How could being brought before authorities be a witness to them that they would not otherwise hear?
2. What should be our attitude if we are ever beaten for being a Christian?

HAULED BEFORE THE AUTHORITIES

One day Jesus told his disciples what they were going to experience in time to come. He said, "On my account you will be brought before governors and kings as witnesses to them and to the Gentiles" (Matt. 10:18). And he was the first to fulfill this prophecy, appearing before Pilate, then Herod, then Pilate again. Pilate knew something unusual was going on because of the manner in which the Jews were trying to get rid of Jesus. He also knew something supernatural was going on because of a message from his wife: "Don't have anything to do with that innocent man, for I have suffered a great deal today in a dream because of him" (Matt.27:19). In John 18:33-38 we read a portion of Jesus' witness to him.

In the book of Acts, it is Paul whom we most often see taken before governors and kings because of his faith. He appeared before the magistrates of Philippi (Acts 16:20), Gallio, proconsul of Achaia (Acts 18:12), Claudius Lysias, chief captain of the Roman garrison at Jerusalem (Acts 21:27-23:22), Felix, the governor (Acts 23:24), Porcius Festus, the governor (Acts 24:27-25:27), King Herod Agrippa II (Acts 26:1-32), Publius, the chief man of the island of Malta (Acts 28:7-10), and finally before Caesar himself (Acts 25:12).

Today many leaders of the world have heard the Gospel through the preaching of Billy Graham, Louis Palau, and others, and there is the indisputable witness of thousands of Christians who will not yield to the godless authorities of their lands who are attempting to crush Christianity. The message is being given, though how much of it is falling on deaf ears, only the Lord knows. But many are hearing it.

BEATEN/SCOURGED

When Herod could get no satisfaction out of Jesus, he sent him back to Pilate, who again tried to release him. But the Jews were adamant, demanding his death. Pilate then had Jesus scourged: stripped and tied down to a pillar (or tied onto a frame), then whipped (Vine, "Scourge," B., pp.327,328, in which he writes about Eusebius, an early Church historian, who lived during the first quarter of the fourth century, who recorded having witnessed the suffering of martyrs who died from Roman scourgings.) The Roman whip consisted of leather thongs (usually nine, known as the "cat of nine tails"), weighted with sharp pieces of bone or lead, which tore open one's flesh (Matt.27:26). It is conjectured that Pilate had him beaten in this way, then presented him so bloodied to the people once again (Jn.19:4,5) with the hope that, seeing him in such a condition, they would be satisfied and let him go. But, seeing him thus, their frenzy for his death was only that much greater!

Christ prophesied that his followers would be flogged in the synagogues (Matt.10:17). Jewish flogging was more humane than the Roman scourging. The Jewish whip consisted of only three leather thongs. The offender received 13 lashes on the bare chest and 13 on each shoulder (the "forty stripes save one"). In 2 Corinthians 11:24, Paul says he was whipped in this way five times. In verse 25 he says he was beaten with rods three times (one time of which occurred in Acts 16:22,23 when he and Silas were severely flogged. The Greek word used here indicates a beating with rods).

Today, in many lands, Christians suffer beatings and scourgings because of their faith. Foxe's Book of Martyrs, Papov's Tortured for His Faith, and other such books report many beatings of believers. I myself have witnessed Christians being beaten on the legs with bamboo rods until they could no longer stand. Allegedly, they had disobeyed some local petty government official and he was out to show them who was boss. Knowing his continued opposition to our work and the Gospel, we suspected that these beatings had some religious overtones, though we could never prove it.

APPLICATION: The best way for us to prepare to appear before authorities is to be in the Word and to trust what the Lord said in

Luke 12:11,12 that the Holy Spirit will give us the right words at the right time. Our attitude in beatings should be like that of the apostles (Acts 5:40,41) who rejoiced because they had been counted worthy to suffer disgrace for the Name [of Jesus].

If you are ever beaten for the sake of Christ, just remember: Jesus was there ahead of you. He took it for you; you can take it for him – and persevere. Again, when the apostles were flogged they rejoiced because they had been counted worthy to suffer for Christ (Acts 5:40,41).

DAY 152
ᶜHE IS THE PERSECUTED ONE, cont.

(Mobbed, Hit, Spit upon)

QUESTIONS TO THINK ABOUT:

1. What is the purpose and power of a mob?
2. How would you feel to be hit in the face and spit upon, especially if you'd done nothing to deserve it?
3. What would that kind of treatment signify?

MOBBED

When Jesus was arrested, the Scriptures say that a large armed crowd followed Judas to the place where Jesus was (Matt.26:47). While Jesus was being examined by Pilate, the Pharisees, elders and teachers of the law incited a near riot among the people clamoring for his death. Mob pressure and fear of another riot were two factors that caused Pilate to yield to their demand.

In Thessalonica, a rioting mob unsuccessfully tried to find Paul and Silas (Acts 17:5-7), but had to be satisfied with Jason and some other brothers. At Berea the same Jews stirred up the crowds against Paul and Silas (Acts 17:13). At Ephesus, the whole city was thrown into an uproar by Demetrius and company because their trade in idols of Diana was being threatened by the Gospel (Acts 19:23-41). Again, when Paul was in Jerusalem, some Jews from the province of Asia saw him in the Temple and immediately stirred up the whole crowd and seized him (Acts 21:27-32). Pretty soon the whole city was in an uproar and Paul was saved from death only by the forceful intervention of the Roman army.

In the first several decades of the Gospel in Colombia, South America, mobs of Catholics, incited by their priests, stoned Protestant churches and murdered Christians. During the cultural revolution in China (and also during the earlier Boxer Rebellion), mobs of Chinese tore down and burned churches, killing all the Christians they could find. Even in Papua mobs of unbelievers have occasionally harassed evangelistic meetings and threatened believers.

HIT IN THE FACE AND SPIT UPON

When the high priest questioned Jesus about his disciples and his teaching, Jesus replied, "I always taught publicly, never in secret. Why question me? Ask those who heard me and know what I said." Then a temple official struck him in the face (Jn.18:20-22). Once they had condemned him, those guarding him blindfolded him and began hitting him in the face, spitting at him (Mk.14:65). In almost any culture, spitting at someone is a sign of the utmost contempt. Later, the soldiers of Pilate took Jesus into the Praetorium, and with all the other soldiers there began to mock him and spit on him and strike him in the face (Jn.19:3).

When Paul was on defense before the Sanhedrin, he said, "My brothers, I have fulfilled my duty to God in all good conscience to this day," at which Ananias, the high priest, ordered him struck on the mouth – in violation of the law (Acts 23:1-3).

Down through the ages, Christians have been treated in the same way. One of our missionaries in language school was spit upon by Muslim school children coming out of a mosque. They were "feeling their oats," just having completed their annual month of fasting, and hearing a pep talk from their Imam. As Christ said in John 15:20, "If they have persecuted me, they will persecute you also."

APPLICATION: There is usually nothing you can do against a mob except to commit yourself to the Lord and ask for his intervention, protection and will to be done. We cannot die before the time appointed by the Lord; and if this is not our time, deliverance will come. If it is our time, then the Lord will give us grace for that hour. Another thought – It could be that the Lord brought all these people to you so that they could hear a clear presentation of the Gospel (if you have a chance to speak)!

To be spit upon is most humiliating, and that is what that action is meant for. Jesus accepted that as part of his humbling himself to become a man. If he took it humbly, so can we.

DAY 153
ᶜHE IS THE PERSECUTED ONE, cont.

(Disfigured, Marred, Pierced, Crucified)

QUESTIONS TO THINK ABOUT:

1. What would happen to one's face and head if his hair was literally pulled away from the skin?
2. How was Christ's body "broken" for us?

DISFIGURED, MARRED

In Isaiah 52:14 we read that "many … were appalled at him – his appearance was so disfigured beyond that of any man and his form marred beyond human likeness – ." Isaiah 50:6 reveals why: "I offered my back to those who beat me, my cheeks to those who pulled out my beard; I did not hide my face from mocking and spitting."

Head wounds bleed profusely. From the crown of thorns, blood streamed down all over him. Patches of beard along with skin were pulled from his face, making him look grotesque. Spit was mingled with blood. His face was probably black and blue from being struck and pummeled. His back and front were torn open and bleeding from the cruel scourging. His garments were blood-soaked. "Many … were appalled." If a true picture were ever painted of Christ's actual appearance on the Cross, it would be so repulsive that the romanticism of the Cross would be forever lost. Christians would finally see the utter horribleness of what sin did to the Son of God and gain a new awe and wonder at the love of God and of the Lord Jesus who willingly suffered all this in order to redeem mankind. None of us would ever again take sin so lightly.

From the time of the Apostles to the present, many Christians have been so tortured as to leave them physically disfigured. I have read where Watchman Nee's arms were broken and set in such a way that he could no longer bring his hands together in prayer. Others were ruined in health as well as body. The Lord Jesus has already been there. He knows that kind of suffering.

PIERCED AND CRUCIFIED

When Pilate handed Jesus over to his soldiers to be crucified, the soldiers plated a crown of thorns and set in on his head. Then they bowed in mockery before him, took the rod "scepter" out of his hand and struck him repeatedly on the head (Matt.27:27-30). Then they took him away to be crucified, and nailed him to the Cross (Jn.20:25). Finally, to see if Jesus was really dead or not, one of the soldiers pierced his side with a spear (Jn.19:34). Again, in Revelation 1:7, he is referred to as the one who was pierced; in Isaiah 53:5 as the one pierced for our transgressions, crushed for our iniquities.

Many early Christians suffered piercing as they were crucified, put to the sword (Acts 12:2; Foxe, p.12), impaled on stakes, or thrown onto the horns of wild bulls (Foxe, p.15). During the Middle Ages they had a special torture called "The Iron Maiden," a body-shaped casket with iron spikes set so as to penetrate the more sensitive parts of the body when closed upon the victim. An MAF pilot in Kalimantan, Indonesia, was nearly killed in a machete attack when protecting his house girl from being raped. He lived, but was disfigured from the attack.

APPLICATION: We can become disfigured through an accident or through persecution; either way, the outcome is the same. What we need to remember is that our disfigurement is only temporary. We await our resurrection bodies which will be entirely whole and even "healthier" than our whole bodies here on earth!

DAY 154
ʿHE IS THE PERSECUTED ONE, cont.

(Property Confiscated, Mocked, Humiliated)

QUESTIONS TO THINK ABOUT:

1. If you lost everything you owned, what would you still have?
2. How would the loss of everything, or of some prized possessions, test what's in our heart?

3. "Sticks and stones can break my bones, but words can never hurt me!" is a saying that I learned as a child. In terms of mocking and humiliation, how true is this statement? In how many ways can we be hurt?

PROPERTY CONFISCATED

During his life on earth, Jesus had very little in terms of possessions, and less during his ministry. But when he was crucified, the last possession he had (his clothes) was taken from him and distributed by lot among the soldiers (Lk.23:34). In Luke 6:29,30 Jesus said to his disciples: "... If someone takes your cloak, do not stop him from taking your tunic... . And if anyone takes what belongs to you, do not demand it back."

The early Christians also suffered loss of property under the Roman Emperor Domitian (Foxe, p.15). The same was true under other Emperors as well. Diocletian (304 A.D.) had one whole town surrounded and burned. In Rome, he confiscated church property (Latourette, p.91). In Hebrews 11:37 we read of believers without adequate clothing and destitute, wandering in the wilderness, everything they had on earth taken from them.

The same story is repeated over and over again in many lands. Churches have been confiscated and used for warehouses, factories and meeting halls. Christians have lost their jobs, their homes, their possessions and their families time and again under all sorts of false charges. And any Christians caught helping those so deprived faced experiencing the same themselves! We refer again to the pastor's wife in Harlan Papov's story, who, after her husband was imprisoned and everything they had taken away, was also rejected by those in the church they had so faithfully served, lest they also be arrested, imprisoned, and suffer the loss of all they had. Informers placed in the church would be sure to report them (Papov, pp.39,62,63).

HUMILIATED

In Matthew 27:29-31,41, Christ was mocked by the soldiers, the chief priests, the teachers of the law and the elders of Israel. He was sneered at and taunted (Lk.23:35), ridiculed (Lk.23:11) and insulted (Matt.27:39) as he hung helplessly on the Cross. As the prophet said, "He was despised" (Isa.53:3). Men do not mock someone they respect.

Stripped of his clothing, hanging openly on a cross, and being mocked and insulted was indeed humiliating to the Lord. In Acts 8:33 we read, "In his humiliation he was deprived of justice. Who can speak of his descendants? For his life was taken from the earth." And yet he endured this humiliation for a higher purpose: "... Who for the joy set before him endured the cross, scorning its shame, and sat down at the right hand of the throne of God" (Heb.12:2b).

When Paul was at Athens proclaiming the "Unknown God" to those gathered in the Areopagus, they listened to him willingly enough until he mentioned the resurrection of the dead (Acts 17:22-32). Upon hearing that, some of them sneered and mocked, humiliating him, but others wanted to hear more about it.

Reports from China tell of Christians being mocked and jeered at in their places of work in an attempt to reclaim them from their "foolishness" to the wisdom of the revolution. If they refused to recant, they often lost their jobs and were reduced to begging or the lowest menial labor. Yet they endured this humiliation for the sake of Christ, and the better hope they have beyond this world (cf. Heb.11:27,35).

There is a principle we find in Scripture: <u>humiliation precedes honor</u>. Philippians 2:8,9a says, "And being found in appearance as a man, he [Jesus] humbled himself and became obedient to death – even death on a cross! Therefore God exalted him to the highest place ... ." First Peter 5:6 says, "Humble yourselves, therefore, under God's mighty hand, that he may lift you up in due time." Sometimes others "help" us along in the process!

DAY 155
ᶜHE IS THE PERSECUTED ONE, cont.

(Cursed, Thirsty)

QUESTIONS TO THINK ABOUT:

1. What does it mean to curse someone?
2. Can Christians be cursed and have it stick? Why or why not?
3. How did Jesus become a curse for us?
4. Have you ever been really, really thirsty? How many kinds of thirst can we experience?
5. How can our thirst be satisfied?

CURSED

We read in Galatians 3:13, "Christ redeemed us from the curse of the law by becoming a curse for us, for it is written: 'Cursed is everyone who is hung on a tree.'" "Cursed" here means to be under God's special condemnation. Christ endured this so that we would never have to!

Yet we find times in Scripture where God's people have been cursed by others. When David was fleeing from Absalom, Shimei, son of Gera, from the tribe of Benjamin, cursed him, denouncing him as a vile man, full of blood, and under God's judgment (2 Sam.16:5-13). Balak, king of Moab, tried to get the prophet Balaam to curse Israel for him so that he could beat them in battle (Num.22:6,17). But the Lord would not permit it, and Balaam had to bless them instead (Num.23:11,12).

Christians today experience cursing from time to time. The Lord anticipated this and said, "... Love your enemies, do good to those who hate you, bless those who curse you, pray for those who mistreat you" (Lk.6:27,28). And Paul adds in Romans 12:14, "Bless those who persecute you; bless and do not curse." The temptation is for us to curse back, but we are to resist that and bless instead.

A friend of ours grew up on the mission field, got married, and had a deformed and retarded first child. She told us later that while she was in boarding school, a witch doctor had cursed her and the group of girls she was with. The first child of each one was not normal. Why did this happen? She and her friends purposely attended a witchcraft convention against their parents' orders. We read in Proverbs 26:2, "Like a fluttering sparrow or a darting swallow, an undeserved curse does not come to rest." Conversely, a deserved curse will take effect. The willful disobedience of these girls put them in the place where this curse could hurt them. However, if they had done nothing deserving of a curse, yet were cursed, the curse would not have taken effect.

However, having said that, I know of a godly missionary family who was cursed by a witch doctor, and from that time on they were plagued with all sorts of physical illness. I don't know what steps they might have taken in terms of spiritual warfare to counter the curse, but obviously the curse remained, so perhaps they just accepted their lot and persevered in spite of it.

But we have at our disposal the authority of the name of the Lord Jesus Christ and the power of his blood to resist and protect ourselves from curses directed our way. But if we passively let the enemy shoot at us without "taking up our arms," I assume we could be hit, no matter how spiritual we are. We must fight Satan with all the weapons at our disposal and not give place or ground to him through purposeful and unconfessed sin (as the girls mentioned above), or passiveness (which might have been the issue with the missionary family) in doing nothing to protect ourselves. James 4:7 says that we are to submit ourselves to God then actively resist the devil; and he will flee from us! That includes curses.

THIRSTY

One of the agonies of crucifixion is that of extreme thirst. The Psalmist prophetically described this in Psalm 22:15 where he writes: "My tongue sticks to the roof of my mouth." Tongue swollen and dry, Jesus cried out, "I am thirsty" (Jn.19:28).

Any Christian who was crucified or left in a cell to rot and die knew thirst. Many forced to wander about in the wilderness (Heb.11:38) knew thirst. Coming back to Harlan Papov – one time he was forced to stand eight inches from a glaringly white wall for two weeks without moving or blinking his eyes, and without food or water! The Lord kept him alive and strengthened him, but he knew thirst! (Papov. pp.29-34).

DAY 156
ʻHE IS THE PERSECUTED ONE, cont.

(Killed, Christ's Attitude)

QUESTIONS TO THINK ABOUT:

1. Why do many of other political and religious convictions want to kill Christians?

2. What was the motivation of Saul of Tarsus in killing Christians?

3. What was Jesus' attitude toward the persecution he experienced?

KILLED

Technically, the Jews and the Romans did not kill Jesus; they could not kill him; but he gave up his spirit by his own volition and died (Lk.23:46). And yet Christ himself said in Matthew 17:22,23, "The Son of Man is going to be betrayed into the hands of men. They will kill him ... ." And Revelation 13:8 calls him "the Lamb that was slain."

He also warned his disciples that "a time is coming when anyone who kills you will think he is offering a service to God" (Jn.16:2). Saul of Tarsus fulfilled this prophecy. He was jealous for his God, the Temple, and the Law, and felt it his sacred duty to exterminate any and all who seemed opposed to them (1 Cor.15:9; Gal.1:13,14). Muslims, in their zeal for Allah (their god), believe they are doing him service by killing infidel Christians and other nonbelievers in holy war, so that only the "true faith" is left. In Hebrews 11:35-37 and Revelation 20:4, we find Christians being put to death by various means, but all killed for the same reason: "For your sake we face death all day long; we are considered as sheep to be slaughtered" (Rom.8:36 quoting Ps.44:22).

More Christians have been killed in the 20th Century than perhaps have been throughout the entire history of Christianity. And the 21st Century is showing no letup. It is said that 20 million Chinese were killed when the communists took over, the majority of whom were Christians. Missionaries and national believers alike have been killed by terrorists, rebels, and governments opposed to the Gospel. Others have been delivered to death by their own families (Matt.10:21). The world continues to try to rid itself of those who bear the only message of deliverance that it needs, wants, and is looking for!

CHRIST'S ATTITUDE

What, then, should be our attitude toward persecution and those causing it? Some will quickly lose heart and fall away, having no spiritual roots (Matt.13:20,21). But Christ gives us the example that we are to follow. We are to expect persecution at one time or another as he said: "If they have persecuted me, they will persecute you also" (Jn.15:20). And Paul told Timothy that "everyone who wants to live a godly life in Christ Jesus will be persecuted" (2 Tim.3:12).

And when it came to Christ? He endured it for the joy set before him (Heb.12:2), forgiving his enemies (Lk.23:34), and not retaliating when they hurled insults at him. "He made no threats. Instead, he entrusted himself to him (God) who judges justly" (1 Pet.2:23).

In regard to facing persecution, the Lord tells us to:

1. Be on guard against men (Matt.10:17).
2. Be shrewd as snakes but innocent as doves (Matt.10:16).
3. Flee persecution if we can (Matt.10:23; cf. Acts 8:1).
4. Rejoice/praise God (Matt.5:11,12; cf. Acts 5:41 and 1 Pet.4:16).
5. Pray for boldness to speak the Word and serve the Lord (Acts 4:24-30).
6. Not to fear them who kill the body but cannot kill the soul; fear God who can destroy both in hell (Matt.10:28).
7. Not to worry about our defense, for the Holy Spirit will give us the words to say. He will speak through us (Matt.10:19,20; cf. Acts 4:8-13).
8. Be faithful to the end (Matt.10:22).
9. Love our enemies, do good to them (Rom.12:20); bless them (Rom.12:14).
10. Forgive them (Acts 7:60).
11. Leave vengeance and retribution in the Lord's hands (Rom.12:17,19).
12. Keep our eyes fixed on heaven and eternity (2 Cor.4:17,18).

Paul aptly summarizes the whole thing in 2 Corinthians 4:17,18 where he writes: "For our light and momentary troubles are achieving for us an eternal glory that far outweighs them all. So we fix our eyes not on what is seen, but on what is unseen. For what is seen is temporary, but what is unseen is eternal."

And lastly, Colossians 3:1-4. "Since, then, you have been raised with Christ, set your hearts on things above, where Christ is seated at the right hand of God. Set your minds on things above, not on earthly things. For you died, and your life is now hidden with Christ in God. When Christ, who is your life, appears, then you also will appear with him in glory." Amen!

APPLICATION: It is neither easy nor pleasant to suffer persecution. But when it falls our lot, God has promised us his peace and eternal reward. He will repay in full for our sufferings for him. He is no man's debtor.

DAY 157
ᶜHE IS THE PERSECUTED ONE, concl.

(Conclusion)

QUESTIONS TO THINK ABOUT:

1. What are some of the positive effects of persecution?
2. How can we "arm" ourselves ahead of time in case persecution comes our way?

This rather long section of our study needs one final word of a more positive and victorious nature, for God does not permit us to suffer persecution for nothing. He promises us positive results and blessings because of it.

Unexpected Transformation / 365

In this world:

Persecution is the worst of hell that we will ever experience and that only for a short time, not for eternity like the unsaved. We actually deserve worse, but God's grace spares us that. So we can then rejoice in his goodness to us in giving us less than we deserve.

Persecution is proof that we are the Lord's as the world reacts against his message through us (Jn.15:18-21). So we have assurance that we are truly saved.

Persecution will refine and purify us (1 Pet.1:6,7). Thus it becomes one more step in God's plan to mold us into Christ's image as we learn to respond to persecution in the way that Christ did.

Persecution is also the guarantee of our inheritance with God (Rom.8:17).

We will be blessed with an extra measure of the Spirit of God for that hour (1 Pet.4:14), for he will give us the words to speak that our enemies cannot refute (Mk.13:11). Thus our persecutors will have to acknowledge God's love for us (and for them) which may, in God's grace, draw some of them to himself (Rev.3:9; Lk.21:12-15).

In heaven:

If we have left houses, lands and family, etc., we will receive 100-fold in repayment plus everlasting life (Matt.19:29).

We will receive a great and eternal reward (Matt.5:12; 2 Cor.4:17), and great joy at the revealing of Christ's glory (1 Pet.4:13). We also will be glorified with him and receive our inheritance (Rom.8:17,18).

We shall reign with him in his kingdom (Lk.22:28,29; 2 Tim.2:12; Rev.20:4).

And we shall receive the Crown of Life (Rev.2:10; Jas.1:2).

This is just the beginning! Paul declares in 1 Corinthians 2:9, "No eye has seen, no ear has heard, no mind has conceived what God has prepared for those who love him." We frequently sing the song, "It will be worth it all when we see Jesus. Life's trials will seem so small when we see Christ. One glimpse of His dear face, all sorrow will erase. So bravely run the race, till we see Christ."

Paul's conclusion to all of this is found in Romans 8:31-39, a statement of assurance and victory: "What, then, shall we say in response to this? If God is for us, who can be against us? He who did not spare his own Son, but gave him up for us all – how will he not also, along with him, graciously give us all things? Who will bring any charge against those whom God has chosen? It is God who justifies. Who is he that condemns? Christ Jesus, who died – more than that, who was raised to life – is at the right hand of God and is also interceding for us. Who shall separate us from the love of Christ? Shall trouble or hardship or persecution or famine or nakedness or danger or sword? As it is written: 'For your sake we face death all day long; we are considered as sheep to be slaughtered.' No, in all these things we are more than conquerors through him who loved us. For I am convinced that neither death nor life, neither angels nor demons, neither the present nor the future, nor any powers, neither height nor depth, nor anything else in all creation, will be able to separate us from the love of God that is in Christ Jesus our Lord."

APPLICATION: Peter admonished his readers in 1 Peter 4:1, saying, "Therefore, since Christ suffered in his body, arm yourselves also with the same attitude, because he who has suffered in his body is done with sin." Suffering or persecution of any kind has a way of refocusing our attention toward that which is pleasing to God and away from that which displeases him. Just as fire refines the metal, so persecution or suffering refines the believer. Above all this, we need to "fix our eyes on Jesus" (Heb.12:2).

DAY 158
ᵇHE IS OUR PROVIDER

◆

QUESTIONS TO THINK ABOUT:

1. What does God expect of us in meeting the needs of others?
2. God has promised to meet our needs. How is it possible for him to provide for our needs, but at the same time, those needs to go unmet?
3. When we meet the needs of others, to whom are we actually ministering?
4. On the basis of Matthew 6:33, what requirements must we fulfill before we can expect God to meet our needs?
5. How does "good stewardship" of our resources govern what we can give to others?

In Psalm 23:1 we read, "The LORD is my shepherd, I shall not be in want." In Philippians 4:19, "And my God will meet all your needs according to his glorious riches in Christ Jesus." In Matthew 6:33 the Lord promises the provision of food, clothing and shelter if we seek first the kingdom of God and his righteousness. In Mark 10:29,30 he promises to those who leave everything for his sake and the gospel's houses, brothers, sisters, mothers, children and lands a hundredfold now in this time. The sons of Korah declare in Psalm 84:11, "No good thing does he withhold from those whose walk is blameless." He promises us wisdom (Jas.1:5), guidance (Isa.30:21), comfort (2 Cor.1:4,5), protection (Ps.34:7; 91), health (Ps.103:3), life (Jn.6:33,47), help (Heb.13:6), spiritual food through his Word (Matt.4:4), the Holy Spirit and everything his presence and ministry includes (Jn.16:7), every spiritual blessing in the heavenly places in Christ (Eph.1:3), and all that we need for life and godliness (2 Pet.1:3). And if these are not enough, Paul writes that "No eye has seen, no ear has heard, no mind has conceived what God has prepared for those who love him" (1 Cor. 2:9).

In Acts 4:34 we find Christians providing for each other so that "there were no needy persons among them." Each one was given or provided for according to his need (vs.35). In Acts 6 one group of widows was being neglected in the daily distribution. A committee of seven godly men was chosen to oversee the distribution and to make sure everyone was provided for. Not to provide for one's relatives, and especially for his own family, was considered to be as bad as apostasy and worse than the sin of unbelief (1 Tim.5:8)!

We find in the above verses that provision must be made in the physical, psychological, emotional, social and spiritual realms. Our own families are first priority, then our needy relatives, then other believers, then non-believers: food, clothing, shelter; comfort, love, acceptance; being a father, mother, brother or sister to those who have no family or are far from their families; talking about, teaching and living spiritual values before our families and others. As Solomon says, "Do not withhold good from those who deserve it, when it is in your power to act. Do not say to your neighbor, 'Come back later; I'll give it tomorrow' – when you now have it with you" (Prov.3:27,28). When we provide for others by sharing from what we have, this is a sacrifice that pleases God (Heb.13:16). Another thing to keep in mind is that when we meet the needs of the least of God's people, the Lord looks on that as being done to himself! (see Matt.25:34-40). Too often we lose sight of this fact in our relationship with others, and thus lose out in eternal reward that would otherwise have been ours. So let us be faithful in providing for the needs of others as the Lord enables us so that we may be found daily serving him.

Just one final thought. Some have asked, "But if I am always giving to the needs of others, how will my needs be met?" The Lord said in Luke 6:38, "Give, and it will be given to you. A good measure, pressed down, shaken together and running over, will be poured into your lap. For with the measure you use, it will be measured to you." As we give to others, the Lord will cause still others to give to us. You see, "God is able to make all grace abound to you, so that in all things at all times, having all that you need, you will abound in every good work" (2 Cor.9:8).

Do you rejoice in meeting the needs of others?

APPLICATION: Giving to meet the needs of others has to be "intentional," i.e. we have to plan for it. If we don't, we will never have enough to give. Part of the culture of Papua, Indonesia, is asking friends/relatives for a loan if one has a need. We encouraged our students to set up a family budget, part of which to be set aside for "loans" (a "public assistance" envelope). Culturally, you're obligated to give even when you don't have it to give. We knew of one person who was asked for a loan, but didn't have it to give. So he went to someone else to ask for a loan so that he could give the loan to the one asking him! God doesn't expect this from us! The Scriptural principle is to give as we have opportunity and resources to give.

So we told our students, "You are responsible first to meet the needs of your family – not outsiders." So, as you set up your budget, plan a certain amount of money to help others; then, when that is gone, you can apologize because you have nothing to give them even though you want to (and have other designated money set aside in your budget). "I'm sorry. We want to help you, but our money [from the public assistance envelope] is gone. But let me pray for you that the Lord would meet your need," and challenge them, on the basis of Matthew 6:33, to seek the Lord first and see what he will do. That way, you guard the needs of your family from those who would take everything you have and force you to beg from others to get your needs met!

We have seen the Lord meet our needs by miraculously providing for them; by taking them away; or by showing us how to get along without them! We must give him that option and be willing to accept whatever he decides.

DAY 159
ᶜHE IS THE REDEEMER

QUESTIONS TO THINK ABOUT:

1. What does it mean to redeem something?
2. How did Jesus redeem us from our sins?
3. How can we serve as a "redeemer" to others?

Amid all his sufferings, Job prophetically proclaimed, "I know that my Redeemer lives, and that in the end he will stand upon the earth" (Job 19:25). Peter declares in 1 Peter 1:18,19, "For you know that it was not with perishable things such as silver or gold that you were redeemed from the empty way of life handed down to you from your forefathers, but with the precious blood of Christ, a lamb without blemish or defect." The Greek word "to redeem" is *lutroo*, signifying the actual deliverance from something by means of the death of Christ.

But in Galatians 3:13 and 4:5, Paul speaks of Christ delivering the Christian Jews from the Law and its curse. Paul here uses the Greek word *exagorazo* which means "to buy" as in "to buy out," especially of purchasing a slave with a view to his freedom. It also includes the concept of substitution. In Acts 20:28 we read that Christ "bought [the church of God] with his own blood." Thus through Christ's death, we are delivered from bondage to sin and from the curse of the Law.

I once translated a film strip script regarding twin brothers. The one was godly; the other a thief. In the process of time the thief murdered someone who had cheated him and had tried to kill him. He fled to his twin brother for refuge. His brother asked him for his bloodstained shirt and gave his shirt to him in exchange. Then he went to the police and turned himself in as the murderer. Since he looked like the murderer, spoke like the murderer and had a bloodstained shirt like the murderer, he was arrested and sentenced to death without a question as to his true identity. Before he was executed, he wrote a letter to his brother, expressing his love for him and Christ's love for him. He wrote explaining how the Lord Jesus exchanged his shirt of righteousness for our bloodstained shirt of sin. Christ, the Son of God, was in the form of man, spoke as a man, and took our sin upon himself. He was executed like a criminal, but through his death, taking our judgment, we were set free to a new life. He "wrote us a letter" explaining what he did and why, encouraging us to trust him and begin to live a new life. Ali's brother, Abdhul, repented and began to live for Christ. His brother had, by his substitutionary death, redeemed him from his old life, delivering him from its bondage and judgment.

The Lord said in John 15:13, "Greater love has no one than this, that he lay down his life for his friends." And John reflects this principle in 1 John 3:16 where he writes, "This is how we know what love is: Jesus Christ laid down his life for us. And we ought to lay down our lives for our brothers."

There are two ways we can lay down our lives for our brothers: by actually dying for them if necessary, thus "redeeming" them from death, or by sacrificing what we have to meet their needs, thus "redeeming" them from physical or other needs (see 1 Jn.3:17).

In what ways have you "redeemed" others from their needs?

APPLICATION: Sometimes "redeeming" others does not mean bailing them out, but counseling them in planning to meet their own needs. I've heard it said that if you give a hungry man a fish, you feed him for one day; but if you teach him to fish, you feed him for the rest of his life. Ask the Lord to give you a heart for the needs of others that will motivate you to sacrifice whatever it takes to meet their needs, whether by giving financially or through giving proper counsel.

If their need is spiritual in nature, then we can "redeem" them through our witness or godly counsel, turning their eyes to Jesus and his Word to meet those needs.

DAY 160
ᵇHE IS OUR REFUGE

QUESTIONS TO THINK ABOUT:

1. What is a refuge and what is its purpose?
2. How was Jesus a refuge for those who knew him?
3. How can we be a refuge to those who are in distress?

In Isaiah 32:1,2 there is a prophecy regarding the Messiah picturing the ideal government over which he will reign: "See, a king will reign in righteousness and rulers will rule with justice. Each man will be like a shelter from the wind and a refuge from the storm, like streams of water in the desert and the shadow of a great rock in a thirsty land." "Refuge," according to Webster, is "the state of being protected, as from danger." Here in Isaiah we seem to have a double picture of refuge; one is protection from the onslaught of a fierce storm, the other as a place of respite and refreshment in the barren wastes. The tempest is an active danger: the wind blowing, branches flying through the air, trees falling, roofs blowing off, boats swamping in high waves; whereas the desert area is deadly silent, dry and empty, very hot, little or no water, and deadly for anyone trying to cross it – a passive danger just sitting there doing nothing but waiting to happen. The first reminds me of giving help and protection to those in distress; the second of providing hospitality to those in need of shelter on their journey. Jesus said, "Come to me, all you who are weary and burdened, and I will give you rest" (Matt.11:28).

Jesus became a refuge for many in distress. Mary Magdalene, who was beset by seven demons, was in deep distress. Jesus delivered her and she followed him ever after. The disciples were in great fear of drowning in a severe storm. Jesus calmed the storm and delivered them from danger. During WWII many Jews were sheltered by Christians from the deadly designs of the German government. Many, many more would have died were it not for these acts of mercy and love.

If Jesus had had a home, it certainly would have been open to anyone passing by – and written above the door would have been Matthew 11:28. He experienced this kind of hospitality, a shelter on his journeys, at the home of Mary, Martha and Lazarus. In 3 John, John writes to Gaius commending him for his hospitality to the servants of God in their travels (vs.5-8) as well as to strangers.

Are we a refuge to whom those in distress can flee and feel safe? Christians need to be in the forefront in establishing crisis centers and counseling services for those who are about to be overwhelmed by the storms of life. Hospitality should be the mark of every Christian home. It was through the hospitality of my parents that I found my wife, and through their hospitality to missionaries passing through that my desire to be a missionary grew and my world vision expanded. Through their hospitality a very troubled young couple found the Savior and relief from their mixed-up life. My parents were always a refuge to which I could go at any time and find shelter and protection. Truly they reflected this characteristic of Christ in their lives, and the command to us is, "Go and do likewise" (Lk.10:37).

Are you a refuge, a shelter for those in distress or need?

APPLICATION: Being a refuge for others is not necessarily a full-time job – it is just being available when the need arises, having a heart open to the needs and stresses of others and a willingness to share what we have in order to make them feel safe with us.

DAY 161
ᵇHE IS THE REPROVER

QUESTIONS TO THINK ABOUT:

1. One of the hardest things I find to do in my Christian life is to reprove a fellow believer. Why is that?
2. What is the purpose of reproof?
3. When we rebuke others, what kind of attitude should we have?

When the Lord and his disciples were on their way to Jerusalem from Galilee, they passed through Samaria. He sent ahead to find lodging for the night, but because he was going to Jerusalem, the Samaritans refused to accommodate him. "When the disciples James and John saw this, they asked, 'Lord, do you want us to call fire down from heaven to destroy them?' But Jesus turned and rebuked them, and they went to another village" (Lk.9:54-56). We read in Hebrews 12:5,6, "My son, do not make light of the Lord's discipline, and do not lose heart when he rebukes you, because the Lord disciplines those he loves, and he punishes everyone he accepts as a son."

"Whom the Lord loves." His reproof is based upon his love for us, not upon disgust for what we have done. If he did not love us, he would not bother to reprove us! But since he knows that correction is necessary if we are to meet his desires for our lives (Heb.12:9-11): life (what is good), sharing in his holiness (becoming Christ-like), and a harvest of peace and righteousness (successful relationships). So he reproves and disciplines us.

There is recorded in Galatians 2:11-14 a situation where Paul rebuked Peter for blatant hypocrisy. In claiming to live free from the Law in Christ among the Gentiles, Peter quickly reverted to the strictures of the Law when Jews came along, evidently not wanting to offend them. Paul publicly rebuked him, forcing him to take his stand one way or the other. Paul did not hate Peter; he loved him as a fellow servant of the Lord but was also jealous for the honor of the Lord's name which Peter was compromising by his actions. Thus the rebuke.

It is not easy to rebuke a fellow believer. We fear rebuke in return, rejection, loss of friendship, or even retaliation. And well we may if our rebuke is not given in genuine love for the offender. But a rebuke is not the "sole occupant" of the house. Paul urges Timothy in 2 Timothy 4:2, "Preach the Word; be prepared in season and out of season; correct, rebuke and encourage – with great patience and careful instruction." "Correct" – showing them the truth from the Word, from God's point of view; "rebuke" – because of the Word, they should do something they're not doing or should not be doing what they are doing; "encourage" – urging them to change their behavior with instruction (teaching) on how to do it: all this done in the context of love _and_ patience (longsuffering – KJV).

Rebuke others like you would want them to rebuke you. Think about that, then couch your rebuke in such words as you yourself would be willing to hear were it you being rebuked. To take and humbly consider a rebuke is a sign of spiritual maturity.

How mature are you?

APPLICATION: Maybe the rebuke will be initially rejected. We may have to wait a long time before the seed of truth finally takes root and grows, and perhaps suffer estrangement in the meantime. But it will be easier for us to be patient toward others when we remember just how patient the Lord is toward us, and how long it has taken us to learn some things from him. A word of caution: Do not rebuke someone when you are angry. It will only come out as bitter criticism. Wait until you have cooled down and prayerfully thought it through. If you can go then to that person in love and with patience, you are ready to rebuke him. If not, then it is best to say nothing.

DAY 162
ᵇHE IS THE RESURRECTED ONE

QUESTIONS TO THINK ABOUT:

1. What does it mean to be "resurrected" from something?
2. What are some proofs of Christ's resurrection?
3. What does Christ's resurrection guarantee for us?
4. How can our salvation be a type of "resurrection" in our lives?

Paul declares in 1 Corinthians 15:20, "But Christ has indeed been raised from the dead, the firstfruits of those who have fallen asleep." In Romans 6:9 he also says, "For we know that since Christ was raised from the dead, he cannot die again; death no longer has mastery over him." The fact of his resurrection was attested to by Peter, the Twelve, 500 believers, James, all the Apostles, and lastly by Paul himself who saw Jesus on the day of his conversion (1 Cor.15:5-8).

There were some obvious changes wrought in Christ's physical body because of the resurrection. Though his appearance was the same, and he could eat and be touched, yet he was able to pass through locked doors and appear and disappear at will (cf. Lk.24:31,36-43; Jn.20:17,19).

There were changes, too, in his disciples because of the resurrection. That they were absolutely convinced of his resurrection, the record is clear. Christ presented himself alive to them during a period of 40 days, with many infallible (unmistakable) proofs (Acts 1:3). He turned their grief into great joy (Jn.20:15,16; Matt.28:8); their fear into boldness (Jn.20:19; Mk.16:20); their disillusionment into renewed hope (Luke 24:19-21,31,32); their unbelief into belief (Mk.16:11-14; Jn.20:25,27); their personal defeat into a renewed call to service (Jn.21:3,15-17). Had Christ not risen from the dead, none of these changes would have taken place.

How do we reflect Christ as the Resurrected One? His resurrection power is seen when he takes those of us who are spiritually dead and makes us spiritually alive. Ephesians 2:1, "As for you, you were dead in your transgressions and sins." And 2 Corinthians 5:17, "Therefore, if anyone is in Christ, he is a new creation; the old has gone, the new has come!" As Paul also says in Romans 6:4, "We were therefore buried with him through baptism into death in order that, just as Christ was raised from the dead through the glory of the Father, we too may live a new life." John Newton is a good example of this change. He was an English slave trader of the most wicked and vile sort. After his conversion, he became a notable preacher and hymn writer. No one who knew him as a vile slave trader could have dreamed possible the change that occurred in his life!

Not only is the character of our life changed, but so is our general outlook on life; our goals and desires are changed. Colossians 3:1-3 emphasizes this new outlook: "Since, then, you have been raised with Christ, set your hearts on things above, where Christ is seated at the right hand of God. Set your minds on things above, not on earthly things. For you died [to your old life], and your [new] life is now hidden [secure] with Christ in God." Thus we fulfill Christ's command in Matthew 6:33 to seek first the kingdom of God and his righteousness. The change in our lives should be such that others who knew us before will see the difference in the way we live now, and that those who didn't know us before will be aware of the difference in our way of life from theirs. Inevitably some will ask us about this difference, thus giving us an opportunity to witness to them (cf. 1 Pet.3:15).

Are you living the resurrection life?

APPLICATION: The resurrected (changed) life is a strong indication that we have truly been saved. If there has not been that kind of change in your life, then you need to seriously consider your relationship with the Lord and make sure of your salvation. The incontrovertible proof of our salvation is a changed life (2 Cor.5:17).

DAY 163
ᶜHE IS THE RESURRECTION

QUESTIONS TO THINK ABOUT:

1. What did Jesus mean when he claimed to be the resurrection?
2. What kind of hope does that give to us in our own lives and ministries?

Not only is Christ the Resurrected One, he also is the Resurrection. When comforting Martha after the death of her brother, Lazarus, he said to her, "I am the resurrection and the life. He who believes in me will live, even though he dies; and whoever lives and believes in me will never die" (Jn.11:25,26). He also declared in John 10:17,18, "The reason my Father loves me is that I lay down my life – only to take it up again. No one takes it from me, but I lay it down of my own accord. I have authority to lay it down and authority to take it up again. This command I received from my Father." Thus as the Resurrection, Jesus has the power of life in himself. So not only did he raise himself from the dead, but he has the power to raise all of his own from the dead as well. As he also claimed in John 6:39,40, "And this is the will of him who sent me, that I shall lose none of all that he has given me, but raise them up at the last day. For my Father's will is that everyone who looks to the Son and believes in him shall have eternal life, and I will raise him up at the last day."

A reflection of Christ as the Resurrection can be seen in the life of Peter. In Acts 9:36-43 we read that he was called from Lydda to Joppa because Dorcas, a disciple, had died. When Peter arrived, all the widows met him crying and showing him the robes and other clothing that Dorcas had sewn for them. "Peter sent them all out of the room; then he got down on his knees and prayed. Turning toward the dead woman, he said, 'Tabitha, get up.' She opened her eyes, and seeing Peter she sat up. He took her by the hand and helped her to her feet. Then he called the believers and the widows and presented her to them alive."

One day in Senggo, Amber called me over to the hospital. A child was critically ill and his parents wanted me to pray for him. Amber and the others had done all they could, medically, and there was nothing more to be done. As I prayed, Amber and the others were watching the child and were sure he had died. Yet as I closed "in Jesus' name," he stirred and began to recover. The Muslim parents knew it was the power of the Lord Jesus Christ that had brought their son through, but they were not willing to acknowledge that or him at the time. I would not go so far as to say that their son was raised from the dead, but he surely was raised from the point of death.

When Christ sent out the Twelve to announce the kingdom of heaven to the lost sheep of Israel (Matt.10:1-8), he said to them, "As you go, preach this message: 'The kingdom of heaven is near.' Heal the sick, raise the dead, cleanse those who have leprosy, drive out demons. Freely you have received, freely give."

Here, the raising of the dead along with the other miracles was to convince the Jews of the truth of the message being proclaimed. In

Peter's case, the raising of Dorcas resulted in the salvation of many people (Acts 9:42).

Whereas most of us will never be used to raise someone from the dead, are we living that new life of those who have been raised spiritually?

APPLICATION: Will the Lord allow his children to do the same today? I believe he will when the need is clearly there and the souls of many people are at stake. And I believe that he will give whatever servant of his is involved the faith and assurance that this is what should be done. We can't just step in and raise the dead arbitrarily; it has to be at his direction.

DAY 164
[a]HE IS THE LAMP

QUESTIONS TO THINK ABOUT:

1. What is the purpose of a lamp?
2. How was Christ God's "lamp" to us?
3. How can we be Christ's "lamp" to others?

In Revelation 21:23 we read, "The city [the New Jerusalem] does not need the sun or the moon to shine on it, for the glory of God gives it light, and the Lamb is its lamp." Here we find Christ as the vehicle through which the glory of God shines. This is further supported in John 1:14 where we read that "the Word became flesh and made his dwelling among us. We have seen his glory, the glory of the One and Only, who came from the Father, full of grace and truth." And in Hebrews 1:3a, "The Son is the radiance of God's glory and the exact representation of his being." Through Jesus Christ the glory of

Unexpected Transformation / 381

God is seen; his holiness and his character are made plain. We read in 1 John 1:5 that "God is light; in him there is no darkness at all."

In and of itself, a kerosene lamp cannot do a thing but sit there. Fuel has to be added and the flame lit. Jesus said in John 5:19, "I tell you the truth, the Son can do nothing by himself." What he sees the Father do, he does (vs.19b); what he "learns" from the Father, he teaches (Jn.7:16), and speaks with authority (Jn.7:17,18). The fuel is the Holy Spirit given to Christ without limit (Jn.3:34). The flame is the glory of God.

The Apostle Paul was given a similar commission. In his testimony before the Jews (Acts 22:14,15) he quoted Ananias who said: "The God of our fathers has chosen you to know his will and to see the Righteous One and to hear words from his mouth. You will be a witness to all men of what you have seen and heard."

Paul knew that he could do nothing in himself, but that if any witness (light) went forth, it would be God's enabling (see 2 Cor.3:5,6). Paul was just a lamp. In Acts 13:47, he addresses the Jews in Pisidian Antioch who had just talked abusively against what he was saying (vs.45). He said, "For this is what the Lord has commanded us: 'I have made you a light for the Gentiles, that you may bring salvation to the ends of the earth.'"

He captured the application of this commission for each of us in 2 Corinthians 4:6,7 where he writes, "For God, who said, 'Let light shine out of darkness,' made his light shine in our hearts to give us the light of the knowledge of the glory of God in the face of Christ. But we have this treasure in jars of clay to show that this all-surpassing power is from God and not from us." For our purposes here, "in jars of clay" could be translated, "in ordinary lamps." But before our lamp can be used, it must be clean, the wick trimmed, and the glass cleaned of soot so that the light can shine clearly from it. The light that God has put in our hearts is the knowledge of his glory as revealed in Jesus Christ. The more we know him, the brighter shines that light for others to see.

How brightly is your lamp shining?

APPLICATION: If our light is to shine brightly, the lamp must be clean. Psalm 119:9,11 tell us how to do that: "How can a young man keep his way pure [keep his lamp clean]? By living according to your word... . I have hidden your word in my heart that I might not sin [smudge my lamp glass] against you." We don't get clean unless we use the soap; our hearts will not become clean apart from the cleansing power of the Word. The more we use it, the brighter will be our light!

DAY 165
ᶜHE IS THE REWARDER

QUESTIONS TO THINK ABOUT:

1. Some say that a reward is nothing but a bribe to get someone to do something you want. How would you evaluate this point of view?

2. How can rewards serve as a motivator toward faithful service and doing a good job?

3. On the other hand, should we work because we want to please our boss or because of the reward he has promised us if we do a good job, or both?

There is a prophecy in Isaiah 40:10 which says, "See, the Sovereign LORD comes with power, and his arm rules for him. See, his reward is with him, and his recompense accompanies him." In Matthew 25:34-40 where we find Christ judging the Gentile nations, he rewards those who were faithful to him in all they did: "Take your inheritance, the kingdom prepared for you since the creation of the world" (vs.34). In Revelation 2:7,10,11,17,26-28 and 3:4, 5,10,12,20,21, Christ promises certain rewards or blessings to those who overcome, to those who are faithful.

Unexpected Transformation / 383

We find during his life, Jesus rewarded the faith of those who came to him in need. Two blind men approached him crying out for mercy. When asked if they believed he could restore their sight, they responded, "Yes!" "Then he touched their eyes and said, 'According to your faith will it be done to you'; and their sight was restored" (Matt.9:29,30a). God is spoken of in Hebrews 11:6 as he who "rewards those who earnestly seek him." Jesus, as the express image of God in human form, could do no less. In fact, he indicates this in John 6:37 where he says, "All that the Father gives me will come to me, and whoever comes to me I will never drive away."

A good example of the reward principle is found in the parable of the talents in Matthew 25:14-30. Jesus uses a situation that is familiar to his listeners in which a master rewards his servants for faithful service, and punishes the one for unfaithfulness. Paul reflects this principle in Colossians 3:23-25 where he writes, "Whatever you do, work at it with all your heart, as working for the Lord, not for men, since you know that you will receive an inheritance from the Lord as a reward. It is the Lord Christ you are serving. Anyone who does wrong will be repaid for his wrong, and there is no favoritism."

Those of us in any kind of leadership position should keep in mind that we are responsible to reward those under our authority according to their faithfulness. It's easy for a boss to give an employee a raise in wages, a bonus, or greater responsibilities in a promotion. But it's a lot harder, for instance, for a husband to reward his wife for her years of faithful service: cooking his food, washing his clothes, cleaning his house, raising his children, enduring his quirks, and so on. One reason for the strength of the feminist movement today is this very thing – after years of faithful service and sacrifice for husband and family, the wife discovers that she is merely taken for granted without a word of thanks or praise from those closest to her. That is humiliating. We husbands should be the first to praise our wives and brag on them to others, to give them unexpected gifts or do special things together to show our love and appreciation. Parents should do the same for their children which will encourage them toward right living.

The Lord has promised us rewards for faithful and obedient service. How are you rewarding those under your authority?

APPLICATION: Stop and think about how others have "served" you in whatever capacity, then purposely plan how you will show your thanks to them for it. It doesn't have to be elaborate; just some creative imagination could serve the purpose. As I was reading the above text, the thought occurred to me to announce to my wife, "Today is Wife Appreciation Day!" and take her out for a meal and/or do something else to make it special just to show her that I "notice." ("Today is Child Appreciation Day!" "Today is Office Worker Appreciation Day!") You get the picture. Nothing blesses and encourages like the feeling that you're appreciated by someone; that you're not taken for granted. Rewards are one way God expresses that to us.

DAY 166
bHE IS THE SAME

QUESTIONS TO THINK ABOUT:

1. What is the value of consistency?
2. Why is that important in terms of our relationship with God?
3. Where in the Bible do we read that God said, "Oops, that didn't work. Let's try something else"?
4. What role does God's sovereignty play in his consistency?

In Hebrews 13:8 we read, "Jesus Christ is the same yesterday and today and forever." In talking about created things, the writer of Hebrews says, "[The earth and heavens] will perish, but you remain ... . They will be changed. But you remain the same, and your years will never end" (Heb.1:11,12). In John 8:58 Jesus claimed to be the God of the Old Testament when he said, "I tell you the truth, ... before Abraham was born, I am!" And God said through the prophet Malachi, "I the LORD do not change" (Mal.3:6a). This implies absolute consistency in his person and work. His methods of operation may differ from age to age, but his character remains the same and the principles governing his work do not change.

In contrast with God's unchanging character, Amber and I have noticed changes in the Church from one Home Assignment to another. What was considered sin last Home Assignment is accepted as all right this one. More and more, the Church is reflecting the world as it neglects God's Word and bows to the standards and rules for behavior that keep changing along with our culture. But God does not change. What he considered sin in Adam's day, he still considers sin today. His judgments on sin and rewards for obedience are just as sure today as they were then. Because the Lord does not change, we can trust him implicitly and unconditionally; he means what he says, and says what he means, and tomorrow will make no difference.

We desperately need to reflect this same consistency in our lives, not only for our own sakes, but also for the sake of our families and those around us. Consistency will give us a sense of direction, a standard of operation in times of doubt or stress; it will give us stability in the face of life's changes; it will give our families a sense of security and stability as well; and even more, consistency will give us credibility before others. My parents always tried to be consistent in their dealings with us kids. We could not play one against the other and win. They were too smart for that, and had already agreed on a teamwork approach. Mom wouldn't accept, "Well, Dad said ..." without first checking with Dad. They agreed together on the punishments we deserved. When they warned us that such-and-such a punishment would be meted out to us if we did thus-and-so, we knew they meant it from past experience. They were clear in what they wanted of us and expected from us, and that gave us a sense of security and stability.

A gyroscope is a good illustration of consistency. When it is spinning you cannot change its angle of rotation. I understand that these have been used in ships to help stabilize them on the high seas so that they can not only maintain their course but also will not rock and bounce around all over the water. So we see that this "consistency" gives the ship a sense of direction and stability.

Consistency is an important ingredient in our relationship with the Lord as well as with others. The more mature we are spiritually, the more consistent we will be. This is the logical outcome from aligning our lives with the Word of him who is unchanging – totally consistent.

Are you being tossed about on the waves of life, or is your heavenly "Gyroscope" in operation?

APPLICATION: It is easy to be consistent as long as we live according to truth because truth never changes. Jesus said that God's Word is truth (Jn.17:17). So there we are! If we are consistent, then we are credible, whether or not others agree with us. They know where we stand on any particular issue and that we will not budge from it as long as it is aligned with the truth. If we are blown back and forth by the winds of culture, and always changing our minds about things in order to "go with the flow," we lose our credibility, our consistency and our witness.

DAY 167
ᶜHE IS THE SECOND MAN (ADAM)

QUESTIONS TO THINK ABOUT:

1. How was Christ compared with Adam? How were they the same? How were they different?

2. How can we reflect Christ as the Second Man, the Second Adam?

In describing the contrasts between Adam and Christ, Paul writes in 1 Corinthians 15:47, "The first man was of the dust of the earth, the second man from heaven." He continues this parallel in verses 48 and 49: "As was the earthly man, so are those who are of the earth; and as is the man from heaven, so also are those who are of heaven. And just as we have borne the likeness of the earthly man, so shall we bear the likeness of the man from heaven."

Here we find two men as the heads of two orders or two races of people: the one earthly, headed by Adam, and the other heavenly, headed by Christ. The contrasts are as literal as the difference between night and day (cf. Col.1:13):

Kingdom of Darkness	Col.1:13	Kingdom of Light
Adam the earthly head	1 Cor.15:22	Christ the Head
1. Death	vs.21-23	1. Resurrection
2. Corruption	vs.42,50,52-54	2. Incorruption
3. Dishonor	vs.43	3. Honor
4. Natural	vs.44,46,50	4. Spiritual
5. Made from dust (earth)	vs.47	5. From heaven
6. Mortal	vs.53,54	6. Immortal

The amazing thing is that we can change "nationality," and though we still bear in our bodies the likeness or image of the earthly man, in our spirit we can bear the image of the heavenly Man! And since it is in our spirit that we shall inherit the heavenly kingdom, the condition of our spirit becomes far more important than the condition of our bodies. Paul emphasizes this truth to Timothy in 1 Timothy 4:7b,8 where he writes, "Train yourself to be godly. For physical training is of some value, but godliness has value for all things, holding promise for both the present life and the life to come."

Christ, as the Second Man, heads a new generation of humanity, people rescued from the fall of the first man and thus possessing the potential of becoming all that God had intended that they should be: a perfect reflection of his own nature and being (Gen.1:26). The clarity with which we reflect his nature and being is directly proportional to the degree of our willingness to be conformed to his image. As we reflect more and more of the Second Man, we will reflect less and less of the first, and it will become increasingly clear to others that we are not of this world, even as he is not of this world (Jn.17:14).

In your character and manner of living, whom do you reflect the most, the first man or the Second?

APPLICATION: Proverbs 23:7a (NKJV) says, "For as he thinks in his heart, so is he." The Lord said that out of the heart proceeds all sorts of evil (Matt.12:34,35). So the key to reflecting the Second Man in our lives is to fill our hearts with God's Word and applying it in our lives – obeying what it says. There is no other way.

DAY 168
ʿHE IS THE SEED OF ABRAHAM

QUESTIONS TO THINK ABOUT:

1. How do we know that Jesus descended from Abraham?
2. Who are Abraham's descendants physically and spiritually?
3. If we are truly Abraham's spiritual descendants, what kind of works will we do?

In Galatians 3:16 Paul writes of Christ, "The promises were spoken to Abraham and to his seed. The Scripture does not say 'and to seeds,' meaning many people, but 'and to your seed,' meaning one person, who is Christ." In Matthew 1:1 we read, "A record of the genealogy of Jesus Christ the son of David, the son of Abraham." This was Christ's genealogy through Joseph. Luke 3:23-38 gives his genealogy through Mary: "... the son of Jacob, the son of Isaac, the son of Abraham ..." (vs.34). Therefore without doubt, Jesus is a descendant of Abraham, even as are all the Jews (cf. Jn.8:37-40), and therefore of Abraham's seed.

But Romans 4:11,12 expand the scope of Abraham's seed/descendants: "And he received the sign of circumcision, a seal of the righteousness that he had by faith while he was still uncircumcised. So then, he is the father of all who believe ... in order that the righteousness might be credited to them ... who also walk in the footsteps of the faith that our father Abraham had ... ." Then, in Galatians 3:29, Paul clearly states: "If you belong to Christ, then you are Abraham's seed, and heirs according to the promise" (see again Gal.3:16). God had said to Abraham, "...And all peoples on earth will be blessed through you" (Gen.12:3). And indeed, this promise was and is fulfilled in Jesus Christ.

Since Abraham is the father of all those who believe, Jew and Gentile alike, then, just as his physical descendants reflect his physical likeness, so his spiritual descendants will reflect his spiritual likeness and will be doing "the works of Abraham" which, according to James 2:21-23, were based on faith and obedience. One day the Jews, who were contesting with Jesus and were ready to kill him, said, "'Abraham is our father ... .' 'If you were Abraham's children,' said Jesus, 'then you would do the things Abraham did. As it is, you are determined to kill me ... . Abraham did not do such things. You are doing the things your own father does ... the devil'" (Jn.8:39-44). Though they were Abraham's physical descendants, they were spiritually of the devil since they did not have the faith of Abraham nor did the works characteristic of Abraham.

What were these works of Abraham that we also must do? Consider: his total, implicit faith in God (Heb.11:8,17), his frequent worship of God (wherever he went, he was building altars – Gen.12:7,8), his unquestioned obedience in submission to the will of God (Gen.22:1-3), his putting God ahead of everything else (Gen.22:16; cf. Matt.6:33), his honoring of God with a tithe (Gen.14:20), his intercessory praying (Gen.18:23-32; 20:17), his faithfulness as spiritual head of his home (Gen.18:19; 24:3,7), his courage in the face of adversity (Gen.14:14-16), his hospitality (Gen.18:1-5), his heavenly vision unclouded by earthly riches (Heb.11:9,10,13-16) which caused him to be unselfish (Gen.13:9) and unwilling to benefit at the cost of others (Gen.23:8,9; 14:21-23), and his patient endurance (Heb.6:15).

If we are the seed of Abraham, we will do the works of Abraham. Of whose seed are you?

APPLICATION: When we consider Abraham's life, that God spoke to him only 15 times (recorded), that is on an average of only once in every 17 years, and how great his faith was, how much more should we be able to exercise our faith when God speaks to us through his Word every day! The question is, "Are we listening?" Then the question is, "Are we, like Abraham, obeying what he says?"

DAY 169
ᶜHE IS THE SEED OF DAVID

QUESTIONS TO THINK ABOUT:

1. How do we know that Jesus descended from David?
2. What did that descent mean to Jesus royally?

3. Christ promised us a kingdom where we will reign with him. But in a very real sense, we can be reigning right now. How can this be?

In his letter to Timothy, Paul wrote, "Remember Jesus Christ, raised from the dead, descended from David" (2 Tim.2:8). In Romans 1:3,4 he writes, "Regarding [God's] Son, who as to his human nature was a descendant of David, and who through the Spirit of holiness was declared with power to be the Son of God by his resurrection from the dead." The cultural proof of his being the seed of David lies in his carefully kept genealogy where he is traced back to David through his mother (Lk.3:31) and through his "father" (Matt.1:1,6,16).

As the seed of David, Christ is of royal lineage and therefore has the right to sit on the throne of David as King over Israel. This was the expectation of the Jews at the time of the Triumphal Entry, and the expectation of his disciples after the resurrection (Acts 1:6). But as there is a time and place for everything, he answered them, "Not yet." That his reign is certain, we read in Scripture the question of the wise men, "Where is the one who has been born king of the Jews?" (Matt.2:2); the promise of the angel Gabriel: "He will be great and will be called the Son of the Most High. The Lord God will give him the throne of his father David, and he will reign over the house of Jacob forever; his kingdom will never end" (Lk.1:32,33); the expectation of Christ himself in Matthew 25:31-46: "When the Son of Man comes in his glory, and all the angels with him, he will sit on his throne in heavenly glory ... . Then the King will say to those on his right ...," etc.; and finally, though not the only remaining proof, the Apostle John sees Christ descending from heaven in great power and glory to strike down the nations and rule them with a rod of iron (Rev.19:15). His name is written on him: "King of kings and Lord of lords" (vs.16).

And the promise to us is that we also shall reign with him if we endure (2 Tim.2:12a), and Christ promised his disciples in Luke 22:28-30, "You are those who have stood by me in my trials. And I confer on you a kingdom, just as my Father conferred one on me, so that you may eat and drink at my table in my kingdom and sit on thrones, judging the twelve tribes of Israel."

But according to Romans 5:17 there is a present reign that we can enjoy now: "For if, by the trespass of the one man, death reigned through that one man, how much more will those who receive God's abundant provision of grace and of the gift of righteousness reign in life through the one man, Jesus Christ." So as we begin to assert our authority and reign in the various areas of our lives (see days 41-49 – HE IS THE KING), we reflect Christ as the royal seed of David.

Are you preparing yourself to reign?

APPLICATION: No king can reign without preparation; neither can we. Days 41-49 (as mentioned above) give us good instruction as to how we should be preparing for our eternal reign by exercising our present reign now. It would be good to review those days and see how our "training" is going.

DAY 170
[a]HE IS SEPARATE FROM SINNERS

QUESTIONS TO THINK ABOUT:

1. How can we live among "sinners" and yet be separate from them?
2. Some believe that we have to become like them in order to reach them. What do you think about that method?
3. Why is it important that we live differently from them?

In Hebrews 7:26 we read of Christ, "Such a high priest meets our need – one who is holy, blameless, pure, set apart from sinners, exalted above the heavens." The word "separate" (*kechorismenos*) means (passive voice) "having been separated from." Although he was in constant contact with sinful men, Christ maintained his absolute purity and perfection. Thus he was separate from sinners. The root form of this Greek word, *chorizo*, means "to put asunder," or, in other words, "to completely separate from."

To illustrate this truth, think for a moment of a fire fighter in an asbestos suit. He can walk unscathed where others would be burned to a crisp. Man is dying in the "fires" of their sin. Jesus comes to walk among them, truly human, but in the "asbestos suit" of his divine holiness. He remains untouched by the fires of sin, though he can see them, and, as a man, be tempted by them. But though human, in his suit of divine holiness, he becomes totally separated from everyone else. Thus he was in the world, but not a part of it. He could associate with sinners, yet not be "burned" by their sin. What's more, in his hand are many "asbestos suits" to give to whoever wants them. Some here, some there receive them and put them on. Now they are safe from the "fire" and likewise separated from those who are dying.

In his High Priestly prayer, Christ prayed, "I have given them your word and the world has hated them, for they are not of the world any more than I am of the world. My prayer is not that you take them out of the world but that you protect them from the evil one" (Jn.17:14,15). Like Christ, we must associate with sinners but not be a part of their sin. This is possible as indicated in the following verses. In Romans 13:14 Paul says, "Rather clothe yourselves with the Lord Jesus Christ, and do not think about how to gratify the desires of the sinful nature." And again in Galatians 5:16 he says, "So I say, live by the Spirit, and you will not gratify the desires of the sinful nature."

This is how we can walk among sinners and still be separate from them: by covering ourselves with (or meditating upon) the Lord Jesus Christ (our protection) and by walking (in obedience to the Word) in the (power of the) Spirit. When we give in to temptation it is because we have entertained it in our thoughts, thus "making provision for it." Christ never did that. We don't have to either. God has given us our "asbestos suit" so that we can walk in this world unscathed by the "fire" of its sin. What's more, he has given us "asbestos suits" to hand out to others who need them. We can only do that by coming into contact with them "in the fire." They must see that our "suits" work before they'll be willing to put theirs on.

Are you using your "asbestos suit"?

APPLICATION: We put on our "asbestos suit" first by confessing our sins to Christ, asking for his forgiveness, and accepting him as our personal Savior. Then we maintain it by obeying the Word of God (Ps.119:9). As long as we live by the truths of God's Word, we can live among unbelievers and not be "burned" by their sins.

DAY 171
ᶜHE IS THE BABE

QUESTIONS TO THINK ABOUT:

1. When we say, "Don't be a baby!" what are we really saying?
2. What are the characteristics of a baby?
3. How can a new Christian be likened to a baby?
4. What are our responsibilities toward new Christians?

In the Christmas story as found in Luke 2:12,16, Christ is called, "The Babe." So he began his human life on earth as a baby, born a baby and treated like a baby. Eight days later, he was circumcised in the Temple according to the Law of Moses. In this same context he is called "the Child" (vs.21, NKJV) and "the Child Jesus" (vs.27, NIV).

On our mission station we had a newborn baby. Even casual observation revealed certain characteristics common to all babies: they are totally dependent upon their parents, and especially their mothers from whom they obtain direct sustenance; they sleep a lot (since they are still developing physically); they are often hungry and waken mother at all hours of the night or distract her from whatever she's doing during the day; they do not like to be left alone, but need the comfort and assurance of someone close, holding them, talking to them, cuddling them; they need proper clothing to protect them from the elements; their protection lies solely with their parents or some other capable person (Matt.2:13).

As we enter the Christian life, we are "born" as babes into God's family. All the characteristics found physically in a baby are present in a "newborn" Christian spiritually. One reason so many fall away after a short time is that we tend to ignore their basic needs as "babes." Initially they are totally dependent on their spiritual parents to feed them (discipleship) the milk of the Word (basic simple teachings – see 1 Pet.2:2) so that they can begin to grow. Often a new Christian will be so fascinated by the Word and so hungry for its truth, that he will be found reading it day and night. A new Christian often is fearful to be left alone. There is so much he doesn't know, so much he is unsure of and even afraid of in this new life. He needs the comfort and assurance more mature Christians can give him, "holding" him, talking to him, "cuddling" him. He needs proper clothing (training) to protect him from the elements (temptation, false teachings, etc.) as well as the protection of his spiritual parents or "uncles and aunts" in difficult circumstances.

Thus as new Christians, as babes in Christ, we reflect Christ as the Babe. He was cared for by his parents until he matured. We must likewise care for spiritual babes until they are mature enough to feed themselves from the Word and stand on their own. Anything less than that is spiritual murder through neglect. We cannot expect a newborn baby to care for himself the day after he is born, yet we often expect this from a newborn Christian! We must be watchful and concentrate on being good spiritual parents so that our "children" will not "die" from neglect but rather grow and become mature, ready to give birth to another generation of spiritual babes.

Are you guilty of spiritual child neglect?

APPLICATON: All of us at one time or another were spiritual "babes." What can we do to protect and nourish the newer Christians in our midst? Discipleship is essential to their eventual maturity. But what they need most is our love and encouragement whenever and at whatever level we can give it.

DAY 172
ᶜHE IS THE YOUNG CHILD, THE BOY JESUS

QUESTIONS TO THINK ABOUT:

1. What are the characteristics of a young child?
2. How does a young child view life in general?
3. How is the faith of a young child an appropriate standard for the faith we must have to be saved?

In Matthew 2:8, Herod says to the Wise Men, "Go and make a careful search for the child." By this time, according to verse 16, Jesus was no longer a baby, but probably nearly two years old. Luke 2:40 continues the narrative: "And the child grew and became strong; he was filled with wisdom, and the grace of God was upon him." This was said of him before he was 12 years old (see vs.42)! When he was 12, he went to the Temple in Jerusalem for the first time with his parents, and stayed behind when his parents left! They found him four days later in the Temple "sitting among the teachers, listening to them and asking them questions" (vs.46). He astonished them with his understanding and answers (vs.47). In vs.49 he showed an awareness of God's purpose for him. In verse 51 we find him in subjection to his parents. And finally, "Jesus grew in wisdom and stature, and in favor with God and men" (vs.52).

There is another young child of whom this was said in Scripture: Samuel (1 Sam.1:26). From the time he was weaned, he served the Lord in the house of the Lord at Shiloh (1 Sam.3:1). And in 3:19 we read, "The LORD was with Samuel as he grew up, and he let none of his words fall to the ground." In other words, Samuel closely heeded what the Lord said, and what he prophesied always came to pass (cf.1 Sam.9:6, "... Everything he says comes true."). Samuel was obedient. Three times, when he thought Eli was calling him, he arose immediately and went to him (1 Sam.3:4-8). And he was willing to hear the Lord's word (3:10).

Timothy was another example. As a child he knew "the Holy Scriptures which [were] able to make [him] wise for salvation through faith in Christ Jesus" (2 Tim.3:15). And Paul responded to what he saw in Timothy.

The Lord further said about little children: "I tell you the truth, unless you change and become like little children, you will never enter the kingdom of heaven. Therefore, whoever humbles himself like this child is the greatest in the kingdom of heaven" (Matt.18:3,4).

From these four passages we find several characteristics that any child can possess. In Matthew 18 we see humility (and faith – implied). Very few children are proud, and very few do not initially believe their parents. In 1 Samuel 1 & 3 and Luke 2 we find the following true of both Samuel and Jesus: respect for authority and obedience (Samuel to Eli; Jesus to his parents), teachable (they listened), inquisitive (they asked questions), desiring the Word of God (awareness of already being involved in God's business), and spiritually wise. Children are potentially far more able and capable of spiritual discernment and service to the Lord than we give them credit for being, thus giving rise to Christ's incredible understatement above, "... unless you change and become like little children, you will never enter the kingdom of heaven."

Do you respond to God as Samuel, Timothy and Jesus did?

APPLICATION: Take another look at the characteristics that any child can possess (in the paragraph above) to see how yosu measure up to them. What steps can you take to strengthen them or begin applying them in your life?

DAY 173
'HE IS THE YOUNG CHILD, THE BOY JESUS, concl.

QUESTIONS TO THINK ABOUT:

What examples can you give for the following questions:

1. Can a child know enough to yield himself fully to the Lord?
2. Is it possible for a child to have an effective ministry for the Lord?
3. Can a child understand enough Scripture in order to live a life pleasing to the Lord and be a testimony to others?

I ask for your indulgence for a few moments, for as I looked back over my childhood, and began to put things together, this is what I discovered: how my childhood reflected Christ as the Young Child.

I accepted Christ as my own Savior when just four years old. I didn't understand very much, but I <u>knew</u> that I was a sinner (for I had already stolen my friend's toys and hid them and myself because I "knew" the police would come and take me off to jail!); and I knew that Jesus died on the cross to take away my sin <u>if</u> I asked him to. So, in very simple <u>faith</u>, I asked him to!

At five, I wanted to serve the Lord as best I could and wanted to be a <u>witness</u> to my school chums, but couldn't find the right words. So I'd bring them home for Mom to witness to them. While she was doing that, I'd sit on the back stairs or in the bathroom praying that my friends would receive Christ.

I can also remember as a child trying to understand my parents when they told me to do something or not to do something; I sensed that they had a good reason for what they said, and wanted to know what that reason was, so listened to them, <u>obeyed</u> them, and learned respect for them and others in authority as a result.

I <u>wanted to please my parents</u> because I loved them, even if it meant doing jobs I didn't like, such as scrubbing the kitchen floor, taking out the garbage, or washing down the front and back inside stairways.

When my parents were there, I had no fear. I <u>knew</u> (faith) that they could handle anything that came along and that I would be safe.

Frequently I would <u>ask</u> my parents <u>questions</u> concerning things I wanted to know about, and most of the time they were able to answer me.

When I was six, at the conclusion of a missionary conference, I <u>gave my life to the Lord</u> for foreign missionary service.

I can remember having a regular <u>Quiet Time</u> with the Lord every day when still in grade school, and writing to mission boards about missionary service when in seventh or eighth grade. (I wrote to the Africa Inland Mission about their work in South America(!) and received a very encouraging reply from them with names of mission boards serving in South America. They took me seriously and I have always appreciated them for that.)

While still young, I <u>grew in spiritual wisdom</u> because I was always reading and memorizing the Word and trying to obey it.

Perhaps we have forgotten, or never even considered the characteristics of a child that God is looking for and wants to see in our lives. And if you are a little child, you <u>can</u> know and serve the Lord even now. You don't need to wait until you are grown up!

As a Christian, are you childlike? Do you respond to God as a child would?

APPLICATION: I began my spiritual journey as a young child. Any young person or adult can begin that same journey – like a little child – humbly coming to the Lord for salvation, then for spiritual growth and understanding. Your journey will not reflect mine, for it is yours! The Lord is only waiting for you to come to him so that you can start your journey together with him.

DAY 174
ᶜHE IS SHILOH

QUESTIONS TO THINK ABOUT:

The meaning of Shiloh is "whose it is." When Jesus indwells our hearts at salvation, we are his ("whose we are"). He is now reigning as Shiloh in our hearts. What does this imply regarding:

1. His righteous kingdom?
2. His overcoming our enemies? and
3. How we reflect him as Shiloh to others?

When Jacob was blessing his sons before his death, he blessed Judah with these words: "The scepter will not depart from Judah, nor the ruler's staff from between his feet, until he comes to whom it belongs and the obedience of the nations is his" (Gen.49:10). This prophecy looks forward to the coming of the Messiah. According to <u>The Bible Knowledge Commentary</u>, the word Shiloh is from the Hebrew *siloh* which means "whose it is"; the scepter will not depart from Judah ... until he comes whose it (the scepter) is (or "to whom it belongs").

There are two aspects to the coming of Shiloh, or the Messiah, which were paramount in Jewish thinking: one was deliverance from their enemies, and the other was the setting up of a righteous kingdom with Israel the head and no longer the tail of the nations. Subsequent blessing will flow out from them throughout the whole earth.

How can we reflect Christ as Shiloh in our lives? Apart from the devil, sickness, sin and death are man's enemies. Yet as Paul declares in 1 Corinthians 15:57, "But thanks be to God! He gives us the victory through our Lord Jesus Christ." We have the victory over:

The devil. Through his death on the cross, Christ destroyed the devil who holds the power of death (Heb.2:14), thus the devil no longer has any authority or power over us. He <u>has</u> to yield to the greater power that is within us, the power of the Holy Spirit himself. We have had no "deliverance" ministry as such, but others have, and have been able to cast out indwelling demons in the name of the Lord Jesus Christ.

Sickness. Through obedience to the Word, the Lord delivers us from much illness. But where he allows illness to come, that very enemy can be turned into a friend as we allow that suffering to conform us to the image of Christ (see Jas.1:2-4).

Sin. Likewise sin is defeated by the sword of the Spirit, the Word of God. As we meditate on it and fill our minds and our hearts with it, we will have little room left for sin. Thus as we encourage others to fill their minds with the Word and obey it, we will be delivering them from three deadly enemies.

Death. In the same way we also deliver them from death. Through the witness of the Word a man is converted. Christ says that when this happens, "he has crossed over from death to life" (Jn.5:24). Paul says that "the wages of sin is death" (Rom.6:23). So it stands that if we turn others from sin, we also turn them from death. As James declares, "My brothers, if one of you should wander from the truth and someone should bring him back, remember this: Whoever turns a sinner away from his error will save him from death and cover over a multitude of sins" (Jas.5:19,20).

Are you reflecting Christ as Shiloh, the Messiah, by delivering others from their enemies?

APPLICATION: We don't have to be "professionals" to share the Word and our spiritual experiences with others. As we do, they will be encouraged to let the Lord rule in each of these areas in their lives. But it is not a passive exercise! Peter wrote in 2 Peter 1:5 that we should "make every effort to add to [our] faith … ." Yes, Jesus is Lord, he is Shiloh, he has the power to gain us the victory; but it is a partnership. We need to take his hand and walk together with him if we expect to overcome our adversaries. This is done as we read, meditate, memorize and obey his Word; as we pray to him and humbly submit ourselves to his headship. He delights in taking small, insignificant people to gain amazing victories (cf.1 Cor.1:26-29). So there is "hope" for all of us!

DAY 175
ᶜHE IS SHILOH, concl.

◆

QUESTIONS TO THINK ABOUT:

1. How can Christ's kingdom be seen in us today?
2. What are the evidences/results of righteousness?

The second expectation of Israel was that the Messiah would set up a righteous kingdom in which Israel would become the head of the nations, no longer the tail, with blessing flowing out from them to the nations. We read in Hebrews 1:8 that righteousness will be the scepter of his kingdom – righteousness, the principal characteristic of his reign. As Christ is reigning in our lives now, righteousness must characterize us in all we do. Our homes, offices, class rooms and churches should be miniatures of the kingdom that is to come. Where we are in positions of authority and leadership, righteousness should characterize our relationships with others, by example first, encouragement second, and decree third. Where we are under the authority of others, righteousness and faithfulness should be the hallmark of our work.

Homes where righteousness prevails (see Day 15 – HE IS RIGHTEOUS) will strengthen the society of a nation; businesses where righteousness reigns will strengthen the nation's economy; classrooms where righteousness is taught and exercised will strengthen the moral fabric of the nation; and churches where righteousness is taught and exemplified will affect everyone in the community in many ways.

As a result, many blessings will be evident individually, in the community and in the nation. To name a few: all the blessings of obedience to the Word of God and helping our fellow man, freedom from a nagging conscience, stability in our families, community and nation, a falling crime rate, easing of the jail crunch, godly leadership and government, economic prosperity enhancing the Lord's work, local and national projects and aid to other countries. With an increase of righteousness comes a corresponding decrease in sin-related disease thus reducing medical expenditures. Lessening of greed will reduce national adventurism and opportunism, check corruption in business and government, and curb inflation bringing a decrease in prices and an increase in both quality and quantity of available goods. The lonely, desolate and poor would be ministered to in such a way as would strengthen their self-respect and feeling of personal worth. All the ills of society would be greatly reduced. This is not idealistic dreaming. Any Christian family can experience the blessings of these principles within the scope of their own home and thus be a savory influence to those around them.

Where does it all begin? In the hearts of those, who, like Daniel, <u>purpose in their hearts</u> not to be defiled by the world's system (see Dan.1:8), but to honor God in all they do and be obedient to his Word. "Shiloh": righteous leadership delivering from the enemy and causing blessing to flow. May the Lord help us all be just that!

APPLICATION: Just a suggestion: Make a list of the results of righteousness above and talk about how each one could be seen in your family, and the steps you might have to take to make it happen. Some may not apply immediately, but some creative thinking might show how the family could be used to make some of these things in your neighborhood and beyond.

DAY 176
ᶜHE IS THE SOIL

QUESTIONS TO THINK ABOUT:

1. What are different kinds of soil; what makes them good or bad?
2. What are the characteristics of good soil?
3. How can we be "planted" in Christ?
4. What does it mean for others to be "planted" in us?

This characteristic of Christ is implied in Colossians 2:6,7 where we read, "So then, just as you received Christ Jesus as Lord, continue to live in him, rooted and built up in him, strengthened in the faith as you were taught, and overflowing with thankfulness." Since Scripture likens a believer to a tree (see Ps.1:1-3; Jer.17:7,8), we will use the same in this passage. The picture here is of a seedling, planted in good soil, sending its roots down (rooted), gaining nourishment for growth (built up) and finally reaching maturity (established in the faith). Without good soil, this kind of growth is impossible.

On the south coast of Papua we had the stark contrasts between good and bad soil. At Senggo, where we lived for eight years, it was impossible to have a good garden without importing much fertilizer at great cost. The soil was so acidic that nothing would grow properly. So we did no gardening. About fifty miles to the south was the village of Nohon, the "garden spot of the south coast." No fertilizer was needed. Throw the seeds on the ground and almost anything would grow! The soil was fertile and productive. Why this difference? Because of the contents of the soil. Nohon's soil contained the various elements and minerals necessary for productiveness.

In the parable of the sower, Christ likened the hearts of men to various types of soil: hard-packed (Lk.8:5), rocky (vs.6), thorny (vs.7) and good ground (vs.8). Only the good ground brought forth fruit. What is it in Christ's life that makes him "good soil" for us to be rooted in? He is truth; he is life; in him are hidden all the treasures of wisdom and knowledge (Col.2:3); learning from him will produce rest in our souls (Matt.11:29). So as we learn from him and absorb his teachings, his character and his way of life, it is like a tree absorbing nutrients from the soil which cause growth and with growth stability and fruitfulness.

We, in turn, become soil from which others can draw forth nutrients for their growth and stability as Christians. One example recently came to mind as I prepared materials for the Hatam Tribe New Year's Conference, 1986-87, on "Indebtedness and Restitution." My parents never lived in debt and always encouraged us children not to live in debt. So that way of life has never been a problem for me. Regarding restitution, whenever we stayed somewhere, and something got broken, my father would always replace that item with something else as good or, frequently, better than what was broken. This was his usual practice and from it I learned respect for other people's property and to be responsible for it if I was using it. This was growth from the nutrients of "good soil." So we can be to others – so we <u>must</u> be to others if we are following Christ as we should.

What kind of soil are you?

APPLICATION: The only way we can become "good soil" is to be "planted" in Good Soil. As we absorb more and more of the character of Christ into our lives, our soil will become good and fruitful as others plant themselves in it (following our example). As Paul said in 1 Corinthians 11:1, "Follow my example, as I follow the example of Christ." And, according to John 15:5, Jesus wants us to bear much fruit. We can only do that if our soil is good!

DAY 177
ʽHE IS THE SON OF ABRAHAM

QUESTIONS TO THINK ABOUT:

1. Describe Abraham's character and works.
2. How could Christ's character and works be said to be similar?
3. So, if we are spiritual children of Abraham, what should our character and works be like?

The Gospel of Matthew starts right out with the following declaration: "A record of the genealogy of Jesus Christ the son of David, the son of Abraham" (Matt.1:1). This term implies descent (since Christ's genealogy follows); but even more than just descent, it implies similarity in character and work. In fact, it was on this basis

Unexpected Transformation / 407

that Jesus refuted the Jews' claim to be Abraham's children. They descended from him, true; but if they were truly his children (sons), they would do his works. Their works, however, indicated that their father (ancestor) was the devil himself (see Jn.8:33,37-41,44).

So Christ, as a son of Abraham, would show the characteristics and works of Abraham in his life. What are these?

Abraham	Characteristic/Work	Christ
Romans 4:19-21	Faith	Hebrews 2:13
Genesis 22:2	Love	John 15:9
John 8:56	Hope	Hebrews 12:2b
Genesis 13:9	Generosity	Ephesians 4:11
Genesis 14:14	Leadership	Isaiah 55:4
Genesis 13:8	Peacemaker	Ephesians 2:14,15
Genesis 14:20	Thankful	John 11:41,42
Genesis 23:4	Temporary resident	John 17:14
John 8:40	Received the truth	John 8:28
Genesis 12:4	Obedient	Hebrews 5:8
Genesis 18:23-32	Intercessor	John 17
Genesis 12:7,8	Worship	John 4:22
Genesis 18:19	Ruled his house well	Hebrews 3:5,6
Genesis 18:3-5	Hospitable	John 14:2,3

These were characteristics not being demonstrated in the Jews' relationship with Christ.

Our national pastor in Papua had a different way of saying, "I'm going witnessing." He would often say, "I'm going out to find sons and daughters of Abraham." Romans 4:11 says that Abraham "received the sign of circumcision, a seal of the righteousness that he had by faith ... [so that he might be] the father of all who believe." Again in Galatians 3:29, "If you belong to Christ, then you are Abraham's seed, and heirs according to the promise."

By our works and character, whom do we declare to be our father, Abraham or Satan?

APPLICATION: For each of the characteristics and works of Abraham listed above, check off in your life which ones are non-existent, weak and needing improvement, moderate but could be strengthened, and strong. Then plan whatever steps are necessary to make needed improvement.

DAY 178
ᶜHE IS THE SOVEREIGN ONE
(of the Universe)

QUESTIONS TO THINK ABOUT:

1. What does it mean to be sovereign?
2. How did Christ demonstrate his sovereignty?
3. How can we reflect his sovereignty in our lives?

In Hebrews 1:2,3,10, we find these statements regarding Christ: "His Son ... made the universe." ... "The Son ... sustain[s] all things by his powerful word." ... "In the beginning, O Lord, you laid the foundations of the earth, and the heavens are the work of your hands." Again in Hebrews 11:3 we read, "By faith we understand that the universe was formed at God's command, so that what is seen was not made out of what was visible."

Christ, as Sovereign of the Universe, created and sustains his creation by the power of his word. As Paul says in Colossians 1:17b, "In him all things hold together." Peter tells us what will happen when the Lord speaks again. "... Long ago by God's word the heavens existed and the earth was formed out of water and with water. By water also the world of that time was deluged and

Unexpected Transformation

destroyed. By the same word the present heavens and earth are reserved for fire, being kept for the day of judgment and destruction of ungodly men ... [in which] the heavens will disappear with a roar; the elements will be destroyed by fire, and the earth and everything in it will be burned up" (2 Pet.3:5-7,10).

We cannot sovereignly create and sustain things out of nothing by our words, but we <u>can</u> create and sustain the "atmosphere" around us by what we say. For instance, Proverbs 15:1 says, "A gentle answer turns away wrath, but a harsh word stirs up anger." James 3:5,6,8 says, "The tongue is a small part of the body, but it makes great boasts. Consider what a great forest is set on fire by a small spark. The tongue also is a fire, a world of evil... . It corrupts the whole person, sets the whole course of his life on fire, and is itself set on fire by hell... . No man can tame the tongue. It is a restless evil, full of deadly poison." See what an atmosphere is created and sustained by an uncontrolled tongue!

I worked in an office once where a fellow employee said, "I wish so-and-so wouldn't come down here. He thinks he owns the place and wants to run everything." After that, it was very difficult for me to see anything else in him than what was told me. Two sentences created a new relationship not easily overcome.

On the other hand, we read in Proverbs 21:23, "He who guards his mouth and his tongue keeps himself from calamity." Proverbs 25:11, "A word aptly spoken is like apples of gold in settings of silver." Proverbs 25:25, "Like cold water to a weary soul is good news from a distant land." Proverbs 26:20, "Without wood a fire goes out; without gossip a quarrel dies down." Proverbs 15:26b, "The [thoughts] of the pure are pleasing... ." Proverbs 12:18, "Reckless words pierce like a sword, but the tongue of the wise brings healing" [the words of the wise soothe and heal].

If we are creating around us an atmosphere of peace, joy and encouragement by the things we say, then we are reflecting Christ as the Sovereign of the Universe who created and sustains all things through the power of his words.

By the power of your words, what are you creating and sustaining?

APPLICATION: We all have problems with our tongues now and again. Sometimes it's intentional, sometimes unintentional. I knew a pastor who often prayed Psalm 141:3, "Set a guard over my mouth, O LORD; keep watch over the door of my lips." Apart from prayer, we need to think before we speak. "Will what I want to say draw that person closer to the Lord, or drive him farther away?" "Will what I want to say help build up and encourage that person, or tear him down and discourage him?" If we practice thinking before speaking, we will save ourselves and others a lot of grief and trouble.

DAY 179
[a]HE VALUES PEOPLE MORE THAN THINGS

QUESTIONS TO THINK ABOUT:

1. When did Jesus not give time to anyone who came seeking him?
2. Some people are "high maintenance, time monopolizers." How can saying, "Yes" to them be harmful whereas saying, "No" could be helpful?
3. Why should people be more important to us than our things?

In considering Christ as the Compassionate One (DAY 13), when he saw the crowds, even at the most inconvenient times, he had compassion on them and taught them many things (Mk.6:34).

Principle: people were more important than rest. Christ could do this because he had already established his priority as found in 2 Corinthians 8:9 which says, "For you know the grace of our Lord Jesus Christ, that though he was rich, yet for your sakes he became poor, so that you through his poverty might become rich." Also Philippians 2:5-7: "Your attitude should be the same as that of Christ Jesus: who, being in very nature God, did not consider equality with God something to be grasped, but made himself nothing, taking the very nature of a servant, being made in human likeness."

Our Western culture emphasizes things rather than people. Daily we are bombarded with advertising trying to convince us of our need for more things. Gifts for people who have everything are common. Soon we find ourselves getting caught up in the materialistic trap. The rich young ruler turned away from Christ because his heart was tied up with his possessions. Christians have turned a deaf ear to the Lord's call to the mission field or to greater involvement in other areas of his work because they didn't want to lose their things. They valued their possessions more than the people Christ wanted them to reach. In Luke 12:15 Jesus warns us about this misplaced sense of values: "Then he said to them, 'Watch out! Be on your guard against all kinds of greed; a man's life does not consist in the abundance of his possessions.'"

The "necessities" of our lifestyle may not be necessities at all! We all could live more cheaply if we had to and get along very well. Amber and I experienced this on the mission field. By American standards, we were living in poverty, but didn't know it! By Indonesian standards, we were very rich! Either way, our needs were being met and we felt content.

Sometimes the "rich American" image gave us problems. But someone counseled us that if our home is open to the nationals, our "riches" wouldn't pose such a problem to them. But that meant inviting in dirty, unwashed people, small babies without diapers, children with runny noses. What about our furniture? What about our varnished floors? What about our beautiful rug? Some ex-pats can't handle that and just shut their homes to nationals lest their things be ruined or contaminated! You see, we carry our "value baggage system" with us wherever we go! What do we put first, people or things?

The value we place on things also directly influences the supply of funds for the Lord's work. Most Christians do not even give a tithe of their income to the church because their "needs" are too great. Inflation and devaluation have continued to cause the missionary support needs to rise. Some have had to stay home because they cannot raise what they need. Many field projects have had to be scrapped because of a lack of finances. The money is there, but it is being used for other things: a second home, a motor boat, additional cars, more lavish home decorating, extended pleasure travel, and so on. Many times on furlough, Amber and I have felt sick at heart to see all the "unnecessary" things in some Christian homes, but hear of the lack of finances in the church for carrying on the Lord's work.

When we were in Singapore, we saw Christians selling their second car, taking out an additional mortgage on their homes, or selling off other possessions in order to give additional funds to the Lord's projects and work. In light of their example, we had to reevaluate our giving. Were we still more preoccupied with our remaining things than we were with the people God was bringing across our path? We need to make people our priority as the Lord did.

When the crunch comes, and you have to choose between the two, do you value people more your things?

APPLICATION: If you're involved in a special project or something else you really want to do, and someone calls or knocks at your door, wanting to speak with you, your priority will be made clear by the degree of aggravation you feel at this "unnecessary interruption."

If someone had a financial need that you <u>could</u> meet if you had "extra funds," but <u>still</u> could meet if you put off buying that new _____ and making do with the old one for a little while longer, your priority will be made clear by the degree of reluctance you feel at meeting this "untimely need."

Perhaps this perspective will help: the soul of the person is eternal – your projects and possessions aren't.

DAY 180
ᵇHE IS THE POSSESSOR OF ALL THINGS

QUESTIONS TO THINK ABOUT:

1. What does it mean for Christ to possess all things?
2. How can it be said of us that we also will possess all things?
3. What steps do we need to take in order to become possessors of all things?

In Colossians 1:16 Paul writes of Christ: "For by him all things were created: things in heaven and on earth, visible and invisible, whether thrones or powers or rulers or authorities; all things were created by him and for him." In Psalm 89:11 we read, "The heavens are yours, and yours also the earth; you founded the world and all that is in it." The Lord possesses or owns everything by virtue of the fact that he created everything (see also Deut.10:14 and Ps.24:1).

Now in 1 Corinthians 3:21-23 we read another declaration from Paul, "So then, no more boasting about men! All things are yours, whether Paul or Apollos or Cephas or the world of life or death or the present or the future – all are yours, and you are of Christ, and Christ is of God." And he says in Romans 8:16,17, "The Spirit himself testifies with our spirit that we are God's children. Now if we are children, then we are heirs – heirs of God and co-heirs with Christ, if indeed we share in his sufferings in order that we may also share in his glory." And in Revelation 21:7, "He who overcomes will inherit all this, and I will be his God and he will be my son."

There is a blanket statement that all things are ours (potentially and actually), yet there seems to be a condition attached to how much of that we shall actually possess – that is, if we suffer with him and overcome. There are those who, according to 1 Corinthians 3:15, will lose everything but their salvation because of adopting a wrong philosophy of life (vs.12,13). The extent of our eternal inheritance depends directly upon our living godly lives (which will bring persecution – 2 Tim.3:12) and overcoming the world and its temptations (see 1 Jn.5:5; Rev.2 and 3). When we fulfill the conditions for inheriting all things, then we will possess them.

But what does this mean for us today? There is a hint found in Mark 10:28-30 where we read, "Peter said to him, 'We have left everything to follow you!' 'I tell you the truth,' Jesus replied, 'no one who has left home [or wife – Luke 18:29] or brothers or sisters or mother or father or children or fields for me and the gospel will fail to receive a hundred times as much in this present age (homes, brothers, sisters, mothers, children and fields – and with them, persecutions) and in the age to come, eternal life.'"

APPLICATION: To be a possessor of all things with Christ, first of all, we have to be Christ's. According to 1 John 5:5, if we believe that Jesus is the Son of God (and, obviously, all that that implies), we will overcome the world (by virtue of our position in Christ). That's step one, our salvation. Step two is to be faithful to him in all we do, including suffering with him. That suffering could be outright persecution, passive persecution, giving up material things or careers in order to serve him, or by being grieved over the unfaithfulness or sins of other believers.

DAY 181
ᵇHE IS THE POSSESSOR OF ALL THINGS, cont.

◆

QUESTIONS TO THINK ABOUT:

1. What does our possession of all things mean for us today?
2. How soon can we claim them?
3. What are some of the conditions that need to be met before we can claim our possessions?

What does our possession of all things mean for us today? Can I walk into my neighbor's beautiful house and claim possession of it? Can I walk into the electric company's office and tear up my bill because I not only own the company but also the resources it uses with which to generate electricity? Hardly! We cannot do that, just as Christ couldn't claim the world's kingdoms as his own during his first advent, even though he possessed them all. That was not the time for him to receive them, even though Satan offered to give them all to him if he would worship him (Matt.4:8-10)! How is this?! In 1 John 5:19 we read, "We know that we are children of God, and that the whole world is under the control of the evil one." When Adam fell into sin by transfer of allegiance from God to Satan, however so temporary, Satan took everything – including Adam's suzerainty over the world. So even though we, as God's children, possess everything, we cannot lay claim to it just yet. But our time will come, when Christ's time comes, to literally possess all things.

Yet again, the Lord will bless us with the meeting of our material needs by giving us part of our possessions now. But there are certain conditions that we must fulfill first. It is like a young child. As he matures, his father can entrust him with more and more of the family wealth. Even though the child possesses it all by virtue of being in the family, yet he can only use those possessions as he matures and shows himself capable of handling them. Certain conditions must be met before his father will trust the family wealth to him. Even so does our heavenly Father do with us. He has laid down certain conditions that we must fulfill if we are to receive our possessions. Consider: Matthew 6:33, [*condition*] "But seek first his kingdom and his righteousness, [*possession*] and all these things [food, clothing, shelter] will be given to you as well." Mark 10:28-30 we read yesterday. [*Condition*] Anyone who has left houses, (wife), brothers, etc. for My sake, [*possession*] shall receive one hundredfold in this world, houses, brothers, etc. Psalm 84:11b, [*possession*] "No good thing does he withhold [*condition*] from those whose walk is blameless."

As we serve him where we are and live lives pleasing to him, we can expect him to meet our needs. When an evangelistic team went into a nearby transmigration settlement to show the "Jesus" film (at about eleven locations), they ran out of money and thought they'd have to cancel the last several showings. But a man who was saved at one showing gave the team 9,700 rupiahs (U.S.$5.00) as a "thank offering" to the Lord. This gift allowed them to purchase gas for the generator and pay taxi fare to the last three or four places! They received that part of their possessions which would allow them to continue in their service for the Lord.

Are you meeting the conditions for receiving portions of your possessions?

APPLICATION: Even though we cannot enter into our possession of all things right now, we can begin to experience them in a limited way as God supplies all our needs as we faithfully live for him. We do not live for him in order to get; we receive because we are living for him.

DAY 182
ᵇHE IS THE POSSESSOR OF ALL THINGS, concl.

◆

QUESTIONS TO THINK ABOUT:

1. What is the difference between possessing all things and possessing all spiritual blessings in Christ?
2. When and how can we make use of those spiritual blessings?

But again, there is another aspect of our possessions which we can enter into fully right now; we don't have to wait for some future date before we can enjoy and use them. These are our spiritual possessions that we have in Christ. Paul says in Ephesians 1:3, "Praise be to the God and Father of our Lord Jesus Christ, who has blessed us in the heavenly realms with <u>every spiritual blessing in Christ</u>." And Peter declares in 2 Peter 1:3, "His divine power has given us <u>everything we need for life and godliness</u> through our knowledge of him who called us by his own glory and goodness" (all underlining mine).

In Christ we possess every spiritual resource that God has provided for godly living and effective service. Thus there is no reason for any Christian not to live a godly life nor to have a fruitful ministry <u>if</u> we use what he has provided.

What are these spiritual resources? Some among the many are:

1. <u>The Holy Spirit</u> – who teaches us and leads us into all truth and empowers us, giving us boldness in our proclamation of the Word; he is the seal of our salvation, assuring us that we are God's.

2. <u>The name of Jesus Christ</u> – the basis of our authority. All that we do is to be done in the name of the Lord Jesus. We are commissioned in his name and are to minister in his name.

3. <u>The blood of Christ</u> – the source of our victory. Through his death the power of sin and Satan over us is broken; we are free!

4. <u>The resurrection</u> – the source of our assurance that our message is true because it proved that Christ's message was true.

5. <u>Prayer</u> – communication with God. His answers assure us of our acceptance with him.

6. <u>Prophecy</u> – removes our fear of the future, thus giving us consistency in our lives.

7. <u>The life of Christ</u> – the example, the blueprint for us to pattern our lives after.

8. <u>Music</u> – for praise, worship, instruction, and comfort.

9. <u>Forgiveness</u> – providing a clear conscience so that we can serve the Lord with our whole heart.

10. <u>Fellowship with other believers</u> – providing strength and security in all we do.

11. <u>The Word of God</u> – providing instruction, direction, correction and comfort for our spiritual maturity.

12. <u>The promises of God</u> – *if we fulfill the conditions*, they are ours and all that goes with them.

Have you entered into the "land" of your spiritual possessions, or are you still on the "other side of the river" looking at them?

APPLICATION: We are truly rich in all that we possess in Christ Jesus. But our possessions are only as good as the use we make of them. Be diligent to make good use of each one.

DAY 183
ᶜHE IS THE POWER OF GOD

◆

QUESTIONS TO THINK ABOUT:

1. How strong do you have to be before God can use you?
2. What is God looking for in the life of the one he wants to use?
3. How can you know when God is calling you to do something?

In 1 Corinthians 1:24 Christ is called "the power of God." Let's pick up the context from verse 22: "Jews demand miraculous signs and Greeks look for wisdom, but we preach Christ crucified: a stumbling block to Jews and foolishness to Gentiles, but to those whom God has called, both Jews and Greeks, Christ the power of God and the wisdom of God." Then follows a comparison of the world's wisdom and power contrasted with God's. Here we will consider the power contrasts. Verse 25 says, "The weakness of God is stronger than man's strength"; (vs.26) "… not many influential (mighty) … are called"; (vs.27) "… God chose the foolish things of the world to shame the strong …" (vs.29) "so that no one may boast before him."

According to Isaiah 53:2b,3a, Christ had "no beauty [stateliness] or majesty [splendor] to attract us to him. He was despised and rejected by men." I take it from this passage that there was nothing in Christ's physical appearance that would naturally draw people to himself. He was just an ordinary-appearing person, not ugly, but perhaps not handsome either. According to the world's standards, he didn't look like a king, nor did he carry a regal bearing about him. He was just a simple, ordinary, poor Israelite carpenter, the perfect candidate for demonstrating the power of God. Men expected nothing more from him than to continue in the trade of his "father" as a carpenter. Suddenly, miracles were being done, teaching was given with authority that even the Scribes and Pharisees didn't demonstrate, and a "nobody" was being followed by an increasing number of people. "'Where did this man get this wisdom and these miraculous powers?' they asked. 'Isn't this the carpenter's son? Isn't his mother's name Mary, and aren't his brothers James, Joseph, Simon and Judas? Aren't all his sisters with us? Where then did this man get all these things?' And they took offense at him" (Matt.13:54b-57a). Christ certainly was not what Israel anticipated in fulfillment of their Messianic hopes!

God worked the same way in Old Testament times. In Judges 6:12,14,15 Gideon is called a man of valor. Yet he was hiding from the Midianites. He was commissioned by God to deliver Israel from the Midianites, but Gideon objected (vs.15): "'But Lord,' Gideon asked, 'how can I save Israel? My clan is the weakest in Manasseh, and I am the least in my family.'" Then when it came to the army, the Lord whittled them down from 30,000 to 300, "in order that Israel may not boast against me that her own strength has saved her" (Judg.7:2). Israel won, but the glory had to go to God.

When the Syrians came against Ahab, their army filled the countryside, whereas the Israelite army was like two little flocks before them (1 Kgs.20:27). Yet the Lord delivered the Syrians into the hands of Ahab so that "[Ahab] will know that I am the LORD" (1 Kgs.20:13).

Asa recognized this principle. When outnumbered two to one by the Ethiopian army, and 300 to nothing in chariots, "then Asa called to the LORD his God and said, 'LORD, there is no one like you to help the powerless against the mighty. Help us, O LORD our God, for we rely on you, and in your name we have come against this vast army. O LORD, you are our God; do not let man prevail against you'" (2 Chr.14:11). And the Lord struck down the Ethiopians (vs.12).

Do you consider yourself small and weak in the face of gigantic adversity? Then you qualify to be used by the Lord!

APPLICATION: "I can't do that!" should never be in the Christian's vocabulary. On the one hand, that is a true statement. We can't, apart from Christ (cf. Jn.15:5). But with Christ, Paul declares that he can do anything (Phil.4:13), that is, anything that God wants him to do, or rather wants to do through him. All we need to do is make ourselves available, then watch him work! He will let us know what he wants us to do.

DAY 184
ᶜHE IS THE POWER OF GOD, concl.

QUESTIONS TO THINK ABOUT:

1. Apart from making ourselves available to God, what is the underlying secret to his power being seen in us?
2. Why does God choose the weak and foolish things anyway to demonstrate his power?

Through Peter and John, two very ordinary, uneducated Galilean fishermen, God's power was demonstrated: a lame man was healed, the Gospel preached with power, and uncharacteristic authority and boldness shown by such men of lowly profession. The rulers, elders and scribes of Israel along with the High Priest called them to task over what they were doing. In Acts 4:13 we read, "When they saw the courage of Peter and John and realized that they were unschooled, ordinary men, they were astonished and they took note that these men had been with Jesus" (cf. Ps.119:97-100).

Paul felt himself weak, but the Lord promised him grace. Paul concludes, "Therefore I will boast all the more gladly about my weaknesses, so that Christ's power may rest on me" (2 Cor.12:9b).

Here is the point. Very few of us are Billy Grahams, D.L. Moodys, John Wesleys or Apostle Pauls. We are just ordinary us: no flash and splash, no news clippings, no name bigger than our circle of acquaintances. So we conclude: "I'm a nobody. I can't possibly be used like these others who are 'somebodies.' Look at all they've done and the multitudes they've reached." So we are sure that God cannot use us. But we couldn't be more wrong! Look at 1 Corinthians 1:27-29 once again: "But God chose the foolish things of the world to shame the wise; God chose the weak things of the world to shame the strong. He chose the lowly things of this world and the despised things – and the things that are not – to nullify the things that are, so that no one may boast before him." If you are a "nothing," a "nobody" in your sight, then you are exactly what God is looking for! He delights in demonstrating his power and goodness and wisdom in those who are nothing so that <u>it will be obvious that he has done it by his power</u>, not yours.

Consider a water channel. It has no power in and of itself. The water flowing through it has the power, but that power is made evident because of the channel. So we need to submit ourselves to the Lord so that he can shape our "channels" to suit his eternal purpose and cause his power to flow through us. He is just waiting for us to make ourselves available to him. In 2 Chronicles 16:9a we read, "For the eyes of the LORD range throughout the earth to strengthen [show himself strong to – KJV] those whose hearts are fully committed to him."

The only qualifications we need for the power of God to flow through us are a loyal and humble heart. Do you qualify?

APPLICATION: James 4:10 says, "Humble yourselves in the sight of the Lord, and he will lift you up." It starts there. God cannot/will

Unexpected Transformation / 423

not use a proud person. The humble person is ready to hear and obey whatever the Lord asks of him. How can we know when God wants us to do something when he doesn't come right out and say it? Usually, there will be a strong, inner, undeniable, inescapable urge/burden for whatever that is. When we sense this urge, pray about it: "Lord, if this is from me, let it pass. But if this is from you, let it remain, and even become stronger." If it remains, then act upon it. And his power, in one way or another, will be demonstrated in your life.

DAY 185
[a]HE IS THE PREACHER

QUESTIONS TO THINK ABOUT:

1. How many ways are there to "preach"?
2. What did Jesus mean when he said that he was anointed to "preach the gospel to the poor"?
3. What did he mean when he said that he was anointed to proclaim freedom to the captives and give sight to the blind?

One Sabbath day in the synagogue, Jesus was given the scroll of Isaiah to read. He opened it to Isaiah 61:1,2 and began to read (Lk.4:18,19), "The Spirit of the Lord is on me, because he has anointed me to preach good news to the poor. He has sent me to proclaim freedom for the prisoners and recovery of sight for the blind, to release the oppressed, to proclaim the year of the Lord's favor."

There are two different Greek words translated "preach" in these verses. The first is from the verb *euaggelizo* which means "to bring good news, to announce glad tidings." We get our word "evangelize" from this term. Hence Christ was anointed to evangelize the poor, to bring them good news concerning Jesus as the Messiah. We must be careful here not to claim that he came only to preach to the economically depressed – for it is obvious that he preached to rich and poor alike. I think Matthew 5:3 carries the point here: "poor in spirit." Among Christ's listeners were both rich and poor, but only those among them realizing their poverty in spirit responded to his glad tidings. "The kingdom of heaven is at hand" was certainly good news for those awaiting it.

The second word used and translated "preach" is *kerusso*, "to herald or proclaim." So Christ was also anointed to proclaim deliverance to the captives and recovery of sight to the blind and to proclaim "the year of the Lord's favor." Again, we see no large-scale exodus of prisoners from Roman jails, nor do we see Jesus proclaiming recovery of sight to the blind such as a herald would do given the announcement. So here again we must understand these words as dealing with the spiritual realm. As Paul says in 2 Timothy 2:25b,26, "… In the hope that God will grant them repentance leading them to a knowledge of the truth, and that they will come to their senses and escape from the trap of the devil… ." In 2 Corinthians 4:4 we read of those who are perishing: "The god of this age has blinded the minds of unbelievers, so that they cannot see the light of the gospel of the glory of Christ." And Jesus himself pronounced the Scribes and Pharisees "blind": "Woe to you, blind guides!" (Matt.23:16); "You blind fools!" (vs.17); "You blind men!" (vs.19); "You blind guides!" (vs.24); "blind Pharisee!" (vs.26). He came to proclaim sight to the blind. Some Pharisees (like Nicodemus and Joseph of Arimathea) believed on him and received spiritual sight, but many did not.

We also have good news to proclaim, not only of salvation in Christ, but also of all that we receive in Christ because of salvation. One day in the seventh grade gym locker room I walked in and someone said, "Watch your language! Here comes the preacher!" I had never once "preached" to them, but I had witnessed many times, sharing with one and another the good news of forgiveness in Christ and freedom from sin through him, etc. So as we share the gospel with others, we reflect Christ as the Preacher.

Just an additional thought. There is the saying that goes, "Your actions speak so loud that I can't hear what you're saying." We don't just preach with our lips, but with our actions as well. Our actions prove that we believe what we say and are willing to live by it. This kind of "preaching" puts <u>all</u> of us in the "pulpit"!

Does your "congregation" believe you?

APPLICATION: Though most of us will never have a seminary education, we all can "preach" by the way we live and by what we share with others. "Sermons in shoe leather" can be some of the most powerful sermons some will ever hear! If we are careful to practice what we say we believe, others will have to "listen" and at least admit that we have "been with Jesus."

DAY 186
ᶜHE IS OUR PROPITIATION
(Atoning Sacrifice)

QUESTIONS TO THINK ABOUT:

1. What is an atoning sacrifice?
2. Christ died as our atoning sacrifice. We cannot do that for others. So how can we reflect his atonement for us in our relationship with them?

In 1 John 2:1,2 John writes, "My dear children, I write this to you so that you will not sin. But if anybody does sin, we have one who speaks to the Father in our defense – Jesus Christ, the Righteous One. He is the atoning sacrifice (propitiation – KJV) for our sins, and not only for ours but also for the sins of the whole world." "Propitiation" means "satisfaction." God's wrath toward us because of sin was satisfied by the atoning sacrifice of Christ. Thus propitiation could be described as I heard it once: "To avert the storm of God's wrath." When Christ died on the cross for our sin, God's wrath was redirected from us to him. And because Christ was a perfect sacrifice, God's wrath was satisfied (which was proved by the resurrection. Had God not been satisfied, Christ would not have risen from the dead!).

I think of another propitiation that occurred during Israel's wandering in the wilderness. Balaam advised Balak, king of Midian, to encourage dialogue and interaction between Midian and Israel, well knowing what it would lead to. Israel fell headlong into Baal worship and all the associated evils, including prostitution. One Israelite prince boldly brought a Midianite woman into his tent right in the sight of Moses and all Israel who were weeping at the door of the Tabernacle. Phinehas was so enraged by this brazen act of sin and defiance of God, that he took a spear and followed the two of them into the tent and "drove the spear through both of them ... Then the plague against the Israelites was stopped" (Num.25:8). In verse 11 the Lord spoke to Moses saying, "Phinehas ... has turned my anger away from the Israelites; for he was as zealous as I am for my honor among them, so that in my zeal I did not put an end to them." And verse 13, "... He was zealous for the honor of his God and made atonement (propitiation – KJV) for the Israelites."

We reflect Christ as our Propitiation whenever we divert God's wrath or judgment on sin through turning ourselves and others from sin to righteousness. James writes, "My brothers, if one of you should wander from the truth and someone should bring him back, remember this: Whoever turns a sinner from the error of his way will save him from death and cover a multitude of sins" (Jas.5:19,20). Had the sinner continued in his evil ways, there would have been much sin committed, and the wrath of God would have descended upon him (cf. Col.3:5,6). But turning him from the error of his way to righteousness will eliminate the sins he otherwise would have committed and thus avert the storm of God's wrath upon him. The same holds true for our community. When we take a stand for righteousness, and people turn to it at least in principle, much sin is eliminated and wrath from God averted.

Do you let sin go on its merry way, or are you standing in the gap to turn men from their sins and away from God's wrath?

APPLICATION: As you see other Christians struggling, pray for them, asking the Lord to give them victory over whatever their issue is. Then be sensitive to that "nudge" from the Lord if he wants you to share something with them to encourage them and perhaps even help resolve that issue.

DAY 187
ʻHE IS THE SON OF MAN

QUESTIONS TO THINK ABOUT:

1. How was Jesus just like us as a man?
2. How was his identity with us an example of how we should relate to others?
3. To what degree should or could we identify with them? (cf. Heb.4:15)

This title Jesus used of himself in Luke 9:44. It emphasizes his humanity. He was born of Mary (Lk.1:30,31), thought to be completely human by others (Matt.13:55-58), and experienced hunger (Matt.4:1,2), exhaustion (Jn.4:3-6), love (Mk.10:21), anger (Mk.10:13,14), grief (Jn.11:35), and poverty (Matt.8:20). Jesus came and fully identified himself with us. Philippians 2:5-8 encourages us to do the same: "Your attitude should be the same as that of Christ

Jesus: who, being in very nature God, did not consider equality with God something to be grasped, but made himself nothing, taking the very nature of a servant, being made in human likeness. And being found in appearance as a man, he humbled himself and became obedient to death – even death on a cross!"

If we expect to be able to minister to people, we must identify with them in some way. It may mean giving up our present lifestyle as we move to where they are: from the suburbs to the inner city; from the U.S. to some other country. It may mean changing some of our cultural biases and thought patterns, even in our own country! But as we make some attempt to identify ourselves with them, they will respond.

I had an interesting experience one Sunday when Matius, the pastor from the village of Tamnim, and I held a service in the village of Epem, some 20 minutes downriver from Senggo. At the close of the message, I gave an invitation to the people to receive Christ (Matius interpreting). No response. Then the chief said, "Tuan, we don't understand this enough yet to make a decision; but we want you to keep coming and telling us God's Word so we'll learn it, and then we will receive Christ."

I appreciated his honesty and their desire to hear more about God, and told him so. He replied, "There was [another religious group] here before you, and they'd beat us and make us feel like stupid ignoramuses. But when you missionaries came, you respected us and treated us like people. That's why we want to hear more of God's Word from you." There are believers in that village now. And I learned that sometimes identifying with others is no more than respecting them as they are and treating them as we would like to be treated.

But the important thing is, we respond to those with whom we can identify. If Christ had come down as an angel, identification with him would have been impossible. If we descend upon others in the guise of a "super saint," "great deliverers from the West," their identification with us is impossible, for in both cases, the one descending lives on a totally different plane than those to whom he intends to minister.

Christ could become our High Priest because he suffered as we suffer, he endured temptation as we endure it (though without sin – Heb.4:15); he knows just how we feel because he has been there. So we can turn to him as one human to another and find comfort, strength and hope.

So those to whom we minister must also realize that we hurt where they hurt, we fall where they fall, we struggle where they struggle. Then when we share with them how they can have victory in this area and that, they respond with, "Hey, he's like me, and he got victory over this thing; if he did, so can I!" So we, in turn, give comfort, strength and hope to them.

Are you a "super saint" or a fellow human struggling with temptation and weakness? It will make a difference in the way others respond to you and your message.

APPLICATION: Our initial plane of identification with others is that we are human just like they are and experience the same temptations (though perhaps with different cultural wrappings). Secondly, we respect them as people, and, by the way, those who can do some things better than we can! (The Citak people could live in the jungle for 6 months and return. I wouldn't last three weeks! They had my respect!). Thirdly, we need to speak their "language." Even in English, we can use words with other English speakers that they cannot understand. Fourthly, we must live humbly (not ostentatiously) among them and welcome them into our habitation however "high" or "low" it may be compared with theirs. If they know that they are welcome, they also know that we respect them – the basis for any witness we may want to share with them later.

DAY 188
ʿHE IS THE SON OF GOD

QUESTIONS TO THINK ABOUT:

1. How does a child reflect his parents' character and actions?
2. How can you know that you are your parents' son or daughter?
3. What does it mean to be someone's child practically and legally?

As the title "Son of Man" asserted the humanity of Christ, so the title "Son of God" asserts his deity. This title was given to him by the angel Gabriel (Lk.1:32a,35), he laid claim to it himself (Jn.11:4), and God called him his Son (Mk.9:7). John testified in John 3:16 that Jesus was God's "one and only Son." Throughout his earthly life, he gave ample proof of his sonship through his teachings and his works (Jn.8:27,28 with 4:34).

Scripture has given us a clear perspective on our relationship to God as his children. We see first that God chose us to sonship before the foundation of the world (Eph.1:4,5)! From among all mankind, before any of us existed, God chose those whom he would adopt into his family. Remember, he didn't have to do this. He could have sent the lot of us to hell because of our sin and rebellion against him. And he would have been no less God had he done so. Then he could have started all over again with a new batch. But he didn't. He chose to save us in spite of ourselves, and to make of us what we could never hope to become. Paul declares that God wants to "make the riches of his glory known to the objects of his mercy (that's us!), whom he prepared in advance for glory" (Rom.9:23). And again, in Ephesians 2:7, "that in the coming ages he might show the incomparable riches of his grace, expressed in his kindness to us in Christ Jesus."

Then came the day when we responded to God's love, repented of our sin and rebellion, and received Christ as our Savior. At that point he gave us "the right to become children (sons, KJV) of God – children born not of natural descent, nor of human decision or a husband's will, but born of God" (Jn.1:12,13). God has chosen us and declared us to be his children through Jesus Christ. This is our position from God's perspective.

What, then, is our position from our perspective? What proofs do we see that we are indeed children of God? There are several:

1. His Holy Spirit indwells us (Rom.8:9) and
2. assures us that we are God's (Rom.8:16).
3. He leads us (Rom.8:14) which he could not do were we not God's (Rom.8:7).
4. He guides us into all truth (Jn.16:13,14); so spiritual perception and growth are good indicators of sonship.
5. So also is our obedience to revealed truth and the Lord's commands (Lk.6:35,36).
6. The chastening of God when we do wrong (Heb.12:5-11) since he only disciplines those whom he has accepted as sons.
7. Later, when we see Christ, our sonship will be perfected, and we shall be like him (1 Jn.3:1-3)! We shall be perfect. Our character shall be like God's, fully restored to his image, but on his terms (cf. Gen.3:5).

Are you a son or daughter of God? If so, how does this relationship with God affect your daily life?

APPLICATION: As children of God, our character and our actions should reflect his. Others should be able to look at us and recognize us as his, just like they look at us and recognize us as our parents' children. That's just the purpose of this study – that our character might more and more reflect that of Christ. Others will be drawn to him by what they see in us; and in coming to him, they come to God the Father. May others see him clearly in us!

DAY 189
ʻHE IS GOD

QUESTIONS TO THINK ABOUT:

1. How did Christ prove himself to be God?
2. In what context are we potentially called gods?
3. Then how can we reflect Christ as God?

Scripture is very clear about Christ's divinity: he is God. The prophets declare it, the apostles declare it, and Christ himself claimed it. Isaiah wrote of the coming Messiah, "And he will be called ... Mighty God" (Isa.9:6). Paul called him, "God over all, forever praised!" (Rom.9:5). John called him, "The Word, ... and the Word was God" (Jn.1:1). Christ, in Revelation 1:8, called himself "the Almighty," and in John 8:58 claimed for himself the Old Testament name that God used to identify himself to Moses: "I AM" (Exod.3:14). The people immediately took up stones to stone him to death for blasphemy (Jn.8:59). They knew who he was claiming to be. The references could easily be multiplied. Jesus Christ is God!

Now how do we reflect Christ as God? How can it be done? Let's look at John 10:34-36 where Christ says, "Is it not written in your Law, I have said you are gods? If he called them 'gods' to whom the word of God came – and the Scripture cannot be broken – what about the one whom the Father set apart as his very own and sent into the world? Why then do you accuse me of blasphemy because I said, I am God's Son?"

It is in Psalm 82 where God called both rulers (vs.1) and congregation (vs.6) "gods": "God presides in the great assembly; he gives judgment among the gods... . I said, You are gods; you are all sons of the Most High."

Those in authority stand as God before those over whom they rule (Zech.12:8). They have the power to use or abuse this authority. They can lead their people in the path of righteousness (Ps.82:3,4) or in the path of unrighteousness (Ps.82:2,5). Rulers bear much responsibility because of their position. James warns against unnecessary assumption of power, saying, "Not many of you should presume to be teachers, my brothers, because you know that we who teach will be judged more strictly" (Jas.3:1; cf. Mk.12:38-40).

Many have asked at one time or another, "How can I know the will of God?" One means of God revealing his will is through those in spiritual authority over us. This puts great responsibility on their shoulders, necessitating a close walk with God on their part, so that they will be open to the Holy Spirit's promptings and sensitive to his leading. Then, as they speak to us and counsel us, it is as if God himself were communicating with us.

But how about the congregation, the average Christian? How are we as God? I think the answer is indicated in DAY 228 – HE IS IMMANUEL. We who know God have become his representatives to the world. As the world sees our reflection of him, so they will evaluate him. This puts a big responsibility on our shoulders and necessitates a close walk with the Lord on our part, so that we will properly respond to his promptings and be open to his leading, thus providing a more accurate reflection of him before the world. When we speak, it should be as if he were speaking (2 Cor.5:20).

We can never be God as Christ is, but we can more and more reflect his character to the world, speaking as he speaks, working as he works, so that they can know him through us.

Are you enough like God to make a difference wherever you go?

APPLICATION: The only way we can properly reflect God to the world is by "abiding in him, and his Word abiding in us" (Jn.15:7). The Sanhedrin took note of the fact that Peter and John "had been with Jesus" (Acts 4:13). Others should be able to come to the same conclusion about us. Jesus chose his disciples, but his disciples also had to choose to remain with him (Jn.6:67,68). We have been chosen by God (Eph.1:4), but it is our choice whether or not to walk in close fellowship with him. If we walk closely to him, then others will see him clearly in our lives, and we will then be as "God" among them.

DAY 190
ᶜHE IS THE SON OF DAVID
(The Offspring of David)

QUESTIONS TO THINK ABOUT:

1. What is the proof that Jesus was the "Son of David" (i.e. the offspring or descendant of David)?
2. What did the name "Son of David" imply Messianically?
3. How can we reflect Christ as the Messiah in our daily lives?

That Jesus Christ was the Son of David, that is, a direct physical descendent from David, was not only proven fact genealogically (see Matt.1:1-17; Lk.3:23-31), but also generally known and accepted by the people of his time. Frequently he was referred to by that name (Matt.9:27; Mk.12:35; Lk.18:38,39; Jn.7:42). The Apostle Paul also declared it as fact in Romans 1:3 and 2 Timothy 2:8. And Christ claimed to be David's offspring in Revelation 22:16.

As the Son of David, Jesus is of royal lineage and heir to David's throne. This is a Messianic title as well, and was used in that way by the people during the Triumphal Entry (Matt.21:9,15). We

Unexpected Transformation / 435

considered his kingship earlier (DAYS 36-41). But what do we see in him, as a royal Son of David, that should be reflected in our lives? He demonstrated the characteristics of what a godly ruler should be like: humble (riding on a donkey instead of a white stallion like a Roman ruler would do – Matt.21:5), sympathetic to the people, having an ear for their cry, and doing all in his power to help meet their needs (Mk.10:47,48; Matt.20:29-34). He even heeded the cry of the foreigner living nearby, delivering the Syrophenician woman's daughter from the power of a demon (Matt.15:21-28). He fulfilled the Old Testament criterion for a good king: "Mercy and truth preserve the king: and his throne is upheld by mercy" (Prov.20: 28 – NKJV). And again: "If a king judges the poor with fairness, his throne will always be secure" (Prov.29:14).

And as is right and good for the king, so it is for his people. We read in Proverbs 29:7, "The righteous care about justice for the poor, but the wicked have no such concern." The truth here is that those of us in authority over anyone must be humble in that position, and open to hear and do something about their needs. It's like the parable of the unforgiving servant (Matt.18:21-35). His master was open to his cry of despair and forgave him a great debt, thus meeting a serious need. But then this servant approached a fellow servant who owed him a pittance, and with a deaf ear to his pleas, demanded immediate payment. His actions were reported to his master, who promptly passed judgment upon him, demanding that he pay the original debt owed, for he had shown no compassion or pity toward his fellow servant (vs.33) as he had been shown by his master.

So we must ask ourselves, "Do we, like Christ as the Son of David, show compassion and pity toward those under our authority? Are we open and receptive to them and aware of their needs? Do we treat them as we ourselves would like to be treated by those in authority over us? We read in Proverbs 21:13, "If a man shuts his ears to the cry of the poor, he too will cry out and not be answered." That's something to think about.

Who are those under your authority to whom your ear should be open?

APPLICATION: In Hebrews 1:1-8 it is written about Jesus, the Messiah, that "righteousness will be the scepter of your kingdom." Thus as we represent him, righteousness must be a central characteristic of our lives (see DAY 15 – HE IS RIGHTEOUS/JUST for more details).

DAY 191
[a]HE IS HUMBLE

QUESTIONS TO THINK ABOUT:

1. What does it mean to be humble in position and in attitude?
2. Is it prideful to lay claim to the truth? Why or why not?
3. How do we become humble?
4. What is the price we pay if we "show off" our humility?

There are two kinds of humility described in Scripture: humility in position and humility in attitude. Both kinds of humility can be arrived at in two ways: by choice or by circumstances.

Christ's position of humility was by both choice and birth (circumstances). In Philippians 2:8 we read: "And being found in appearance as a man, he humbled himself and became obedient to death – even death on a cross!" And again in 2 Corinthians 8:9, "For you know the grace of our Lord Jesus Christ, that though he was rich, yet for your sakes he became poor, so that you though his poverty might become rich." He was also humble by birth. His parents were so poor that they had to offer "the poor man's sacrifice," a pair of turtledoves, or two young pigeons (Lk.2:24).

Christ's attitude of humility was by choice: "... for I am gentle and humble in heart ..." (Matt.11:29b). He did nothing through pride. At one time he said, "The words I say to you are not just my own. Rather, it is the Father, living in me, who is doing his work" (Jn.14:10b). Christ claimed nothing as of himself but gave all the credit to the Father. And when he made a claim for himself, it was a true statement consistent with his humility (see Jn.8:28).

Some of us are humble by birth, like Christ, being born in lower economic circumstances. Others of us are humble by choice, choosing to live on a lower level, or going to another country whose standard of living is much lower than ours. But all of us can choose to adopt a humble attitude. Scripture abounds with urgings toward humility and promises of blessing if we become so. The problem is that so many of us turn an unintentionally deaf ear to the Word!

The Lord has been exercising my conscience to discern what I do or say out of pride and what I do or say from humility. To date, it has been an exercise of discovery and of some shock to realize just how much is done from pride. My heart says, "Well, if I don't blow my horn, who will?" We have a "need" to be recognized and appreciated and so take it upon ourselves to gain that recognition, be it through good works or bad. We do something well, so plan to do it when people are around to notice. We drop hints of our supposed greatness or spirituality when others can hear. We help others, all the while hoping for praise. Pharisee-ism anyone? Christ said in Matthew 6:1-4 that our good deeds should be done quietly and will be rewarded by God himself publicly: "Be careful not to do your 'acts of righteousness' before men, to be seen by them. If you do, you will have no reward from your Father in heaven. So when you give to the needy, do not announce it with trumpets, as the hypocrites do in the synagogues and on the streets, to be honored by men. I tell you the truth, they have received their reward in full. But when you give to the needy, do not let your left hand know what your right hand is doing, so that your giving may be in secret. Then your Father, who sees what is done in secret, will reward you [openly]" – NKJV).

Peter tells us in 1 Peter 5:6, "Humble yourselves, therefore, under God's mighty hand, that he may lift you up in due time." And Paul urges us in Colossians 3:23,24, "Whatever you do, work at it with all your heart, as working for the Lord, not for men, since you know that you will receive an inheritance from the Lord as a reward. It is the Lord Christ you are serving."

How well used is your horn?

APPLICATION: Our hearts are naturally prideful. Jesus chose to be humble; so must we. That is the starting point.

DAY 192
ªHE IS HUMBLE, cont.

QUESTIONS TO THINK ABOUT:

1. How can we overcome our pride?
2. Describe the tension between the American attitude of "We can do anything" and our ministry.
3. What is the difference between seeking men's praise and seeking God's praise?

What is the answer to overcoming pride and being truly humble? There are several steps we can take as a beginning. The first is that of obedience. We are commanded to humble ourselves (1 Pet.5:6), so it's not an option. In fact, Proverbs 6:16,17 and 8:13 say that the Lord hates pride. So when we are proud, we are doing something the Lord hates. Hardly a good basis for continued fellowship! So, in faith, we renounce our pride and choose to humble ourselves before God.

But how do we do that? By changing our perspective on ourselves. "I'm really a very nice guy and quite capable to handle most problems." Really? What does the Bible say? "The heart is deceitful above all things, and desperately wicked; who can know it?" (Jer.17:9 – NKJV). "For out of the heart come evil thoughts, murder, adultery, sexual immorality, theft, false testimony, slander" (Matt.15:19). Look into your heart as I have mine. Each of these is there. Are we really that nice? Or is it the Holy Spirit, rather than us, that is controlling and checking the expressions of evil that would otherwise freely flow out from our hearts?

Are we really capable of handling most problems? (Beware of religious humanism: in attitude, the same as secular humanism, thinking that man is capable of handling anything himself. He doesn't need God. Religious humanism transfers this same attitude into the Christian life.) In Lamentations 3:37 we read, "Who can speak and have it happen if the Lord has not decreed it?" We can say anything we want, but only the Lord will permit it to come about. Christ said in John 15:4,5, "Remain in me, and I will remain in you. No branch can bear fruit by itself; it must remain in the vine. Neither can you bear fruit unless you remain in me. I am the vine; you are the branches. If a man remains in me and I in him, he will bear much fruit; <u>apart from me you can do nothing</u>" (underlining mine). But we tend not to believe that. We must recognize ourselves for what we really are and admit it, if for no other reason that God says that's what we are like. We must empty ourselves of our inflated self-esteem and humbly admit that we are nothing except for the grace and enabling of God.

Secondly, we must <u>consciously submit to God</u> and to the circumstances he sends along our way to help in the humbling process. He knows we need help to become humble, and in his sovereignty and love, sends us those experiences that will accomplish this. James 4:6,7 is encouraging here: "But he gives us more grace. That is why Scripture says: 'God opposes the proud but gives grace to the humble.' Submit yourselves, then, to God. Resist the devil, and he will flee from you."

Thirdly, we must place more value on God's recognition than on man's, trying to please him rather than man. Man's plaudits are temporary; God's are eternal (see Col.3:23,24 with Matt.6:1-4).

And lastly, we must be willing to give credit where credit is due. "Rather, it is the Father, living in me, who is doing the work" (Jn.14:10b).

Are you willing to humble yourself before God?

APPLICATION: We all suffer from pride to varying degrees at different times. Sometimes it's worse than at other times. It may be well to remember what pride actually is: the root cause of all sin! Pride says, "I know better than you do what's best for me, and that's what I'm choosing to do!" You know, that's not the best thing to say to God! Rather, ask him to help you hate what pride actually is, and not give in to it.

DAY 193
[a]HE IS HUMBLE, concl.

QUESTIONS TO THINK ABOUT:

1. What are some examples of false humility?
2. How could false humility actually be considered "reverse pride"?
3. How could false humility actually be a cover for unbelief?
4. How can an accurate self-evaluation go hand-in-hand with humility?

Something also needs to be said regarding false humility. In a sense this could be called "reverse pride" since, in effect, we put on a humble air in order to avoid something that might make us look foolish and thus injure our self-esteem, our pride! "Oh, I could never teach a Sunday School class. I'm just not good enough. I don't know enough. There are others far more qualified than I am, and could do a much better job." Is this humility? He certainly is putting himself below others. Or is it really pride? It could be that he is too proud to take a chance on making a fool of himself before those who might know more than he does. Or too proud to change his private lifestyle, and fearful that it might be revealed if he were to take this position, and thus damage his self-image, or the humble image he wants others to think he has. It could be this ... or ... the false humility of unbelief. "I could never do that!" when asked to fill a new role, the request coming through God's chain of authority over you. We don't believe that if we abide in Christ, we will be fruitful (Jn.15:4,5). We don't believe that we can do all things (that God has asked us to do) through Christ who strengthens us (Phil.4:13). And so, in false humility disguising unbelief, we say, "I can't possibly do it. There are others far more able than I am." Thus we don't even give God a chance to work through us. I was asked once to become office manager of our field office for a couple of years. I do not have the gift of administration, nor do I enjoy administration. But it was either me, or someone else having to be pulled out of their ministry to do the job. I knew I couldn't do it, but I also knew that with God's enablement, I could. So I trusted him and he helped me do the job that needed to be done. Looking back, I am still amazed at how he worked it all out.

Let's look again at Christ. Part of humility is the ability to make an accurate assessment of one's self and abilities in light of his relationship with God. Christ made many claims about himself, which, if not true, would have been the words of a very proud egotistical man. But his assessment of himself in relationship to his Father was true and accurate. In Romans 12:3 Paul says, "For by the grace given me I say to every one of you: Do not think of yourself more highly than you ought [We err most in this direction, but it could be written, "not to think of yourself more lowly than you ought to think"!], but rather think of yourself with sober judgment, in accordance with the measure of faith God has given you." We are to consider ourselves soberly, realistically, in terms of the faith God has given us. So when he directs us to do something for which we feel totally inadequate, true humility will respond with something like this: "God has given me the ability to do this job up to such and such a point (realistic evaluation of one's ability); but beyond that point I'm a wipeout. But since he has obviously directed me to do this job, I must trust him in faith to supply me with both the wisdom and the ability to do it. Whether I fail or succeed, I must humbly submit myself and my work to him, and learn the lessons he has for me in this." Let me say, that's a lot easier said than done! It's a struggle, no doubt about it. But if our sovereign God taps us on the shoulder for something, that means he's going to see us through it too (cf. Judg.6:11-16 where Gideon was given an impossible job to do). Our part is to humbly submit to him and his wisdom (see also 1 Cor.1:26-31).

Is your humility based upon your inability or God's sovereignty?

APPLICATION: We grow when we're stretched beyond what we think we can do. Don't "short-change" God by saying, "No!" before giving him a chance to work through you. Remember, he delights in using the weak things to confound the mighty, the foolish things to confound the wise. The "smaller" we are, the more glory God receives when the job gets done. May I suggest a change of mindset? The next time he obviously asks you to do something you feel totally inadequate to do, accept that assignment with eager anticipation as to how he's going to work through you to bring it about.

By the way, he will not ask you to be a bookkeeper if you have no mathematical ability! On the other hand, if he did ask you to do that, he would also give you the mathematical ability to accomplish it. Wouldn't that be exciting, amazing and mind-blowing? As described above, he did that with me in terms of administration. He gave me the gift I needed to do the job required, and I learned a "new skill"!

DAY 194
[a]HE IS THE SELF-DENYING ONE

QUESTIONS TO THINK ABOUT:

1. In our culture of commercialism, why is the concept and practice of self-denial so difficult?
2. How would Matthew 6:33, "Seek first the kingdom of God and his righteousness" change our focus?
3. Can you give some real-life examples of self-denial?
4. What can be some of the results/benefits of self-denial?
5. What could be some of the results from refusing to deny self?

A good definition of self-denial is "deliberately giving up something for a purpose." Philippians 2:5-7 and 2 Corinthians 8:9 again bring this out. Christ denied himself his heavenly riches so that we might become rich. He denied himself his heavenly glory so that we might become glorious (Jn.17:5,22). He gave up his right to live so that we might have life (1 Thess.5:9,10).

In Matthew 16:24-27 Christ extends this principle to us. "Then Jesus said to his disciples, 'If anyone would come after me, he must deny himself and take up his cross and follow me. For whoever wants to save his life will lose it, but whoever loses his life for me will find it. What good will it be for a man if he gains the whole world, yet forfeits his soul? Or what can a man give in exchange for his soul? For the Son of Man is going to come in his Father's glory with his angels, and then he will reward each person according to what he has done.'"

On the surface, denying oneself would seem to involve a denial or resigning oneself to a place of lesser importance than we consider essential for a full life here on earth. In the States, perhaps it would be bypassing that better paying job in order to have more time for the Lord's work and church involvement. For us missionaries in Papua it was putting ourselves in a place with little or no adequate medical help, especially in case of emergency. We had go to Jakarta, Singapore, Australia or the States in order to get the type of emergency medical help we considered essential in the States. We could have literally lost our lives for his sake in this situation.

Others might have to change to a lower standard of living in order to keep up with their tithe commitments to the Lord's work. Inflation, devaluation and recession are tightening many purse strings and it takes more and more money for Christians to maintain their present lifestyle. That means less and less money for the Lord. But what happens when economic depression strikes? Their present lifestyle is decimated, their wealth and possessions are suddenly gone, and they have nothing to show for all their efforts. Further, there is little or no fruit in their "eternal bank account" – thus occasioning a double loss.

Self-denial is the deliberate choice to give up our life and our rights to God for his purpose of making us like Christ and reaching a lost world with the Gospel. It is seeking first the kingdom of God and his righteousness, with his promise that all we need will then be given to us (Matt.6:33). It is a step of faith. But we have the promise of our sovereign, loving God that he will take care of us. What more could we ask?

In Philippians 4:19 Paul writes, "And my God will meet all your needs according to his glorious riches in Christ Jesus." This Paul promises to those who sacrificed to meet his needs. They denied themselves in order to help him and further the Lord's work. Let's not throw our lives away through self-indulgence, but invest them in eternal dividends through self-denial, willing sacrifice, even as our Lord Jesus Christ has done.

How can you simplify your lifestyle in order to have more resources to give to the Lord's work and the needs of others?

APPLICATION: I've often wondered why it is so easy for me to put off doing something important when a friend shows up and needs my help. Yet when the Lord asks me to do something, it's often a real struggle to put aside what I'm doing in order to do what he is asking. It may boil down to our love for him. When we genuinely love someone, no sacrifice is too great to make. If we really loved the Lord, doing what he asks of us would not be a problem. It also may be an issue of being able to see the one and not the other. We respond more readily to what we see than to what we don't see. Either way, whatever the reason, we need to ask the Lord to help us love him unconditionally and be ready to respond to him regardless of what we have to lay aside to do it.

DAY 195
ᶜHE IS THE LIFE-GIVING SPIRIT

◆

QUESTIONS TO THINK ABOUT:

1. What is the difference between a life-giving being and a life-giving spirit?
2. In referring to Jesus as a "life-giving spirit," what does that mean for us personally?
3. How can we reflect Jesus as the "life-giving spirit" in our relationship with others?

In 1 Corinthians 15:45 we read, "So it is written: 'The first man Adam became a living being; the last Adam, a life-giving spirit.'"

In John 5:21 Jesus told his listeners: "For just as the Father raises the dead and gives them life, even so the Son gives life to whom he is pleased to give it." To be given life is to be set free from the law of sin and death (Rom.8:2). In setting us free from the law of sin (spiritual death), the Lord Jesus also freed us from the results of sin (physical death: either in that physical death will not be able to hold us, or that we would not die as the result of committing some sin). To be free from spiritual and physical death is to have life! And because of the death and resurrection of Jesus Christ, he has the authority to give life to those who ask him for it.

Paul demonstrates this truth in Ephesians 2:1-7 where he writes: "As for you, you were dead in your transgressions and sins, in which you used to live when you followed the ways of this world and of the ruler of the kingdom of the air, the spirit who is now at work in those who are disobedient. All of us also lived among them at one time, gratifying the cravings of our sinful nature and following its desires and thoughts. Like the rest, we were by nature objects of wrath. But because of his great love for us, God, who is rich in mercy, made us alive with Christ even when we were dead in transgressions – it is by grace you have been saved. And God raised us up with Christ and seated us with him in the heavenly realms in Christ Jesus, in order that in the coming ages he might show the incomparable riches of his grace, expressed in his kindness to us in Christ Jesus."

In John 7:37-39a we read: "On the last and greatest day of the Feast, Jesus stood and said in a loud voice, 'If anyone is thirsty, let him come to me and drink. Whoever believes in me, as the Scripture has said, streams of living water will flow from within him.' By this he meant the Spirit, whom those who believed in him were later to receive." We reflect Christ as the life-giving Spirit as we permit his Spirit to work in and through us. As he says in John 6:63, "The Spirit gives life; the flesh counts for nothing. The words I have spoken to you are spirit and they are life." The Holy Spirit not only gives us life, but gives others life through us as we give them the Word of

God. Unbelievers are dead in their sins; many Christians are "dead on their spiritual feet." Both need a touch from the life-giving Spirit. There is no greater joy than to see the light of understanding flash in their eyes as that spark of life ignites their souls. And as they begin to follow that new light, they are freed from spiritual death and cease following the ways of sin that would also bring on physical death. Wherever we go, we can be spreading life to those around us as we share the Word with them, counsel and encourage them, or just be helpful to them in the name of our Lord Jesus Christ.

Are you a life-giver?

APPLICATION: We cannot give to others what we do not possess ourselves. Jesus came to give us abundant life. If we are living defeated lives, we have nothing to share with others. The abundant life begins with a daily submission to the lordship of Jesus Christ and a willingness to obey him. Then he can work in and through us, and then we can be a "life-giving spirit" to others.

DAY 196
ᶜHE IS THE LION

QUESTIONS TO THINK ABOUT:

1. When you think of a lion, what comes to mind?
2. This is a mixed metaphor, but how is the lion's ferociousness tempered by truth and justice as seen in Jesus?
3. At what or to whom should our "ferociousness" be directed?
4. What is the difference between combating the sin and combating the sinner?

In Revelation 5:5 Christ is called "the Lion of the tribe of Judah." Judah evidently adopted the lion as its symbol because of

Jacob's prophecy found in Genesis 49:8-12 where Judah is pictured as strong as a young lion having eaten its prey, and as secure as a mature lion whom no one would dare rouse. There were plenty of lions around at that time, so Israel had many opportunities to observe their behavior and appearance.

Of all mentions of the LORD in Scripture in connection with lions, the symbolism is frightening, for the LORD is pictured as a lion on the hunt (Job10:16), lying wait in ambush (Lam.3:10), catching its prey, tearing it apart (Hos.13:7,8), breaking its bones (Isa.38:13), carrying it away (Hos.5:14,15) and devouring it (Hos.13:8). He also is pictured as a fearless lion defending its own territory no matter what the odds against him (Isa.31:4). And when he "roars," men quake in fear and obey him (Hos.11:10; Amos 3:8).

As a lion, Christ shows no mercy on his enemies, but is ferocious and deadly. In Revelation 19:11 we read: "I saw heaven standing open and there before me was a white horse, whose rider is called Faithful and True. With justice he judges and makes war." In the following verses he deals out death to those who oppose him. But according to John 8:16, he judges according to truth. So the lion-like ferociousness and deadliness in which he deals with sin is not dealt with in hate, arrogance or vengefulness, but in righteousness and according to truth.

We reflect Christ as a ferocious and deadly lion as we fight sin, both in ourselves and in society. In Hebrews 12:1-4 we read, "Therefore, since we are surrounded by such a great cloud of witnesses, let us throw off everything that hinders and the sin that so easily entangles, and let us run with perseverance the race marked out for us. Let us fix our eyes on Jesus, the author and perfecter of our faith, who for the joy set before him endured the cross, scorning its shame, and sat down at the right hand of the throne of God. Consider him who endured such opposition from sinful men, so that you will not grow weary and lose heart. In your struggle against sin, you have not yet resisted to the point of shedding your blood."

In society, Christians should become actively involved in combating crime, supporting law enforcement. Not only should we obey the laws, but should teach our children to do the same, respecting and honoring the police officers. I know of one church that gives one Sunday a year especially to honor the policemen of their community and express appreciation for the job they're doing. We should encourage our young people to consider some branch of law enforcement as a vocation: policemen or women, lawyers or judges. We need godly men and women in these positions. We ourselves can participate in jury duty, not as a duty, but as an opportunity to reflect Christ as a lion against sin. We also can become involved in or support various organizations that fight against pornography, child abuse, corruption and other kinds of vice and sin in the community and in our nation. If all the 50 million Christians in America would suddenly rise up against sin, there would be a tremendous "house cleaning" in this nation, and we would likely become a nation truly "under God."

APPLICATION: We cannot do everything or be involved in everything. Some of us will be involved full-time in social-political issues; others of us full-time in spiritual ministry; yet others in domestic and work-related pursuits, etc. It is often hard not to "judge" others when they don't share the same burden that we have regarding the area of activity in which we feel most driven. But we need to remember that not all members of the body have the same function, but must be fully committed to the functions given to them. The nose must not judge the hands because they are not fully committed to smelling. Both are essential to the smooth functioning of the body. So we need to give ourselves fully to the burden God has given us and not be judgmental of others for not sharing the same burden.

DAY 197
ᶜHE IS THE LION, cont.

QUESTIONS TO THINK ABOUT:

1. What is the function of a male lion in his pride?
2. How does Christ fulfill that function?
3. How can we fulfill that function in the body of believers?

One function of the male lion is to look after the pride's safety. He will show no mercy toward other lions who trespass onto his territory. In just such a way the Lord is our defender. It is his responsibility to keep us safe. We read in Psalm 5:11, "But let all who take refuge in you be glad; let them ever sing for joy. Spread your protection over them, that those who love your name may rejoice in you." In John 10:27,28 Jesus says, "My sheep listen to my voice; I know them, and they follow me. I give them eternal life, and they shall never perish; no one can snatch them out of my hand." In John 17:12 we read part of Jesus' prayer to the Father where he says, "While I was with them [the disciples], I protected them and kept them safe by that name you gave me. None has been lost except the one doomed to destruction so that Scripture would be fulfilled."

There is another lion prowling about toward whom the Lord shows no mercy. We read in 1 Peter 5:8, "Be self-controlled and alert. Your enemy the devil prowls around like a roaring lion looking for someone to devour." But the word God has about this situation is clear: Satan will bruise Christ's heel (cause him to suffer), but Christ will crush Satan's head (the deathblow dealt him at the Cross – cf. Gen.3:15); and if we submit ourselves to God and resist Satan, we enter into Christ's victory and Satan will have to flee from us (Jas.4:7).

We reflect Christ as the defending lion as we study the Word of God, then proclaim its truths and principles to others, encouraging them to remain faithful to the Lord and grow in their Christian lives. It also involves intercessory prayer on the behalf of others – in a sense becoming a shield between them and Satan. It means taking our stand against Satan and his demons, in the authority given to us in the name and through the blood of our Lord Jesus Christ, on their behalf, that they might be delivered from "the mouth of the lion."

Perhaps the best way to defend or be a defense for fellow believers is through the example of our own lives. Many turn away from the Faith or fall into sin or suffer defeat because of the failure of those to whom they looked for an example. As we are faithful and demonstrate the truth and reality and practicality of Biblical principles in our lives, so that others can see that they "work," then they also will be encouraged in their faith and, hopefully, remain faithful to the Lord. I remember when a pastor friend of ours ran off with another man's wife. I was devastated and thought in my heart, "If such a godly man as he can do that, what hope is there for me?" But my ultimate example is the Lord Jesus Christ, who will <u>never</u> fail. So even as we encourage others to follow our example (see 1 Cor.11:1), we must caution them that we are apt to fail. Thus they should always look to Christ as their ultimate example, not us.

Are you, as a defending lion, jealously guarding the Lord's "pride"?

APPLICATION: If our "pride" is attacked, let it not be the result of our doing. Daily, if not several times a day, I pray, "Lord, keep me faithful." I do not want to be the cause of others' faith failing because of sin in my life. We do not live to ourselves. Someone is always watching us. Let us strive to live in such a way that their faith is protected by what they see in us, that we give Satan no foothold from which to attack the faith of others.

DAY 198
ᶜHE IS THE LION, concl.

QUESTIONS TO THINK ABOUT:

1. How is our response different from hearing a lion roar in the zoo and hearing it roar in the wild?
2. In what way can we sound the "roar" of Christ before others?

The third aspect of Christ as the Lion is alluded to in Hosea 11:10 and Amos 3:8 where we find him speaking and men responding. In Hosea 11:10,11 we read: "They will follow the LORD; he will roar like a lion. When he roars, his children will come trembling from the west. They will come trembling like birds from Egypt, like doves from Assyria. I will settle them in their homes, declares the LORD." When he gives a directive, his people obey it. Then in Amos 3:8 we read: "The lion has roared – who will not fear? The Sovereign LORD has spoken – who can but prophesy?" When he gives a message it MUST be proclaimed. Jeremiah faced this dilemma during his ministry. We read of it in Jeremiah 20:7-9 where he prays: "O LORD, you deceived me, and I was deceived; you overpowered me and prevailed. I am ridiculed all day long; everyone mocks me. Whenever I speak, I cry out proclaiming violence and destruction. So the word of the LORD has brought me insult and reproach all day long. But if I say, 'I will not mention him or speak any more in his name,' his word is in my heart like a fire, a fire shut up in my bones. I am weary of holding it in; indeed, I cannot." When the Lord commands, people move and his messengers speak.

As the Apostle Paul spoke God's Word, the Christians at Rome and Philippi obeyed. Romans 6:17, "But thanks be to God that, though you used to be slaves to sin, you wholeheartedly obeyed the form of teaching to which you were entrusted." And Philippians 2:12,13

"Therefore, my dear friends, as you have always obeyed – not only in my presence, but now much more in my absence – continue to work out your salvation with fear and trembling, for it is God who works in you to will and to act according to his good purpose."

The Lion roared. His people obey with fear and trembling. Notice that it is not we who roar, but God; it is his Word that causes fear and trembling and that produces obedience, not our word. So as we give forth God's Word, we can expect results; the Lion will roar in their hearts, producing fear and hatred in the hearts of some, fear and obedience in the hearts of others, and trembling in all. We need to call God's people to a life of obedience. But they also need to speak. I have found that when God gives me a message, <u>I must</u> speak, and I yearn for as many opportunities as possible to share it. Whether or not anyone receives it is not the point; it is God's message and it <u>must</u> be given. The Lion has roared; who can but speak?" So as we reflect Christ as the Lion, we will give forth his Word in boldness and confidence and with authority in full assurance that it will produce results.

Have you "roared" lately as the Lord's mouthpiece?

APPLICATION: When the Lord has shown you something special from his Word, or blessed you in an unusual way, share it with others. When you speak to them in this way, it may seem like just a purr to you, but to them more like a lion's roar as it does God's work in their hearts.

DAY 199
ᶜHE IS THE FEARED ONE

QUESTIONS TO THINK ABOUT:

1. What is the difference between positive fear and negative fear?
2. What are some causes of fear?

In Mark 11:18, after Jesus purified the Temple, upsetting the status quo, we read, "The chief priests and the teachers of the law heard this and began looking for a way to kill him, for they feared him, because the whole crowd was amazed at his teaching." Again in Mark 1:21, 22, "They went to Capernaum, and when the Sabbath came, Jesus went into the synagogue and began to teach. The people were amazed at his teaching, because he taught them as one who had authority, not as the teachers of the law."

What was the difference between his teaching and that of the teachers of the law? "He taught with a direct authority from God and had the power to evoke decisions. This contrasted sharply with the teachers of the law (lit. "scribes") who were schooled in the written Law and its oral interpretation. Their knowledge was derived from scribal tradition, so they simply quoted the sayings of their predecessors" (Walvoord, N.T. ed, p.109). The Jewish leaders feared "Him because of His authoritative appeal to the crowds" (Ibid., p.158). In John 12:17-19 we read, "Now the crowd that was with him when he called Lazarus from the tomb and raised him from the dead continued to spread the word. Many people, because they had heard that he had given this miraculous sign, went out to meet him. So the Pharisees said to one another, 'See, this is getting us nowhere. Look how the whole world has gone after him!'" I suspect the Pharisees feared their loss of prestige and power to Jesus more

Unexpected Transformation / 455

than anything else. They also feared the erosion or abrogation of the "doctrines" that they had held for centuries. When Jesus said on several occasions, "You have heard that it was said ... but I say to you ...," the Pharisees just couldn't take it.

On several occasions Jesus evoked fear in the hearts of those around him. Each time it was because of an unusual miracle: the unusual draught of fish (Lk.5), the raising of the widow of Nain's son (Lk.7), the calming of the storm (Mark 4), the healing of the paralytic (Lk.5), the deliverance of the Gadarene maniac (Lk.8), his walking on the water (Matt.14), and the Transfiguration (Matt.17). People fear the unusual and the supernatural because it is something that happens totally outside their experience and control.

We find the same thing happening whenever the disciples wrought a miracle. In Acts 2:43 we read, "Everyone was filled with awe, and many wonders and miraculous signs were done by the apostles." Upon the judgment of Ananias and Saphira before Peter, many feared (Acts 5:5). The incident of the seven sons of Sceva (Acts 19:17) caused many to fear. We find also in the Old Testament that those who walked with the Lord were feared by others. Of the prophets, specific mention is made of Samuel (1 Sam.12:18; 16:4). Then Saul greatly feared David just because the Lord was with him and he behaved himself very wisely (1 Sam.18:12,15).

As we live close to the Lord and teach authoritatively from his Word, others will be brought to him; lives will be changed, and the authority of the leaders of other religions or nominal Christianity will become fearful that their religion is "losing out," their power is being eroded, and that we are "stealing their sheep." They fear our success and will oppose it even as the Lord continues to bless.

Does your way of life evoke this kind of fear in others?

APPLICATION: Occasionally the Lord might use us to work a miracle, but most often he will use us to speak authoritatively from his Word. But that presupposes that we are first in his Word! We cannot speak authoritatively about that which we don't know. "I think somewhere ..." just doesn't cut it. Some people fear the truth, but the truth is its own best defense because it works; in the end, it will prove them false. But they will still oppose it because it shows up their false presuppositions and beliefs, and few like to admit that they are wrong!

DAY 200
ᶜHE IS THE FIRSTBORN FROM THE DEAD, THE FIRSTFRUITS OF THE DEAD

◆

QUESTIONS TO THINK ABOUT:

1. What does it mean for Jesus to be the "firstborn from the dead"?

2. What did the word "firstfruits" mean to Israel? So when Christ is called "the firstfruits of the dead," what would come to mind in Jewish thinking?

In Revelation 1:5, and I Corinthians 15:23 we read two descriptive phrases about Christ which imply the same truth: he is the firstborn from the dead, and he is the firstfruits of the dead.

The term "firstborn," to the Jews, carries with it all the inherited rights, blessings and responsibilities given to the firstborn son of a family. He would become the head of the family upon his father's death and would carry on in his place with full authority. So as Christ is referred to as the firstborn from the dead, we understand that he not only was the first one to rise from the dead never to die again, but also that he is sovereign; he has full authority in this whole new order. Thus in Christ "the old has gone, the new has come!" (2 Cor.5:17).

Others were raised from the dead, only to die again. But Jesus was raised with an immortal body never to die again. As such, he became the firstfruits (of the dead), the symbol of or sample of the full harvest that is yet to come. The Jews would present a sheaf of grain to the Lord as the firstfruits of their harvest (Lev.23:10,11), then they would commence their harvest. The grain was already there in the field. So, in God's sight, the grain is already fully developed, ready to be harvested, Christ being the first "harvested" of what is already there.

As the firstborn from the dead, Christ becomes the heir of all things (Heb.1:2). In Romans 8:17 we read that if we are children of God, then we are "heirs – heirs of God and co-heirs with Christ, if indeed we share in his sufferings in order that we may also share in his glory." So not only has Christ been appointed heir of all things, but we also have been appointed as co-heirs with him!

In Colossians 1:15 we read that Christ is "the firstborn over all creation." This title states his sovereign right over all creation. Not only will we be glorified together with Christ as we suffer with him, but we will also reign with him (2 Tim.2:12). As we yield to him, even now the Holy Spirit will endue us with power and authority to serve God and his kingdom as his representatives. And though we suffer, men will not be able to deny the source of our power and authority.

As heirs of God, reflecting Christ's rights as the firstborn, we have received "everything we need for life and godliness through our knowledge of him who called us by his own glory and goodness" (2 Pet.1:3).

Are you living out and using your inheritance? (For further discussion about this, see DAY 217 – HE IS THE HEIR).

APPLICATION: Everything we need for life and godliness is found in God's Word. We need to be reading it so that we will know what his provisions are for us, then act on them. An "inheritance" is of no value to us if we keep it hidden away somewhere.

DAY 201
ᵇHE IS THE FORERUNNER

QUESTIONS TO THINK ABOUT:

1. What is the meaning of the term "forerunner"?
2. How then does that term refer to Christ in relationship to us?
3. How can we become a "forerunner" for other believers?

Have you ever found yourself wishing that someone else had done this before you? Or wondering if anyone else has ever experienced what you are going through? In both cases, the answer is, "Yes, someone else has, and his name is Jesus, "The Forerunner," the one who has gone before us, the one who has already gone through what we are going through.

In Hebrews 6:19,20a we read, "We have this hope as an anchor for the soul, firm and secure. It enters the inner sanctuary behind the curtain, where Jesus, <u>who went before us</u>, has entered on our behalf" (underlining mine). Before Jesus, only the High Priest could enter the presence of God, and that only once a year with incense and the blood of a sacrifice. Now, because Jesus has entered the presence of God with the final sacrifice, he has opened the way for us to "approach the throne of grace with confidence, so that we may receive mercy and find grace to help us in our time of need" (Heb.4:16). We can come daily, hourly, at need into the very presence of God, not with fear, but with confidence, because <u>Jesus has gone before us</u>.

A second question: Have you ever felt that no one has ever been tempted like this before? Well, someone has – Jesus. We read in Hebrews 4:15, "For we do not have a high priest who is unable to sympathize with our weaknesses, but we have one who has been tempted in <u>every way</u> just as we are – yet was without sin." And it wasn't a breeze for him either. In Hebrews 2:18 we read: "Because he himself <u>suffered</u> when he was tempted, he is able to help those who are being tempted" (all underlining mine).

Thirdly, have you ever felt panic-stricken at the thought of death? As we saw yesterday, Jesus has already been there and back! He arose from the dead thus guaranteeing our resurrection which removes the dreaded fear of death from us. Again we turn to Hebrews 2:14,15 which says: "Since the children have flesh and blood, he too shared in their humanity so that by his death he might destroy him who holds the power of death – that is, the devil – and free those who all their lives were held in slavery by their fear of death." It doesn't remove the grief and uncertainty of death, but it does remove the fear – and the Lord has promised to comfort us in our grief as well. Paul says in 2 Corinthians 1:3-5, "Praise be to the God and Father of our Lord Jesus Christ, the Father of compassion and the God of all comfort, who comforts us in <u>all</u> our troubles, so that we can comfort those in any trouble with the comfort we ourselves have received from God. For just as the sufferings of Christ flow over into our lives, so also through Christ our comfort overflows" (underlining mine).

In this sense, we too reflect Christ as The Forerunner. As we suffer and are comforted by our heavenly Father, we can then turn to others who are suffering or enduring a trial and say, "I've been there myself. I know exactly what you're going through." And then share God's comfort with them.

Are you sharing the comfort you have received from God with others? (More tomorrow.)

APPLICATION: There's a certain satisfaction when we can "show the ropes" to others – we've been there, done that and "got the t-shirt!" Sharing our experiences with others and seeing them profit by them is a rich blessing that God has given us, even as Christ shared in our experiences and we profit by what he went through. Perhaps a good question to ask when "going through an experience" is, "What can I learn from this to share with others?"

DAY 202
bHE IS THE FORERUNNER, concl.

QUESTIONS TO THINK ABOUT:

1. Is it egotistical or proud on our part to encourage others to follow our example? Why or why not?

2. Why is it important for us to share spiritual truth with one another?

There is another way in which we reflect Christ as the forerunner, and that is by forging ahead in our spiritual lives, testing and trying new spiritual truths, and applying the Word in new areas. The Apostle Paul did this and at one time he wrote to the Philippians (4:9), "Whatever you have learned or received or heard from me, or seen in me – put into practice. And the God of peace will be with you." How could he say this? Isn't he a bit egotistical to claim that if they do what he does, God will be with them? Not if it's true! That's no more egotistical than a trail guide saying, "If you carefully follow this map I've drawn for you, you won't get lost or sidetracked. I've been there before, many times. This is the way and you will arrive safely as long as you follow this map."

What Paul is saying, in essence, is: "Look, what I've taught and preached to you is the Word of God, which I also make every attempt to put into practice. I have discovered that it works every time, that there is blessing in doing and being what God says (even along with hardship and heartaches). I have experienced God's peace, God's deep peace, in spite of my circumstances. God is entirely consistent. He doesn't change. If I have experienced his peace by obeying his Word and trusting him, then so will you. So you do what I have taught you and shared with you from my own experience, and the God of peace will be with you!" No, not an egotistical statement, but just a statement of fact.

So as we experience new spiritual truths and find out that they "work," we can encourage others to forge ahead in the same direction and to expect certain results. We become their "forerunners." But the fascinating thing about this is that, as they forge ahead, the Holy Spirit will show them things that he has not chosen to show us, and they, in turn, become our "forerunners" as they share these new insights with us! In this way, no one ever gains a monopoly on spiritual truth, and we can truly help and encourage one another along in our Christian lives.

This is why love and unity in the Body is so important, for a fragmented body is unable to nourish and care for itself or even function properly. But with love and good communication, we will be able to encourage and challenge fellow believers in their walk with God, thus nourishing and strengthening the Church, and increasing its overall effectiveness.

So let's be faithful in sharing with others what God is teaching us, so that they too will be encouraged to forge ahead in their Christian experience.

In what ways have you been a forerunner of spiritual truth for others?

APPLICATION: In order to be a "forerunner" in this sense, it is absolutely essential that we are in the Word daily so that the Lord can speak to us and show us new and wonderful things from his Word that we can share with others. But spending time in the Word doesn't come automatically – it has to be planned, prioritized, or we will never do it. The amount of time and frequency is up to us, but the Lord will bless us as we spend that time with him.

DAY 203
ᵇHE IS THE FOUNDATION

QUESTIONS TO THINK ABOUT:

1. Why is a foundation for any building needed?
2. What are the characteristics of a good foundation?
3. Why is it important to pay attention to the type of ground upon which the foundation is laid?

In the business of construction there are many different types of foundations that can be used, some better than others. The Lord mentioned two of these in Matthew 7:24-27: solid rock and sand. While in Chicago one furlough, I saw a large hole in the ground where a construction company was building a skyscraper; but first they dug down to solid rock where they would begin laying the foundation of the building itself. That building will be around for a while!

I can't imagine anyone building directly on the sand, though I suppose in the course of history, some have tried. While in Manokwari (Papua, Indonesia), we often went to the beach with another missionary family. Sand castles were the order of the day, and we tried to build them up with protective sand walls against the incoming tide. Had we returned that evening, we'd have been hard-pressed to find where we had made that castle!

I've read of floating foundations, where large buildings are built on floats in order to withstand earthquakes. So when an earthquake strikes, they just wobble around a bit, but otherwise remain in mint shape. (I've wondered what would happen if the water-holding tank over which the building is built sprung a leak! But maybe the engineers have thought of that too.)

Another foundation is mud. In Agats, Papua, I saw a team of men sink a 40 foot long, 15 inch thick tree trunk (for a house support) 30 feet into the mud, and they could have kept right on going! It sort of gave me a sinking feeling. For if the combined structural weight was heavy enough, the building would gradually sink into the mud. It did happen to a road there. A copper company built a road from the south coastal area all the way up into the mountains to the mine site. In the coastal swamp, they built the road to a height of 15 feet, taking three dump truck loads of gravel just to lengthen the road one foot! About 10 years later the road was a mere three feet above the swamp floor!

Another foundation is gravel and loose rock. Some missionaries, locating in mountain areas, and not having the equipment available to dig foundation holes in the rock, built their solid homes on house pilings just set and braced on top of the gravel and rock. However, when earthquakes came, those houses went sliding!

APPLICATION: The ground underneath any foundation is absolutely critical to the safety and durability of the building above it. But this principle is also applicable to any endeavor we undertake. If the foundation is poorly thought through, no matter how noble our endeavor, it will fail.

DAY 204
ᵇHE IS THE FOUNDATION, cont.

◆

QUESTIONS TO THINK ABOUT:

1. Why is it important for us to have a good spiritual foundation?
2. What is our spiritual foundation?

There is yet another type of foundation I have seen. I was in and out of a house once which was built half over the river and half over the river bank, with rather smallish poles underneath stuck into both in order to hold the house up. We were to have a Sunday service there, but as people kept coming in, my worry factor kept rising. And sure enough, even before we started, there went up a scream from where the women were seated and everybody but me made a fast exit. I couldn't figure out what was going on until I looked up at the rafters and saw them moving – toward the river!! Then I made my fast exit, and we had our service sitting on fallen trees on the river bank. (By the way, the house didn't fall completely. Several men held it back while others tied new bracing underneath. Then, with one shove, they righted and secured it in place once again!)

In 1 Corinthians 3:11 we read of Christ, "For no one can lay any foundation other than the one already laid, which is Jesus Christ." Everything that Jesus Christ was and is, is foundational to our faith. As the Cornerstone, he had to be flawless and without a crack (see DAY 88 – HE IS THE CORNERSTONE). So as the Foundation, he can be nothing less. That is why he said in Matthew 7:24, "Therefore everyone who hears these words of mine and puts them into practice is like a wise man who built his house on a rock." The intimation is not lost. "My teaching (hence I) is like a solid rock foundation. Any life built upon this foundation will not fall." One of the favorite names of God to the psalmist was "Rock" (see DAY 93 – HE IS

THE ROCK OF OFFENSE). Time and again he refers to God as his Rock, which, to the Jew, meant not only a place of refuge, but also a solid foundation upon which to stand unshaken (see Ps.28:1; 31:2,3; 42:9; 62:2,6,7; 78:35, and more).

As we move from unbelief to faith in Christ, we experience what the psalmist did in Psalm 40:2. "He lifted me out of the slimy pit, out of the mud and mire [a change of foundation]; he set my feet on a rock and gave me a firm place to stand."

A strong foundation bears the entire weight of the building and will not move be there earthquake, flood, fire or storm. We read in Hebrews 13:8 that "Jesus Christ is the same yesterday and today and forever." He is unchanging. No cracks or flaws develop in him over a period of time. He is as solid and dependable now as he has been from eternity past. We can count on him to hold us up regardless of the blast of the storm. There are times when our superstructure is totally demolished and we have to return to our Foundation and begin to rebuild. He is always there, though sometimes we have to dig through the rubble to find him. And he will always be that sure foundation upon which we can build again.

APPLICATION: Without the firm foundation of the Word of God in our lives, our "spiritual houses" will crumble and fall at the least provocation. The endurance of our "spiritual houses" depends solely upon our abiding in the Word and the Word abiding in us. If we don't know the Word, then we won't know how to weather the storms that come our way, and our "house" will fall.

DAY 205
ᵇHE IS THE FOUNDATION, concl.

QUESTIONS TO THINK ABOUT:

1. How does our consistency in spiritual matters become a sure foundation for others?
2. How does our conformity to Christ's image make us a foundation for others to build their lives upon?

How do we reflect Christ as the Foundation? In two ways at least. First I think again of the older people at church when I was a boy. They loved the Lord and served him faithfully where they were. They came to prayer meeting, and often would pair off with us younger ones when it came time to pray. Their consistency and encouragement to me gave me a sense of security, of standing on a firm foundation. I saw Christ at work in their lives, which showed me that Christianity was something real and not just put-on.

Secondly, we reflect Christ as the Foundation by becoming like him and thus revealing him to others. Christians who are solid in their faith and reflect the character of Christ give a sense of stability and security to others around them. Sometimes we refer to such people as pillars of the Church. In Galatians 2:9 Paul refers to James, Peter (Cephas) and John "who seemed to be pillars." (This James was the brother of the Lord Jesus, and now head of the Church Council.) These three men had a very close, personal relationship with the Lord, which gave them a solidness around which others could build.

This leads us to the means by which we reflect Christ as the Foundation. How close is your personal relationship with the Lord? A close walk with him can only be developed over a long period of time. There are no shortcuts. We begin with a growing knowledge and familiarity with the Word of God. As we increase in the knowledge of the Word, we increase our potential to know Christ. As we seek to know him better, he takes us step by step through various experiences where we have to apply the principles we've learned and discover that they actually work! This increases our faith and confidence in the Lord. We learn to measure our reactions and responses by Christ's. As we get to know him better, our actions and reactions will reflect his, his thoughts will become ours, his desires our desires (cf. Ps.37:4).

The disciples felt a certain stability and security in Christ's presence. They were standing upon an unshakeable rock. So as our faith and confidence in Christ grows, and as we reflect more and more of him in our daily lives, and as others see for themselves that the principles of Scripture actually work, they will gain a sense of stability and security around us, and we will be providing them a sure foundation on which to build.

"On Christ the Solid Rock I stand, all other ground is sinking sand. <u>All</u> other ground is sinking sand" (underlining mine). Mud, sand, loose rock and gravel, floats, solid rock. Which of these characterize the foundation of your life?

APPLICATION: Review the third paragraph above which deals with the means by which we can reflect Christ as the Foundation and become a foundation for others to build upon.

DAY 206
[a]HE IS THE HARMLESS ONE

◆

QUESTIONS TO THINK ABOUT:

1. When you think of the word "harmless," what comes to mind? What does that word imply?

2. How could one be harmless and weak, or harmless and strong? Which one would characterize Christ?

In Hebrews 7:26 we read of Christ as our High Priest: "Such a high priest meets our need – one who is holy, blameless [harmless – KJV], pure, set apart from sinners, exalted above the heavens." The Greek word used here for blameless is *akakos*, "void of evil," the negative of *kakos* which means bad or evil. In Romans 16:19 (RV) *akakos* is translated "innocent." Webster defines "harmless" as "free from power to harm, inoffensive." Here we have the Lord's gentleness coming out, completely void of evil; there is no threat of danger in his presence. We can fully trust him and not even give it a thought that he might "stab us in the back" as soon as we turn around.

My parents were good examples of this characteristic. They always had the welfare of us children at heart, and never once did they ever give us cause to doubt it. We could trust them implicitly. This is the way God intended all men to live. But when sin entered the picture, this relationship was destroyed, trust was broken, and suspicion and fear began to reign.

But the Lord is going to change all that back again when he comes to set up his kingdom. Trust will be restored and what is harmful now will become harmless then. In Micah 4:2-4 we read: "Many nations will come and say, 'Come, let us go up to the mountain of the LORD, to the house of the God of Jacob. He will teach us his ways, so that we may walk in his paths.' The law will go out from Zion, the word of the LORD from Jerusalem. He will judge between many peoples and will settle disputes for strong nations far and wide. They will beat their swords into plowshares and their spears into pruning hooks. Nation will not take up sword against nation, nor will they train for war anymore. Every man will sit under his own vine and under his own fig tree, and no one will make them afraid, for the LORD Almighty has spoken."

Are our lives characterized by acts of kindness that engender trust? Or are people afraid of our anger and tempestuousness? When we are around others, do they feel secure from threat of harm, or are they worried and suspicious of our motives? Paul illustrates this attitude in 1 Thessalonians 2:7,8 where he writes: "But we were gentle among you, like a mother caring for her little children. We love you so much that we were delighted to share with you not only the gospel of God but our lives as well, because you had become so dear to us."

Is this your attitude toward others as well?

APPLICATION: Harm can be inflicted physically, emotionally or mentally. We must relate to others in such a way that they will have no fear of harm in any manner. They must know that we have their best interest at heart (*agape* love) and that they can trust us implicitly.

DAY 207
cHE IS THE HEAD OF THE CHURCH

QUESTIONS TO THINK ABOUT:

1. What is the function of the head in relation to the rest of our body?
2. What does it mean to be the head of something?
3. As the head, what are one's functions and responsibilities?

We find this title of Christ given to him in Colossians 1:18a where Paul writes: "And he is the head of the body, the church." And again in Ephesians 1:22,23, "And God placed all things under his feet and appointed him to be head over everything for the church, which is his body, the fullness of him who fills everything in every way."

Following the progression of these verses is Ephesians 4:15,16 and Colossians 2:19. "Instead, speaking the truth in love, we will in all things grow up into him who is the Head, that is, Christ. From him the whole body, joined and held together by every supporting ligament, grows and builds itself up in love, as each part does its work." "He has lost connection with the Head, from whom the whole body, supported and held together by its ligaments and sinews, grows as God causes it to grow."

The function of the head is to govern the body. The brain directs the whole operation. Sever the head from the body and everything stops. In a properly functioning body, the brain receives thousands of stimuli every minute, sorts through and evaluates them, and gives direction to the various parts of the body as to how they should react. From the neck comes a message: "There's an itch here that needs scratching." The brain almost simultaneously sends a message down the arm: "Rise up and bend toward the neck"; then on to the fingers: "Start moving back and forth across the spot that itches." The neck sends back the message: "That's enough, thanks." Then the brain responds by commanding the fingers to cease their motion and the arm to return to its original position. If you stop to think about all that actually goes on, it's an amazingly complex process!

In God's economy, he has appointed men and women to become heads over various areas, to give direction to the various parts of the body of people under their control. In government, in the military, in business, in any organization, in the clan and in the family, there is headship. In the Church we find it as well. In every case, leadership is provided and direction is given. If the head is sick or disoriented, the body will not function properly. For this reason every Christian in a position of authority must maintain his spiritual health through prayer and the Word. Then the body will function properly and be fruitful.

In what area(s) are you the head? What indications are there that you are leading effectively?

Unexpected Transformation / 471

APPLICATION: Being the head doesn't mean that you have to know everything; but it does mean that you know when to call others in who can do the work you can't. In a sense, the head is sort of like a switchboard: organizing what needs to be done, then making the right connections to carry it out. But being a good head also means that you are watching out for the best interests and welfare of the rest of the body. If our head makes bad choices, the rest of the body suffers! Above all, we must remember that we are accountable to our Head, the Lord Jesus Christ, and will be called upon to answer for how we carried on our headship responsibilities (cf. Col.4:1).

DAY 208
ᶜHE IS THE HEALER

QUESTIONS TO THINK ABOUT:

1. How did Jesus use healing in his ministry?
2. What was the purpose of the gift of healing as given to the Church?

In Malachi 4:2 we find a prophecy regarding the coming Messiah: "But for you who revere my name, the sun of righteousness will rise with healing in its wings. And you will go out and leap like calves released from the stall." In Matthew 4:23,24 we find Jesus fulfilling this prophecy: "Jesus went throughout Galilee, teaching in their synagogues, preaching the good news of the kingdom, and healing every disease and sickness among the people. News about him spread all over Syria, and people brought to him all who were ill with various diseases, those suffering severe pain, the demon-possessed, those having seizures, and the paralyzed, and he healed them."

In Luke 9:1,2 we read where Jesus gave his disciples the power to heal the sick: "When Jesus called the Twelve together, he gave them power and authority to drive out all demons and to cure diseases, and he sent them out to preach the kingdom of God and to heal the sick." According to I Corinthians 12:9, the Holy Spirit has given "gifts of healing" to the Church along with many other gifts by which everyone might benefit and be edified (see also 12:7; 14:12). According to Hebrews 2:4, the gifts of the Holy Spirit were one set of several proofs sent by God to authenticate the message of the Gospel: "God also testified to it by signs, wonders and various miracles, and gifts of the Holy Spirit distributed according to his will." So the gifts are given with a twofold purpose: to edify and strengthen the Church and to authenticate its message.

I believe that all the gifts of the Spirit (excepting that of Apostleship) are as valid and useful today as they were when they were given to the Church. But through misuse by some, and overemphasis by others, the gift of healing has been rejected as a valid gift, and the Church has turned to medicine as an alternative – helpful, to be sure, but strictly limited to the wisdom of man which at times is grossly inadequate to deal with the sickness or injury – not to mention the expense involved in the meantime.

If we have a headache, we go straight to the aspirin bottle; if our nose is reacting to something around us, to the antihistamines; if our stomach is acidic, the antacids. I have found that many times, though not always, these symptoms disappear when rebuked in the name of the Lord Jesus Christ (see DAY 43 – HE IS THE KING [over Sickness] for more detailed discussion of this issue.)

Generally, we should check out possible spiritual causes of an illness before trying to treat the physical symptoms, for many physical afflictions have a spiritual or emotional cause and will disappear as soon as the precipitating problem is resolved. I remember my frequent visits to the university clinic with all sorts of strange symptoms. I was worried about my pre-med studies and worried

Unexpected Transformation / 473

about getting sick and uptight about some family matters. I would feel faint, my arms would tingle and feel weak, my stomach was nauseated, and so on. But once my worries were adequately dealt with, and that wasn't for some time, these other symptoms vanished. The medicines I was given at the clinic didn't help a bit other than mask the symptoms for a short time. But as long as the basic problems were unresolved, the symptoms kept returning.

So before taking medicine, check out what might be other than a physical cause of your affliction, and you may not have to be medicated at all!

APPLICATION: I suppose most of us have been turned off of healing as a gift because of what we have seen of "faith healers" on T.V. or in other venues. Their theatrics have made a mockery of the gift of healing that the Holy Spirit has given the Church. But just because there are quacks in the medical profession, that doesn't mean that we must stop going to the doctor any more than the misuse of the gift of healing means that we must deny its validity and stop practicing it. People still get sick today, and the message we bring still needs validation as many have never read the Bible or have rejected its message as irrelevant. Those who have that gift have a vital ministry to perform, even today.

DAY 209
bHE IS THE GIFT OF GOD

◆

QUESTIONS TO THINK ABOUT:

1. What is the nature of a gift? What does it signify?
2. What can a gift accomplish?

In Isaiah 9:6 we read, "For to us a child is born, to us a son is given... ." And again in John 3:16, "For God so loved the world that he gave his one and only Son, that whoever believes in him shall not perish but have eternal life." Jesus, and everything we have in him, is God's gift to us.

What is the nature of a gift? It is something given to express the feeling of the giver toward the receiver. It springs from a heart of love wanting to show gratitude; it springs from a heart of compassion desiring to meet a need; it originates in the heart of the giver, totally independent of the actions or needs of the receiver; for if the receiver had done something to "deserve" it, then the gift would no longer be a gift, but a reward or even considered as wages. This is what Paul says in Romans 4:3-5: "What does the Scripture say? 'Abraham believed God, and it was credited to him for righteousness.' Now when a man works, his wages are not credited to him as a gift, but as an obligation. However, to the man who does not work, but trusts God who justifies the wicked, his faith is credited for righteousness." Thus, when God so loved the world that he gave them his only Son, it wasn't because of anything the world had done to deserve that gift – for the world was wicked and deserved nothing but eternal judgment. Rather, God gave his Son because he chose to do so, loving his created images and having compassion for their need.

This is one reason why Christ told us to love our enemies, for only a heart of love and compassion will prompt us to share the Gospel with them in order that they also might be saved. Only a heart of love and compassion will prompt us to respond to their needs and do good toward them, even as God has done toward all men: "For he causes his sun to rise on the evil and the good, and sends rain on the righteous and the unrighteous" (Mat.5:45).

And as God has given to us, so he expects us to give to others. Jesus said to his disciples in Matthew 10:8, "Heal the sick, raise the dead, cleanse those who have leprosy, drive out demons. Freely you have received, freely give." And he adds: "Give, and it will be given to you. A good measure, pressed down, shaken together and running over, will be poured into your lap. For with the measure you use, it will be measured to you" (Luke 6:38).

God gave us his Son (Jn.3:16); Jesus gave us his life (Mk.10:45); and the Holy Spirit gave us gifts for the ministry (1 Cor.12:7-11). We likewise must be willing to give to others, even as Paul expressed in 1 Thessalonians 2:8, "We loved you so much that we were delighted to share with you not only the gospel of God but our lives as well, because you had become so dear to us."

Do you reflect the Lord's love and compassion as you give yourself to others? "Freely you have received, freely give."

APPLICATION: God does not expect us to give to others from what we do not have, but from what we do have, which might not be monetary but time, attention, helping with work, a good word or praying with them. Just like Peter said to the lame beggar in Acts 3:6 (paraphrased), "I don't have any money, but what I do have, that I will give you. In the name of Jesus Christ of Nazareth, get up and walk!" Sometimes all we have to give is our attention, and, in the end, that might be just what they need!

DAY 210
'HE IS THE BRANCH

QUESTIONS TO THINK ABOUT:

1. What is the significance of the tree in Jewish thought?
2. In that light, what is the "promise" of a shoot or branch springing up from the roots of the tree?

To the Jews, a tree often symbolized a kingdom (Israel, Ps.80:8-11; Assyria, Ezek.31:1-9; Babylon, Dan.4:14) and a branch symbolized that from which the kingdom has sprung, hence a figure of life and growth. Water is also prominent in connection with these figures (cf. Ps.1:3; Jer.17:7,8; Ezek.31:4), nourishing and strengthening the tree.

In the same way, the taking away of water from the tree, cutting off or striping the branches of their bark (cf. Ezek.19:12,13; Joel 1:7; Isa.18:5), and burning them (Ezek.19:14; Job 15:30; Jer.11:16), symbolized judgment.

The symbol of the flourishing tree was often applied to individuals who delighted in the Lord and were obedient to him (cf. Ps.1:1-3; 128:1-4; Jer.17:7,8).

Prophetically, the Branch refers to Christ as the reigning Messiah, and the prosperity of a revived Israel (Isa.4:2-6). When Judah returned from exile, the Lord told Joshua, the high priest, and those sitting with him, that they were symbolic of things to come pertaining to Israel's future when he would bring to Israel his Servant, the Branch (Zech.3:8). In what way? Zech.6:11-13 answers that question. "Take the silver and gold and make a crown, and set it on the head of the high priest, Joshua son of Jehozadak. Tell him this is what the LORD Almighty says: 'Here is the man whose name is the Branch, and he will branch out from his place and build the temple of the LORD. It is he who will build the temple of the LORD, and he will be clothed with majesty and will sit and rule on his throne. And there will be harmony between the two.'"

Joshua symbolized Christ, the Branch, in two ways: first, his name means "Jesus," Savior (lit. "Jehovah is Salvation." Variations appear, all meaning the same thing: Hoshea, Oshea, Jehoshua, Jeshua and Jesus.) Secondly, he combines royalty and the priesthood. Jesus combines them also as Priest and King.

Now we have the situation where Israel became unfaithful to the Lord and he pronounced judgment upon them. In Jeremiah 11:16 we read, "The LORD called you a thriving olive tree with fruit beautiful in form. But with the roar of a mighty storm he will set it on fire, and its branches will be broken." In essence, the tree is dead. But it does not remain dead, for there is still life in its roots.

As you look at your life, are you like a tree cut down, or a new shoot springing up into new life? Tomorrow we will see how this life springs forth.

APPLICATION: Do not despise "small things," for out of them can come something "big." Great works often begin with the seeds of small thoughts of what might be possible.

DAY 211
ᶜHE IS THE BRANCH, concl.

QUESTIONS TO THINK ABOUT:

1. For Israel, what is the promise of the sprouting shoot or branch from the roots of the tree?
2. We are referred to as grafted-in branches (Rom.11). What are the implications of this picture?
3. What is the purpose of a grafted branch?

According to Job 14:7-9 it is the nature of a tree stump to send forth new shoots and grow into a new tree. This principle God uses to show that he is not yet finished with Israel as a nation. So the prophets declare: "From the roots of Jesse a Branch will bear fruit" (Isa.11:1); "I will raise up to David a righteous Branch" (Jer.23:5); "I will make a righteous Branch sprout from David's line" (Jer.33:15). Thus the stump sending forth new branches represents Israel brought back to life by Christ, her Messiah. Right now there is only a remnant that believes. But they are the "firstfruits" of Israel (Rom.11:16) indicating that a national resurrection and returning to the Lord in faith is yet coming (see Rom.11:1-32).

God's promises to Israel are still valid (see Jer.31:37), and will be fulfilled in full as the living, righteous Branch grows into a tall and mighty tree, and Israel becomes the blessing to the world that God intended her to be.

As Christ is the Branch that grows into a tall tree, we also are likened to both. In Romans 11:17-21, we are called wild olive branches, grafted contrary to nature into the cultivated olive tree. Jesus said of his disciples, hence all believers, "I am the true vine and my Father is the gardener. He cuts off every branch in me that bears no fruit, while every branch that does bear fruit he trims clean so that it will be even more fruitful. You are already clean because of the word I have spoken to you. Remain in me, and I will remain in you. No branch can bear fruit by itself; it must remain in the vine. Neither can you bear fruit unless you remain in me" (Jn.15:1-4).

David, in Psalm 1:1-3, refers to the man who spurns worldly wisdom but delights and meditates in the law of the LORD as "a tree planted by streams of water, which yields its fruit in season, and whose leaf does not wither. Whatever he does prospers." Jeremiah 17:5-8 reflects the same attitude. The central idea in all these passages is fruit-bearing. Jesus continues in John 15:5 saying, "If a man remains in me and I in him, he will bear much fruit... ." And in verses 7 and 8, "If you remain in me and my words remain in you, ask whatever you wish, and it will be given you. This is to my Father's glory, that you bear much fruit... ." And again in verse 16 he says, "You did not choose me, but I chose you to go and bear fruit – fruit that will last... ."

As we abide in Christ, his life will be infused into us as branches or new shoots, and we will grow and bear fruit to the glory of the Father. What kind of fruit? Among others: love, joy, peace, patience, kindness, goodness, faithfulness, gentleness and self-control (Gal.5:22,23), nothing less than the very character of Christ which we have been discussing all along.

What kind of fruit are you bearing as you grow in him?

APPLICATION: As the shoot from the roots bears a promise of better and greater things to come, so we, as grafted branches into the tree of Israel, bear the promise of better and greater things to come as we bear the fruit for which we were intended. That is one reason why it is necessary for us to know what our spiritual gift is, so that we will know what kind of fruit we should be bearing and can work to that end. (See APPENDIX III on discovering what your spiritual gift is.)

DAY 212
ʻHE IS THE BREAD OF LIFE

QUESTIONS TO THINK ABOUT:

1. How many uses of the word "bread" can you think of?
2. What does bread symbolize generally?
3. What did Jesus mean when he said that he was the Bread from heaven?

To quote from ISBE from its article on bread: "All life was seen to be dependent upon the grain harvest, this in turn depended upon rain in its season, and so bread, the product at bottom of these Divine processes, was regarded as peculiarly 'a gift of God,' a daily reminder of his continual and often undeserved care. Bread became a symbol of hospitality and friendship, and thus rated very high in the esteem of Jews and Arabs alike. Thus physically and socially, bread became the staff of life, the central pillar around which everything else revolved. So the significance of Christ's response to Satan in Matt.4:4 is not lost on the eastern believer: 'It is written: "Man does not live on bread alone, but on every word that comes from the mouth of God"'" (The International Bible Encyclopedia, Vol. I, p.516). There is something more important in life and more central to life than bread, and that is the Word of God. Job said it well in Job 23:12b, "I have treasured the words of his mouth more than my daily bread."

After the feeding of the 5,000, many of them sought Jesus, not because of what he taught them, but because they were after another free meal (Jn.6:26). He told them not to work for food that spoils, but for food that endures to eternal life, which he would give them (vs.27). Then, while they were still thinking "physical" (vs.52), Christ began to talk to them "spiritual" (vs.63), and the result was quite a misunderstanding and thinning of the ranks (vs.66,67). He taught them, or tried to, that there was something more central to life than bread: the Word of God – himself. In verse 35 "Jesus declared, 'I am the bread of life. He who comes to me will never grow hungry, and he who believes in me will never be thirsty.'" And he had just said that "the bread of God is he who comes down from heaven and gives life to the world" (vs.33).

Keeping with the figure of speech, Jesus continues by telling the people that they must eat of this bread, his flesh, if they would live forever (vs.51). Physical bread was necessary for sustaining temporal life; but the spiritual bread, Jesus himself, was absolutely essential for sustaining eternal life. Whatever he heard the Father say, that is what he taught (Jn.8:28). In this same way, whatever he teaches us in the Word, we must pass on to others, for this Word will sustain them and lead them to eternal life. All men must eat of this spiritual food if they expect to have eternal life. And as we faithfully give them the Word of God, it is even as if we came down from heaven to give life to the world, since we have in our hands that life-giving message, the Bread of God.

When it comes to preparing and distributing the Bread of God, how good a "baker" are you?

Unexpected Transformation

APPLICATION: Just as a good baker must know the recipe for his bread, so we must know the "recipe" for ours – the Word of God. If you don't know the "ingredients," you won't know how to prepare and serve it!

DAY 213
ᶜHE IS THE BRIDEGROOM

QUESTIONS TO THINK ABOUT:

1. In Jewish culture, what was the responsibility of the bridegroom?
2. What was the responsibility of the bride?
3. How do these responsibilities reflect the relationship of Christ to the Church?

In Matthew 9:15 Jesus referred to himself as the bridegroom. The Church is frequently referred to as his Bride (see Rev.19:7). Understanding the cultural significance of the bridegroom to the Jewish mind will clarify some aspects of Christ's relationship to the Church, his Bride. (Some of the following material is taken from the book, Manners and Customs of Bible Lands, by Fred. H. Wight, pp.129-134).

First comes the promise of marriage carried out between the families of the boy and girl. This promise could be canceled or broken off at any time for many reasons. Then comes betrothal, when a spoken covenant forever bound the man and woman together. After the exile, a written document of marriage was signed in addition. Then the bridegroom would leave his bride for one year to prepare a home for her. Sometime near the end of that year, the bride would prepare herself for the coming of the bridegroom, knowing that he is coming, but not when, though it seems that the wedding procession usually took place after dark since lamps or torches are frequently referred to as lighting the way of the procession. The bridegroom would arrive at the bride's home amid shouts announcing his arrival, and the bride, having heard of his coming once he was on his way, was ready to meet him. Then he would take her to their new home where the wedding feast would be held for at least a week with much joy and celebration.

This same pattern appears in our relationship with the Lord. First came the promise of marriage in Psalm 2:7,8 where the Son says, "I will proclaim the decree of the LORD: He said to me, 'You are my Son; today I have become your Father. Ask of me, and I will make the nations your inheritance* (see ***NOTE** below), the ends of the earth your possession.'" The "friend of the bridegroom" was often the one designated by the bridegroom's father to act as mediator in securing the girl desired for his son. Such was John the Baptist. He was designated by God to "make the arrangements" in preparation for the "marriage" between Christ and his people (Jn.3:27-29). However, in this case, the "promise" was broken as his people rejected him (Jn.1:11). So he had to seek another bride, the Gentile nations, who gladly came to him (Acts 13:46-48). Verse 48 says, "When the Gentiles heard this [the message of salvation], they were glad and honored the word of the Lord; and all who were appointed for eternal life believed."

The second step in the marriage process was the betrothal, where a solemn verbal covenant was spoken, or a written marriage document signed. This step was considered final. An example of this is found in Ezekiel 16:8b where Ezekiel pictures God as marrying Jerusalem. "I gave you my solemn oath and entered into a covenant with you, declares the Sovereign LORD, and you became mine." In 2 Corinthians 11:2, Paul brings up the same principle, signifying himself as the spokesman for the bride: "I am jealous for you with a godly jealousy. I promised you to one husband, to Christ, so that I might present you as a pure virgin to him." The only way one could be released from this pledge was through divorce, for once the covenant was entered into, they were as good as married. Matthew 1:18,19 demonstrates this: "This is how the birth of Jesus Christ came about. His mother Mary was pledged to be married to Joseph, but before they came together, she was found to be with child through the Holy Spirit. Because Joseph her husband was a righteous man and did not want to expose her to public disgrace, he had in mind to divorce her quietly."

APPLICATION: If you, perchance, have never made a personal decision for Christ, then you are not a part of his Bride. Now is the time for you to make that decision so that when he returns, you will be ready to meet him. All you need to do is express to him the faith in your heart in praying something like this: "Dear Lord Jesus, I believe that you died on the cross for my sins so that I might be forgiven and accepted by God. I ask you to forgive me of my sins, come into my life, and be my Lord and Savior. Thank you! Amen." You don't need to wonder if he will accept you or not. He said in John 6:37, "… The one who comes to me I will by no means cast out" (NKJV). If you have prayed in this way, expressing your faith in him, you are forgiven (saved), and are now a part of Christ's Bride (the Church) and, as such, are "betrothed" to him in the Jewish understanding.

***NOTE:** i.e. first interpretation: believers from every nation; second interpretation: when he shall literally rule the nations.

DAY 214
ᶜHE IS THE BRIDEGROOM, cont.

QUESTIONS TO THINK ABOUT:

1. What is Christ doing between his ascension and his return for us?
2. What are we as believers supposed to be doing until he returns?

After the betrothal, there came an interval of a year before the actual wedding took place. During this time the bridegroom prepared a house in which he and his bride would live, and cared for other things in preparation for taking her as his wife. She also would be getting herself ready to be his wife, learning and boning up on wifely duties and responsibilities. Then the Bridegroom would come for his bride at or near the end of that year. The exact date was unknown to the Bride, so as the time approached, she had to be ready to meet him at any time.

Using this imagery, Christ says to his disciples, "In my Father's house are many rooms; if it were not so, I would have told you. I am going there to prepare a place for you. And if I go and prepare a place for you, I will come back and take you to be with me that you also may be where I am" (Jn.14:2,3). Christ made our betrothal permanent. Now he has gone to prepare a place for us, his Bride. In the meantime, we must prepare ourselves to meet him, for we must be pure and ready. In I John 3:2,3 we read: "... But we know that when he appears, we shall be like him, for we shall see him as he is. Everyone who has this hope in him purifies himself, just as he is pure." (See DAY 21 – HE IS THE PURE ONE for further discussion on this). Christ's teachings abound with exhortations to watch – to be looking for the coming of the Bridegroom: "No one knows about that day or hour, not even the angels in heaven, nor the Son, but only the Father" (Matt.24:36); "Therefore keep watch, because you do not know on what day your Lord will come" (Matt.24:42).

The coming of the Bridegroom was heralded by the shouts of his friends coming before him: "Here's the Bridegroom! Come out to meet him!" (Matt.25:6). Before leaving her house, the bride, adorned and perfumed, with a crown on her head, would receive the blessing of her relatives. When the Bridegroom arrived, she was ready to proceed with him to their new home.

When our Bridegroom comes, it also will be with a shout, with the voice of the archangel, and with the sound of the trumpet of God. The Bride will then rise to meet him in the air, and so will be with the Lord forever (1 Thess.4:16,17).

The Bridegroom usually came at night for his Bride, the darkness emphasizing the beauty of the candlelight procession. Upon arriving at their home, a week-long wedding feast was begun. Only those invited guests who had torches or lamps, could join the wedding procession and take part in the wedding feast.

In John 9:4 Jesus said to his disciples, "As long as it is day, we must do the work of him who sent me. Night is coming, when no one can work." As long as it is "day," the Bride should be preparing herself for the coming of her Bridegroom. For the "night" is coming, in which the world's condition will deteriorate, and it will be very difficult to carry on the Lord's work. Then, I believe, he will come (if not before) and take us home, and the world will plunge headlong into great tribulation.

Are you ready were he to come right now?

APPLICATION: How do we prepare ourselves for his coming? By doing that which he has commanded us (cf. Matt.28:18-20); by learning what pleases him (1 Jn.3:22); by gaining victory over sin (1 Jn.3:3). That also means spending time in the Word, for it is the

Word that cleanses us, keeps us from sin (cf. Eph.5:26 and Ps.119:9-11) and prepares us to meet our Lord.

DAY 215
ʿHE IS THE BRIDEGROOM, concl.

QUESTIONS TO THINK ABOUT:

1. If we live our life here on earth how and when we want to with little regard to what the Word of God says about it, what does that say about our faith and our relationship with the Lord?

2. Read Revelation 19:6-9a. How should this prophecy regarding us as the Lamb's Bride affect our life on earth now?

"Then I heard what sounded like a great multitude, like the roar of rushing waters and like loud peals of thunder, shouting: 'Hallelujah! For our Lord God Almighty reigns. Let us rejoice and be glad and give him glory! For the wedding of the Lamb has come, and his bride has made herself ready. Fine linen, bright and clean, was given her to wear.' (Fine linen stands for the righteous acts of the saints). Then the angel said to me, 'Write: "Blessed are those who are invited to the wedding supper of the Lamb!"'" (Rev.19:6-9a).

One question that is often asked is, "When will the Wedding Supper of the Lamb take place?" Part of the answer is, "Whenever the Lord returns for his Bride." Those believing in a pre-trib rapture hold that the Wedding Supper will take place in heaven during the seven years of tribulation on earth. They claim support for this view from the prophetic week of seven years as found in Dan.9:24-27. Others take the position of a mid-trib rapture, saying that Revelation clearly states that the Bride has prepared herself and is ready for the Wedding Supper immediately upon the destruction of the Apostate

Church which occurs at the close of the first three-and-a-half years of the Tribulation (see Rev.19:1-10 with 14:8 in the context of chs.12 and 13). Post-trib proponents say that the Wedding Supper will actually be the Millennium. Based upon the Jewish marriage customs as the Lord alluded to in John 14:1-3, I would tend to hold to the pre-trib view. But perhaps our focus should be less on that than how we should be preparing ourselves for his coming, whenever it happens.

After the wedding feast was over, the husband was escorted by his friends into the place where his wife has previously been conducted, and they became "one flesh." Even so, we are one with Christ and once our salvation is completed and sin is totally done away with, we will enjoy that oneness to the full. Even as he prayed in John 17:24, "Father, I want those you have given me to be with me where I am, and to see my glory, the glory you have given me because you loved me before the creation of the world." And in verses 20,21 he prays, "My prayer is not for them [his disciples] alone. I pray also for those who will believe in me through their message, that all of them may be one, Father, just as you are in me and I am in you." What that final unity will be like, we cannot know now; but are you preparing yourself diligently for it, so that you will be able to enjoy it to the fullest? We reflect Christ's character as the Bridegroom as we return his love, remain faithful to him during this "waiting" period, prepare ourselves for life with him, and keep our promise of fidelity to him, even as he does to us. And the promise is that once he comes, we shall be with him forever (1 Thess.4:17).

"For the Lord himself will come down from heaven, with a loud command, with the voice of the archangel and with the trumpet call of God, and the dead in Christ will rise first. After that, we who are still alive and are left will be caught up together with them in the clouds to meet the Lord in the air. And so we will be with the Lord forever" (1 Thess.4:16,17). "Even so, Come, Lord Jesus!"

APPLICATION: In our daily Christian lives, we often take the world's cue: the "short view," how will this benefit me now? What we need to do is take the "long view": how will this benefit me then (in heaven)? "Now" is only temporary – just a few years; "then" is eternal – forever! We need to carry on the details of living now in terms of how what we are doing will prepare us for then – our eternal relationship with the Lord, our Bridegroom, in heaven.

DAY 216
'HE IS THE BUILDER OF THE HOUSE

QUESTIONS TO THINK ABOUT:

1. What are the responsibilities of the builder of a house?
2. What does he have to do with the raw materials provided for that house?
3. If those materials could speak, what might they say?
4. How would the builder answer them?

There are several passages of Scripture which picture Jesus Christ as a builder. Hebrews 3:3, "Jesus has been found worthy of a greater honor than Moses, just as the builder of the house has greater honor than the house itself." Ephesians 4:11-13, "It was he [Jesus] who gave some to be apostles, some to be prophets, some to be evangelists, and some to be pastors and teachers, to prepare God's people for works of service, so that the body of Christ <u>may be built up</u> until we all reach unity in the faith and in the knowledge of the Son of God and become mature, attaining to the whole measure of the fullness of Christ" (underlining mine). In Matthew 16:18 he says, "I will build my church, and the gates of Hades will not overcome it."

Unexpected Transformation / 489

How does he build his Church? First he provides the building materials (as seen in Eph.4:11-13 above). Then he provides the "Contractor," the Holy Spirit, who puts all the pieces together by teaching us all things regarding Christ and our relationship with him and to each other.

Then, through circumstances, the Holy Spirit begins to "put us together." There is digging, scraping, cutting, chipping, smoothing off, forming, nailing, mixing, cementing and finishing. Sometimes one or another of these processes is quite painful. It's no fun to be left out in the sun to be dried! "The Builder has gone off and left me! It's HOT out here! I'm drying up! Useless! What am I doing here? O Lord, why have you left me?!" Yet the Builder knows that a dried brick is stronger than a brick full of moisture. A dried brick will not crack and break under pressure. A brick with moisture in it will give out and crumble under pressure. It's no fun to be chipped, planed and sanded. "Why can't I just remain a plank of wood? Why does the Builder have to dig into me so with his chisel, skin me with his planer and scrape me with his sandpaper? O Lord, why are you doing this to me?"

"Be patient, dear one. I'm making you into a beautiful, sculptured beam for all to see my glory in you. As a rough plank, you do not fit into the scheme of my house. But you must be formed, carved and fitted so that you can fulfill your function as I have planned."

So with his help, we are being built for God's dwelling place. Peter says: "You also, like living stones, are being built into a spiritual house" (1 Pet.2:5). And Paul calls us "God's temple" (1 Cor.3:16).

Scripture also says that we are builders of our own houses as well as of the Church (1 Cor.3:10-13; 12:7; 14:3,4; Eph.4:11-13). The word "edify" found in some of these passages means "to build up." How do we build up? In our own lives (our own "house") we build up through obedience to the Word, doing those things and developing those attitudes that are pleasing to the Lord, striving to become more like him. We build up others by being a good example for them to follow, by encouraging them in their Christian walk, spurring them on to good works (Heb.10:24), and exercising our spiritual gifts (I Cor.12:7).

The building materials have been provided. Now it is up to us to choose what we will use in our construction. How are you using your materials?

APPLICATION: Any good builder reads the blueprints and follows them. They tell the builder not only the design of the house, but also where the plumbing and electricity need to be installed. The style of the design may even indicate the type of materials needed to complete it. If we are to be good builders, we must read and follow the "blueprints" that God has given us (his Word). If we do, we will have good success in building the structure that God has intended for us.

DAY 217
[b]HE IS THE HEIR

QUESTIONS TO THINK ABOUT:

1. What does it mean to be an heir of something? a co-heir of something?
2. When does one become an heir?
3. What is the guarantee that you will receive all your inheritance and not just a part of it?

In Psalm 2:8 God says to Christ, "Ask of me, and I will make the nations your inheritance, the ends of the earth your possession." In Romans 8:17 we are mentioned as being co-heirs with Christ. Again in Hebrews 1:2 we read, "But in these last days he [God] has spoken to us by his Son, whom he appointed heir of all things... ." That means that Christ is heir of the cosmos, a unique inheritance. Everything is his!

When does one become an heir? Usually when he is born or adopted into a family. Christ was declared legally as Son and Heir of God at the resurrection. In Acts 13:32,33 Paul says, "We tell you the good news: What God promised our fathers he has fulfilled for us, their children, by raising up Jesus. As it is written in the second Psalm: 'You are my Son; today I have become your Father.'"

In the Old Testament days, the eldest son received his inheritance from his father and all that goes with it: the family land, title, money, and authority (signet ring, etc.). Whatever that man owned, whatever honor he had, was passed on to his chosen son through the inheritance. So Christ, as God's firstborn Son ("first-born" in terms of position rather than generation), is his legal heir. He "inherits" everything that is his Father's, and his Father owns the universe! As heir, Christ could speak with his Father's authority, having been sent by his Father (see Jn.5:19,20,43a; 7:16-18). He claimed that "All authority in heaven and on earth" had been given to him (Matt.28:18). That's part of his inheritance.

We also are God's inheritance when we are born/adopted into his family by receiving Jesus Christ as our Savior (cf. Eph.1:18 where we are said to be "God's inheritance." By extension then, we become Christ's inheritance as he inherits all things from his Father, which includes us!). But, at that same time, we also are made his heirs, receiving the Holy Spirit who indwells us, leads us, and witnesses to our spirit that we indeed are the children of God (Rom.8:14-16). "Now if we are children, then we are heirs – heirs of God and co-heirs with Christ ..." (vs.17). (If your head is "spinning" like mine, you might want to read and digest this paragraph over again!)

When will we receive our inheritance? Usually it is received upon the death of one's parents. But in this case, our Father cannot die. We will enter fully into our inheritance when we die, or are caught up to be with Christ in the Rapture. But we can begin to enjoy our inheritance right now in at least two ways: in God's blessings to us when we obey him, and in enjoying the "relational aspect" of eternal life as we get to know him better (Jn.17:3). In Mark 10:28-30 we read, "Peter said to him, 'We have left everything to follow you!' 'I tell you the truth,' Jesus replied, 'no one who has left home or brothers or sisters or mother or father or children or fields for me and the gospel will fail to receive a hundred times as much in this present age (homes, brothers, sisters, mothers, children and fields – and with them persecutions) and in the age to come, eternal life.'" Then in John 17:3 Jesus prayed, "And this is eternal life, that they may know You, the only true God, and Jesus Christ whom You have sent" (NKJV). What we enjoy here on earth is a mere shadow of the inheritance that awaits us in heaven.

How much are you enjoying your inheritance right now?

APPLICATION: A willingness to obey and a desire to get to know God better are the two keys to enjoying a portion of our inheritance right now. It is accomplished by choosing to fully surrender all that we are and have to him, then following through with obeying what we know he wants us to do and by taking as much time as we want to prioritize getting to know him through his Word. You might say, "It's all ours for the choosing!"

DAY 218
[a]HE IS OUR HELPER

QUESTIONS TO THINK ABOUT:

1. How would you define being a help to someone?
2. How can helping someone actually become a detriment to their well-being?

3. What does and does not constitute a true need deserving of our help?

4. How can you help others when you don't have the means to help them?

5. If we close our eyes to the needs of others, what can we expect as a result?

Wherever the Lord went in his ministry, he helped people. Mostly we read of him healing the sick and delivering those who were demon possessed. But we also find him replenishing the supply of wine at the wedding at Cana (Jn.2), supplying the tax money for himself and Peter (Matt.17:24-27), and helping his disciples catch fish (Lk.5:4-7). At least twice he fed large groups of people (Mk.6:32-44; 8:1-9). In Matthew 28:20 he promised that he would be with us until the end of the age; in John 14:16 that the Holy Spirit would be with us forever. The writer to the Hebrews (13:5,6) recalls the promise of God to Israel in Deuteronomy 31:6,8 when he writes: "Be content with what you have, because God has said, 'Never will I leave you; never will I forsake you.' So we say with confidence, 'The Lord is my helper; I will not be afraid. What can man do to me?'"

The New Testament is full of illustrations of how Christians helped others: giving food and drink to the hungry, clothing to the needy, visiting the sick and imprisoned (Matt.25:35,36); spurring one another on to good deeds, encouraging each other, standing beside those falsely accused and persecuted (Heb.10:24,25,33); contributing money to the poor and needy (Rom.15:26); meeting each other's needs (Acts 4:32); healing the sick and even raising the dead! (Acts 5:15,16; 9:36-42). And the list could go on. Paul urges us in Galatians 6:10, saying, "Therefore, as we have opportunity, let us do good to all people, especially to those who belong to the family of believers." And Solomon adds this bit of advice: "Do not withhold good from those who deserve it, when it is in your power to act. Do not say to your neighbor, 'Come back later; I'll give it to you tomorrow' – when you now have it with you" (Prov.3:27,28).

To be an effective helper, we need to have a servant heart (see DAYS 37,38 – HE IS THE KING [the Servant]) which places the welfare and needs of others ahead of our own. As long as we have our own plans and interests, and feel irritated when the needs of others interrupt them, we will not be good helpers. As Paul again writes: "Each of you should look not only to your own interests, but also to the interests of others" (Phil.2:4). When we are able to help someone, our attitude should not just be willing but eager, for as we help others, we are expressing that part of Christ's character to them, bringing encouragement and stimulation toward further growth if they are Believers or opening a door to a witness if they are not. Let us ask the Lord to make us more sensitive in situations where we can be of help, and then obedient to the urgings of his Spirit to be helpful.

There is a promise to the helpful found in Luke 6:38 where Christ says, "Give, and it will be given to you; good measure, pressed down, shaken together, running over, they will pour into your lap. For whatever measure you deal out to others, it will be dealt to you in return."

I dated a young lady once who had a servant heart. No matter where we were, she always paid attention to the people around us to see if there was someone she could help. Her example taught me to be more mindful of others than myself and be ready to help those in need if I was able to. Come to think of it, wouldn't we appreciate someone like that if <u>we</u> were in trouble and needed a helping hand? I guess the principle, "Do unto others as you would have them do unto you," would apply here too!

What kind of helper are you?

Unexpected Transformation / 495

APPLICATION: Helping others begins with a mind-set: we must want to help them. Then we must look for ways to help them according to the resources we have. If we don't have the resources, we at least can pray for them. That shows our concern for their need, and they will appreciate that. But here's an additional thought: Jesus said that whatever good we do to other believers, he takes it personally as being done to himself (Matt.25:40)! So, when we help others, we are actually ministering to Christ! What an honor!

DAY 219
ᶜHE IS THE HORN OF SALVATION

QUESTIONS TO THINK ABOUT:

1. Throughout history, what is the significance of the horn? (Ex. When the cavalry comes!)
2. If a horn blows an uncertain sound, what will be the results?

In Luke 1:68,69 the priest Zacharias prophesied regarding Christ in these words: "Praise be to the Lord, the God of Israel, because he has come and had redeemed his people. He has raised up a horn of salvation for us in the house of his servant David." In this context as well as in 2 Samuel 22:3 and Psalm 18:2 the deliverance from one's enemies is in view. Literally, Zacharias was looking forward to deliverance from the Romans, which he and Israel firmly believed the Messiah would accomplish. David was praising the Lord for deliverance from Saul. The word "horn" metaphorically stands for strength or power, and many times is used in that way. So we find Christ as the Horn of Salvation, our Power of Deliverance from all our enemies. Paul claims that the gospel of Christ (good news) "is the power of God for the salvation of everyone who believes" (Rom.1:16).

Not only do we have physical enemies whom we can see, but the New Testament also enumerates our spiritual enemies whom we cannot see: Satan and his demons (1 Pet.5:8; Eph.6:11,12), sin and death (1 Cor.15:26,54-57). Christ, as the Horn of our Salvation, delivers us from <u>all</u> our enemies. That doesn't mean that we will not experience attacks and persecution, but it <u>does</u> mean that we will be delivered through those things, and because of the resurrection, even death, when it comes, cannot hold us!

The Apostle Paul testifies to this truth in 2 Timothy 3:10-12 and 4:17,18 saying, "You, however, know all about my teaching, my way of life, my purpose, faith, patience, love, endurance, persecutions, sufferings – what kinds of things happened to me in Antioch, Iconium and Lystra, the persecutions I endured. Yet the Lord rescued me from all of them. In fact, everyone who wants to live a godly life in Christ Jesus will be persecuted... . But the Lord stood at my side and gave me strength, so that through me the message might be fully proclaimed and all the Gentiles might hear it. And I was delivered from the lion's mouth. The Lord will rescue me from every evil attack and will bring me safely to his heavenly kingdom. To him be glory for ever and ever. Amen."

We reflect Christ as the Horn of Salvation when we feed the starving, rescue those in physical danger, protect the weak from harm, and so on. On the spiritual and psychological level, we can give a word of encouragement, exhortation from the Word of God, instruction on how to wage spiritual warfare and claim the promises of God for daily needs and situations. As we share materially and spiritually with others, we will see them delivered from many kinds of "enemies," and we will become to them as a horn of salvation.

Do you "blow your horn" before men, or use it to deliver them from their "enemies"?

APPLICATION: Those who "toot their own horn" are focused upon themselves and how they can deliver themselves from various problems. We need to follow Christ's example and focus on others as we "blow our horn" on their behalf to deliver them from the problems they are facing. Also, the "horn" of our witness can be the means by which they are delivered from Satan, sin and death if they receive Christ as their Savior.

DAY 220
ᶜHE IS THE HUNGRY ONE

◆

QUESTIONS TO THINK ABOUT:

1. How does it feel to be really, really hungry?
2. If you had an urge to eat and as strong an urge to study the Bible and pray, which would you do, and why?
3. How can Bible study or sharing the Word with others be "just as filling" as having a good meal?

In Matthew 4:2 we read of Christ in the wilderness: "After fasting forty days and forty nights, he was hungry." In Mark 11:12 we read: "The next day as they were leaving Bethany, Jesus was hungry." And in Matthew 25:35, he identifies himself with his people as being hungry because there is no food. Jesus knows what it is to be hungry.

The Apostles and the early Church knew this as well. They fasted (Lk.5:35; Acts 14:23), they became hungry as a matter of course (Matt.12:1; Acts 10:10), and they also went without food when none was available (Phil.4:12; 2 Cor.6:5; 11:27). Some of us have experienced hunger through fasting; all of us have experienced it as a natural phenomenon; but few if any of us have experienced it because no food was available.

In the matter of natural hunger, we need not belabor the point. Actually, in that, the Lord was identifying himself with us. But in the matter of fasting, we can reflect his character in two ways. To fast is go without food, purposely or because of one's circumstances. At the beginning of Christ's ministry, he chose not to eat for a period of forty days and nights (Matt.4:2). He taught fasting as an accepted activity (Matt.6:16-18). There were times in the ministry when he and his disciples did not eat (Mk.8:1,2), probably for three days. We read in Mark 6:31, "Then, because so many people were coming and going that they did not even have a chance to eat, he said to them, 'Come with me by yourselves to a quiet place and get some rest.'" In John 4:32-34 when Jesus' disciples were urging him to eat something, he said to them, "I have food to eat that you know nothing about.' Then his disciples said to each other, 'Could someone have brought him food?' 'My food,' said Jesus, 'is to do the will of him who sent me and to finish his work.'" Job put it this way in Job 23:12b, "I have treasured the words of his mouth more than my daily bread." Paul chose to be faithful in the ministry given him from the Lord, and many times he went without food because of his circumstances. In 2 Corinthians 11:27 he said that he often went without food. Are we willing to do the same? Do we put such priority on the Word and the ministry God has given us that we are willing to miss a meal or more if necessary in order to spend time with him or accomplish something he wants us to do?

In the summer of 1960 I was having a real struggle with my Quiet Time. I'd get up late and just have no time to meet with the Lord. One morning I read Job 23:12, and Job's attitude toward the words of God really hit me. That morning I vowed before the Lord that I would eat nothing any day until I had had my Quiet Time with him. That got me back on track – and I only missed breakfast twice! May the Lord help us decrease our emphasis on food and increase our emphasis on his Word and his work!

Are you willing to be hungry for his sake?

APPLICATION: Sometimes I have been so involved in my Bible study that I literally lost track of time and forgot to eat! Other times, as other believers and I were sharing the Word together, mealtime passed without our noticing, and none of us felt hungry at all! That's a bit different than choosing not to eat in order to be able to spend time with the Lord or make time for serving him in some way. Some of us are so busy, it wouldn't hurt to plan to skip a meal just so we can "kick back and relax" in the Word and in prayer. Who knows? The Lord just might respond by giving us an "appetite" for more times like that on a regular basis!

DAY 221
ᶜHE IS THE HUNGRY ONE, concl.

QUESTIONS TO THINK ABOUT:

1. How can hunger, thirst and riches be used as spiritual metaphors?
2. How is hunger a sign of life, and spiritual hunger a sign of spiritual life?
3. Fasting can be a good spiritual discipline, but how can it become an avenue for Satan's temptations?

There is another aspect of hunger that we need to consider, and that is the metaphorical use of the word and its implications. When Mary visited Elizabeth and received her blessing, Mary's heart was moved to praise the Lord. In Luke 1:53 she said: "He has filled the hungry with good things but has sent the rich away empty." When Jesus was speaking to the people following him, he said (Jn.6:35): "I am the bread of life. He who comes to me will never go hungry, and he who believes in me will never be thirsty." And again in Matthew

5:6 he says: "Blessed are those who hunger and thirst for righteousness, for they will be filled."

One sign of life is hunger (see DAYS 8,9 – HE IS THE LIFE). If we truly know the Lord, there will be a hunger for spiritual food, a hunger for God's Word, and a hunger for fellowship with God's people. And the Lord has promised that if we hunger (implying that eating will follow), we will be filled, satisfied. A healthy person is one who eats the right foods regularly. Likewise, a healthy Christian will be eating good spiritual food regularly, daily, watching out for "spiritual junk food" that is so readily available. He gets hungry and eats, physically _and_ spiritually. Usually we have our spiritual breakfast, but what about lunch and supper? It is always good to carry a New Testament or memory verses with us wherever we go so we can "snack" at odd moments or sit down and "eat" if we feel "hungry." Our smart phones even have Bible apps that we can readily access.

Something else I noticed. In Matthew 4:3, after Jesus had fasted and was physically weak and hungry, the Devil hit him with temptation. But the Lord overcame him by using the Word of God. Likewise, when we are spiritually hungry, having that "feeling" or "sense" that something is missing or not quite right, and there's that desire to go deeper into the Word, to spend more time with the Lord – Satan will also come to us with his tasty goodies promising to satisfy that hunger. If we seek satisfaction from all that he offers, we will discover that his water is laced with salt, only increasing our thirst; and the delicious food he provides evaporates before we can swallow it, increasing our hunger. Unless we have that wisdom from above, we will return again and again to the Devil's banquet table, seeking the satisfaction of our increasing hunger and thirst that can _only_ come from the Word of God.

Is your spiritual hunger and thirst being satisfied or are you seeking your satisfaction from food that evaporates?

APPLICATION: When there is that sense of "hunger" inside, don't turn on the TV or read that magazine, don't go out seeking something, anything to fill that void, but open the Word of God, and you will be filled, satisfied. And your hunger will increase! But each time you eat, you will feel full and satisfied, not empty and still craving more.

DAY 222
ᶜHE IS THE INCARNATE ONE

QUESTIONS TO THINK ABOUT:

1. What does it mean to be "incarnated"?
2. What do we understand about Christ in his incarnation?
3. How can we "incarnate" ourselves to the people we minister to?
4. How far should we go in identifying with them?

The word "incarnate" is derived from the Latin *in* (meaning "in") and *caro*, from *carnis* ("flesh"), with the resultant meaning "to be made flesh." This is exactly what we find in John 1:14, "The Word became flesh and made his dwelling among us. We have seen his glory, the glory of the One and Only, who came from the Father, full of grace and truth." In Hebrews 2:14,15 we read, "Since the children have flesh and blood, he too shared in their humanity so that by his death he might destroy him who holds the power of death – that is, the devil – and free those who all their lives were held in slavery by their fear of death." In Philippians 2:7, Christ took upon himself "the very nature of a servant, being made in human likeness." In John 1:1 and Philippians 2:6 it is clear that before Christ became flesh, he was God, and God is Spirit (Jn.4:24); so Christ was in Spirit-form as part of the triune Godhead.

There were two reasons for Christ's incarnation. The first was to reveal the Father to us (Jn.14:9); the second was to provide reconciliation for us with the Father through his death and resurrection (Jn.14:6; 2 Cor.5:18,19).

The Apostle Paul catches the meaning of the incarnation in his ministry when he writes: "Though I am free and belong to no man, I make myself a slave to everyone, to win as many as possible. To the Jews I became like a Jew, to win the Jews. To those under the law I became like one under the law (though I myself am not under the law), so as to win those under the law. To those not having the law I became like one not having the law (though I am not free from God's law but am under Christ's law), so as to win those not having the law. To the weak I became weak, to win the weak. I have become all things to all men so that by all possible means I might save some" (1 Cor.9:19-22). Paul identified with his listeners in order to effectively communicate the gospel to them.

In describing his sufferings because of the gospel on their behalf, Paul wrote to the Philippians: "But even if I am being poured out like a drink offering on the sacrifice and service coming from your faith, I am glad and rejoice with all of you" (Phil.2:17). He was willing to sacrifice himself on their behalf. Today there is little of this kind of love even among Christians, let alone that sacrificial love for the unsaved that will win them to the Lord. But to willingly identify ourselves with others and sacrifice ourselves on their behalf means death to self, and few among us are willing to go that far. Yet this is the example Christ gave to us, and Paul also. Jesus said in Mark 8:34,35, "... If anyone would come after me, he must deny himself and take up his cross and follow me. For whoever wants to save his life will lose it, but whoever loses his life for me and for the gospel will save it."

Are you willing to "incarnate" yourself in the lives of others?

APPLICATION: "Incarnating" ourselves to the people to whom we minister demands studying their culture, their language and all you can learn about them as people (or a people group). Missionaries encounter these issues daily as they minister cross-culturally in other lands. However, I have noticed that even in our home state of Maine, we have to be aware of the same issues! There are three distinct cultural milieus: down east, southern Maine, and Aroostook County. And in each area there are layers of sub-cultures. If you're not "from here," or have some pretty strong connections to that area, you will have a difficult time ministering there. How do you establish credibility among these peoples? By respecting them, by learning their ways, by showing genuine interest in what they are doing and by loving them unconditionally, as a start. Then, in time, you can minister to them; but you will always be an outsider, and many times treated that way. So even ministry in the United States can be culturally difficult!

DAY 223
ᶜHE IS THE INCARNATE ONE, concl.

QUESTIONS TO THINK ABOUT:

1. As Christ revealed the Father to us, how can we reveal Christ to others?
2. What does that responsibility demand from us?

Yesterday I mentioned two reasons for Christ's incarnation: to reveal the Father to us and to reconcile us with the Father. The Lord has passed these responsibilities on to us!

Jesus said, "I am the way to the Father... . He who has seen me has seen the Father" (Jn.14:6,9). Everything that Jesus taught, said and did came from the Father and was done in the Father's name. Likewise, everything that we as Christians teach, say and do should come from our Lord Jesus Christ and should be done in his name. This is staggering, but that is why he has given us his Holy Spirit to enable us to live lives that are pleasing to him and that reflect his character.

I remember just snatches of a story that I heard about a soldier in World War II who showed kindness to a little boy. In his innocence and gratitude, the little boy looked up at him and asked, "Mister, are you Jesus Christ?" "Let the Beauty of Jesus Be Seen in Me" and "O To Be Like Thee!" are two prayer songs that should become a daily reality in each of our lives. But that reality will only come as we meditate on his character and in his Word and then apply what we have learned. It is imperative that others see Christ in us; otherwise our witness will have no meaning.

Then Jesus Christ came to reconcile us with the Father, and, as Paul writes in 2 Corinthians 5:18-20, he has given to us the ministry of reconciliation, to plead with men to be reconciled to God. His plan is for us to be witnesses for him "in Jerusalem [our home town], and in all Judea [our county] and Samaria [the next county], and to the ends of the earth [everywhere else]" (Acts 1:8). We cannot go everywhere, but everywhere we go we can be a witness. If every Christian was a witness everywhere he went, the Great Commission would be fulfilled before we knew it. Then we could move from the making of disciples of all nations to the teaching them to obey everything Christ commanded us.

We need to pray that the Lord will open up opportunities for us to witness, and then open our mouths to speak the right words. We need to have a New Testament and some good tracts with us to help us as we witness and to have something to leave with the person to whom we spoke. But there is one other thing: we must be willing to identify with those to whom we witness; we must try to see life from their perspective and attempt to identify with some aspect of it to form that common bridge that will allow us to convey that which will meet their real need. We must be willing to get involved in their lives, if need be, in order to coax them along to faith and then to nourish them once faith has bloomed. We will not have many contacts witnessing this way, but if every Christian were doing it … .

Do your character and actions reveal the Father to others and give them a desire to be reconciled to him?

APPLICATION: God wants to use us to be a witness and a light for him wherever we are, and he will place us just where he wants us to be. Our responsibility is to live for him, to speak for him whenever he opens up the opportunity, and to reflect his character to all whom we meet. We don't need to worry about anyone else – just us, that we will be all that he wants us to be right where we are.

DAY 224
ᶜHE IS JESUS

QUESTIONS TO THINK ABOUT:

1. What is the function of a savior? Why is he or she called that?
2. Jesus came to save his people from their sins. How can we "save" others from their sins?

When the angel Gabriel came to Mary to tell her that she was to be the mother of the Messiah, he said that she should call his name, Jesus (Lk.1:31). A while later, an angel appeared to Joseph in a dream, giving him the same name with an explanation: "You are to give him the name Jesus, because he will save his people from their sins" (Matt.1:21). The name "Jesus" means "Savior." Scripture is clear that on the cross, Jesus took all our sins upon himself as the perfect sacrifice for our sins, reconciling us to God and giving us eternal life. Because the wages of sin is death (Rom.6:23), and because we all are sinners (Rom.3:23), we must die. But when Jesus came to take our place, dying as our Substitute, we were released from death and given life (provided, of course, that we acknowledge him as our Savior – Jn.1:12).

There are two groups of people to whom we can reflect Jesus Christ as Savior: the unsaved and the saved. We cannot die for them as Jesus did for us, but we <u>can</u> share the gospel with the unsaved and the message of victory over sin with the saved. To the unsaved, we read in Ezekiel 3:18,19 what God told Ezekiel at the beginning of his ministry: "When I say to a wicked man, 'You will surely die, and you do not warn him or speak out to dissuade him from his evil ways in order to save his life, that wicked man will die for his sin, and I will hold you accountable for his blood. But if you do warn the wicked man and he does not turn from his wickedness or from his evil ways, he will die for his sin; but you will have saved yourself." Conversely, if we warn the wicked, and he turns from his sin and believes in Christ, we have delivered his soul, and, in a very real sense, have "saved" him from the sins he would have otherwise committed had he continued on in his godless ways.

The same principle applies to a fellow believer who wanders from the truth. James 5:19,20 says, "My brothers, if one of you should wander from the truth and someone should bring him back, remember this: Whoever turns a sinner from the error of his way will <u>save him</u> from death and cover over a multitude of sins" (underlining mine). Again, the wages of sin is death no matter who does the sinning, Christian or non-Christian. Christians at Corinth were judged with physical death for their sins against the Lord's Table so that they would not be judged later with the world (1 Cor.11:30-32). But as we warn Christians from the error of their ways and they heed that warning and turn back to the truth, we have "saved" them from the many sins they would otherwise have committed. Thus we reflect Jesus Christ as the one who saves his people from their sins and restores them into a right relationship with God and with each other.

Are you "saving" dying souls and deceived saints?

APPLICATION: In order for God to use us in "saving" others, we must know two things: first, the message of the Gospel – Jesus died on the Cross in our place for our sins. Through him we can be forgiven and be brought into a right relationship with God. Secondly, we need to know how to express that message, how to "give a reason for the hope that is in us (1 Pet.3:15). A review of DAY 26, "He Is the Witness," might be helpful here.

DAY 225
aHE IS THE JOYFUL ONE

QUESTIONS TO THINK ABOUT:

1. What verses of Scripture can you recall which tell us that Christ was joyful?
2. Some Christians believe that being joyful, or even laughing, is sin. If Christ was a human being like us, would this attitude be characteristic of him?
3. How can we increase the Lord's joy?

It is never mentioned in Scripture where Jesus laughed, though we may assume that he did just because he was human and there are many funny things in life that will make us laugh. But there are several places where Christ is described as having joy, an emotion much deeper than laughing at something funny or even feeling happy. The most explicit statement in found in Luke 10:21. Earlier, Christ had commissioned the seventy to go, two by two, into every city and place where he himself was about to go (vs.1). He told them to heal

508 / *Unexpected Transformation*

the sick "and say to them, 'The kingdom of God has come near to you'" (vs.9). In verse 17 the seventy returned and reported that even the demons were subject to them in his name. Christ confirmed this in verse 19, saying, "Behold, I give you the authority to trample on serpents and scorpions, and over all the power of the enemy, and nothing shall by any means hurt you." Then "Jesus <u>rejoiced in the Spirit</u> and said, 'I praise you, Father, Lord of heaven and earth, that You have hidden these things from the wise and prudent and revealed them to babes... . For so it seemed good in your sight'" (underlining mine).

What were "these things" hidden from the wise and prudent and revealed to babes? I believe the answer is found in verses 23 and 24 where Christ says: "Blessed are the eyes that see what you see. For I tell you that many prophets and kings wanted to see what you see but did not see it, and to hear what you hear but did not hear it." What was it they saw but the miracles of Christ, and what was it they heard but the messages of the kingdom from the lips of the Messiah himself! They saw, they heard, they believed, they acted, they saw results, they rejoiced, and Christ was full of joy. The "wise and prudent" of Israel saw and heard, but did not believe, nor did they understand.

That Christ himself was filled with joy is also indicated in John 15:11 and 17:13 where he says, "I have told you this so that <u>my joy</u> may be in you and that your joy may be complete... . I am coming to you now, but I say these things while I am still in the world, so that they may have the full measure of <u>my joy</u> within them" (underlining mine). What was the source of his joy? 1. He was filled with the Holy Spirit (Lk.4:1); 2. He always did the will of the Father (Jn.6:38); 3. He rejoiced in the Father's wisdom (Lk.10:21); 4. He could see himself reproduced in the lives of others (Lk.10:17); and 5. He knew that his mission would succeed (Heb.12:2).

So as we learn more about the character of Jesus Christ and increase in conformity to it, we increase his joy. He prayed that his joy might be fulfilled in us. Thus as his joy is increased, so ours will be also.

Are you a joyless or joy-filled Christian?

APPLICATION: As parents' hearts are filled with joy when seeing their children doing something well, so the Lord's heart is filled with joy when we "do things well." Choose to excel in doing those things which please him. As you do, his joy will bubble over upon you!

DAY 226
[a]HE IS THE JOYFUL ONE, concl.

QUESTIONS TO THINK ABOUT:

1. How is it possible to be truly joyful in all our trials?
2. How should our knowledge of Jesus Christ give us inexpressible joy?
3. What are the things that can take our joy away from us?

Briefly, we must answer the question: "What can take away our joy?" Simply, by doing the opposite of those things which will bring us joy, i.e. willful sin, unbelief, a life of disobedience, rebellion against God's will, selfishness, a poor understanding of who our God actually is, busyness (being distracted by everything around us), etc.

The Scriptures are full of those things that will bring us joy. Consider:

1. Psalm 16:11b – "You will fill me with joy *in your presence*, with eternal pleasures at your right hand (emphases mine).

2. John 15:11 – Jesus says, "I have told you this so that my joy may be in you and that your joy may be complete." One reason for *the Word of God* is to bring us joy.

3. John 16:24 – Another source of joy is in *answered prayer*: "Until now you have not asked for anything in my name. Ask and you will receive, and your joy will be complete."

4. John 16:22 – There is joy in seeing/*knowing the risen Christ*: "Now is your time of grief, but I will see you again and you will rejoice, and no one will take away your joy."

5. 1 Peter 1:8,9 – From *believing in Christ and all he has done for us*, we experience inexpressible joy. "Though you have not seen him, you love him; and even though you do not see him now, you believe in him and are filled with an inexpressible and glorious joy, for you are receiving the goal of your faith, the salvation of your souls."

6. Acts 5:40,41 – *Persecution* for the sake of Christ can bring us joy. The Apostles were imprisoned, beaten, and warned/commanded that they should no longer speak in the name of Jesus; then they were released. "The apostles left the Sanhedrin, rejoicing because they had been counted worthy of suffering disgrace for the Name."

7. Galatians 5:22,23 – There is joy from *the presence and fruit of the Holy Spirit* in our lives. "But the fruit of the Spirit is love, joy, peace, patience, kindness, goodness, faithfulness, gentleness and self-control. Against such things there is no law."

8. James 1:2-4 – There is *joy in our trials*, knowing their ultimate purpose. "Consider it pure joy, my brothers, whenever you face trials of many kinds, because you know that the testing of your faith develops perseverance. Perseverance must finish its work so that you may be mature and complete, not lacking anything."

9. Philippians 4:1 – There is joy *in our fellowship* with and love for other Christians. "Therefore, my brothers, you whom I love and long for, my joy and crown, that is how you should stand firm in the Lord, dear friends!"

10. 1 John 1:4 – *The testimony of other Christians* gives us joy. "We write this to make our joy complete." There is joy in sharing what the Lord has done, etc. (see Jn.15:11 above, no.2).

11. 1 Thessalonians 2:19,20 – There is joy *when we see results from our work* and souls saved. "For what is our hope, our joy, or the crown in which we will glory in the presence of our Lord Jesus when he comes? Is it not you? Indeed, you are our glory and joy."

12. 3 John 4 – And finally, there is joy *when we see our spiritual children living and walking in the truth*. "I have no greater joy than to hear that my children are walking in the truth."

Thus the joy of the Lord is our strength, our encouragement. And that joy, welling up in our inner being, will be reflected on our faces and in what we say and do. Paul says in Philippians 4:4, "Rejoice in the Lord always. I will say it again: Rejoice!" What reason do we have not to?

On a scale from 1 to 10, where would you rate your joy factor?

APPLICATION: Settling on who your God is is probably the most important key to your personal joy. If you are convinced that he is working out all things for your good and bringing you into conformity to the image of his Son through them (Rom.8:28,29), then you will have joy deep down inside in spite of your circumstances. (You might want to review DAYS 1-3 dealing with God's Loving Sovereignty, God's Goal for Humanity and Our Reaction to God's Goal for Humanity, to reaffirm in your own mind why we can implicitly trust him in all of life's circumstances.)

DAY 227
ʻHE IS OUR GUILT OFFERING

◆

QUESTIONS TO THINK ABOUT:

1. What is the meaning of a "guilt offering"?
2. How can we fulfill the intent of the guilt offering on the behalf of someone else?
3. How would you feel if someone said, "I'm sorry!" but made no attempt to right the wrong done?

In speaking prophetically about his Servant, God said that "the LORD makes his life a guilt offering" (Isa.53:10). The guilt offering was required in the case of ignorant sin, such as unwittingly trespassing in the holy things, or anything which the Law forbade depriving God or the priest of their due (I.S.B.I., Reeve, 2645), or purposeful sin regarding the rights of property or money of others. Thus this offering not only required the death of a ram (two rams and a ewe in the case of a cleansed leper), making atonement toward God, but also restitution in full plus 20% toward whoever suffered loss at the guilty person's hands.

Through his life, death, and resurrection, Christ performed both of these functions of the guilt offering. Because his life was perfect (Jn.8:46), he fulfilled the conditions of a "ram without defect" (Lev.6:6). Thus his sacrifice as our guilt offering was sufficient in making atonement for us before God, so bringing peace between God and man. God's holiness and justice were satisfied in that the price for sin was fully paid. This is the second aspect of the guilt offering – restitution to give satisfaction to the offended one.

The 20% assessed the offender was directed toward him as a fine, a punishment, so that he would be more careful in the future and not repeat this sin. But we were so bankrupt before God that there was no

Unexpected Transformation / 513

way we could pay this assessment. Christ himself assumed that debt as well, paying not just 20%, but 100% as he gave his life for us. That is why Romans 5:1 states that we have peace with God through our Lord Jesus Christ. After his sacrifice, there was nothing but peace left. Hebrews 10:17,18 states this truth from another perspective: "Then he adds: 'Their sins and lawless acts I will remember no more.' And where these have been forgiven, there is no longer any sacrifice for sin." Where there is forgiveness, there is peace.

Paul demonstrated this characteristic in his relationship with Philemon. In his letter to him, he wrote: "If he [Onesimus] has done you any wrong or owes you anything, charge it to me. I, Paul, am writing this with my own hand. I will pay it back – not to mention that you owe me your very self." Paul was willing to suffer loss in order to restore peace between Philemon and Onesimus. He was willing to make restitution on behalf of the offender.

In talking to my students about forgiveness and restitution one day, I asked them about the Indonesian custom of asking forgiveness to "patch" things up. At farewell dinners, it is always said, "<u>If</u> I have done anything or said anything that has upset you or made you angry at me, I ask your forgiveness." One day a year, Muslims are supposed to walk about from one house to another asking forgiveness, <u>if</u> they perchance did anything that made one upset during the year. I remember one occasion when I felt very upset with another person for a number of things in which he had offended me and others. When he left the area, he gave the same "If I have done" speech, and I had a miniature internal "Vesuvius eruption." "What does he mean 'if'? He knows good and well that he has offended us and has never even tried to make it right!" I was rankled, irritated and completely put out with his hypocrisy.

So I asked my students how they felt in similar situations when forgiveness is asked, but no restitution made. They said that their hearts still did not feel at peace; they still felt the wrong done to them, even though culturally they answered, "Sure. No problem." They said that when restitution is made, then they <u>know</u> that the person is truly sorry and, as far as they are concerned, the situation is resolved.

Do you have restitution to make in regard to some past wrongs you have done? Are you, like Paul, willing to help others do what is necessary so as to secure peace between them and the offended parties?

APPLICATION: If you have been guilty of wronging someone, make every effort as quickly as possible to right that wrong and make whatever restitution is necessary to cover the actual or felt loss. The credibility of your testimony and witness is at stake, not to say the name and honor of our Lord Jesus Christ.

DAY 228
ᶜHE IS IMMANUEL (GOD WITH US)

QUESTIONS TO THINK ABOUT:

1. What does it mean to us for Christ to be called Immanuel?
2. How could it be that we also could be called "Immanuel" for those around us?

In Matthew 1:23 is written a prophecy by Isaiah concerning Christ that he shall be named Immanuel, God with us. In John 1:1-14 and again in Philippians 2:5-8 we find declarations of this truth. John says, "The Word became flesh and made his dwelling among us. We have seen his glory, the glory of the One and Only, who came from the Father, full of grace and truth" (Jn.1:14). God actually came to earth in the person of Jesus Christ so that we might know him (John 14:9) and that he might provide salvation for those who would receive it (1 Tim.1:15). Christ, in a manner of speaking, spoke and worked just like God would have, had he been here visibly.

Unexpected Transformation / 515

When we receive Christ as our Savior, the Holy Spirit comes to live in us and work through us. In this way we literally become "Immanuel, God with us" to others; for wherever we are, God himself is in us and with us, and thus is also among those about us (cf. Acts 27:21-25). Christ told his disciples, "If you have seen me, you have seen the Father" (Jn.14:9). As others see us, can we say to them, "If you have seen me, you have seen Christ"? This is not an egotistical statement, for the better we know Christ, the more like him we will become in character, action and word. As others say on the human level, "You are just like your father," so they should be able to say on the spiritual level, "You are just like Christ." That is what the Sanhedrin had to say about Peter and John in Acts 4:13. "When they saw the courage of Peter and John and realized that they were unschooled, ordinary men, they were astonished and they took note that these men had been with Jesus."

During our days as house parents at TEAM's Hostel, we were intrigued as we watched how the mannerisms, actions and manner of speech of each child reflected in miniature that of their parents. They lived with their parents. They had a close relationship with them. Thus they were like them, and the spirit and influence of their parents was among us through the children. So it stands that if we live with Christ and have a close relationship with him, we will become like him, and through us his Spirit will be among and exerting his influence upon those around us.

So wherever we are, if we are among unbelievers, we become "Immanuel" to them. We are as God coming into their presence, and he will be judged by them according to what they see in us. As God sent Christ into the world, so Christ has sent us into the world (Jn.17:18) to be his ambassadors and his representatives (2 Cor.5:20) to speak and work on his behalf as he would do were he here in person.

By what we are, by what we say and do, do others sense God's presence when we are with them?

APPLICATION: The sobering realization is that because God indwells us, we literally "take him" wherever we go (acknowledging, of course, that he is already omnipresent!). As such, people will then evaluate him by what they see in us. What kind of God do they see by our words and actions?

DAY 229
'HE IS THE GIFT-GIVER

QUESTIONS TO THINK ABOUT:

1. What is a gift and how do we earn it?
2. How can someone be said to be a gift to someone else?
3. How is a gift not always giving something tangible to someone?

Paul describes Christ as the Gift-Giver in two ways: as giving himself for us (Gal.2:20) and as giving us specific gifts (Eph.4:7-12). In giving himself for us, he provided for our salvation and all that pertains to it. In giving us gifts, he provided for the growth and maturing of his Body, the Church. Beyond these things, we receive daily gifts from him in forms of answered prayer (1 Jn.5:14,15), the meeting of our needs (Matt.6:25-33), spiritual insight (Jn.14:26), and much more.

We will not all have to give our lives in death for someone else as Christ did (cf. 1 Jn.3:16), but we are commanded to give up our lives to God (Rom.12:1) and our rights to the Lord (Mk.8:34,35). And as we obey, which means willingly giving of ourselves to others (such as husbands to wife, parents to children, missionaries to the people of other lands, etc.) we will be able to invest and multiply ourselves in them, resulting in much blessing here as well as in heaven. As Christ said in John 12:24-25, "I tell you the truth, unless a kernel of wheat falls to the ground and dies, it remains only a single seed. But if it dies, it produces many seeds. The man who loves his life will lose it, while the man who hates his life in this world will keep it for eternal life."

We cannot give spiritual gifts to others; only the Lord can do that. But we <u>can</u> give them the "gift" of being aware of their spiritual gifts, identifying those gifts and encouraging their development. It is important for us to know the spiritual gifts of others, not only so that these gifts can be orchestrated for the growth and maturity of the Church, but also that we may live and work harmoniously with our fellow believers.

For example: when a person on the church board says, "We should have more emphasis on soul-winning and have more evangelistic services," and keeps making this an issue, understanding that his spiritual gift is probably evangelism (Eph.4:11) will help the others be patient toward him. This is especially important when the Christian Ed. director responds with, "No, I don't agree. That's important, to be sure. But what we really need is a stronger teaching and discipleship ministry." Reaction from several others follows. But this man's gift, and therefore his main interest and thrust, is in teaching or exhortation/encouragement (Rom.12:7,8). Another responds that greater emphasis should be given to social outreach in meeting people's physical needs, indicating the gift of mercy or perhaps giving (Rom.12:8). The truth is that we need all of these as operative gifts in the Church, but <u>the key is balance</u>; we must not emphasize one to the exclusion of the others.

Finally, as Christ meets our daily needs, even so we also should meet the daily needs of others, first of all, those of our own family, then of those outside our family as we have opportunity (cf. 1 Jn.3:17). Truly, "It is more blessed to give than to receive" (Acts 20:35), but sadly it seems that most of us would rather receive.

What can you do today to give yourself to others and encourage the use of their spiritual gifts?

APPLICATION: Perhaps it would be useful to make a list of ideas that come to mind on how you could give yourself more to others, then act on it. You might be surprised at the results!

DAY 230
ᵇHE IS THE JUDGE

QUESTIONS TO THINK ABOUT:

1. In Scripture, the word "judge" has two definitions: to judge between (as a judge); to rule over (as a king). How are these two definitions interrelated?

2. How do these two definitions affect our interpretation of Scripture where they appear?

3. How do these two definitions affect our judgment in spiritual matters?

In John 5:22 and Acts 10:42 we find two statements regarding Christ as Judge: "Moreover, the Father judges no one, but has entrusted all judgment to the Son." "… He is the one whom God appointed as judge of the living and the dead." Yet having authority as Judge, he did not exercise that authority while on earth, for he "did not come to judge the world, but to save it" (John 12:47).

Likewise we have been given authority to judge, but that authority is for the future, not the present. "Do you not know that <u>the saints will judge the world</u>? … Do you not know that <u>we shall judge angels</u>?" (1 Cor.6:2,3). To the disciples Christ said, "… You … will also sit on twelve thrones, judging the twelve tribes of Israel" (Matt.19:28; underlining mine). James and John tried to exercise their authority too early: "Lord, do you want us to call fire down from heaven to destroy

Unexpected Transformation / 519

[these Samaritans]?" and received a sound rebuke from the Lord (Luke 9:54,55). Now is the time for us to witness, not judge (Acts 1:8).

Yet we see Christ judging in spiritual matters during his ministry. In John 9:39-41 he said, "'For judgment I have come into this world, so that the blind will see and those who see will become blind.' Some of the Pharisees who were with him heard him say this and asked, 'What? Are we blind too?' Jesus said, 'If you were blind, you would not be guilty of sin; but now that you claim you can see, your guilt remains.'" In Matthew 23 Christ had obviously made a character judgment about the Scribes and Pharisees calling them hypocrites.

Both Apostles John and Paul have made it clear that we are to judge spiritual matters within and as they affect the Church. John tells us to "test the spirits to see whether they are from God" (1 John 4:1-3), and in the same vein Paul says, "Test everything" (1 Thess.5:21). Sin in the Church, personal matters between Christians, and our own selves must be judged by ourselves and/or by those in authority in the Church (1 Cor.5:1-5,12; 6:1-5; 11:28,31; Heb.13:17).

By what standard do we judge? Christ himself said, "That very word which I spoke will condemn him at the last day" (Jn.12:48). He will judge by his spoken word. This word we now have in written form; it is true (Jn.17:17) and therefore absolutely trustworthy and reliable in its use. The alternative, judging after the flesh (Jn.8:15), is unacceptable and condemned. [Scripture gives several illustrations of wrong judgment: 1. according to appearance – (Jn.7:24); 2. hypocritically – (Matt.7:3-5; Rom.2:1,3); with partiality and wrong motives – (Jas.2:1-4); and 4. arbitrarily (as on disputable matters unclear in Scripture – Rom.14:1-13 with Col.2:16,17).] We are urged to be in unity in regard to judgment (1 Cor.1:10), and that unity can only be attained if we all follow the same "law book" – the Word of God.

There are a number of stern warnings in Scripture about judging others (Matt.7:1-5 with Jas.2:1-4,12,13; 4:11,12; Rom.14:1-4). So it is not a thing to be done lightly or without due consideration, for we in turn will be judged according to how we judge others (Matt.7:1-5).

When you must judge, do you judge by the Word of God or by what <u>you</u> think is just?

APPLICATION: Apart from ruling, the biggest danger we face in judging others is judging by assumption. We all have that tendency. It's a real exercise of the will to seek out the truth before "saying" anything. If we did that more and said less, a lot of unnecessary rumors would never be given birth, and our relationship with others would greatly improve. So would our ability to judge correctly. We must seek to be truth seekers, not rumor mills.

DAY 231
ªHE IS THE GENTLE ONE

[The basic outline for this subject came from a sermon given by Jim Larkin, UFM, at the Newman Memorial Chapel, Sentani, Irian Jaya, Indonesia.]

QUESTIONS TO THINK ABOUT:

1. How would you define a "gentle" person?
2. How does "gentleness" imply or not imply "weakness"
3. How can one be "gentle" when a firm or sharp rebuke is needed?

In describing Christ as the Gentle One, we encounter a slight problem in terms, for we meet with four synonyms which not only mean the same thing, but include many other closely related characteristics as well:

Unexpected Transformation / 521

a. Gentleness – mildness, fairness, softness in manner and disposition, kindness, courteous, considerate, gracious, merciful, compassionate.

b. Meekness – (freely interchanged in various translations with gentleness): submissive, obedient, humble, unexcitable, patient under injuries, gentle, mild in temper, kind.

c. Kindness – benevolent, loving, showing a gentle, considerate character or disposition, to be helpful.

d. Graciousness – good, kind.

In Matthew 11:29 Christ invited the weary and burdened to come to him, saying, "I am gentle [meek] and humble in heart." Paul called him meek and gentle (2 Cor.10:1). And many examples could be cited to show Christ's gentleness. Consider his gentleness to Zacchaeus, the hated tax collector (Lk.19:1-10); to the Pharisee Nicodemus (Jn.3:1-21); to the woman at the well, many times divorced (Jn.4:7-29); to the hungry multitude (Mk.6:30-37); and to Peter who denied him three times (Jn.21:15-19). In each case, he could have derided, chided, scolded, "preached" or ignored them. But he didn't. They knew their problem and didn't have to be told. As Jesus spoke with each person, his words were to the point, but gracious, kind, gentle. And they responded. How tender and gentle he must have been to the children who came to be blessed by him (Mk.10:13).

Paul urges Timothy to kindness (gentleness) as the Lord's servant. In 2 Timothy 2:24 he writes, "And the Lord's servant must not quarrel; instead, he must be kind to everyone, able to teach, not resentful." And in 1 Timothy 6:11 he urges Timothy to "pursue ... gentleness," to seek after it eagerly. Then he exhorts Titus "... to be ready to do whatever is good, to slander no one, to be peaceable and considerate, and to show true humility toward all men" (Tit.3:1,2). And again, in Ephesians 4:2, Paul exhorts the Ephesians, saying, "Be completely humble and gentle; be patient, bearing with one another in love." And finally, in Colossians 3:12, we find several characteristics involved in gentleness: "Therefore, as God's chosen people, holy and dearly loved, clothe yourselves with compassion, kindness, humility, gentleness and patience."

Are you eagerly seeking after gentleness? Are you clothing yourself with it? Gentleness is a trait only seen in our actions toward others in kindness, courteousness, consideration, graciousness – our tone of voice, the way we say things (not just what we say) – that look we give someone. There is a place for sharp rebuke, but 98% of the time we should demonstrate that gentle spirit that characterized Christ when he was with people.

Are you gentle toward others, or are there yet many rough edges in your dealings with them?

APPLICATION: Some people relish "vigorous fellowship"; others "strong debate." I suspect that that may be a "cover" for a bad temper or the desire to speak one's mind and let the chips fall where they may. Proverbs 15:1 might be a good reminder here for all of us: "A gentle answer turns away wrath; but grievous words stir up anger." Let us strive for the gentle answer, even when it has to be somewhat forceful at times.

DAY 232
ᶜHE IS THE LAST ADAM

◆

QUESTIONS TO THINK ABOUT:

1. Why is Christ called "the Last Adam"?
2. What does that term imply as attributed to him?

Unexpected Transformation

3. As physical descendants of the First Adam and spiritual descendants of the Last Adam, how is this conflict played out in our lives?

4. What kind of control do we have in this contest?

In 1 Corinthians 15:45 we read, "... The first man Adam became a living being; the last Adam, a life-giving spirit." The context of this verse shows the "last Adam" to be Christ himself. "As the last Adam, he has been made head of a new race (of people), because all who believe in His shed blood become new creatures (2 Cor.5:17)" (Green, p.27).

When Adam was created, he was created in God's image and after his likeness (Gen.1:26), and was given power to rule the earth. This image was greatly marred by the entrance of sin. As Adam's descendants, we also have received this sin-corrupted nature, and thus reflect his condition in ourselves (1 Cor.15:49).

When Christ came as "the man from heaven" (vs.49), he came offering a new birth, a spiritual birth, that would answer the problem of the sin-corrupted nature passed down to us through our physical birth (Jn.3:3-8). Thus as we are born spiritually after the Last Adam, we also shall reflect or bear his likeness. It was this likeness that God intended for Adam to bear. Romans 5:14 says that he "was a pattern of the one to come." Again from the context, we understand this "one" to be Christ. Furthermore, we see that all that Adam should have been (as that pattern and as head of the human race), Christ was.

How much of an effort is it for us to accurately reflect the nature of Adam? None at all. We come by it naturally, for we who "walk in the flesh" will naturally do those things typical of the flesh. <u>That</u> we do not have to be taught; but what we learn from others are the finer points of expressing the character traits already there.

How much of an effort is it for us to accurately reflect the nature of Christ? <u>None at all</u>! If we walk by the Spirit in the spiritual life, we will express Christ's nature naturally as it flows out through us. For, those who walk in the Spirit will not fulfill the desires of the flesh (Gal.5:16,17; see also 1 Jn.3:9).

But here is the point of unresolved tension: As descendants of Adam, we still reflect his likeness in every way; as spiritual descendants of Christ, we bear his likeness, spiritually, in every way. Everything is already there in both natures for the full expression of either. Possessing both puts us in the dilemma of having to choose which one to express: the (old) nature of Adam, energized by Satan, or the (new) nature of Christ energized by the Holy Spirit.

Added to this problem is the fact that both natures are actively fighting against each other (Gal.5:17)! At this point, our spiritual training takes place, learning to die to the sin-corrupted nature and to live to the new spiritual nature (Romans 6 tells us how to make that change successfully. [See also DAY 41 – HE IS THE KING OF KINGS, where we can reign over sin.]

I remember as a child hearing the story of the two dogs in our hearts who are always fighting: one black (the old, sinful nature); the other white (our new nature in Christ). "The dog we feed is the dog that will win," we were told. We need to learn to feed the "white dog" and let the "black dog" go hungry. "So always feed the white one!" We got the picture.

To which nature are you permitting full expression? Or, in other words, which "dog" are you feeding?

APPLICATION: We reflect Christ as the Last Adam when we live in the way God intended the First Adam to live. He was living in unbroken fellowship with his God, untainted by sin and all that goes with it – until he fell into sin and broke that bond of fellowship. Because of the resulting sin nature passed on to us, we cannot live untainted by sin, but we can have victory over it and we can enjoy close fellowship once again with the Lord as we walk in the Spirit, i.e. live in obedience to the Word of God. That puts us in "agreement" with the Lord, and allows us to "walk together" (see Amos 3:3).

DAY 233
'HE IS THE I AM

QUESTIONS TO THINK ABOUT:

1. Since we are not divine, how can we possibly reflect the qualities of the I AM that Christ shares with God?

2. What provisions has God made for us so that we can reflect his unity with Jesus and the Holy Spirit?

One day while talking with the Jews, Christ laid claim to his divinity and eternalness saying, "I tell you the truth ... before Abraham was born, I am!" (Jn.8:58). At this, they picked up stones to stone him for blasphemy in making himself equal with God (vs.59).

Again, in John 10:30, Christ said, "I and the Father are one." And again the Jews picked up stones to stone him because he was "blaspheming" (vs.33). Yet Christ is one with the Father in essence, character and purpose. He told Philip, "Anyone who has seen me has seen the Father" (Jn.14:9b).

The very night Christ was arrested, he prayed, "Holy Father, protect them by the power of your name – the name you gave me – <u>so that they may be one as we are one</u>" (Jn.17:11b, underlining mine). And again in verses 20,21, "I pray also for those who will believe in me through their message, that all of them may be one, Father, just as you are in me and I am in you. May they also be in us so that the world may believe that you have sent me."

Paul expresses our oneness with Christ this way: "For you died [when you were saved], and your life is now hidden with Christ in

God" (Col.3:3). Positionally, we have become one with God, though experientially, we are far from it. [**NOTE:** We will never be like him in essence, but we will be in character and purpose!]

We have already considered Christ's eternalness and divinity in some detail (See DAYS 234-236 – HE IS ETERNAL and 189 – HE IS GOD). But here we find another aspect of his relationship with the Father: similarity in essence, character and purpose. Our oneness with one another in essence (our humanity), character (Christ-likeness) and purpose (to do his will) reflects Christ's oneness with the Father in each area. And this oneness (not carbon copy clones) is to be a witness to the world that God indeed sent Christ into the world (Jn.17:21), and that his message that he brought actually works (Jn.13:35)!

Paul urges us on to this characteristic in Phil.2:2, saying, "Make my joy complete by being likeminded, having the same love, being one in spirit and purpose." The world needs to see the same oneness between Christians as it saw demonstrated between Christ and the Father. This is entirely possible since we are in Christ (Eph.2:6) and in God (Col.3:3), and they (including the Holy Spirit – Jn.14:16,23) are in us!

What's more, when we were saved, God gave to us his divine nature (cf. 1 Jn.3:9; 2 Pet.1:3,4). So with the Triune God indwelling us and we indwelling him and his divine nature becoming ours, we cannot help but reflect the I AM unity and oneness of the Father and the Son. Sin, of course, will mar and distort this reflection. But as we grow in Christ-likeness, sin will become less and less a problem and our expression of the Divine nature will become more and more of a reality. And this, indeed, is God's intention.

Is it yours?

APPLICATION: Striving for unity in the Body means that we are seeking unity in our essence, character and purpose. As we grow in these three areas, we will reflect the unity in the essence, character and purpose of the Son with the Father (and hence, the Holy Spirit).

DAY 234
ᶜHE THE IS MIGHTY, POWERFUL ONE

◆

QUESTIONS TO THINK ABOUT:

1. What is the difference between our position in Christ and our practice on earth?
2. How should our position influence our practice?

In Isaiah 9:6 we read another name of Christ, "The Mighty God." This characteristic is easily seen throughout Christ's life in the physical realm as he healed the sick (Jn.9:1-7), fed multitudes (Jn.6:1-14), walked on the water (Jn.6:15-21), stilled the raging storm (Mk.4:35-41), and arose from the dead (Jn.20:9).

In the spiritual realm, Christ's power is also seen as he had victory over Satan (Matt.4:1-11), sin (Jn.8:46), and death (Heb.2:14,15; 1 Cor.15:20-23). And in Matthew 28:18 he declares: "All authority in heaven and on earth has been given to me."

Where on occasion the Holy Spirit empowers a Christian to work a miracle in the physical realm, the usual area of our might is shown and experienced in the spiritual realm. We see this in several ways.

First of all, we are in a *position of might* in Christ according to Romans 6:3-5 and must reckon on this. Paul declares in Romans 8:37 that "... in all these things we are more than conquerors through him who loved us." Christ said in John 15:5b, "Apart from me you can do nothing." Conversely, together with him, we can do anything God wants us to do (Phil.4:13)! So, to begin with, we need a change of attitude from a position of defeat to one of victory: "With Christ, I can do it!"

Secondly, throughout his life, Christ resisted Satan and overcame him by *using God's Word*. So may we. Psalm 119:11 says, "I have hidden your word in my heart that I might not sin against you." James 4:7 says, "Submit yourselves, then, to God. Resist the devil, and he will flee from you." We submit to God by obeying him, and we learn how to obey him by knowing his Word (which is our sword in spiritual warfare – Eph.6:17). Then, as is promised, we can resist the devil successfully. The Word of God also contains our spiritual armor to be used in this battle, and our use of that armor directly depends on our knowledge of the Word (Eph.6:10-18; see APPENDIX VIII for an outline of this passage). One cannot effectively use a weapon that he has not trained for. Submitting ourselves to God and his authority will give us boldness and courage to resist the devil and our knowledge of the Word will help us gain the victory over him.

Thirdly, *we are dead to sin's power* (our position based on Romans 6:6,7). We must live like it and not let sin rule any longer in our lives (our works based upon our position as in Romans 6:11-14). However, the choice is ours whether or not to resist sin. But in every case, God has provided the way out if we want to take it (1 Cor.10:13 – the very reason we are tempted means that we can overcome it!). So there is no compelling reason for us to sin apart from our choice to do so (Jas.1:13-15). Therefore, let us choose godliness and resist sin!

Lastly, in effect, we also have overcome death, in that *we already possess eternal life* (Jn.5:24). This is our position of victory which will be realized at the rapture (1 Cor.15:51-56) when our bodies will be changed to be like Christ's (1 Jn.3:2), and we will be able to enjoy eternity physically. Thus the fear and dread of death itself is gone, and we can turn our full attention to setting our minds on things above where Christ is (Col.3:1-4).

A good summary statement is found in 1 Cor.15:57, "But thanks be to God! He gives us the victory through our Lord Jesus Christ."

Are you living in the victory Christ has given you or in defeat caused by the Devil's lies denying that victory?

APPLICATION: To avoid critical misunderstandings of various Scriptural passages, we must know the difference between our position in Christ and our practice on earth. When we confuse the two, our doctrine will get mixed up, and we will end up teaching things that just aren't so. Just as reminder: In Christ, (Heb.10:14) we are *already perfect* (position); but we *still sin* and have to be made holy (practice). In Christ, (Eph.2:6) we are *already seated* in the heavenlies (position); but we are *still living on earth* awaiting the Rapture (practice). Be careful not to mix the two!

DAY 235
ᶜHE IS ETERNAL

◆

QUESTIONS TO THINK ABOUT:

1. If I offered you something, but didn't actually possess it, what would your response be?
2. Usually we think of eternal life as "living forever." But how does Christ's definition of eternal life in John 17:3 modify that definition? How is it different from the usual one?

In Isaiah 9:6 and other passages (Jn.1:1-3; 8:58; Heb.13:8), we find declarations of Christ's eternalness. We find also in John 10:27-30 where Christ gives eternal life to his sheep. He says, "My sheep listen to my voice; I know them, and they follow me. I give them eternal life, and they shall never perish; no one can snatch them out of my hand. My Father, who has given them to me, is greater than all; no one can snatch them out of my Father's hand. I and the Father are one."

One cannot give to others what he does not already possess himself! Many times we had Irianese come to us wanting to sell us some land. Since most of the time they did not own that land, they could not legally sell it to us. But the fact that Christ <u>is</u> eternal means that he <u>can</u> give eternal life to his sheep.

Those who know Christ as their Savior possess eternal life now (Jn.5:24). If this is true, then how can we, as possessors of eternal life, pass it on to others? Two other questions we could ask as well are: "What does possession of eternal life mean to our present lifestyle?" And, "How do we prepare for the eternal life to come?"

To answer the first question, we pass on eternal life to others through our witness to them. We give them the Gospel (1 Cor.15:1-4), and if they choose to believe it and receive Christ as their Savior, they receive eternal life. In John 17:2,3 Jesus prayed, "For you [God] granted him [Christ] authority over all people in that he might give eternal life to all those you have given him. Now this is eternal life: that they may know you, the only true God, and Jesus Christ, whom you have sent."

Technically, it is always the Lord who gives people eternal life, but we who possess it are the ones who tell them about it so that they also can possess it if they will (Acts 1:8).

I just saw an interesting thing in John 17:3 which I had never noticed before: a definition of what eternal life is. Usually when we think of eternal life, we think of it in terms of time (<u>quantity</u>), living without the bonds of time (Gen.3:22), in an ever-present existence (as alluded to by Christ in John 8:58).

But what is the <u>quality</u> of eternal life which gives it meaning? Let's look at verse three again: "Now this is eternal life: <u>that they may know you, the only true God, and Jesus Christ</u>, whom you have sent" (underlining mine). Eternal life will not only be characterized by living in timelessness, but also by an ever-increasing knowledge of who God is, who Christ is, and what they have done, are doing, and are going to do. That is why Christ says in John 5:24 that those who believe in him already possess eternal life, for they are already in a position to begin knowing God and Christ whom he has sent. Now we begin to realize just how imperative it is for us to be reading from and studying God's

Unexpected Transformation / 531

Word daily, for only there do we find the revelation of who he is, what he is doing, and what he wants to do both in the world and in our lives.

So the quality aspect of our life with the Lord in heaven will be a mere continuation of our life with him on earth. The quantity aspect of eternal life will begin at death, or the Rapture, when we will actually experience life that is no longer bound by time.

Are you taking advantage right now of the eternal life you possess?

APPLICATION: A side-benefit of the quality aspect of eternal life that we possess right now is that it becomes a very strong evidence of our salvation. It is impossible for an unsaved person to read the Word of God and grow in his knowledge of God and of Jesus Christ (apart from the divine intervention of the Holy Spirit!) because it's all foolishness to him (cf. 1 Cor.1:18). The fact that we, as believers, can grow in this knowledge implies the presence of the Holy Spirit in our lives as our Teacher and Guide into all spiritual truth. He is only there if we are saved.

DAY 236
ᶜHE IS ETERNAL, cont.

◆

QUESTIONS TO THINK ABOUT:

1. How does possession of eternal life (thinking especially of the quality aspect) change our focus?
2. What does this possession of eternal life mean to our present lifestyle?

We come now to the second question: "What does possession of eternal life mean to our present life style?"

First of all, it means that we will begin giving priority to those things which really matter. This involves a change of attitude. Colossians 3:1-3 says, "Since, then, you have been raised with

Christ, set your hearts on things above, where Christ is seated at the right hand of God. <u>Set your minds</u> on things above, not on earthly things. For you died, and your life is now hidden with Christ in God" (underlining mine).

"Set your minds" – this is an act of our will in conformity to the eternal life we possess. Christ warns us of materialistic attitudes in Luke 12:15, saying, "Watch out! Be on your guard against all kinds of greed; a man's life does not consist in the abundance of his possessions."

Our perspective on life is now determined in terms of eternity, and we set our priorities in that direction (Matt.6:33). But if there were no eternal life, then our Christian life would be subordinated to other desires; other things would easily take priority, and we would fall prey to the philosophy expressed in 1 Corinthians 15:32b which says, "If the dead are not raised [i.e. if there is no eternal life], 'Let us eat and drink, for tomorrow we die.'" But Christ <u>is</u> risen from the dead, and we are guaranteed a resurrection too (1 Cor.15:20)! And so, with this prospect in mind, we can adjust our priorities toward that which is eternal. [We will take up this subject tomorrow when we consider how to prepare for the life to come.]

Now, what are some of the changes we can expect as we restructure our priorities?

1. We lose the need "to keep up with the Joneses," resulting in a more reasonable standard of living, extra money to put into the Lord's work or give to those in need, time saved, and emotional and psychological stability.

2. No longer do we worry about the prosperity of the wicked, knowing that "our time" will come after they have lost everything.

3. The dread and fear of dying is gone because we know that we possess eternal life.

4. We develop an unselfish life, realizing that we have something that others should have and want to give it to them.

5. Consciously or unconsciously, we begin to evaluate decisions, projects, and plans in light of eternity: "What will produce lasting, eternal results? What will in any way contribute to our witness and the Lord's work?" and so on.

6. What we watch, what we read, what we think, will now be influenced by God's standard of holiness (Phil.4:8 – which now is accepted as a help rather than rejected as a restriction), no longer by man's standard.

Other things will change too. The problem is, many, if not most Christians, are living as if there were no eternity!

How does your possession of eternal life reveal itself in your lifestyle? Is eternal life a reality to you?

APPLICATION: There is no other way to effect the changes that possession of eternal life offers than to sit down and consciously weigh your lifestyle now in terms of what it should be, or could be, according to the eternal life we possess. Then make those changes necessary to bring your life into line with those principles. That is a decision you will never regret!

DAY 237
ᶜHE IS ETERNAL, concl.

QUESTIONS TO THINK ABOUT:

1. How do we prepare for the life to come, quantitatively and qualitatively?

2. What does "laying up our treasures in heaven" have to do with eternal life?

3. How do our priorities affect our preparation for eternal life?

We come now to the final question: "How do we prepare for the life to come?"

First and foremost, we prepare for it by receiving Christ as our personal Savior, asking him to forgive us of our sins and be the Lord of our lives. We read in 1 John 5:12, "He who has the Son has life; he who does not have the Son of God does not have life." It's as black and white as that!

Secondly, we prepare for eternal life by getting to know God better while here on earth (Jn.17:3). This involves faithful church attendance, reading, studying, memorizing and meditating on the Word of God, prayer and an active interest in missions at home and abroad (since this will put us in touch with what God is doing around the world). It involves reading Christian literature to gain insights from others about God and the Christian life. It is essential that we get to <u>know him</u>.

Thirdly, Christ commands us to lay up treasure in heaven rather than on earth (Matt.6:19-21). How? By doing good works (Eph.2:10) which are pleasing to him (Col.1:10), by being faithful to him in all we do (Matt.25:14-23), by doing all we do in the name of the Lord Jesus (on his authority and according to his will – Col.3:17), and so on. 1 Corinthians 3:11-15 makes it very clear that our good works will bring eternal reward and our bad works (those done in the power of the flesh, and other sins), eternal loss. There are rewards also for loving his appearing (2 Tim.4:8), overcoming sin (Rev.2:7,11,17,26-28; 3:5,12,21), and martyrdom (Rev.2:10). We should be seeking to do those things which will please God and gain us eternal reward.

Along with these comes the fourth type of preparation: a changing of our priorities in terms of the use of our time, money and possessions. The priority we assign to each of these items will determine directly what we will receive in heaven. One step back, our attitudes

Unexpected Transformation / 535

will determine our priorities: what we really want to be or do will receive our full attention. Remember, God's primary goal for us is to make us like Christ (Rom.8:29). If this also becomes our goal, then the stage is set for changed attitudes, reordered priorities, and reward for faithful service. Then as our character is changed to reflect more and more of his character, we will find ourselves doing those things which are pleasing in his sight and worthy of eternal reward.

I often think back to my school days. At the beginning of each semester, I would picture myself at the end of that semester having just taken my finals. Then ask myself, "How do you want to feel when finals are over: shame in failure, or 'Whew! I made it! Boy, am I <u>glad</u> I studied'"? Right then I set my priorities and studied, letting other things of lesser priority go.

In the same way we need to think about the end of life's "semester," just having met the Lord face to face. "How do I want to feel when I see Jesus: shame in failure, or 'Whew! I made it! Boy, am I <u>glad</u> I was faithful.'"?

What is your answer?

What changes, then, do you need to make?

APPLICATON: Have you received Christ as your Savior? If not, now is the time to do it, asking him to come into your life and forgive you of your sins.

What are you doing to get to know God better? How much of a priority is he in your life? Begin to do those things which will increase your knowledge of him! What are you doing to lay up treasures in heaven? We need to pay more attention to that than the Stock Market! How are you arranging your priorities? Do they center on being made like Christ (God's goal for our lives) or on living as comfortable a life as you can under the circumstances? Contemplate the message of the first verse of "O to Be Like Thee."

> O to be like Thee! Blessed Redeemer
> This is my constant longing and prayer;
> Gladly I'll forfeit all of earth's treasures,
> Jesus Thy perfect likeness to wear.
> — Thomas O. Chisholm

DAY 238
ʽHE IS A FATHER

QUESTIONS TO THINK ABOUT:

1. When you think of a father, what kind of qualities would you hope to see in him?
2. What are the responsibilities of a father toward his family?
3. How is it possible for any of us to be like a father to someone?

In Isaiah 9:6 Christ is referred to as the Eternal Father. He told Philip, "Anyone who has seen me has seen the Father" (Jn.14:7-9). He declared to the Jews, "I and the Father are one" (Jn.10:30), and they understood him to be claiming to be God (Jn.10:33). Throughout his ministry, Christ demonstrated fatherly characteristics, meeting both the physical and spiritual needs of people to whom he ministered.

In the physical realm, he provided food (Jn.6:1-4), mediated problems (Lk.12:13-21), healed the sick (Lk.14:1-4), and helped give success (Jn.21:3-8). In the spiritual realm, he taught a godly outlook on life (Lk.12:22-34), provided an example for others to follow (Jn.13:2-15), and gave a sense of security (Jn.6:67-69), comfort (Jn.14:1-3) and motivation (Matt.28:18-20). He also provided opportunities for practicing the lessons being learned (Mk.6:7-13), and loved his own (Jn.13:1).

The term "father" in itself implies a physical maturity, bodily development to the point where reproduction is possible. It also implies spiritual, emotional and psychological maturity, the ability to face life, make decisions, and relate successfully to both God and man. Not all of us can or will become physical parents, but we all can become spiritual parents, reproducing (winning others to Christ) and nurturing (discipling) spiritual babes toward maturity. In 1 John 2:13,14, John states that our spiritual maturity (becoming a father) depends upon our knowledge of God. The more we know him, the more like him we become; hence the more we mature spiritually and become capable of leading others into spiritual growth and maturity.

Now how does this all work out in everyday life? In the physical realm, we should be mature enough, and unselfish enough to help others in need (Jas.2:14-16; 1 Jn.3:17,18), even as a parent would help his own children. As Paul urges us in Galatians 6:10, "Therefore, as we have opportunity, let us do good to all the people, especially to those who belong to the family of believers."

Spiritually, we should be growing day by day in our knowledge of God and of Christ, and putting into practice that knowledge. Our value system and outlook on life should be changing into a more godly direction. Our lives should more and more become an example for others to follow. We should grow in love toward others, and grow in our ability to comfort and motivate them. Young Christians should be able to feel secure in our presence. Spiritual fathers are the ones who should become leaders in the church (in all areas), who should most exhibit the character of Christ, the ability to discipline the wayward, wisdom, spiritual insight, and provision of opportunities for younger Christians to grow. They should love and care for the Church as parents would their own children.

In a letter to her older brother, a sister once wrote the following: "Yesterday being Father's Day, [the pastor] preached on what fathers should be to their children. On one hand, I was sad, because I never had what he was talking about with Dad. I do appreciate the good things that Dad gave us – his wisdom, choosing our spouses, and his honesty, but I missed having the kind of relationship I heard about. As I was thinking over [pastor's] message, I realized that God <u>did</u> provide for me in my need. He said fathers should spend time with their children teaching them what they know, playing with them, and praying for them. You are the one that God used to do this for me. Thank you for teaching me about having a quiet time, about loving God, about morality. Thank you for teaching me to write poetry. Thank you for being a godly model for me... . Thanks for being the kind of big brother I could follow, and know that you wouldn't lead me wrong."

Are you a spiritual father (mother)? Can others look to you in the same way this sister looked to her older brother?

APPLICATION: Think about the stages of a child's growth into an adult and make a parallel list for spiritual growth. At what point are you? Fortunately, spiritual growth can happen a lot faster than physical growth. So, wherever you are on the growth chart, mark out the steps it will take you to move on to the next growth level and begin moving toward that direction such as having a Quiet Time, personal projects from your Quiet Time, informal Bible study (personal or church-related), formal Bible study (online or school campus) specific ministry-related training, etc.

DAY 239
ᵇHE IS THE GLORIOUS, ᶜTHE TRANSFIGURED, EXALTED, MAJESTIC ONE

◆

QUESTIONS TO THINK ABOUT:

1. What does it mean to be "glorious"?
2. How can we possibly reflect the Lord's glory?

In Scripture, the word "glory" has many meanings: heaven, praise, high position, boastfulness, fame, honor (Isa.45:4), reward, awesomeness, power, beauty, our witness (1 Pet.4:14), splendor, brightness, and the nature of God (Rom.3:23 – or as someone once said to me, "Glory is God's excellence [Jer.2:11] and our recognition of his excellence [Jer.4:2])." The problem is, when we speak of Christ's glory, which definition are we to use? In what way or ways is he glorious? I think we can come closest to it from three directions: first, his appearance on the Mount of Transfiguration; secondly, the moral and spiritual character of his nature; and thirdly, his exalted position.

In appearance on the Mount of Transfiguration, he was glorious. "His clothes became dazzling white, whiter than anyone in the world could bleach them" (Mk.9:3). In Matthew 17:2, "His face shone like the sun, and his clothes became as white as the light." That this was nothing less than a direct reflection of God's glory is illustrated for us by Moses himself. According to 2 Corinthians 3:7, when Moses came down from Mount Sinai, "he was not aware that his face was radiant because he had spoken with the LORD. When Aaron and all the Israelites saw Moses, his face was radiant, and they were afraid to come near him."

In like manner the angels also reflect the glory of God as they come out from his presence to do his bidding: at the announcement of Christ's birth (Lk.2:9), at the resurrection (Matt.28:3,4), in appearance to Daniel (Dan.10:5,6), and to John (Rev.10:1).

In every account, the manifestation of God's glory evoked fear in the hearts of the onlookers (see ***NOTE** on next page): the disciples were terrified (Mk.9:6), Israel was afraid (Exod.34:30), the shepherds were terrified (Lk.2:9), the grave guards became as dead men for fear (Matt.28:4), the women at the grave were terrified (Matt.28:5), Daniel became faint (Dan.10:8), and John fell as one dead from fear before the Lord's glory (Rev.1:17 – **NOTE:** After that experience, he was "immune" to the glory of the angels as far as fear was concerned – Rev.10:1ff).

The more time one spends in the presence of the Lord, the more he will reflect the Lord's glory. A missionary friend of mine told me once of a personal experience in which he had attended a most unusually blessed prayer meeting. Returning to work, he began to share this with a friend there. "I know," his friend replied, "Your face is glowing."

A literal glow is unusual, yet there is a sensed aura about such a person which inspires respect and trust in the hearts of Believers, and fear in the hearts of unbelievers. This same missionary said, "Unbelievers will not touch a Believer around whom is this aura because they are too afraid to come near him." Perhaps so, but Steven's face was "like that of an angel" before the Sanhedrin (Acts 6:15), yet they stoned him to death because of what he told them (Acts 7:54-60).

God has ordained that we should fully reflect Christ's glory.

Is your reflector polished or tarnished?

APPLICATION: The only way we can reflect another's glory is to be with them and become like them. There is no other way. It stands to reason, then, that the more time we spend with the Lord and become like him, the more his glory will be seen in us.

[***NOTE:** For this reason, I am highly skeptical of people who claim to have had a dream or vision of the Lord but showed no awe or fear in his holy presence. I don't doubt they had a dream or vision, but I do doubt that it was the Lord they saw.]

DAY 240
ᵇHE IS THE GLORIOUS, ᶜTHE TRANSFIGURED, EXALTED, MAJESTIC, cont.

◆

QUESTIONS TO THINK ABOUT:

1. How is it possible for us to begin to measure up to God's holy character?
2. Some say that it is possible for a Christian to live a sinless life. What do you think?
3. If we possess the New Nature (God's nature) that cannot sin, then why do we still sin?

In terms of the moral and spiritual character of his nature, Christ reflected God's glory. In Romans 3:23 we read that "… all have sinned and fall short of the glory of God." Here "the glory of God" refers to his sinless, holy nature; his holy standard by which everything is measured. In every situation where God spoke directly to man regarding his Son, he had nothing but praise for him, an impossibility had Jesus not wholly reflected and partaken of the very nature of God. We find these words of praise prophetically in Isaiah 42:1, audibly at his baptism (Matt.3:17) and the Transfiguration (Matt.17:5), and by observation in Luke 2:52 and Eph.1:6.

Our daily experience, however, is different from this, for we often sin and must seek God's forgiveness. But by our position in

Christ, God has made every provision available to us for moment by moment victory over sin and for partaking of his divine, sinless nature. Second Peter 1:3,4 says: "His divine power has given us everything we need for life and godliness through our knowledge of him who called us by his own glory and goodness. Through these he has given us his very great and precious promises, so that through them you may participate in the divine nature and escape the corruption in the world caused by evil desires."

Let's look at 1 John 3:6,9. Following the Greek tenses we read: "No one who lives in him keeps on [habitually] sinning. No one who [habitually] continues to sin has either seen him or known him... . No one who is born of God will [habitually] continue to sin, because God's seed remains in him; he cannot go on [habitually] sinning because he has been born of God." The present tense in Greek indicates continuous, linear action. It would seem to follow then, that when we are walking in fellowship with the Lord, we will not be habitually sinning; and when we do sin, it is only a temporary fall. Christ walked in continuous, unbroken fellowship with God, and never committed a sin, even though tempted. Thus he fully reflected the glorious moral character of God. As we walk with the Lord, we also will be tempted to sin. Then we're faced with a choice: to continue abiding in Christ and refuse to yield to the temptation, or to yield to the temptation and thus break our fellowship with him until repentance and confession restore that fellowship (1 Jn.1:7,9).

As we saw in DAY 41 – HE IS THE KING OF KINGS, Romans 6:6,7 clearly states that we are dead to sin. That means that sin no longer has any legal or moral authority over us! So, if we're dead to sin, then we are alive to God (vs.10) and living _positionally_ in 1 John 3:9 where, being born of God and partaking of his nature, we cannot sin. The fact that this perfection has not yet been fully realized in our experience and that we still give in to temptation and sin, makes it no less true than Paul's assertion in Eph.2:6 that we are _already_ seated in heavenly places together with Christ; yet here we are still here on earth!

Our position before the Lord thus makes sin even worse in our lives; for at that point we are deliberately choosing to abrogate our new position of sinlessness in Christ in order to degrade ourselves to the old position of being alive to sin and dead to righteousness! This situation is totally unnecessary in the light of Romans 6 and 2 Peter 1:3,4. Put in other words, "There is no compulsion for the Christian to sin apart from his choice to do so!"

It would be well to meditate on these passages, remembering that we are positionally dead to sin, and that through the knowledge of God, we receive all things that pertain to life and godliness, holiness and victory. Thus we also can more and more clearly reflect the glorious nature of God's character as we gain more and more victory over sin.

Even though none of us can live in continuous, unbroken fellowship with God, it's something we can strive toward. This side of heaven, we will never reach it, but spiritual growth implies moving closer and closer to it so that when we reach heaven, the change won't be that much!

APPLICATION: Basically, the only thing that stands between us and victory over sin is our will not to sin! God has given us every provision in order to help us make the right choice. We just have to choose to appropriate those provisions.

DAY 241
ᵇHE IS THE GLORIOUS, ᶜTHE TRANSFIGURED, EXALTED, MAJESTIC, cont.

QUESTIONS TO THINK ABOUT:

1. What is the pathway to exaltation or glory?
2. How did Christ achieve exaltation and glory?

3. How was that different from the world's way to get there?

In Philippians 2:9-11 we read of Christ's glorified position at the right hand of God: "... God exalted him to the highest place and gave him the name that is above every name, that at the name of Jesus every knee should bow, in heaven and on earth and under the earth, and every tongue confess that Jesus Christ is Lord, to the glory of God the Father." In Mark 16:19 we read that "... he was taken up into heaven and he sat at the right hand of God," the place of glory. Thus we see the answer to Christ's prayer in John 17:5, "And now, Father, glorify me in your presence with the glory I had with you before the world began."

Why was Christ glorified? There are at least three reasons: because he was faithful, he was humble, and he suffered.

He was faithful in finishing the work God gave him to do. In John 17:4 he prayed, "I have brought you glory on earth by completing the work you gave me to do." And God glorified him. In Matthew 25:23, we read of the faithful servant rewarded by his master: "His master replied, 'Well done, good and faithful servant! You have been faithful with a few things; I will put you in charge of many things. Come and share your master's happiness!'" God demands faithfulness from us, and in exchange for our faithfulness, he will exalt us to greater responsibilities.

Because Christ humbled himself as a servant, God exalted him. Philippians 2:5-9a says, "Your attitude should be the same as that of Christ Jesus: Who, being in the very nature God, did not consider equality with God something to be grasped, but made himself nothing, taking the very nature of a servant, being made in human likeness. And being found in appearance as a man, he humbled himself and became obedient to death – even death on a cross! Therefore God exalted him to the highest place." He humbled himself and became a servant. He demands the same of us, saying that whoever among us wants to be number one, must be the slave of all (Matt.20:27; 23:11)! He also warned us in Matthew 23:12, "For whoever exalts himself will be humbled, and whoever humbles himself will be exalted." James repeats this principle in James 4:10 saying, "Humble yourselves before the Lord, and he will lift you up." We do the humbling (see DAYS 191-193 – HE IS HUMBLE as to how we do it); God does the exalting!

Again we meet this principle in the Sermon on the Mount. In Matthew 6:2,6,17,18, Christ says that what we do, we should do secretly, quietly (the spirit of humility), and God will reward us openly (Matt.6:4,6,18 – KJV). This honor we may or may not receive here on earth. Often we do receive it here, and are exalted before others either in recognition or in added responsibilities or promotions. We have heard stories from missionaries of another country where Christians are preferred as employees because they are faithful (not absent because of drunkenness), honest (don't steal), and are good workers (not lazy, trying to get something for nothing). This is their glory, their exalted position on earth. This is also their Father's glory as they reflect his character before men, thus fulfilling Matthew 5:16, "... Let your light shine before men, that they may see your good deeds and praise your Father in heaven."

Solomon says in Proverbs 15:33, "The fear of the LORD teaches a man wisdom, and humility comes before honor."

Are you faithful in all you do, and willing to humble yourself before God and men? If so, then you will be exalted in due time.

APPLICATION: I have found one good way to remain humble is to meditate on John 15:5 where Jesus says, "For without me, you can do nothing." And then on John 16:8 where Jesus says, "When he [the Holy Spirit] comes, he will convict the world of guilt in regard to sin, and righteousness and judgment." It's not our cleverness, knowledge or piety that are going to win others, it is the Holy Spirit himself, and sometimes in spite of us! We are merely the conduit through which God's Word passes. It's our job to keep the conduit clear of debris; it's God's job to "make the water flow."

DAY 242
ᵇHE IS THE GLORIOUS, ᶜTHE TRANSFIGURED, EXALTED, MAJESTIC, concl.

QUESTIONS TO THINK ABOUT:

1. How is suffering a way to exaltation and glory?
2. What does looking into Scripture and looking into a mirror have in common? (see Jas.1:23-25)
3. How does that concept help us reflect the glory of the Lord?

The third way to exaltation is that of suffering. We also read in Philippians 2:8,9 that when Christ humbled himself, he because obedient to death. He suffered the death of the cross. Therefore God exalted him. Consider the following verses in this context: Romans 8:17, "Now if we are children, then we are heirs – heirs of God and co-heirs with Christ, if indeed we share in his sufferings [see also Phil.1:29,30] in order that we may also share in his glory." First Peter 4:13, "But rejoice that you participate in the sufferings of Christ, so that you may be overjoyed when his glory is revealed." Second Corinthians 4:17,18, "For our light and momentary troubles are achieving for us an eternal glory that far outweighs them all. So we fix our eyes not on what is seen, but on what is unseen. For what is seen is temporary, but what is unseen is eternal." And finally, 1 Peter 2:20b-21, "But if you suffer for doing good and you endure it, this is commendable before God. To this you were called, because Christ suffered for you, leaving you an example, that you should follow in his steps."

The way to glory/exaltation is faithful, humble service and suffering. There is no other way.

Our future exalted position remains for us to experience. It is stated in Ephesians 2:6, "And God raised us up with Christ and seated us with him in the heavenly realms in Christ Jesus." And in Revelation 5:10, "You have made them to be a kingdom and priests to serve our God, and they will reign on the earth."

Christ also promised an exalted position "to him who overcomes." In Revelation 2:26,27 he says, "To him who overcomes and does my will to the end, I will give authority over the nations – he will rule them with an iron scepter; he will dash them to pieces like pottery – just as I have received authority from my Father." And again in Revelation 3:21, "To him who overcomes, I will give the right to sit with me on my throne, just as I overcame and sat down with my Father on his throne." Overcoming involves suffering: death to self (Mk.8:34,35), struggle against sin (Heb.12:4), and warfare against Satan (Rev.12:11).

The actual experience of this glorified, exalted position we find recorded in Revelation 19:7,8 where the Church is glorified as Christ's Bride: "Let us rejoice and be glad and give him glory! For the wedding of the Lamb has come, and his bride has made herself ready. Fine linen, bright and clean, was given her to wear. (Fine linen stands for the righteous acts of the saints.)" Also Revelation 20:4,6: "I saw thrones on which were seated those who had been given authority to judge. And I saw the souls of those who had been beheaded because of their testimony for Jesus and because of the word of God. They had not worshipped the beast or his image and had not receive his mark on their foreheads or their hands. They came to life and reigned with Christ a thousand years... . Blessed and holy are those who have part in the first resurrection. The second death has no power over them, but they will be priests of God and of Christ and will reign with him for a thousand years."

Positionally, our exalted state is a fact; but practically, it is an ongoing process as we behold the Lord's glory. Second Corinthians 3:18 says, "And we, who with unveiled faces all reflect the Lord's glory, are being transformed into his likeness with ever-increasing glory, which comes from the Lord, who is the Spirit."

How much of the Lord's glory do you see from day to day? Only that much can you reflect.

APPLICATION: As we glance quickly at ourselves in the mirror, then go our way, it is impossible to recall which hair is out of place, or what blemish needs the help of a bit of makeup, etc. Those things can only be corrected as we carefully look at ourselves and pay attention to what we see. The same is true regarding the Scriptures. A quick or casual "glance" at them will be of no use to us. Any "character corrections" will come only from a careful examination of ourselves in the light of Scripture so that our moral "hairs and blemishes" will be properly cared for. Only then will we reflect the Lord's glory in its true light.

DAY 243
ᶜHE IS THE LORD

QUESTIONS TO THINK ABOUT:

1. What does the word "Lord" imply?
2. What did the Lord exercise his lordship over?
3. How is it possible for us to reflect the lordship of Christ?

In John 13:13, Jesus said to his disciples, "You call me 'Teacher' and 'Lord,' and rightly so, for that is what I am." The Greek word for Lord, *kyrios*, means "supreme in authority, i.e. controller." We find that Scripture supports this definition as applied to Christ. In

Matthew 28:18 Jesus said, "All authority in heaven and on earth has been given to me." In Colossians 1:17 we read, "He is before all things, and in him all things hold together" (Gk. *synesteken*, means "to cohere, hold together"). Christ, by his great power, literally holds the universe together! He is Lord!

Others testified of his lordship. Peter declared: "This is the message God sent to the people of Israel, telling the good news of peace through Jesus Christ, who is Lord of all" (Acts 10:36). Paul called him "Lord" in Acts 9:6 (NKJV): "So he, trembling and astonished, said, 'Lord, what do you want me to do?'"

And his works proved his lordship. Not only did he create the world (Col.1:16,17), but he demonstrated his power over it in the animal kingdom (Mk.11:2), in the natural world (Lk.8:22-25), and over man (Jn.17:2; Lk.10:19). He also exercised authority in spiritual matters (Matt.7:29; Lk.4:32; Mk.2:28), in giving eternal life (Jn.17:2), in forgiving sin and healing sickness (Matt.9:2-8), and death (Jn.6:39,40; 10:18). He is supreme over all evil spirits (Matt.10:1) and the Devil himself (1 Jn.3:8b; Matt.4:1-11). The final judgment is also under his control (Jn.5:22; Matt.25:31-34,41,46).

In every one of these areas, we find Christians, with the Lord's help, reflecting his lordship: power over animals and man (Lk.10:19; Acts 28:3-5), over the weather (Jas.5:17,18), in spiritual matters (Acts 15:1-27), in passing on (not giving) eternal life (John 17:20), in forgiving sin (on the human level – Matt.18:35), and healing the sick (Lk.10:9), over death (Acts 20:9,10; Rom.6:5,8), over evil spirits (Lk.10:17), over Satan (Rev.12:10,11), and power in judgment (Matt.18:18; 1 Cor.6:2,3).

Not every Christian will reflect all these aspects of Christ's lordship at any given time, but his Body, the Church, will. And at one time or another, each of us will reflect more and more of them; for many of these demonstrations of lordship hinge upon our circumstances. For instance:

Exercising our Lordship over Satan

One day my sister and her husband grew aware of the fact that every time the school where their daughter attended had a special program, inevitably she got sick and couldn't take part. She had missed all but one program since she had begun school. She was otherwise healthy. Sure enough, the next program came along and she became sick with a fever. Suspecting demonic involvement, they first prayed, then rebuked the spirit or spirits involved in causing their daughter's sickness. They said afterwards, "We never saw anyone recover from a fever as fast as she did." She took her part in the program.

APPLICATION: We have already seen where we have victory over Satan in the name of the Lord Jesus Christ (see DAY 42 – HE IS THE KING [over Satan]). James 4:7 is still there: "Submit yourselves, then, to God. Resist the devil, and he will flee from you." We submit, knowing that it is his power, not ours; then we resist the Devil in God's authority and the promise is that he will flee from us.

DAY 244
ᶜHE IS THE LORD, concl.

QUESTIONS TO THINK ABOUT:

1. When we exercise our lordship over things such as weather and in areas of judgment, what must we keep in mind?
2. How is prayer a "tool" in the expression of our lordship?

Exercising our lordship over weather

One day, Amber and I were flying through bad weather on the south coast of Irian Jaya. We got lost. The pilot and I were scouring his maps to try to locate ourselves. The folks at the station we were headed for heard us far to the north and radioed our position. We landed safely. But on the next leg of our flight, we had to cross the mountains. They were shrouded with clouds. The pilot tried and tried to penetrate the cloud barrier, but with no success. Meanwhile, back in the States, my mother had a strong urge to pray for our safety. She urgently prayed for a way through the clouds to be opened even though she didn't know we were flying. Suddenly, an alleyway opened in the clouds, not much wider than the wings of the Cessna, and the pilot flew through it and out over the exact place where he wanted to be!

Exercising our lordship in judgment

On one occasion at the Bible school, I was confronted by an angry father accusing one of our married students of trying to have an affair with his daughter. I was shocked. The character of this student was such that I had to doubt the accusation. But as I talked with various ones involved, I began to have a nagging feeling that maybe he did try something. Some things just didn't fit the "innocent" picture. But there was no real proof; and the man's daughter was not known for her truthfulness. So I prayed much for wisdom to know what to do. In my heart, the Lord confirmed that the student indeed was guilty. Now what to do? I shared with him some of my own problems in the area of impure thoughts and asked him if he had experienced anything similar. He immediately opened up, confessed his sin, and expressed genuine repentance for what he had tried to do. When I brought him and the father together to settle the affair, I didn't have to declare the verdict. The student made an open confession of the whole thing, shared how the Lord had been working in his heart regarding it, and asked the father to forgive him. I just sat there praising the Lord for the gracious spirit in both of them as forgiveness was given and friendship restored.

We need to remember that in Christ, our position is that of lords over all that he is lord of (cf. Eph.2:6 with Rev.3:21), reflecting his authority through our circumstances and responsibilities. We also should not short-change ourselves, saying, "In such and such a situation, I could never demonstrate his lordship," for, depending upon him, in just such a situation he may very well choose to work that miracle that will show his lordship through us in that area. The key is always to trust him, be available to him in any given situation, and consciously try to reflect his lordship when and where we can.

APPLICATION: Exercising our reflected lordship in Christ is further discussed in DAYS 43-49 – HE IS KING. As we "reign in life," we reflect his lordship over all aspects of our lives.

DAY 245
ªHE IS THE APOSTLE,
ᵇTHE SENT ONE

QUESTIONS TO THINK ABOUT:

1. What does it mean to be "sent" by someone?
2. What is the function of an ambassador?
3. As ambassadors for Christ, what should we be doing?

In Hebrews 3:1 we read, "... Fix your thought on Jesus, the apostle and high priest whom we confess." The word "apostle" comes from the Greek word *apostolos*, meaning "a delegate; specifically, an ambassador of the Gospel"; "messenger, one who is sent." An ambassador has one major responsibility: to represent his country and its interests in a foreign state. He reflects the character of his country and speaks on behalf of his government. He is his government's mouthpiece in a foreign land.

In such a way, God sent Christ into the world as his Ambassador of the kingdom of heaven. Representing the interests of that kingdom, Christ came with the message of peace and reconciliation to God (Jn.17:8,18,21,23,25; 20:21). He communicated to us the character of that kingdom (Rom.14:17) and spoke on its behalf with full authority. He could do that because he was always in constant communication with his Father (Jn.5:19,30; 6:38; 7:16; 8:28,38). He was truly the mouthpiece of the kingdom. He told Philip in John 14:9b, "Anyone who has seen me has seen the Father." It stands, then, that anyone who has heard him has also "heard the Father."

After his resurrection, Jesus told his disciples, "Peace be with you! As the Father has sent me, I am sending you" (Jn.20:21; see also 17:18). As Jesus was sent by the Father into this world to represent the kingdom of heaven, so he is sending us into this world to represent his kingdom. We, then, are not of this world, just as he is not of this world (Jn.17:16; Phil.3:20), but are ambassadors, representatives in this world of another world to which we belong.

To us has been given the message of peace and reconciliation (2 Cor.5:18-20). To us also has been given the responsibility of reflecting the character of the kingdom, as seen in Jesus Christ. So our chief occupation is two-fold: to preach the message of peace and reconciliation with God, and to reflect the character of Christ so as to persuade others to "change their nationality" and be conformed to his image. If we are doing this, then we are speaking heaven's message and can speak with full authority.

Many times on furlough we have said, "Anyone who tells someone else about Christ is a missionary." The only real difference between us is our geographical location. On one occasion we received a letter that began something like this: "Dear Fellow Workers for Christ. Now that's some way to begin a letter, for you are doing so much for the Lord and we are doing so little here." The first part of this statement is true. As Christians, we are all fellow workers in Christ because we are all ambassadors of the kingdom of heaven. The second part is purely relative to the individual, not his geography; for geography doesn't determine what we do for the Lord. But rather it is our attitude of heart and the seriousness with which we take our ambassadorial responsibilities wherever we are that makes the difference.

As others listen to us, do they hear the message of peace and reconciliation that we were sent to give? Do they see in us a true picture of our heavenly kingdom, or merely another reflection of their own "kingdom"? Are we, as heaven's ambassadors, being diligent about heaven's interests: the reconciliation of man to God and the revealing of the character of the kingdom, or are we leaving that to "more professional" ambassadors? One day all of us are going to be "recalled" to give an account of our ambassadorship. May we hear, "Well done!" from the lips of our King.

Do those around you know that you are an ambassador from heaven, or have you so adapted to the kingdom of this earth that they have no idea as to your true identity?

APPLICATION: Any good ambassador has to be well-versed in the affairs, attitudes and goals of his country so that he can represent those issues in the country to which he has been sent. He must also be well-versed in the needs of the country to which he has been sent so that the resources available in his home country might be applied to helping meet those needs. Just so, we must be well-versed in the details of our "handbook" so that we can represent our kingdom well to others and know what resources are available to help them in their need.

DAY 246
ᵇHE IS THE AMEN

◆

QUESTIONS TO THINK ABOUT:

1. What does the word "amen" mean?
2. What does it imply as applied to Christ?
3. What should it imply as applied to us?

In Revelation 3:14 Jesus claims for himself the title of "Amen, the faithful and true Witness." Along with our familiar usage of "amen" as "so be it," the Greek term, *amān*, also means "firmness, trustworthiness." Christ, as "The Amen," is firm and trustworthy in everything he says and does. It is as James says of the Father in James 1:17, "… with whom there is no variation, or shifting shadow." Our Lord is not wishy-washy, changing his mind at every turn, nor unfailing to keep his promises of judgment and blessing. What he says, we can be sure that he will do. Hebrews 13:8 declares that he "is the same yesterday and today and forever." He is totally consistent, which gives us great security in Christ as "The Amen."

As Christians, we generally have a real problem with this kind of credibility in our own lives. One cause is that we so often act before we think or consult the Lord about what we should do or say. Then we get backed into a corner and have to retract what we have said or try to come up with a good excuse; or adverse circumstances force us to change hastily-made plans, and we come out looking foolish, disorganized and perhaps dishonest (see ***NOTE** on the next page). What is worse, our inconsistencies often appear to be hypocrisy to outsiders, and this, as we have seen, drives people away from the Lord (see DAY 6 – HE IS THE WAY).

The cure for this problem is found in Romans 15:5,6: "Now may the God who gives perseverance and encouragement grant you to be

556 / *Unexpected Transformation*

of the same mind with one another <u>according to Christ Jesus</u>; that with one accord you may with one voice glorify the God and Father of our Lord Jesus Christ" (underlining mine). A knowledge of the truth enables us to be firm, consistent, and therefore trustworthy. Jesus Christ <u>is</u> the truth (Jn.14:6), as is his Word (Jn.17:17), and thereby becomes our standard for living and making decisions. Therefore, as you and I live according to the standard of Jesus Christ, we will be likeminded in all we do, and will thereby glorify God with one mind and one mouth. We get into trouble when we seek like-mindedness according to our own wisdom, philosophy of life, or experiences; for we all differ considerably in each of these areas. So it is imperative that our unifying standard be the Lord Jesus Christ himself, as only in him can we be certain of the truth and live consistently in our practice of it.

One further step is always to pray first before planning and acting, consciously seeking the Lord's help and direction. This is in fulfillment of Proverbs 3:5,6 and has God's promise of assistance: "Trust in the LORD with all your heart, and do not lean on your own understanding. In all your ways acknowledge him, and <u>he will make your paths straight</u>" (underlining mine).

When others comment about us, can they say, "Whatever he does is sure and trustworthy. He's as good as his word"? If so, then we have grown into this characteristic of Christ as "The Amen."

APPLICATION: Nowadays it seems like many people don't care whether or not they fulfill a promise. It just doesn't seem to matter to them that much. Christians should not be that way! They should be as good as their word. If, for any reason, they cannot fulfill a promise, they should let the persons involved know so that they're not "left hanging." The credibility of our witness hangs on others knowing that we are as good as our word. If not, how will they know that what we tell them about the Lord is true? So, always strive to keep your promises; and if you can't, do your best to let those involved know.

[*NOTE: We experienced this problem at times on the mission field. At our annual Field Conference one year, we'd make decisions based on the "leading" of one individual (for whatever reason) only to have to reverse that decision the following year. Or some missionaries with a special interest, push their agenda through the Conference floor without majority agreement, which backfires and has to be withdrawn the following Conference. At best, this was poor stewardship of our time and resources.]

DAY 247
ᶜHE IS THE ALPHA AND OMEGA, ᶜTHE FIRST AND THE LAST, ᶜTHE BEGINNING AND THE END

◆

QUESTIONS TO THINK ABOUT:

1. Why is it important to finish a job that we begin?
2. What is the significance of the saying, "The job begun is the job finished"?

In Revelation 1:8,17; 21:6 and 22:13, Christ declares that he is the alpha and omega, the first and the last, the beginning and the end. These three phrases are saying the same thing in three different ways: alpha and omega are the first and last letters of the Greek alphabet. Between them are all the other letters. Thus Christ is saying that he encompasses everything that is.

As the First and the Last, if there were a first, he would be it; if there were a last, that would be him. In other words, if there was a beginning, he would precede it; if there were an end, he would outlast it! Nothing could come before him, nor could anything come after him. As the First, he has primal authority; and as the Last, ultimate authority.

As the Beginning and the End, we see Christ as the originator and concluder of all things. The Greek word for "beginning" is *arche* which denotes "the person or thing that commences something; the first person or thing in a series, the leader" (Thayer, p.77. This and following definitions are not exact quotes, but compilations of the information found there. The same follows for the Thayer footnote that follows). In Revelation 3:14 he calls himself, "the beginning (chief) of the creation of God," or "that by which anything begins to be, the origin or active cause of something." As the Apostle John wrote: "Through him all things were made; without him nothing was made that has been made" (Jn.1:3).

The Greek word for "end" is *telos*: "so set out for a definite point or goal; the point aimed at as the limit; the conclusion of an act of state; the last in any succession or series" (Thayer, pp.619,620). Thus when Christ declares himself to be the "end," he is stating that everything in the universe is targeted toward and will ultimately be wrapped up in him (see Eph.1:10).

How do we reflect Christ as the Alpha and Omega, the First and the Last, the Beginning and the End? A common thread that suggests itself in these three titles is, "The job begun is the job finished."

For example, Christ came to earth to secure man's redemption. What he began with his birth, he finished with his death (and resurrection). On the cross he cried out, "It is finished!" Man's redemption was now provided for with nothing lacking.

Paul stated his confidence in God's completing what he has begun: "Being confident of this, that he who began a good work in you will carry it on to completion until the day of Christ Jesus" (Phil.1:6).

Paul says of his own ministry: "I have fought the good fight, I have finished the race, I have kept the faith. Now there is in store for me the crown of righteousness, which the Lord, the righteous Judge, will award to me on that day – and not only to me, but also to all who have longed for his appearing" (2 Tim.4:7,8).

When given a job to do, do we stick with it until it is finished? Frequently I find that when a job I'm doing is almost done, I have the strongest urge to quit at that point. It is a real effort to force myself to continue on until it is finished. But the Lord always finishes his work and expects us to do the same.

Do you finish what you begin? Or is your life a strung-out series of unfinished projects?

APPLICATION: We need motivation to finish a job. Sometimes it's wages; sometimes it's the praise of others as they look at what we've done; sometimes it's just because we want to please someone; but other times (and this is the most difficult), it's just something we want to do for our own benefit, and that's where we can quickly lose our enthusiasm if our motivation is no more than, "I'd like to do that." So, before you consider doing a job or project, ask yourself what your motivation is, and if the job is worth finishing or not. If the motivation is uncertain, and, in the end, it may not be worth finishing, then don't start it.

DAY 248
ᶜHE IS THE MIRACLE-WORKER

QUESTIONS TO THINK ABOUT:

1. Why were spiritual gifts given to the Church?
2. Why is it that some of the gifts no longer seem to be functional today?

3. So why would the Holy Spirit withdraw some of the gifts he gave the Church? (cf. Rom.11:29)

In John 2:3-11 we find recorded the first of many miracles that Christ performed turning water into wine at the wedding in Cana. Nicodemus was convinced that Jesus was a teacher come from God because of the many signs he performed (Jn.3:2). When John the Baptist's disciples came to Jesus bearing the question as to whether Jesus was really the Messiah or not, he answered them, saying, "Go back and report to John what you have seen and heard: The blind receive sight, the lame walk, those who have leprosy are cured, the deaf hear, the dead are raised, and the good news is preached to the poor" (Lk.7:22).

When Jesus sent the 70 out to preach, he gave them power to heal the sick and cast out demons as confirmation of the message they proclaimed (Lk.10:9,17). After Pentecost, the apostles wrought many miracles, empowered by the Holy Spirit – miracles which not only met the needs of people, but authenticated the apostles as God's messengers bringing glory to the Lord (Acts 3:8; 5:12-14). When the Holy Spirit came, he gave gifts to the Church, which, if exercised, would bring benefit and blessing to all (1 Cor.12:7). Not everyone received the same gifts, but these were given to each one individually according to the Holy Spirit's will (vs.11). Among these gifts were the working of miracles and gifts of healings (vs.9,10).

But in the course of time, these gifts disappeared along with others for many reasons, like, "This disappearance of gifts always occurs when God's Spirit is grieved and thus ceases to work." It is not unlike the plethora of books we see on the market today dealing with one problem after another: How To (this) and How To (that), when most of those problems could be resolved through simple obedience to the Scriptures! Every explanation is offered on resolving them except obeying the Word!

Another reason offered is: "As the Church gradually became more aligned with the world, the Spirit was grieved and ceased working as in earlier days." This should have caught the attention of the Church; but instead, they turned more and more to the world and less and less to Christ to meet their needs. What gifts remained were tainted, if not corrupted, and were largely, if used, carried on in the power of the flesh rather than in the power of the Spirit. This situation resulted in a dichotomy of the gifts that we see nowhere in Scripture, i.e. "ordinary" gifts and "sign" gifts, the latter considered as "especially empowered" by the Holy Spirit, and the former not so much. But any gift of the Spirit is useless unless exercised in his power. The fact that the Church is generally ignorant of the spiritual gifts today is no proof that they are no longer valid or that the Lord has thrown them out. They were <u>all</u> given for the edification and building up of the Church. We are the same as they were then, and need just as much help from one another in encouragement, teaching and meeting of our needs.

APPLICATION: The Lord has given each of us spiritual gifts to use in the building up of his Church. He expects us to use them! Do you know what yours is, and are you using it? (See APPENDIX III for Identifying Your Spiritual Gift).

DAY 249
ᶜHE IS THE MIRACLE-WORKER, cont.

QUESTIONS TO THINK ABOUT:

1. If some of the spiritual gifts ceased, when does Scripture say they did?

2. Paul speaks of the cessation of some of the gifts "when that which is perfect has come" (1 Cor.13:10). Which gifts are those, and to what time is he referring?

3. What are the uses of those gifts and why would they cease "when the perfect has come"?

Permit me to suggest an example of why I believe all the gifts are still valid for today. Take healing, for example. When we went to the Citak (CHEE-tuck) people in Senggo (Papua), there were less than a handful of believers. We went in with medicine to treat their illnesses and to demonstrate our love for them. Now after a time many believed in Christ, and they were sure of our love and concern for them. So we then said, "O.K. You're believers now in Christ, and you know that we love you, so we're not going to give you any more medicine." ... So when the Church reached a certain point in its history, the Lord said, "O.K. My revelation to you is complete and now authenticated, so you don't need these gifts of healing anymore." How do you respond to this statement? Does this attitude jar you as it does me? Apart from the gift of Apostleship (the Twelve plus the Apostle Paul), I don't see in Scripture where any of the other gifts are said to be temporary. Paul's teaching about the gifts in 1 Corinthians was to an ongoing church, and the whole tenor of his teaching was, "These gifts are important for ministering to each other."

Some have said that, based on 1 Corinthians 13:8-12, the "sign" gifts are no longer valid because the canon of Scripture is now completed ("when perfection comes, the imperfect disappears"). This is an assumption that I find very difficult to accept for the context itself does not allow for it. Let's test it. Verses 8-13: "Love never fails. But where there are prophecies [communication from God to man], they will cease; where there are tongues [communication from man's spirit to God], they will be stilled; where there is knowledge [the knowing of certain things only through the power of the Spirit], it will pass away. For we know in part and we prophesy in part, but when perfection

Unexpected Transformation / 563

comes [?], the imperfect disappears. When I was a child, I talked like a child, I thought like a child, I reasoned like a child. When I became a man, I put childish ways behind me. Now we see but a poor reflection as in a mirror; then [when?] we shall see face to face. Now I know in part; then [when?] I shall know fully, even as I am fully known."

Now "when the perfection comes," we will know ourselves fully even as we are known, and we will see face to face. Commentators write that this is a description of our glorification before the throne of God. But others say, "No, this occurred at the completion of the canon of Scripture." O.K. We have the entire Bible in our hands. Let's test that assumption. Do you know yourself as God knows you? Hardly. Many times I wonder why I did that stupid thing – I can't understand why I reacted in that way. Jeremiah 17:9 says that man's "heart is deceitful above all things and beyond cure. Who can understand it?" With God's completed Word, I know more about my heart than perhaps the Old Testament saints did, but I still can't fully understand it. Test two: "Then we will see face to face." Have we seen God face to face yet? No. So that view fails the test also. The gifts mentioned here are communication gifts between God and man. As long as we are on earth and God in heaven (spatially speaking), there is the need for communication. But once we are in heaven before the throne of God, such communication gifts as we had need of here on earth are no longer necessary, for we will speak face to face with the Lord. The difference between our earthly and heavenly lives is likened to that of a child becoming an adult. Once adulthood [heaven] is reached, there is no further need for childish [earthly] things.

APPLICATION: Following the rules of hermeneutics (interpretation of Scripture), we must let the Scriptures interpret themselves and be careful not to reinterpret them in terms of what we see or don't see around us. What we see is always changing; the Scriptures don't change. Since they don't seem to declare the cessation of the spiritual gifts during the Church Age, then we are amiss to say that they have ceased based on what we see around us. Just because they don't seem to be operating here in the United States doesn't mean that they are not operating elsewhere (in fact, they are!). So the question we need to ask is, "Why are these gifts not operating here in the States as they are elsewhere? Noting the general apathy and materialism of the Church, lack of teaching about and therefore the ignorance of what the spiritual gifts are and the tendency to deny the relevance of a group of them, the answer may not be that difficult to find!

DAY 250
ᶜHE IS THE MIRACLE-WORKER, cont.

QUESTIONS TO THINK ABOUT:

1. How are we to exercise our spiritual gifts?
2. Why is it not possible to rightly exercise them at our own whim?
3. How much of the Holy Spirit do we possess at salvation? What does that mean, potentially, for the use of our spiritual gifts?

Assuming then, from yesterday's discussion, that all the gifts are still valid for today, what can we say about the gift of miracles? There are at least two principles that I see in Scripture regarding this gift.

PRINCIPLE #1: <u>God must direct it and empower the worker by his Holy Spirit</u>. It is clear in Scripture that miracles cannot be performed at our own whim. Even the Lord Jesus didn't work miracles except as he was empowered by the Spirit of God and at the direction of the Father! (Matt.12:28; Jn.14:10,31. See also Exod.7:5 where it is emphasized that the LORD did the miracle, not Moses; Lk.5:17; Acts 19:11 and Gal.3:5.) Nicodemus and John the Baptist both recognized this truth:

"For no one could perform the miraculous signs you are doing if God were not with him" (Jn.3:2); "A man can receive only what is given him from heaven… . For the one whom God has sent speaks the words of God, for God gives the Spirit without limit" (Jn.3:34). "The Father loves the Son and has placed everything in his hands" (Jn.3:35).

According to verse 34 above, when God gives the Spirit to anyone, he gives him without limitations. When we are saved and receive the gift of the Holy Spirit, we don't receive just one-third of him, or one-half of him, but 100 per cent of him! The only difference between the Lord Jesus and us is that Jesus was sinless and therefore had nothing in his life to hinder the full flow of the Spirit's power. Sin grieves the Spirit and limits his power in our lives. The more godly we become, the more the power of the Spirit will be evidenced in us because the less hindrance of sin will be there. So any miracles performed must be done as directed by God and empowered by the Holy Spirit. This necessitates that the human channel through whom God desires to work must be in close fellowship with him so that he can be sensitive to God's leading in any given situation.

But why miracles at all? What is their purpose? Some say that "their only purpose was to authenticate God's message and his messenger. Therefore there's no more need for miracles today since we have the full body of revelation in the Scriptures." The first statement is partly true, but incomplete. But the second is Scripturally unfounded. To be sure, Moses, Elijah, Elisha, Jesus Christ and the Apostles were all authenticated as prophets and messengers of God by the miracles they performed. But there were many more prophets who weren't. Their only "authentication" came, not through miracles, but only as their prophecies were fulfilled, sometimes not for hundreds of years after they were made (see Joel 2 as an example – see ***NOTE** below).

The Scriptures themselves give us many more purposes for the working of miracles than just the authentication of God's message and messenger. On DAY 251 we will consider them in brief detail.

APPLICATION: Regardless of our spiritual gifts, the bottom line in exercising them is that we are to be pure vessels in God's hands for him to use however he will. Unconfessed or purposeful sin in our lives will grieve God's Spirit and hinder if not block entirely the expression of our spiritual gifts in his service.

[***NOTE:** Other means of authentication: 1. the irrefutable evidence of a changed life (2 Cor.5:17); 2. applied Scripture works (2 Tim.3:16,17); 3. fulfilled prophecy (Matt.1:22; Acts 3:18); 4. the life of Christ himself (Jn.8:46); 5. boldness of Christians in the face of opposition (Acts 4:29-31); 6. good works (Matt.5:14-16); and 7. love for and unity with fellow believers (Jn.13:35; 17:21).]

DAY 251
ᶜHE IS THE MIRACLE-WORKER, cont.

QUESTIONS TO THINK ABOUT:

1. What other purposes for miracles, other than authentication of God's message and messengers, can you think of?
2. What would be the overall impact on the witness of the Church if the gift of miracles was deleted from the list of gifts given to it?

There are at least twelve Scriptural purposes for miracles:

1. For the glory of God, revealing his character (Jn.9:3); to fulfill his promises (Exod.15:13-17); to show his wrath in judgment (Matt.8:28-34); and to convince men that he is the LORD (Exod.7:5).

2. To show forth Christ's glory (Jn.2:11), demonstrating his characteristics of mercy and compassion in meeting the needs of

others (Matt.9:27,36; 14:15-20); to show that he is a Rewarder of those who seek him (Matt.9:29); and that he has power over nature (Mk.6:48-51) and death (Jn.11:43,44).

3. To fulfill prophecy (Matt.8:16,17).

4. To provide a situation or opportunity to teach spiritual truth: regarding faith and the kingdom of heaven (Matt.8:10-13); to strengthen another's faith (Mk.5:33-36); as a warning against false doctrine (Mk.8:1-21); and as a parable of Israel's immediate future, but more immediately to encourage faith among his disciples (Matt.21:18-22).

5. To restore others to service. Peter's mother-in-law (Matt. 8:14,15); Peter (Jn.21:6,15-19) and Paul (Acts 9:18).

6. To call someone to service. Moses saw the burning bush that was not consumed (Exod.3:2-10), and God called him from the bush to deliver his people from Egypt; Peter, Andrew, James and John were astounded at their catch of fish at Jesus' command (Lk.5:4-11) and responded to his invitation to "catch men" from then on.

7. To save someone from danger. The parting of the Red Sea so that Israel could escape the Egyptian army (Exod.14:21,22,27,30); the calming of the sea which threatened the lives of the disciples (Lk.8:23,24); the release of the apostles from jail (Acts 5:18,19,23), and Peter also (Acts 12:1-11).

8. The separation of believers from unbelievers (Lk.11:14-16). Those who believed marveled; those who didn't blasphemed and tested the Lord. The sides were very clearly marked by their reactions.

9. Just to meet a need (2 Kgs.6:6). One of the student prophets had borrowed an ax. The ax head fell off into the water causing the

student much anxiety. Elisha caused the ax head to float, restoring it to the student so that he could return it to its owner.

10. To authenticate the messenger (Exod.4:1-9,30,31; Jn.6:14; Acts 8:6,7): Moses (Exod.14:31), Elijah (1 Kgs.17: 24), Elisha (2 Kgs.2:14,15), Christ (Acts 19:17; Matt.9:2-8; Mk.1:27) and the Apostles (Acts 5:12,13).

11. To authenticate the message preached (Mk.6:12,13; Acts 14:3): to gain people's attention (Matt.9:8,34,35; Acts 3:9-11) so that they would hear the message (Acts 3:12ff); to eliminate hindrances to the Gospel (Acts 16:17,18); to inspire faith (2 Kgs.5:15; Exod.14:31; Jn.2:11; Acts 5:14); and to convince men that they are sinners (Jn.15:24).

12. To prove to Jewish believers that God had accepted the Gentiles (Acts 15:12).

APPLICATION: Where we don't look for miracles every day, don't be surprised when the Lord works one when the need is there.

DAY 252
ᶜHE IS THE MIRACLE-WORKER, concl.

◆

QUESTIONS TO THINK ABOUT:

1. What is the context in which we can expect miracles to occur?
2. How can the "miraculous" be seen in every-day ministry?

From the above twelve purposes for miracles, emerges PRINCIPLE #2: Miracles must be done in the context of ministry to others with the intent of glorifying God through the teaching of spiritual truth and in giving a witness to the unsaved. If the messenger is glorified, the message is lost (cf. Acts 14:7-18).

Returning to the statement of some that, because of the completed Word of God, miracles are no longer needed today as authentication of its truth, there is a problem this statement ignores: the vast majority of the world's population is ignorant of God's Word and the Gospel message. How are they to know that our God is <u>the</u> God, the Almighty Creator of the universe and Savior of all who call upon him? How are they to be convinced that he is greater and more powerful than their gods and the spirits they worship? In many cases, sooner or later, there must be a power confrontation where God's power is shown to be greater than Satan's. This power confrontation will often include a miracle, some kind of supernatural manifestation.

When I was a child, I heard a story about a missionary couple trying to reach a jungle tribe with the Gospel. For some reason, they were in mortal danger. One night the angry chief and his warriors surrounded their house, planning to kill them. The missionaries, aware of their danger, spent the night in prayer until the warriors left. When morning came, the chief, seeing just the two of them about, came to the house asking, "Where are all those men who were with you last night?" "There wasn't anyone with us," replied the missionary. "We were alone in the house praying." "No," said the chief, "we came to kill you, but your house was surrounded by men dressed in white holding spears, and we were afraid of them." Then the missionary couple realized that God had sent his angels to protect them. When they shared this fact with the chief, he was convinced that the Lord's power was greater than anything he had ever seen. Soon he and his entire village came to know the Lord.

As I look over the American scene, I am increasingly aware of the fact that the vast majority of Americans are ignorant of the Bible. In fact, many people attending evangelical churches and claiming to know the Lord are functionally illiterate in the Scriptures, being content to be "fed" each Sunday and leave it at that. Thus America is becoming a heathen land in which God's message once again must be authenticated. The use of miracles is one of several means to do that (see below for others). Also in the Church there is room for miracles in the edification and strengthening of Believers (cf. Acts 9:36-42; 1 Cor.12:7-10).

But the overriding PRINCIPLE #3 in the use of miracles is found in Colossians 3:17, "<u>And whatever you do, whether in word or deed, do it all in the name of the Lord Jesus, giving thanks to God the Father through him</u>" (underlining mine). Is there room in your Christian life for the miraculous?

APPLICATION: Most of the time, the miraculous will be seen in the little things we do: "Where did that thought come from?" "I didn't know the answer to that question. How could I answer it the way I did?" "I've read that passage a thousand times and never could figure it out. This time it was as clear as could be!" But once in a while the miraculous will be something big, an unusual answer to prayer, being healed from a severe illness or injury, some impossible situation "just working out," and whatever else the Lord might have for that particular situation. It's his call; just be ready for it!

DAY 253
aHE IS ONE WITH THE FATHER

QUESTIONS TO THINK ABOUT:

1. How is it possible for us to be one with the Father?
2. Why is that important in our daily lives and witness?
3. How can we be "one" with other believers with whom we disagree?

In John 10:30 Jesus claimed: "I and the Father are one," at which the Jews took up stones to stone him for blasphemy (vs.33) "because you, a mere man, claim to be God." Jesus Christ was one with his Father in spirit, in purpose and in will. In spirit, he was of the same nature and essence as God, equal with him in power and glory (see Jn.1:1-4,14). That is why he could say to Philip in John 14:9, "Anyone who has seen me has seen the Father."

Christ also was <u>one in purpose</u> with the Father. Whatever the Father does, the Son does (Jn.5:19,20); he speaks what he has seen with his Father (Jn.8:38); and he felt compelled to "… do the work of him who sent me" (Jn.9:4). The Father did his work through the Son, and the Son always did what pleased the Father.

And he was <u>one in will</u> with the Father, always seeking to do the Father's will (Jn.5:30). And in John 4:34 he told his disciples, "My food … is to do the will of him who sent me and to finish his work." That this was done is recorded for us in John 19:30 where Jesus cried out on the cross, "It is finished!" (see also Jn.17:4).

More than anything else, Christ wanted his followers to enter that same oneness that he enjoyed with the Father. In John 17:11, he prayed "that they may be one as we are one." And again in vs.20-23 regarding all who would believe in him through their word, "… that all of them may be one, Father, just as you are in me and I am in you. May they also be in us… . I have given them the glory that you gave me, that they may be one as we are one: I in them and you in me. May they be brought to complete unity… ."

Amos asks the question, "Do two walk together unless they have agreed to do so?" (Amos 3:3). The answer to this rhetorical question is, "No." If we are to walk together we must be <u>agreed in spirit</u>, desiring each other's company; <u>agreed in purpose</u>, to go for a walk; and <u>agreed in will</u>, choosing to go in the same direction. It has struck me that if we are indeed one in spirit, as Christ is with the Father, that that would preclude any differences in purpose and will. Yet among Christians, who have the same Spirit, there are so many differences. Why is this? I believe the answer lies in our different backgrounds and experiences. Christ and the Father are of identical background and experience, therefore are one in purpose and will. Each of us bring differing backgrounds and experiences into our salvation which influence our interpretation and practice of Scripture. So where we are one in spirit (enjoying one another's fellowship) and purpose (desiring to do the Lord's work), we can differ greatly in will about how to accomplish that purpose (heading in opposite directions). So we part ways, unable to "walk" together, for we are not agreed. But I see here the wisdom of God and the foolishness of man. In our foolishness, we say, "Since we cannot walk together with Christian so-and-so, we are right and he is wrong." Yet God, in his wisdom, has ordained us to reach and minister to one group of people, and our "rejected" fellow believer to reach and minister to another group that we, by our background, could not reach. Thus the function of the Body continues, each member performing its own work. So let us who are the fingers take care that we do not falsely judge those who are the toes! Let us rejoice that the Lord's work is being accomplished by a variety of ways and determine to be faithful to Him in ours.

APPLICATION: I recall an illustration of the relationship between a husband and wife and God – a triangle. The closer the husband and wife become to God (moving up the triangle), the closer they come to one another. I believe it is the same between us and other Christians. The closer we all come to God, the closer we will become to one another. We may differ in methodology and some secondary doctrinal issues which make it difficult to work together, but we can enjoy closer fellowship on a personal level because of our common faith and desire to know God better. In this way, we can more and more reflect the oneness that we have with God.

DAY 254
ᵃHE IS ONE WITH THE FATHER, cont.

QUESTIONS TO THINK ABOUT:

1. How can we be men and women after God's own heart?
2. What will that mean in our fellowship with one another?
3. What is the guarantee that we will have fellowship with one another?

Paul strikes at this issue of oneness from another angle in 2 Corinthians 6:14-18 where he exhorts the believers: "Do not be yoked together with unbelievers. For what do righteousness and wickedness have in common? What harmony [oneness in spirit] is there between Christ and Belial? What does a believer have in common [oneness in purpose] with an unbeliever? What agreement [oneness in will] is there between the temple of God and idols? For we are the temple of the living God... . Therefore [since there is no oneness at any level] come out from them and be separate ... and I will receive you. I will be a Father to you, and you will be my sons and daughters."

Now Jesus prayed that we would be one with him and with the Father. Obviously we cannot be one with him in essence, but we can be one with him in spirit (and character). Through his indwelling Spirit, we become one in spirit, and as we become more and more like Christ, we become one in character. Even as Peter writes in 2 Peter 1:3,4, "His divine power has given us everything we need for life and godliness through our knowledge of him who called us by his own glory and goodness. Through these he has given us his very great and precious promises, so that through them you may participate in the divine nature... ." The writer of Hebrews states that God chastens us "for our good, that we may share in his holiness" (Heb.12:10b). David was one in spirit with the Lord, being described as "a man after my own heart; he will do everything I want him to" (Acts 13:22). Caleb was described by the Lord as "my servant [who] has a different spirit and follows me wholeheartedly" (Num.14:24). "Delight yourself in the LORD and he will give you the desires of your heart" (Ps.37:4). The Lord desires us to be one in spirit with him, and if we are one in spirit with him, we'll be one in spirit with one another.

We read in Philippians 2:13 that God sovereignly works in our lives in order to accomplish oneness with him in purpose and will: "For it is God who works in you to will and to act according to his good purpose." In Ephesians 2:10 we read that "we are God's workmanship, created in Christ Jesus to do good works, which God prepared in advance for us to do." As the Father sent the Son into the world, so the Son has sent us into it; and as the Son only did the works he saw the Father doing, so we should only be doing the works we see the Son doing (Jn.20:21; 1 Jn.2:6). This demands diligence on our part: in the Word to see what kind of works Jesus did, and in the Spirit, to be sensitive to his promptings when to act and when not to. If we are doing what the Lord Jesus is doing, then we'll be walking in the light. And 1 John 1:7 says that "… if we walk in the light, as he is in the light, we have fellowship with one another … ."

In John 7:16,17 Jesus said, "My teaching is not my own. It comes from him who sent me. If anyone chooses to do God's will [going in the direction in which he is going], he will find out whether my teaching comes from God or whether I speak on my own." The Lord Jesus has promised that if we want to do God's will, we will not be led astray by false doctrine, people speaking on their own authority, but will know the truth. And if we are walking in the same direction as God, and that we can plainly know from his Word, then we will be in oneness with him and with one another.

Are you one with the Lord in spirit, purpose and will?

APPLICATION: In The Tales of Narnia, when Shasta asked Aslan why he wounded Aravis, he replied, "Child, I am telling you your story, not hers. I tell no one any story but his own" (Lewis, p.139). And that should be our focus as well – to be sure that we are doing what the Lord wants, and not be worrying about others. They have to live their story – we ours. And all of us will have to give account to him on how we lived it. But, in the meantime, let us be sure that we are growing in oneness with the Lord in spirit, purpose and will.

DAY 255
[a]HE IS ONE WITH THE FATHER, concl.

QUESTIONS TO THINK ABOUT:

1. Why is oneness with the Lord and with one another important?
2. What role does *agape* love play in our oneness with one another?
3. Why is it important to God that we be made in the likeness of his Son?

Why is oneness with the Father and with one another so important? I find at least three reasons mentioned in Scripture. The first is that God takes pleasure in our fellowship and obedience and singleness of heart and purpose with him. In Revelation 4:11 we read, "You are worthy, our Lord and God, to receive glory and honor and power, for you created all things, and by your will they were created and have their being." God made us and all creation for his pleasure, his pleasure in fellowship and his pleasure in work (see Phil.2:13). He had perfect fellowship with Adam and Eve and desires the same with us: "The LORD delights in those who fear him, who put their hope in his unfailing love" (Ps.147:11). That is why making us into the image of Jesus Christ is so important to him.

The second reason is found in Christ's prayer in John 17:21,23: "... That the world may believe that you have sent me... . To let the world know that you sent me" (underlining mine). Our invisible unity with the Lord and our visible unity with other believers is intended to be a witness to the world, proof that God indeed did send Christ into the world. Some have said that church splits and schisms are good and necessary, for by this means pure doctrine has been preserved. In some cases, yes; but in most cases, no. The majority of church splits occur over personality clashes, personal preferences, administrative conflict, and lack of church discipline (allowing sin to go on unchecked). When churches split because two families can't get along, or because the church kitchen was painted the wrong color, or because someone came into the service wearing jeans instead of suit and tie, or because of who knows what else, the Church becomes a target of laughs and derision in the community, not a witness. And you hear: "If that's Christianity, I don't want any part of it!" Frankly, neither would I!

The third reason why oneness with the Father is so important is found in John 17:23b, "To let the world know that you ... have loved them [believers] even as you have loved me" (underlining mine). This love is *agape* love, the love of choice, the same love mentioned in John 3:16 that God has for the world. As the world sees this kind of love in operation among believers, and the oneness there in spite of great diversity, they will have to acknowledge that a greater Power than man has achieved that. "By this all men will know that you are my disciples, if you love [*agape*] one another" (Jn.13:35). They will say, "Then if Christians, for all their weaknesses and differences, can love one another and be loved by God with this kind of love, so can we!" And many will be drawn to him. Then they will also realize that this is the same kind of love that is shared in the Godhead: love for whom the person is rather than being based on what he has or has not done or what he looks like, etc.

Unexpected Transformation / 577

David sums it up for us in Psalm 133:1,3b, saying, "How good and pleasant it is when brothers live together in unity! ... For there the LORD bestows his blessing, even life forevermore."

Are you one with the Father and with your fellow believers?

APPLICATION: As love [*agape*] covers a multitude of sins (Prov.10:12), so it becomes the "cement" that binds us together (Col.3:14), making us one. Let us seek to excel in showing *agape* love to one another (see DAYS 78,79 – HE IS THE LOVING ONE).

DAY 256
ᵇHE IS THE OVERSEER (BISHOP OF OUR SOULS)

QUESTIONS TO THINK ABOUT:

1. What does it mean to oversee something?
2. How are we overseers in the church and in our families?

In 1 Peter 2:25 we read, "For you were like sheep going astray, but now you have returned to the Shepherd and Overseer of your souls." The word "overseer" comes from the Greek *episkopos* (*piskop* = bishop), lit. "an overseer, one who is appointed to watch over the interests of the Church." Lockyer translates Peter's description of Christ here as "the great Guardian and Superintendent of His Church" (Lockyer, p.246). The Lord jealously guards and watches over his own. In his prayer in John 17:12a he says, "While I was with them, I protected them and kept them safe by that name you gave me." We read in 1 Peter 3:12, "For the eyes of the Lord are on the righteous and his ears are attentive to their prayer...." And again in 2 Chronicles 16:9, "For the eyes of the LORD range throughout the earth to strengthen those whose hearts are fully committed to him." In the end of time, the Lord Jesus will surrender everything over which he has had oversight to the Father, giving an account to him of his oversight. First Corinthians 15:24 says, "Then the end will come, when he hands over the kingdom to God the Father after he has destroyed all dominion, authority and power."

In Hebrews 13:7,17 we see that church leaders have a similar role: "Remember your leaders who spoke the word of God to you. Consider the outcome of their way of life and imitate their faith ...Obey your leaders and submit to their authority. They keep watch over you as men who must give an account. Obey them so that their work will be a joy, not a burden, for that would be of no advantage to you." Just as the welfare of the Church Universal is in the hands of the Lord, so the welfare of the Church Local is in the hands of its leaders. The assumption here is that their character reflects that of the Lord Jesus (see 1 Tim.3:1-7): blameless. Men of such character we can emulate in faith and conduct, we can obey them and submit to them with full confidence that they will lead us in the way of truth. Thus if we become rebellious, they will still have to give an account of their oversight to the Lord, but it will be with grief, not with joy; and we will be the losers.

When we were in Senggo, I had oversight of ten young men who were in my church leaders' training class. Upon returning from a village visitation, one of them commented, "You know, what I enjoy the most is visiting these villages and telling them about Jesus." If I had to give an account for these men right now, it would be with joy. And that would be profitable for them because it means that they would receive the reward for faithful service. But we too must be faithful in providing the kind of examples that can be followed and that kind of faith that brings positive results, and at the same time attending to the spiritual needs of those under our oversight, providing every opportunity for them to grow in their Christian lives and service for the Lord.

How is your oversight?

APPLICATION: Apart from any administrative aspects of oversight, there are two other aspects that are of utmost importance: discipling those under us in Christian growth and service and being a godly example for them to follow. If we're not doing the latter two well, then the first will end up looking no more than just an organized religion."

DAY 257
ᶜHE IS THE HORN OF DAVID

QUESTIONS TO THINK ABOUT:

1. What is the significance of a horn politically and militarily?
2. What does a horn symbolize?

We read in Psalm 132:17, "Here I will make a horn grow for David and set up a lamp for my anointed one." In this verse, the "horn ... for David" refers to the coming Messiah and subsequent government. The strength of a bull is in its horns, as is the strength of a stag. Thus "horn" came to mean power and strength for whatever it was applied to. In this case, the Messiah will embody all the power granted to David's family in order to rule the people fully and effectively. In the verse above, God promised to increase David's power, making it grow. In Daniel 2:34,35 we see another image of the same promise, a stone cut out of the mountain became a great mountain (the Messiah's kingdom) and filled the whole earth (see also Ezek.29:21).

In Acts 1:8a Jesus told his disciples, "But you will receive power when the Holy Spirit comes on you; and you will be my witnesses." And indeed they did receive power. On the Day of Pentecost about

3,000 souls were saved. The Apostles wrought miracles which provided further witnessing opportunities (Acts 3). Their defense before the religious authorities was with power that they otherwise would not have had (Acts 4:8,13), and their boldness and power in their witness was indisputable (Acts 4:31,33).

Part of Paul's prayer for the Ephesian Christians was that they might know what is "his incomparably great power for us who believe. That power is like the working of his mighty strength, which he exerted in Christ when he raised him from the dead and seated him at his right hand in the heavenly realms" (Eph.1:19,20). How is this power released in our lives? I picture God's power as a huge dam, holding back the waters of the Holy Spirit. Below are the three floodgates of prayer (Jas.5:16b), the Word (Isa.55:11) and meditation (Josh.1:8), opening into the channel of our lives. The degree to which we open those floodgates measures the degree of obedience in our lives and directly affects the measure of power that will flow through our "channel" to others. Each of the above verses promise us results if the respective floodgates are opened. But there is another factor to consider as well. A channel cluttered with debris and clogged with mud is useless. We need confession and repentance (turning away from sin) in order to keep the channel clean (1 Jn.1:7,9) so that the power of the Holy Spirit can freely flow through us in ever-increasing volume. The song "Channels Only" reflects this picture. The fourth verse and refrain reads: "Jesus, fill now with Thy Spirit/ Hearts that full surrender know;/ That the streams of living water/ From our inner man may flow./ Channels only, blessed Master,/ But with all Thy wondrous power/ Flowing through us/ Thou canst use us/ Every day and every hour." (<u>Living Hymns</u>, Alfred B. Smith, Mus. Doc., Encore Publications, Inc., 1984, p.477.) May God's power in our lives continually grow!

How wide are your floodgates opened? How clear is your "channel"?

APPLICATION: We will only know the power (horn) of God in our lives as we surrender to him and keep our channels clear of debris. Psalm 66:18 is a clear warning to us in this regard: "If I had cherished sin in my heart, the Lord would not have listened." Also, we read in Leviticus 11:44, "… consecrate yourselves and be holy, because I am holy." What rings clear in my mind is the word the Lord spoke to me in my heart one day as I lay sick with malaria and unable to fulfill my ministry responsibilities: "My child, my servants must be holy, but you are not holy because you are holding onto [this sin]. As long as you do, you cannot serve me!" We need to keep short accounts with him and keep our channels clean. Only then will we see his power flowing through us to the blessing of others.

DAY 258
ᶜHE IS OUR PASSOVER

QUESTIONS TO THINK ABOUT:

1. What was the significance of the Passover in Jewish history?
2. Why did they have to make their bread without leaven (yeast)?
3. What did leaven come to signify for them and for us?

In 1 Corinthians 5:7 Paul writes, "Get rid of the old yeast that you may be a new batch without yeast – as you really are [as the result of the following fact]. For Christ, our Passover lamb, has been sacrificed." For the Jewish Christians, this title would have immediate significance. Their minds would immediately go back about 1,500 years to that first Passover, the night before Israel came out of Egypt. Unleavened bread (bread without yeast) was baked and eaten (no time to wait for it to rise). A lamb without blemish, one for each household, was slain, its blood applied to the lintel and two doorposts of the house, its flesh eaten after being roasted.

The New Testament takes this event and applies it to Christ (as it was intended to be). In John 1:29 John the Baptist introduced him as the Lamb of God who takes away the sin of the world; he takes away that which demands God's righteous judgment. In 1 Peter 1:19 Christ is described as a lamb without blemish or spot (cf. Exod.12:5). In John 12:24,27, Christ revealed to his disciples that he must die (cf. Exod.12:6). And in Hebrews 9:22, we see that his blood had to be applied for the purpose for which it was shed (see Exod.12:7). The sacrificial blood applied meant deliverance from death. Israel and all believing Egyptians were spared. Elsewhere, the firstborn of every household died.

Israel was a redeemed and delivered people, special to God, holy, set apart from all other nations on earth. That is why Paul says to get rid of the old yeast (yeast or leaven in Scripture symbolizes sin – here our old way of life) that we may become in practice a new batch of dough (since our position is that of a new batch already – all this resulting from the sacrifice of our Passover Lamb).

As a result of Christ's sacrifice, we are passed over if we apply his blood to the "lintel and doorposts" of our hearts. Every house had its own lamb. Each of us must make his own decision to receive Jesus Christ as our Passover Lamb, our Savior, or to reject him. Having received him, we have become without yeast (unleavened), pure (see Heb.10:14), a new batch (see 2 Cor.5:17).

We cannot die to bring salvation to others as Christ did, but we can be living sacrifices in our service to God as we die to ourselves each day (see Mk.8:34,35 and 1 Cor.15:31). When our lives and witness prove the effectiveness of Christ as our Passover Lamb, others will, in effect, join our household, applying the blood to their hearts, and thus escape sure judgment.

As the lamb was without blemish, so our lives also must be holy, without blemish. That this is possible is indicated in 1 Timothy 3:1-7 where we find the qualifications for a church leader listed, among which are being blameless and having a good testimony before those outside the church.

Would you qualify as a Passover Lamb?

APPLICATION: Just as the Passover lamb had to be without blemish and whose blood guaranteed the life of the firstborn, so we must live sacrificial lives of integrity before others so that there would be nothing in our lives that would hinder them from coming to Christ, our true Passover Lamb, and be given life.

DAY 259
bHE IS THE ANGRY ONE

QUESTIONS TO THINK ABOUT:

1. What situations can you remember from Scripture where it is recorded that Christ became angry?

2. What was the common thread in each situation that caused his anger?

Have you ever thought of Christ as being angry? Do you know what makes him angry? There are several passages of Scripture which reveal his anger and the cause of it.

Chronologically, *the first time* is found in John 2:14-17 where Christ found the Temple turned into a commercial enterprise. He made a whip and proceeded to overturn tables and throw merchants and animals off the premises. [**NOTE:** In Matthew 21:12-13 we again find Christ throwing over tables and casting out merchants and animals from the Temple. Obviously, the first lesson didn't "take."]

The second time, it is stated that he was angry. In Mark 3:1-5, the Jews were eyeing him to see if he would break their traditions and heal on the Sabbath Day. They didn't care a whit about the suffering of the man with the withered hand. Verse 5a: "He looked around at them in anger ..., deeply distressed at their <u>stubborn hearts</u>" (underlining mine).

In Matthew 23:1-36, *the third time*, he delivers a scathing blast at the Scribes and Pharisees for their <u>hypocrisy</u>, spiritual callousness, greed in the guise of spirituality, following the letter but not the spirit of the Law, bound by tradition but knowing nothing of obedience to God nor of love and mercy toward others, and totally lacking in faith.

The fourth time we see Jesus angry is found in Mark 10:13-16 where parents were bringing little children to him to bless them. The disciples interfered, no doubt trying to spare the Master an unnecessary nuisance. Verse 14 says, "When Jesus saw this, he was indignant. He said to them, 'Let the little children come to me, and <u>do not hinder them</u>, for the kingdom of God belongs to such as these'" (underlining mine).

What is the common thread in all four passages that arouses Christ's anger?

In the first instance, Jesus accused the merchants of making his House a den of thieves when it should have been a House of Prayer (Matt.21:13). The purpose of his House was to have a special place where people could come to pray and worship God. Commercializing the Lord's House for profit not only engendered thievery through greed and dishonesty, but also robbed others of their right to meet God there. Both money and opportunity were robbed from would-be worshippers, causing them double loss, and many were turned away from God in the very place where they should and could have met him!

Then there is hypocrisy (Matt.23:13) which shuts up the kingdom of heaven to those who want to enter. How many times have we heard people say, "I'd become a Christian, except for one thing: there are too many hypocrites in the church." Though this is usually just an excuse, many have been turned away from the Lord because of hypocrisy. "He says he's a Christian, but he's no different than I am. What has he got in Christianity that I haven't got the way I am now? Nothing. So I don't see any valid reason why I should become a Christian." And the Lord is angry!

Had the stubborn, hard-hearted traditionalists had their way, the man with the withered hand would have remained that way until it was "a proper time" for him to seek healing. By their traditions, they blocked the way to God for those wanting to come to him to have their needs met. The Lord said in Mark 7:9, "You have a fine way of setting aside the commands of God in order to observe your own traditions."

And with indignation, he rebuked his disciples for trying to keep children from coming to him: "Do not hinder those who want to come to me!" (Mk.10:14).

So we see that in each case where Christ became angry, someone was hindering someone else from coming to him. When we, by our lifestyle, actions and words, hinder others from coming to the Lord, we are making ourselves the objects of Christ's anger – a very dangerous thing to do!

Does what makes Christ angry make us angry?

Or are we, like the disciples, the objects of his anger?

APPLICATION: Occasionally, it would be good to ask ourselves the question: "Is what I am doing or saying helping or hindering others from coming to the Lord? Am I holding so tightly to my religious traditions that there is no room for others who don't hold those same traditions to enter the place where they can find and worship God?"

DAY 260
[b]HE IS THE BRIGHTNESS OF THE FATHER'S GLORY

◆

QUESTIONS TO THINK ABOUT:

1. How is it possible to look at a child and almost know instinctively who his parents are?
2. How does our expression, "Like father, like son" apply to Christ?
3. How should it apply to our relationship with Christ?

In the grand description of the Son of God in Hebrews 1:3a, we read, "The Son is the radiance of God's glory and the exact representation of his being." God is a Spirit, therefore invisible. Christ told his disciples, "Anyone who has seen me has seen the Father" (Jn.14:9b). He was the visible manifestation of the invisible God.

Now the glory of a man lies in what he has done or accomplished, which are the visible manifestations of inward character and ability, things that cannot otherwise be seen, therefore invisible. So also with God. Through Christ he made the world (Heb.1:2) in which, according to Romans 1:20, "God's invisible qualities – his eternal power and divine nature – have been clearly seen, being understood from what has been made." In his works, Christ revealed God's righteous character (Jn.14:10,11). And as the brightness of the Father's glory, there was nothing that Christ said or did that had to be hidden because it was sinful.

On the Mount of Transfiguration Christ literally radiated this glory, even as Moses did to a lesser degree when he came down from Mount Sinai after having talked with God face to face (see Exod.34:29,30).

Since God's glory is shown in what he has done, then we each stand in line to show forth his glory as his works are revealed in us. The change in our character is the <u>first</u> revelation of his glory (2 Cor.5:17): "Therefore, if anyone is in Christ, he is a new creation; the old has gone, the new has come!" The change in our works is the <u>second</u> (Eph.2:10): "For we are God's workmanship, created in Christ Jesus to do good works, which God prepared in advance for us to do." The things created of necessity glorify the creator! So as our new life and good works stand out in contrast to our old life and old works, the glory of our Creator is shown forth. <u>Third</u>, there is a change in our attitude (Jn.3:20,21): "Everyone who does evil hates the light, and will not come into the light for fear that his deeds will be exposed. But whoever lives by the truth comes into the light, so that it may be seen plainly that what he has done has been done through God." Or, as Christ says in Matthew 5:16, "Let your light shine before men, that they may see your good deeds and praise your Father in heaven."

The more our works, our character and our attitudes reflect the works, character and attitudes of Christ, the more we also will show forth the brightness of the Father's glory.

How bright is your light shining?

APPLICATION: Children reflect their parents because of heritage and from spending so much time with them. We, as children of God, have that heritage (the Divine nature within us – 2 Pet.1:4) which will be more and more reflected in our lives as we spend time with him.

DAY 261
'HE IS THE COMING ONE

QUESTIONS TO THINK ABOUT:

1. What situations can you recall in which you were eagerly awaiting the coming of something or someone?
2. What did you do in preparation for that "coming"?

"When John [the Baptist] heard in prison what Christ was doing, he sent his disciples to ask him, 'Are you the one who was to come, or should we expect someone else?'" (Matt.11:2,3). John was puzzled. He knew that he was the forerunner of the Messiah. He knew that Christ was the Lamb of God and the Messiah. And yet here he was in prison and there seemed to be no movement toward the establishment of the kingdom that John announced. Christ sent an answer back to him, quoting from Isaiah 29:18 and 35:4-6: "Go back and report to John what you hear and see: The blind receive sight, the lame walk, those who have leprosy are cured, the deaf hear, the dead are raised, and the good news is preached to the poor. Blessed is the man who does not fall away on account of me" (Matt.11:4-6).

"Are you the Coming One?" "Yes, I am, but don't judge me by your expectations. I have my own agenda."

Just before this, Jesus had commissioned his disciples to go out and preach that "the kingdom of heaven is near" (Matt.10:7). And as a sign of the authority of this message, the Lord gave them power to cast out demons and heal the sick (Matt.10:1). In verse 8 he says, "Heal the sick, raise the dead, cleanse those who have leprosy, drive out demons. Freely you have received, freely give." So with this general proclamation throughout Galilee and Judea, along with the accompanying signs, it is no wonder that John the Baptist had doubts when nothing more seemed to come of it.

These same signs accompanied the conception of the Church: the sick were healed, demons were cast out (Acts 5:15,16), the dead raised (Acts 9:36-41), and the poor had the gospel preached to them (Acts 3:11-16). This stands to reason since the outward form of the kingdom and its inward form are the same. It's just the wrappings that are different. The outward form was wrapped in the nation of Israel, but rejected. The inward form was wrapped in the Church and accepted. We enjoy in our hearts many of the blessings of the kingdom that Israel could have enjoyed as a nation had they accepted Christ as their Messiah.

But now the question remains, "How do we or can we reflect Christ as the Coming One"? Can we do the same signs as he did in our proclamation of the Gospel, thus demonstrating his power and authority to those who hear? I believe we can, but only as we are yielded to and energized by the Holy Spirit. Many claim that the "sign gifts" are no longer valid today since they were basically functional to establish the authority of the completed Word of God. Now that it has been completed, there is no longer any need for these special gifts (For a fuller discussion of this see DAYS 248-252 – HE IS THE MIRACLE-WORKER). Yet in my own ministry as well as in the ministry of others, we have seen miracles happen.

I believe we are not seeing more miracles for at least two reasons. First, we are not putting ourselves out in the forefront as witnesses for the Lord, so we are not necessarily where miracles are needed. Secondly, because of sin, compromise and apathy in our lives, we are no longer in touch with our Power Source as we should be. If the appliance is not plugged in, it won't work! Therefore it's no wonder we don't see anything happening, and therefore mistakenly conclude that it shouldn't happen! In principle, it's not unlike what Christ experienced at Nazareth. We read in Matthew 13:58 that "he did not do many miracles there because of their lack of faith."

Miracles aside, is your life such that others would respond to Christ by what they see in you?

APPLICATION: Our lives should be such that, as others see Christ in us, they would eagerly anticipate his coming into their own lives. That would be a miracle in and of itself!

DAY 262
ᶜHE IS THE COMING ONE, cont.

QUESTIONS TO THINK ABOUT:

1. How can one know when a "sign" or miracle is needed? They are not there for the asking!
2. What is the role of a sign or miracle in our witness to others?

I cannot testify to having experienced, seen or heard of all these signs Jesus mentioned as happening today too. But I can mention some that are well documented.

"*The poor have the gospel preached to them.*" There are missionaries and national evangelists in nearly every underdeveloped country, countries "poor" by most economic standards, preaching the Gospel of Jesus Christ to them.

"*The blind receiving their sight.*" One day a young man by the name of Nahor Leo (LAY-o) in the village of Soe (SO-ā), Timor, was deeply stirred by a dynamic challenge to Christian service given by the headmistress of a Soe school (Crawford, <u>Miracles in Indonesia</u>, Tyndale House, pp.22,23). While studying in a local pastor's home, he suddenly went blind. After resting for a few minutes he seemed to be wrestling with an invisible force and talking to someone. He drew out a fetish from among his clothes and confessed it. Another student asked him what was going on. Leo replied, "It was the Lord.

He made me reveal the [fetish] I had never given up. He told me he wanted me to serve him alone. And he told me I must have Pastor Daniel pray for me – or I will die." After a prayer of confession, the fetish was burned, and Leo's sight was restored.

Another incidence of blindness was reported in the Evangelical Missions Quarterly, (vol.23, No.3, July 1987, "Global Report" by Sharon E. Mumper, p.316). "Eye specialists turn away a blind woman whose condition is 'hopeless.' A Christian friend prays, her eyesight is restored, and her family and 30 other villagers accept Christ."

"The dead are raised up." "An elderly woman among the mourners at the funeral of a young boy felt a strong impression to pray for the lad's life. At first she resisted the impulse. The boy had been dead for several hours and in that climate it was imperative that an unembalmed body be buried soon after death. But her feeling persisted. When it came time to put the lid on the wooden coffin in place, she felt compelled to act. She asked if she could offer a prayer. The ceremony was stopped to humor the old woman. While she was praying, the boy stirred, then rose up" (Crawford, Miracles in Indonesia, pp.26,27). Many came to faith in Christ as a result.

"Cast out demons." From the same source (Ibid., pp.63,64) comes another account. "One day the pastor of a local church was called "to come and pray for a fifteen-year-old Chinese girl. When he arrived with a deacon at the home, he found the girl stretched out on her bed, her eyes open but her body absolutely still. She did not respond to the pastor's words, spoken to her in Indonesian. Perplexed, Pastor Wirijantoe (Wir-ee-JAN-toe) spoke softly to his helper in his native Javanese. To their surprise the girl suddenly sat up and started talking in Javanese, a tongue she did not normally use, and in a voice much different from her own.

"'Who are you?' the bewildered pastor asked. The name the girl uttered was not her own.

"'Where do you come from?' the pastor wanted to know.

"'I live at the cemetery,' the voice replied.

"After prayer, the pastor told the demon that he had no right to this person since she was a Christian, to which the spirit replied that he knew that and was not going to stay long.

"For two more hours the girl lay in a coma while the pastor and her parents continued their prayer vigil. Then she spoke in Indonesian with her own voice. She was delivered.

"Addressing a group on the small southern island of Roti (RO-tee), Detmar [Scheunemann] was talking about the spiritual development of King Saul, who at one point contacted demonic powers (1 Sam.28). Suddenly a listener jumped from his seat with a wild cry and started toward the pulpit. The startled congregation stirred but made no move to stop the man. Detmar learned later that the people were desperately afraid of the person who was known as one possessed by ninety-nine spirits and seeking one more.

"'You cannot do anything in this room!' Detmar shouted to the man as he advanced menacingly up the aisle. 'In the name of Jesus, sit down!'

"As Detmar voiced the name of Jesus, the attacker fell to the floor. Students from the Batu (BAA-too) team carried him to the rear of the church, where they and the local pastor ministered to him as the sermon continued. That night the man was relieved of the many demons who had ruled him.

"The following evening in front of the astonished congregation, the man openly confessed his faith in Christ... . Through his testimony, many ... accepted Christ or recommitted their lives to him" (Ibid., pp.70-72).

APPLICATION: In the end, it is the Word of God, not signs or miracles, that is the essential element in our witness. But on occasion, a miracle can create a receptive atmosphere for a presentation of the Gospel. Are you in the place where a miracle could happen if needed?

DAY 263
ʿHE IS THE COMING ONE, concl.

QUESTIONS TO THINK ABOUT:

1. What role does prayer play when a sign or miracle is needed?
2. What happens when we "conjure up" a sign or miracle for our own benefit? (cf. Acts 19:13-16)

"The deaf hear." In southern Sumatra "the leader of an area Mosque had lost his hearing. When he was visited by the local Christian pastor and an evangelist from Batu, the Muslim priest challenged the two: 'If Christ is the Son of God, let him heal me.' The evangelist placed his hands on the priest's ears and prayed for healing. When the 'Amen' was spoken, the Muslim heard wind blowing past his ear! He is now a staunch member of the local Christian fellowship" (Ibid., pp.111,112).

We have just noted several modern day illustrations of the "signs" that Jesus gave to prove his Messiahship to John the Baptist: the Gospel preached to the poor, healing of the blind, the raising of the dead, the casting out of demons, and healing of the deaf. What remains is the healing of the sick and the lame.

"Heal the sick." While we were in Senggo, a Muslim family brought their four-year-old boy to the hospital seriously ill. We had no doctor there, so the nurses did what they could for the little fellow day and night around the clock. But he grew steadily worse. Finally there was absolutely nothing more they could do. Responding to their suggestion, the family agreed to have me come and pray for him. Even as I was praying, the nurses were sure the child had died. But when I finished, he stirred and began to recover. The Lord's power was demonstrated to that family. After that, they began to

show some interest in the Lord. We don't know if any decisions for Christ were made, but the seed was definitely planted.

"The lame walk" (if we can be granted the liberty to include all those suffering from some physical abnormality as follows). Our Indonesian pastor made regular visits to the two hospitals in Manokwari (MAHN-o-KWA-ree). He learned of a pregnant woman who was unable to give birth after three days of labor. When he went to visit her, he found some local "Christian practitioners" anointing her with "holy water" and laying the Bible on her stomach and doing all sorts of things to help her deliver her baby. Thadeus just stood there and watched.

After several hours of frustration and continued suffering for the woman, the "practitioners" gave up. Then Thadeus stepped forward and said, "Let's pray." He then prayed for the woman, for the safe delivery of her child, and for those who tried to help her. Five minutes after he prayed, she delivered a healthy baby. The "practitioners" were dumbfounded and not a little upset. "Why did you wait so long before praying for her. You saw the way she was suffering!" "Yes," he replied, "but I had to wait until you were finished with your magic so that there would be no confusion as to which power caused her to give birth. Now you see that your ways are futile, and that only the power of Christ can bring healing and help when we need it." And he continued to witness to them.

Thus we as a body of believers can reflect Christ as the Coming One by proclaiming the Gospel and, when led by the Holy Spirit, working miracles that will serve as a springboard to sharing Christ with others.

Is Christ "coming" to others through you?

APPLICATION: Just a word of caution here. Don't go out looking for a miracle to perform. Our responsibility is to be filled with the Holy Spirit, to walk close to the Lord and to seek to win the lost. If a miracle is needed, the Lord will do it as we respond to his leading in faith. Then his name will be glorified before those to whom we are ministering, and, hopefully, they will be saved.

DAY 264
ᶜHE IS THE CONSOLATION OF ISRAEL

QUESTIONS TO THINK ABOUT:

1. What does the word "consolation" mean?
2. How can we be a consolation to others?

Eight days after Jesus was born, his parents took him to the Temple in Jerusalem to be circumcised. "Now there was a man in Jerusalem called Simeon, who was righteous and devout. He was waiting for the consolation of Israel, and the Holy Spirit was upon him" (Lk.2:25). The Greek word *paraklesis* here means "consolation." *Para* = beside; *kaleo* = to call. Hence a calling to one's side for comfort or consolation.

The history of Israel had been tumultuous, a series of one upheaval and disaster after another. Satan, knowing the prophecy of the coming Messiah (Gen.3:15), bent all his efforts at destroying the nation from which the Messiah would come, thus assuring his own survival. He had Abel killed outright. Then Seth was born. He corrupted mankind to such wickedness that God had to destroy them with a flood. But Noah was saved. Then came the Tower of Babel where he tried to destroy all faith. Abraham was chosen and responded in faith to God. But Sarah was barren, threatening an end to the line. Isaac was born. Rebekah was barren. Jacob and Esau were born. Esau tried to kill Jacob, but Jacob fled. Laban would have tried to keep Jacob's family to himself thus occasioning their assimilation with the surrounding populace, but Jacob, by stealth, slipped away with his family intact. All male babies in Egypt were commanded to be killed, threatening an end to the race. Moses was born and protected in Pharaoh's own household! Balaam was hired by Moab's King Balak to curse Israel in the wilderness. But God caused him to bless Israel instead.

The next really serious threat came when the ten northern tribes were decimated and the few survivors scattered to the four winds. Then Judah followed in destruction with only a little over 4,000 people carried off to Babylon. In Babylon, Haman hatched a plot to kill them all, but was foiled by Queen Esther and her cousin, Mordekai. Then the upheaval during the Maccabean Revolt securing the Jews from annihilation.

And, after all else had failed, Satan engineered numerous attempts on Jesus' life beginning with King Herod's attempt to kill him, then the people of Nazareth, then the Scribes and Pharisees, a violent storm on the Sea of Galilee – and finally SUCCESS! The crucifixion! – only to be confounded once again by the RESURRECTION which ended the matter once and for all. Satan's power was crushed and he now awaits his doom. He lost the battle, but Israel suffered greatly and earnestly longed for and anticipated the consolation of the Messiah's coming. The greatest tragedy of history occurred when he came and they neither recognized him nor received him!

As Jesus entered Jerusalem less than a week before his death, he wept over the city, saying, "If you, even you, had only known on this day what would bring you peace – but now it is hidden from your eyes" (Lk.19:42). After waiting so many centuries for their consolation, they rejected it once it appeared, and plunged themselves back into the abyss of suffering and national disaster. Depressing, isn't it? Yet how often do we ourselves read the promises of help, comfort and strength in the Word only to reject them for self-pity and worry and our own plans to find a way out? So you see, we're not that much different from the Jews who rejected their Consolation!

Where are you looking for your consolation?

APPLICATION: We find our consolation in the promises of God. Meditate on them as you find them, then claim them as needed. Then a delightful surprise awaits you! Second Corinthians 1:3,4 says, "Praise be to the God and Father of our Lord Jesus Christ, the Father of compassion and the God of all comfort, who comforts us in all our troubles, so that we can comfort those in any trouble with the comfort we ourselves have received from God." And we thus reflect Christ as the Consolation of Israel.

DAY 265
ʻHE IS THE CONSOLATION OF ISRAEL, concl.

QUESTIONS TO THINK ABOUT:

1. What was the consolation that Christ offered to Israel?
2. In what way or ways can we be a consolation to Israel?

What was the consolation that Christ offered to Israel? It was double-pronged: deliverance from their enemies (national) and deliverance from sin (personal).

Israel had long awaited the day when the kingdom of the Messiah would be set up, freeing them from the oppression of their enemies and giving them peace in place of the frequent calamities they have experienced. They longed for the time when they would be the head, not the tail, among the nations. I suppose there was as well some spirit of revenge in their hope where they would take the rod of iron and crush those who have crushed them. They were certainly ready to take up arms against the Romans when Christ came the first time. But a kingdom established on hatred and revenge cannot long endure. So before the nation could be delivered, there had to be a change of heart among the Jews.

It was this change of heart that Christ came to effect but which the Jews resisted. They wanted war and freedom with no postponement. Yet Christ came to deliver them from sin first. Otherwise his kingdom would not be characterized by righteousness. But the national peace and personal peace he came to offer is truly the consolation and comfort that Israel has long sought for and long rejected!

Paul recognized this and devoted three chapters of Romans to the necessity of a new heart before a renewed nation is possible (Rom.9-11). Peter bent all his Apostolic efforts at winning the Jews. But gradually the pendulum swung to the Gentiles who soon far outnumbered Jewish converts, for the Jews by and large still rejected Christ as their Messiah.

Paul makes a statement in Romans 1:16 that would be good for us to ponder. He says, "I am not ashamed of the gospel, because it is the power of God for the salvation of everyone who believes: first for the Jew, then for the Gentile." "First for the Jew." Indeed, the Gospel was given to the Jews first and rejected, then taken to the Gentiles. But the problem is that ever since then, any consistent and serious program of witness to the Jews has never been made until now (with such organizations as Jews for Jesus and Friends of Israel, and a few others). Yet I read somewhere where only 3% of all monies given to missions is directed toward Jewish evangelism. Doing a bit of research, there are approximately 14.4 million Jews in the world today (Yahoo.com, "Jewish World Population" as of 2016) out of a total world population of 7.4 billion. That comes out to about 0.2% of the world population receiving 3% of the money for missions. So proportionately, they're doing O.K., though admittedly more could be done. In the end, Israel will be saved nationally and personally (Rom.11:26). But in the meantime we should take every advantage to witness to them and support those who are on a regular basis so that more and more Jews will experience the consolation they are longing for. Psalm 122:6 says, "Pray for the peace of Jerusalem." But as we pray, we also should put feet to our prayers.

Are you bringing consolation to Israel?

APPLICATION: There are four ways we can be a consolation to Israel:

1. by praying regularly for the peace of the nation of Israel;
2. by giving to organizations working with Jewish people;
3. by befriending Jewish people around us to build a bridge of communication for the Gospel;
4. by going to Israel itself and ministering there part-time or full-time.

DAY 266
ᶜHE IS THE DESIRE OF ALL NATIONS

QUESTIONS TO THINK ABOUT:

1. For what things are the nations seeking?
2. Where are they going to find their ultimate fulfillment?
3. What role can we play in the process?

About 520 years before Christ, the prophet Haggai wrote the following words: "This is what the LORD Almighty says: 'In a little while I will once more shake the heavens and the earth, the sea and the dry land. I will shake all nations, and the desired of all nations will come, and I will fill this house with glory,' says the LORD Almighty" (Hag.2:6,7). This is an interesting title, especially in light of the fact that the nations willfully reject him. Psalm 2:1-3 speaks of their rebellion. Psalm 14:1-3 speaks of mankind as a whole with no desire to seek after God. And Romans 1:18-23 declares that even when men knew God, they rejected him. So what or who is it that the nations desire?

In these troubled days they want peace, but reject the Prince of Peace. They want prosperity, but reject him from whom all blessings flow. They want unity among the nations, yet reject the one Lord who can give them unity. They want freedom, but reject the truth that will set them free. They want a healthy environment, yet refuse to go to him who alone can lift the curse. In short, what they are seeking for and longing for is <u>Utopia</u>. And everything they want in that Utopia is to be found in Christ. Therefore, though they don't and will not recognize it, they are actually desiring him! Ironic, isn't it? <u>He</u> is the Desire of All Nations.

Now how can we reflect Christ in this regard? First of all, by demonstrating these "desires" of the nations in the arena already prepared by God: the Church. And yet the Church is troubled by those very things the nations desire but cannot find! Down through history, the Church has had no internal peace, no real prosperity, been troubled by immoral and corrupt leadership, disunity and party spirit, slavery to sin, and a spirit of selfishness that destroys its "environment." Just look at the Corinthian Church for a prime example of this gross failure. So if the nations cannot see in practice in the Church what they are seeking in principle in the world, they will never come to a knowledge of the truth, and will continue seeking their Utopia everywhere but where it can be found. That, then, becomes our fault and sets the stage for the reception of the Antichrist who will show himself powerful and promise all these things and more.

We, obviously, cannot influence the entire world, yet we <u>can</u> and <u>must</u> influence our community, our nation. We must seek to live out these "Utopian" principles of Christ in the Church, then carry them over into our places of work and community involvement. We must become miniatures of what the world is seeking so that they can find through us the Source of their desire. We become those miniatures as we obey the Word in our daily living and as we become more and more like Jesus Christ.

APPLICATION: Is your family, is your church a miniature of the Utopia for which all nations seek? If not, what steps can be taken to make you the miniatures you should be?

DAY 267
[a]HE IS THE ENDURER

QUESTIONS TO THINK ABOUT:

1. What does it mean to endure something?
2. Why would we want to?

Have you ever had to face an unpleasant situation knowing that you must go through it? There is no joy in it, but you plan to endure it in order to get it over with and move on to better things beyond. Christ experienced this feeling. He did not want to die on the cross. He did not want to suffer. He was in great agony of soul in contemplating what he was about to go through (Lk.22:44). He prayed for God to change his mind (Lk.22:41,42), yet put God's will ahead of his own. There was no other way. Christ had to go through death by crucifixion so that God's plan of redemption might be accomplished.

We anticipated our second term in Irian Jaya in similar fashion. I particularly did not want to go back. I'd had it. In fact, my aversion toward returning was so great that I began having memory blackouts. That scared me! But we put God's will ahead of our own (since he had not opened any other doors for us) and prepared ourselves to return and endure our second term. We went and began working out of obedience, not out of joy. Our situation became worse and worse, and we wanted to leave in the worst way, not wanting four more years of this.

Then one day I read Hebrews 12:2,3 and made a startling discovery: Christ had already been in our position! "Let us fix our eyes on Jesus, the author and perfecter of our faith, who for the joy set before him <u>endured</u> the cross, scorning its shame, and sat down at the right hand of the throne of God. Consider him who <u>endured</u> such opposition from sinful men, so that you will not grow weary and lose heart" (underlining mine). What an encouragement! We were in good company!

But then I saw something else. The endurance of hard situations is only possible if we have a higher goal beyond them. Christ endured the cross "for the joy set before him" – the provision of salvation for mankind and restoration to his former glory with the Father after accomplishing his will. The joy set before us was the establishment of a strong, missionary-minded Citak (CHEE-tuck) Church reaching out with the Gospel. So I became willing to endure so that that goal might be reached. Then, as I willingly chose to trust God's loving sovereignty in our situation, and leave behind my bitterness and complaining spirit, I began to experience his peace and had joy in serving him, even though our circumstances grew worse.

So as you may be enduring one situation or another, keep these things in mind:

1. Christ has already been there. He knows how you feel.
2. Choose to submit your will to God's. In his loving sovereignty, he has permitted this time of trial and you must trust him in it.
3. Ask yourself, "What is God's purpose for me or for others in this?" His primary purpose, remember, is to make us like Christ. So if there is no other reason, this is enough to help us endure.

"You therefore must endure hardship as a good soldier of Jesus Christ" (2 Tim.2:3, KNJV).

APPLICATION: A useful clue in any trial or situation is to ask yourself, "What is my attitude in this situation?" Your attitude will be a clue as to what God wants to accomplish in you to make you more like Christ. In other words, "Is my attitude reflecting what Christ's would be in similar circumstances, or not?" If it is, then this trial is probably either a test of that attitude or a joyful confirmation of the change that has already taken place. If not, then this trial is pointing once again to where we are not like Christ and showing us what we still have to work on to become like him.

DAY 268
ªHe IS THE ENDURER, concl.

QUESTIONS TO THINK ABOUT:

1. How does the Lord use what we must endure to make us more like Christ?

2. How does having a "goal" beyond the situation we're enduring help us get through it?

As Christians, we have the resources to live above our circumstances and respond positively, in faith, to what God wants to accomplish in our lives through them. One time I was being falsely accused for lying to the national believers, breaking my promises, and generally not working together with them, misusing mission funds, etc. This went on for months and was really disturbing me. I'd answer anger with anger trying to defend myself. One day I read Proverbs 15:1, "A gentle answer turns away wrath, but a harsh word stirs up anger." Then I remembered that when the Lord was reviled, he didn't revile in return, but committed himself to him who judges justly (1 Pet.2:23). So I confessed my anger and self-justification to the Lord and asked him to help me give a gentle answer the next time an accusation came. I didn't have long to wait! In about 15 minutes the phone rang and we were "off and runnin'." While that person was talking to me, I was talking to my heavenly Father: "Lord, help me give a gentle answer. Help me not blow it again." (I really needed victory, for every time I got angry, I had to go to this person to ask for forgiveness in order to clear my conscience! This was getting embarrassing. I was the one being falsely accused, yet I had to keep going to ask for forgiveness because of my anger!) So when a pause came, I gave a gentle answer when anger was expected. Surprise! Silence. "Well, uh, guess that's it. Goodbye." And we have been good friends ever since. Lesson learned. Trial finished. And I consciously became more like Christ in my attitude toward others.

Keeping this goal in mind, then, we can endure our trials for the joy set before us, knowing that they will shortly be through and we will have an eternity completely free from them all, and that in the meantime we will be conformed more and more into Christ's image.

From another perspective, I can remember times of sickness when I was a child, down flat in bed feeling as miserable as one can feel. Yet deep in my heart there was always a song, a sense of deep joy. God doesn't promise that we won't hurt; he doesn't promise that we will not weep. Even Christ wept (Jn.11:35), and experienced emotional agony (Lk.22:44). But God has promised us strength for our trials to take us through them (Lk.22:43; 1 Cor.10:13). Christ was victorious because he could see the end result of his sufferings rather than just the immediate circumstances surrounding them (Heb.12:2).

Paul had this viewpoint as well. In 2 Corinthians 4:17,18 he writes, "For our light and momentary troubles are achieving for us an eternal glory that far outweigh them all. So we fix our eyes not on what is seen, but on what is unseen. For what is seen is temporary, but what is unseen is eternal."

Thus when we face life's temptations and sins with victory, and life's adverse situations with faith, patience and joy even when hurting deeply, others will see the life of Christ at work in our lives and we will have opportunities to share the Gospel with them. If we respond in anger and bitterness toward the Lord and others, then that opportunity for a witness is gone, that step toward becoming more like Christ is lost, and we put ourselves in the position of having to learn the same lesson all over again another time. I <u>don't</u> like repeats. I'd far rather learn it the first time around. How about you?

APPLICATION: Again, in any trial, we need to take the "long view." "How will my response/reaction to this trial affect my witness now? How will these things make me more like Christ? How will it affect things down the road? How will it affect my relationship with the Lord now and my rewards in eternity?" Answering these questions will cause us to pause and think, and perhaps save us from having wrong attitudes and making wrong choices in the heat of the moment.

DAY 269
[a]HE IS THE FAITHFUL ONE

QUESTIONS TO THINK ABOUT:

1. What does it mean to be faithful?
2. What kind of situations would test our faithfulness?
3. What role do our priorities play in faithfulness?

Closely aligned to the quality of endurance is faithfulness, for having a clear goal toward which we are striving will help us overcome adverse circumstances and obstacles in the way. Thus we remain faithful in whatever we are doing.

In Revelation 3:14, Christ is described as "the faithful and true witness." In the mind of God, faithfulness is a high quality. In Hebrews, Christ is described as being faithful to the one who appointed him and faithful in all God's house (Heb.3:2,6). In the parable of the talents (Matt.25:14-30), the faithful servants were the ones rewarded. In 1 Corinthians 4:1,2 Paul writes: "So then, men ought to regard us as servants of Christ and as those entrusted with the secret things of God. Now it is required that those who have been given a trust must prove faithful."

Just as Christ was faithful, enduring the cross for the joy set before him, so are we to be faithful, enduring life's circumstances and adversities for the joy set before us – becoming like Christ (1 Jn.3:2), receiving a full reward (1 Cor.3:14), and living eternally with our Lord (Jn.17:24).

In thinking about adversities, one furlough we were asked to share the three hardest things and the three greatest things we had experienced as missionaries. Amber found leaving family and friends very difficult; adapting to and learning to be comfortable in another culture; and learning to fight spiritual warfare. Mine were different. I sorely missed not having someone to "talk theology" with; not initially being able to teach in a Bible School (my dream); and having to do jobs for which I was unqualified and untrained.

These trials continued into our second term and were nearly our undoing. But God kept encouraging us through his Word (1 Chr.28:20; Prov.20:24) and people's letters, to be faithful and learn the lessons he wanted to teach us in order that we might become more like Christ. The knowledge of his loving sovereignty and that he had all the circumstances of our lives in his control, gave me the encouragement I needed to choose to leave behind my own bitterness over our circumstances and believe God's promises to us. Our circumstances didn't change in the least, but my attitude toward them did, and that made all the difference. My bitterness changed to joy. I finally had a goal beyond our circumstances which put them in proper perspective.

I've often wondered, if we had quit and come home, would the Citak (CHEE-tuck) Christians have reached the point where they were willing to give up their witchcraft? Or would it have been delayed due to their discouragement over our unfaithfulness? Praise God, this question need not be answered. But we ourselves have experienced the discouragement and disheartening effect that unfaithfulness among fellow believers can cause. When we are unfaithful, we place an unnecessary burden on others that may never be lifted, for they will always hurt inside as they remember us.

Does faithfulness characterize your life in everything you do?

APPLICATION: I have found that my priorities really set the stage for being faithful. I do what I really want to do! Prayerfully consider what your present priorities are, and what you think they should be. Then discipline yourself to follow what they should be. It may be difficult at first, but repeated choosing to keep at them will soon change into a habit that comes automatically without thought. The end results will be less personal guilt, you will become known as a person who can be counted upon, and finally, you will hear those words from the Lord, "Well done, good and faithful servant!"

DAY 270
ªHE IS THE FAITHFUL ONE, concl.

◆

QUESTIONS TO THINK ABOUT:

1. What role does the Word of God play in our faithfulness?
2. How does our love for the Lord affect our faithfulness? (cf. 2 Cor.5:14,15)

To keep the balance with the three hardest things about being a missionary, we were also asked to share the three greatest things about being a missionary. Amber found great delight in seeing others coming to know Christ personally; making new friends both here and on the field; and knowing that we were in the will of God. For myself, I thoroughly enjoyed furlough ministry: sharing with people what God is doing elsewhere, making new friends, and seeing what God is doing in the lives of friends from previous furloughs; growth in my own faith toward God; and being able to share God's Word with the national believers and seeing it take root in their lives.

One evening, just before our Church Leaders' Training Class, Matius, the main church leader from the village of Tamnim (TAHM-neem) across the airstrip, came to talk. He had had a dream the night before and wanted me to interpret it for him! Normally, when it comes to seeing symbolism in things, I just don't. Even in my university English classes, when my professors would point out the "deep and hidden" meanings in various works we read, I was amazed and totally puzzled as to how anyone could know so well what the author really meant. Sometimes I wondered if the authors themselves knew these things! But as Matius began telling me his dream, its meaning became clear.

He related how he was walking in Tamnim one day and saw a circular garden filled with beautiful flowers and grass loaded with grass seed (representing God's Word in its eternal character – the circle; its beauty – the flowers; and its reproductive ability – the grass seed). Then he looked up and saw me sitting in the doorway of a house. A man (the Holy Spirit) was standing beside me, and as Matius came up the stair pole, this man gave him some of the flowers and grass with the grass seed (only the Holy Spirit can give us the Word of God with understanding so that we can give it to others), while I wrote down what was given (each week I would write out the Bible lesson for the men to preach the following Sunday).

Then he left the house and met the village chief from Epem (eh-PEM) and asked him where Wapet (wa-PET), the Tamnim chief, was (representing the people of Tamnim). He indicated a house beyond a large, thick swath of grass (obstacles in our lives) through which the path went. Matius thought that he would rather wait for Wapet to come to him than to try getting through that grass, so turned around to go back to his house in the village. Almost immediately he noticed that all the grass seed was gone! (loss of effective ministry).

I told him the meaning of the symbols, then the application. This dream was both a warning and an encouragement: a warning that if he turned back from the ministry due to hard circumstances, he would lose it; but an encouragement that if he would "go through the grass," there would be fruit.

Several months later, a sickness went through Tamnim and Senggo (seng-GO) killing about 20 infants, including Matius's 2-month-old baby. A year later, Jim Lynn, an MAF pilot and good friend was killed when his plane crashed. Shortly after that, Matius's 18-year-old step brother fell from a slippery tree branch and broke his neck, dying instantly. The next day, Matius, deeply grieved, came to me in tears asking, "Tuan, what is the Lord doing?!" "Matius, I don't know. But do you remember the grass in your dream?" "Yes." "Well, you've come to it. Go through it." We talked a while longer and had prayer together before he left for home. The next day he came to me, smiling from ear to ear. "Tuan, I just wanted to come to thank you for your encouragement and for praying for me yesterday. After I got home, the Lord showed me these passages from the Old Testament that greatly encouraged and comforted my heart." And he showed them to me. I was totally amazed. Matius was 98% illiterate in Indonesian and knew nothing of the Old Testament beyond Genesis (where our current lessons were taken from), yet the Lord led him elsewhere to five passages he didn't even know to comfort his heart! So we prayed again, thanking the Lord for his goodness to Matius and the comfort he had given him.

APPLICATION: We need to "go through the grass" when adverse circumstances come, for there will be much blessing on the other side – if we are faithful.

DAY 271
ʽHE IS GREATER THAN THE TEMPLE/ LORD OF THE SABBATH

QUESTIONS TO THINK ABOUT:

1. How could Christ be said to be greater than the Temple, hence also Lord of the Sabbath?
2. In the same way, how can we be said to be "greater" than the church building in which we worship?
3. What does it mean for us to be "Lords of the Sabbath"?

One day the Pharisees contested with Jesus about his disciples' breaking the Sabbath Day when they plucked heads of grain to eat. "According to the Pharisees, plucking wheat from its stem is reaping, rubbing the wheat heads between one's palms is threshing, and blowing away the chaff is winnowing!" (Walvoord, Zuck, The Bible Knowledge Commentary, Victor Books, p.45).

Jesus replied to their "hair-splitting" legality with three statements. The first, where David and those with him ate of the showbread from the house of God, which is lawful only for the priests to eat, and was not blamed for it. Secondly, the temple priests worked on the Sabbath, yet they were considered blameless. And thirdly, he said to them, "I tell you that one greater than the temple is here" (Matt.12:6) ["and I do not condemn these men"]. "If you had known what these words mean, 'I desire mercy, not sacrifice,' you would not have condemned the innocent" (vs.7). The principle here is that "mercy supersedes law," especially where law is carried far beyond its original intent as the case with the Pharisees. And then he adds another title for himself in verse 8, "For the Son of Man is Lord of the Sabbath" (underlining mine). Then he promptly entered their synagogue and healed a man with a withered hand to demonstrate his authority and the principle of showing mercy and doing good on the Sabbath as over against strict adherence to a merciless, legalistic interpretation of the law.

The Pharisees were infuriated at Christ's "arrogance," his claim to authority even over the temple, his "flagrant and willful violation" of the Sabbath and even holding others blameless for "breaking" it. So for blasphemy and rebellion there was but one judgment: death. They took council as to how they could effect this judgment. This was particularly difficult since the multitudes accepted Christ as a prophet and he did many mighty works. Putting him to death would be no easy matter.

Now how is it that Jesus is greater than the Temple? Hebrews 3:3,4 gives us one part of the answer. "Jesus has been found worthy of greater honor than Moses, just as the builder of the house has greater honor than the house itself. For every house is built by someone, but God is the builder of everything." So by virtue of the fact that the Lord himself built the Temple (he gave wisdom and ability to the builders and supplied all the materials for it – see Exod.31:1-6; 1 Chr.29:14), he is greater than the Temple. Another reason he is greater is that the Temple is merely a building. The only thing that gives it value is the One indwelling it: God. Christ claimed to be God in the flesh, so his claim to be greater than the Temple naturally follows. It also naturally follows that if he is greater than the Temple, he also is Lord of the Sabbath, for it was he that originated it and he had the right to interpret the spirit of that regulation.

How do we reflect Christ as Greater than the Temple? By recognizing that the church buildings in which we worship have no meaning in and of themselves. They are mere physical structures. It is <u>we</u> who give them meaning by what we do inside them. Therefore, we are "greater" than the church building. As "Lords of the Sabbath"– we should do good and show mercy, even on our day of rest, and should always remember that mercy supersedes law.

Are you so tied down by laws and regulations that you cannot minister at any time to the needs of others?

APPLICATION: It would be well for us to remember that whether we worship in a church building, a school or a home, it is not the building itself that gives it meaning, but those who worship in it. Also, it is right and honorable to do good on the Lord's day just as much as on the other six days of the week. We must be aware of the first and doers of the second, thus reflecting Christ as Greater than the Temple and Lord of the Sabbath.

DAY 272
[b]HE IS OUR HABITATION

◆

QUESTIONS TO THINK ABOUT:

1. What is a "habitation"?

Unexpected Transformation

2. How is the Lord a habitation for us?
3. How can we be a habitation for others?

The scripture referring to the LORD as our habitation is Psalm 91:9. But since it is here referring to the LORD Jehovah rather than specifically to Christ, I nearly "crossed it off." But then I thought of Ephesians and Colossians where we find the phrase "in Christ" a good number of times. Now if we are "in Christ" then he can be nothing other than our spiritual dwelling place, or habitation (John 15:7, "... If you abide in me ...," Jesus said). Psalm 91:9,10 says, "If you make the Most High your dwelling – even the LORD, who is my refuge – then no harm will befall you, no disaster will come near your tent." Paul said to the Athenians in Acts 17:28, "For in him we live and move and have our being." He says to the Corinthians, "Therefore if anyone is <u>in Christ</u>, he is a new creation" (2 Cor.5:17a – underlining mine). Then he speaks of our being rooted and built up in him (Col.2:7). In other words, Jesus is our home!

Now what do you think of when the word "home" is mentioned – or, what would you like to think of when "home" comes to mind? I think of family, those whom I'm closest to, those who understand me best and still love me. I think of security, nothing can harm me while Mom and Dad are there. "Please, make yourself at home," we have all heard. So we kick off our shoes, go to the fridge for a snack and something to drink, and sit down to read a book or watch T.V. Home is a place of welcome, comfort, relaxation, refreshment. Home is a place of peace at the end of a hectic day. If I am away from home and become ill, my first thought is, "I want to go home," for there is security and there is healing.

Christ is our home, our habitation, and we reflect this characteristic as we create the same kind of atmosphere in our homes. We have been in homes where we could cut the atmosphere with a knife and were only too glad to leave. A number of years ago we stayed a few days with a church family. As we sat down for some good fellowship we suddenly were subjected to harsh criticism of this church and that church. We were told how this pastor was falling into sin, and that one teaching wrong doctrine, and another causing division, etc., etc. The spirit of criticism in that place weighed heavily upon us and sapped our emotional and spiritual energy. We left feeling whipped, beaten down and only too glad to get away.

But we have been in other homes where we just didn't want to leave. There we experienced genuine love, generosity, hospitality, heart-felt care and concern, peace and welcome. There was genuine sharing of spiritual things, and a refreshing spirit of godliness and concern for the Lord's work. At the end of a week we felt refreshed, our batteries recharged, and ready to continue on in our ministry.

As we learn to dwell in our Habitation each day, we will be refreshed and strengthened for each day's tasks. Then, as we are ministered to by the Lord himself, we will learn how to minister to others in the same way, becoming a pleasant "habitation" for them.

APPLICATION: "Home is where the heart is." If our hearts are with Christ, then he is our home. If the hearts of others are with us, then our home becomes their home, our family their family, where they can always feel safe, secure and welcome. What kind of atmosphere are you creating in your home?

DAY 273
bHE IS OUR HABITATION, concl.

◆

QUESTIONS TO THINK ABOUT:

1. Christ is our Habitation, but so are we his! How can that be?
2. As we look at ourselves, what kind of habitation does he have?

There is an interesting twist to consider here. Not only is Christ our Habitation, but we are his! Consider the following verses: "If you love me, you will obey what I command. And I will ask the Father, and he will give you another Counselor to be with you forever – the Spirit of truth. The world cannot accept him, because it neither sees him nor knows him. But you know him, for he <u>lives with you and will be in you</u>... . If anyone loves me, he will obey my teaching. My Father will love him, and we will come to him and <u>make our home with him</u>" (Jn.14:15-17,23 – underlining mine).

In Ephesians 2:21,22 we read that in Christ "the whole building is joined together and rises to become a holy temple in the Lord. And in him you too are being built together to become a dwelling in which God may dwell in your hearts through faith" (Eph.3:17a). We also read in Psalm 22:3 that God inhabits the praises of his people. With Christ as the foundation of our house (1 Cor.3:11), our works done in obedience, faith and love for him become the walls and superstructure of the house, and the roof is our praise, covering all that is below. [A lot of us have very leaky roofs!]

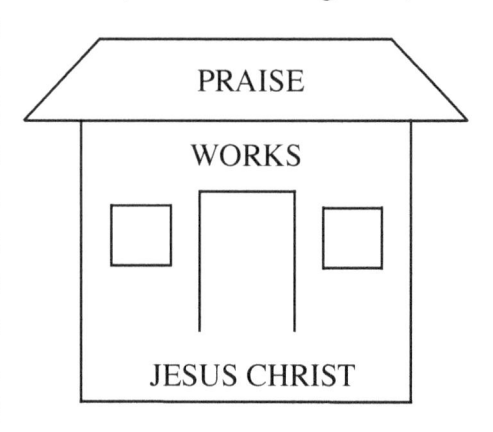

Have you ever consciously considered how you could make Christ feel at home in your heart? What changes would you make? What kind of atmosphere would you create so as to make him feel comfortable? What would you quickly get rid of before he came in? When he enters, would he feel safe and secure? Would he sense a genuine love and concern for what concerns him? Could he "make himself at home," go to the fridge and get a snack and something to drink and relax with any book or magazine from our library or any movie from our DVD collection? Would he feel free to join in with our family chatter and laugh with us? Would he feel at one with us, thoroughly enjoying our fellowship, and desiring to stay on forever?

OR...?

Would he sense a tense atmosphere because of things we're trying to hide from him and we really wish he wouldn't stay very long. We find it very inconvenient, even embarrassing for him to be here. Awkward. We make a few polite inquiries about how he is and how his work is progressing, but aren't really interested. When he tries to talk about deeper spiritual things, we find ourselves quickly out of our depth so try to politely change the subject without trying to be too obvious. He gets the message, so desires to cut his visit short, to his relief and ours, though he is very disappointed, even heartbroken, as he leaves. He has been cheated of the fellowship he created us to have with him, and we have cheated ourselves with the substitute of powdered chaff and dry grass. Is this what we really want?

So we need to ask ourselves, "Would Christ feel at home in my heart right now the way it is? Or do I need to do some house cleaning first?"

APPLICATION: Before partaking in Communion, the Apostle Paul urges us to examine ourselves to take care of any unconfessed sin that we are aware of. That's not unlike a woman cleaning her house before her guests come for dinner. She wants the place spotless! Let's keep short accounts with others and with the Lord, so that his dwelling is as clean as we can make it.

DAY 274
ᶜHE IS THE HOPE OF ISRAEL

QUESTIONS TO THINK ABOUT:

1. How is Christ the hope of Israel?
2. By extension, how, then, does he become our hope?
3. How can we become a hope to others?

In Acts 28:20 Paul tells the Jewish leaders at Rome that he was bound "because of the hope of Israel." In what way does this phrase refer to Christ? In Acts 26:6 Paul refers to "my hope in what God has promised our fathers." Then, in verse 7, he says that it is because of this hope that the Jews are accusing him. In verse 8 he further clarifies this hope as God raising the dead. In Acts 13:32,33, he brings it all together saying, "We tell you the good news: What God promised our fathers he has fulfilled for us, their children, by raising up Jesus. As it is written in the second Psalm: 'You are my Son; today I have become your father.'" So whatever was promised, it was fulfilled at the resurrection of Jesus Christ from the dead.

What was promised can be found in Gen.3:15, 22:18 and 49:10. The hope of Israel was for Satan to be crushed, the world to be blessed, and the Messiah to set up the kingdom. Consider:

1. At the resurrection, Satan was crushed, his power broken. Thus we read in James 4:7 that if we submit to God and resist the devil, he will flee from us.

2. At the resurrection, the world was blessed, for our salvation then became an accomplished fact. The penalty for sin was paid in full, and we were given the right to enter into it if we so desired. In Revelation 5:9 we find people from every kindred, tongue, people,

and nation before the throne of God. Truly in Christ, all nations of the earth are blessed.

3. At the resurrection, Jesus established the kingdom in its invisible form, reigning in the hearts of those who believe in him. He told Pilate that his kingdom was not of this world (Jn.18:36), that is, not "out of" or "according to" this world. It is based on different principles than the world's kingdoms. There will yet be the thousand year reign of Christ on the earth; but for now, his kingdom is in seed form in the hearts and lives of those who believe in him.

Simeon spoke of these three areas of hope when he took the baby Jesus in his arms and praised God (Lk.2:30-32): "For my eyes have seen your salvation [Satan crushed], which you have prepared in the sight of all people, a light for revelation to the Gentiles [all nations blessed] and for glory to your people Israel" [the kingdom].

So how can we reflect Jesus Christ as the Hope of Israel? First of all, <u>by using our God-given authority over Satan</u> to gain daily victory. We give in too much and too readily without a struggle. The Lord overcame him with the Word (Matt.4:1-11), and at other times with a rebuke (Matt.16:23); so may we (but in <u>his</u> power, not our own!). Secondly, <u>by our witness</u>. We also are supposed to be lights in the world (Matt.5:16) and communicators of God's revelation of salvation to others. As we witness to them, the hope of salvation from sin and the prospect of eternal life should be made clear, so that they will know what they are receiving or rejecting. Thirdly, <u>by making Christ Lord and King of our lives</u> now, living as subjects of his kingdom, showing others that there is an alternative to the world's system that is far better and more fulfilling. Thus we reflect Christ not only as the Hope of Israel, but also the hope of the world based upon the promises of God.

Is your life an open channel for God's hope to flow out to others?

APPLICATION: We give hope to others as we share with them our victories in spiritual warfare, the Gospel of salvation in Jesus Christ, and his lordship in our lives as we obey his Word and find out that it works! We cannot take others where we have not been; but as they see the reality of these things in our lives, they will have hope that it can be experienced in their lives too. Thus we reflect Christ as the Hope of Israel, and of the entire world as well!

DAY 275
ᶜHE IS THE MINISTER OF THE SANCTUARY

QUESTIONS TO THINK ABOUT:

1. Of what Sanctuary is Christ the minister, and what is the nature of his ministry?

2. Of what "sanctuary" can we become ministers, thus reflecting this aspect of Christ's character?

In Hebrews 8:1,2 we read of Christ: "The point of what we are saying is this: We do have such a high priest, who sat down at the right hand of the throne of the Majesty in heaven, and who serves in the sanctuary, the true tabernacle set up by the Lord, not by man." As a Minister of the Sanctuary, he serves both man and God. He is the Mediator between God and man (see DAY 68– HE IS THE MEDIATOR), and the High Priest representing man to God (see DAY 69– HE IS OUR HIGH PRIEST). He cares for the interests and concerns of both God and man.

In Matthew 20:28 Christ declared his purpose for coming to earth: "Just as the Son of Man did not come to be served, but to serve, and to give his life as a ransom for many." Thus the word "minister" also carries with it the connotation of Servant (see DAYS 37,38 – HE IS THE KING). As Christ also told his disciples, "Whoever wants to become great among you must be your servant [minister]" (Matt.20:26b).

In Matthew 4:11 we find angels ministering to Christ after his 40-day fast and temptation. In Matthew 8:15 we see Peter's mother-in-law ministering to Christ and his disciples, evidently providing them with a meal. In Luke 8:3 we find a group of women ministering to Jesus and his disciples over a longer period of time, supporting them, as it were, from their substance. In Acts 20:34 Paul says, "You yourselves know that these hands of mine have supplied [ministered to] my own needs and the needs of my companions." And an interesting statement is found in Acts 13:2 (NKJV) where certain prophets and teachers in Antioch "ministered to [worshipped] the Lord and fasted."

So we minister to others (as well as ourselves) when we meet their needs. In the Sanctuary, Christ met our need of a High Priest, a Mediator and a Sacrifice. He met God's need to satisfy his justice and wrath on sin, but at the same time to show forth his love and mercy to sinners. It is no problem for us to figure out how to minister to others. There are more opportunities than we can know what to do with even without looking for them. But how do we minister to the Lord? What are <u>his</u> needs? Does he, the Almighty, All-encompassing, All-sufficient God even <u>have</u> needs?

Well, one doesn't necessarily have to have needs in order to be ministered to. According to Revelation 4:11, the Lord created all things for his own pleasure and, according to Romans 9:22-24, he created to express his nature or character. Now Satan came along and saw God's "painting." Being jealous, Satan got some paint of his own and threw it all over God's masterpiece, marring it beyond recognition. But this picture was different than others, for it came alive and became a vast mural of the history of the world. Many remained besmirched by the Devil's paint. But some God cleaned up, repainted, and gave the power to restore other parts of the canvas. So as we go about restoring our part of the canvas through praise, worship and the good works God has given us to do (see Eph.2:10), through the winning back of bespattered humanity to the Master Painter, God is pleased, his heart rejoices, and we minister to him! When the 70 disciples returned to Jesus and reported success in their ministry (much to their own amazement), it filled Jesus' heart with joy and thanksgiving (Lk.10:17-24). Thus he was able to take pleasure in that much more of his "painting" that had been restored (see also Ps.149:4).

Are you a "splotcher" or a restorer of the Lord's canvas?

APPLICATION: As we seek to serve other believers, the Lord takes that as ministering to him too (see Matt.25:40). As we intercede for them, seek to meet their needs and sacrifice ourselves on their behalf, we become Ministers of the Sanctuary and reflect this characteristic of Christ.

DAY 276
ᶜHE IS THE ONE

QUESTIONS TO THINK ABOUT:

1. How would you feel about being singled out from among the others: "You are the one!"

2. How would we qualify for God to single us out? What would he be looking for?

"Now [Judas] had arranged a signal with them: 'The one I kiss is the man; arrest him.' Going at once to Jesus, Judas said, 'Greetings, Rabbi!' and kissed him" (Matt.26:48,49). And we know the rest of the story. Jesus was singled out for special attention: "He is the man," and was arrested. What made him so special? He was the chief antagonist to the Scribes and Pharisees, challenging their authority, revealing their hypocrisy, exposing their sin by his righteousness, and he claimed Deity. Thus he became the focal point of their jealousy and hatred. He became the main topic of conversation in Galilee and Judea, pro and con. He was "the One."

In the Old Testament we find a man named Job. He "was blameless and upright; he feared God and shunned evil" (Job 1:1). At set times, evidently, the angels come before God to report on their activities or to receive direction for work to be done, and Satan also came among them. God asked Satan from where he had come, to which he replied: "From roaming through the earth and going back and forth in it" (Job.1:6,7).

Then God asked him if he had seen Job, his servant. "There is no one on earth like him; he is blameless and upright, a man who fears God and shuns evil" (Job.1:8; see also Prov.8:13). Satan scoffed: "Sure I've seen him, but I couldn't get close to him because of the hedge of protection you've put around him. Sure he serves you well, for you've given him everything he could ever want or hope for. But take it away from him and he will curse you to your face!" (paraphrased from verses 9-11). And the stage was set for the vindication of God's grace to Job and of Job's faith toward God, neither of which Satan was capable of understanding. "Job is the one," said God. "There's no one else like him in the whole earth." What a statement! What a commendation!

What did Jesus and Job have in common? They feared God and shunned evil. No one could bring an accusation of wrong-doing against either of them. Satan is called "the Accuser of our brothers, who accuses them before our God day and night" (Rev.12:10). But he couldn't find a thing against Job! God had to point out Job to him, not vice versa. Now this is not to say that Job was not a sinner. He was. But when he sinned, he took care of it so fast that Satan never had opportunity to accuse him. Had David confessed his sin straight off, Nathan would never have had to say, "You are the man!" (2 Sam.12:7).

Unexpected Transformation / 623

If we really feared God, as Job did, we also would shun evil (sin). But if we enjoy a sin or two, and find pleasure in watching others sin the sins we'd like to do but are afraid to, then we open up ourselves to Satan's accusations before God and God's discipline to correct us.

In the long run, which is better: Satan's condemnation or God's commendation? "Lord, help us to hate sin as you hate sin. Help us to fear you even as Job did, so that Satan will not be able to point us out in accusation before you, but that you will be able to point us out in commendation to Satan: 'Have you noticed my servant _____?' Amen."

APPLICATION: Being "the one" is not something we strive for. It comes as a result of closely following the Lord and living a life that is pleasing to him. That should be our goal. The other will care for itself in due time.

DAY 277
ᶜHE IS THE PHYSICIAN

QUESTIONS TO THINK ABOUT:

1. What is the role/work of a physician?
2. What does the saying, "Physician, heal yourself" imply?
3. In what two ways can we be "physicians" to others?

With tongue in cheek, the Lord turned a proverb of the Jews upon himself in a rebuke to the people of Nazareth. He said to them, "Surely you will quote this proverb to me: 'Physician, heal yourself! Do here in your home town what we have heard that you did in Capernaum'" (Lk.4:23). What is it that they heard? That which characterized Jesus' ministry as a whole: the sick were healed, demons cast out and the kingdom of heaven preached. What is it that they asked him to do? "If you are a doctor, prove it!" They had no heart to believe; they, like Herod, just wanted Jesus to perform – and he refused. They were infuriated at the contents of his refusal and tried to kill him on the spot.

On another occasion, Jesus and his disciples were eating and drinking with tax collectors and sinners in Levi's (Matthew's) house. The self-righteous scribes and Pharisees complained as usual. Jesus answered them, saying, "It is not the healthy who need a doctor, but the sick. I have not come to call the righteous, but sinners to repentance" (Lk.5:31,32).

Jesus healed the physically sick as well as the spiritually sick. We don't need to look far in the book of Acts to see the early Christians doing the same. At Pentecost 3,000 people were saved – spiritual healing. And daily many more were saved (Acts 2:39,47). In Acts 3:2-8, we see the healing of a lame man. And in Acts 2:43 the general statement: "And many wonders and miraculous signs were done by the apostles." In Acts 14:8-10 Paul and Barnabas healed a crippled man. In Acts 16 Paul and Silas cast out a demon from a slave girl (vs.16-18), and the Philippian jailer and his family were saved early the next morning (vs.30-34).

I recently read of an elderly Chinese woman who had an untreatable illness. The doctors had given up on her. A Chinese evangelist or pastor (I can't remember which, for unfortunately the article was thrown away) came and prayed for her, and she was immediately healed. As a result, she and her entire village became believers. So she was healed in body, and they were all healed in soul.

Paul teaches that gift of healing is one of the gifts given by the Holy Spirit to the Church for the profit (edification) of all (1 Cor.12:7,9,28). But healing in and of itself is of no profit if spiritual truth does not accompany it. With physical healing, the unsaved need to hear the Gospel to understand that God wants to complete the process that he has begun (by his power) by saving their souls as well. With physical healing the believer needs to hear about the need of repentance of sin, God's chastening, and his sovereignty in working through the sickness for his glory (when healing doesn't occur). But we must beware of a dangerous attitude: Just because the gift of healing is grossly misused by some or totally ignored by most, that does not mean that the gift has been discontinued. It just means that a good thing is being misused or disused, but it is still there for the Church to use as God intended it to be. The evidence for this observation worldwide is too overwhelming to be casually dismissed or rationalized away.

May the Lord, through his power, enable us to be physicians of bodies as well as of souls.

APPLICATION: We will more often be "physicians" of the soul through our witness than "physicians" of the body since the gift of healing is not given to everyone. Sometimes healing will occur by a word, sometimes through prayer, sometimes through confession of sin, other times through the Word of God itself. God is not limited as to how he will heal someone. We need to give him that option, and just be ready to do our part if and when he asks us.

DAY 278
[b]HE IS THE REAPER

QUESTIONS TO THINK ABOUT:

1. What is necessary before any reaping can be done?
2. Who is more important, the planter or the reaper? Why do you think so?
3. What kind of reaping will Jesus do? What kind are we to do?

At the end of the Great Tribulation period there will be a harvesting of the earth to judgment. We read in Revelation 14:14-16, "I looked, and there before me was a white cloud, and seated on the cloud was one 'like a son of man' with a crown of gold on his head and a sharp sickle in his hand. Then another angel came out of the temple and called in a loud voice to him who was sitting on the cloud, 'Take your sickle and reap, because the time to reap has come, for the harvest of the earth is ripe.' So he that was seated on the cloud swung his sickle over the earth, and the earth was harvested."

This passage speaks of judgment (the sickle). The time for reaping has come because the earth has run its course (harvest). The word for "ripe" in the Greek is *xeraino* which means "over-ripe, dried up, rotten on the vine." The rest of this chapter (vs.17-20) takes us through the Battle of Armageddon. At this time the seven bowl judgments are poured out one after another in quick succession. The sixth bowl is the gathering of the armies of the world to Armageddon (16:12-16) where "the great winepress of the wrath of God" will be trampled (14:19,20).

God has committed judgment to the Son (Jn.5:27) of which the above reaping is a part. But the Son has committed to us a different kind of reaping, not to judgment but to salvation. When the woman at the well in Samaria went running back to town with the news of the Messiah (Jn.4:28,29), Jesus took the opportunity to teach his disciples about reaping (vs.35-38). He told them: "Do you not say, 'Four months more and then the harvest'? I tell you, open your eyes and look at the fields! They are ripe for harvest. Even now the reaper draws his wages, even now he harvests the crop for eternal life, so that the sower and the reaper may be glad together. Thus the saying, 'One sows and another reaps' is true. I sent you to reap what you have not worked for. Others have done the hard work, and you have reaped the benefits of their labor."

Seldom do we sow spiritual seed and also reap the harvest. Others reap where we have sown and we reap where others have sown. I think of our work in Senggo. For several years before our arrival there, there was a Christian school teacher who sowed the Seed. When we arrived and began teaching the Citakers (CHEE-tuckers) in more depth from the Word and through their own language, they began to respond and receive Christ.

I think of a college buddy whom I led to the Lord one day. He had begun attending a Navigator's Bible study with me where the Seed was sown. Finally the harvest was ready, and it was I who reaped, not the leader of our study. Yet, true to verse 36, "The sower and the reaper [will be] glad together." We were, and he who was "reaped" also rejoiced!

We see this in God's promise in Psalm 126:5,6. "Those who sow in tears will reap with songs of joy. He who goes out weeping, carrying seed to sow, will return with songs of joy, carrying sheaves with him."

Are you sowing <u>and</u> reaping?

APPLICATION: In order to sow, you must know your seed (Bible study, reading the Word, etc.); in order to reap, you must know what the harvest looks like (cf. Matt.13:24-30) and what implements to use to bring it in (see DAYS 25-30 – HE IS THE WITNESS). We must remember that this is a "group effort." No one person will sow and reap. Sometimes it's years between the two! And sometimes the reaping involves many workers along the way. If we are faithful in doing our part, the Lord of the Harvest will do his, and we will come "rejoicing, bringing in the sheaves."

DAY 279
ᶜHE IS THE REFINER

QUESTIONS TO THINK ABOUT:

1. Why do precious metals need to be refined?
2. How often do they need to be "passed through the fire"? Why?
3. How does God's "smelting process" help us become more like Christ?

In prophesying of the Messiah, Malachi said of him: "But who can endure the day of his coming? Who can stand when he appears?

For he will be like a refiner's fire or a launderer's soap. He will sit as a refiner and purifier of silver; he will purify the Levites and refine them like gold and silver. Then the LORD will have men who will bring offerings in righteousness" (Mal.3:2,3).

Ezekiel details the process even more, saying: "Then the word of the LORD came to me: 'Son of man, the house of Israel has become dross to me; all of them are the copper, tin, iron and lead left inside a furnace. They are but the dross of silver. Therefore this is what the Sovereign LORD says: "Because you have all become dross, I will gather you into Jerusalem. As men gather silver, copper, iron, lead and tin into a furnace to melt it with a fiery blast, so will I gather you in my anger and my wrath and put you inside the city and melt you. I will gather you and I will blow on you with my fiery wrath, and you will be melted inside her. As silver is melted in a furnace, so you will be melted inside her, and you will know that I the LORD have poured our my wrath upon you"'" (Ezek.22:17-22).

Isaiah prophesies with the same imagery in Isaiah 1:25,26, telling of restoration after judgment. He says, "I will turn my hand against you; I will thoroughly purge away your dross and remove your impurities. I will restore your judges as in days of old, your counselors as at the beginning. Afterward you will be called The City of Righteousness, The Faithful City."

In Psalm 12:6 we learn of the thorough process of refining: "The words of the LORD are flawless, like silver refined in a furnace of clay, purified seven times."

The process involved here is that of smelting. To use iron as an example, the iron ore is first "washed" with chemicals, water and heat to remove dirt and other impurities adhering to it. Then the smelting process is begun in which the iron ore is melted in such a way as to remove impurities within it. A blast furnace is lined with coke and limestone and then fired to a great heat. The coke burns and produces carbon monoxide (CO) which combines with oxygen molecules in the iron ore, removing them to form carbon dioxide (CO_2). Other impurities melt to combine with the limestone to form a liquid collection of refuse (dross or slag) which is lighter than the iron. This slag rises to the top of the molten metal and is siphoned off. However, the metal is still impure, so must be refined further. As the Psalmist indicates above, silver, to be really pure, must be smelted "seven times." [However, I suspect that this might be a figure of speech, since "seven" is the number of perfection. So God's words are as pure as silver would be if it were refined seven times.] But at any rate, any metal ore requires several times in the smelting process before it is really pure.

Have you ever wondered why, once you've been through a certain trial, it is repeated another time, perhaps in a different form or perhaps in the same way as before? Not all "impurities" or "imperfections" are removed the first time through!

APPLICATION: The "impurities" or "imperfections in our lives are those things which keep us from conformity to Christ's image. So God has to take us through various experiences and trials in order to remove them from our lives so that the reflection of Christ's image will be more clearly seen. The faster we learn, the less "smelting" we will have to go through.

DAY 280
cHE IS THE REFINER, cont.

QUESTIONS TO THINK ABOUT:

1. What kind of things constitutes God's refining fire in our lives?
2. What is the overall purpose of his refining us?
3. What happens if we resist his refining process?

The prophets indicated that God and the Messiah had a goal in mind as they refined Israel through the smelting fires of judgment and trials: to make them righteous, to purify them, and to make them like God himself in character.

Job recognized this in his very severe trials. He told his three accusing friends: "But he knows the way that I take; when he has tested me, I will come forth as gold" (Job 23:10).

James reflects this view in his letter to the scattered tribes, saying what our attitude should be when being refined: "<u>Consider it pure joy</u>, my brothers, whenever you face trials of many kinds, because you know that the testing [purifying] of your faith develops perseverance. Perseverance must finish its work so that you may be mature and complete, not lacking anything" (Jas.1:2-4, underlining mine). We read in verse 12: "Blessed is the man who perseveres under trial, because when he has stood the test, he will receive the crown of life that God has promised to those who love him."

Remember that each of us is a different kind of "metal ore," so the Lord has to suit the smelting process accordingly. Some of us want to hold on to the impurities of our lives, refusing to yield them up to become slag that will be washed away. So the smelting process has to be repeated again and again and again until we yield them up. Keep in mind that this is not to judge us, but to purify (discipline) us so that we can become all that God has created us to be: like himself. This is what Hebrews 12:10,11 says: "Our fathers disciplined us for a little while as they thought best; but God disciplines us for our good, <u>that we may share in his holiness</u>. No discipline seems pleasant at the time, but painful. Later on, however, <u>it produces a harvest of righteousness and peace</u> for those who have been trained by it" (underlining mine).

As a child, I would become very angry if I lost a game. It got to the place where no one wanted to play games with me anymore, because if I lost, I'd get furious. An "impurity" in the "metal ore." So the Lord kept smelting me in the blast furnace of "lost games" until I learned to lose with grace. But then there was still anger against situations that didn't go my way, or things breaking down that I couldn't fix. Anger and selfishness combined. So the smelting process continued to remove these impurities. The worst of it is over, but the Lord still has need to re-stoke the furnace now and then. It has taken a <u>lot</u> longer and much hotter flame to smelt these out than the original anger at losing a game. But the Lord is patient, and he will keep right on smelting us until we readily yield up the sludge and slag in our lives to his refining fires.

By the way, the faster we give up the sludge, the sooner he can turn down the fire! There will always be areas in our lives needing purifying, but if we respond quickly to his promptings, the refining process will not be nearly so painful; and we will find our trials not so much a purifying from impurities as a strengthening of our faith and character. However, the choice is ours depending on how badly we want to hold on to our impurities, or what we are willing to throw off at any cost in order to become like Christ.

What is your choice?

APPLICATION: Think of difficulties/trials you have gone through. What was your attitude was in them? As you look back, can you see how they strengthened your faith or helped you become more like Christ by getting rid of sinful sludge in your life? If not, can you discern what God might have been trying to accomplish in your life through them? Take some time to pray, thanking the Lord for what he has done, or confessing your resistance to what he was trying to do, and make whatever attitude adjustments necessary for the "next round." Pray for a teachable spirit and a willingness to change, always keeping in mind God's ultimate goal for your life – to make you like Christ – and using these trials to get you there.

DAY 281
ᶜHE IS THE REFINER, concl.

QUESTIONS TO THINK ABOUT:

1. How does the Lord use us, negatively and positively, in the refining process in the lives of others?
2. What qualifies us to be refiners in their lives?
3. How can a sharp rebuke be given with a gentle spirit?

The Lord has engaged us also in the refining process in the lives of others, both negatively and positively. Negatively (*passive, unintended refining*), we have all experienced personality clashes. I have been in a leadership position where a fellow believer resented my authority and made life miserable for me in general. The Lord was using this person in my life to refine the qualities of patience, endurance, humility and really committing my trials to him without harboring resentment, anger and a spirit of revenge against the offending party. It's always a lot harder to take "guff" from a fellow Christian than from an unbeliever. I know of times when I've rubbed others the wrong way as well. So it works both ways.

<u>Positively</u> (*active, intentional refining*), there are many commands in Scripture about how we are to encourage others into a more godly lifestyle. Consider the following:

Proverbs 27:6 – "The kisses of an enemy may be profuse, but faithful are the wounds of a friend."

Proverbs 27:17 – "As iron sharpens iron, so one man sharpens another."

Unexpected Transformation / 633

Titus 2:15 – "These, then, are the things you should teach. Encourage and rebuke with all authority. Do not let anyone despise you."

2 Timothy 4:2,3a – "Preach the Word; be prepared in season and out of season; correct, rebuke and encourage – with great patience and careful instruction. For the time will come when men will not put up with sound doctrine."

Hebrews 3:12,13 – "See to it, brothers, that none of you has a sinful, unbelieving heart that turns away from the living God. But encourage one another daily, as long as it is called Today, so that none of you may be hardened by sin's deceitfulness."

Hebrews 10:25 – "Let us not give up meeting together, as some are in the habit of doing, but let us encourage one another – and all the more as you see the Day approaching."

Many other such references could be used, but these are sufficient to show that we also are responsible to encourage our Christian brothers and sisters to godly living. Some will hear, others will become angry and reject our encouragements, even as we often do to the Lord. But even as the Lord perseveres, so must we, in persistent love and patience. There will come the right time when they will respond.

APPLICATION: To be a refiner, we must know what the Word says and have experienced the refining process personally, responding to it in a godly way. In other words, don't try to refine others unless you are being refined yourself and applying it in your own life!

DAY 282
ᵇHE IS THE SEALED ONE

QUESTIONS TO THINK ABOUT:

1. What is the significance of a seal?
2. Is it possible for the contents of a sealed document to be changed?
3. What does it mean to be sealed for something?

Many people were seeking Christ because of the food he had given them. In John 6:27, he admonished them, "Do not work for food that spoils, but for food that endures to eternal life, which the Son of Man will give you. On him God the Father has placed his seal of approval."

In Christ's day, the seal was a pad of soft wax imprinted with the ring of the wearer, unique to him only. Thus any letter or document bearing a seal of wax with that imprint would immediately be recognized as originating from that person, and would carry with it all the authority that he possessed or was recognized as having (see Esth.8:8). So Christ, saying that God had sealed him, was declaring that he had come to earth to work with the full authority and power of God himself. God had fully approved him for the task to be done.

A seal was also the sign of ownership. In 2 Timothy 2:19 we read: "Nevertheless, sealed with this inscription: 'The Lord knows those who are his' and, 'Everyone who confesses the name of the Lord must turn away from wickedness.'" The 144,000 in Revelation 7:2-4 and 14:1 are sealed with the name of the Father written on their foreheads. No doubt the seal itself is invisible, but not to the Lord. He knows those who are his. However, there is an outward sign of the seal, the righteous life (2 Tim.2:19b). This anyone can see. We are also said to be "marked in him with a seal, the promised

Holy Spirit, who is a deposit guaranteeing our inheritance until the redemption of those who are God's possession to the praise of his glory" (Eph.1:13b,14).

Christ taught and worked with full authority. We read in Matthew 7:28,29 that "... the crowds were amazed at his teaching, because he taught as one who had authority, and not as their teachers of the law." Another time he was challenged by the chief priests and elders of the people who asked him, "By what authority are you doing these things? ... And who gave you this authority?" (Matt.21:23b). In Luke 9:1,2 Jesus gave his disciples "... power and authority to drive out all demons and to cure diseases and he sent them out to preach the kingdom of God and to heal the sick." In Matthew 28:19,20 he commissions them with authority to make disciples of all nations, teaching them to do all the things he commanded them.

In 2 Corinthians 5:18-20, we read where God has committed to us the ministry of reconciliation. So we labor as "Christ's ambassadors, as though God were making his appeal through us. We implore you on Christ's behalf: Be reconciled to God." An ambassador is one who speaks on behalf of his government to another government. He has the seal of authority, the approval of his government to so speak. Christ has this seal of authority from God, and we have it from Christ. So as long as we stick to the "policy manual" of our heavenly Government, we will be able to teach and work with the full authority of God.

Are you stamped with the seal of God's approval?

APPLICATION: To be sealed and approved by God, we first have to have received Christ as our personal Savior. Then we have to read and study the Word of God (our "policy manual") in order to know what the message is that he wishes to convey through us to the world. People will judge God and his kingdom by what they see in us. If we are hypocritical and dishonest in our dealings with others, that will be their evaluation of God and his kingdom;

if we are ambassadors of honesty and integrity, then they will be much more inclined to believe our message and, hopefully, "change their citizenship."

DAY 283
ᶜHE IS THE SEED OF THE WOMAN

QUESTIONS TO THINK ABOUT:

1. What does it mean that Christ is the Seed of the Woman? Which woman?
2. What was the implication of this title in his life and ministry?
3. How would this title apply to us?

The first promise of the Messiah and indication of his birth (and work) was given by God to none other than Satan himself! Since Satan had set himself up to ruin everything that God had made, it was most appropriate for God to declare to him that his efforts had already failed. He said: "I will put enmity between you and the woman, and between your offspring and hers; he will crush your head, and you will strike his heel" (Gen.3:15). [**NOTE:** This verse explains, by the way, the "unreasonable" persecution of Jews and Christians around the world and the blind acceptance and toleration of all other -isms, for there is enmity, deep hatred, between Satan's seed and the woman's. The two representative systems are deeply antagonistic and Satan will energize his seed to oppose the woman's at every turn, whether they realize or not what they are doing.]

Paul again emphasizes Christ's virgin birth in Galatians 4:4, saying, "But when the time had fully come, God sent his Son, born of a woman, born under the law." He was born of a woman, not of a man and a woman. Matthew records the angel's message to Joseph when he was contemplating divorcing Mary on grounds of adultery: "But after he had considered this, an angel of the Lord appeared to him in a dream and said, 'Joseph son of David, do not be afraid to take Mary home as your wife, because what is conceived in her is from the Holy Spirit'" (Matt.1:20).

As the Seed of the Woman, Christ would suffer at the hands of Satan ("You will strike his heel"), but Satan will be totally defeated by Christ ("He will [utterly – Greek *suntribo*] crush your head"). We understand that this "crushing" took place at the Cross where the principalities and powers were disarmed and made a public spectacle in their defeat (Col.2:15). The resurrection was the seal of Satan's doom, the removal of the sting of death, and the final word on victory over sin (see 1 Cor.15:25,26,55-57).

If we are in Christ, then we are also a part of his victory over Satan. Paul declares in Romans 6:5 that "If we have been united with him in his death, we will certainly also be united with him in his resurrection." This whole passage (6:1-14) is a declaration of our victory over sin, death and Satan in Christ.

In encouraging the Roman Christians to stand for the truth and righteousness (Rom.16:17-19), Paul gives them this promise (vs.20): "The God of peace will soon crush Satan under your feet." How will this be done? How can we crush Satan? For the answer, let's look at Revelation 12:11. "They [our "brothers" from vs.10] overcame him [Satan, the Accuser from vs.9,10] by [1] the blood of the Lamb [Calvary – this is our foundation] and by [2] the word of their testimony [their witness to others in both winning the lost and standing up for righteousness before the unsaved]; [3] they did not love their lives so much as to shrink from death" [They were willing to die for what they believed, so they witnessed boldly without fear of death]. A willingness to die for what we believe has not yet been tested, but a bold witness and a willingness to stand up for righteousness is on the decrease as very few Christians are willing to do either. Thus the Church that should be victorious over the Devil seems to be being slowly strangled to death by him!

Have you also thrown away your victory by laying down your arms before our defeated foe?

APPLICATION: If we are in Christ, then we are already in the place of victory over Satan who can harass us, but can't defeat us! Ultimately, Christ will send him to his final and already determined doom. Often we forget our position in Christ and try to face our battles on our own. That doesn't work! It is only in Christ's power and authority that we can overcome in the skirmishes and look forward to ultimate victory. So, as the writer of Hebrews encourages us, "Fix your eyes on Jesus" (Heb.12:2).

DAY 284
ᵇHE IS THE SOWER

QUESTIONS TO THINK ABOUT:

1. How is the sharing of the Gospel like sowing seed?
2. What is it that actually causes the seed to sprout and grow?
3. Apart from the Gospel, what else in our lives is referred to as seed?

Having given the parable of the wheat and the tares to the multitudes (Matt.13:24-30), Christ explained its meaning to his disciples (vs.36-43). In verse 37 he says, "The one who sowed the good seed is the Son of Man." In verse 19 he defines the "good seed" as the "word of the kingdom," the kingdom message. What was that? It was what John the Baptist, Jesus and his disciples preached everywhere: "Repent, for the kingdom of heaven is at hand!" (see Matt.3:2). So this parable of the Sower has immediately to do with Israel's

Unexpected Transformation / 639

rejection of the kingdom through the rejection of their King. But wherever he went, Christ sowed the seeds of the kingdom message and confirmed it with miracles through the power of the Holy Spirit.

Later on, Paul applies the same imagery to his own work in spreading the Gospel of Christ. In 1 Corinthians 3:6 he writes: "I planted the seed, Apollos watered it, but God made it grow." No longer is it the kingdom message which the Jews heard and rejected, but it is the message of salvation through faith in Christ which the Gentiles have received. But first there needs to be the sowing of the seed. This takes place as we initially give the Word to others through our witness or through lessons from the Word (as in Sunday School, VBS, kids' clubs, adult Bible studies, etc.). The reapers are often, but not always, those who have the gift of evangelism. But before they can reap, the seed must be sown, and that is something we all can and must do regardless of our spiritual gifts. We go where most others will never go; we meet those whom most others will never meet. So it is up to us to be light and salt to those around us and thus plant the seed of the Word in their lives.

But the Gospel is not the only "seed" we sow. There are varieties of seeds of righteousness and sin that we can sow in our own lives. We can sow trouble (Job.4:8), discord among others (Prov.6:16,19), strife (Prov.16:28), iniquity (Prov.22:8), rebellion (Hos.8:7); and will reap trouble, the Lord's anger, perversity, sorrow and the whirlwind. On the other hand, we can sow to ourselves righteousness (Prov.11:18b), and the fruits of righteousness (Jas.3:18) along with "spiritual things" (1 Cor.9:11). These are pretty general terms, but the fruits of righteousness and the fruit of the Spirit are easily one and the same: "love, joy, peace, patience, kindness, goodness, faithfulness, gentleness and self-control" (Gal.5:22,23). Peter lists other like seed for us to sow in 2 Peter 1:5-7 promising a fruitful harvest (vs.8): "… Make every effort to add to your faith goodness … knowledge … self-control … perseverance … godliness … brotherly kindness … love. For if you possess these qualities in increasing measure, they will keep you from being ineffective and unproductive in your knowledge of our Lord Jesus Christ."

There are two principles to remember in our sowing. These are found in 2 Corinthians 9:6 and Galatians 6:7,8: "Remember this: Whoever sows sparingly will also reap sparingly, and whoever sows generously will also reap generously." "Do not be deceived: God cannot be mocked. A man reaps what he sows. The one who sows to please his sinful nature, from that nature will reap destruction; the one who sows to please the Spirit, from the Spirit will reap eternal life."

In everything we do, we reap what we have sown, and the abundance of our harvest is directly proportional to how much we have sown.

Is your seed still in the bag?

APPLICATION: Before the farmer sows his seed, he plans how it will be done. This principle applies to us as well. I use teaching and preaching as my primary "seed sowing," but also have Gospel tracts that I give to those who serve me or with whom I have had some conversation. Seed sowing has to be intentional or it won't get done. Pray, asking the Lord how he would have you do it, then take steps (make plans) how you will go about it. He said in Acts 1:8, "You will be my witnesses when the Holy Spirit has come upon you." That's our commission and our enablement to fulfill it! Let's get it done!

DAY 285
[b]HE IS THE STAR

QUESTIONS TO THINK ABOUT:

1. In what different ways are the stars used by us here on earth?
2. How do we use the word "star"? What does it signify?

Unexpected Transformation

When Israel reached the plains of Moab (Num.22), Balak, king of Moab, hired Balaam to curse Israel. But the Lord would only allow him to bless Israel instead. In this blessing came also a prophecy regarding the Messiah. In Numbers 24:17 we read: "I see him, but not now; I behold him, but not near. A star will come out of Jacob; a scepter will rise out of Israel. He will crush the foreheads of Moab, the skulls of all the sons of Sheth."

In Revelation 22:16 Jesus told John, "... I am the Root and the Offspring of David, and the bright Morning Star," paralleling Balaam's prophecy.

The "morning star," usually the planet Venus, is the brightest of "stars" shining just before sunrise. Thus it "announces" the beginning of a bright, new day. So when Christ claimed to be the Bright and Morning Star, he was saying that his coming will be the announcement of a bright, new day in the history of man, the day of his kingdom on earth full of righteousness, peace and the blessing of God. No wonder the immediate response of the Holy Spirit and the Bride in verse 17 is, "Come!" In Revelation 2:28 Christ promises the morning star (himself) to those who overcome.

I cannot resist a slight diversion at this point. Another reference to the morning star is found in 2 Peter 1:19. "And we have the word of the prophets made more certain, and you will do well to pay attention to it, as to a light shining in a dark place, until the day dawns and the morning star rises in your hearts." From <u>The Bible Knowledge Commentary</u> (Walvoord & Zuck. Victor Books, Wheaton, IL. pp.868,869), the following comments (adapted) are made: The prophetic word is God's Word, the Scriptures, as a light (Gk. *luchno*, an oil-burning lamp – cf. Ps.119:105 "Your word is a lamp to my feet," etc.) shining in a dark place (this world full of sin and spiritual darkness), until the day dawns (Christ's return, when lamps are no longer needed) and the morning star (Christ Himself as the Light-Bringer) rises in (illuminates) your hearts (though the light which it brings on that great day will be greatly exceeded by the understanding which will be <u>in</u> their <u>hearts</u>).

At that time, Christ himself will be shining in our hearts with an illumination that we have never known before. With this in mind, let's turn to 1 Corinthians 13:9-12, "For we know in part and we prophesy in part, but when perfections comes, the imperfect disappears... . Now we see but a poor reflection; then we shall see face to face. Now I know in part; then I shall know fully, even as I am fully known." When the Morning Star rises in our hearts, then the Lamp of God will not need to shine where the glory of the True Light is radiating. (We do not need our Sweetheart's letters any longer when we are in his/her presence!). <u>Then</u> we shall know even as we are known, as the Morning Star shines in our hearts and all around us. We shall see him with unveiled eyes, beholding the splendor of his glory with an unsoiled heart.

In Daniel 12:3 the wise are said to "shine like the brightness of the heavens, and those who lead many to righteousness, like the stars for ever and ever." As the coming of the Lord heralds the New Day of his kingdom, so our coming into the lives of the unsaved with the message of the Gospel can herald a "new day" for them right now. Second Corinthians 5:17 declares: "Therefore, if anyone is in Christ, he is a new creation; the old has gone, the new has come!" For that person, the New Day has dawned.

How brightly is your star shining?

APPLICATION: Our lives should radiate the brightness of the Lord's presence in our hearts. There should be an aura about us that others will recognize as "different, and good." This will only happen as we grow in our relationship with the Lord and become more like him. As we make this our priority, many, if not all of the characteristics of Christ that we have studied will be there also.

DAY 286
ᶜHE IS OUR SUBSTITUTE

QUESTIONS TO THINK ABOUT:

1. What does the word, "substitute" imply?
2. How was Christ a "substitute" for us?
3 How can we be a "substitute" for others?

Have you ever considered taking on yourself some else's punishment for the wrong he has done? Not many of us are called upon to do that, and fewer would volunteer! But we read in Isaiah 53:6 that Christ took our sins on himself, as if he had done them, and then died because of them. Romans 5:8 says that "While we were still sinners, Christ died for us" [died in our place]. The Jews were very familiar with this concept through their sacrificial system. Every day a lamb or goat died because of the worshiper's sins, though the lamb or goat did nothing to deserve that fate.

One day I was called upon to translate a script for a film strip into Indonesian. The story was about two brothers, one a Christian, the other a thief. The thief refused to listen to his brother's witness. One day he was cheated by his crime boss, so he killed him. The police came after him, so he ran to his brother for protection. His brother took his twin's torn and blood-spattered shirt and gave him his new, fresh one. Then, after writing a note to him containing a final witness about how Jesus Christ became our Substitute to die in our place so that we might live, he went to the police station to "give himself up." He was convicted of murder and shot. This demonstration of Christ's love and compassion won his brother's heart and he surrendered himself to Christ, determined to take his brother's place as a servant of God.

The Apostle Paul reflects this same attitude in Romans 9:3 where he writes: "For I could wish that I myself were cursed and cut off from Christ for the sake of my brothers … ." Moses pleaded with God, after the incident with the golden calf at Mount Sinai, "But now, please forgive their sin – but if not, then blot me out of the book you have written" (Exod.32:32). Epaphroditus, a fellow worker with Paul, was honored by Paul with this commendation: "Welcome him in the Lord with great joy, and honor men like him, because he almost died for the work of Christ, risking his life to make up for the help you could not give me" (Phil.2:29,30). He was willing to be a substitute for the Philippian Christians in meeting Paul's needs, and nearly died in the process.

I heard of a father once who was so exasperated with his rebellious child that he had his child spank him for the child's misbehavior! It worked. The child became like a new person after that.

There are many ways we can become a substitute for others: by actually dying for them, by taking on ourselves their punishment because of their wrong, by giving ourselves in service on behalf of someone else, by assuming another person's debts, and so on.

Are you willing to be a substitute?

APPLICATION: Being a substitute for someone else is perhaps the greatest sacrifice we could ever make. It would really test our dying to self and loving someone else with that agape love that would compel us to act on their behalf. The best preparation for this eventuality, at whatever level it presents itself, is to deal with our basic selfishness and the prioritizing of our own plans, hopes and schedules, and submitting ourselves to God's loving sovereignty – for it is he who is orchestrating these events for his glory and our blessing!

DAY 287
ʽHE IS THE SUFFICIENT ONE

QUESTIONS TO THINK ABOUT:

1. If we think, "I can do that!" why can't we?
2. How can the use of our spiritual gifts and talents serve as a supply for the needs of others?

Paul wrote in 2 Corinthians about the Lord's sufficiency in our suffering, in our giving, and in our daily lives and ministry. He writes: "Three times I pleaded with the Lord to take [my thorn in the flesh] way from me. But he said to me, 'My grace is sufficient for you, for my power is made perfect in weakness'" (12:8,9a). And again in 2 Corinthians 9:8 we read: "And God is able to make all grace abound to you, so that in all things at all times, having all that you need [sufficiency], you will abound in every good work." Again in 2 Corinthians 3:5,6a, "Not that we are competent [sufficient] to claim anything for ourselves, but our competence [sufficiency] comes from God. He has made us competent [sufficient] as ministers of a new covenant."

We recently read a part of the testimony of E. Stanley Jones, Methodist missionary to India. When he was old, he suffered "a debilitating stroke that left him immobile and virtually speechless. But not faithless. 'I need no outer props to hold up my faith,' he wrote, 'for my faith holds me'" (<u>Ordering Your Private World</u>, by Gordon MacDonald, Nashville, Oliver Nelson, 1984, p.125). He found the Lord's sufficiency in his suffering.

The Lord also gives us sufficient abundance in order to perform every good work that he desires us to do once we have set our hearts on doing it. Some time ago we began praying that the Lord would give us $10,000 so that we could give it to a particular work of God.

We were asking for a one-time amount, but the Lord has chosen to answer in small increments. As of this writing, we have more than exceeded that amount! The Lord has answered above and beyond what we originally asked for.

In our ministry, the best that we can do is to present the truths of God's Word to our students. But there is no way we can touch their hearts and minds to bring about conviction of the truth and a willingness to obey it apart from the ministry of the Holy Spirit in our lives and theirs, giving us faith to believe and power to obey. So as God gives us the means for carrying on our ministries and the power to do it through the Holy Spirit, our sufficiency becomes an extension of his sufficiency toward meeting the needs of others. Thus as he meets our needs through his sufficiency, we can meet the needs of others through ours and they, in turn, to others.

I am encouraged by what Paul wrote in 2 Corinthians 9:8,10,11 in this regard: "And God is able to make all grace abound to you, so that in all things at all times, having all that you need, you will abound in every good work. …Now he who supplies seed to the sower and bread for food will also supply and increase your store of seed and will enlarge the harvest of your righteousness. You will be made rich in every way so that you can be generous on every occasion, and through us your generosity will result in thanksgiving to God." Our sufficiency is of him!

As Jesus commissioned the 12 disciples and sent them out to announce the kingdom of God and to minister to the needs of the people, he sent them with these words: "Freely you have received, freely give" (Matt.10:8b). So may we do also.

How sufficient is your God?

APPLICATION: God, in his sufficiency, meets our needs and supplies what we need in order to help others. The first thought is that through our sharing from our substance we can meet the material needs of others. But in another way, in terms of ministry, as we use whatever spiritual gifts and talents we have in service, that could free up others to serve according to their spiritual gifts and talents. In other words, our "sufficiency" enables them to use their "sufficiency" in serving still others. We need to be faithful in both areas as the Lord enables us.

DAY 288
ᶜHE IS THE SUN OF RIGHTEOUSNESS

◆

QUESTIONS TO THINK ABOUT:

1. What is the definition of righteousness?
2. What common characteristics do the sun and righteousness share?
3. How can these characteristics apply to Christ?

In Malachi 4:2a there is a prophecy which some take as a reference to Christ as the coming Messiah and others take to be the Day of the Lord in general where righteousness will pervade the kingdom as the sun's rays pervade throughout the earth: "But for you who revere my name, the son of righteousness will rise with healing in its wings."

In Revelation 1:16c we read John's description of Christ: "His face was like the sun shining in all its brilliance." And of his people we read in Matthew 13:43, "Then the righteous will shine like the sun in the kingdom of their Father." So the title for Christ as the "Sun of Righteousness" is very apropos.

We have already dealt with Christ as the Righteous One (see DAY 15), defining and describing righteousness, so we will not repeat that here. But what we now need to look at is this additional title, "Sun," to find out how it relates to righteousness.

"Righteousness" was defined as "conformity to God's standard," and Christ conformed 100% to it. That standard is the perfect, holy nature of God himself. Thus as we speak of righteousness, we speak of the character of Christ, as pictured and demonstrated here by the sun. Consider the following:

1. As the sun's rays penetrate everywhere, so will righteousness. Righteousness will be the scepter of Christ's kingdom (Heb.1:8) and the guiding rule of his judgments. We read in Isaiah 26:9b, "When your judgments come upon the earth, the people of the world learn righteousness." John puts it this way: "Christ the true light that gives light to every man was coming into the world" (Jn.1:9).

2. Sunlight contains all the colors of the rainbow blending together to form white light. All of God's promises, as signified by the rainbow, emanate from his righteous character and purpose. Christ is the embodiment of God's promises to us, for in him the greatest promises of God have been fulfilled.

3. The thermonuclear fusion occurring in the sun releases sufficient amounts of energy to keep the sun shining for billions of years. Two things here we notice: 1. the sun is its own source of light and energy. So is Christ. In the New Jerusalem, according to Revelation 21:23, "the city does not need the sun or the moon to shine on it, for the glory of God gives it light, and the Lamb is its lamp." 2. "Billions of years" is long enough to indicate eternity by our standard of time. Christ is eternal. He will keep shining for eternity as his inexhaustible righteousness will keep his light burning brightly.

APPLICATION: Jesus said that we are lights in the world and should let our light shine revealing God's glory and the sin of mankind. Our light shines as we obey God's Word (cf. Matt.5:14,16). Because the Church is world-wide, so will be the light that shines forth from us.

DAY 289
ᶜHE IS THE SUN OF RIGHTEOUSNESS, cont.

◆

QUESTIONS TO THINK ABOUT:

1. How can a sense of Christ's presence encourage spiritual life in us?

2. What do heat and light from the sun and consistency in Christ's life have in common?

4. We continue from yesterday considering the fourth aspect of Christ as the Sun of Righteousness. Life on earth depends on the sun for food and air (oxygen). Green plants create their own food and grow through the process of photosynthesis, by which the plant cells combine energy from sunlight with CO_2 from the air and water in the ground. Oxygen is given off as a by-product, thus enabling other life forms to breathe. Many of these plants are also edible, thus providing food for other living things. In John 5:21 we read, "For just as the Father raises the dead and gives them life, even so the Son gives life to whom he is pleased to give it." Paul says in Acts 17:28a, "For in him we live and move and have our being." Thus as we depend upon sunlight for physical life, we also depend on "Sonlight" for spiritual life.

5. Sunlight is useful for many things: 1. we can see by it, 2. tell time by it, 3. get direction from it and even 4. calculate our position on earth by it. As the light of the world, Jesus revealed the works of God for all to see clearly (Jn.9:5). The Jews could have recognized "the time of God's coming to [them]" (Lk.19:44) had they accepted Christ as their Messiah. The Lord gave direction to his disciples through his teaching (cf. Matt.5-7) by which they could order their

lives in a way pleasing to the Father. And our position in the spiritual realm is also clear: if we keep his commandments (equal to doing "correct calculations"), we will abide in his love, even as he kept his Father's commandments and thus abides in his Father's love (Jn.15:10).

This positional relationship is described even fuller by Paul in Colossians 3:3 where he writes: "For you died and your life is now hidden with Christ in God." And again in 1 Corinthians 3:23, "And you are of Christ, and Christ is of God." In conclusion, we read in Revelation 21:23,24, "The city does not need the sun or the moon to shine on it, for the glory of God gives it light, and the Lamb is its lamp. The nations will walk by its light, and the kings of earth will bring their splendor into it."

6. Heat and light from the sun makes the development of life on earth possible. As the sun's light and energy strike the earth, the earth's atmosphere traps in the heat, thus making the earth a giant greenhouse conducive to life and growth. We have in our hearts a God-created "atmosphere" that will trap and hold the warmth of Christ's love and the light of his countenance which will make possible the development of our spiritual lives. If the heat and light of the sun varied, life would be endangered (see Rev.16:8 and 8:12 that hint of this), but the sun's output is totally consistent. Hebrews 13:8 says that "Jesus Christ is the same yesterday and today and forever." His total consistency guarantees our spiritual life and health.

On a practical level, righteousness always creates a healthy environment for progress and growth since progress and growth depend on honesty and trust, integral factors of righteousness (see Prov.14:34 and 21:21).

APPLICATION: Truthfulness, honesty and consistency are crucial factors in developing trusting relationships with others. In developing these characteristics, people will believe you even if they don't agree with you!

DAY 290
ᶜHE IS THE SUN OF RIGHTEOUSNESS, cont.

◆

QUESTIONS TO THINK ABOUT:

1. As the sun is a source of energy, how can Christ "energize" us in our personal lives and in his work?

2. An appropriate amount of sunlight brings healing. How does this picture the way the Lord brings healing to us?

7. Too much sunlight is harmful to men and beast alike. It can burn the skin, blind the eyes, cause skin cancer and death. When John saw the glorified Christ (Rev.1:16b,17), whose face "was like the sun shining in all its brilliance," he fell at his feet as dead. John could not bear the full glory of Christ. As God told Moses in Exodus 33:20, after Moses had requested to see his glory (vs.18), "You cannot see my face, for no one may see me and live." God's glory would kill us outright in our physical state; it is too bright, too intense, too powerful, too holy. Only when we have our resurrection bodies will we be able to see the fullness of God's glory and live. Too much sunlight is synonymous with too much heat from the sun. In James 1:10,11a we read, "But the one who is rich should take pride in his low position, because he will pass away like a wild flower. For the sun rises with scorching heat and withers the plant; its blossom falls and its beauty is destroyed." In Revelation 16:8,9 "the fourth angel poured out his bowl on the sun, and ... they were seared by the intense heat and ... cursed the name of God... ." So the heat of the sun speaks of judgment. Man cannot stand before the light of his glory or the intense heat of his wrath. As the writer of Hebrews says in 12:29, "... our God is a consuming fire."

8. The sun is also a source of energy. Solar energy creates wind, which in turn, drives windmills, fills the sails of ships, and sends refreshing breezes for our comfort. It evaporates water which then forms in clouds which, when "too heavy" with moisture, drop rain on the earth, forming rivers from which energy is taken to drive hydroelectric plants to produce electricity. It heats water causing it to circulate in pipes heating homes and providing hot water without using expensive fuels. Solar energy is used to recharge batteries – and so on – a multitude of uses. So the Lord, through his Holy Spirit, energizes us in a multitude of different ways to do his work here on earth (Acts 1:8a, "But you will receive power when the Holy Spirit comes on you").

9. We read in Malachi 4:2 that "the sun of righteousness will rise with healing in its wings." Whereas too much heat from the sun is deadly, just the right amount of heat promotes healing. A distant friend of ours once suffered from rheumatoid arthritis in a wet, tropical climate. His doctor recommended a warm, dry climate where he should live, and in a short time he was off all medication and no longer suffering from his arthritis. Christ went about healing and doing good. No sick person ever went away from him still sick. They were all healed who came to him.

10. Finally, the sun is also an object of worship (for some – see Ezek.8:16). Christ is our "sun," the focus of our worship. Because of all that he is, he is worthy of our praise and adoration. We sing to him, pray to him and seek to serve him. He is our Sun of Righteousness. Without him we could not exist.

APPLICATION: As you read and study the Word, pay attention to things that you could share with others for their encouragement. Nothing "brings life" like sharing the Word together. Since "a joyful heart does good like a medicine" (Prov.17:22), there will be many side benefits to this activity, among which we will be like the good amount of sunlight in their lives.

DAY 291
ᶜHE IS THE SUN OF RIGHTEOUSNESS, cont.

◆

QUESTIONS TO THINK ABOUT:

1. What effect will or should our good works have before others?
2. If we are living according to the promises of God and others see that, what effect will that have on them?
3. How is it possible for us to create a spiritually life-sustaining environment for other believers as well as for unbelievers?

Now we come to the main questions I've been asking myself throughout the last three days: "How can we reflect Christ as the Sun of Righteousness?" Let's consider each description of the sun again and try to answer this question as we go along.

1. Its rays penetrate everywhere. So will righteousness in Christ's Kingdom. We are to let the light of our righteousness "shine before men, that they may see [our] good deeds and praise [our] Father in heaven" (Matt.5:16).

2. Sunlight contains all the colors of the rainbow, which symbolizes God's promises to us. Christ is the embodiment of God's promises to us both in living them out in his life and in opening the way for us to experience them. As other believers see the reality of God's promises lived out in our lives, our message to them will take on new credibility and they also will be encouraged to trust his promises. As we witness to unbelievers, sharing the Gospel, we open up the way for them to experience God's promises as well. This is implied in 2 Corinthians 5:18 where "… God … reconciled us to himself through Christ and gave us the ministry of reconciliation."

Reconciliation is the making of peace between two or more parties. God's promise of peace through our Lord Jesus Christ is one of his greatest promises to man.

3. The sun is its own source of light and energy, with sufficient energy to keep it shining for billions of years. Christ is his own source of light and energy ("God is light" – 1 Jn.1:5b) and he is eternal. Christ is described as the "image of the invisible God" (Col.1:15) and "… the radiance of God's glory and the exact representation of his being, …" (Heb.1:3). As Christ reflected the glory and righteous character of God, so we can reflect the glory and righteous character of Christ – by becoming like him and acting like him. So as the Lord himself indwells us, our source of light is from within, a Source with sufficient energy to keep us shining for eternity! And, according to 1 Peter 5:10, it is to this that we have been called: "… God … called you to his eternal glory in Christ… ."

4. The sun provides a life-giving environment. Christ gives life to whomever he will. Here we find an environment created which sustains life. In our homes, our churches, and other places we can create or provide the kind of environment that will sustain spiritual life as well as physical life – keeping in mind that one's spiritual health always affects one's physical health. As parents and church leaders "practice what they preach" and others see that Christianity really "works," an environment of receptivity is created in which weak Christians will become strong and non-believers will receive spiritual life as they are drawn to the Savior. Thus we reflect the life-giving, life-sustaining ministry of Christ with resulting growth and stability of the Church. Paul hints at this in Ephesians 4:11-13 where he writes: "It was he who gave some to be apostles, some to be prophets, some to be evangelists, and some to be pastors and teachers, to prepare God's people for works of service, so that the body of Christ may be built up until we all reach unity in the faith and

in the knowledge of the Son of God and become mature, attaining to the whole measure of the fullness of Christ."

APPLICATION: The only way we can develop these characteristics of Christ as the Sun of Righteousness, is by having a close relationship with him. If we are walking close to him, these characteristics will be so much a part of our being that we won't have to "try" to do them, they will flow out of our hearts as naturally as water flowing down a stream.

DAY 292
ᶜHE IS THE SUN OF RIGHTEOUSNESS, cont.

QUESTIONS TO THINK ABOUT:

1. How important is our example as a light for others to follow?
2. Why is it important that others see consistency in our lives?
3. What is the role of truth in the progress and growth of an economy, not to say one's own life?

5. The light from the sun helps us see things, tell time, direction and geographical position. Through Christ we can see spiritually, discern the signs of the times, receive direction for our lives, and be aware of our position before God. The writer to the Hebrews indicates that spiritual leaders can and should provide the same light for those under their authority. Hebrews 13:7 says, "Remember your leaders, who spoke the word of God to you. Consider the outcome of their way of life and imitate their faith." Paul said in 1 Corinthians 11:1, "Follow my example, as I follow the example of Christ." By our lives and through the Word, we can provide light for others to see by and gain direction in their lives.

6. The light from the sun is consistent. It does not vary. Even so Christ is consistent, the same yesterday, today and forever (Heb.13:8). He doesn't change. We always do, either from fickleness, change of circumstances, just plain cantankerousness, or gaining of new understand or maturity. Consistency and mankind have little in common. To be consistent we need a rule or standard that is consistent, and that standard is the Word of God! As we align our lives to its precepts, we will begin to live more and more consistently. Consistency provides a healthy environment for growth, for it gives stability to whatever we endeavor to do. One reason for the lack of progress in underdeveloped countries is the lack of trust. Lying is a way of life, truthfulness is not important. But lying creates instability, and instability uncertainty, and uncertainty caution. This is no way to build a country's economy. There must be trust, but in order to establish trust there must be the consistency of truth. So James writes, "… Do not swear … by anything… . Let your 'Yes' be yes, and your 'No' be no, or you will be condemned" (Jas.5:12). Having to swear that what we are saying is true indicates an inconsistent environment of untruth where neither physical or spiritual progress will be made. But consistent truthfulness will create an atmosphere of trust and that will enable great progress in every area.

7. Because of the sun's brightness, man cannot look at it directly with the naked eye. The effect of too much light and heat from the sun is dangerous to one's health! No man can look upon Christ's glory and live. He must be judged as one unworthy to behold the Lord's glory. Thus the heat of the sun can symbolize judgment. We as believers, having the Sun of Righteousness indwelling us, should be able to judge various matters with the wisdom of God. In 1 Corinthians 6:2 Paul writes, "Do you not know that the saints will judge the world? And if you are to judge the world, are you not competent to judge trivial cases?" We will never have the overpowering glory of Christ here on earth, but the closer we are to him, the

stronger will be the aura of God's presence about us and the sense of authority in what we do and say. Thus as we judge with righteous judgment, no one will be able to stand against it.

APPLICATION: As exemplars of light, consistency and truth, what James said (as quoted above) applies fully: we must be men and women of our word. If we say, "Yes," that is what we should mean. If we say, "No," then that is what we should mean. If we are known as men and women of our word, then we will have the credibility to minister in all these other areas.

DAY 293
"HE IS THE SUN OF RIGHTEOUSNESS, cont.

◆

QUESTIONS TO THINK ABOUT:

1. How does your Christian life compel others to action?
2. How does one discern the cause of an illness as to a physical cause, a psychological cause, a spiritual cause (sin) or because of spiritual warfare? Then, how does one go about "treating" it?

8. We also saw that the sun is a source of energy. The Lord, through his Holy Spirit, energizes us to do his will in serving him. In the same way, we can often serve as catalysts to start things and get people moving in a desired direction. We just finished reading a book about Martin Luther. Talk about being a catalyst, his writings set the whole of Europe in motion and began the Reformation. Paul and Silas were accused of "turning the world upside down" (Acts 17:6). Wherever they went, people had to make a choice whether or not to receive Christ as Savior and leave their old religions. Paul and Silas's message got them moving one way or the other. So we can be

a challenge to those around us in their lives to make a decision for Christ and to grow in their walk with him.

9. The right amount of heat from the sun promotes healing. Christ healed literally multitudes of sick people. So may we in a number of ways. Much sickness results from emotional and spiritual problems. But healing can come through words of encouragement. Consider the following: Proverbs 12:25, "An anxious heart weighs a man down, but a kind word cheers him up." Proverbs 12:18b, "But the tongue of the wise brings healing," or, as the Living Bible says, "The words of the wise sooth and heal." Proverbs 15:1a, "A gentle answer turns away wrath." Proverbs 25:11, "A word aptly spoken is like apples of gold in settings of silver."

There is also healing power in prayer. James 5:14-16a: "Is any one of you sick? He should call the elders of the church to pray over him and anoint him with oil in the name of the Lord. And the prayer offered in faith will make the sick person well; the Lord will raise him up. If he has sinned, he will be forgiven. Therefore confess your sins to each other and pray for each other so that you may be healed."

While we were at the TEAM Hostel in Sentani (sen-TAH-ni, Papua), there was a time when I was experiencing extreme physical weakness and much discomfort and pressure in my chest. I felt like I could hardly breathe. I mentioned my distress to the leader of our prayer fellowship and he immediately called together several others to come and pray for me. As they prayed, the feeling of pressure in my chest vanished. I could breathe easily and began to feel refreshed. Gradually my strength returned. I will be forever grateful for their loving concern and effectual prayers. James 5:16b, "The prayer of a righteous man is powerful and effective."

A third way we can be involved in bringing health to others is through the proper use of medicine. The danger in medicine is in its use to treat the symptoms rather than the causes – treating the physical with no regard to the spiritual. The two must be combined, and often the need for medicine will be alleviated by the resolution of the underlying spiritual/emotional problems. As one example, one time I had a terrible headache. Aspirin didn't even touch it. After about five hours and two more aspirins with no let up, I confessed the sin I knew was in my heart, and within ten minutes my headache was gone! Another time I had a headache that again did not respond to medication, nor did it let up when I confessed what sin I could find in my heart. But it <u>did</u> respond immediately to a rebuke in the name of the Lord Jesus Christ. Other times confession of sin and a rebuke didn't help at all, but aspirin did!

APPLICATION: We, of ourselves, cannot compel others to action. That can only come as they see the presence and power of the Holy Spirit in our lives and surrender themselves to the Lord as a result. When it comes to healing others, again, that is the Lord's doing, not ours; but he often graciously involves us in the process. As you read through the Gospels and Acts, pay particular attention to places where Jesus or Luke mentioned the cause of someone's sickness. List them, then determine under which category mentioned above that particular sickness falls and how it was dealt with. I believe the Lord will give us discernment for each situation as we minister to the sick so that we will know how to help them or how to get them help.

DAY 294
ᶜHE IS THE SUN OF RIGHTEOUSNESS, concl.

QUESTIONS TO THINK ABOUT:

1. How should we handle the honor and praise from others for what we have done? How does God get the glory because of it?

2. What kind of life will compel unbelievers to acknowledge that Christ loves us?

10. Finally, we see the sun as an object of worship: men worshiping the symbol rather than the One symbolized. The Triune God alone is to be worshiped. Worship involved praise, adoration, honor and a sense of unworthiness on the part of the worshiper compared with the one worshiped. As we serve the Lord here on earth, there will be times when men will honor us for what we have done. They will "sing our praises" to others. This reflects the worship that must be given to the Lord, and when we are thus honored, we must direct the praise to him, remembering what he said to his disciples in John 15:5b, "Apart from me, you can do nothing." In Revelation 3:7-13, the Lord praises the church at Philadelphia and gives them a promise (vs.9): "I will make those who are of the synagogue of Satan, who claim to be Jews though they are not, but are liars – I will make them come and fall down [worship] at your feet and acknowledge that I have loved you." In this "worship" is the acknowledgement of the truth of the faith we possess, and acknowledgement of the Lord who loves us. Thus because of us, the Lord is ultimately worshiped by those who do not believe. This should provide a strong motivation toward a holy, God-honoring lifestyle so that when men honor us, they are actually honoring and worshiping the Lord!

One time when Corrie ten Boom was being honored for her tireless work, she was given a huge bouquet of roses. She immediately raised them up "to the Lord" giving him the credit for all she had done.

In Matthew 13:41-43 we read that in the Day of Judgment, when the wicked are cast into hell, "Then the righteous will shine like the sun in the kingdom of their Father." In that day we will not only reflect Christ's glory as the sun, but we will share that very glory having been made complete in his image (cf. Rom.8:18; 2 Cor.3:18). Our righteousness will be perfect righteousness, our service untarnished, our worship pure and undefiled, our love for the Lord unclouded, our surrender to him complete and unreserved. We will walk in the light of his glory and reflect that glory as a perfect mirror. What a perfect and glorious day that will be!

Are you getting ready for it? How bright is your sun shining?

APPLICATION: Regarding praise from others, we just have to remember that without Christ, we can do nothing; so we must die to the pride that would be so easily stoked by what others say. As to unbelievers "worshiping" at our feet, what we need to concentrate on is the same thing the Philadelphia Church was noted for: keeping Christ's word, not denying his name and patient endurance. Whatever honor comes from that will be the Lord's doing.

DAY 295
[a]HE IS OUR SUPPORTER

◆

QUESTIONS TO THINK ABOUT:

1. What does it mean to give or lend support to someone?
2. What does Solomon imply when he says that a three-fold cord cannot be broken? (cf. Eccl.4:9-12)

Lazarus was dead. Mary and Martha, his sisters, were crushed. Jesus had not come in time to heal him. He had not heeded their urgent plea for help. When he finally arrived, Martha met him with a mixture of grief and faith and perhaps accusation as well. "When Martha heard that Jesus was coming, she went out to meet him, but Mary stayed at home. 'Lord,' Martha said to Jesus, 'if you had been here, my brother would not have died. But I know that even now God will give you whatever you ask.' Jesus said to her, 'Your brother will rise again.' Martha answered, 'I know he will rise again in the resurrection at the last day.' Jesus said to her, 'I am the resurrection and the life. He who believes in me will live, even though he dies; and whoever lives and believes in me will never die. Do you believe this?' 'Yes, Lord,' she told him, 'I believe that you are the Christ, the Son of God, who was to come into the world'" (John 11:20-27).

Jesus came to Martha with words of comfort, support and hope, and she acknowledged the truth of what he said based on who she believed him to be. Yet she had no idea about what was going to happen to her brother within the next hour. Where she felt the comfort of Christ's support in her grief, she was totally unprepared for what was about to happen. Upon arriving at the tomb, "Jesus wept" (vs.35), then ordered the stone to be removed from the grave's mouth. Martha was shocked. "But, Lord," [she said,] "by this time there is a bad odor, for he has been there four days" (vs.39). "Then Jesus said, 'Did I not tell you that if you believed, you would see the glory of God?'" (vs.40). Then he prayed, commanded Lazarus to come out, and grief gave way to joy and utter amazement.

Most of us will never have such a dramatic experience as this. In fact, many of us will have to bear grief or physical affliction for years without relief. It is in these situations where we need the Lord's support – and that support is assured to us in Deuteronomy 33:27a where we read, "The eternal God is your refuge, and underneath are the everlasting arms." Here lies the foundation of our support for all situations, the arms of the eternal God are <u>always</u> under us to support us and keep us from falling. If we have a continuing trial, he has promised us grace to endure it (see 2 Cor.12:7-9). He has also promised that he would never permit us to be tested beyond our endurance (1 Cor.10:13), but when that point is reached, he will open a door of relief, a door of deliverance. And sometimes that deliverance comes from unexpected quarters. Martha certainly didn't expect her brother to be raised that same hour. Yet he was. A surprise deliverance to be sure! And the Lord's promise in Hebrews 13:5, "Never will I leave you; never will I forsake you," assures us that those everlasting arms will always be there to support us.

As Martha, we can be supported and sustained by the very words of Jesus himself through his written Word or through a word of prophecy (a word of encouragement from the Lord through someone for any given situation). As an example (as referred to in DAY 293 – HE IS THE SUN OF RIGHTEOUSNESS, but in more detail here), when I was sick in Sentani, and the folks from our prayer fellowship came to pray for me, not only was I physically suffering, but I was worried that I might die – and there was so much yet to do and responsibilities to fulfill. During our time of prayer, a word of prophecy was given that greatly encouraged my heart and changed my worry to confidence. The Lord assured me that he was going before to prepare the hearts of the students at the Bible School for his Word as I taught them. He challenged me to walk close to him and be sensitive to the voice of his Spirit. "Surely he wouldn't be speaking like this if I was going to die," I reasoned. Thus I was greatly encouraged and healed psychologically and soon physically.

Another time, shortly after we arrived in Sowi (SOW-ee, Irian Jaya), to teach in the Theological College there, once again I was suffering from extreme physical weakness. It was an effort to breathe – I just couldn't seem to get that deep, refreshing breath that we take for granted every time we breathe. I was desperate and pleaded with the Lord for someone to come and pray for me, or somehow something be done to deliver me from this weakness. "Lord, I can't teach and fulfill all my other responsibilities feeling this way!" I had just been reading in Psalm 68 (NKJV) and had gotten to verse 27, stopped to pray and plead with the Lord as a wave of weakness came over me, then resumed my reading at verse 28: "Your God has commanded your strength; strengthen, O God, what You have done for us." I read it again and realized that the Lord was answering my prayer immediately. Just that fast, the feeling of weakness left me and my physical strength and stamina improved. I have never stopped praising him for this miracle.

Likewise we can support, encourage and meet the needs of the Lord's people through **hospitality** ("you ... have refreshed the hearts of the saints" – Philm.7b), **prayer** ("pray for each other so that you may be healed" – Jas.5:16b), and **compassion** ("For I was hungry and you gave me something to eat, I was thirsty and you gave me something to drink, I was a stranger and you invited me in, I needed clothes and you clothed me, I was sick and you looked after me, I was in prison and you came to visit me... . Whatever you did for one of the least of these brothers of mine, you did for me" – Matt.25:35,36,40b).

After my father died, my mother was very much at loose ends trying to adjust and frustrated with the mechanics of maintaining a house. When the men of the church realized her need, and the needs of other widows in the church, they set up a committee to monitor and meet these needs as they were made known. This support went a long way in helping Mom adjust to living alone as she knew she could call on someone anytime she needed help. In our support of one another, we will strengthen the body of believers and thus reflect Christ as our Supporter.

APPLICATION: Before we can give or lend support to others, we have to be aware of their needs. You can obtain that information from your pastor or others involved with them. Pray, asking the Lord whom he wants you to help and in what way. Then do it.

DAY 296
ᶜHE IS OUR SURETY

QUESTIONS TO THINK ABOUT:

1. What does the word "surety" mean?

2. How can we become a surety for someone?
3. In what way is Christ our surety?

In Hebrews 7 the superiority of Melchizedek's priestly order is emphasized over that of Aaron's. Christ is declared to be a priest forever in the order of Melchizedek (vs.17). The Aaronic priesthood was based upon lineal descent (vs.13-16), but Christ's priesthood was by an oath (vs.20,21). This oath became the foundation of the New or Better Covenant, and Christ, being made High Priest of the New Covenant, thus became its "surety" or guarantee that this Covenant indeed will be fulfilled. We read in verses 20-25, "And it was not without an oath! Others became priests without any oath, but he became a priest with an oath when God said to him: 'The Lord has sworn and will not change his mind: "You are a priest forever."' Because of this oath, Jesus has become the guarantee of a better covenant. Now there were many of those priests, since death prevented them from continuing in office; but because Jesus lives forever, he has a permanent priesthood ... because he always lives to intercede for them." Thus because of God's oath and because Christ lives forever, the New Covenant is guaranteed forever. As W. E. Vine puts it (Vol. IV, "Surety," p.97), "As the Surety He is the personal guarantee of the terms of the new and better covenant, secured on the ground of His perfect sacrifice (vs.27)."

In Scripture we find only three instances where someone has declared himself surety for someone else or something else. In Genesis 44:32, Judah declares to Joseph regarding Benjamin: "Your servant guaranteed the boy's safety to my father. I said, 'If I do not bring him back to you, I will bear the blame before you, my father, all my life!'" Thus Judah guarantees Benjamin's safety as far as is humanly possible. In Israel the guaranteeing of another's debt must have been common, for in Proverbs Solomon warns against this practice several times. In Proverbs 6:1-3 we read, "My son, if you have put up security for your neighbor, if you have struck hands in pledge for another, if you have been trapped by what you said, ensnared by the words of your mouth ... then ... free yourself" (slightly paraphrased). Again in Proverbs 17:18 he says, "A man lacking in judgment strikes hands in pledge and puts up security for his neighbor." The third example is that of Paul when interceding for Onesimus to Philemon. In Philemon 18,19a he writes: "If he has done you any wrong or owes you anything, charge it to me. I, Paul, am writing this with my own hand. I will pay it back ... ." Paul was willing to assume Onesimus' debt in order to make peace between him and his master. Paul's promise based on his character and relationship with Philemon became the guarantee that the debt would be paid. This is exactly Christ's position as our surety. We owed God a debt we couldn't pay. Christ assumed that debt, based on his character and relationship with the Father, so making peace and thus assuring our acceptance with the Father.

We can reflect this characteristic of Christ as we promise to meet the needs of others as our resources allow. A national fellow-worker had a motor bike that needed repairs. We had the money to pay for it; he did not. So we told him to find out how much it would cost and we would guarantee payment. Thus we became his "surety" that the motor bike repairs would be paid for and that he need not worry about it.

APPLICATION: Becoming surety for someone is very risky unless you have the resources to back it up. Even promises to pay it back can fail to be met, so be sure you can stand the loss if it comes to that. You must also be sure that by becoming surety for someone, you are not just enabling them to continue in an unhealthy financial pattern, "knowing" that you will always be there to bail them out.

DAY 297
ᵃHE IS THE TEMPLE

QUESTIONS TO THINK ABOUT:

1. What is the significance of the Temple?
2. How can we be considered the temple of the Living God?

In describing the New Jerusalem in Revelation 21, John says, "I did not see a temple in the city, because the Lord God Almighty and the Lamb are its temple" (vs.22). The Temple was the focal point of prayer, praise, sacrifice and worship resulting in a sense of God's presence and glory. All these things come together in Jesus Christ. The New Jerusalem will be the physical manifestation of that glory, emanating from Christ himself.

A precursor of that glory was seen at the erection of the Tabernacle and the dedication of the Temple where the Shekinah Glory Cloud so filled both places that no one could enter either one to serve (see Exod.40:34,35; 2 Chr.5:13,14). That was physical.

There also is a spiritual temple. The Lord said in Matthew 18:20, "For where two or three come together in my name, there am I with them." Here is an "invisible, spiritual temple" formed by the union of several believers with Christ in their midst. The New Testament imagery regarding this temple likens each believer to a brick or building stone, each being placed in his own spot in the wall. This temple is still unfinished, yet Christ indwells it and jealously guards its purity. Taken from two passages, we read: "You also, like living stones, are being built into a spiritual house …" (1 Pet.2:5a), "built on the foundation of the apostles and prophets, with Christ Jesus himself as the chief cornerstone. In him the whole building is joined together and rises to become a holy temple in the Lord. And in him you too are being built together to become a dwelling in which God lives by his Spirit" (Eph.2:20-22).

To the Jew, the Temple was a physical building where God dwelt among his people, thus it became the focal point of their faith, the place where God was "located." The key concept here is, "God is among his people." The same can be said about the New Jerusalem, the Bride of Christ, in which or among whom the Lamb dwells. Thus the Bride, the Church, also is the Lord's temple. This gets mind boggling: Jesus is the temple in which we dwell, but we are the temple in which he dwells! (cf. Jn.17:21,23; 14:23).

Then comes a stern warning regarding the use of this temple. In 1 Corinthians 3:16,17 Paul writes: "Don't you know that you yourselves are God's temple and that God's Spirit lives in you? If anyone destroys God's temple, God will destroy him; for God's temple is sacred, and you [plural] are that temple." As an example of this warning, while we were in Papua, there was a national pastor who had lost all of his spiritual perspective. He'd preach beautifully from his vast knowledge of Scripture, then go home and treat his wife "like a chair," she said. He took to himself ungodly men as assistant pastor and head elder, and these three caused nothing but grief to the National Church. Then he began to harp on the same subject month after month. If people got bored, they were bored with the Word of God, and that was sin! If he didn't feel properly honored, or if there was any doubt cast upon his views, he would throw a temper tantrum, ranting and raving wherever he might be. "If anyone destroys God's temple, God will destroy him." A year or two later he died of a heart attack at 45.

Can others sense God's presence and glory through you as his temple?

APPLICATION: The Temple was the focal point of prayer, praise, sacrifice and worship resulting in a sense of God's presence and glory. If these graces are not a part of or are weak in your life, what

Unexpected Transformation / 669

steps could you take to institute them or strengthen them? Under each focal point, list the steps you need to take in order to strengthen each one. It would be helpful to get the input of others as well since "talking things out" can more easily clarify what needs to be done.

DAY 298
HE IS THE TEMPLE, concl.

QUESTIONS TO THINK ABOUT:

1. Why must the Temple of God be holy?
2. How should the holiness God demands for his Temple affect the way we live?

Not only is the union of believers considered a temple, but each individual believer, indwelt by the Eternal God is a temple. In a strong exhortation to holiness, Paul writes to the Corinthian believers: "Do you not know that your body is a temple of the Holy Spirit, who is in you, whom you have received from God? You are not your own; you were bought at a price. Therefore honor God with your body" (1 Cor.6:19,20).

Nothing that defiled was permitted to enter God's Temple. It was the place of undefiled worship from which undefiled and undiminished glory emanated. As Paul again reminded his readers: "For God, who said, 'Let light shine out of darkness,' made his light shine in our hearts to give us the light of the knowledge of the glory of God in the face of Christ. But we have this treasure in jars of clay to show that this all-surpassing power is from God and not from us" (2 Cor.4:6,7). It wasn't the gold, silver, cedar wood and beautiful embroidered hangings that made the Temple dazzling. These are mere earthly elements. What made the Temple dazzling was the glory of God. We are just ordinary us! Nothing flashy, of little note, and of limited ability. But put the glory of God inside us and the temple becomes a dazzling display of God's power and grace. The challenge is this: Who will be that ordinary one who will so purge his temple of all that defiles outwardly and inwardly, so that God's full glory will be displayed for all to see?

So, to summarize, we see three temples in which God dwells: the temple of our bodies, the temple of the local church and the completed Temple (the New Jerusalem) joining together all believers from all ages. And yet it is all one Temple!

The purpose of God's Temple was to provide a place of worship in which and from which his glory and power could be seen. Through Christ, God's power and glory are clearly demonstrated. As we cleanse our temples, individually and corporately, more and more of God's power and glory will be seen through us.

APPLICATION: God's Temple must be holy because he is holy (cf. Lev.11:45b). The challenge for us to keep the Temple "clean." We want to make it a place where he is not ashamed to "live" and where others can "come" to worship him unhindered. And we need his help to do it.

DAY 299
ᶜHE IS THE TESTATOR

QUESTIONS TO THINK ABOUT:

1. Who is a testator and what does he/she do?
2. How did Christ fulfill this role?
3. How can we reflect him in this role?

A testator is one who makes out a will or testament on behalf of those for whom he is responsible if they survive his death. The will is a legal guarantee that such-and-such possessions are the testator's and that upon his death, these are to become the property of his stated heirs. Without a will, there is no legal proof as to what is the person's property, and upon his death, the State confiscates everything and sells it, leaving the person's survivors with little or nothing of what the testator wanted. Those who could have been adequately provided for for many years could potentially be reduced to poverty.

We find that both the Old and New Covenants (Testaments) only took effect upon the death of the Testator, God himself in the person of Jesus Christ. The Old Testament sacrifices merely prefigured the death that would "legalize" everything. We read in Hebrews 9:13-18, "The blood of goats and bulls and the ashes of a heifer sprinkled on those who are ceremonially unclean sanctify them so that they are outwardly clean. How much more, then, will the blood of Christ, who through the eternal Spirit offered himself unblemished to God, cleanse our consciences from acts that lead to death, so that we may serve the living God! For this reason Christ is the mediator of a new covenant, that those who are called may receive the promised eternal inheritance – now that he has died as a ransom to set them free from the sins committed under the first covenant. In the case of a will, it is necessary to prove the death of the one who made it [the testator – KJV]. Because a will is in force only when somebody has died; it never takes effect while the one who made it [the testator] is living. This is why even the first covenant was not put into effect without blood." So Christ died that we might receive the provisions of our spiritual inheritance. We have been well cared for in every way. And best of all, he didn't stay dead, but arose from the dead in order to administer the provisions of his will to us.

There are two ways we can reflect Christ as the Testator. One, on the physical level, is to draw up a will for the benefit of our families.

Some have neglected this, saying, "The Lord will care for my family after I'm gone," but failing to realize that he will do that initially through a will. In light of what happens to the heirs when there is no will (as mentioned above), not having a will could be regarded as criminal negligence and a total disregard of one's family.

On the spiritual level there are two wills we can leave for those who survive us. One is the will of our memory. Something no one could ever take from our heirs. From my father, I have the memory of common sense, faithfulness and basic honesty. From my grandmother the memory of fellowship as we often played games together. From my grandfather the memory of an unfailing humor, quiet patience, and a total, simple trust in God.

The other will is that of the spiritual lessons we pass on to others through our example, our teaching, and what we write down in books, journals or diaries. Don't be loathe or lazy to write down the blessings you receive from the Word, for they may prove to be key turning points in the lives of others later on.

Have you written your wills for your physical and spiritual heirs?

APPLICATION: Our lives are a legacy of influence that will affect others as they remember us. May we live in such a way as will continue to bring growth to the kingdom of God after we are no longer on the scene.

DAY 300
HE IS THE TREASURE HOUSE

QUESTIONS TO THINK ABOUT:

1. What does it mean that in Christ are hidden all the treasures of wisdom and knowledge?

Unexpected Transformation / 673

2. How can we become a repository of wisdom and knowledge?

We read in Colossians 2:3 of Christ, "In whom are hidden all the treasures of wisdom and knowledge." Wisdom (Greek, *sophia*) means, "The all-encompassing insight into the true nature of things." Knowledge (Greek, *ginosko*) means, "A personal and true relation between the person knowing and the object known." And these are hidden (Greek, *apokruphoi*), meaning, "To conceal from, to keep secret" in Christ. All – There is not a single aspect of wisdom or knowledge that has not originated in Christ. So to be truly wise and knowledgeable, we have to begin with him.

The people who heard him were continually amazed, having known his background, and questioned, "'Where did this man get these things [teachings]?' they asked. 'What's this wisdom that has been given him, that he even does miracles!'" (Mk.6:2). In John 2:24,25 we read, "But Jesus did not entrust himself to them, for he knew all men. He did not need man's testimony about man, for he knew what was in a man."

In Acts 4:13 we find Peter and John confounding the educated elite of the day. "When they saw the courage of Peter and John and realized that they were unschooled, ordinary men, they were astonished and they took note that these men had been with Jesus" [the source of all knowledge and wisdom]. Of Stephen we read in Acts 6:10, "But they could not stand up against his wisdom or the Spirit by which he spoke." He was a man full of faith (vs.8), the Holy Spirit and wisdom (vs.3).

Like Peter, John and Stephen, the Lord says that we also are treasure houses. In Matthew 12:35, he says, "The good man brings good things out of the good stored up in him, and the evil man brings evil things out of the evil stored up in him." Apart from the Lord himself indwelling and the treasury of our heart, Peters suggests some of the jewels and gems that we are to store there (2 Pet.1:5-8): faith, goodness, knowledge, self-control, perseverance, godliness, brotherly kindness and love, with the promise that "if [we] possess these qualities in increasing measure, they will keep [us] from being ineffective and unproductive in [our] knowledge of our Lord Jesus Christ."

When the door of a treasury is opened, every time the glitter and splendor of the riches within it are seen. The "door" to our treasury is our mouth. Each time we open it, what do others "see"?

APPLICATION: The Temple had its gatekeepers to guard what was inside. The Psalmist prayed in Psalm 141:3, "Set a guard over my mouth, O LORD; keep watch over the door of my lips." Jesus said in Matthew 12:34b (NKJV), "For out of the abundance of the heart the mouth speaks." Prov.23:7 (NKJV), "For as [a man] thinks in his heart, so is he." And Paul says in Philippians 4:8, "Finally, brothers, whatever is true, ... noble, ... right, ... pure, ... lovely, ... admirable – if anything is excellent or praiseworthy – think about such things." So what we think about the most is what will make up the treasures in our "storehouse." And from those "treasures" our mouth will speak. Will others then discover the treasures of wisdom and knowledge, or tarnished metals of self-delusion and foolishness? As we follow Paul's exhortation in Philippians 4:8, our treasure house will be filled with that which will bring blessing to others.

DAY 301
HE IS THE UNDEFILED

QUESTIONS TO THINK ABOUT:

1. What would it mean to a Jewish person to be considered "undefiled"?

2. What is the difference between being undefiled outwardly and undefiled inwardly?

In Hebrews 7:26, Christ's character as our High Priest is set forth: "Such a high priest meets our need – one who is holy, blameless [undefiled – NKJV], pure, set apart from sinners, exalted above the heavens." "Undefiled" (Greek, *amiantos*) means, "to be free from contamination." In the Jewish mind, to be defiled was to be ceremonially unclean, and therefore unfit to come into God's presence either for worship or for service. There were many things by which a person could be defiled. **Eating**: with unwashed hands, what dies naturally or is torn by beasts, food offered to idols or improperly prepared (according to the Law). **Cooking**: using human waste as fuel. **Agriculture**: sowing of two kinds of seed in one's vineyard. **Bodily contact**, **touching**: creatures that crawl about on the ground, someone who has a bodily discharge or something that that person has touched, or a corpse (human or animal). **Sickness**: leprosy, or a bodily discharge of any kind. **Sex**: sexual impurity and perversity. **Idolatry**: worshiping idols, sacrificing one's children to them, taking part in sorcery and the occult. **Social**: entering a Gentile's house, murder, marrying unbelievers. **Economic**: dishonest trade practices, working on the Sabbath. **Sin**: all iniquity and sin, presuming to enter God's presence with unconfessed sin, changing and manipulating God's laws, stealing what belongs to God, entering his presence unclean. These things and many others would come to a Jew's mind when the term "defiled" was used. An undefiled person is one who has either been cleansed from these defilements or never did anything to defile himself in the first place.

But they basically dealt with externals, ignoring the internal state of the heart. This fact is clear in the response of the Pharisees and Scribes when they found Jesus' disciples eating without having washed their hands first (see Mk.7:1-5). Jesus had a few choice words about the Pharisees' treatment of the Word of God, then answered the hand-washing problem, saying, "Nothing outside a man can make him 'unclean' by going into him. Rather, it is what comes out of a man that makes him 'unclean.' ... For from within, out of men's hearts, come evil thoughts, sexual immorality, theft, murder, adultery, greed, malice, deceit, lewdness, envy, slander, arrogance and folly. All these evils come from inside and make a man 'unclean'" (Mk.7:15,21-23).

Thus when Jesus is described as being "undefiled," he was ceremonially undefiled, according to the Law, and he was inwardly undefiled, since he had no sin. Perhaps the closest Biblical example of this characteristic is Daniel, who, as a teenager, purposed in his heart not to defile himself (Dan.1:8). Eighty-some years later, when the governors and satraps of the Medo-Persian Empire "tried to find grounds for charges against him in his conduct of government affairs, ... they were unable to do so. They could find no corruption in him, because he was trustworthy and neither corrupt or negligent" (Dan.6:4). What a testimony!

In our society everything militates against undefilement and it is only getting worse. It is becoming increasingly difficult not to let ourselves become defiled. Yet God's command remains the same: "Be holy, because I am holy" (1 Pet.1:16). And the only way we are going to make an impact on our society is by being different, undefiled, and true to the Lord. That was Daniel's choice in a very corrupt and pagan society, and the Lord marvelously used him. That must be our choice also if we are to reflect Christ as the Undefiled.

The glove is thrown down. Do you accept the challenge?

APPLICATION: Daniel "purposed in his heart not to defile himself." That's where it begins. Philippians 4:8 is our guideline to accomplish what we "purpose," and it will be a continuous daily battle.

Unexpected Transformation

DAY 302
ᵇHE IS THE WARRIOR

◆

QUESTIONS TO THINK ABOUT:

1. In defending our faith, when is it right to take revenge and carry on physical warfare?
2. What did the Lord say should be our attitude toward our enemies?
3. What was the basis for God saying, "Vengeance is mine, I will repay"?

In Revelation 19:11,15 John says, "I saw heaven standing open and there before me was a white horse, whose rider is called Faithful and True. With justice he judges and makes war…. Out of his mouth comes a sharp sword with which to strike down the nations. 'He will rule them with an iron scepter.' He treads the winepress of the fury of the wrath of God Almighty." Perhaps a better title would be, "He Is the Invincible Warrior." No one, be he devil or man, can withstand him.

In Genesis 3:15 it was prophesied that Christ would crush Satan's head with a lethal blow. 1 John.3:8 declares that Christ came to "destroy the devil's work." Hebrews 2:14 carries it further: "… that by his death he might destroy him who holds the power of death – that is, the devil."

The Lord has reserved the sole right of physical warfare to himself alone. Paul tells us in Romans 12:19, "Do not take revenge, my friends, but leave room for God's wrath, for it is written: 'It is mine to avenge; I will replay,' says the Lord." Unlike the Muslims who have their Jihad (Holy War) against all infidels, we have no right to bear arms against those who refuse faith in Christ. The Lord has not called us to fight, but to bear witness to the truth.

There will come the time for physical warfare (see Rev.19:11-16), but even then it will be Christ, not us, doing it, even though we may be accompanying him. The key difference between him and us is that he makes war in righteousness, knowing everything involved. In our physical state, hatred and vengeance would quickly overcome any initial righteous motives we might have had, and there is no way we could rightly judge the attitudes and motives of our enemies. So we would end up killing the wrong people! We would have killed the Apostle Paul before he had a chance to be converted! Yet Christ saw his motives and had mercy on him.

In prophesying of Paul (and perhaps others too), Jesus said to his disciples, "A time is coming when anyone who kills you will think he is offering a service to God" (Jn.16:2). Paul himself testified to Timothy, "I thank Christ Jesus our Lord, who has given me strength, that he considered me faithful, appointing me to his service. Even though I was once a blasphemer and a persecutor and a violent man, I was shown mercy because <u>I acted in ignorance and unbelief</u>" (1 Tim.1:12,13 – underlining mine). Ask any persecuted Christians of that time if they knew this, and to a man they would say, "No!" There was no way they could judge the motives of Saul's heart. All they could see was his violent hatred and the destruction of the Church at his hands.

So Christ commands us, saying, "You have heard that it was said, 'Love your neighbor and hate your enemy.' But I tell you: Love your enemies and pray for those who persecute you, that you may be sons of your Father in heaven" (Matt.5:43-45a).

APPLICATION: Before we respond/react in any way toward our enemies (be they believers or unbelievers), we should ask this question: "Will my reaction draw them closer to the Lord, or drive them farther away?" Then act in such a way as will secure the first and keep us from the second.

DAY 303
ᵇHE IS THE WARRIOR, concl.

◆

QUESTIONS TO THINK ABOUT:

1. Is suing for our "rights" under the Constitution something Christians can do without violating God's command of non-retaliation?

2. What should constitute the main theater of our warfare, and how should that be waged?

3. How is our spiritual warfare different from warfare waged by our nation?

Yesterday we saw that physical retaliation and warfare in defending our faith is not an option for the Christian. That is, if someone or some group chooses not to believe in Christ as we do, and persecutes us as well, we have no right to retaliate.

Paul reminds us in 2 Corinthians 10:3-5, "For though we live in the world, we do not wage war as the world does. The weapons we fight with are not the weapons of the world. On the contrary, they have divine power to demolish strongholds [the demonic powers energizing our enemies]. We demolish arguments and every pretension that sets itself up against the knowledge of God, and we take captive every thought to make it obedient to Christ." Our warfare is spiritual, not physical.

In Papua (Indonesia) there was a man who declared himself to be of our church, but set himself up to be head over all in spite of gross sin in his life. When he was opposed, he began to hinder the church at every turn and at one point tried to kill the church president (a kite string in his face as he rode his motorbike deterred him from that attempt!). Our hearts were filled with thoughts of fighting fire with fire or worse. But instead we prayed and saw the Lord remove him again and again at crucial times so that his influence would not hinder the Lord's work. I guess we prayed <u>against</u> him more than we prayed <u>for</u> him!

Our real warfare is decidedly in the spiritual realm, not in the physical (see DAY 42 – HE IS THE KING [over Satan], II. for an example). Christ emphasized this point before Pilate in John 18:36 when he said, "My kingdom is not of this world. If it were, my servants would fight to prevent my arrest by the Jews. But now my kingdom is from another place."

Paul describes this spiritual warfare in Ephesians 6:10-18 (see APPENDIX VIII), describing our <u>position</u> in the Lord, the <u>promise</u> of victory, the <u>problem</u> we face, and the <u>provision</u> of God's armor for the battle. Along with the hymnist, we should ask, "Am I a soldier of the Cross?" Can we say with Paul, "I have fought the good fight, I have finished the race. I have kept the faith" (2 Tim.4:7)?

APPLICATION: God has provided everything we need for victory in our spiritual battle. We just have to use it! Taking the Ephesians 6 outline, go through each point to consider what each piece of armor is, what it means, and how it is used (what is its application?). Then incorporate that into your Christian life.

DAY 304
ᶜHE IS THE WORTHY ONE

QUESTIONS TO THINK ABOUT:

1. What does it mean to be "worthy"?
2. What is Christ worthy of?
3. What is the core characteristic of being said to be worthy?

To be worthy is to be considered of equal value or worth based upon the evaluation of others. The Greek word, *axios*, is translated "worthy" as of a person and his deeds. He is worthy of something, is highly valued in the sight of others, because of what he has done. Therefore, what he has done makes him of equal value (worthy) to the reward he receives.

Looking at Christ in Revelation 4:11; 5:9,10,12, we find him three times declared worthy, and as such to receive praise or reward commensurate with his worthiness: "You are worthy, our Lord and God, to receive glory and honor and power, for you created all things, and by your will they were created and have their being. You are worthy to take the scroll and to open its seals, because you were slain, and with your blood you purchased men for God from every tribe and language and people and nation. You have made them to be a kingdom and priests to serve our God, and they will reign on the earth.... . Worthy is the Lamb, who was slain, to receive power and wealth and wisdom and strength and honor and glory and praise!"

These verses could be charted as follows:

Ref.	Person	Deed	Declaration	Reward
Rev. 4:11	Jesus	Creator	Worthy	Of glory, honor, power.
Rev. 5:9, 10,12	"	Died to redeem & elevate man	"	To take the scroll, open its seals, receive power, riches, wisdom, strength, honor, glory and blessing.

Because of what he has done, he is worthy to receive our worship and praise. Because of what we do, we also will receive reward and commendation from him. Using the same chart as above:

Ref.	Person	Deed	Declaration	Reward
Matt. 10:37,38	Christians	Love Christ more than anything else.	Worthy	Christ himself and life.
Luke 21:36	"	Watching for his return	"	Escape tribulation and stand before the Son.

Unexpected Transformation / 683

Ref.	Person	Deed	Declaration	Reward
Eph.4:1-3	Christians	Lowliness, gentleness, longsuffering character, bearing with one another in love, striving for unity and peace in the Spirit	Worthy	The calling of God.
Col.1:10	"	Fruitful in every good work; increasing in the knowledge of God.	"	The Lord's pleasure
Rev.3:4	"	Rev.3:4	"	To walk with Christ in white

Thus from these few examples we see that, like Christ, we also will be declared worthy to receive honor and reward if we are faithful, the ultimate commendation being, "Well done, good and faithful servant! You have been faithful with a few things; I will put you in charge of many things. Come and share your master's happiness!" (Matt.25:21).

By your character and works, will you be declared "worthy"?

APPLICATION: Our goal should not be to be declared worthy, but to please our Master and leave the declarations up to him. By

Christ's blood we have been made acceptable to God and worthy to live with him forever. In the end, that is reward enough; everything else is grace!

DAY 305
[a]HE IS THE WISE ONE

QUESTIONS TO THINK ABOUT:

1. What is the Scriptural understanding of "wisdom"?
2. From where did Jesus get his wisdom since it seems he never went beyond Synagogue school?
3. From what sources do we get our wisdom? God's wisdom? Which source works best? Why?

Again from Colossians 2:3 we read that in Christ "are hidden all the treasures of wisdom and knowledge." We looked at him as the Treasure House of God's wisdom and knowledge (DAY 300). But today we want to look at him as the Wise One. From where did he get his wisdom? – for we read in Luke 2:52 that he "grew in wisdom and stature, and in favor with God and man."

Proverbs gives us as good an answer as we can find anywhere, and we can assume that these things are true of the Lord in his humanity as well. Quoted from the Living Bible (all following underlining mine):

1. 1:7 "How does a man become wise? The first step is to trust and reverence the Lord!"
2. 2:6 "For the Lord grants wisdom!" (cf. Dan.1:17)
3. 9:10 "For the reverence and fear of God are basic to all wisdom. Knowing God results in every other kind of understanding."

Unexpected Transformation / 685

4. 2:3,4   "Yes, if you want better insight and discernment, and are <u>searching for them</u> as you would for lost money or hidden treasure, then wisdom will be given you and knowledge of God himself."
5. 9:9   (<u>A teachable spirit</u>) "Teach a wise man, and he will be the wiser; teach a good man, and he will learn more."
6. 19:25b   (<u>Reproof</u>) "Reprove a wise man and he will be the wiser."
7. 23:22   "Listen to your <u>father's advice</u> and don't despise an old <u>mother's experience</u>."
8. 13:20a   "<u>Be with wise men</u> and become wise."
9. 6:6   (Heeding the world of nature) "<u>Take a lesson from the ants</u>, you lazy fellows. Learn from their ways and be wise."

I think the passage in Luke 2:46-51 answers to most of these elements in Christ's life as a twelve-year-old boy. Verse 46: "… They found him in the temple courts (#1,3), sitting among the teachers (#8), listening to them and asking them questions (#5). Everyone who heard him was amazed at his understanding and his answers (#2 implied). When his parents saw him, they were astonished. His mother said to him, 'Son, why have you treated us like this? Your father and I have been anxiously searching for you' (#6). 'Why were you searching for me?' he asked. 'Didn't you know I had to be in my Father's house?' (#4)… . Then he went down to Nazareth with them and was obedient to them" (#7).

Jesus probably had no further education beyond the local Nazareth Synagogue, yet he continually amazed his listeners with all he said and did (Matt.7:28,29) and never lost a verbal confrontation with those more highly educated (Matt.22:41-46).

I suppose that the greatest proof of his wisdom lies in the fact that what he taught worked, if followed and practiced. As he said in

John 8:32, "Then you will know the truth, and the truth will set you free." And he promises in Matthew 7:24,25 that if anyone hears him and does what he says, he will be like a wise man who builds his house on a rock, a house that will not fall in life's storms.

APPLICATION: Meditate on the nine sources of wisdom above and determine which ones need more attention; then work on them.

DAY 306
[a]HE IS THE WISE ONE, concl.

◆

QUESTIONS TO THINK ABOUT:

1. What do God and his Word have to do with our gaining of wisdom?

2. What role does the fear of the Lord play in our gaining of wisdom?

Daniel was the wisest man in the whole of the Babylonian Empire as well as that of the Medo-Persian. The details of his life are not chronicled as those of Christ's but key elements are there to support the means of his gaining wisdom.

In Psalm 111:10 we read: "The fear of the LORD is the beginning of wisdom; all who follow his precepts have good understanding." Even as a teenager, Daniel had distinguished himself in wisdom, knowledge and understanding (Dan.1:3,4). He continued in his convictions in Babylon. "But Daniel resolved not to defile himself with the royal food and wine" (1:8). The fear of the Lord. Step number one.

Then we read in verse 17 that God gave Daniel and his three friends "knowledge and understanding of all kinds of literature and learning. And Daniel could understand visions and dreams of all kinds." He obviously sought wisdom with a teachable spirit, for at the end of

Unexpected Transformation / 687

three years of intensive training in all areas, King Nebuchadnezzar found him "ten times better than all the magicians and enchanters in his whole kingdom!" (1:20).

I once knew a Midwestern farmer who never went beyond the eighth grade, yet he was always winning people to the Lord and when he preached, it was with power. From where did he get this wisdom? He was a diligent student of the Word and determined to put God first in all he said and did. Need more be said? Well, perhaps just a bit more.

Let's listen to what the Psalmist says in Psalm 119:97-100: "Oh, how I love your law!" [Today many of us say, "Oh, how I love romance novels!" or "Oh, how I love Sports Illustrated!" or "Oh, how I love the Wall Street Journal!"] "I meditate on it all day long." [When the Psalmist daydreamed, the Word of God was central in his thoughts.] "Your commands make me wiser than my enemies, for they [God's commands] are ever with me. I have more insight than all my teachers, for I meditate on your statutes. I have more understanding than the elders, for I obey your precepts." Look at verses 104 and 105. "I gain understanding from your precepts; therefore I hate every wrong path. Your word is a lamp to my feet and a light for my path" [guidance].

Today the Word of God is just one of the many choices of things with which we fill our time and minds. Most of the time, it seems to get crowded out, not because we don't have the time, but because we don't value the Word enough to make it a priority over other things. It does take time to study it and meditate upon it. Yet the truth is, we always make time for what we really want to do. So if the Word of God is crowded out of our lives, or given very little space, it's because we have chosen to treat it so. Thus it seems the Church in general has failed to gain wisdom and to reflect Christ as the Wise One because it has generally neglected the one source from which God's wisdom is gained.

God's wisdom is for the taking. It's all in his Word. How interested are you in gaining it?

APPLICATION: Daniel chose; the Psalmist meditated; the Midwest farmer applied. They prioritized God's Word in their lives, and God blessed them. The amount of wisdom you have will be directly proportionate to the amount of time you spend in the Word and applying it. There is no other way. Consider Proverbs 2:1-6 as a final word: "My son, if you accept my words and store up my commands within you, turning your ear to wisdom and applying your heart to understanding, and if you call out for insight and cry aloud for understanding, and if you look for it as for silver and search for it as for hidden treasure, then you will understand the fear of the LORD and find the knowledge of God. For the LORD gives wisdom, and from his mouth come knowledge and understanding."

DAY 307
bHE IS THE WISDOM OF GOD

QUESTIONS TO THINK ABOUT:

1. How is God's wisdom different from ours?
2. How should God's sovereign will affect our world view?
3. How did God use the current world situation of that day to prepare for the coming of Christ?

In Paul's classic wisdom passage in 1 Corinthians 1, he writes of Christ, "But we preach Christ crucified: a stumbling block to Jews and foolishness to Gentiles, but to those whom God has called, both Jews and Greeks, Christ the power of God and the wisdom of God" (vs.23,24). In Christ, we see the full wisdom of God at work bending all his means to the task of reconciling men to himself. In verse 30 he says, "It is because of him that you are in Christ Jesus, who has become for us wisdom from God … ." Christ is the one who shows us how we ought to live and work and what we should be like.

Consider God's wisdom in Christ's **birth**.

1. He prepared the **right vehicle**. (Hebrews 10:5b) "Sacrifice and offering you did not desire, but a body you prepared for me."
2. In Galatians 4:4 we see that "when the time had fully come (the **right timing**), God sent his Son, born of a woman (the **right means**), born under the law" (the **right circumstances**).

So everything concerning Christ's birth was totally in God's hand and totally apart from man's. God prepared Christ's body. In Matthew 1:20b we read, "Because what is conceived in her is from the Holy Spirit." Everything about his physical appearance he took care of in the womb. It was also important for Christ to have a human body (the **right vehicle**) so that he could fully identify with us in our physical weaknesses and temptations. As Hebrews 2:14,15,17,18 says, "Since the children have flesh and blood, he too shared in their humanity so that by his death he might destroy him who holds the power of death – that is, the devil, and free those who all their lives were held in slavery by their fear of death… . For this reason he had to be made like his brothers in every way, in order that he might become a merciful and faithful high priest in service to God, and that he might make atonement for the sins of the people. Because he himself suffered when he was tempted, he is able to help those who are being tempted."

Christ was born at the **right time**. Rome had conquered most of the known world, giving it a common language, culture and transportation system, thus making possible the spreading of the Gospel in a very short time a number of years later.

And the **means** of his birth, being conceived by the Holy Spirit and born of a virgin (Matt.1:20,23), guaranteed his sinless nature and acceptability as God's perfect sacrifice for our sins. Any human involvement in his birth and he would have been disqualified, having a sinful nature.

And finally, he was born under the Law (the **right circumstances**) so that he could fulfill it as God's perfect Man (Matt.5:17), thus paving the way for the New Covenant and a better way (see Heb.8:6-13).

APPLICATION: No matter how bleak the world situation may look, God is always in control, moving or allowing events to take place that will bring his plan for world history to an eventual end. Since we know that we are secure in him, we can look optimistically to the future and trust him for whatever comes, knowing that, in the end, **he wins**!

DAY 308
ᵇHE IS THE WISDOM OF GOD, cont.

◆

QUESTIONS TO THINK ABOUT:

1. When we minister to others, how much leeway does God give us in using our own thoughts and imagination?
2. If we submit ourselves to God's will, what does that do to our "freedom"?
3. Why does it make sense to submit to his will anyway?

God not only planned the details of Christ's birth, but also of his life and ministry. In Matthew 1:21 the angel said to Joseph: "You are to give him the name Jesus, because he will save his people from their sins." Thus the purpose or direction of Christ's life was determined.

Christ's teachings and works originated straight from the throne of God's wisdom. He told his listeners in John 8:28b,29b, "I do nothing on my own but speak just what the Father has taught me ... for I always do what pleases him." Thus he reflected and demonstrated God's wisdom in all that he said and did.

His death and resurrection were no different. God had planned them from the beginning. In Revelation 13:8 we read of Christ as being "the Lamb that was slain from the creation of the world." In Psalm 16:10,11a we find one of the many prophecies concerning his resurrection: "Because you will not abandon me to the grave, nor will you let your Holy One see decay. You have made known to me the path of life... ."

And what was Jesus' attitude through all this? Was he like a robot going through the motions of God's predetermined plans? No way! By an act of his will he humbled himself and submitted to God's plan (see Phil.2:5-11). As he is quoted in Hebrews 10:7, "I have come to do your will, O God." (And where God's will is the best and wisest thing going, rejecting it results in eternal loss!)

We see a similar pattern in the birth, life and death of John the Baptist. First of all, the **right vehicle**. God prepared John's body. (Luke 1:15) "For he will be great in the sight of the Lord. He is never to take wine or other fermented drink, and he will be filled with the Holy Spirit even from birth."

Then the **right timing**. God answered Zacharias' prayer so that John would be born about six months before Christ and thus be able also to carry out the purpose of his ministry before Christ appeared on the scene 30 years later (see Lk.1:26,36,39).

The **right means**. A godly couple was chosen for this special child. Not just any parents could handle this assignment. And Elizabeth gave birth to John (Lk.1:57). Though John was filled with the Holy Spirit from the womb (which makes for some interesting theological wonderings), John was born of a human union, thus totally man with a sin nature.

The **purpose** of his work was clear (Lk.1:17b) – he had to "make ready a people prepared for the Lord." And his **work** was aligned with that purpose (vs.16,17a) – "Many of the people of Israel will he bring back to the Lord their God. And he will go on before the Lord, in the spirit and power of Elijah, to turn the hearts of the fathers to their children and the disobedient to the wisdom of the righteous... ."

John's death came only when his purpose was completed. As his ministry and Christ's overlapped, there began to be some competition between his disciples and Christ's (Jn.3:25-28), so Jesus distanced himself from John and returned to Galilee. Very shortly after this, Herod the Tetrarch imprisoned and beheaded John (Lk.3:19,20; Matt.14:1-10). Upon his death (Matt.14:13), the multitudes turned to Jesus and began to follow him as God had planned.

John's attitude in all of this? "He is the one who comes after me, the thongs of whose sandals I am not worthy to untie" (Jn.1:27). "He must become greater; I must become less" (Jn.3:30). Humility. He knew his position and purpose of his ministry and submitted himself completely to God's will.

In looking at God's role in the birth of Jesus and of John the Baptist, what does that make you think about his role in your own birth?

APPLICATION: You might want to ponder Psalm 139 in preparation for the conclusion of DAY 309.

DAY 309
ᵇHE IS THE WISDOM OF GOD, concl.

QUESTIONS TO THINK ABOUT:

1. How much involved is God in the timing of our birth, life and ministry?

2. If we are unhappy or dissatisfied with ourselves the way God made us, what are we actually saying to Him?

Unexpected Transformation / 693

3. What should be our response when his ways just don't seem to make sense (including how and when we were born)?

Before going to the field, I attended a Men's Retreat sponsored by one of our supporting churches. On the way to the Retreat, I confided my feelings of gross inadequacy to the pastor, especially in the area of mechanics. I will never forget his reply. "Bob, God made you just the way you are, with your abilities and inabilities. He has called you to a specific ministry. And if, in that ministry, you come up against mechanical problems, he knows about that too, and will show you how to fix it, bring someone else along who can fix it, will fix it himself, or show you how to get along without it." What a salve to my troubled soul!

Then I remembered Psalm 139, that special, personal creation Psalm that God put into his Word just to encourage people like me when I feel depressed about myself.

First, he prepared the **right vehicle** for his purpose. Verses 13-16a: "For you created my inmost being; you knit me together in my mother's womb. I praise you because I am fearfully and wonderfully made; your works are wonderful, I know that full well [I know it, but often forget it!]. My frame was not hidden from you when I was made in the secret place. When I was woven together in the depths of the earth [euphemism for the womb], your eyes saw my unformed body." So God is intimately involved in our formative stage in the womb. As the Psalmist says in Psalm 119:73a, "Your hands made me and formed me."

Our length of life is also predetermined (vs.16b): "All the days ordained for me were written in your book before one of them came to be." We've often heard the phrase (though lived as if we didn't believe it) that we are immortal until our work is done. Well, this is the passage upon which that phrase is based. It's worth stopping to meditate upon ...

The **purpose** and **work** God has for us to do is wrapped up in his thoughts (plans) toward us (vs.17,18): "How precious to me are your thoughts, O God! How vast is the sum of them! Were I to count them, they would outnumber the grains of sand. When I awake [birth, or perhaps the resurrection], I am still with you [You're still thinking about me]."

With these truths in mind, we can trust him that he has caused us to be born at the **right time**, by the **right means**, and under the **right circumstances** – all of which will directly influence all that we are and what we will do in life.

And our **attitude** in all this? Verses 23,24: "Search me, O God, and know my heart; test me and know my anxious thoughts. See if there is any offensive way in me, and lead me in the way everlasting." Humble submission to the will of God.

Let's put our common, everyday selves in proper perspective. None of us will ever be as well-known as the Lord Jesus, nor as great as John the Baptist (Matt.11:11). And God obviously took great pains regarding the details of their births, lives and deaths. So by comparison, we really don't count for much. Right? Well, consider this. On DAY 107 we dealt with the believer as a living stone, fitted into the structure of the Temple of God along with Christ as the cornerstone. As beautiful and as important as the cornerstone may be, of what use is it if there are no other stones (bricks) to tie together? Again, if you have a beautiful temple, but here and there are missing bricks creating holes in the façade, that beauty is marred. Every "common" brick is vital to the overall beauty and appearance of the temple. Get the picture?

In Acts 15:18 (NKJV) we read, "Known to God from eternity are all his works." You know, I think we can trust him then to do what is good and wise concerning us – every aspect of us!

Are we, as Christ, reflectors of God's wisdom in the way he has made us, or are we (by our attitude) detractors from it?

APPLICATION: Take time to thank God for the way he made you, the family he put you in, and the work he created you to do. Then gratefully submit to his will, to be used in any way he sees fit in accordance to how he made you.

DAY 310
ᵇHE IS THE WEEPING ONE

◆

QUESTIONS TO THINK ABOUT:

1. Can you recall the three times in Scripture where it recorded that Jesus wept?
2. What makes you weep?

There are only three times in Scripture where we read of Jesus weeping. Once was at the grave of Lazarus (Jn.11:35) as he shared the grief of a loved one gone, and the other the following week as he entered Jerusalem just days before his crucifixion, weeping over the city's spiritual blindness (Lk.19:41-44). A third time is recorded in Hebrews 5:7, most likely occurring in the Garden of Gethsemane, though the verse reads as a frequent occasion during his brief life. Here he was crying because of his personal anguish and the death that was to come upon him. No doubt he cried many other times during his ministry as he faced the frustration of hearts hardened and calloused by unbelief that would not respond to the truth.

Paul often wept over the churches he planted and tried to bring to maturity. When meeting with the elders from Ephesus he said, "You know how I lived the whole time I was with you, from the first day I came into the province of Asia. I served the Lord with great humility and with tears, although I was severely tested by the plots of the Jews" (Acts 20:18,19). He also had warned them night and day for three years with tears about the false teachers that would come in to destroy them (vs.31). The Corinthian Church was a church beset with every problem in the books. In 2 Corinthians 2:4 he wrote: "For I wrote you out of great distress and anguish of heart and with many tears, not to grieve you but to let you know the depth of my love for you." Had Paul not deeply loved them, he would not have been so troubled at their condition.

Some people are afraid to love or become deeply involved in the lives of others for fear of being betrayed, hurt, disappointed or grieved. So they climb into their protective shells and try to isolate themselves from everyone and everything that might cause them grief. Christ didn't do that. Paul didn't. Neither should we. The rewards of love and involvement in the lives of others far exceed the occasional griefs and hurts we receive because of that love.

One day we learned that an unmarried daughter of some friends of ours was pregnant. They were devastated and we deeply felt and shared their grief, praying, crying and grieving as if she were our own daughter. When I wrote my Master's Thesis on Zionism, half my time was consumed in tears and crying out to God to deliver his people from their spiritual bondage and blindness. It broke my heart to see them miss out on all the promises and blessings God has for them. Betrayal and double-dealing by a trusted national worker brought tears, as did the rejection of another of 16 years of friendship after he was caught in adultery. Willingness to become involved with others will assuredly bring heartache and tears. But there is a promise from God in Psalm 126:5,6 for those who weep: "Those who sow in tears will reap with songs of joy. He who goes out weeping, carrying seed to sow, will return with songs of joy, carrying sheaves with him." And again is Psalm 30:5b, "Weeping may remain for a night, but rejoicing comes in the morning."

Do you weep? If not, you are robbing yourself of great joy!

APPLICATION: Any relationship will cause grief and tears at some point. God took that risk when he created us in the first place to have fellowship with him; Christ took that risk when he came to earth as one of us and to die for our sins. If we are to reflect Christ fully, we have to be willing to take that same risk by involving ourselves in the lives of others. As we bring grief and tears to the Lord by what we say and do, so they will bring grief and tears to us. But we persevere anyway knowing or hoping toward what they will eventually become in Christ, and doing our best to help them get there. If they repent and submit themselves fully to him, he will have great joy, and so will we!

DAY 311
ᶜHE IS THE WEARY ONE

QUESTIONS TO THINK ABOUT:

1. How do you handle being tired when others make requests of you?

2. How important are "our rights" when others have needs that we could meet?

3. On the other hand, how does one balance the need for rest with the unending needs of others?

On the way from Judea to Galilee, Jesus and his disciples journeyed through Samaria. This was most unusual, for the Jews always went around Samaria on the east side of the Jordan River when going north or south because of their intense hatred for the Samaritans, half-breeds: half-Jews, half-Gentiles originating from the time of the scattering of the ten northern tribes (see 2 Kings 17:24-34). Thus they were considered corrupted and worse than dogs. Yet Jesus "had to go through Samaria" (John 4:4) because he "had an appointment" with a certain woman that had to be kept, though she was totally unaware of it. They arrived at the town of Sychar where Jacob's well was. "Jesus, tired as he was from the journey, sat down by the well. It was about the sixth hour [12:00 noon]" (Jn.4:6).

Another time, at the end of a long day of healing and teaching, Jesus said to his disciples, "Let us go over to the other side" (Mk.4:35). So they got into their boats and began to cross over. Jesus, tired out, lay down in the stern of the boat with his head on a pillow, and was out like a light.

We also see that even though he was weary, he used his weariness as an opportunity to minister and teach. In his weariness he ministered to the woman at the well, then taught his puzzled disciples about the will and work of God being more important than food. In the boat, he was in a sudden, raging storm that was already swamping the boat. He rebuked the wind and the waves, then rebuked his disciples because of their fear and unbelief.

Now we don't have to practice being weary; that comes naturally! What we need to work on is our <u>attitude</u> when weary. Christ wasn't always interrupted when he was tired out. Neither will we be. But when he was called on, he ministered and even went beyond what was "required" of him. When I am tired, I don't want to be disturbed. I "have a right" to uninterrupted peace and quiet, and if I don't get it, I become irritable in order to let others know that I'm tired and don't want to be bothered. Or I only half-heartedly listen to what they are asking, then try to put them off until I feel like responding to their need. Most if not all of us have reserves of strength that we aren't even aware of. One reason that we are not aware of them is because we so often close the door to them through a selfish attitude. If Christ had had his own way, the woman would have ministered to <u>his</u> thirst and gone away still empty in soul, and the boats would have been lost in the storm with all their occupants except him. No, Paul rather urges us in Galatians 6:9 saying, "Let us not become weary in doing good, for at the proper time we will reap a harvest if we do not give up."

There is a reward in doing good, unselfishly, even when physically weary. Let's not lose it!

APPLICATION: We can easily become too involved in the needs of others to the point of burnout. We need to ask the Lord what our priorities should be, set "boundaries" where needed, then ask him to order our days and our interruptions. Only then will we know that we will have the energy and wisdom to do whatever he brings to us.

DAY 312
ᶜHE IS THE WORD

QUESTIONS TO THINK ABOUT:

1. What is the importance of speech?
2. How does that apply to God revealing himself to us through Jesus Christ?
3. How does that apply to our witness about Jesus Christ to others?
4. If we view ourselves as what we are, Christ's mouthpiece to those around us, how will this fact change our speech?

John opens his Gospel with these words: "In the beginning was the Word, and the Word was with God, and the Word was God" (1:1). The name "Word" comes from the Greek word *logos*, meaning "the spoken word ... the word spoken manifests the invisible thought, so he manifests to us the invisible Deity and Godhead" (Dillenger, A Critical Lexicon and Concordance to the English and Greek N.T., Zondervan, p.896.) Were it not for God's spoken word, first through his prophets and finally through his Son (see Heb.1:1), we would not know who he is nor would we have any idea who we are! But, "Thus says the LORD" clarifies all that and more.

Jesus claimed to be speaking to us just as the Father himself would were he here and visible. In John 7:16 he says, "My teaching is not my own. It comes from him who sent me." Again in John 8:28b,38a he says, "I do nothing on my own but speak just what the Father has taught me... . I am telling you what I have seen in the Father's presence." And again in John 14:10b, "The words I say to you are not just my own. Rather, it is the Father, living in me who is doing his work." In John 14:9 he said to Philip, "Anyone who has seen me has seen the Father." Or, as the Word, "He who has heard me had heard the Father."

Peter declared that the contents of the Old Testament did not originate "in the will of man, but men spoke from God as they were carried along by the Holy Spirit" (2 Pet.1:21). The Holy Spirit was speaking through them. They were God's mouthpiece to man. Paul also claims the same thing for New Testament times. In 1 Corinthians 2:13 he says, "This is what we speak, not in words taught us by human wisdom but in words taught by the Spirit, expressing spiritual truths in spiritual words." And also in 2 Corinthians 5:20, "We are therefore Christ's ambassadors, as though God were making his appeal through us. We implore you on Christ's behalf: Be reconciled to God."

The Apostle John says in 1 John 4:17b, "Because in this world we are like him [Christ]." We are an extension of Christ in this world, thus as we work and as we speak, others should sense God's presence and hear his voice. Our words will be the only words of God that many will initially hear. Do our words reflect his love and his concern for those around us? In Colossians 4:5,6 Paul urges us to "be wise in the way you act toward outsiders; make the most of every opportunity. Let your conversation be always full of grace [pleasant to the heart], seasoned with salt [healthful, edifying], so that you may know how to answer everyone." If we view ourselves as what we are, Christ's mouthpiece to those around us, how will this fact change our speech? Would Christ make suggestive comments? Tell off-color stories? Gossip to his neighbor? Color the truth to his own advantage? Boast of himself before others (even in a humble manner)? Speak in anger to cause hurt because of some wrong done? If not, then how dare we, as his mouthpiece, presume to "put words in his mouth" that are so contrary to his nature?

By the words you speak, whose mouthpiece are you?

APPLICATION: We need to make Psalm 19:14 the sincere prayer of our heart: "May the words of my mouth and the meditation of my heart be pleasing in your sight, O LORD, my Rock and my Redeemer." Amen!

"O to Be Like Thee"

O to be like Thee! Blessed Redeemer.
This is my constant longing and prayer.
Gladly I'll forfeit all of earth's treasures,
Jesus, Thy perfect likeness to wear.

O to be like Thee! Full of compassion,
Loving, forgiving, tender and kind;
Helping the helpless, cheering the fainting.
Seeking the wandering sinner to find.

O to be like Thee! Lowly in spirit,
Holy and harmless, patient and brave;
Meekly enduring cruel reproaches,
Willing to suffer others to save.

O to be like Thee! Lord, I am coming
Now to receive th'anointing divine.
All that I am and have I am bringing,
Lord, from this moment all shall be Thine.

O to be like Thee! While I am pleading,
Pour out Thy Spirit, fill with Thy love;
Make me a temple meet for Thy dwelling,
Fit me for life and heaven above.

Refrain:
O to be like Thee! O to be like Thee,
Blessed Redeemer, pure as Thou art!
Come in Thy sweetness, come in Thy fullness;
Stamp Thine own image deep on my heart.

– Thomas O. Chisholm

NOTE: See APPENDIX IX for additional characteristics of Christ and where they can be found.

May the Lord bless you as you continue your study on conforming to the character of Christ.

APPENDIX I
PRINCIPLES IN HELPING US DEAL WITH THE WORLD SYSTEM AND HOW TO OVERCOME IT

(from DAY 20 – HE IS SUBMISSIVE TO THE FATHER)

We must begin with our POSITION IN CHRIST.

PRINCIPLE #1   We are dead to the world, but alive to Christ.

(Rom.6:6-8) "For we know that our old self was crucified with him so that the body of sin [which responds to the world system] might be rendered powerless, that we should no longer be slaves to sin – because anyone who has died has been freed from sin. Now if we died with Christ, we believe that we will also live with him."

(Gal.6:14) "May I never boast except in the cross of our Lord Jesus Christ, through which the world has been crucified to me, and I to the world."

(Col.2:20-23) "Since you died with Christ to the basic principles of this world, why, as though you still belong to it, do you submit to its rules: 'Do not handle! Do not taste! Do not touch!'? These are all destined to perish with use, because they are based on human commands and teachings. Such regulations indeed have an appearance of wisdom, with their self-imposed worship, their false humility and their harsh treatment of the body, but they lack any value in restraining sensual indulgence."

Then we must SETTLE IN OUR MINDS WHO GOD IS.

PRINCIPLE #2   We must be certain who our God is before we will have the faith to make the necessary changes. Once we know who he is, faith will be no problem.

(2 Pet.1:2-4) "Grace and peace be yours in abundance through the knowledge of God and of Jesus our Lord. His divine power has given us everything we need for life and godliness through our knowledge of him who called us by his own glory and goodness. Through these he has given us his very great and precious promises, so that through them you may participate in the divine nature and escape the corruption in the world caused by evil desires."

(Lk.1:37) "For with God nothing is impossible."

Now we are ready to begin claiming his promises rather than the world's.

PRINCIPLE #3   Claim the sure, clear-cut promises of the Word that God will do something (especially as these are tied in with his names – such as Jehovah Ropheka, "God Is My Healer"; or Jehovah Jireh, "God Will Supply," etc.). We must also pay close attention to conditions that must be met before God will fulfill his promises to us.

How can we know if something is of the world or not?

PRINCIPLE #4   Anything that panders to the lust of the flesh, the lust of the eyes and pride (self-glory, etc.) is of the world (cf. 1 Jn.2:15,16).

PRINCIPLE #5   Anything violating Philippians 4:8 (especially re: all media forms and gossip) must be rejected. Whatever is true, noble, right, pure, lovely, admirable, excellent, praiseworthy – think about these things.

PRINCIPLE #6   Anything that transfers your affection and dependence upon God to something else in the world is highly suspect.

PRINCIPLE #7   Anything that would cause us to give glory to other than God is highly suspect.

PRINCIPLE #8   Use the things of the world without being used or controlled by them.

(1 Cor.7:29-31) "What I mean, brothers, is that the time is short. From now on those who ... use the things of the world [should live] as if not engrossed in them. For this world in its present form is passing away."

(Lk.16:9-12) "I tell you, use worldly wealth to gain friends for yourselves, so that when it is gone, you will be welcomed into eternal dwellings. Whoever can be trusted with very little can also be trusted with much, and whoever is dishonest with very little will also be dishonest with much. So if you have not been trustworthy in handling worldly wealth, who will trust you with true riches? And if you have not been trustworthy with someone else's property, who will give you property of your own?"

PRINCIPLE #9   DETERMINE to set your heart on things above.

(Col.3:1-3) "Since, then, you have been raised with Christ, set your hearts on things above, where Christ is seated at the right hand of God. Set your minds on things above, not on earthly things. For you died, and your life is now hidden with Christ in God."

A Very Brief Comparison between the Worldly System and the heavenly System

The World says ...	God says ... References
1. Hate your enemies	1. Love your enemies (Matt.5:43,44)
2. Curse your persecutors	2. Bless your persecutors (Rom.12:14)
3. Limit your forgiveness	3. Forgive unconditionally (Matt.18:21,22)
4. Revenge wrongs	4. Give place to vengeance (Rom.12:19)
5. Look out for #1	5. Look out for others first (Phil.2:3)
6. When in need: borrow	6. When in need: pray (Prov.22:7; Rom.13:8)
7. Deceit & treachery are noble	7. Honesty & sincerity are noble (Deut.25:13-15)
8. The end justifies the means	8. The end never justifies the means (1 Sam.15:21-23)
9. Worship whatever will benefit you the most	9. Worship only the Lord (Rom.1:25; Exod.20:3-5)
10. Go immediately to the medicine bottle	10. Go immediately to the Lord when ill, then take medicine as needed (2 Chr.16:12; Isa.38:1-5,21)
11. Insure against every eventuality	11. Insure only for basic needs and leave all "eventualities" to the Lord (Matt.6:21,31; Phil.4:19)

The World says ...	God says ... References
12. P.R. is all-important	12. Prayer is all-important (Jas.4:2,3; Lk.18:1)
13. Help God out whenever you can	13. Trust God implicitly to work things out (Prov.14:12; 3:5,6)
14. Save your life	14. Lose your life (Mk.8:35-37)
15. Exhibit your good deeds	15. Hide your good deeds (Matt.6:1-4)
16. Sex is O.K. if you love the other person	16. Purity is essential if we are to see God (1 Cor.7:2; Heb.12:14)
17. Money is everything	17. Heavenly riches are everything (1 Tim.6:10; Matt.6:20)
18. Take all you can get	18. Give away all you can (Matt.6:19; Acts 20:35)
19. Form (appearance) is important	19. Content is what counts (2 Tim.3:5)
20. To be great, you must be boss	20. To be great, you must be a servant (Mk.10:42,43)
21. It's O.K. to lie to get yourself out of trouble	21. Always speak the truth (Judg.16:6-14; Col.3:9)
22. Do unto others before they do unto you	22. Do unto others what you would have them do unto you! (2 Kgs.6:20-22; Matt.7:12)
23. We must keep up with the Joneses!	23. Be content with what you have (1 Tim.6:9; Heb.13:5)

... and the list goes on.

Unexpected Transformation / 709

But this is sufficient to show how diametrically opposed the two systems are and how it is impossible for a Christian to serve both. A major aspect of Christian growth is moving from what the world says to doing what God says (Rom.12:2). Today, many Christians are sliding back into what the world says, and are pulling the Church with them.

In which direction are you moving in your Christian life?

APPENDIX II
ONE WAY TO SET UP A PRAYER DIARY

(from DAY 23 – HE IS THE MAN OF PRAYER)

Someone asked me once, "Do you pray for the whole list at the same time?" No, it usually take us at least two weeks to work through it, taking several pages each day. I go through it consecutively. Amber takes a bit from each section every day.

We have noted three different types of prayers, what I call short-term, long-term and general continuous.

Short-term (S or ST) requests are those for which we desire an immediate answer. Someone is sick and needs healing, or there is a problem for which an answer is needed very soon.

Long-term (L or LT) requests cover those requests which, by their nature, will not be answered until some time has passed. In November, a missionary asked prayer for evangelistic meetings coming up next March. Or in September, we pray that a college student will do well in his studies (two answers being implied here: one at the end of the first semester and another at the end of the second).

General Continuous (G or Gen. Cont.) requests are those which, by nature, are continuous requests with yearly answers. Praying for someone's spiritual growth is a continuous request which will have many answers along the way. Praying for a certain country to remain open to the Gospel will have yearly answers noted.

When entering a request, say from a friend, we open the FRIENDS section, find his name, and write down the request, followed by the date it was entered. Then we decide whether it is a short-term, long-term or general continuous request and put an S, L, or G in front of the request.

Unexpected Transformation / 711

EXAMPLE:

(The following columns are narrowed because of page width. Using 8½ x 5½ notebook paper, the ANSWERED column is 2" wide; the DATE column is as wide as the longest date [12/15/19]; and the request column as long as what space is left.

FRIENDS	DATE	ANSWERS
Mike and June Mueller ^{S}That their house might sell soon.	6/12/87	

When a request is answered, the date is noted along with the answer in the ANSWERED column, and a red or green check marks off the request. If the answer happens to be "No," then a red or green check with a line through it (✓) is made. Red indicates a request answered and not needing further prayer. Green means it has been partially answered, but needs more prayer. Thus the "Continuous" requests would have the abundance of green checks, though occasionally an S or L request may have one.

EXAMPLE:

FRIENDS	DATE	ANSWERED
Mike and June Mueller		
(red check) ✓ That their house might sell soon	6/12/87	8/7/87 Sold.
(grn check) ✗ Continued spiritual growth	6/12/87	6/12/88 Yes.

The following pages show a more detailed picture of how we set up our prayer list.

Periodically, we go through our list to cull out "dead wood" – requests for which we no longer have a burden to pray, people with whom we have lost contact, or requests which, due to changing circumstances, no longer need prayer.

Every day we must have time set aside specifically for prayer. If we make it a priority, we will do it. Sometimes it becomes hard work. But the results that come make that work worthwhile.

SUGGESTED FORMAT FOR A PRAYER LIST

We have found a loose-leaf notebook that takes lined, 3-ring notebook paper (8 1/2" x 5 1/2") to be the most convenient for our use. On the top line of each page is the section title (FAMILY, FRIENDS, MISSIONARIES, etc.), below which is the name of the person being prayed for, as follows:

TITLE	ANSWERS
NAME	CHILDREN'S NAMES

Below the name are listed the prayer requests from that individual/family/organization, with the date the request was entered. In the right column are recorded the answers to each request along with the date recorded.

FAMILY	DATE	DATE
Name	(began praying)	(prayer answered)
REQUESTS		ANSWER RECORDED
Type of request (in pencil so that it can be erased) → C S L		

A running monthly record of requests and answers at page bottom (in pencil because of monthly updates).

ANS.	UNANS.	GEN.
Yes No	LT ST	CONT.

714 / *Unexpected Transformation*

EXAMPLE OF A PRAYER LIST PAGE

MISSIONARIES	DATE	ANSWERS
Chuck & Betty Doe - S.Asmat Mis. - Peru		Brian
(grn cks)| ✓✓ ᶜCont. spiritual growth	11/10/78	11/15/79 Much progress 11/13/18 Yes.
(red ck. ✗ Salvation of Pedro with \ through it)	1/8/79	11/15/79 Killed in a bus accident: no decision made
(red ✓) ✓ Safe preg. & del. for Betty	3/1/79	1/7/80 A boy, Brian Allan, b. 12/20/7
(red ✓)✓ Rains to end the drought	3/1/79	8/20/79 Drought ended. Good rains.
(grn ck) (red ck) ✓✓ Soon del. of printing materials	8/20/79	11/3/79 Part of order arrived. 1/10/80 All in hand
(dash) – Salvation of Miguell & Julianna	8/20/79	10/27/80 Lost contact (delete fr. prayer list.)
ˢMany area missionaries sick	10/27/80	
ᴸEvangelistic campaign in March	10/27/80	
ᴸWisdom revising primmer series	12/1/80	

ANS.		UNANS.		GEN.		
Yes	No	LT	ST	CONT.		
6	1	1	2	1		(Page #) 15

Unexpected Transformation / 715

APPENDIX III
IDENTIFYING YOUR SPIRITUAL GIFT(S)

(from DAY 31 – HE IS THE PEACEFUL ONE)

In general:

How do you find out what your spiritual gift(s) is? Most Bible book stores or other book outlets have materials on knowing and discovering one's spiritual gifts. As a starting point, ask yourself, "If I could do anything I wanted in the church, what would that be?" (Visitation, be on a church board, teach Sunday School, preach, etc.) Your answer to this question will indicate what your spiritual gift might be. Ask your pastor where he thinks you might fit in best; ask him what he thinks your spiritual gift might be, then test it in those areas of ministry that use it. A sense of joy, a feeling that this is "just right," and fruit from your ministry will confirm that this is most likely your spiritual gift. Then keep on serving and developing in that area (or those areas) until the Lord leads otherwise.

It is important to realize that the process of spiritual growth involves learning to use and develop other spiritual gifts than your own. So don't be afraid to try new things and stretch yourself in other areas of ministry. As example, my basic, motivational spiritual gift is exhortation, but I use teaching and preaching to express it even more than counseling. From other Christians I have learned how to express the gifts of helps and mercy. So always keep yourself open to learning new expressions of your faith through the use of different gifts.

In greater detail:

There are five steps to take in discovering your spiritual gift:
1. You have to know what the gifts are that God has given us.
2. You have to know what the function of each gift is.
3. You must pray, asking God to make clear to you what your gift is.
4. You must test various gifts (if you think it could be one or another) to see which one best "fits."
5. Ask others what they think your spiritual gift is.

LIST OF SPIRITUAL GIFTS

A. Personal Gifts:

1. **Administration** = Knowing how to organize things and to get jobs done efficiently (Rom.12:8; 1 Cor.12:28).

2. **Helps** = The ability to come alongside someone in need, knowing exactly how to meet that need in practical ways (Rom.12:7; 1 Cor.12:28).

3. **Mercy** = Showing compassion to those who are hurting; bringing comfort to them (Rom.12:8).

4. **Giving** = The desire and ability to give, even beyond one's means, to help meet the needs of others (Rom.12:8).

5. **Discernment** = The ability to tell the difference between what is true and what is false. This gift would especially, but not exclusively, apply to those in the field of Apologetics (1 Cor.12:10).

6. **Wisdom** = The ability to know practically and Biblically what to do in any given situation (1 Cor.12:8).

7. **Knowledge** = The ability to know what others do not know, e.g. to know the hidden sins/motives of someone and bring it to light (1 Cor.12:8; cf. Acts 5:1-4).

B. Public Gifts:

1. **Apostle** = "one sent." Originally the 12 Apostles given authority to establish the Church and its doctrines (Eph.4:11; 1 Cor.12:28). Now sometimes used of missionaries as "ones sent to establish the Church in other lands" (see **NOTE 1** on next page).

2. **Teacher** = One who has a deeper understanding of the Word of God and able to teach it clearly (Eph.4:11; Rom.12:7; 1 Cor.12:28).

3. **Pastor** = The gift of shepherding God's people; a "shepherd's heart" (Eph.4:11).

4. **Leadership** = Knowing how to set the example for others to follow and gain their support. Being able to present a clear objective/vision for the work that needs to be done (Rom.12:8; 1 Cor.12:28).

5. **Faith** = The ability to believe (possessing firm assurance about) what God will do in any given situation (1 Cor.12:9).

6. **Evangelism** = The ability to effectively share the Gospel with others so that many receive Christ (Eph.4:11).

7. **Exhortation** = The ability to effectively counsel others so as to bring resolution to their problems/issues (Rom.12:8).

8. **Prophet** = The ability to foretell the future (Isa.7:14; Acts 11:28)
>
> The ability to proclaim God's Word:
> Spoken (Mal.3:16; 1 Cor.14:1,3)
> Sung (1 Chr.25:1)
> (cf. NOTE 1)

NOTE 1: Somehow I sense that the current "redefinition" of Apostle (to include missionaries) is more of a theological compromise for the present day, which makes me very uncomfortable since the new definition takes away from the original meaning of the word.

The same can be said for the gift of prophecy being redefined as "a word from God regarding any particular situation." But this use of that gift needs to be tested (cf. 1 Jn.4:1) since there are many confirmed false "prophecies" that have been given in the name of the Lord.

9. **Healing** = The God-given ability to heal the sick, cast out demons, even raise the dead (1 Cor.12:9,28 – see **NOTE 2** on next page).

10. **Miracles** = The God-given ability to perform special signs/wonders when needed. Originally used to authenticate/validate the Gospel message being given. The same holds true today in places where the Gospel has never been proclaimed.

11. **Tongues** = The ability to speak spiritual truth in an unknown language (to the speaker). It could include both angelic as well as human languages (as indicated in 1 Cor.13:1). But since the speaker does not know what he is saying, this gift especially needs to be tested (cf. 1 Jn.4:1), for he could be speaking blasphemy as well as what is praiseworthy without knowing it. His gift needs to be totally Spirit-controlled (see **NOTE 3** below).

12. **Interpretation** of Tongues = The ability to correctly interpret an unknown language (1 Cor.12:10). This also needs to be tested since this speaker likewise doesn't know the language he's interpreting. He could give a totally wrong interpretation without the Spirit's control.

NOTE 2: As with the other "sign gifts" (an arbitrary designation not found in Scripture except for tongues in 1 Cor.14:22), their cessation has not so much to do with the completion of the Canon of Scripture, as some proclaim (but seems to be contradicted in 1 Cor.13:8-12), as it does with the lack of faith to accept and use them as given to the Church by the Holy Spirit. Rom.11:29 says that "the gifts and the calling of God are irrevocable." If this is true, then there must be a better explanation for the assumed cessation of certain spiritual gifts while others continue. God does not change his mind.

NOTE 3: I know of an instance in which someone spoke in an unknown tongue, blaspheming the name of Jesus, but someone else got up and interpreted it as a paean of praise to Jesus! Someone else in the congregation knew that language and called it for what it was!

NOTE 4: (General observation): Natural Talent is not a spiritual gift as it is not mentioned in any N.T. listing of spiritual gifts. However, natural talent can be and often is energized by the Lord for a special work (cf. Ex.31:1-5; 35:31-33).

* * * *

C. Praying about One's Gift(s): You must pray to the Lord, asking him to make clear what his gift to you is.

D. You must test the gifts to see which one fits you best.

1. Look at the definitions of the various gifts and ask yourself, "Which one(s) seem to fit me best?"
2. Think about this: If you could choose just one ministry in the church (or church-related ministry) to do, which one would that be? Which ministry would truly motivate and energize you to serve? Your choice will indicate the possibility of what your gift is.
3. Get active in church ministry and pay attention to that which is fruitful for you.

4. Ask more mature Christians what they think your spiritual gift is.

5. You also may ask, "What is my attitude toward others?" Since your spiritual gifts are given in the context of serving others. Your attitude toward them could be a strong indicator as to what your gift is. Following are two examples of how this type of interaction could occur.

a. Example: <u>At the dinner table</u>, little **Mark** didn't pay attention to what he was doing and spilled his glass of water on the table. The resulting reactions of the various family members could very well reveal what their spiritual gifts are.

1) **Adriana** "Oh dear! I will get a dish towel and dry the wet area!" (gift of *helps/service*)

2) **Father** "Mark! That's the results of your playing around! Pay more attention to what you are doing so that it won't happen again!" (gift of *exhortation*)

3) **John** "Mark, listen! If you put your glass to the right of your plate, it's easy to knock it over. It's safer to put it behind your plate where it won't be so easily hit." (gift of *teaching*)

4) **Suzie** "Oh, Mark! Don't cry! Here, my glass is still full. I don't need it all. You can have some of mine." (gift of *giving*)

5) **Margaret** "Oh, Mark! Don't cry! Don't feel embarrassed! We've all done that before. Come here and sit by me where it's dry and don't worry anymore about the spilled water." (gift of *mercy*)

6) **Mother** "Adriana, get a dish towel and dry Mark's place. Mark, don't worry about it! Suzie, help Mark change his wet shirt. Mark, stop crying! Sit beside Margaret where it's dry." (gift of *administration*)

b. Example: <u>In an Elder Board meeting</u> called to discuss and form an effective outreach program that would result in church growth.

1) **Pastor** "What we really need is the full proclamation of the Word of God in all its truth from the pulpit. If God's Word is given in that way, surely there will be growth. (gift of *prophecy*)

2) **Elder #1** "True, Pastor. But many children don't attend our services, so we need to guard our future by emphasizing our Sunday School ministry where our children can be taught to become our next generation of leaders. Their spiritual education is paramount to our church growth. (gift of *teaching*)

3) **Elder #2** "That may be so, but if we really want our church to grow, we must put together an effective evangelistic program, training the church people how to witness, perhaps using "The Four Spiritual Laws," so that they will know what to say when talking with others. If we don't do that, our Sunday School will fail for lack of students, and our overall church attendance will decline." (gift of *evangelism*)

4) **Elder #3** "All of you are wrong in your emphases! None of that will work unless it's properly organized. We must carefully list the programs we need and form committees to organize and run them. After all, the Bible says, 'Do all things properly and in order'!" (gift of *administration*)

[**NOTE:** Being unaware of each other's spiritual gift, the groundwork is laid for a knock-down, drag-out fight over how best to develop an effective church outreach program. Elder 3's response provides the ignition of the potential dispute. The question is: Who is right? The answer is, they all are! They were just looking at the issue from the perspective of their spiritual gift. The resolution of the potential conflict is found in the recognition of each other's spiritual gift, understanding their comments in that context, and recognizing that all four views must be coordinated in order to achieve their objective.]

APPENDIX IV
HELPFUL BOOKS ON ADMINISTRATION

(from DAY 35 – HE IS THE KING [Governor/Ruler])

◆

The following books I have found helpful in developing a sense of administration and gaining of useful principles in working with others.

Bennis, Warren and Burt Nanus. Leaders. New York. Harper and Row, 1985.

Hersey, Paul and Kenneth B. Blanchard. Management of Organizational Behavior. 5th ed. Englewood Cliffs. Prentice-Hall, 1988.

Johnson, David W. and Frank Johnson. Joining Together: Group Theory and Group Skills. 3rd. ed. Englewood Cliffs, NJ. Prentice-Hall.

Jones, Bruce R. Ministerial Leadership in a Managerial World. Wheaton. Tyndale, 1988.

McSwain, Larry L. and William C. Treadwell, Jr. Conflict Ministry in the Church. Nashville. Broadman, 1981.

Peters, Tom. Thriving on Chaos. New York. Harper and Row, 1987.

Tillapaugh, Frank R. Unleashing the Church. Ventura. Regal Books, 1982.

Wakefield, Norman. Solving Problems Before They Become Conflicts. Grand Rapids. Zondervan, 1987.

APPENDIX V
HELPFUL BOOKS ON SPIRITUAL WARFARE

(from DAY 42 – HE IS THE KING [over Satan])

These are some books that I have found particularly helpful in the area of spiritual warfare. If you must choose which ones to read first, I would suggest the two by Neil Anderson and Piretti's book. The latter is fiction, but demonstrates the power of prayer in the Christian's spiritual warfare. The book by Jessie Penn-Lewis is a bit "far-fetched" in some areas (in my opinion) but will give some idea of how Europeans have dealt with spiritual warfare in time past.

Anderson, Neil T. <u>The Bondage Breaker</u>. Eugene, OR: Harvest House, 1990.

_____. <u>Victory Over the Darkness</u>. Ventura, CA: Regal, 1990.

Bubeck, Mark I. <u>The Adversary: The Christian Verses Demon Activity</u>. Chicago: Moody Press, 1975.

_____. <u>Overcoming the Adversary</u>. Chicago, Moody Press, 1984.

Dickason, C. Fred. <u>Demon Possession and the Christian</u>. Chicago. Moody Press, 1987.

MacMillan, John. <u>The Authority of the Believer</u>. Harrisburg. Christian Publications, 1980.

Penn-Lewis, Jessie. <u>War on the Saints.</u> Fort Washington, PA. The Christian Literature Crusade, 1984.

Piretti, Frank. <u>This Present Darkness</u>. Westchester, IL. Crossway, 1986.

Reisser, Paul C., Teri K. Reisser, and John Weldon. <u>New Age Medicine: A Christian Perspective on Holistic Health</u>. Downers Grove, IL. IVP, 1987.

Unger, Merrill F. <u>Demons in the World Today</u>. Wheaton. Tyndale House, 1976.

APPENDIX VI
EIGHT REASONS WHY WE GET SICK

(from DAY 43 – HE IS THE KING [over Sickness])

◆

There are just a couple of additional thoughts that need to be mentioned here. I said, "When the Lord has accomplished his purpose, then healing will come." What purpose? I see from Scripture at least eight purposes/reasons for our suffering sickness or physical disability:

1. Discipline because of sin (1 Cor.11:29,30)

2. As a trial of our faith – toward maturity (Jas.1:2-4; 1 Pet.1:6,7)

3. Direct Satanic attack (Lk.13:10-16; 1 Pet.5:8-11)

4. For the glory of God (Jn.9:1-3; 1 Pet.1:6,7 – Consider for a moment the tremendous ministries of Helen Keller, Fanny Crosby and Joni Eareckson Tada because of their infirmities that were not healed.)

5. To teach us how to comfort others – sensitivity, compassion (2 Cor.1:3,4)

6. As a result of the Fall – we are in and part of a fallen world; therefore our bodies are subject to viruses, etc. (1 Tim.5:23; 2 Cor.4:16). The purpose? To develop hope (Rom.8:22-25) as we look forward to having new bodies not subject to sickness, etc.

Some say that this is not a reason for Christians getting sick since Christ took the curse of sin for us on the Cross (Gal.3:10-14).

But a careful reading of that passage shows that we are redeemed "from the curse of the law" (not from the curse of sin), the curse being having to do everything written in the Book of the Law, which no man could do, in order to be accepted by God, with the prospect of death for failure! God says in Ezekiel 18:4, "The soul who sins is the one who will die." His promise in Exodus 15:25,26 was that he would put none of the diseases of Egypt upon Israel if they obeyed. In Romans 8:2 we are said to be free from the law of sin, not the curse of sin. So where we still suffer from its general curse, we are no longer under its domination or power.

7. Personal carelessness – 1 Tim.5:23. If we fail to take proper hygienic measures or safety precautions, we will inevitably reap the results of sickness and/or injury.

8. So that others might grow in their Christ-likeness as they minister to us in our infirmity. Amber had a great aunt who was downed by a stroke. She lay for a number of years in the nursing home bed and I often asked, "Why? What is she accomplishing for the Lord just lying there? Can she think? Can she pray? What is God's purpose in letting her linger like this?"

One answer is, "I don't know." Another answer is that God was using her in this passive condition to develop Christ's character in the lives of those ministering to her. Amber's parents no doubt grew in the areas of compassion, faithfulness, willingness to sacrifice, and patience as they visited Aunt Myrtle week by week. I have no doubt that she will receive a reward because of the work accomplished in their lives through her condition.

Any one or a combination of several of these purposes can be at work each time we become sick. Our problem is discerning which one or ones they are, so that we can respond properly each time. I usually make a mental check list of the possibilities from the above list, and then go through it in prayer:

1. Is this discipline because of sin? Check my heart, mind, etc. If I find sin there that is unconfessed, then I confess it. Sometimes the sickness immediately disappears; other times it stays on.

2. Is this a training session for the glory of God and maturing of my faith? Then I submit myself and my condition to the Lord for the accomplishment of his higher purposes.

3. Is this an attack from Satan? Having taken the first two steps, then, based on James 4:7, I can rebuke the sickness in the name of the Lord Jesus Christ; if this is an attack, it will then cease. If it continues, then I assume that the second area is where I should concentrate my attention and begin learning what the Lord wants to teach me.

APPENDIX VII
POINTERS FOR PERSONAL BIBLE STUDY

(from DAY 85 – HE IS THE ROOT OF DAVID/ THE NAZARENE)

To set yourself up for personal Bible study, the following materials are essential (in order of importance):

a. Good modern language Bible (I personally prefer the NIV, 1985 ed.; the ESV is also good)

b. Notebook and pen (for jotting down your thoughts and findings)

c. A good concordance (Cruden's – cheapest, or Strong's – most thorough, including Greek and Hebrew sources; see the bibliography)

d. A good Bible commentary (particularly useful for background material – I highly recommend the two volume set by Walvoord and Zuck entitled, <u>The Bible Knowledge Commentary</u>, O.T. and N.T. editions; see the bibliography.)

e. A good word study book (Vine's is excellent; Zodhiates is superb for explanation of various Greek words and their meanings; see the bibliography.)

f. Perhaps you would want some colored pencils for marking particular verses or passages. Using a color code will help you find verses quickly that have to do with particular topics. The following is what I use:

black	=	sin (cf. Jas.1:15)
black-orange	=	"life is but a vapor"-type passages (cf. Jas.1:10,11)
black pencil	=	numbers, dates (cf. Ezek.1:1,2)
blue-green	=	purpose (of Christ's coming, etc. – cf. Jn.5:19,20,30)
dark blue	=	occult (cf. Ezek.13:18); proverbial sayings (cf. Ezek.16:44)
light blue	=	godly actions (cf. Jas.1:22a)
brown	=	special blessing (cf. 2 Cor.10:3-5)
brown-orange	=	"The word of the LORD came to me" (cf. Ezek.1:3)
dark green	=	direction indicators: "out of the north" (cf. Ezek.1:4)
light green	=	character of God/Christ/Holy Spirit (cf. Jas.1:13b); miracles (cf. Acts 12:7,10)
orange	=	judgment (cf. Jas.1:6b-8,15b)
purple	=	knowledge of God (cf. Ezek.11:10,12)
red	=	general items of interest: names (cf. 1 Chr.6:60-66); periods of time kings reigned (cf. 2 Sam.5:4)
violet	=	special item of interest – progressive departure of the glory of the Lord from Jerusalem (cf. Ezek.9:3; 10:4,18; 11:23)
yellow	=	God's sovereignty (cf. Jas.2:5)
green star	=	fulfilled prophecy (cf. Ezek.26:3)
red star	=	Messianic prophecy (cf. Ezek.34:23,24)
light blue and red	=	promise (red) based on certain conditions (lt. blue) (cf. Jas.1:5,12)

APPENDIX VIII
OUTLINE OF EPHESIANS 6:10-18

(from DAY 234 – HE IS MIGHTY, POWERFUL)

◆

I. **Our Position** – *one of strength* (vs.10).

"Be strong in the Lord and in his mighty power."

II. **The Promise** – *you will stand* (vs.11).

"Put on the full armor of God so that you can take your stand against the devil's schemes."

III. **The Problem** – *the struggle against spiritual powers* (vs.12).

"For our struggle is not against flesh and blood, but against the rulers, against the authorities, against the powers of this dark world and against the spiritual forces of evil in the heavenly places."

IV. **Our Provision** – *the whole armor of God* (vs.13).

"Put on the full armor of God ... so that ... you may be able to stand your ground ...."

A. **What you:**

1. **Know** –*truth* (vs.14a).

"Stand firm then, with the belt of truth ...

2. **Do** – *righteousness* (vs.14b)

... with the breastplate of righteousness in place ...

3. **Communicate** – *the gospel of peace* (vs.15).

...and with your feet fitted with the readiness that comes from the gospel of peace."

4. **Exercise** – *faith* (vs.16). "In addition ... take up the shield of faith with which you can extinguish all the flaming arrows of the evil one."

5. **Possess** – *the helmet of salvation* (vs.17a). "Take the helmet of salvation ...

6. **Use** – *the word of God* (vs.17b). ... and the sword of the Spirit ... the word of God."

B. **How you:**

1. **Prepare** – *pray in the Spirit on all occasions* (vs.18a). "And pray in the Spirit on all occasions with all kinds of prayers and requests."

2. **Persevere** – *by being alert* (vs.18b). "Be alert and always keep on praying for all the saints."

APPENDIX IX
ALPHABETICAL LISTING OF CHRIST'S CHARACTERISTICS, NAMES AND TITLES

C/N/T	Scripture	Day
A		
Accredited (Approved) of God	Acts 2:22	
Acknowledged One, The	Matt.16:16; Ps 2:12; Heb.3:1	95
Adam, The Last	1 Cor.15:45	
Advocate, Our	1 John 2:1	66
Afflicted One, The	Isa.53:7	138-157
Alpha and Omega, The, etc.	Rev.22:13	247
Amen, The	Rev.3:14	246
Angel, An	Exod.23:20 with 1 Cor.10:4; Rev.8:3-5	102
My...	Exod.23:23	
...of His Presence, The	Isa.63:9	
...of the Lord, The	Exod.3:2	
Angry One, The	Mark 3:5	259
Anointed One, The	Luke 4:18; 7:38; Ps.2:2	96
Apostle, The (The Sent One)	Heb.3:1	245
Appointed One, The	Heb.3:2	97
Approved (Accredited) One, The	Acts 2:22	
Author and Finisher of Our Faith, The	Heb.5:9; 12:2	98
Author of their Salvation, The	Heb.2:10	
B		
Babe, The	Luke 2:12,16	171
Banner for the Peoples, A	Isa.11:10	
Baptizer, The	Luke 3:16	
Battle Bow, The	Zech.10:4	
Beaten, The	John 19:1	151

C/N/T	Scripture	Day
Beautiful One, The	Isa.33:17	
Beginning and the End, The	Rev.22:13	247
Beginning of God's Creation, The	Rev.3:14	130,131
Beloved One, The	Eph.1:6	133
Benevolent, The	Acts 10:38	16
Betrayed, The	Luke 22:48	147
Bishop of Our Souls, The (see Overseer)		256
Blessed One, The	Luke 19:38	135
Boy Jesus, The	Luke 2:43	172,173
Branch, The	Isa.4:2; Zech.3:8; 6:12	210,211
a Righteous...	Jer.23:5	
...from the root of Jesse	Isa.11:1	
Bread: of God	John 6:33	
...of Life, The	John 6:35	212
...from heaven, The True	John 6:32,33,41	
Bridegroom, The	Matt.9:15	213-215
Bright and Morning Star, The (see Star)		285
Brightness of the Father's Glory, The	Heb.1:3	260
Broken-Hearted One, The	Luke 19:41,42	81
Brother of James, et.al.	Mark 6:3	
Builder of the House, The	Eph.4:8-13; Heb.3:3	216
Burden-Bearer, The	Ps.55:22; Isa.53:4	55-57

C

Captain, The (see Author and Finisher)		98
Carpenter, The	Mark 6:3	
Carpenter's Son, The	Matt.13:55	
Chief Shepherd, The	1 Pet.5:4	161,62
Child, The (see The Young Child)		172,173
Chosen One, The	Isa.42:1; 1 Pet.2:6	89
Christ:	Matt.1:16	117
...Jesus	Gal.3:26	

C/N/T	Scripture	Day
...Jesus our Lord	Rom.8:39	
...Jesus my Lord	Phil.3:8	
The...	John 1:41	117
The...of God	Luke 9:20	
...the Lord	Luke 2:11	
The Lord's...	Luke 2:26	
Comforter, The (see Burden-Bearer)	Luke 8:48	55-57
Coming One, The	Matt 11:3	261-263
Commander, The	Josh.5:14; Isa.55:4	118
Compassionate	Mark 6:34	13
Confessor, Our	Matt.10:32; 1 Jn.1:9	129
Consolation of Israel, The	Luke 2:25	264,265
Cornerstone, The Chief	Eph.2:20; 1 Pet.2:6	88
Counselor, A	Isa.9:6	58
Covenant, The	Isa.42:6	119
Creator, The (see Beginning of God's Creation)	John 1:1-3; Heb.1:10	130,131
Criticized, The	Luke 15:2	141
Crucified, The	John 19:16; 1 Cor.1:23	153
Cursed, The	Gal.3:13	155

D

David	Ezek 34:23	120,121
Day Star, The	2 Pet 1:19	123
Dayspring (Sunrise), The	Luke 1:78	122
Dead One, The	Rev 1:17	
Defender, Protector, Our	Ps 5:11	109,110
Deliverer, Our	Luke 4:18; Rom 11:26	104
Denounced One, The	Matt 9:3	148
Dependent One, The	John 8:28	
Deserted One, The	Matt 26:56	82,83,144
Dew, The	Hos 14:5	124
Desire of All Nations, The	Hag 2:7	266
Despised One, The	Isa 53:3	141

736 / *Unexpected Transformation*

C/N/T	Scripture	Day
Disappointed One, The	John 6:67; 14:9	125
Disfigured One, The	Isa 50:6; 52:14	153
Dishonored One, The	Isa 53:2	
Door/Gate of the Sheep, The	John 10:9	126

E

Elect, My (see Chosen)		89
Elder Brother, Our	Rom.8:29; Heb.2:11,12	
End, The (see Beginning and the End)		247
End of the Law, The	Rom.10:4	
Endurer, The	Heb.12:2,3	267,268
Envied, The	Matt.27:18	149
Eternal	Isa.9:6	235-237
...Life	1 John 5:20	
Everlasting Father, The	Isa.9:6 (see Eternal)	235-237
Exalted One, The (see Glorious)	Phil.2:9	239-242
Example, Our	1 Pet.2:21	5

F

Faithful One, The	Rev.1:5	269,270
Falsely Accused, The	Matt.9:34	143
Father, A	Isa.9:6	238
Faultless One, The (see Holy One)	John 8:46; 19:4	18-20
Feared One, The	Mark 11:18	199
Finisher of Our Faith, The (see Author and Finisher)		98
First and the Last, The	Rev.1:17; 22:13	
Firstborn, The:	Heb.1:6	
The...among many brothers	Rom.8:29; Matt.1:25	
The...from the Dead	Rev.1:5, Col.1:18	200
The...over all creation	Col.1:15,18	
Firstfruits, The	1 Cor.15:23	200
The...of those who have fallen asleep	1 Cor.15:20	162,200
Forerunner, The	Heb.6:20	201,202
Forgiving One, The	Luke 23:34	11,12

Unexpected Transformation / 737

C/N/T	Scripture	Day
Forsaken One, The	Matt.27:46	148
Foundation, The Sure	Isa.28:16; 1 Cor.3:11	203-205
Friend, Our	John 15:13,14	91
...of tax collectors and "sinners," The	Matt.11:19	
Fullness of the Deity, The	Col.2:9	

G

C/N/T	Scripture	Day
Gentle One, The	2 Cor.10:1	231
Gift-Giver, The	Eph.4:11	229
Gift of God, The	Isa.9:6	209
Glorious One, The	John 1:14; 17:5,24	239-242
Glory of Thy People Israel (see Glorious	Luke 2:32	239-242
God	Isa.9:6; Heb.1:8	189
Great...and Savior (see God; Savior)	Titus 2:13	
my...	John 20:28	
...with Us (see Immanuel)	Matt.1:23	228
The Only...	1 Tim.1:17	
The True...	1 John 5:20	
Good/Benevolent	John 10:14	16
Governor/Ruler, The	Matt.2:6	36
Gracious One, The	Luke 4:22; 1 Pet.2:3	
Great One, The:	Isa.53:12	
The...High Priest (see High Priest)	Heb.4:14	
The...Shepherd of the Sheep (see Good Shepherd)	Heb.13:20	61,62
Greater than:		
...the Temple/Lord of the Sabbath	Matt.12:6,8,12	271
...Jonah	Matt.12:41; Luke 11:32	
...Solomon	Matt.12:42; Luke 11:31	
Grieved One, The	Mark 3:5	80
Guide, Our	Luke 1:79	
Guilt Offering, Our	Isa.53:10	227
Guiltless One, The (see Holy One)	Matt.12:7	18-20

C/N/T	Scripture	Day
H		
Habitation, Our	Ps.91:9	272,273
Harmless, The	Heb.7:26	206
Hated One, The	John 15:18	143
Head, The:		
...of every man	1 Cor.11:3	
...of the Body, the Church	Col.1:18	207
...of the Corner	Matt.21:42	
...over all things	Eph.1:22	
Healer, The	Mal.4:2; Luke 8:43,44	208
Heir, The	Ps.2:8; Rom.8:17; Heb.1:2	217
Helper, Our	Heb.13:6	218
High Priest, Our	Heb.3:1; 7:26	69-76
...forever	Heb.7:17	
...of our confession (see Acknowledged)	Heb.3:1	95
Holy Child, The (see Holy; Young Child)	Acts 4:27 (KJV)	18-20, 172,173
Holy One, The	Luke 1:35; Acts 3:14	18-20
The...and Just/Righteous	Heb.7:26	15
(see Holy One; Just)		18-20
The...of God (see Holy One)	Mark 1:24	18-20
Homeless One, The	Matt.8:19,20	144
Honored One, The	Honored One, The	111,112
Hope: of Glory, The	Col.1:27	
...of Israel, The	Acts 28:20	274
Our...	1 Tim.1:1	
Horn: of David	Ps.132:17	257
...of Salvation, The	Luke 1:69	219
Humble One, T	Phil.2:8	191-193
Humiliated One, The	Acts 8:33	154
Hungry One, The	Matt.4:2	220,221
Husband	Rev.19:7	

Unexpected Transformation / 739

C/N/T	Scripture	Day

I

I AM, The	John 8:58	233
Illuminator, The	Isa.9:2	
Image of God, The	Col.1:15	4
Immanuel/Emmanuel (God with Us)	Isa.7:14; Matt.1:23	228
Immortal One, The (see Eternal)	1 Tim.1:17; 6:16	235-237
Incarnate One, The	John 1:1,14; Phil.2:5-8	222, 223
Innocent One, The (see Holy One)	Luke 23:14,15	18-20
Insulted One, The	1 Pet.2:23	
Intercessor, The	Heb.7:25	67
Invisible One, The	1 Tim.1:17; 6:16	
Israel	Isa.49:3	

J

Jesus	Matt.1:21	224
...Christ	1 John 1:7; 4:2	
...Christ Our Lord	Rom.1:3	
...Christ, the Righteous One	1 John 2:1	
(see Righteous)		
...of Nazareth		
Joyful One, The		
Judge, The		
...of all the earth (see Judge)		
...of Israel		
...of the living and the dead (see Judge)	Acts 10:42	230
The Righteous...	2 Tim.4:8	
(see Judge; Righteous)		15, 230
Just:		
Man (Person), That...	Matt.27:19,24 (NKJV)	
(see Just One)		15
...One, The	Acts 3:14; 22:1	15

C/N/T	Scripture	Day
K		
Keeper, Our	John 17:12 with 6:37	
...of the Keys	Rev.1:18; 3:7	
Kind One, The	1 Cor.13:4	
King, The:	Zech.9:9	
(see also Governor/Ruler; Servant; Scepter; Prince)		36-40
...Eternal (see Eternal)	1 Tim.1:17	235-237
...Everlasting (see Eternal)	Luke 1:33	235-237
...of Glory	Ps.24:7	
...of Israel	John 1:49	
...of the Jews	Matt.2:2	
...of Kings	1 Tim.6:15; Rev.19:16	41
...over circumstances	Luke 4:28-30	44
...over all the earth	Zech.14:9	
...over Satan	Heb.2:14	42
...over self	Mark 7:37	45
...over sickness	Luke 4:38,39	43
...over sorrow	John 11:40-45	49
...over the Gentiles/nation	Rom.15:12	
...over the world	John 16:33	46,47
King, The, cont.		
...of Righteousness	Isa.32:1	
...of Saints	Rev.15:3	
...of Zion	Ps.2:6	
...with authority	John 5:26,27	48
L		
Lamb, the		63-65
The...without spot or blemish	1 Pet.1:19	
(see Holy One)		18-20
The...of God	John 1:29	
The...slain from the creation of the world (see Crucified)	Rev.13:8	

C/N/T	Scripture	Day
Lamp, The	Rev.21:23	164
Last Adam, The	1 Cor.15:45	232
Laughed At, The	Matt.9:24	142
Leader/Commander of the people, The	Isa.55:4	
Liberating One, The	Isa.42:7 with John 8:32	
Life, The	John 14:6	8,9
Our...	Col.3:4	
Life-giving Spirit, The	1 Cor.15:45	195
Light:		99-101
The...of the Gentiles	Isa.42:6	
The...of Life	John 1:4	
The...of the World	John 8:12; 9:5;	
The True...	John 1:9	
Lion of the Tribe of Judah, The	Rev.5:5	196-198
Living One, The	Rev.1:17.	
The...Bread	John 6:51 (see Bread)	212
The...Stone	1 Pet.2:4	107
The...Water	John 4:10 with 7:38	
Lonely One, The (The Deserted)	Matt.26:56	82,83
Longsuffering One, The	2 Pet.3:9	108
Lord, The	Matt.3:3; 1 Cor.2:8; Rev.19:16	243,244
...and My God, My	John 20:28	
...and Christ	Acts 2:36	
...and Savior Jesus Christ	2 Pet.2:20	
...and Teacher, Your	John 13:14	
...from heaven	1 Cor.15:47	
...Jesus	Rom.5:1,11; Rev.22:21	
...Jesus Christ	Rom.5:1,11; Rev.22:21	
...of All	Acts 10:36	
...of Glory	1 Cor.2:8	
...of Lords	1 Tim.6:15; Rev.19:16	
...of Peace	2 Thess.4:16	

C/N/T	Scripture	Day
...of Sabaoth (Lord of Hosts)	Jas.5:4	113
...of the Dead and Living	Rom.14:9	
...of the Sabbath	Matt.12:8	271
(see Greater than the Temple)		
Lord, The, cont.		
...Our Righteousness, The	Jer.23:6	
...over all	Rom.10:12	
Loving One, The	John 13:1	78,79

M

Majestic One, The (see Glorious)	2 Pet.1:16	239-242
Male Child, A	Rev.12:5	
Man, The:		114
...Approved of God, A	Acts 2:22	
(see Approved)		
...of Prayer, A (see Prayerful)		24
The...	Acts 17:31	
...of Sorrows, A	Isa.53:3	
The...Christ Jesus	1 Tim.2:5	
The heavenly...	1 Cor.15:48	
The Second...	1 Cor.15:47	
Marred One, The	Isa.52:14	153
Master in heaven, Your (see Lord)	Col.4:1; Eph.6:9	
Master/Teacher, The	John 11:28	77
Mediator, Our	1 Tim.2:5	68
Mediator, Our	Matt.11:29; Isa.53:7	
Merciful One, The	Matt.9:27; Heb.2:17; Jas.5:11	115
Messenger of the Covenant, The	Mal.3:1; Luke 22:20	103
Messiah, The Prince	Dan.9:25	
...The Christ, The	John 1:41	117
Mighty:		
...God/Powerful, The	Isa.9:6	234
...to save	Isa.63:1	

Unexpected Transformation / 743

C/N/T	Scripture	Day
Minister, The:		
...of the Circumcision	Rom.15:8	
...of the Sanctuary	Heb.8:2	275
Miracle-Worker, The	John 2:9	248-252
Misunderstood, The	John 6:47-63	140
Mocked, The	Matt.27:29-31,41	154
Most Holy (see Holy)	Dan.9:24	
Mourned For, The	Zech.12:10; Rev.1:7	
Morning Star, The (see Star)	Rev.22:16	
Mystery of God	Col.2:2	

N

Nazarene, The	Matt.2:23	84,85

O

Obedient One, The	Rom.5:19; Heb.5:8	134
Offering, Our (see Sacrifice)	Eph.5:2	
Offspring of David, The	Rev.22:16	190
One, The	Matt.26:48	276
One with the Father	John 10:30	253-255
Only Begotten Son, The	John 3:16	116
Only Savior	Acts 4:12	
Only Wise God	1 Tim.1:17	
Opposed One, The	John 5:16	144
Oppressed, The	Isa.53:7	147
Overcomer, The	Rev.3:21	
Overseer, The	1 Pet.2:25	256

P

Passover, Our	1 Cor.5:7	258
Patient One, The	2 Pet.3:9	136
Peaceful One, The	Isa.9:6; Eph.2:14,15	31-35
Peacemaker, The (see Peaceful One)		31-35
Persecuted One, The/The Afflicted One		138-157
(Background)	John 15:20	138

744 / *Unexpected Transformation*

C/N/T	Scripture	Day
(Lack of Privacy, Hangers-on)	Mark 6:31; John 6:26	139
(Misunderstood, Rejected)	John 6:60,63; John 1:11	140
(Criticized, Despised/Ridiculed)	Matt.9:10,11; Isa.53:3	141
(Laughed at)	Matt.9:23,24	142
(Hated, Falsely Accused)	John 7:7; Matt.12:24	143
(Homeless, Deserted, Overtly Opposed)	Matt.8:19,20; John 6:66; Luke 4:28	144
(Satanic Attack)	Mark 1:12,13	145
(Psychological/Emotional Turmoil, Fear and Dread of the Worst Possible Thing Happening)	John 12:27,28; Mark 14:33,34	146
(Oppressed, Betrayed)	Isa.53:7; Matt.27:3-5	147
(Seizure and Arrest, Denounced, Forsaken)	John 18:12; Matt.26:63-66; Mark 14:50	148
(Falsely Tried, Accused and Condemned)	Mark 14:55-61	149
(Target for Jealousy/Envy)	Matt.27:18	149
("Imprisonment," Treated as a Curiosity piece)	Matt.25:36; Luke 23:7-11	150
(Brought before the Authorities, Beaten/Scourged)	Matt.10:18; John 18:33-38; Matt.27:26	151
(Mobbed, Hit in the Face and Spit upon)	Matt.26:47; John 18:20-22; Mark 14:65	152
(Disfigured/Marred, Pierced and Crucified)	Isa.52:14; Matt.27:27-30; John 20:25	153
(Property Confiscated, Mocked and Humiliated)	Luke 23:34; Matt.27:29-31,41	154
(Cursed, Thirsty)	Gal.3:13; John 19:28	155
(Put to Death/Killed, Christ's Attitude)	Matt.17:22,23; 1 Pet.2:21-23	156
Persevering One, The	Isa.42:4	
Physician, The	Luke 4:23	277
Pierced One, The	Rev.1:7	153
Possessor of All Things, The	Col.1:16	180-182

Unexpected Transformation / 745

C/N/T	Scripture	Day
Potentate, The Blessed and Only	1 Tim.6:15	
Powerful One, The	Matt.28:18	234
Power of God, The	1 Cor.1:24	183,184
Prayerful One, The	Luke 5:16	24
Preacher, The	Luke 4:18	185
Precious One, The	1 Pet.2:6,7	90
Preeminent One, The	Col.1:18	86
Preserver, The	2 Tim.4:18	105
Priest, The (see High Priest, Our)		69-76
Prince, The:	Acts 5:31	40
...of Kings	Rev.1:5	
...of Life	Acts 3:15	
...of Peace	Isa.9:6	
Prophet, The:		
...Mighty in Word and Deed	Luke 24:19	106
...from Nazareth	Matt.21:11	
...of the Highest	Luke 1:76	
Propitiation, Our	1 John 2:2	186
Protector, Our (see Our Defender)	John 17:12	109,110
Provider, Our	Ps.23:1; Phil.4:19	158
Purifier, The	Mal.3:3	22,23
Pure One, The	Prov.30:5; John 15:3; 1 John 3:3	21
...of Kings	Rev.1:5	
...of Life	Acts 3:15	
...of Peace	Isa.9:6	
Prophet, The:		
...Mighty in Word and Deed	Luke 24:19	106
...from Nazareth	Matt.21:11	
...of the Highest	Luke 1:76	
Propitiation, Our	1 John 2:2	186
Protector, Our (see Our Defender)	John 17:12	109,110

C/N/T	Scripture	Day
Provider, Our	Ps.23:1; Phil.4:19	158
Purifier, The	Mal.3:3	22,23
Pure One, The	Prov.30:5; John 15:3; 1 John 3:3	21

Q

Quiet One, The (see The Silent One)	1 Cor.5:7	258

R

Rabbi (see Master)	John 1:49	77
Rabboni (see Master)	John 20:16	77
Radiance of God's Glory (see Glorious)	Heb.1:3	239-242
Ransom, Our	Matt.20:28; 1 Tim.2:6	127
Reaper, The	Rev.14:15	278
Reconciler, The	2 Cor.5:18-20	17
Redeemer, The	Job 19:25	159
Redemption, Our	Rom.3:24; Eph.1:7	
Refiner, The	Mal.3:3	279-281
Refuge, Our	Isa.32:1,2	160
Reflector of God's Glory, The	Heb.1:3	239-242
Rejected One, The	Luke 20:17; Jn.1:11; Acts 4:11; 1 Pet.2:7	140
Reprover, The	Luke 9:55	161
Resurrected One, The	1 Cor.15:20	162
Resurrection, The	John 11:25	163
Rewarder, The	Matt.9:29; Isa.40:10	165
Ridiculed One, The	1 Pet.2:23	141
Righteous/Just One, The	1 John 2:1,29; Mal.4:2	15
The...servant (see Servant)	Isa.53:11	37,38
Righteousness, Our	1 Cor.1:30	
Rock, The (Spiritual) (see Unchangeable)	1 Cor.10:4	87

Unexpected Transformation / 747

C/N/T	Scripture	Day
Rock of Offense, The (see Stumbling Stone)		93
Rod, The (see Branch)	Isa.11:1	210,211
Root, The:		
...of David/The Nazarene	Rev.5:5	84,85
...of Jesse	Isa.11:10	
...out of Dry Ground	Isa.53:2	
Ruler, The	Mic.5:2; Zech.10:4	

S

C/N/T	Scripture	Day
Sacrifice, Our	Heb.9:26	127
Salvation, Your	Luke 2:30	
Same, The	Heb.13:8	166
Sanctification, Our (see Holy)	1 Cor.1:30	18-20
Savior, The/The Deliverer	Matt.1:21	104
Scepter, The	Num.24:17	39
Scourged One, The	John 19:1	151
Sealed One, The	John 6:27	282
Second Man, The	1 Cor.15:47	167
Seed, The		
...of Abraham	Gal.3:16	168
...of David	2 Tim.2:8	169
...of the Woman	Gen.3:15	283
Self-Denying One, The	Phil.2:7	194
Sent One, The	John 20:21	245
Separate from Sinners	Heb.7:26	170
Servant, The	Matt.12:18; Phil.2:7	37,38
...of Rulers	Isa.49:7	
Shepherd, The (see Good Shepherd for all of the below)		
My...	Zech.13:7	61,62
The...and Bishop of Our Souls	1 Pet.2:25	61,62
The Chief...	1 Pet.5:4	61,62
The Good...	John 10:11	61,62

C/N/T	Scripture	Day
The Great…	Heb.13:20	61,62
Shiloh	Gen.49:10	174,175
Shoot, A…from the stump of Jesse (see Branch)	Isa.11:1	210,211
Sign Spoken Against, A	Luke 2:34	
Silent One, The	Isa.42:2; 53:7	
Sin-Bearer, The	2 Cor.5:21	128
Sinless One, The	Heb.4:15; Isa.53:9	
Slain One, The	Rev.13:8	156
Smitten One, The	Mic.5:1	151,152
Soil, The	Col.2:6,7	176
Son, The:		
…of Abraham	Matt.1:1	177
…of David (The Offspring of David)	Matt.9:27	190
…of God	Matt.3:17	188
…of Man	Matt.8:20	187
…of Mary	Mark 6:3	
…of the Highest	Luke 1:32	
…of the Living God	Matt.16:16	
…over His Own House	Heb.3:6	
…Well-pleasing…	Mark 1:11	
Sorrowful, The	Matt.26:38	
Sought After, The	Mal.3:1; Mark 1:37	
Sovereign One (of the Universe), The	Heb.1:3	178
Source (Author) of Eternal Salvation, The	Heb.5:9	
Sower, The	Matt.13:37	284
Spotless One, The	Heb.9:14	
Spring of Living Water, The	Jer.17:13 with John 4:13,14	
Star, The	Num.24:17; Rev.22:16	285
Stone,		
The…Rejected	Matt.21:42	94

Unexpected Transformation / 749

C/N/T	Scripture	Day
The Stumbling..., The Rock of Offense	Rom.9:33; 1 Pet.2:8	93
The Tried...	Isa.28:16	
The Elect...	1 Pet.2:6	
The Living...	1 Pet.2:4	107
Submissive One, The	Luke 22:42	10
Substitute, Our	Isa.53:6; Rom.5:8	286
Suffering One, The	Heb.5:8	
Sufficient One, The	2 Cor.12:9	287
Sun of Righteousness, The	Matt.13:43; Mal.4:2	288-294
Supporter, The	John 11:21-27	295
Surety of a Better Covenant, A	Heb.7:22	296
Sustaining One, The	Col.1:17; Heb.1:3	132

T

Taunted One, The	Luke 23:35-37	
Teacher, The (see Master)	John 13:13 [ASV]	77
Temple, The	Rev.21:22	297,298
Tempted One, The	Heb.4:15	53,54
Tenderhearted, The	Luke 13:34; Mark 10:13-16	14
Tender Plant, A	Isa.53:2	
Tent Peg, The	Zech.10:4	
Testator, The	Heb.9:16,17	299
Thirsty, The	John 19:28	155
Transfigured, The (see Glorious)	Mark 9:2-9	239-242
Treasure House, The	Col.2:3	300
Triumphant, The (see Victorious One)	Col.2:15	50-52
Troubled One, The	John 12:27,28	
Trustworthy One, The	John 17:4	137
Truth, The	John 14:6	7

C/N/T	Scripture	Day
U		
Unchangeable One, The; The Rock	Heb.1:12; 13:8	87
Undefiled, The	Heb.7:26	301
Undiscouraged One, The	Isa.42:4	
Unfailing One, The	Isa.42:4	
Unifying One, The	Col.3:11	
Unrecognized One, The	Matt.14:22-27	
Unspeakable Gift, The	2 Cor.9:15	
V		
Values People More than Things	2 Cor.8:9	179
Victorious, The; The Triumphant	1 Cor.15:57	50-52
Vine, The	John 15:5	
The True...	John 15:1	
W		
Warrior, The	Rev.19:11	302,303
Way, The	John 14:6	6
Weary One, The	John 4:6	311
Weeping One, The	Luke 19:41,42; John 11:35	310
Wisdom of God, The	1 Cor.1:24	307-309
Wise, The	Col.2:3	305,306
Witness, The Faithful	Rev.1:5	25-30
The Faithful and True...	Rev.3:14	
...to the People	Isa.55:4	
Wonderful	Isa.9:6	59,60
Word, The	John 1:1	312
...of God	Rev.19:13	
...of Life	1 John 1:1	
Worshipped One, The	Matt.8:2	
Worthy One, The	Rev.4:11; 5:12	304
Wounded One, The	Isa.53:5	

Unexpected Transformation / 751

C/N/T	Scripture	Day
Y		
Young Child, The (see Boy Jesus)	Matt.2:8	172,173
Z		
Zealous One, The	John 2:17	92

REFERENCE LIST

Aldwinckle, Russell F. 1976. *More than a Man: A Study in Christology*. Grand Rapids: Eerdmans.

Anderson, Neil T. 1990. *The Bondage Breaker*. Eugene, OR: Harvest House.

_____. 1990. *Victory over the Darkness*. Ventura: Regal.

Bachman, Evelyn. 1991. "Names and Character of My Saviour and My Lord." A poem written to a sick friend on 8 January.

Baillie, Donald. 1948. *God Was in Christ*. New York: Scribner's.

Bennis, Warren, and Burt Nanus. 1985. *Leaders*. New York: Harper and Row.

Berkhouwer, G.C. 1955. *The Person of Christ*. Grand Rapids: Eerdmans.

Blackaby, Henry T., and Claude V. King. 1994. *Experiencing God, Knowing and Doing the Will of God*. Nashville: Lifeway Press.

Bosley, Harold A. 1967. *The Character of Christ*. Nashville: Abingdon.

Bryant, T. Alton, ed. 1967. *The New Compact Bible Dictionary*. Grand Rapids: Zondervan.

Bubeck, Mark I. 1975. *The Adversary: The Christian Verses Demon Activity*. Chicago: Moody.

_____. 1984. *Overcoming the Adversary*. Chicago: Moody.

Bullinger, Ethebert W. 1975. *A Critical Lexicon and Concordance to the English and Greek New Testament*. Grand Rapids: Zondervan.

Bushnell, Horace. 1908. *The Character of Jesus*. New York: Charles Scribner's.

Crabb, Lawrence J. 1977. *Effective Biblical Counseling*. Grand Rapids: Zondervan.

Crawford, Don. 1972. *Miracles in Indonesia*. Wheaton: Tyn-dale House.

Cruden, Alexander. 1930. *Cruden's Complete Concordance to the Bible* Philadelphia, Universal Book and Bible House.

Cruden, Alexander. 1991. *Cruden's Handy Concordance to the Bible*. Grand Rapids: Zondervan.

Cullmann, Oscar. 1963. *The Christology of the New Testament*. Rev. ed. Philadelphia: Westminster.

Dickason, C. Fred. 1987. *Demon Possession and the Christian*. Chicago: Moody.

Eareckson, Joni. 1978. *A Step Further*. Minneapolis: World Wide Publications.

Fitzjerrell, Glen. 1994. Juvenile Justice Ministry. Metro Chicago Youth for Christ. Oral mission report. Calvary Memorial Church. Oak Park, IL.

Forsyth, P.T. 1909. *The Person and Place of Jesus Christ*. Boston: Pilgrim.

Foxe, John. 1975. *Foxe's Book of Martyrs*. Edited by Marie Gentert King. Old Tappan: Revell.

Fugate, J. Richard. 1980. *What the Bible Says about Child Training*. Garland: Aletheia Publishers.

Gallagher, Steve. 1990. *Conformed to His Image*. Crittenden, NY: Pure Life Press.

Gariepy, Henry. 1987. *Portraits of Christ*. Wheaton: Victor Books.

Greene, Oliver. 1966(?). *The Epistle of Paul to the Hebrews*. Greenville: The Gospel Hour.

Hersey, Paul, and Kenneth B. Blanchard. 1988. *Management of Organizational Behavior*. 5th ed. Englewood Cliffs: Prentice-Hall.

Howard, Clinton N. 1925. "The names of our Lord." Wheaton: Greater Europe Mission. Pamphlet.

Jefferson, Charles Edward. 1910. *The Character of Jesus*. New York: Thomas Y. Crowell.

Johnson, David W., and Frank Johnson. 1982. *Joining Together: Group Theory and Group Skills*. 2d ed. Englewood Cliffs: Prentice-Hall.

Jones, Bruce R. 1988. *Ministerial Leadership in a Managerial World*. Wheaton: Tyndale House.

Kempis, Thomas à. 1910. *The Imitation of Christ*. New York: Dutton.

Latourette, Kenneth Scott. 1953. *A History of Christianity*. New York: Harper & Row.

Lewis, C.S., 1965 *The Horse and His Boy*, London: Puffin Books.

Lockyer, Herbert. 1975. *All the Divine Names and Titles in the Bible*. Grand Rapids: Zondervan.

MacDonald, Gordon. 1984. *Ordering Your Private World*. Nashville: Oliver Nelson.

Mackintosh, H.R. 1962. *The Doctrine of the Person of Christ*. Edinburgh: T. & T. Clark.

MacMillan, John. 1980. *The Authority of the Believer*. Harrisburg: Christian Publications.

Marshall, I. Howard. 1977. *I Believe in the Historical Jesus*. Grand Rapids: Eerdmans.

McDonald, H.D. 1968. *Jesus–Human and Divine*. Grand Rapids: Zondervan.

McSwain, Larry L., and William C. Treadwell, Jr. 1981. *Conflict Ministry in the Church*. Nashville: Broadman.

Moody, D.L. _____. *Inspiring Quotations*. Nashville: Thomas Nelson Publishers. Quoted in Steve Gallagher. *Conformed to His Image*, lesson 8:1. Crittenden, NY: Pure Life Press. 1990.

Morris, Leon. 1958. *The Lord from heaven*. London: Inter-Varsity.

Mumper, Sharon E. 1987. Global Report. Evangelical Missions Quarterly 23, no.3: 314-20.

Orr, James, gen. ed. 1939. *The International Standard Bible Encyclopedia 1*. Grand Rapids: Eerdmans. S.v. "Anointing," no.4, by George B. Eager.

_____. 1939. *The International Standard Bible Encyclopedia 4*. Grand Rapids: Eerdmans. S.v. "Sacrifice (O.T.) guilt offering," by J.J. Reeve.

Pannenburg, Wolfhart. 1968. *Jesus–God and Man*. Philadelphia: Westminster.

Papov, Haralan. 1971. *Tortured for His Faith*. Grand Rapids: Zondervan.

Peabody, Francis. 1905. *Jesus Christ and the Christian Character*. New York: Macmillan.

Penn-Lewis, Jessie. 1984. *War on the Saints*. Fort Washington: Christian Literature Crusade.

Peters, Tom. 1987. *Thriving on Chaos*. New York: Harper and Row.

Pink, Arthur W. 1975. *Exposition of the Gospel of John*. Grand Rapids: Zondervan.

Piretti, Frank. 1986. *This Present Darkness*. Westchester: Crossway.

Reisser, Paul C., Teri K. Reisser, and John Weldon. 1987. *New Age Medicine: A Christian Perspective on Holistic Health*. Downers Grove: Inter-Varsity.

Rockstad, Ernest B. 1982. "Praise the Lord by Confessing His Name!" Andover, KS: Faith and Life Publications. Pamphlet.

Soteriologi. ____. Yogyakarta: Evangelical Seminary of Indonesia.

Spear, Charles. 1842. *Names and Titles of the Lord Jesus Christ*. Boston: Privately printed.

Stonehouse, N.B. 1951. *The Witness of Luke to Christ*. Grand Rapids: Eerdmans.

Strong, James. 1944. *Exhaustive Concordance of the Bible*. New York: Abingdon-Cokesbury.

Tada, John Eareckson. 1986. *Choices, Changes*. Grand Rapids: Zondervan.

Taylor, Vincent. 1958. *The Person of Christ in New Testament Teaching*. London: Macmillan.

Thayer, Joseph Henry. 1966. *Thayer's Greek-English Lexicon of the New Testament*. Grand Rapids: Zondervan.

Thayer, Joseph Henry. 1977. *Thayer's Greek-English Lexicon of the New Testament*. Grand Rapids: Baker Book House.

Tillapaugh, Frank R. 1982. *Unleashing the Church*. Ventura: Regal Books.

Towns, Elmer L. 1991. *My Father's Names*. Ventura: Regal Books.

Trench. ____. Quoted in *Soteriologi*. ____. Original source and dates not given.

Unger, Merrill F. 1976. *Demons in the World Today*. Wheaton: Tyndale House.

Vine, W.E., M.A. 1966. *Vine's Expository Dictionary of New Testament Words*. Old Tappan: Revell.

Vos, G. 1926. *The Self Disclosure of Jesus*. New York: Doran.

Wakefield, Norman. 1987. *Solving Problems before They Become Conflicts*. Grand Rapids: Zondervan.

Walvoord, John F., and Roy B. Zuck, eds. 1978. *The Bible Knowledge Commentary, Old Testament Edition*. Wheaton: Victor Books.

_____. 1983. *The Bible Knowledge Commentary, New Testament Edition*. Wheaton: Victor Books.

Warfield, Benjamin B. 1974. *The Lord of Glory*. Grand Rapids: Baker.

Webster, Noah. 1984. *Webster's II New Riverside Dictionary*. New York: Berkley Books.

Wooding, Dan. 1989. *Secret Missions*. Harderwijk, Holland: Open Doors International.

Zodhiates, Spiros. 1992. *The Complete Word Study Dictionary: New Testament*. Chattanooga: AMG.

ABOUT THE AUTHOR

Dr. Robert J. Leland, the oldest of five children, was born in 1942 to Gordon and Edith Leland, and grew up in Oak Park, Illinois. He accepted the Lord as his Savior when just four years old and dedicated his life to foreign missions when he was six.

He received his B.A. degree in Secondary English Ed. from Northern Illinois University in 1966; his M.A. in Biblical Ed. from Columbia International University in 1971; and his D.Min. from Trinity International University in 1994.

He and his wife, (Ruth) Amber (married in 1966), served in Papua, Indonesia from 1971-2002 as church planters in the Citak (CHEE-tuck) tribe on the south coast, house parents at TEAM's hostel for missionary children in Sentani (Sen-TAH-nee) on the north coast near the Papua New Guinea border, office administrator (Bob) and bookkeeper (Amber) in Manokwari (MAH-no-KWAH-ri), and the last nineteen years of their service at the Erikson-Tritt Theological College near Manokwari. They also spent nine months in Singapore (1996) teaching at the Asian Cross-Cultural Training Institute while awaiting their visa renewal for Indonesia.

His Major Project for his D.Min., Conformed to His Image (now retitled, Unexpected Transformation), was translated into Indonesian and published in Indonesia. Upon return from the field in 2002, he translated Mounce's The Analytical Lexicon to the Greek New Testament from English into Indonesian, which has since been published in Indonesia for use in Bible schools and seminaries where Greek is taught.

He and Amber have also been teaching extension courses from the Grace Evangelical College and Seminary (located in Bangor, Maine) up in Aroostook County, Maine, where they now reside.

CPSIA information can be obtained
at www.ICGtesting.com
Printed in the USA
LVHW052050120421
684250LV00023B/2914